RESEARCH HANDBOOK ON SECURITIES REGULATION IN THE UNITED STATES

RESEARCH HANDBOOKS IN FINANCIAL LAW

Series Editor: Rosa Lastra, *Queen Mary, University of London, UK*

This important new *Handbook* series presents high quality, original reference works that cover a range of subjects within the evolving field of financial law. National, regional and global financial markets are at the epicenter of economic, political and social developments. They are shaped by their own intrinsic dynamics, but are also at the receiving end of potent external forces, including monetary developments, state regulation and policies towards international and regional financial integration and free trade areas.

Under the general editorship of Rosa Lastra, these *Handbooks* are edited by leading scholars in their respective fields, and comprise specially commissioned contributions from distinguished academics, who critically, innovatively and substantially analyze a wide range of current issues in financial law.

Each of the individual handbooks is a definitive reference work, essential for both scholars of financial law as well as for practicing lawyers. The comprehensive coverage and thorough examinations of the significant topics and ideas in financial law signify the *handbooks*' position as authoritative and scholarly information resources.

Titles in the series include:

Research Handbook on International Insurance Law and Regulation
Edited by Julian Burling and Kevin Lazarus

Research Handbook on Hedge Funds, Private Equity and Alternative Investments
Edited by Phoebus Athanassiou

Research Handbook on Securities Regulation in the United States
Edited by Jerry W. Markham and Rigers Gjyshi

Research Handbook on Securities Regulation in the United States

Edited by

Jerry W. Markham

Professor of Law, Florida International University at Miami, USA

Rigers Gjyshi

Senior Compliance Associate, The PNC Financial Services Group, Inc., USA

RESEARCH HANDBOOKS IN FINANCIAL LAW

Edward Elgar

Cheltenham, UK • Northampton, MA, USA

Published by
Edward Elgar Publishing Limited
The Lypiatts
15 Lansdown Road
Cheltenham
Glos GL50 2JA
UK

Edward Elgar Publishing, Inc.
William Pratt House
9 Dewey Court
Northampton
Massachusetts 01060
USA

A catalogue record for this book
is available from the British Library

Library of Congress Control Number: 2014937779

This book is available electronically in the ElgarOnline.com Law Subject Collection, E-ISBN 978 1 78254 007 6

MIX
Paper from responsible sources
FSC® C013056

ISBN 978 1 78254 006 9

Typeset by Columns Design XML Ltd, Reading
Printed and bound in Great Britain by T.J. International Ltd, Padstow

Contents

Contributors

EDITORS

Jerry W. Markham – Professor of Law, Florida International University at Miami

Rigers Gjyshi – Senior Compliance Associate, The PNC Financial Services Group, Inc.

AUTHORS

Barbara Black – Charles Hartsock Professor of Law and Director, Corporate Law Center, University of Cincinnati College of Law

Leslie A. Blau – Blau & Malmfeldt, Partner

Roel C. Campos – Partner at Locke Lord LLP in Washington, DC; former Commissioner at the Securities and Exchange Commission

Peter Evans – Attorney at Law

James Fanto – Gerald Baylin Professor of Law and Co-Director of the Center for the Study of Business Law & Regulation, Brooklyn Law School

José Gabilondo – Professor of Law, Florida International University at Miami

Zachary J. Gubler – Associate Professor Law, ASU Sandra Day O'Connor College of Law, Arizona State University

Thomas L. Hazen – Cary C. Boshamer Distinguished Professor of Law, UNC School of Law

Wulf A. Kaal – Associate Professor, University of Saint Thomas School of Law (Minneapolis)

Arthur B. Laby – Professor of Law, Rutgers University School of Law

Mark Liston – Kokoszka & Janczur, P.C.

Joan MacLeod Heminway – W.P. Toms Distinguished Professor of Law, The University of Tennessee College of Law; J.D., New York University School of Law; A.B., Brown University

Marlon Q. Paz – Partner at Locke Lord LLP, Adjunct Professor at Georgetown University Law Center; former senior member of the staff at the Securities and Exchange Commission

Preface

This Handbook was created for the purpose of providing a broad overview of the federal securities laws. There are many treatises that examine those laws in detail, and the number of law review articles that examine every minutiae of those statutes is staggering. This Handbook seeks to fill a void in that literature by providing ready access to the scope of the federal securities laws, while also providing the reader with the basic information needed to understand their reach.

The Handbook's initial chapter provides a description of the federal securities laws and the operation and structure of the agency charged with their enforcement – the Securities and Exchange Commission ("SEC"). Subsequent chapters focus on the definition of a security and registration requirements under the Securities Act of 1933, the underwriting process, and the continuous reporting requirements under the Securities Exchange Act of 1934 Act (1934 Act).

The regulation of secondary markets under the 1934 Act is the subject of other chapters. Price manipulation concerns are considered in another chapter. The Handbook also addresses the rules governing the operations of broker-dealers, including compliance and capital requirements. Other chapters describe the arbitration of disputes between broker-dealers and their customers, and private rights of action for self-regulatory organization rule violations. Still another chapter addresses the regulation of investment advisers under the Investment Advisers Act of 1940.

The Handbook also includes a chapter on corporate governance issues under the Sarbanes-Oxley Act of 2002. Another chapter addresses provisions in the Dodd-Frank Wall Street Reform and Consumer Protection Act of 2010, which broadened regulation of the securities markets and brought the regulation of derivative instruments into the realm of the SEC. The international regulation of financial instruments, which followed the Financial Crisis of 2008 and which are now affecting U.S. traders, is the subject of still another chapter.

Part of the strength of this Handbook is the diverse background of its contributors, including securities litigators, former regulators and academics. Each contributor has provided their unique style and experience, and the editors have exercised care in preserving that style while bringing together a broad overview of the complex provisions of the federal securities laws. The contributors to this Handbook have done a remarkable job capturing and describing the existing regulatory arena while setting up the framework for further analysis of the ever-evolving financial regulations. Indeed, with the Dodd-Frank Act, regulators are still hard at work finalizing a substantial portion of the rules that Act requires.

1. Overview

Jerry W. Markham

THE FEDERAL SECURITIES LAWS—AN OVERVIEW

The federal securities laws that now govern the regulation of securities markets in the U.S. are largely based on legislation that was passed in the wake of the Stock Market Crash of 1929 and in the midst of the Great Depression. The passage of those statutes was preceded by lengthy Congressional investigations that uncovered numerous abusive trading practices and widespread fraud.[1]

Those congressional investigations resulted in the passage of five statutes that now comprise the legislation that, after many amendments, still regulates the securities markets. The statutes are commonly referred to as the "federal securities laws" and include the Securities Act of 1933 ("1933 Act"),[2] the Securities Exchange Act of 1934 ("1934 Act"),[3] the Investment Advisers Act of 1940 ("1940 Act"),[4] the Investment Company Act of 1940,[5] and the little noticed Trust Indenture Act of 1939.[6]

The 1933 Act

The 1933 Act regulates public offerings of securities. That statute is modeled after earlier English legislation that sought to regulate public companies through the disclosure of their operations and finance. The federal securities laws also embrace the views of Justice Louis Brandeis who stated that "publicity is justly commended as a remedy for social and industrial diseases. Sunlight is said to be the best of disinfectants;

---

[1] Ferdinand Pecora, Wall Street Under Oath (1939) (describing those congressional investigations).

[2] 15 U.S.C. § 77a *et seq.*

[3] 15 U.S.C. § 78a *et seq.*

[4] 15 U.S.C. § 80b-1 *et seq.*

[5] 15 U.S.C. § 80a-1 *et seq.*

[6] 15 U.S.C. § 77aaa *et seq.* Another of these statutes, the Public Utility Holding Company Act of 1935, was largely repealed by the Energy Policy Act of 2005.

electric light the most efficient policeman."[7] The 1933 Act also added "to the ancient rule of caveat emptor, the further doctrine 'let the seller also beware.'"[8]

The 1933 Act prohibits the public sale of securities that are not registered with the Securities and Exchange Commission ("SEC"), unless they are exempted from that requirement. In brief, the registration statement required by the 1933 Act must contain information fully disclosing the financial circumstances of the company and all other material information about the company. The 1933 Act and SEC rules specify the information that must be disclosed and the format for such disclosure. The 1933 Act provides for a waiting period before the registration statement becomes effective. That waiting period allows the public to assess the information disclosed in the registration statement. It is intended to avoid the need for hurried, uninformed investment decisions.[9]

The 1933 Act prohibits fraud in connection with the sale of securities, as defined in that statute.[10] The 1933 Act also contains private rights of actions for investors who are injured by violations of the Act or SEC regulations. Such actions may be brought against underwriters, brokers and company insiders who signed the registration statement. There are, however, limitations on the damages that may be claimed and the actions that may be brought.[11]

The 1934 Act

The 1934 Act regulates the secondary market in securities transactions. The 1934 Act thus picks up where the 1933 Act leaves off by requiring public companies to provide current information about their finances and operations. This assures that the information provided during the registration process under the 1933 Act remains up to date and allows

---

[7] Louis Brandeis, Other People's Money and How the Brokers Use It, 4 (1932).

[8] H.R. Rep. No. 85, 73d Cong. 1st Sess. 2 (1934).

[9] *See* 1 Thomas L. Hazen, Treatise on the Law of Securities Regulation, ch. 3 (4th ed. 2002) (describing the registration process).

[10] Section 17 of the 1933 Act is an antifraud provision that allows the SEC to bring civil enforcement cases and which also provides for criminal penalties. 15 U.S.C. § 77q.

[11] Section 12 of the 1933 Act provides purchasers of a security sold under a misleading prospectus with a right of recession. 15 U.S.C. § 77. Section 11 of the 1933 Act imposes liability on those who prepare and sign misleading registration statements. 15 U.S.C. § 77k.

investors to make informed decisions about securities traded on exchanges or in the over-the-counter market.

The 1934 Act also governs the proxy process for shareholder voting companies registered under the 1933 Act (public companies).[12] The 1934 Act includes a requirement that securities exchanges register with the SEC as a "national securities exchange." Those exchanges must fulfill a 1934 Act mandate of a "self-regulatory organization" ("SRO"). They are required to police the conduct of their members in order to insure that they do not harm the public. That SRO role is largely carried out by the Financial Industry Regulatory Authority ("FINRA").

The 1934 Act also broadly regulates the operations of broker-dealers. Broker-dealers must register with the SEC. Once registered, a broker-dealer is subject to a broad range of regulatory requirements.[13]

Broker-dealers must keep customer funds and securities segregated from the broker-dealer's own funds.[14] To insure financial stability, broker-dealers are subject to a complex net capital requirement, which is designed to shut down failing broker-dealers before they become bankrupt and endanger customer funds insured by the Securities Investor Protection Corporation ("SIPC").[15]

The Dodd-Frank Wall Street Reform and Consumer Protection Act of 2010 ("Dodd-Frank") regulated swaps and other over-the-counter derivative instruments for the first time. That legislation divided regulation of those instruments between the SEC and the Commodity Futures Trading Commission ("CFTC").

The 1940 Act

In brief, the 1940 Act applies to investment advisers, i.e., persons who provide investment advice to customers and who manage customer funds. Among other things, the 1940 Act has an anti-fraud provision that prohibits investment advisers from even negligently defrauding their clients. The SEC has adopted a number of rules under that provision that seek to assure that investment adviser activities do not conflict with those

---

[12] 15 U.S.C. § 78n.

[13] *See* 23A Jerry W. Markham & Thomas Lee Hazen, Broker Dealer Operations Under Securities and Commodities Law: Financial Responsibilities, Credit Regulation, and Customer Protection (2012) (describing in detail the regulation of broker-dealers under the 1934 Act).

[14] *Id.*

[15] *Id.*

of their customers.[16] SEC rules also impose custody requirements for customer assets held by registered investment advisers.[17]

An SEC rule requiring hedge funds to register as investment advisers under the 1940 Act was stricken by a court of appeals. However, the Dodd-Frank Act included a provision overturning that decision.

The Investment Company Act of 1940

The Investment Company Act of 1940 ("Investment Company Act") regulates mutual funds and other investment companies. "It regulates virtually every aspect of the operations of investment companies; their valuation of assets, their governance and structure, their issuance of debt and other senior securities, their investments, sales and redemptions of their shares, and, perhaps most importantly, their dealings with service providers and other affiliates."[18]

The Investment Company Act classifies investment companies into the following categories: "face amount certificates"[19] and "unit investment trusts,"[20] which are not actively managed, and "management companies," which are actively managed.[21] Management companies are further classified into "closed" and "open-end" investment companies.[22]

Trust Indenture Act of 1939

The Trust Indenture Act of 1939 regulates the public offering of debt securities in excess of $1 million. The title of this legislation is a reference to "trust indentures," which are master agreements that govern the terms and conditions of the issuance and payment of interest and principal on corporate bonds, a.k.a., "debentures." The Trust Indenture

---

16 15 U.S.C. § 80b-6.

17 SEC Rule 206(4)-2 (17 C.F.R. § 275.206(4)-2).

18 Paul F. Roye, Remarks Before American Law Institute/American Bar Association Investment Company Regulation and Compliance Conference (Oct. 16, 2003).

19 *See* SEC v. Mount Vernon Mem'l Park, 664 F.2d 1358 (9th Cir. 1982) (describing these instruments).

20 *See* Investment Company Institute v. Camp, 401 U.S. 617, 625 (1970) (describing these instruments).

21 15 U.S.C. § 80a-4.

22 *See* Jerry W. Markham, *Mutual Fund Scandals—A Comparative Analysis of the Role of Corporate Governance in the Regulation of Collective Investments*, 3 Hastings Bus. L. J. 67, 75–79 (2006) (describing the companies regulated by the Investment Company Act of 1940).

Act sets forth requirements of independence and the responsibilities of indenture trustees. It provides for certain protections for investors when there has been a bond default.

THE SECURITIES AND EXCHANGE COMMISSION

Created by the 1934 Act, the SEC is an independent federal agency that is responsible for the enforcement of the federal securities laws. The SEC has responsibility for regulating the securities exchanges and the over-the-counter market. It also regulates approximately 35,000 regulated entities including some 12,000 investment advisers, 10,000 mutual funds and exchange traded funds ("ETFs"), 4,500 broker-dealers and 9,100 public companies.[23]

The SEC is composed of five commissioners who are appointed by the President with the advice and consent of the Senate for five-year terms. No more than three members may be members of the same political party. The SEC is headquartered in Washington, D.C., but it also has several regional offices across the country.

The SEC's work is largely carried out by its staff, which is divided into various divisions and offices. The SEC's Division of Enforcement is staffed by some 1,500 employees and is responsible for investigating potential violations and recommending to the SEC whether an enforcement action should be brought.[24] If approved by the Commission, the Enforcement Division will prosecute the case as a civil matter in federal court or before an SEC administrative law judge. It may also make criminal references to the Justice Department if deemed warranted.

The SEC's Division of Trading and Markets is responsible for the oversight of the securities exchanges. The SEC Division of Economic and Risk Analysis is responsible for integrating risk and data analysis into the SEC's processes. The SEC Division of Corporate Finance is responsible for reviewing disclosure documents and financial statements filed with the SEC by public companies. The SEC Division of Investment Management oversees the regulation of investment companies and investment advisers.

The SEC also has several other offices, including the Office of General Counsel, which defends the SEC in court, handles appeals and advises

---

[23] SEC, *In Brief, FY 2013 Congressional Justification*, at 2 (Feb. 2012), available at http://www.sec.gov/about/secfy13congbudgjust.pdf (accessed on Oct. 10, 2013).

[24] *Id.*

the SEC as its lawyer. The SEC's Office of Compliance and Inspections is responsible for conducting compliance inspections of investment advisers and broker-dealers. Other offices include an Office of Municipal Securities, Office of International Affairs, Office of Credit Ratings and the Office of Chief Accountant.

THE DODD-FRANK ACT

Adopted in the wake of the Financial Crisis in 2008, the Dodd-Frank Act made several changes to the SEC's regulatory duties. Among other things, the SEC was subjected to oversight by the Office of the Comptroller General, who must report on the SEC's effectiveness every three years.[25] That change reflected a concern that the SEC had not been an effective regulator during and before the Financial Crisis in 2008.

Dodd-Frank subjected hedge funds to regulation by the SEC.[26] That legislation also addressed the regulation of rating agencies because the ill-advised high ratings given to securitized subprime loans was thought to have contributed to the intensity of the Financial Crisis. The SEC was ordered to establish an Office of Credit Ratings and the SEC was to conduct examinations of credit rating agencies at least once a year. Disclosure of rating methodologies was also required. At least 50 percent of the directors of the rating agencies were required to be independent directors.[27]

In response to the massive Madoff Ponzi scheme,[28] the Dodd-Frank Act directed the SEC to conduct a study of how it could enhance its examinations of investment advisers.[29] A new Office of Investor Advocate was created at the SEC and it was to be assisted by the appointment of an ombudsman to act as an investor advocate.[30] The SEC was authorized to restrict mandatory arbitration of retail customer claims.[31] Whistleblower bounties were addressed for persons reporting violations of the federal securities laws.[32]

---

[25] Dodd-Frank § 962.

[26] Dodd-Frank § 401 *et seq.*

[27] Dodd-Frank § 931 *et seq.*

[28] *See* Diana B. Henriques, The Wizard of Lies: Bernie Madoff and the Death of Trust (2011) (describing that fraud).

[29] Dodd-Frank § 914.

[30] Dodd-Frank § 915.

[31] Dodd-Frank § 921.

[32] Dodd-Frank § 922.

Dodd-Frank gave shareholders a say on executive pay in the form of the right to vote approval or disapproval on executive pay and golden parachutes.[33] The SEC was given authority to allow shareholders proxy access to nominate directors. Compensation committees were required to include only independent directors who would have authority to hire compensation consultants in order to strengthen their independence.[34]

Public companies are now required to adopt claw-back provisions for executive compensation that was based on inaccurate financial information.[35] Regulators were required to adopt rules prohibiting compensation practices in the form of excessive compensation that encourages excessive risk taking.[36] Broker voting restrictions on board votes were adopted.[37] Public companies are also required to disclose why they have or have not decided to split the role of chairman and CEO.[38]

Advisers on municipal securities are now required to register with the SEC and are subject to regulation and fiduciary duties. The industry is also required to fund the Governmental Accounting Standards Board, which is tasked with establishing standards of financial accounting and reporting recognized as generally accepted accounting principles applicable to State and local governments.[39] The SEC was directed to conduct a study of whether customers of broker-dealers should be given the same protections of fiduciary duties as those of investment advisers. The SEC was authorized to impose such a requirement, but there was to be no continuing fiduciary duty after personalized advice is given.[40]

The Dodd-Frank Act directed the SEC substantively to regulate the previously unregulated market in securities-based swaps and security-based swap dealers.[41] Dodd-Frank gave the SEC broad and exclusive jurisdiction over "security-based swaps," while the CFTC was given jurisdiction over other swaps, and joint jurisdiction was declared for the SEC and CFTC over "mixed swaps."[42] The goal of that legislation was to move swaps from the over-the-counter market to central exchanges where

---

[33] Dodd-Frank § 951.

[34] Dodd-Frank § 952.

[35] Dodd-Frank § 954.

[36] Dodd-Frank § 956.

[37] Dodd-Frank § 957.

[38] Dodd-Frank § 972.

[39] Dodd-Frank § 975. *See* SEC Staff, Study on Investment Advisers and Broker-Dealers (Jan. 2011) (recommending uniform fiduciary duties for broker-dealers and investment advisers).

[40] Dodd-Frank § 913.

[41] Dodd-Frank § 762.

[42] Dodd-Frank § 712.

they would be cleared like futures and options contracts. That regulation reversed a decision by Congress in legislation enacted in 1992 and 2000 to allow these instruments to trade without substantive regulation. However, concerns over energy price manipulations and losses from credit default swaps led to their regulation. The bankruptcy of the American International Group, which the federal government had to bail out as the result of losses from credit default swaps, was a key factor in the demand for legislation that led to the passage of Dodd-Frank.

SEC ENFORCEMENT PROCEEDINGS

As described above, the SEC Division of Enforcement ("DOE") is responsible for investigating potential violations of the federal securities laws and SEC regulations.[43] These investigations are conducted privately and may be "informal" or "formal." An informal investigation involves a request for information by the DOE that is voluntary on the part of the person receiving the request. A formal investigation is conducted pursuant to an order of investigation. A formal investigation carries with it the power to subpoena witnesses and documents. A court may enforce those subpoenas.[44]

If the DOE concludes that a violation has occurred and that enforcement action is appropriate, notice of that conclusion is given to the targeted party. That party is then normally provided the opportunity to submit a "Wells Submission" to the SEC to explain why such an enforcement action should not be undertaken.[45] Such notices frequently result in settlements in which the party neither admits nor denies the SEC's findings of violations. However, in recent months, the SEC has

---

[43] *See, e.g.*, 15 U.S.C. § 78(a) for the SEC's authority to conduct such investigations.

[44] For a description of formal and informal SEC investigations, see Colleen P. Mahoney, *et al.*, The SEC Enforcement Process: Practice and Procedure in Handling an SEC Investigation, 77–4th (C.P.S. BNA).

[45] *See* SEC v. Sands, 902 F. Supp. 1149, 1167 (C.D. Cal. 1995), aff'd sub nm.; SEC v. First Pacific Bancorp, 142 F.3d 1186 (9th Cir. 1998), *cert. denied*, 525 U.S. 1121 (1999) ("A Wells submission is a document filed with the SEC in which a defendant presents the evidence and legal theories he believes the SEC should consider in deciding whether to file an enforcement action.").

begun a campaign of requiring at least some parties to admit wrongdoing.[46]

If settlement cannot be reached, and if the SEC concludes that such an action should be taken over the objections of the targeted party, the DOE will be authorized to bring enforcement proceedings. Such a proceeding may take the form of an injunctive action in federal court[47] or an administrative proceeding before an SEC administrative law judge.

As one author notes:

> First, the SEC has the power to bring actions in federal court to seek temporary and permanent injunctive relief against possible violators, to request that a court prohibit persons from serving as officers or directors of registered companies, to seek civil monetary penalties for securities law violations, and to request equitable relief. Second, the SEC can bring administrative action against alleged violators. In these administrative proceedings, the SEC may impose monetary penalties after notice and opportunity for a hearing. An administrative law judge (ALJ), who is independent of the SEC, presides over these hearings. The ALJ issues an initial decision, which can be appealed to the Commission. The Commission's decision can be appealed to federal circuit courts. Third, the SEC can refer cases to the Department of Justice for criminal prosecution.[48]

In order to establish that injunctive relief is appropriate, the DOE need not show irreparable injury or the inadequacy of other remedies, as is the case for private injunctive relief. Instead, the DOE must show that there is a "realistic likelihood" of future violations. As one court held:

> Several factors are to be considered in determining the probability of future violations: "(1) the degree of scienter involved, (2) the isolated or recurring nature of the fraudulent activity, (3) the defendant's appreciation of his wrongdoing, and (4) the defendant's opportunities to commit future violations." Where the defendant's misconduct involves "systematic wrongdoing"

---

46 SEC, *JPMorgan Chase Agrees to Pay $200 Million and Admits Wrongdoing to Settle SEC Charges*, available at http://www.sec.gov/News/PressRelease/Detail/PressRelease/1370539819965#.UmFB5xam5GA (accessed on Oct. 18, 2013).

47 15 U.S.C. § 78u(d).

48 Matthew P. Wynne, *Note: Rule 10b-5(B) Enforcement Actions In Light Of Janus: Making The Case For Agency Deference*, 81 Fordham L. Rev. 2111, 2118–2119 (2013) (footnotes omitted).

> rather than an isolated incident, courts have found that there is a greater probability that the defendant will commit future violations of the securities laws.[49]

The SEC often seeks "ancillary" equitable relief in its enforcement actions, including disgorgement from defendants of their ill-gotten gains and civil penalties may be imposed.[50] As one court noted:

> Although injunctive relief is the only relief that the statutes expressly authorize, we have held that federal courts have "inherent equitable authority to issue a variety of 'ancillary relief' measures in actions brought by the SEC to enforce the federal securities laws." In particular, a court may impose a receivership, freeze assets, and order the disgorgement of the proceeds of fraud held by defendants, and by third-party nominal defendants.[51]

A receiver may be appointed in SEC injunctive actions to take control of a company found to have defrauded investors.[52] Alternatively, a "corporate monitor" may also be appointed to assure future compliance.[53] The SEC may also seek to bar individuals from serving as an officer or director of a public company if they are shown to be unfit to serve in such a capacity.[54]

The maximum amount of civil penalties that may be imposed in SEC enforcement proceedings may vary based on the level of seriousness of the violations found. Those penalties range from $7,500 to $150,000 for each violation committed by an individual and from $75,000 to $725,000 for corporate entities.[55] In actions for insider trading, the civil penalty may not exceed three times the insider's trading benefits.[56]

In administrative proceedings, a respondent may be subject to a cease and desist order, revocation of registration, monetary penalties and bars

---

49 SEC v. Blackout Media Corp., 2012 U.S. Dist. LEXIS 134330 (S.D.N.Y. 2012) (citations omitted).

50 The 1934 Act states that: "In any action or proceeding brought or instituted by the Commission under any provision of the securities laws, the Commission may seek, and any Federal court may grant, any equitable relief that may be appropriate or necessary for the benefit of investors." 15 U.S.C. § 78u.

51 Sherman v. SEC, 491 F.3d 948, 959 (9th Cir. 2007).

52 *See generally* Warfield v. Byron, 436 F.3d 551 (5th Cir. 2006).

53 *See* In re Worldcom, Inc., 311 B.R. 151 (S.D.N.Y. 2004) (describing role of a corporate monitor).

54 15 U.S.C. § 78u.

55 15 U.S.C. § 77h-1 and 15 U.S.C. § 78u-2.

56 15 U.S.C. § 78u-1.

from the securities industry.[57] The decision of an SEC administrative law judge is appealable to the SEC and from there to a federal court of appeals.[58]

57 *See* 15 U.S.C. §§ 78u-2 and 78u-3.
58 15 U.S.C. § 78y.

2. The definition of "security" under the federal securities laws

Arthur B. Laby

INTRODUCTION

Definitions are essential in any regulatory regime and the federal regulation of securities is no exception. The application of multiple statutes and hundreds of administrative rules turns on the definition of a single term, such as "offer," "sale," "issuer," or "underwriter." The most fundamental of those terms under the federal and state securities laws is the term "security." Without the presence of a security, federal and state securities laws are unavailing. This Chapter provides a brief overview of the definition of "security" under the federal securities laws.

The definition of "security" appears in securities statutes, case law, and numerous interpretations by the U.S. Securities and Exchange Commission ("SEC" or "Commission"), the primary regulator with responsibility to implement and enforce the federal securities laws. Whether a security exists has far-reaching consequences for issuers and promoters offering financial arrangements to customers or clients. Under the Securities Act of 1933, the first of the federal securities laws passed in the aftermath of the Great Crash of 1929, an investment offered to the public generally must be registered with the SEC if the investment being offered is a security.[1] Moreover, the Securities Act provides a private right of action against anyone who offers or sells a security in violation of the registration provision. The damages are a return of the purchase price of the security to the purchaser.[2] As a result, if an investment loses value, an investor can sue for a return of his or her funds if the investor can demonstrate that the investment should have been registered as a security.

The meaning of "security" is a complex area of law. The definition is a tangled web and often yields no clear answers. Several reasons account for the complexity. First, there are a voluminous number of cases

---

[1] Securities Act § 5, 15 U.S.C. § 77e (2012).

[2] Securities Act § 12(a)(1), 15 U.S.C. 77l(a)(1); *see generally* THOMAS LEE HAZEN, THE LAW OF SECURITIES REGULATION 289–91 (rev. 5th ed. 2006).

defining the term "security" or applying the definition in novel ways, including twelve U.S. Supreme Court cases. There are over 1,000 federal cases, which cite to the leading Supreme Court case of *SEC v. W.J. Howey Co.*, discussed below.[3] The classic treatise in the field, *Securities Regulation* by Louis Loss, Joel Seligman, and Troy Paredes, devotes nearly 300 pages to the definition.[4] The Supreme Court has recognized this complexity, writing with understatement that cases have not been "entirely clear" on the proper method for determining when an instrument is a security.[5]

As a result of this complexity, it is not possible to cover all of the salient issues regarding the definition of "security" in this Chapter. The goal of the Chapter is to provide an overview of the law, introduce key themes, and raise several controversial topics to give the reader a flavor for some of the debates that arise over the definition.

Several themes will emerge in this Chapter. The definition of "security" exemplifies the broader tension regarding the scope of federal regulation of securities and the securities laws. Debates over whether to expand or contract the definition of "security" are really debates over the scope of securities regulation itself. As one might imagine, the SEC and private plaintiffs often argue for an expansive definition of the term. The SEC seeks a broad definition in the name of investor protection, but an expansive definition also augments the SEC's regulatory and enforcement jurisdiction. Private plaintiffs seek a broad definition because investors, upset with performance, often try to characterize an investment as a security to obtain relief under the securities laws. Businesses resist attempts to expand the definition, trying to convince courts and regulators that a particular investment is not a security. As will become clear, however, generalizations regarding who seeks a more or less expansive definition of security are prone to exception.

Another theme that will emerge is that the definition of "security" is dynamic. Malefactors have an impressive capacity to hatch new schemes, or revise old ones, to convince investors to part with their savings. Thus, lawyers, regulators, and courts often look to the definition of "security" to determine if a newly-minted investment scheme is covered by the securities laws. Moreover, securities markets are themselves dynamic. Products and services that did not exist twenty years ago are now ubiquitous. A prime example is the advent of exchange-traded funds with

---

[3] 328 U.S. 293 (1946).

[4] II Louis Loss, Joel Seligman & Troy Paredes, Securities Regulation 855–1143 (4th ed. 2007).

[5] Landreth Timber Co. v. Landreth, 471 U.S. 681, 688 (1985).

over $1.3 trillion in assets, which are considered securities.[6] Another example is Bitcoin, the digital currency not backed by any government, which commentators have argued should not be considered a security.[7] New products and services call for a careful review of the definition of "security" to determine whether it should be modified or adapted.

The plan for this Chapter is to begin with the statutory definition of "security" and the definition of "investment contract," a term included in the definition. The Chapter then discusses interests in various business organizations, such as corporations and partnerships. It then moves to a discussion of notes, derivative instruments, insurance products, and bank products, each presenting different problems. The Chapter then has a short discussion of the state law definition of "security" primarily as a point of contrast with the federal definition. The Chapter concludes with emergent themes to bear in mind when analyzing whether a security exists.

The best place to begin is with the statutory definition. Although the securities statutes seldom provide a clear answer, a careful review of the statutory definition is unavoidable.

THE STATUTORY DEFINITION OF "SECURITY"

The term "security" is defined in each of the federal securities laws, the Securities Act of 1933, the Securities Exchange Act of 1934, the Investment Advisers Act of 1940, the Investment Company Act of 1940, and the Trust Indenture Act of 1939 (by cross-reference to the Securities Act of 1933). Because the term is defined similarly, courts interpreting the definition under one statute refer to interpretations of the term under other statutes.[8] Moreover, although there are exceptions, the Supreme Court has stated that coverage under the Securities Act and the Securities Exchange Act "may be considered the same."[9] The Securities Act defines a "security" as follows:

> [a]ny note, stock, treasury stock, security future, security-based swap, bond, debenture, evidence of indebtedness, certificate of interest or participation in

---

[6] Investment Company Institute, 2013 Investment Company Fact Book, available at http://www.icifactbook.org/fb_ch3.html#total.

[7] *See, e.g.*, Reuben Grinberg, *Bitcoin: An Innovative Alternative Digital Currency*, 4 HASTINGS SCI. & TECH. LAW J. 159, 194–99 (2012).

[8] Tcherepnin v. Knight, 389 U.S. 332, 335–36 (1967).

[9] United Housing Foundation, Inc. v. Forman, 421 U.S. 837, 847 n.12 (1975).

> any profit-sharing agreement, collateral-trust certificate, preorganization certificate or subscription, transferable share, investment contract, voting-trust certificate, certificate of deposit for a security, fractional undivided interest in oil, gas, or other mineral rights, any put, call, straddle, option, or privilege on any security, certificate of deposit, or group or index of securities (including any interest therein or based on the value thereof), or any put, call, straddle, option, or privilege entered into on a national securities exchange relating to foreign currency, or, in general, any interest or instrument commonly known as a "security", or any certificate of interest or participation in, temporary or interim certificate for, receipt for, guarantee of, or warrant or right to subscribe to or purchase, any of the foregoing.[10]

Although this definition is detailed and lengthy, it is not particularly helpful to understand what sorts of relationships constitute securities.

There are several reasons the statute provides no clear answers. First, there are approximately thirty terms packed into the definition, each of which calls for its own definition and analysis. What qualifies as a note, stock, bond, or evidence of indebtedness? Second, the definitional section in the Securities Act contains a qualifier. Congress inserted the words "unless the context otherwise requires" before the definitions begin.[11] Thus, courts, regulators, and others may depart from the statutory definition when the context requires a departure. The "context" clause should not be taken lightly; the Supreme Court has invoked it at least twice.[12] Third, courts tend to put substance over form. Thus, even if parties to an investment agreement state in writing that an investment is not a security, courts might deem one to exist. The Supreme Court has stated on several occasions that one must analyze the "economic reality" of an investment to determine whether a security exists.[13]

Finally, the definition of security includes an "investment contract." Courts have described the term "investment contract" as a "catch-all" to cover interests with the functional attributes of stock but not called stock.[14] Indeed, a complex body of case law addresses whether an agreement constitutes an investment contract, the next topic.

---

[10] Securities Act § 2(a)(1), 15 U.S.C. § 78b(a)(1).

[11] Securities Act § 2(a), 15 U.S.C. § 78b(a).

[12] Int'l Brotherhood of Teamsters v. Daniel, 439 U.S. 551, 567 n.22 (1979); Marine Bank v. Weaver, 455 U.S. 551, 556 (1982).

[13] Forman, 421 U.S. at 848 (quoting Tcherepnin, 389 U.S. at 336); SEC v. W.J. Howey Co., 328 U.S. 293, 298 (1946).

[14] Peoria Union Stock Yards Co. Ret. Plan v. Penn Mut. Life Ins. Co., 698 F.2d 320, 324 (7th Cir. 1983).

"INVESTMENT CONTRACT" AND THE *HOWEY* TEST

After nearly seventy years, the classic case defining an "investment contract" is still *SEC v. W.J. Howey Co.*[15] The importance of *Howey*, however, extends far beyond the definition of investment contract. The Supreme Court has written that the *Howey* analysis embodies the "essential attributes" that run through all decisions defining a security.[16] As a result, even if an instrument meets the definition of "security" on its face, such as stock or treasury notes, the *Howey* analysis could color a court's determination of whether the instrument is in fact a security.[17]

W.J. Howey Company owned several tracts of citrus acreage in Lake County, Florida.[18] The company planted groves and offered them to the public. A sister corporation, Howey-in-the-Hills Service, Inc., cultivated and developed the groves and sold the crops. The Howey Company offered customers a land sales contract and a service contract. Once the customer paid, land was conveyed by warranty deed. Howey-in-the-Hills, however, kept possession of the land; the owner had no right to enter the property or market the crop. Instead, the owner received an allocation of net profits based on his or her ownership interest. The customers were predominantly out-of-towners; they were businesspersons with no knowledge or skill regarding citrus cultivation and care.[19] The issue in the case was whether the sales contract, the warranty deed, and the service contract together constituted an "investment contract."[20]

Drawing on a definition under state law, the Court set forth a four-part test to define investment contract.[21] Under *Howey*, an investment contract under the Securities Act is a contract whereby a person (1) invests money, (2) in a common enterprise, (3) with the expectation of profit, (4) derived solely from the efforts of a third party.[22]

A careful reading of *Howey* suggests that the Court was concerned about investor protection. The Howey Company had "full discretion and

---

[15] 328 U.S. 293, 298 (1946).

[16] Forman, 421 U.S. at 852. A later Supreme Court case limited the force of this dicta. *Landreth Timber*, 471 U.S. at 691–92.

[17] *See* James D. Cox, Robert W. Hillman & Donald C. Langevoort, Securities Regulation: Cases and Materials 40 (7th ed. 2013).

[18] Howey, 328 U.S. at 294–95.

[19] *Id.* at 295–96.

[20] *Id.* at 297.

[21] *Id.* at 298–99.

[22] *Id.* at 299.

authority" over the groves.[23] The service contract lasted ten years with no option to cancel.[24] The Court focused on the vulnerability of persons from "distant localities" who lacked the experience to market citrus groves and were attracted purely by a return on investment.[25] Indeed, the purchasers were patrons of a hotel adjacent to the groves operated by the Howey Company, and purchasers were subject to a marketing and sales campaign during their stay.[26] Moreover, the Court indicated that the four-part test was meant to be flexible in order to capture the variety of schemes that can be devised by those seeking to use other people's money with the promise of profits down the road.[27] Each *Howey* factor has generated substantial case law. Because the definition of "investment contract" is so important, this Chapter discusses each factor in turn.

Investment of Money

Perhaps the most fundamental of the four *Howey* factors is an investment of money. An investment of money is not limited to a cash investment. As the Supreme Court stated in another case, an investment of money can take the form of an investment of goods or services.[28] According to an often-cited test for an investment of money, it requires no more than that an investor "commit his assets to the enterprise in such a manner as to subject himself to financial loss."[29]

Common Enterprise

If an investment of money is the most fundamental of the *Howey* factors, the one that has generated most litigation is likely the requirement of a common enterprise. The Supreme Court gave little indication in *Howey* of what it meant by common enterprise. The Court stated that the term investment contract was construed by state courts to protect the investing public. But this provides little guidance of what the Court had in mind. The state court opinion referenced by the Supreme Court in formulating

---

[23] *Id.* at 296.
[24] *Id.* at 296.
[25] *Id.* at 299–300.
[26] *Id.* at 196–97.
[27] *Id.* at 299.
[28] Daniel, 439 U.S. at 560 n.12.
[29] Hector v. Wiens, 533 F.2d 429, 432 (9th Cir. 1976) (*per curiam*) (cited in Warfield v. Alaniz, 569 F.3d 1015, 1021 (9th Cir. 2009)).

its test refers to multiple purchasers, not a single investor.[30] As a result, perhaps the Supreme Court assumed that an investment contract would entail more than one investor. With no clear guidance, it is unsurprising that multiple interpretations of commonality have appeared in the federal case law. Courts refer to both horizontal and vertical commonality. Within vertical commonality, there are two variations, broad vertical commonality and narrow vertical commonality.

Horizontal commonality

Horizontal commonality generally requires a pooling of investor funds and a sharing of the profits of the enterprise. The First, Second, Third, Fourth, Sixth, Seventh, Ninth, and D.C. Circuits have accepted or required horizontal commonality to demonstrate a common enterprise.[31] Horizontal commonality emphasizes commonality between or among multiple investors as opposed to commonality between an investor and a promoter. Even in the case of horizontal commonality, however, it is possible to have just one investor. This result is not necessarily intuitive; it is unclear how a single investor could lead to horizontal commonality because with a single investor there can be no pooling among investors or a division of profits among multiple investors. Courts, however, appear unconcerned with this anomaly. One court explained that the character of the investment, not the presence of multiple investors, determines commonality.[32] This court, relying on common sense, stated that otherwise a person could perpetuate a fraud and be immune from the federal securities laws by limiting the number of investors to one – a result not contemplated by cases that require horizontal commonality.[33]

Vertical commonality

Vertical commonality requires no pooling of funds. Vertical commonality looks to the relationship between the investors and the promoter as opposed to the relationship between or among investors. It examines whether the activity of a promoter is the controlling factor in the success

---

[30] *See* State v. Gopher Tire & Rubber Co., 177 N.W. 937, 938 (Minn. 1920) (quoted in Howey, 328 U.S. at 298).

[31] *See, e.g.*, SEC v. SG Ltd., 265 F.3d 42, 49–51 (1st Cir. 2001); SEC v. Lauer, 52 F.3d 667, 670 (7th Cir. 1995); *see generally* James D. Gordon III, *Defining Common Enterprise in Investment Contracts*, 72 OHIO ST. L. J. 59, 66–70 (2011) (reviewing Circuit Court cases).

[32] Lauer, 52 F.3d at 670.

[33] *Id.*

of the enterprise. Are the investor's fortunes somehow tied to the success of the promoter and not to the success of other investors?

Just when it appears that matters could not get more complex, courts have developed two variations of vertical commonality, broad vertical commonality and narrow vertical commonality. Broad vertical commonality, adopted by the Fifth and Eleventh Circuits, requires only a loose connection between the promoter's efforts and the success of the enterprise. To determine whether broad vertical commonality exists, courts look to whether investors depend on the promoter's expertise or efforts for their return.[34] The broad vertical commonality test has evoked sharp criticism. If broad vertical commonality is the legal test, the "efforts of others" requirement, discussed below, would arguably be unnecessary. Both tests would collapse into a single inquiry of whether the success of the investment depends on a third party.[35]

Narrow vertical commonality is not as forgiving. Narrow vertical commonality, adopted by the First and Ninth Circuits, requires that the investor's fortune be "interwoven with and dependent upon" the success of the promoter.[36] As several courts have put it, the fortunes of the investor and the promoter must be linked so they "rise and fall" together.[37]

Discretionary accounts as securities

The internecine conflict among the circuits over the appropriate test for commonality recurs in the context of determining whether a discretionary brokerage or advisory account may itself be considered a security and, therefore, subject to Securities Act registration and other legal requirements. Normally when an investor opens a securities account, the investor has the final word on the investments purchased for the account. When the investor grants discretion to a financial advisor, however, the financial advisor has the authority to invest funds without consulting the investor about the particular security purchased or sold, or about price, amount, or timing of the trades for the account.[38] In the case of a

---

[34] SEC v. ETS Payphones, Inc., 408 F.3d 727, 732 (11th Cir. 2005).

[35] *See* Revak v. SEC Realty Corp., 18 F.3d 81, 88 (2d Cir. 1994).

[36] SG Ltd., 265 F.3d at 49 (quoting SEC v. Glenn W. Turner Enterprises, 474 F.2d 476, 482 n.7 (9th Cir. 1973)).

[37] Dooner v. NMI Ltd., 725 F. Supp. 153, 159 (S.D.N.Y. 1989); Savino v. E.F. Hutton & Co., 507 F. Supp. 1225, 1237 (S.D.N.Y. 1981).

[38] *See* FINRA, What to Expect When You Open a Brokerage Account, available at http://www.finra.org/Investors/SmartInvesting/GettingStarted/OpeningaBrokerageAccount.

discretionary account, a financial advisor typically is paid on a fee basis calculated as a percentage of assets under management. As a result, in the case of a discretionary account, the financial advisor is making key decisions regarding management of the account and the advisor will be paid regardless of whether the account is increasing or decreasing in value. The advisor receives a fee calculated as a percentage of assets under management even when the account is declining in value.

The different tests for commonality lead to different results regarding whether a discretionary account is a security. Under horizontal commonality, a discretionary account would not be a security because the investor's funds are not pooled with others' funds – they are simply placed in an account managed by the advisor. No pooling means no horizontal commonality and no security. Similarly, under a narrow vertical commonality test, a discretionary account would not be considered a security because the profits of the customer and the financial advisor do not necessarily rise and fall together: the investor may be losing money year after year in the account, but the financial advisor would continue to collect the asset-based fee. Thus, under narrow vertical commonality, this account could not be considered a security. Under broad vertical commonality, however, a discretionary account could be considered a security because the investor depends on the advisor's efforts and expertise for the investor's success. Under broad vertical commonality, there is no requirement that the investor's fortunes rise and fall with the promoter's. Thus, the account could be considered a security under broad vertical commonality whether losing or gaining in value.

For many years, the SEC's position was that commonality could be satisfied by horizontal commonality or narrow vertical commonality, but not by broad vertical commonality. In 2001, the SEC stated that this was the Commission's "long-held view."[39] The SEC's reasoning was that broad vertical commonality, as discussed, collapses the common enterprise element into the "efforts of others" element, discussed below.[40] The SEC took a consistent position under the Investment Company Act. In a release regarding the status of investment advisory programs under that statute, the Commission stated that an investment advisory program would satisfy the common enterprise requirement of *Howey* only if the account was discretionary *and* investors received substantially the same advice. If investment advice were individualized, commonality would not

[39] Brief of the Securities and Exchange Commission, Appellant at 28 and n.11, SEC v. SG Ltd., 265 F.3d 42 (1st Cir. 2001) (Nos 01–1176, 01–1332), 2001 WL 36006429.

[40] *Id.*

be met.[41] Under this analysis, a discretionary account managed on an individualized basis would not constitute a security.

In 2004, the SEC quietly changed its view. In supplemental briefing in *SEC v. Edwards*,[42] after the Supreme Court decided the case, the SEC strongly endorsed broad vertical commonality.[43] This represents a sea change from the Commission's "long held view." In *Edwards*, the Court held that profit under *Howey* refers to both variable returns and fixed returns, such as the lease payments in the case, and that a specific right to payments under a contract does not mean the payments cannot be derived from the efforts of others.[44]

In its supplemental brief, the SEC reversed its earlier view and stated that the Supreme Court's decision confirmed the "correctness" of broad vertical commonality.[45] In a surprising move, the SEC also stated that not only did the Supreme Court confirm broad vertical commonalty as the correct interpretation of common enterprise, but in addition the *Edwards* case, the SEC stated, also supports the SEC's original interpretation of investment contract first articulated in 1941.[46] According to the SEC, the common enterprise requirement is not a separate requirement for the existence of an investment contract.[47] In its brief, the SEC argued that the substance of an investment contract is an investment of money with the expectation of profit derived from the efforts of others, thereby striking the commonality element from the test.[48] The SEC concluded, "Nothing in *Howey* suggests that 'common enterprise' imposes a separate requirement for an investment contract."[49]

The SEC's new approach is contrary to the leading view outside the Commission. According to *Securities Regulation*, the leading treatise by Loss, Seligman, and Paredes, an approach that accepts horizontal commonality and narrow vertical commonality is preferable. When two or more investors pool funds, a common enterprise would exist regardless of

---

41 Status of Investment Advisory Programs Under the Investment Company Act of 1940, Investment Company Act Release No. 21,260, [1995 Transfer Binder] Fed. Sec. L. Rep. (CCH) ¶85,646, 86,969 n.15 (July 27, 1995).

42 540 U.S. 389 (2004).

43 Brief of Securities and Exchange Commission, Appellee at 13–20, SEC v. Edwards, 540 U.S. 389 (2004) (No. 01–10107-DD), 2004 WL 3459066.

44 Edwards, 540 U.S. at 395–97.

45 Brief of Securities and Exchange Commission, *supra* note 43, at 13.

46 *Id.* at 14.

47 *Id.* at 15; *see also* Anthony H. Barkate, Securities Exchange Act Release No. 49542, 2004 WL 762434 (Apr. 8, 2004).

48 Brief of Securities and Exchange Commission, *supra* note 43, at 16.

49 *Id.* at 17.

how the promoter was paid. Moreover, when the income of a single investor and a promoter depends on the profits of the undertaking, a common enterprise would exist. A conventional discretionary investor account, however, absent a sharing of profits, should not result in a security according to leading writers in the field.[50]

Expectation of Profits

Far less need be said about the "expectation of profits" element. By profit, the Supreme Court has meant either "capital appreciation" growing out of an initial investment or "participation in earnings" that result from use of the investor's funds.[51] The key to profits is that the investor be attracted by the prospect of return on his or her investment.[52] According to *United Housing Foundation, Inc. v. Forman*, one can contrast a desire to achieve a return with a desire to consume the item acquired.[53] In *Forman*, the investors were residents of Co-op City in New York. They bought so-called stock in the enterprise to have a place to live, not for the prospect of financial return.[54] Moreover, the element of an expectation of profit is not defeated merely because a promoter offers a fixed rate of return. As discussed, in *Edwards*, the Supreme Court held that profit refers to both variable and fixed returns.[55] The fact that investors negotiated for a specific return does not mean that the return does not derive from the efforts of others.[56] This view of the profits element of *Howey* seems to blend the profits element and the "efforts of others" element. The Court is suggesting fixed returns can be considered profit because they derive from the efforts of others. Thus, it is to the "efforts of others" element that this Chapter now turns.

Efforts of Others

When setting forth the "efforts of others" element of the *Howey* test, the Court used the phrase, "solely from the efforts of the promoter or a third party … ."[57] The first emendation of the *Howey* formulation is that the

---

50 *See* LOSS, SELIGMAN & PAREDES, *supra* note 4, at 937.
51 Forman, 421 U.S. at 852.
52 *Id.*
53 Forman, 421 U.S. at 853.
54 *Id.* at 853.
55 Edwards, 540 U.S. at 395–97.
56 *Id.* at 397.
57 Howey, 328 U.S. at 299.

word "solely" no longer means solely. In *Forman*, the Supreme Court formulated this element using the phrase, "expectation of profits to be derived from the entrepreneurial or managerial efforts of others."[58] The Court omitted the word "solely" and prepared a footnote stating that although the original test used "solely," the Ninth Circuit has held that the word "solely" should not be read as a literal limitation on the definition of investment contract.[59] Recall that in the context of horizontal commonality, courts were concerned that limiting investors to one would defeat commonality. So too here are courts concerned that a rigid requirement of efforts being "solely" the efforts of others could be evaded by a promoter requiring the investor to contribute some small degree of effort on his or her own.[60] This result would be unacceptable; the "solely" requirement therefore had to be purged from the test.

If efforts of others must not necessarily be *solely* efforts of others, to what extent must efforts be performed by third persons? One answer is that efforts of others must be "undeniably significant," essential efforts, which "affect" the success or failure of the enterprise.[61] Another formulation is that efforts must be "predominantly" efforts of others.[62] Regardless of the specific formulation, the key point is that something less than "solely" now satisfies the legal standard.

The *Edwards* case, as mentioned, is also relevant to the "efforts of others" requirement. The offer of a fixed rate of return does not eliminate efforts of others. A return, even if fixed, is still expected to arise from efforts of others. As the *Edwards* Court wrote, the fact that investors will receive a fixed return does not mean that the return does not come from the efforts of others.[63]

One final consideration to bear in mind when considering whether an investment satisfies the efforts of others element is *timing* of the efforts. Courts distinguish between pre-purchase efforts (those that occur before the investor decides to invest) and post-purchase efforts (those that occur after the investor has parted with his or her funds). If investors' profits depend on post-purchase efforts, the investor is more likely to benefit from disclosure and other requirements incident to securities registration

---

[58] Forman, 421 U.S. at 852.

[59] *Id.* at 852 n.16.

[60] SEC v. Glenn W. Turner Enterp., Inc., 474 F.2d 476, 482 (9th Cir.), *cert. denied*, 414 U.S. 821 (1973).

[61] *Id.*

[62] SEC v. International Loan Network, Inc., 968 F.2d 1304, 1308 (D.C. Cir. 1992).

[63] Edwards, 540 U.S. at 397.

and the applicability of the securities laws. By contrast, if the efforts of others take place before the purchase occurs, and there is no expectation of additional efforts post-purchase, then the efforts of others have likely been impounded into the promoters' fees or the purchase price of the investment, and there is less need for the protections of the securities laws.[64] Other courts reject the distinction over the timing of the efforts of others.[65] The Eleventh Circuit wrote that although it may be true that the "efforts of others" prong is more easily met through post-purchase efforts, it saw no basis for excluding pre-purchase activities in determining whether an investment satisfied the "efforts of others" test.[66]

INTERESTS IN BUSINESS ORGANIZATIONS

To what extent does an interest in a business organization, such a corporation, partnership, or limited liability company ("LLC") constitute a security? The answer is not obvious and often depends on a variety of factors. In some cases, this inquiry refers back to the *Howey* analysis.

Stock

Although stock appears in the statutory definition of security, stock is not always considered a security. The general rule is substance over form. In determining the scope of the definition of "security," the Supreme Court has written that "form should be disregarded for substance and the emphasis should be on economic reality."[67] In the *Forman* case, discussed above, the Court explicitly rejected the suggestion that the transaction at issue, which was a sale of interests called "stock," must be deemed a security merely because the statutory definition of security contains the magic words, "any … stock."[68] The economic reality test, which has its roots in the definition of "investment contract," has limits. The Supreme Court formulated the economic reality test to determine whether an instrument is an investment contract under *Howey*, not whether it satisfies any of the statutory definitions of security, such as stock.[69]

---

[64] *See* SEC v. Life Partners, Inc., 87 F.3d 536, 545–48 (D.C. Cir. 1996).
[65] SEC v. Mutual Benefits Corp., 408 F.3d 737, 743 (11th Cir. 2005).
[66] *Id.*
[67] Tcherepnin, 389 U.S. at 336.
[68] Forman, 421 U.S. at 848.
[69] *See* Landreth Timber, 471 U.S. at 691.

When stock might not be a security is addressed by the so-called "sale of business" doctrine. Under this doctrine, when a buyer acquires 100 percent of a closed corporation's shares, the stock is not considered a security because managerial control passes directly into the buyer's hands.[70] In *Landreth Timber Co. v. Landreth*,[71] the Supreme Court stated that the label "stock" is not sufficient to qualify an instrument as a security. Rather, one must examine whether the instrument has characteristics typically associated with stock, such as payment of dividends, negotiability, ability to be pledged, voting rights, and possibility of appreciation.[72] The Court refused to apply the sale of business doctrine and stated that the sale of stock is exactly the context to which the federal securities laws were meant to apply.[73]

Partnership Interests

The term "partnership" is not listed in the definition of security. Thus, whether a partnership interest constitutes a security likely depends on whether a partnership interest is considered an investment contract. An empirical study of reported federal cases on the definition of "security" showed that a general partnership interest typically is not considered a security but a limited partnership interest typically is.[74] This division makes sense as a result of the control that a general partnership typically reposes in general partners as opposed to the lack of control characteristic of limited partners in a limited partnership. A limited partner's lack of control means that he or she tends to rely on the efforts of others (the general partners) to achieve a return on his or her investment.

Similarly, a general partnership that places control in the hands of certain managing partners may result in an investment contract with respect to the non-managing partners.[75] And partnership interests sold to a large number of the general public typically would not provide much control to the partners. In that case, at some point, a partnership vote is

---

70 Landreth Timber, 471 U.S. at 685–86.

71 471 U.S. 681.

72 *Id. at* 686.

73 *Id. at* 687, 693.

74 Theresa A. Galbadon, *A Sense of a Security: An Empirical Study*, 25 J. Corp. L. 307, 334–35 (2000).

75 Williamson v. Tucker, 645 F.2d 404, 424 (5th Cir.), *cert denied*, 454 U.S. 897 (1981).

more akin to a shareholder vote than a vote by general partners, and the partnership interest would be considered an investment contract.[76]

One court set forth three non-exclusive factors to determine when a partnership interest or joint venture might result in a security. First, the partnership agreement leaves little authority in the hands of the partners and distributes power more as a limited partnership would distribute power. Second, the investor is inexperienced and unknowledgeable in the field of business. Third, the investor depends on particular skills or abilities of the manager, who cannot easily be replaced.[77] That this court focused attention on the vulnerability of the investors, such as on the extent of their power and control and on their level of experience and knowledge in business, is consistent with a similar undercurrent in *Howey*. As mentioned, the *Howey* Court referenced the vulnerability of persons from far off localities who lacked experience to market citrus groves and who were attracted solely by a return on investment.[78]

Finally, case law regarding when a partnership interest will constitute a security is consistent with general limited partnership doctrine. The law of limited partnerships addresses when a limited partner will exercise control sufficient to deem the limited partner a general partner. A limited partnership must have at least one general partner and one limited partner. The general partner has unlimited liability but the limited partner has the benefit of limited liability, much like a corporate shareholder. If a limited partner has too much power and responsibility, however, the limited partner will be deemed a general partner and lose the benefit of limited liability. Thus, one question bedeviling limited partnerships is how much power in the hands of a limited partner is enough to tip the scales and turn the limited partner into a general partner in the eyes of the law. In both the investment contract analysis and in the general partner versus limited partner context, the answer turns on the amount of power exercised by the limited partner.[79]

Limited Liability Company Interests

A limited liability company, or LLC, is a business vehicle whereby owners can benefit from the limited liability of a corporation and, at the

---

[76] *Id.*

[77] *Id.* at 424.

[78] Howey, 328 U.S. at 299–300.

[79] *See* Liberty Prop. Trust v. Republic Prop. Corp., 577 F.3d 335, 339–41 (D.C. Cir. 2009), *reh'g en banc denied* (Mar 3, 2010).

same time, avoid the double taxation of a corporation.[80] LLC interests are not shares of stock; they resemble partnership interests. A key feature of LLCs is that they provide the parties significant flexibility in developing rules regarding management and control. An LLC can be managed by members, like a general partnership, or by a group of managers, like a corporation. The managers might be LLC members, but they need not be.[81] As a result, LLC interests are non-uniform and determining whether they meet the investment contract definition must be on a case-by-case basis.[82] To determine whether LLC interests were securities in *U.S. v. Leonard*, the court assessed members' control, and how active they were in the management of the enterprise.[83]

Leonard is an interesting case because the organizational documents reposed control with the members. Each member was required to participate in management and received one vote for each LLC unit acquired. Important decisions were submitted to a member vote.[84] As discussed, however, courts put substance over form. The members in *Leonard*, in reality, were inexperienced and unlikely to exercise their rights. They were passive. They seldom voted on LLC matters. Few served on the management committee or other committees. The court concluded that notwithstanding the language of the agreements, there was no reasonable expectation of investor control in the enterprise.[85] *Leonard* demonstrates that a court will look beyond the "bare terms" of a legal agreement to determine whether rights granted to members or partners are meaningful.[86]

This discussion of LLC interests raises the issue of whether the status of an instrument as a security should be elective. Should investors and promoters be permitted to contract around the application of the securities laws by choosing whether an investment is deemed a security? Several of the securities laws, including the Securities Act, contain an anti-waiver provision, which provides that waiver of compliance with any provision of the act, or rules under the act, shall be void.[87] At the same

---

80 James D. Cox & Thomas Lee Hazen, Corporations 16 (2nd ed. 2003).

81 William A. Klein, J. Mark Ramseyer & Stephen M. Bainbridge, Business Associations: Cases and Materials on Agency, Partnerships, and Corporations 268 (8th ed. 2012).

82 U.S. v. Leonard, 529 F.3d 83, 89 (2d Cir. 2008).

83 *Id.* at 89–90.

84 *Id.* at 89.

85 *Id.* at 89–90.

86 *See* SEC v. Merchant Capital, LLC, 483 F.3d 747, 760 (11th Cir. 2007).

87 Securities Act § 14, 15 U.S.C. § 78n.

time, for reasons discussed above, courts hold that member-managed LLC interests are typically not considered securities while limited partnership interests and manager-managed LLC interests are considered securities.[88] Consequently, promoters might be able to choose whether the securities laws will apply by varying the amount of control exercised by LLC members.

This type of election might be appropriate because the decisions are based on economic substance. Establishing a member-managed LLC results in different relationships than those in manager-managed LLCs. The former might not give rise to the same need for the protections of the federal securities laws as the latter. Although it is true that in the former case the promoters avoid the application of the securities laws, LLC members in the former case are engaged in the management of the business and can monitor their interests, thereby obviating the need for further protections.[89]

Real Estate

Ordinary real estate investments, such as the purchase of a home, are generally not considered securities. The facts of each transaction, however, determine whether particular real estate investments could qualify as securities.[90] The offer of post-sale income to buyers, for example, could give rise to an investment contract.[91] The SEC long ago stated that investments in condominium units could be considered securities. Condominiums coupled with rental arrangements, for example, will be considered securities if marketed to highlight the benefits to the purchaser derived from the managerial efforts of a promoter or a third party designated to rent the units.[92] The same is true today. A leading case finding that a sale of a condominium could be a security is *Hocking v.*

---

[88] *See* COX, HILLMAN & LANGEVOORT, *supra* note 17, at 63.

[89] *See generally* Park McGinty, *The Limited Liability Company: Opportunity for Selective Securities Law Deregulation*, 64 U. Cin. L. Rev. 369 (1996); Larry E. Ribstein, *Form and Substance in the Definition of a "Security": The Case of Limited Liability Companies*, 51 WASH. & LEE L. REV. 807 (1994).

[90] Kosnoski v. Bruce, 669 F.2d 944, 947 n.3 (4th Cir. 1982).

[91] *See* COX, HILLMAN & LANGEVOORT, *supra* note 17, at 64. For a state law example, see Mathews v. Cassidy Turley Maryland, Inc. 2013 WL 6182531 *8–9 (Md. Nov. 26, 2013).

[92] Guidelines as to the Applicability of the Federal Securities Laws to Offers and Sales of Condominiums or Units in a Real Estate Development, Securities Act Release No. 5347, 1973 WL 158443 (Jan. 4, 1973).

Dubois.[93] The inability of the real estate agent in *Hocking* to make a binding offer of a rental pool arrangement to the customer did not mean that the arrangement could not be considered part of a package offered to determine if the arrangement was a security.[94] The Ninth Circuit sitting *en banc* concluded that there was an issue of fact as to whether the arrangement was a security. Summary judgment was not appropriate.[95]

Other circuits came to different conclusions, albeit based on different facts. The Second Circuit, for example, has held that a condominium offer is an investment contract only if it has one or more of the following characteristics: (i) a rental arrangement combined with a sales effort to rent the condominium through the condominium manager or its agents; (ii) a rental pool arrangement; or (iii) restrictions on the owner's rights to occupy or rent the unit him or herself, such as requiring that it be available for rental to others for a part of the year.[96] In another case, the Seventh Circuit held that a condominium investment was not an investment contract because it did not provide for an undivided share of the assets and profits of an enterprise.[97]

NOTES AS SECURITIES

Securities Act section 2(a)(1) defines a security as "any note."[98] Thus, one might think that a note would not entail problems of analysis with respect to whether a note is a security. The analysis of a note as a security, however, is equally as thorny as the investment contract analysis.

Short-Term and Long-Term Notes

Although the Securities Act definition of security includes a note, section 3(a)(3) exempts short-term notes from the Act. A note is exempt if it "arises out of a current transaction" or if the proceeds "have been or are

---

93 885 F.2d 1449 (9th Cir. 1999) (en banc), *cert. denied*, 494 U.S. 1078 (1990).

94 *Id.* at 1457.

95 *Id.* at 1458.

96 18 F.3d 81, 89 (2d Cir. 1994).

97 Wals v. Fox Hills Development Corp., 24 F.3d 1016, 1019 (7th Cir. 1994); *see generally* Robert C. Art, *Sell a Condominium, Buy a Securities Lawsuit: Unwarranted Liabilities in the Secondary Market*, 53 OHIO STATE L. J. 413 (1992).

98 Securities Act § 2(a)(1), 15 U.S.C. § 77b(a)(1).

to be used for current transactions" and if the maturity of the note at the time of issuance is not greater than nine months.[99] So far, so good. Notes are securities, but short-term notes are excluded from the definition. The first complexity comes as a result of Securities Act section 17, the general antifraud provision. Section 17 states that the exemptions in section 3 do not apply to section 17.[100] In other words, even if a note under the Act is not considered a security for registration and other purposes, it is still considered a security for antifraud purposes.

This differential treatment of notes in the registration and antifraud provisions of the Act might strike a reader as peculiar. In other contexts, however, courts and regulators apply the antifraud provisions of the securities laws more broadly than the registration provisions. The SEC staff has recognized in another context that the antifraud provisions of the securities laws have broader effect than "purely regulatory" provisions.[101]

There is yet another complexity with respect to notes: the Securities Exchange Act does not provide for this differential treatment. As discussed above, each of the federal securities laws defines the term security, and the definition in the Exchange Act is similar to the definition in the Securities Act.[102] In Exchange Act section 3(a)(10), security is defined as "any note" just as in the Securities Act. Unlike the Securities Act, however, the Exchange Act definition of security expressly excludes short-term notes (notes with a maturity not over nine months). Moreover, the Exchange Act contains no provision stating that short-term notes shall be considered securities for purposes of the Exchange Act's antifraud provision. In the Exchange Act, unlike the Securities Act, short-term notes are excluded from the statute entirely.[103]

This technical difference in definition could have tremendous implications in practice. Both the Securities Act and the Exchange Act contain general antifraud provisions.[104] Only the Exchange Act's antifraud provision, however, has an implied private right of action; most courts have

---

[99] Securities Act § 3(a)(3), 15 U.S.C. § 77c(a)(3).

[100] Securities Act § 17, 15 U.S.C. § 77q (2012).

[101] SEC. & EXCHANGE COMM'N, DIV. OF INV. MGMT., PROTECTING INVESTORS: A HALF CENTURY OF INVESTMENT COMPANY REGULATION 228 (1992), available at http://www.sec.gov/divisions/investment/guidance/icreg50–92.pdf.

[102] *Compare* Securities Exchange Act § 3(a)(10), 15 U.S.C. § 78c(a)(10) (2012), *with* Securities Act § 2(a)(1), 15 U.S.C. § 77b(a)(1).

[103] *See* Reves, 494 U.S. at 80–81 (Rehnquist, C.J., concurring in part and dissenting in part).

[104] *See* Securities Act § 17, 15 U.S.C. § 77q; Exchange Act § 10(b), 15 U.S.C. § 78j(b).

denied a private right of action under the antifraud provision of the Securities Act.[105] Thus, the technical difference discussed here presents a barrier to a private action with regard to a short-term note. Although the Securities Act covers fraud in the offer and sale of a short-term note, the Securities Act provides no clear private right of action under the antifraud provision. And although the Exchange Act provides an implied private right of action for fraud, short-term notes are excluded from the definition of "security" under the Exchange Act in their entirety.

Long-term notes present different types of issues than short-term notes. Long-term notes fit more easily into the statutory definition of security and do not possess the complexity of the exemption for short-term notes. Notwithstanding the clarity of the definition, many believe that certain long-term notes, like mortgages, should not be considered securities.[106] The determination of when a note will be considered a security was taken up by the Supreme Court in *Reves v. Ernst & Young*.[107]

The *Reves* Analysis

The Supreme Court clarified in *Reves* that each word of the statutory definition of "security" must be considered separately.[108] One should not wrap the entire definition of "security" in the *Howey* test for investment contract, notwithstanding the U.S. Supreme Court's language in *Forman*, mentioned above, that the *Howey* analysis contains the critical attributes in all decisions defining a security.[109] In *Reves*, the Supreme Court explicitly rejected using *Howey* to determine if a note is a security. Using the *Howey* test would render superfluous the enumeration of the types of instruments that qualify as securities.[110]

In *Reves*, the Farmers Cooperative of Arkansas and Oklahoma sought to raise money for general business purposes.[111] The co-op had 23,000 members. It sold uncollateralized and uninsured promissory notes, payable on demand, and which paid a variable rate of interest adjusted monthly to keep the rate higher than that paid by local banks. The notes

---

105 *See* Stoneridge Inv. Partners, LLC v. Scientific Atlanta, 552 U.S. 148, 157 (2008) (Exchange Act); Schlifke v. Seafirst Corp., 866 F.2d 935, 943 (7th Cir. 1989) (Securities Act).

106 *See* Cox, Hillman & Langevoort, *supra* note 17, at 73.

107 494 U.S. 56 (1990).

108 Reves, 494 U.S. at 64.

109 Forman, 421 U.S. at 852.

110 Reves, 494 U.S. at 64 (quoting Landreth Timber, 471 U.S. at 692).

111 *Id.* at 58.

were offered to members and non-members alike and marketed as an "Investment Program." Ultimately, 1,600 people held notes worth approximately $10 million when the co-op went bankrupt. The plaintiffs sued the auditor, Arthur Young & Co., later Ernst & Young, alleging deficiencies in the co-op's audit.[112]

In *Reves*, the Court explained that unlike stock, which was more self-evidently a security, not all notes are investments. The term "any note," therefore, should not be interpreted literally. The term must be understood in the context of what Congress was trying to accomplish in the Securities Act.[113] According to *Reves*, several tests have emerged to determine which notes should be considered securities. The first is the "investment versus commercial" test, used by a majority of the courts of appeals. This test attempts to distinguish notes issued in the investment context from those issued in a consumer context. Only the former would be securities.[114] The second is the "family resemblance" test, developed by the Second Circuit.[115] This approach permits an issuer to rebut a presumption that a note is a security by showing that the note has a "strong family resemblance" to items courts generally hold are not securities.[116] Last is the *Howey* test used by the Eighth Circuit and the D.C. Circuit. This approach determines whether an instrument is a note by determining whether it is an investment contract under *Howey*.[117]

The *Reves* Court adopted the family resemblance test.[118] There are several types of notes usually not considered securities, such as consumer financing notes and notes secured by a mortgage on a home.[119] To further refine what makes those notes *not* securities, the *Reves* Court identified four additional factors. The first is the motivation for entering into the transaction. If the motivation is to raise money for the general use of a business or to finance an investment, and the buyer is seeking a profit, it will result in a security; if the motivation is to facilitate the purchase of an asset or pay off short-term debt, it will not.[120] The second is the plan of distribution to assess whether there is common trading for speculation

---

112 *Id.* at 59.
113 *Id.* at 62–63.
114 *Id.* at 63.
115 *Id.* at 63.
116 *Id.* at 63–64.
117 *Id.* at 64.
118 *Id.* at 64–65.
119 *Id.* at 65.
120 *Id.* at 66.

or investment.[121] The third factor examines the reasonable expectations of the investing public. Even if an economic analysis of an instrument suggests it is not a security, a court might be persuaded if the public expects an instrument to be a security.[122] The final factor is risk reduction. This examines whether a mitigating factor, such as the existence of another regulatory scheme, reduces risk and decreases the need for the federal securities laws.[123]

The *Reves* Court applied the four factors and held that the co-op notes were securities. The co-op raised capital for general business purposes and the buyers bought the notes to earn a profit. The notes were offered to 23,000 members and 1,600 people held them. The advertisements held out the notes as "investments." And there was no risk-reducing factor.[124]

Another issue presented by *Reves* harkens back to the question of timing and what qualifies as a short-term note. Recall that the notes in *Reves* were demand notes. They were payable on demand. Notwithstanding this feature, the Court did not consider the notes to have a maturity of less than nine months. If notes are payable on demand, how should one treat them? The *Reves* Court focused on the legislative intent of the securities laws.[125] Although a note payable on demand could be considered a short-term note of less than nine months duration, it could also be paid over a period greater than nine months. Given the ambiguity, the Court resorted to the legislative intent of the securities laws, which was to prevent fraud and abuse across a wide spectrum of investments, and it held that notes payable on demand were not excluded.[126]

Loan Participations

Although bank loans to customers are not securities, banks often market and sell loans to third persons. Thus, a question arises regarding whether loan participations can constitute securities. A leading case is *Banco Español de Credito v. Security Pacific National Bank* from the Second Circuit.[127] The court applied the *Reves* factors discussed above, holding that the loan participations were not securities. The issuer sought to increase lines of credit to the borrower and the borrower needed

---

121 *Id.*
122 *Id.* at 66–67.
123 *Id.* at 67.
124 *Id.* at 68–69.
125 *Id.* at 60–61.
126 *Id.* at 73.
127 973 F.2d 51 (2d Cir. 1992), *cert. denied*, 509 U.S. 903 (1993).

short-term credit to finance current operations. Only institutional and corporate entities were solicited to participate, and the plan of distribution-prohibited resales. The buyers were given notice that the instruments were loan participations and not investments. The Comptroller of the Currency provided additional regulation.[128]

This result, however, was not uncontroversial. It drew a strong dissent sharply criticizing the majority for misreading the facts and making bad banking law and bad securities law.[129] Among other things, the dissent pointed out that 843 entities had purchased loan notes in the program.[130] Two years later, in another Second Circuit case where the investors were not sophisticated, the court came to the opposite result. Applying the *Reves* factors, the court held that mortgage participations were notes.[131]

DERIVATIVES

Owners of options and futures have different rights and responsibilities than owners of traditional stock or debt. Options give the options buyer the right, but not the obligation, to buy or sell an asset at a specific price during a specified time in the future. A futures contract obligates the futures purchaser to buy a specific asset at a specific date in the future, and it obligates the seller to sell and deliver the asset at a specific date unless the position is closed before the contract's expiration. Treatment of these derivative contracts and other derivative instruments under the securities laws is complex and subject to change, particularly in light of the Dodd-Frank Wall Street Reform and Consumer Protection Act of 2010.[132]

The general rule with respect to derivatives has been that options, such as puts and calls, were considered securities, but futures were not. This was the case since 1973, when the SEC began to require options to be registered with the Commission.[133] For a long time, this regulatory treatment made sense. Options, such as puts and calls, were regulated by the SEC while futures were regulated by the U.S. Commodity Futures

---

128 *Id.* at 55.

129 Banco Español, 973 F.2d at 56 (Oakes, C.J., dissenting).

130 *Id.* at 58.

131 Pollack v. Laidlaw Holdings, Inc., 27 F.3d 808, 812 (2d Cir.), *cert. denied*, 513 U.S. 963 (1994).

132 Pub. L. No. 111–203, 124 Stat. 1376 (2010) (codified in scattered sections of 7, 12, 15, 18, 22, 31, and 41 U.S.C. (Supp. IV 2010)).

133 Loss, Seligman & Paredes, *supra* note 4, at 1112.

Trading Commission ("CFTC"), an independent agency created in 1974 to regulate certain derivative instruments.

Derivatives in the United States were primarily focused on futures and forward contracts on agriculture and commodities. The CFTC was created to regulate such products. But as financial products and arrangements grew in complexity, the line of separation between the responsibilities of the SEC and CFTC began to blur.[134] The SEC and CFTC announced in 1981 that they reached agreement with respect to their jurisdictions.

The agreement allocated securities options to SEC regulation. It allocated futures and futures options to CFTC regulation. And foreign currency options were allocated to the regulator of the exchange on which the option traded.[135] The agreement was codified by Congress in 1982.[136]

In 2000, Congress passed the Commodities Futures Modernization Act ("CFMA") to promote innovation in the derivatives market. As a result of the CFMA, over-the-counter derivatives and credit default swaps were largely unregulated.[137] The CFMA amended the definition of security to include security futures, to bring those instruments within the definition of security.[138] But the overall effect of the legislation was deregulatory, precluding the SEC from regulating over-the-counter derivative transactions.[139] Thus, in the years leading up to the financial crisis of 2007 and 2008, over-the-counter derivatives largely escaped regulation by either the SEC or CFTC.[140] The failure of regulation of OTC derivatives bore much of the blame for the financial crisis of 2007 and 2008 and, as a result, the Dodd-Frank Act authorized the SEC and CFTC to limit the systemic risk that derivatives can cause.[141]

A prime example of the expanded regulation brought about by Dodd-Frank is the regulation of swap agreements. The CFMA largely prohibited the SEC and CFTC from regulating the OTC swap markets. Although the SEC had antifraud authority over security-based swap agreements, such as credit-default swaps, the SEC was prohibited from

---

134 Roberta Romano, *The Political Dynamics of Derivative Securities Regulation*, 14 YALE J. ON REG. 279, 357–58 (1997).

135 *Id.* at 357; LOSS, SELIGMAN & PAREDES, *supra* note 4, at 1121.

136 LOSS, SELIGMAN & PAREDES, *supra* note 4, at 1122.

137 *See* COX, HILLMAN & LANGEVOORT, *supra* note 17, at 566.

138 LOSS, SELIGMAN & PAREDES, *supra* note 4, at 857.

139 *Id.* at 1133.

140 *See* COX, HILLMAN & LANGEVOORT, *supra* note 17, at 566.

141 *See id.* at 568.

imposing reporting, record-keeping, or disclosure requirements on such agreements. Dodd-Frank filled this gap by providing for regulation of the OTC swaps market.[142] Under Dodd-Frank, the SEC has authority over security-based swaps and the CFTC has authority over all other swaps, such as agricultural swaps. The two agencies share authority over mixed swaps – those that are security-based but also have a commodity component.[143] Moreover, the SEC has antifraud authority over swaps that are related to securities but that do not fall within the definition of a security-based swap. Dodd-Frank requires the SEC and CFTC to act together to define terms and adopt certain joint rules.[144] These rulemaking initiatives are ongoing as of 2014.

INSURANCE PRODUCTS

The Securities Act in section 3(a)(8) exempts from the definition of "security" insurance policies and annuity contracts issued by a regulated insurance company.[145] As in the context of notes described above, the exemption for insurance contracts is effectively a registration exemption – the exemption is not applicable for purposes of the Securities Act antifraud provision. (As discussed, Securities Act section 17, the antifraud provision, states that the exemptions in section 3 from the definition of "security" do not apply to section 17.)

There is significant support for the proposition that insurance products are altogether exempt from the federal securities laws and that the insurance exemption is merely supererogation, meant to confirm the exemption lest there is any doubt. The Securities Act legislative history states that the exemption "makes clear what is already implied in the act, namely, that insurance policies are not to be regarded as securities subject to the provisions of the act."[146] The House Committee explained that the "entire tenor" of the statute, even without the specific exemption, would lead to exclusion of insurance policies from the Act, and that the specific exemption was included "to make misinterpretation impossible."[147] Moreover, the Supreme Court has noted that "the exemption from

[142] SEC, Dodd-Frank Rulemaking: Derivatives, https://www.sec.gov/spotlight/dodd-frank/derivatives.shtml.
[143] *Id.*
[144] *Id.*
[145] Securities Act § 3(a)(8), 15 U.S.C. § 77c(a)(8).
[146] H.R. Rep. 85, 73d Cong., 1st Sess. 15 (1933).
[147] *Id.*

registration for insurance policies was clearly supererogation."[148] The D.C. Circuit has stated that insurance contracts are "altogether exempt from coverage under the federal securities laws."[149]

The supererogation thesis, however, is not consistent with the statute, which, in section 3, exempts insurance policies and annuity contracts from the definition. As the authors of a leading securities law casebook have explained, although the legislative history may have been clear, the statutory structure leads to a different result. Just as in the case of short-term notes, the section 3 exemption for insurance policies is relevant only for Securities Act registration purposes. The implication, however, is that insurance policies are covered by the antifraud provision.[150]

Another difficulty is determining which products are considered insurance or annuities, which are securities, and which qualify for the registration exemption. The development of variable annuities in the 1950s put this question squarely before the SEC and the courts. In a variable annuity, the annuitant's payments are used to purchase assets in a range of investment options, such as a fund of securities, much like a mutual fund. As a result, the annuitant's account value will vary depending on the performance of the investment options chosen.[151] Whether variable annuities should be considered securities was particularly nettlesome, not only because of the exemption in Securities Act section 3(a)(8), but also because the McCarran-Ferguson Act enacted in 1945 gave the states authority to regulate "the business of insurance" without federal interference, unless federal law provides otherwise.[152]

The issue arose when the SEC tried to enjoin a life insurance company, Variable Annuity Life Insurance Company of America ("VALIC"), from selling variable annuity contracts without SEC registration. Both the district court and the court of appeals sided with VALIC, but the U.S. Supreme Court reversed.[153] The Court recognized that, absent a fixed guarantee, a variable annuity places investment risk on the annuitant. "The holder gets only a pro rata share of what the portfolio of equity

---

148 Tcherepnin, 389 U.S. at 342 n.30.

149 Life Partners, Inc., 87 F.3d at 541.

150 *See* COX, HILLMAN & LANGEVOORT, *supra* note 17, at 472–73.

151 *See* SEC, Office of Investor Education and Advocacy, Variable Annuities: What You Should Know 3 (Sept. 2007), http://www.sec.gov/investor/pubs/sec-guide-to-variable-annuities.pdf.

152 McCarran-Ferguson Act § 2, 15 U.S.C. § 1012 (2012).

153 SEC v. Variable Annuity Life Ins. Co. of Am., 359 U.S. 71 (1959).

interests reflects – which may be a lot, a little, or nothing."[154] Moreover, this case gave rise to other questions about the application of the Investment Company Act to variable annuities. A structure evolved whereby an insurance company would incorporate an investment fund, registered under the Investment Company Act, whose shares were held by the insurance company, although voting power would pass through the insurance company to the contract holders. This separate account was an investment company separate from the insurance company. The security issued was not the variable annuity contract but rather the interest in the investment company separate account.[155]

In a subsequent Supreme Court case, *SEC v. United Benefit Life Insurance Company*,[156] the issue was whether a Flexible Fund Annuity contract was a security. Part of the Flexible Fund was invested in common stock. The contract, however, also guaranteed a fixed payment of a substantial amount.[157] The Supreme Court rejected the lower courts' assumption that the contract must be characterized in its entirety.[158] Once the Court considered the contract separable, it had little problem characterizing the accumulation portion of the Flexible Fund contract as a security. The product competed with mutual funds and was marketed to provide professional investment management.[159]

The insurance industry continues to evolve with new products and services offered each year. In many cases, the products are hybrids with traditional insurance, such as term life insurance, married with traditional investments, such as mutual funds, in novel ways. These products fall on a spectrum. The challenge for courts and regulators will be to analyze such products to determine the extent to which investment risk passes from the insurance company to the contract holder and what regulation is appropriate.[160]

BANKS AND BANK PRODUCTS

In addition to notes and insurance, there are other instruments that would be securities but they are exempt from the definition by the Securities Act section 3(a)(2). As should now be clear, these instruments are still

---

154 *Id.* at 71.
155 *See* LOSS, SELIGMAN & PAREDES, *supra* note 4, at 1039–41.
156 387 U.S. 202 (1967).
157 *Id.* at 205–06.
158 *Id.* at 207.
159 *Id.* at 210–11.
160 *See id.* at 1054.

covered by the antifraud provision of the Securities Act. One example is any security "issued or guaranteed by any bank."[161] A bank is defined as any national bank or banking institution organized under the laws of any state, territory, or the District of Columbia, whose business is "substantially confined" to banking and is supervised by the state, banking commission, or similar body.[162] This definition suggests that securities issued or guaranteed by bank holding companies are not exempt.[163] What about institutions similar to banks, such as industrial loan companies? In some cases, the SEC staff has written no-action letters to give relief based on the entities' functional equivalence to banks.[164]

A similar problem arises with U.S. branches of foreign banks. This issue is doubly hard because the International Banking Act of 1978 prohibits discriminatory treatment of U.S. branches of foreign banks. On many occasions, the SEC staff provided no-action relief allowing the exemption for banks to apply to foreign banks as long as certain conditions were met. In 1986, the SEC codified this treatment in a Securities Act release.[165] The SEC stated that for purposes of the registration exemption in Securities Act section 3(a)(2), the Commission would deem a branch or agency of a foreign bank located in the United States to be a bank as long as the "nature and extent" of federal or state regulation and supervision of the branch or agency was "substantially equivalent" to domestic banks doing business in the same jurisdiction.[166]

Certificates of deposit or other notes that might not be considered securities can be repackaged and sold, thereby transforming an instrument that was not a security into one. Certificates of deposit are not typically considered securities. Although the term "certificate of deposit" appears in the definition of "security," in *Marine Bank v. Weaver*, the Supreme Court held that "certificate of deposit" in the definition of "security" does not refer to bank-issued certificates of deposit.[167] The Court held that certificates of deposit are issued by banks and subject to

---

161 Securities Act § 3(a)(2), 15 U.S.C. § 77c(a)(2).

162 *Id.*

163 *See* Hewlett-Packard Financing Co., SEC No-Action Letter, 1992 WL 335320 (Oct. 7, 1992).

164 *See, e.g.,* Morris Plan Co. of Calif., SEC No-Action Letter, 1990 WL 286795 (May 7, 1990); *see* COX, HILLMAN & LANGEVOORT, *supra* note 17, at 459.

165 Securities Issued or Guaranteed by United States Branches or Agencies of Foreign Banks, Securities Act Release No. 6661 (Sept. 23, 1986), 1986 WL 703870.

166 *Id.*

167 455 U.S. at 557–59.

comprehensive regulation.[168] They are different from long-term debt obligations; holders are virtually guaranteed payment. Certificates of deposit and other notes, however, can become securities when repackaged by a broker-dealer or other intermediary. Merrill Lynch, for example, offered customers bank certificates of deposit. In doing so, Merrill Lynch played key roles screening the banks, negotiating with them, and monitoring their creditworthiness. In a case challenging the broker-dealer's conduct, the court concluded that the sale of the certificates of deposit depended on Merrill Lynch's financial and managerial expertise and, therefore, the instruments were transformed to securities.[169]

STATE REGULATION

Although the focus of this Chapter has been federal regulation of securities and the definition of security as applied by the SEC and the federal courts, state law remains important, particularly in the antifraud context. A glance at state law is illuminating because of contrasts with federal law.

State courts often define "security" more broadly than federal courts. Many state courts view the role of state securities regulation as different from the role of federal regulation. State courts view state securities regulation primarily as promoting investor protection. By contrast, states view federal regulation as protecting the integrity of the securities markets that have become increasingly nationalized over the years.[170] Thus an early definition of "investment contract" offered by a state court appears broader than the *Howey* formulation. In 1920, years before the federal Securities Act was enacted, the Minnesota Supreme Court stated, "The placing of capital or laying out of money in a way intended to secure income or profit from its employment is an 'investment' as that word is commonly used and understood."[171]

Indeed, state courts criticized the *Howey* test as too rigid. One leading state case, *State v. Hawaii Market*, explained that the "primary weakness" of *Howey* is that it has led courts to analyze investments mechanically,

---

[168] *Id.* at 557.

[169] Gary Plastic Packaging Corp. v. Merrill Lynch, Pierce, Fenner & Smith, 756 F.2d 230, 240–41 (2d Cir. 1985).

[170] *See* King v. Pope, 91 S.W.3d 314, 319–20 (Tenn. 2002).

[171] State v. Gopher Tire & Rubber Co., 177 N.W. 937, 938 (Minn. 1920).

"based on a narrow concept of investor participation."[172] The criticism was that courts have become "entrapped in polemics" over the word "solely" and lost site of the fundamental value of investor protection, even in those situations where an investor actively participates in the business.[173]

As a result, *Hawaii Market* attempted to focus attention on economic realities. The court set forth a four-part test for investment contract, with strong echoes of *Howey*. The test is as follows: an offeree furnishes value, a portion of which is subject to the risks of the enterprise, the offeror makes promises or representations that create an understanding that the offeree will receive a benefit, and the offeree has no right to exercise practical or actual control over management of the enterprise.[174] This test focuses on *risk capital*, the idea that the investor was induced to risk his or her capital in the enterprise and did so based on promises and representations of the offeror.[175] In *Forman*, the Supreme Court was urged to adopt the "risk capital" approach and declined.[176] State courts seem to recognize that the U.S. Supreme Court reassessed the *Howey* definition of "investment contract" in its post-*Howey* cases and in *Forman*, articulated a better, broader test.[177] Still many state courts view the *Hawaii Market* formulation as more apt to protect investors.[178]

EMERGENT THEMES IN THE DEFINITION OF "SECURITY"

The definition of the term "security" has so many facets and complexities that it is difficult to arrive at generally applicable trends. Are there broad themes or principles that one can bring to bear when trying to discern whether a security exists? This section draws from the previous sections of the Chapter and discusses three themes one should bear in mind when trying to decide whether a given instrument will be considered a security. The three themes are the amount of risk posed to the investor, the presence of alternative regulation, and the SEC's prosecutorial discretion.

---

172 State v. Hawaii Market, 485 P.2d 105, 108 (Haw. 1971).

173 *Id.* at 108–09.

174 *Id.* at 109.

175 *See* Silver Hills Country Club v. Sobieski, 361 P.2d 906, 907–09 (Cal. 1961).

176 Forman, 421 U.S. at 857 n.24.

177 *See* King, 91 S.W.3d at 321.

178 *Id.* at 324.

Risk

The first theme is the risk of the investment. If one were to focus on the concluding language of *Howey*, risk should matter little in the calculus of whether a security exists. Toward the end of the opinion, the Supreme Court wrote that it is "immaterial" whether an enterprise is speculative or non-speculative, or whether the property has no intrinsic value.[179] Thus, according to *Howey*, the risk and speculative nature of an investment is irrelevant. Other cases, however, suggest that risk is important. In *Edwards*, the Court was worried about the risk of the investment scheme to unsophisticated investors.[180] Investments marketed as low risk are particularly attractive to older and less sophisticated investors, who are more vulnerable to fraud.[181] And, as discussed above, the *Howey* Court focused on the vulnerability of investors visiting Florida from out of town and who lacked the necessary skills and tools for the cultivation, harvesting, and marketing of citrus.[182]

Perhaps the resolution of the apparently conflicting language in *Howey* is that the risk about which courts are concerned is risk of fraud, not necessarily the speculative nature of an investment. It may be hard to separate the two because the more speculative an investment, the greater the chance that an investor, through misrepresentations or omissions, might be misled to believe the investment is safer than it really is. But given that the securities laws are based on a philosophy of full disclosure, it makes sense that courts would worry less about pure speculation, which can be addressed through disclosure, than about how an investor might be deceived regarding the investment's characteristics.[183]

Alternate Regulation

The second theme to bear in mind is the presence of another regulatory scheme. This factor has appeared in a sufficient number of Supreme Court cases defining a "security" that it cannot be ignored. As discussed, in *Reves*, the Court included the presence of another regulatory scheme as the fourth factor to help determine which notes should not be considered securities.[184] In *International Brotherhood of Teamsters v.*

---

179 Howey, 328 U.S. at 301.
180 Edwards, 540 U.S. at 394–95.
181 *Id.* at 394.
182 Howey, 328 U.S. at 299–300.
183 *See* SEC v. Capital Gains Research Bur., Inc., 375 U.S. 180, 186 (1963).
184 *See supra* note 123 and accompanying text.

Daniel, the Court pointed to comprehensive regulation by the Employee Retirement Income Security Act ("ERISA") to demonstrate that pension fund interests were not securities.[185] According to the Court, the enactment of ERISA "put the matter to rest" because ERISA dealt explicitly with pension plans. Since Congress was filling a regulatory void with ERISA, it must be the case that the securities laws were not applicable or there would have been no void to fill.[186]

Similarly, in *Marine Bank v Weaver*, the Court stated that the certificate of deposit was issued by a federally regulated bank and subject to comprehensive banking regulation.[187] What's more, in *Marine Bank*, the Court acknowledged that the reason the pension plan interest in *Daniel* was not considered a security was the existence of an alternative regulatory scheme. Thus, the *Marine Bank* Court not only invoked alternative regulation in its decision not to impose securities regulation, it went further and endorsed a previous court's use of alternative regulation as a key reason to avoid securities regulation.[188]

Courts are sensitive to the fact that too much regulation might be overly burdensome and that regulation of certain transactions, particularly certain note transactions, is better left to other regulatory schemes.[189] The First Circuit explained that note transactions often involve loan agreements, sales agreements, deeds of trust, mortgages, and personal security agreements. These agreements are governed by other federal laws such as the Truth in Lending Act, the Magnuson-Moss Warranty Act, and the antitrust laws, and by state laws, such as the Uniform Commercial Code and unfair and deceptive acts and practices statutes. As a result, regulation of certain transactions should be left to these other laws, particularly since the securities laws are onerous. Subjecting the maker of every note to the Securities Act's reporting requirements would "paralyze the business community rather than assist in the free flow of capital as Congress intended."[190]

Similarly, some courts have held that even the presence of a foreign regulatory scheme can sufficiently protect investors to obviate the need for federal securities regulation. When a bank, for example, is sufficiently regulated that there is almost no risk of insolvency that would prevent the

---

185 439 U.S. 551, 569–70 (1979).

186 *Id.*

187 455 U.S. 551, 558 (1982).

188 *Id.* at 558 n.7.

189 *See* Futura Dev. Corp. v. Centex Corp., 761 F.2d 33, 39 (1st Cir. 1985), *cert. denied*, 474 U.S. 850.

190 *Id.*

bank from repaying a holder of its certificates of deposit, the certificate of deposit will not be considered a security. Can foreign regulation qualify? The answer for some courts is yes. In *Wolf v. Banco Nacional de Mexico, S.A.*, the Second Circuit explained that the parties conceded that Mexico's regulation provided certificate holders with the same degree of protection as U.S. law.[191] Because Mexican regulation provided protection equivalent to that in the United States, the certificates of deposit were not considered securities under the Securities Act.[192]

Prosecutorial Discretion

Finally, one should consider prosecutorial discretion in trying to determine when the SEC or another regulator will take an interest in whether an instrument is a security. As one might imagine, regulators tend to be concerned with securities law violations in cases of fraud or where investors have been injured. Although selling unregistered securities is itself a violation of law,[193] regulators are less likely to devote resources to a case where the only violation is the sale of unregistered securities. A review of the SEC's 2013 Annual Report discussing Major Enforcement Cases suggests that registration cases are not a high priority. The SEC highlighted actions related to the financial crisis, market structure cases, Foreign Corrupt Practices Act cases, financial fraud cases, insider trading matters, and other cases alleging fraud, manipulation, or investor harm. The report, however, is shorn of reference to cases focusing on the failure to register instruments that should be considered securities.[194] In a 2013 speech, SEC Chair Mary Joe White set forth enforcement priorities for the agency. Even where Chair White discussed the breadth of coverage desired, she focused on four areas: advisors and funds, accounting fraud, insider trading, microcap securities fraud. It is no surprise that registration violations did not make the list.[195]

The *Howey* case was an example of an SEC action for failure to register securities sold to investors. A closer look at *Howey*, however,

---

[191] 739 F.2d 1458, 1463 (9th Cir. 1984), *cert. denied*, 469 U.S. 1108 (1985).

[192] *Id.* at 1463–64.

[193] *See supra* note 2 and accompanying text.

[194] *See* Securities and Exchange Commission, Fiscal Year 2013 Agency Financial Report, Appendix B: Major Enforcement Cases 127–144 (2013), http://www.sec.gov/about/secpar/secafr2013.pdf.

[195] SEC Chair Mary Joe White, Deploying the Full Enforcement Arsenal, SEC Speech, Sept. 26, 2013, http://www.sec.gov/News/Speech/Detail/Speech/1370539841202#_ftnref11.

suggests that, even there, the SEC may well have been concerned about possible fraud. There are at least five reported decisions that pre-date *Howey* where plaintiffs allege fraud against W.J. Howey or related entities.[196] There can be little doubt that the SEC was aware of these matters when it pursued its case. In its brief in the *Howey* matter, the SEC wrote that it was not suggesting that the program in *Howey* was adopted for an improper purpose. Then the SEC continued, "The fact remains, however, that the sale of property in conjunction with a contract for its development has been and still is a rather common device by which fraudulent promoters have sought to escape the applicability of securities laws."[197] Thus, *Howey* was a registration case but the potential for fraud was not far off.

CONCLUSION

The definition of the term "security" is rich in complexity and nuance. There is much ground to cover and this Chapter provided an overview of some main topics. The definition of "security" begins with the securities statutes but moves quickly to case law, particularly for the definition of "investment contract." The definition of the term "investment contract" is itself a vast topic with nuances surrounding the variations of horizontal and vertical commonality. Moreover, this topic is in flux as is clear by the SEC's changed view regarding whether broad vertical commonality should satisfy the requirement. The variation in the circuit courts regarding commonality suggests that the Supreme Court, at some point, will address the issue and provide clarity.

Aside from the term "investment contract," there are many other areas where courts are called on to define "security," such as when notes are securities, or when business interests, such as stock, partnership interests, or LLC interests qualify as securities. One consideration is that, in some cases, other legal doctrines help with the definition of "security." In the context of limited partnerships, for example, the same general analysis used to determine whether a limited partner should be deemed a general partner can be applied to determine whether a partner has sufficient

---

[196] Brite v. W.J. Howey Co., 81 F.2d 840 (5th Cir. 1936); Cowan v. Orange Belt Sec. Co., 194 So. 489 (Fla. 1940); Patzman v. Howey, 100 S.W.2d 851 (Mo. 1936); Pepple v. Rogers, 140 So. 205 (1932); Stoltzfus v. Howey, 54 S.W.2d 501 (Mo. App. 1932).

[197] Brief of the Securities and Exchange Commission, Appellant at 39–40, SEC v. W.J. Howey Co, 328 U.S. 293 (1946), 1946 WL 50582.

control so that the partner does not rely on the efforts of others and, therefore, no security exists.

Although one can try to arrive at broad themes governing the definition of "security," doing so is not necessarily fruitful because decisions are often made on a case-by-case basis. A case-by-case analysis is unavoidable particularly because the Supreme Court has admonished that substance prevails over form and economic realities are what matter most. Still, one might consider the relative risk of an investment and whether investors are protected through an alternative regulatory structure. When deciding whether regulators will have an interest in bringing an action alleging that a security exists, one should also consider that regulators generally are most concerned with fraud or investor harm.

3. The integrated disclosure system

Rigers Gjyshi

INTRODUCTION

The Securities Act of 1933[1] ("1933 Act") followed the economic collapse of 1929 that led to the Great Depression. The goal of the 1933 Act was to ensure transparency in the financial system by mandating disclosures of material information to prospective investors through required securities registrations. The 1933 Act represented the first major involvement of the federal government in the regulation of securities offered for sale to the public, though certainly not the last.

As the securities industry evolved, so did the regulatory arena under the 1933 Act. Generally speaking, the 1933 Act enables buyers and sellers of securities to make an informed decision by ensuring adequate disclosure of information and preventing purposeful manipulation of that information. In 1982, the SEC formally adopted the concept of integrated disclosure, which combined disclosures under the 1933 Act with those required under the Securities Exchange Act of 1934 ("1934 Act"). Some scholars had advocated for some time, with the main goal of revising or eliminating duplicative disclosure requirements with the hope of reducing the burden on registrants while still ensuring that market participants had access to adequate information.[2]

---

1 15 U.S.C. § 77a *et seq.*

2 *See* Adoption of Integrated Disclosure System, SEC Release No. AS-306 (Mar. 3, 1982) [hereinafter 1982 Release]. The 1982 Release was the culmination of a series of SEC releases designed to modernize the disclosure system under the 1933 and 1934 Acts. *See, e.g.*, Reproposal of Comprehensive Revision to System for Registration of Securities Offerings, SEC Release No. 33–6331 (Aug. 18, 1981); Proposed Revision of Regulation S-K and Guides for the Preparation and Filing of Registration Statements and Reports, SEC Release No. 6276 (Dec. 23, 1980); Proposed Revision of Regulation C, Registration and Regulation 12B, Registration and Reporting, SEC Release No. 6333 (Aug. 6, 1981); Delayed or Continuous Offering and Sale of Securities, SEC Release No. 6334 (Aug. 18, 1981); Circumstances Affecting the Determination of What Constitutes Reasonable Investigation and Reasonable Grounds for Belief Under Section 11 of the

In 2005, the SEC adopted sweeping changes to registration and other requirements under the 1933 Act designed to further modernize the securities offering and communication processes.[3] The goal behind the 2005 reforms was to shift the attention away from specific transactions and focus instead on company registration. Under the concept of company registration, the 1933 Act's registration and disclosure burdens would move from transactions to issuers, and individual issuers would take additional steps as necessary for disclosure and registration of individual offerings.[4] For example, larger companies that are active market participants and that continually provide information to regulators and the public, could leverage existing disclosures and supplement those disclosures with transaction-specific information to meet the requirements under the 1933 Act.

The crux behind the 2005 reforms was the leveraging of 1934 Act disclosures to facilitate the capital raising process. Congress enacted the 1934 Act to ensure continuous disclosure of material information after the registration statement filed under the 1933 Act becomes stale.[5] The main goal of the 1934 Act was thus the regulation of securities trading after the initial offering. The 1934 Act accomplishes this goal predominantly by regulating industry professionals who trade these securities, for example brokers and dealers of securities, the markets in which this secondary trading takes place, and by requiring companies to disclose continuously material information for specific periods. To ensure compliance with these goals, the 1934 Act created the Securities and Exchange Commission ("SEC") and gave it broad powers over the securities industry, including the power to require companies whose securities are traded on an exchange on a continuous basis to report material information through periodic filings with the SEC.

The information contained in these disclosures is the type that market participants would need to make an informed decision regarding the

---

Securities Act Treatment of Information Incorporated by Reference Into Registration Statements, SEC Release No. 6335 (Aug. 6, 1981); Disclosure of Security Ratings in Registration Statements, SEC Release No. 6336 (Aug. 6, 1981); Integrated Disclosure: Proposed Implementing Amendments to Rules and Forms Under the Securities Act of 1933 and Rescission of Obsolete Forms, SEC Release No. 6337 (Aug. 6, 1981).

[3] *See* Securities Offering Reform, SEC Release No. 75, 2005 WL 1692642, (Aug. 3, 2005) [hereinafter 2005 Release].

[4] *Id.* at *6.

[5] The 1934 Act (as amended) regulates numerous areas of the securities industry that are beyond the scope of this Chapter, which focuses mainly on the continuous disclosure requirements under the 1934 Act.

value of the securities sold in the marketplace. Like the disclosure requirements under the 1933 Act, the SEC does not guarantee that the information contained in the 1934 Act disclosures is accurate, but companies face stiff penalties, as well as civil and administrative liability, for failing to disclose material information or for disclosing inaccurate information.

The upside of required disclosure under the 1934 Act is the ability of certain issuers to leverage said disclosures to comply with the 1933 Act registration requirements when they issue new securities in a secondary offering. Certain issuers who have already complied with 1934 Act disclosure requirements have a lesser registration burden when it comes to offering new securities to the public. An added benefit to relying on the 1934 Act information is that it requires prompt disclosure of the material changes in the financial condition or operations of the issuer, which is not the case under the 1933 Act. This concept of integrated disclosure recognizes the reality that most new public offerings come from companies that already disclose substantial information under the 1934 Act, giving investors sufficient information to make an informed decision on the value of the company.

MANDATORY DISCLOSURE OF INFORMATION UNDER THE 1933 ACT

The 1933 Act aims at providing adequate information to investors so they can make an informed decision regarding the value of a particular class of securities that a company sells or offers for sale to the public. It accomplishes this goal by: (i) requiring issuers to file a registration statement containing full and fair disclosures of all material facts necessary to an accurate determination of the value of the securities; and (ii) requiring issuers to furnish potential investors with a statutory prospectus designed to disclose sufficient material information to enable an informed decision. This approach covers in impressive thoroughness material information about the offering (e.g., price, intended use of proceeds, underwriters, etc.) and material information about the issuer (e.g., its business, property, contracts, lawsuits, etc.), which in tandem provide a full picture to prospective investors.[6]

---

[6] Milton Cohen, *Truth in Securities Revisited*, 79 Harv. L. Rev. 1340 (1966).

The 1933 Act, however, does not guaranty the information disclosed is accurate. It merely requires disclosure and allows investors to recover in case of inadequate or misleading disclosure.

Required Filings with the SEC

Section 5 of the 1933 Act sets forth the registration framework for public securities. Section 5 prohibits any person from offering to either buy or sell a security while making use of the instrumentalities of interstate commerce before the issuer files a registration statement.[7]

Section 5(a) prohibits the sale[8] of a security using the channels and instrumentalities of interstate commerce, through a prospectus or otherwise, unless a registration statement is in effect.[9] Section 5(a) has evolved to accommodate trading realities of an evolving securities market place. Under the original version, Section 5(a) prohibited sales or actual sales of a security prior to the registration statement becoming effective. This imposed an undue burden on issuers who were unable to create sufficient initial interest as they were unable to communicate with underwriters and other parties who actually carry out the offering. In 1954, Congress amended Section 5 to allow communications with professionals who were involved in carrying out the offering.

Generally, once a company files a registration statement, it must wait for it to become effective. This known as the "waiting period" and companies are subject to specific rules during this period. Once the registration statement is filed, Section 5(b) prohibits sales of securities without first providing a statutory prospectus that meets the requirements of the 1933 Act.[10] However, during the waiting period, companies can make oral solicitations of interest, but written offers are only allowed if

---

[7] 15 U.S.C. § 77e. *Accord* Offers and Sales of Securities By Underwriters and Dealers, SEC Release No. 33–4697 (May 28, 1964).

[8] Section 2(a)(3) defines "sale" or "sell" to include every contract of sale or disposition of a security or interest in a security, for value. 15 U.S.C. § 77b(a)(3).

[9] 15 U.S.C. § 77e(a).

[10] 15 U.S.C. § 77j. *See also* Thomas Hazen, Securities Regulation 109 (2003).

they are in the form of a "red herring" or preliminary prospectus,[11] a summary prospectus,[12] or a tombstone ad.[13]

The prospectus is usually the only part of the registration statement that goes to the investors, and it serves the dual (and often conflicting) objective of providing sufficient disclosures to and creating interest from investors about the offering.[14] Section 2(a)(10) defines the term "prospectus" to include any communication, written or by radio or television, which offers any security for sale or confirms the sale of any security.[15] However, a communication provided after the effective date of the registration is not considered a prospectus if it is shown that prior to or at the same time with such communication the seller sent or gave a written prospectus meeting the requirements of Section 10(a).[16] In 2005, the SEC adopted the "access equals delivery" model through Rule 172, pursuant to which there is a presumption that investors have access to the internet, and issuers and intermediaries can satisfy the delivery requirements by posting the documents on a website and informing buyers of the website's address.[17] Note, however, that the "access equals delivery" model only applies to the final prospectus, and not to delivery obligations for preliminary prospectuses for initial offers.

To complement Rule 172, the SEC adopted Rule 173, which requires each underwriter or dealer participating in a registered offering to provide, within two days of a sale, a copy of the final prospectus, or a statement that the sale was part of a registered offering pursuant to which a final prospectus would have been delivered were it not for Rule 172.[18]

---

[11] Rule 433 (17 C.F.R. § 230.433). Rule 433 contains specific conditions depending on the type of issuer. The "red herring" refers to the red disclaimer on the front page informing investors that the registration statement is still not effective and that the prospectus is not yet final.

[12] 15 U.S.C. § 77j(b). SEC Rules 434, 434A (17 C.F.R. §§ 230.434 and 230.434a).

[13] SEC Rule 134 (17 C.F.R. § 230.134).

[14] *See* Carl W. Schneider, Joseph M. Manko and Robert S. Kant, *Going Public—Practice, Procedure and Consequences*, 27 Villanova L. Rev. 1 (1981).

[15] 17 U.S.C. § 77b(a)(1).

[16] *Id.*

[17] 17 C.F.R. § 230.172. Under this rule, the SEC will deem a final prospectus to precede or accompany a security for sale for purposes of Section 5(b) as long as a final prospectus, as defined under Section 10(a), is filed as part of the registration statement.

[18] 17 C.F.R. § 230.173. An investor can also request a prospectus, which the underwriter or dealer must provide by the settlement date. *Id.*

Since 1954, Section 5(c) of the 1933 Act prohibits offers to sell or buy a security prior to the issuer filing a registration statement with the SEC. Section 2a(3) defines "offer to sell" or "offer for sale" to include every attempt or offer to dispose of, or solicitation of an offer to buy, a security or interest in a security, for value.[19] However, the definition excludes communications between the issuer and underwriters with whom they are in privity of contract.[20] Moreover, once the registration statement becomes effective, offering participants can only make written offers through a statutory prospectus; however, they may use additional written offering materials as long as they are accompanied by a final prospectus that satisfies Section 10(a).[21]

An issue that comes up with some frequency, especially in high profile IPOs, is excessive publicity during the prefiling period, which may constitute an "offer to sell" under the 1933 Act.[22] For example, in *SEC v. Arvida Corp*, the SEC sought to enjoin the IPO of a company where the issuer, control person and underwriters had issued a press release disclosing the IPO plan, including the target share price, location and extent of the corporation's holding and future business plans, as well as

---

[19] 15 U.S.C. § 77b(a)(3). It quickly became clear that the definition of the term "offer" was much broader than its common law definition. *See* Diskin v. Lomasney & Co., 452 F.2d 871 (2d. Cir. 1971); SEC v. Cavanagh, 1 F.Supp. 2d 337 (S.D.N.Y. 1998). *See also* Guidelines for the Release of Information by Issuers Whose Securities are in Registration, SEC Release No. 33–5180 (Aug. 16, 1971) (the publication of information and publicity efforts, made in advance of a proposed financing which have the effect of conditioning the public mind or arousing public interest in the issuer or in its securities constitutes an offer).

[20] *Id. Accord* Offers and Sales of Securities by Underwriters and Dealers, SEC Release No. 33–4697 (May 28, 1964) (this means that discussion of financing the offering is allowed between the issuer and the underwriter or underwriters, but neither the issuer nor the underwriter may offer the security to investors or dealers, and dealers are prohibited from offering to buy the securities during this period). *See also* S.E.C. v. Cavanagh, 1 F.Supp.2d 337, 368 (S.D.N.Y. 1998). ([The definition of an "offer"] has been interpreted as going well beyond the common law concept of an offer. Thus, "sale of unregistered, unlegended shares of corporate participant in merger by management shareholders of such corporation violated registration requirements of Securities Act.").

[21] *See* 15 U.S.C. § 77b(a)(10); Section 5(b)(1) (15 U.S.C. § 77e(b)(1)).

[22] *See* Publication of Information Prior to or After the Filing and Effective Date of a Registration Statement Under the Securities Act of 1933, SEC Release No. 5009 (Oct. 7, 1969).

the estimated size of the offering, without filing a registration statement.[23] The SEC found that the press release had generated enough support from brokers, dealers and the investing public to generate at least $500,000 on behalf of the issuer, and it constituted an "offer to sell" under Section 5(c) the 1933 Act.

SEC's tolerance for pre-filing communications has changed over the years. In 1995, the SEC issued a proposed rule allowing Regulation A issuers to "test the waters" before engaging in the expensive and time consuming effort of filing a registration statement as part of an IPO for offerings by small companies.[24] There was an industry push to apply this test-the-waters provision beyond Regulation A offerings, signaling a shift in the approach to the registration process under the 1933 Act.

Participants who violate the preceding rules are said to engage in "gun jumping." Moreover, the distinction between a sale and an offer to sell, though nuanced, becomes important when it comes to the liability that may attach to defective or fraudulent registration statements under Section 11 of the 1933 Act.

Modern Communication Rules

The "gun jumping" provisions of the 1933 Act were created at a time when communication tools were different from current ones. Technological advances, however, have changed the availability of information significantly, with the average investor having wide access to information that a company discloses voluntarily or pursuant to regulatory requirements. Recognizing this change, the SEC shifted its attention from the availability of the information toward ensuring the information was materially accurate and complete. Today, the focus is on the type of issuer, the issuer's reporting history and its market capitalization.

As part of these changes, the SEC defines all methods of communications, with the exception of oral communications, as written communications for purposes of the 1933 Act.[25] Under the modern rules, internet

---

[23] 169 F.Supp. 211 (S.D.N.Y. 1958). The defendants unsuccessfully argued that the press release was not an offer to sell but a legitimate news item of general financial news interest that furthers the 1933 Act's goal of full and fair disclosure, and such disclosure was necessary to enable the issuer to procure interim financing for the offer.

[24] *See* Solicitations of Interest Prior to an Initial Public Offering, Release No. 33–7188 (Jun. 27, 1995).

[25] 2005 Release, *supra* note 3, at *19.

communications are considered graphic communications,[26] bringing it under the definition of written communications.[27] This, however, excludes real time communications through the use of a phone or other means in front of a live audience, e.g., internet video presentations.[28]

Generally, communication rules consist of the following subcategories:

---

[26] The SEC defines "graphic communications" to include any form of electronic media, such as audiotapes, videotapes, facsimiles, CD-ROM, electronic mail, Internet websites, computers, computer networks, and other forms of computer data compilation. *See* Use of Electronic Media, SEC Release No. 33–7856 (Apr. 28, 2000).

[27] The SEC defines "written communications" as communications that are written, printed, or television or radio broadcast (regardless of the transmission means), or graphic communications. 2005 Release, *supra* note 3, at *19. All other communications that fall outside of this definition are considered "oral communications."

[28] The SEC explained that while written communications do not include an individual voicemail, they would include voicemails that are disseminated to a broad audience contemporaneously: so-called "blast" voicemails. 2005 Release, *supra* note 3, n. 97. The crux of the issue appears to be whether participant communicated the information to a live audience. The SEC provides the following examples:

> A live telephone call is not a written communication;
>
> A live telephone call that is recorded by the recipient is not a written communication;
>
> E-mails, facsimiles and electronic postings on web sites are graphic communications.
>
> A live, in-person road show to a live audience is not a written communication
>
> A live, in real-time road show to a live audience that is transmitted graphically is not a graphic communication even if it is transmitted to an overflow room;
>
> A webcast or video conference that originates live and in real-time at the time of transmission and is transmitted through video conferencing facilities or is webcast in real-time to a live audience is not a graphic communication, even if an audience member can record the webcast or video conference;
>
> A live telephone call or video or webcast conference that is recorded by or on behalf of the originating party or parties and then transmitted, or is otherwise transmitted other than live and in real-time, will be a graphic communication and therefore a written communication;
>
> A live telephone call or video or webcast conference that is recorded by the recipient and then re-transmitted by the recipient is a graphic communication by the recipient when it is re-transmitted; and
>
> An interview with an issuer's chief executive officer conducted live as part of a television program is a written communication regardless of how the television signal is transmitted (whether over the airwaves, or through cable,

1. Regularly released factual business information;
2. Regularly released forward-looking information;
3. Communications made more than 30 days before filing a registration statement;
4. Communications by well-known seasoned issuers during the 30 days before filing a registration statement;
5. Written communications made in accordance with the safe harbor in Rule 134; and
6. Written communications (other than a statutory prospectus) by any eligible issuer after filing a registration statement.[29]

To accommodate operational realities, the SEC allows prefiling communications by issuers regarding important business and financial developments. Thus, Rule 135 exempts from the definition of an "offer" communications regarding proposed rights offerings, proposed exchange offerings and proposed offerings of a security if it includes a legend (i.e., a notice that the communication is not an offer of securities for sale).[30]

Under the modern regulatory framework, certain issuers are allowed additional leeway from the gun-jumping provision. For example, well-known seasoned issuers filing for automatic shelf registration are free to engage in any communication (oral or written), even if it is by virtue of a free-writing prospectus.[31]

Moreover, all reporting issuers can publish regularly released factual business information, including forward-looking information under Rule 168.[32] For non-reporting issuers, the SEC allows publication of regularly released business information as long as it is intended for use by non-invertors.[33]

---

satellite, or Internet) and regardless of how it is received by the recipient (whether a television set or a computer). 2005 Release, *supra* note 3, at *20.

[29] 2005 Release, *supra* note 3, at *21.

[30] 17 C.F.R. § 230.135. The notice must have limited content, which depends on the type of the offering.

[31] Rule 405 defines a "free-writing prospectus" as any written communication that constitutes an offer to sell or a solicitation of an offer to buy the securities in a registered offering that is used after the registration statement is filed. 17 C.F.R. § 230.405. Rules 164 and 433 allow all issuers to use free-writing prospectuses after filing a registration statement, subject to certain conditions. *See* 17 C.F.R. §§ 230.164 and 230.433.

[32] 17 C.F.R. § 230.168. Rule 168 does not allow technical compliance with its provisions if it is a part of efforts to evade the registration requirements, thus the SEC will look through the form of the transaction to its substance.

[33] 17 C.F.R. § 230.169.

Under Rule 163A, communications by issuers more than 30 days before filing a registration statement are not prohibited offers as long as they do not reference a securities offering that is or will be the subject of a registration statement.[34] Additionally, under Rules 164 and 433, all issuers and offering participants can use free-writing prospectuses after the filing of the registration statement, with some conditions.[35]

Table 3.1 provides a summary for modern communication rules.[36]

Table 3.1 Summary of modern communication rules governing IPOs

	Could it be an offer?	Is it a prospectus?	Is it a prohibited pre-filing offer for purposes of Section 5(c)?	Is it a prohibited prospectus for purposes of Section 5(b)(1)?
Regularly Released Factual Business Information	Yes..........	No..........	Rule defines it as not an offer for Section 5(c) purposes	Section 5(b)(1) relates only to "prospectuses"—it is not applicable
Regularly Released Forward-Looking Information	Yes..........	No..........	Rule defines it as not an offer for Section 5(c) purposes	Section 5(b)(1) relates only to "prospectuses"—it is not applicable
Communications Made More than 30 Days Before Filing of Registration Statement	Yes..........	Possibly, based on facts and circum-stances	Rule defines it as not an offer for Section 5(c) purposes	Section 5(b)(1) does not apply in the pre-filing period—it is not applicable
Well-Known Seasoned Issuers—Oral Offers Made Within 30 Days of Filing of Registration Statement	Yes..........	No..........	Is exempted from prohibition of Section 5(c)	Section 5(b)(1) does not apply in the pre-filing period—it is not applicable

34 17 C.F.R. § 230.163A.

35 *See* 17 C.F.R. §§ 230.164 and 230.433.

36 2005 Release, *supra* note 3, at *21.

	Could it be an offer?	Is it a prospectus?	Is it a prohibited pre-filing offer for purposes of Section 5(c)?	Is it a prohibited prospectus for purposes of Section 5(b)(1)?
Well-Known Seasoned Issuers—Written Offers Made Within 30 Days of Filing of Registration Statement	Yes.........	Yes. It also is a free-writing prospectus	Is exempted from prohibition of Section 5(c)	Section 5(b)(1) does not apply in the pre-filing period – it is not applicable
Well-Known Seasoned Issuers—Free Writing Prospectuses Used Before Filing of Registration Statement	Yes.........	Yes.........	Is exempted from prohibition of Section 5(c)	Section 5(b)(1) does not apply in the pre-filing period—it is not applicable
Identifying Statements in Accordance with Rule 134	Yes.........	No.........	Section 5(c) is not applicable, as Rule 134 relates only to the period after the filing of a registration statement	Section 5(b)(1) relates only to "prospectuses"—it is not applicable
All Eligible Issuers—Free Writing Prospectuses Used After Filing of Registration Statement	Yes.........	Yes.........	Section 5(c) is not applicable, as it does not apply in the post-filing period	Section 5(b)(1) will be satisfied, as the free writing prospectus will be a permitted Section 10(b) prospectus

Types of Issuers

As already mentioned, the modern disclosure system shifted the focus away from the transaction in the offering toward the issuer and its history in the market place. To accomplish this, the SEC created a tiered system that gives preferential treatments to certain issuers.

Well-Known Seasoned Issuers

As technological advances made the spreading of information easier, it became clear that the largest issuers were the ones about whom investors, the press and financial analysts seek information on the financial health on a continual basis. These large issuers make regular and thorough disclosures to regulators and the public of material events that affect their financial condition.

The 2005 reforms added a new category of issuer, the so-called "Well-Known Seasoned Issuer" ("WKSI"). WKSIs have preferential treatment under the 1933 Act when it comes to the "gun jumping" provisions.[37]

To qualify as a WKSI, an issuer must:

1. Be a registered broker-dealer under Section 15(a) of the 1934 Act or a regular filer of periodic reports under Section 13(a) of the 1934 Act;
2. Must have filed Forms S-3 or F-3; and
3. Must have a market capitalization of $700 million or more, or must have issued at least $1 billion aggregate principal amount of nonconvertible securities (other than common equities) in primary offerings for cash that are registered under the 1933 Act.[38]

For issuers seeking to qualify under the $1 billion threshold, the SEC provides the following additional guidance:

1. Issuers may aggregate the amount of non-convertible securities, other than common equity, issued in registered primary offerings during the prior three years;
2. Issuers may include only such non-convertible securities that were issued in registered primary offerings for cash—they may not include registered exchange offers in this aggregation; and
3. Parent company issuers only may include in their calculation the

[37] The preferential treatment for these types of issuers is in large part due to their disclosure requirements outside of the offering process, e.g., under the 1934 Act.

[38] 2005 Release, *supra* note 3, at *11. Affiliates of a WKSI can qualify as such for their own offerings if they meet certain conditions. The determination of public float is based on a public trading market … . Therefore, an entity with $700 million of common equity securities outstanding but not trading in any public trading market would not be a WKSI based on market capitalization. *Id.* at n. 50.

principal amount of their full and unconditional guarantees, within the meaning of Rule 3–10 of Regulation S-X, of non-convertible securities, other than common equity, of their majority-owned subsidiaries issued in registered primary offerings for cash during the three-year period.[39]

The streamlined process for WKSIs reflects an acknowledgement of the reality that such issuers are responsible for 95 percent of equity market capitalization. Qualifying as WKSI provides important benefits as it allows an issuer to make use of the automatic shelf registration to register securities being offered. However, WKSI status is not available to voluntary filers, ABS issuers or Schedule B issuers.[40]

Other types of issuers

In addition to the WKSI designation, the SEC has identified the following types of issuers: seasoned issuers, unseasoned 1934 Act reporting issuers and non-reporting issuers.

The SEC defines a seasoned issuer as:

> [a]n issuer that is eligible to use Form S-3 or Form F-3 to register primary offerings of securities pursuant to General Instruction I.B.1 of such Forms or is registering securities in reliance on General Instruction I.B.2, I.B.5, or I.C. of Form S-3 or General Instruction I.A.5 or I.B.2 of Form F-3. Majority-owned subsidiaries registering offerings of their securities on Form S-3 or Form F-3 pursuant to General Instruction I.C. of Form S-3 or I.A.5 of Form F-3 also are considered seasoned issuers. As commenters requested, we are clarifying that issuers of asset-backed securities eligible for registration on Form S-3 also are considered seasoned.[41]

Unseasoned issuers, on the other hand, are ones that are required to file reports under Sections 13 or 15(d) of the 1934 Act, but that do not meet the conditions in Form S-3 or Form F-3 for a primary offering of securities.[42] Lastly, a non-reporting issuer is one that does not have to file reports under Sections 13 or 15(d) of the 1934 Act, and they may not make use of the lesser reporting requirements.[43]

---

39 2005 Release, *supra* note 3, at *13.
40 2005 Release, *supra* note 3, at *16.
41 2005 Release, *supra* note 3, at *17.
42 2005 Release, *supra* note 3, at *17.
43 2005 Release, *supra* note 3, at *17.

The Registration Process

Section 6 of the 1933 Act governs the registration process.[44] It provides for a disclosure framework whereby issuers must submit with the SEC information that will form the basis of the prospectus, which the issuers will send to prospective investors. In addition, Section 6 requires disclosure of additional information that even though it is not part of the prospectus, it is available to the public through the SEC's EDGAR system. Section 6 lays out the method of registration. At the very least, issuers must file a registration statement (in triplicate), that contains the signature of the issuer, principal executive officer, principal financial officer, comptroller or principal accounting officer, and the majority of the board of directors.[45] Section 6 also sets forth the required fee schedule, the review and effective date, and the time the registration is effective.

Section 7 gives SEC authority to determine what information issuers must submit. As discussed more fully below, offering-related filings fall into two main categories, information about the issuer and information about the terms of the offer. Disclosure requirements under each category include descriptions of the issuer's business, past business performance, information about the issuer's officers and managers, audited financial statements of past business performance, executive compensation, risks of the business, tax and legal status, and the terms and information about the securities issued.[46]

Section 8 of the 1933 Act dictates that a registration statement shall become effective 20 days after the filing.[47] The SEC can accelerate this date for certain issuers or based on the information provided. If the SEC identifies incomplete or inaccurate information in the registration statement, it will notify the filer through a phone call (for minor mistakes) or a comment letter within 10 days of receipt. Generally, issuers must take action on SEC comments, which usually means amending the registration statement. At times, issuers may disagree with the staff's comments, at

---

44 *See* 15 U.S.C. § 77f.

45 *Id.*

46 *See* 15 U.S.C. § 77j.

47 15 U.S.C. § 77h(a). Amendments before the effective date will reset the effective date to the date of when the amendment was filed, unless the issuer files the amendment with the SEC's consent or pursuant to an SEC order.

which time they can seek review from senior staff.[48] Issuers have an incentive to resolve any disagreement with the SEC, especially in light of the requirement in Regulation S-K that they disclose any such disagreements to the public. Moreover, if an issuer does not comply, the SEC has the power to issue a refusal or stop order, which prevents the issuer from proceeding with public offering.

Forms to be used when registering securities

Companies seeking to offer securities to the public must register them by filing a registration statement pursuant to specific SEC forms. These forms are described below in some detail; however, it is important to note that these are not forms with blank spaces that one fills out. Instead, the forms contain items calling for specific disclosures as detailed in specific items of Regulations S-K and S-X (discussed below). In other words, even though issuers must follow the requirements of the registration statements, they must really comply with the framework set forth in regulations S-K and S-X.

Generally, a registration statement has two components. The first is the prospectus, under which issuers must disclose specific information required by regulations S-K and S-X. The second part of the registration statement contains business-specific information that must be filed with the SEC.[49]

If a company is unable to use one of the many exemptions, it must register its issuance with the SEC. To do so, companies must file a registration statement on SEC designated forms disclosing the information required therein. In 1982, the SEC adopted a simplified registration system by adopting three forms that would constitute the basic framework for registration statements under the 1933 Act.[50] Moreover, it expanded and reorganized Regulation S-K to institute uniform disclosure requirements for registering companies.

The 1933 Act registration forms provide the starting point for registrants to comply with the integrated disclosure system. The main forms under the 1982 reform were Forms S-1, S-2 and S-3. These forms

---

48 SEC staff expect some pushback on their comments. It is important, however, that companies go through each level of review instead of trying to go around the initial reviewing staff and seek directly senior review.

49 Though they do not have to be sent to prospective investors, they are available to the public through the SEC's public access portal.

50 *See* the 1982 Release, *supra* note 2. *See also* Reproposal of Comprehensive Revision to System for Registration of Securities Offerings, SEC Release No. 33–6331 (Aug. 6, 1981).

established three categories of registrants. All three required registrants to disclose the same information, whether contained in a prospectus or incorporated by reference, but they differed as to how this information is presented.[51] It should be noted that there are numerous forms that the SEC has issued that apply to different/specific issuers, and the discussion below is intended only as a primer on the primary forms that apply to issuers.

The first type of the registration statement must be presented on Form S-1. This is the main form that all registrants for which no other form is authorized or prescribed must file to register their offering with the SEC. It requires issuers to set forth complete disclosures in the prospectus, and it only allows issuers that have filed at least one annual report on Form 10-K to incorporate by reference information disclosed in previous 1934 Act reports and documents.[52] However, incorporation by reference is not available to reporting issuers who are not current with their 1934 Act reports, and issuers who, during the past three years, have been blank check issuers, shell companies or issuers for offerings of penny stocks.[53] Issuers that can incorporate by reference must make the reports being incorporated available on their website. Moreover, Form S-1 does not allow for forward incorporation by reference (i.e., information filed with the SEC after the registration statement is effective).

Issuers that incorporate by reference must include the following information in the prospectus accompanying the registration statement: (i) a list of the incorporated reports and materials; (ii) a statement that the filer will provide copies of any incorporated reports or materials on request; (iii) an indication that the reports and materials are available from the SEC through the EDGAR system or the SEC's public reference room; (iv) an identification of the issuer's website address where buyers can access the incorporated reports and other materials; and (v) the required disclosures regarding material changes in or updates to the information that is incorporated by reference from a 1934 Act report or other material required to be filed. Lastly, issuers using Form S-1 must

---

[51] *See* the 1982 Release, *supra* note 2. Much of the information relating to the company is already available on Forms 10-Q and 8-K, allowing for incorporation by reference; information about the offering, however, is not available in those forms, which means that registrants must fully disclose it in the prospectus in all cases. *Id.*

[52] Form S-1 allows successor registrants to incorporate by reference if the predecessors were eligible.

[53] 2005 Release, *supra* note 3, at *98.

disclose information in accordance with the rules of Regulation S-K and Regulation S-X.[54]

The second type of the registration statement had to be presented on Form S-2. Form S-2 combined incorporation by reference of 1934 Act reports with delivery of streamlined information to investors to ensure disclosure of required information.[55] This form was available to issuers who had participated in the 1934 Act reporting system for at least three years. Form S-2 allowed such issuers to: (i) deliver a copy of their annual report to security holders as well as a copy of the prospectus describing the offering; or (ii) present issuer-oriented information in the prospectus that is comparable to the information in the annual report along with the description of the offering.[56] Independently of which option an issuer chose, the prospectus would incorporate by reference the more complete information in Form 10-K. The SEC rescinded Form S-2 in 2005 as part of its continued streamlining of the disclosure system.

The third type of registration statement must be presented on Form S-3, which is the least burdensome and most simplified of the forms. Based on the efficient market theory, it allows for maximum use of incorporation by reference of information on 1934 Act reports and requires the least disclosure to be presented in the prospectus and delivered to investors.[57] The main feature of Form S-3 is the absence of issuer-specific information, unless there is a material change in the issuer's affairs not reported in a related filing, but issuers must still present the same transaction-specific information that Forms S-1 requires.[58] However, before using Form S-3, issuers must meet specific transaction-related and registrant-related requirements set forth in the form.

Shelf registration

Rule 415 provides for continuous or delayed offerings, otherwise known as "shelf registration," in which an issuer registers securities that it has no present intention of selling immediately.[59] Shelf registration is appealing

---

54 2005 Release, *supra* note 3, at *99.

55 1982 Release, *supra* note 2.

56 *Id.*

57 1982 Release, *supra* note 2.

58 *Id.*

59 17 C.F.R. § 230.415. In a continuous offering, the issuer offers the securities immediately after the shelf registration becomes effective, and continues the offering in the future; for delayed offering, the issuer signals that it has no immediate plans of offering the securities covered in the shelf registration

because it allows an issuer to register securities for sale and sell them at any time, thus using the same registration statement for multiple offerings.[60] A registrant may use shelf registration only for specific products listed in Rule 415.[61]

Generally, under Rule 415, when an issuer decides to take the securities off the shelf ("takedowns"), it must offer them with the base prospectus (filed at the time of the registration statement) and the prospectus supplement (designed to make the old prospectus current) in accordance with Item 512 of Regulation S-K.[62]

If a shelf registration statement is based on Form S-3, it will incorporate by reference all the reports that the issuer has filed with the SEC under the 1934 Act. This is an appealing feature, because it allows issuers to act quickly to take advantage of favorable market conditions without having to wait for SEC review of information contained in any supplements.

Before being able to use shelf registration, issuers must:

1. Have a class of securities registered under the 1934 Act (or have to file reports under Section 15(d) of the 1934 Act);

---

statement. The distinction is important because only certain seasoned issuers may make use of primary offerings on a delayed basis.

[60] 17 C.F.R. § 230.415(a)(2). For the following two classes, the shelf registration statement is effective for three years: (i) securities the offering of which will be commenced promptly, will be made on a continuous basis and may continue for a period in excess of 30 days from the date of initial effectiveness, and (ii) securities registered on Form S-3 or Form F-3 which are to be offered and sold on an immediate, continuous or delayed basis by or on behalf of the registrant, a majority-owned subsidiary of the registrant or a person of which the registrant is a majority-owned subsidiary. 17 C.F.R. § 230.415(a)(1)(ix)–(x).

[61] Under the old rules, the automatic shelf registration was only effective for two years, but that is no longer the case as long as issuers file new shelf registration statements within three years of the original statements. Issuers may continue to offer the securities for six months after the three-year period until the new shelf registration statement becomes effective.

[62] *See* 17 C.F.R. §§ 230.415(a) and 229.512(a). *See also* Rule 430B (17 C.F.R. § 230.430B) and Rule 424(b) (17 C.F.R. § 230.424(b)). Many of the takedowns can be accomplished using only a prospectus that was complete at the time the registration became effective, thus not requiring a supplement or post-effective amendment. However, a base prospectus that omits statutorily required information would not be considered a "final prospectus" without a prospectus supplement or a post-effective amendment to the registration statement. *See* 2005 Release, *supra* note 3.

2. Have filed timely reports pursuant to Section 12 or Section 15(d) of the 1934 Act for at least 12 months immediately before the filing; and
3. Have not failed to pay dividends, sinking fund installments on preferred stock, or defaulted on indebtedness installments since the end of the preceding year.[63]

In 2005, the SEC began allowing automatic shelf registration for WKSIs, which allowed issuers to register an unspecified amount of securities to be offered without indicating whether the securities would be offered in primary or secondary offerings, with the shelf registration statement becoming effective right away without requiring SEC review.[64] Automatic shelf registration is available in connection with Form S-3 registration statements for all primary and secondary offerings of securities for WKSIs.[65] Moreover, under shelf registration, WKSIs can add additional classes of securities and majority-owned subsidiaries as additional registrants after the registration is effective. The new rules also gave WKSIs a "pay as you go" option to pay filing fees at the time they file the prospectus supplement instead of paying all filing fees up front.

Moreover, the 2005 changes allowed WKSIs filing for automatic shelf registration to omit more information from the base prospectus than Rule 430B requires for a regular shelf registration offering. Specifically, the base prospectus may omit information that is unknown and not reasonably available under Rule 409,[66] as well as information on whether it is a primary or secondary offering, the description of securities to be offered (other than an identification of the name or class of securities), the names of any selling security holders, and disclosures regarding any plan of distribution.[67] The base prospectus, however, must identify in general terms the names or class of the securities being registered.

To address concerns about providing adequate information to investors, the 2005 changes provided several mechanisms through which issuers

---

63 For more information for requirements for eligible issuers, see General Instructions of Form S-3.

64 Once filed, issuers can rely on the automatic shelf registration statement to offer securities unless the SEC objects to the shelf registrations, in which case the issuer must amend the registration to reflect the appropriate category.

65 *See* 2005 Release, *supra* note 3, at *92. WKSIs, moreover, can amend a registration statement via a post-effective filing to add an eligible subsidiary as an issuer. *Id.*

66 17 C.F.R. § 230.409.

67 2005 Release, *supra* note 3, at *92.

would add information to the base prospectus, including through a post-effective amendment to the registration statement, incorporation by reference of information disclosed in 1934 Act reports, or a prospectus/ prospectus supplement that would be deemed part of and included in the registration statement.[68] The main exception to this flexibility is the requirement that issuers add new types of securities or new eligible issuers (including guarantors and securities they may issue) through a post-effective amendment effective immediately upon filing.

Liability for Violation of Registration Requirements

Under Section 11, offering participants are liable for registration statements that contain an untrue statement of a material fact or that omit a material fact necessary to make the statements therein not misleading.[69] Those subject to liability include every person who signed the registration statement, every person who was a director or partner in the issuer at the time of the filing of the part of the registration statement giving rise to the liability, every person who was (or about to become) a director or partner, every accountant, engineer, appraiser, or other such professional who prepared or certified any report/valuation used in connection with the registration statement, and every underwriter with respect to such security. Section 11, however, limits damages to the difference in price between the amount paid and the present value of the securities.[70] Section 11 also allows for a due diligence defense to liability arising under it.

To establish a prima facie case of violation of Section 5 of the 1933 Act, plaintiffs must prove the following three elements: (i) no registration statement was in effect as to the securities; (ii) the defendant sold or offered to sell the securities; and (iii) that there was a use of interstate transportation, or communication, or of the mails in connection with sale or offer of sale.[71] Violation of registration requirements for securities

---

[68] 2005 Release, *supra* note 3, at *94. Through these mechanisms, issuers can add information about the public offering price, updating information regarding the issuer, add a description of securities including information not contained or incorporated by reference in the base prospectus, information about the identity of underwriters and selling security holders, and the plan of distribution of the securities.

[69] 15 U.S.C. § 77k(a).

[70] 15 U.S.C. § 77k(e).

[71] SEC v. Cavanagh, 1 F.Supp.2d 337 (S.D.N.Y. 1998); *See also* SEC v. Softpoint, Inc., 958 F.Supp. 846, 859–60 (S.D.N.Y. 1997).

offering can expose one to aiding and abetting liability as well. In *SEC v. Universal Major Indus.*,[72] the appellant argued against Section 5 aiding and abetting liability. The court held that "in order to accomplish the broad remedial purposes of the [1933 Act] … there are compelling reasons to impose secondary liability in Section 5 actions … [t]he heart of this prohibition would be cut away if the only person covered by its provisions was the individual who actually consummated the sale."[73]

Specific Disclosure Requirements—Regulation S-K

The S.E.C. adopted Regulation S-K in 1977, and it has since evolved into the main regulation for required disclosures in forms and reports required under the 1933 and 1934 Acts. Generally, Regulation S-K is not self-executing, meaning that registrants do not have to automatically disclose information required therein, but only information that a report or form requires by directing a registrant to an Item of Regulation S-K. In 1980, the SEC proposed extensive revisions to Regulation S-K as part of the ongoing effort to adopt the integrated disclosure system and to avoid duplicative, unnecessary or impractical reporting requirements, making Regulation S-K the main source of uniform disclosure items under the 1933 and 1934 Acts.[74]

The current Regulation S-K has nine parts containing items that together cover every aspect of the integrated disclosure system.[75]

Part 1—general

Part 1 only contains Item 10, which provides a general description of Regulation S-K, as well as its purpose and general requirements.[76] Item 10 provides that Regulation S-K contains the requirements applicable to

---

72 546 F.2d 1044 (2d Cir. 1976).

73 *Id.* at 1046–1047. *See also* SEC v. Management Dynamics, Inc., 515 F.2d 801 (2d Cir. 1975); SEC v. Spectrum, Ltd., 489 F.2d 535 (2d Cir. 1973); SEC v. North American Research & Development Corp., 424 F.2d 63 (2d Cir. 1970) (finding that injunctive relief is proper against aiders and abbeters [sic] of Section 5 violators).

74 *See* Proposed Revision of Regulation S-K and Guides for the Preparation and Filing of Registration Statements and Reports, SEC Release No. 6276 (proposed Dec. 23, 1980).

75 The actual numbering of Regulation S-K is somewhat peculiar. The first part is designated as Part 10 and is followed by Parts 100, 200, etc. Thus, to ensure ease of reference, this section refers to the parts as used in Regulation S-K.

76 17 C.F.R. § 229.10.

the content of the non-financial statements portions of registration statements required under the 1933 Act and the 1934 Act, as well as periodic reports filed thereunder.[77] Moreover, Item 10 encourages management's projections of future economic performance as long as they have a reasonable basis and are presented in an appropriate format.[78]

Moreover, Item 10 provides the conditions the SEC considers important in making projections. The goal here is to present information in such a way that facilitates investor understanding of the information and that avoids misleading the average investor. For example, if a company relies on third party reviews of management's projections instead of or in addition to the history of performance or operations, it must disclose information about the third party on whom they are relying.[79] Generally, although projections focus on three main areas thought to be most important to investors—revenues, net income (loss), and earnings (loss) per share—management may choose to provide other information as long as it is not misleading (i.e., the additional terms reported are not selectively in favor of the company).[80] Moreover, if management decides to include in its projections ratings by professional ratings agencies, it must do so based on specific conditions the SEC provides in Item 10, and if the information provided relies on non-GAAP accounting principles, the projections must disclose certain information.[81] To make disclosure less burdensome, Item 10 allows incorporation by reference of information disclosed on a previous SEC filing.[82]

Part 100—business

Part 100 covers description of the business, property and legal proceeding in which the business is involved.[83] Item 101 sets forth guidelines for providing a description of the business.[84] Registrants must describe the

---

77 17 C.F.R. § 229.10(a).

78 17 C.F.R. § 229.10(b). *See also* Williamette Industries, Inc., SEC No Action Letter (Mar. 22, 2001) (denying no action relief for projection of projects based on the potential form of future legislation).

79 *Id.*

80 *See generally* S.E.C. v. Black, 2008 WL 4394891 (N.D. Ill. 2008).

81 17 C.F.R. § 229.10(c). *See also* In re Netflix Securities Litigation, 2005 WL 3096209 (N. D. Cal. 2005) (discussing allegation that defendants violated Item 10 of Regulation S-K, which requires an issuer disclosing non-GAAP information to state why that information is useful to investors).

82 *See* XL Capital Assurance, Inc., SEC No Action Letter (July 23, 2002).

83 17 C.F.R. § 229.100 e*t seq.*

84 17 C.F.R. § 229.101.

general development of the business (as well as subsidiaries and predecessors) for the preceding five years (if applicable), with particular attention given to year and form of organization, bankruptcy or material changes in the registrant or significant subsidiaries, nature and result of any material reclassification, merger or consolidation of the registrant or of its significant subsidiaries, the acquisition/disposition of material assets made not in the ordinary course of business, and any material changes in the way the registrant conducts business.[85] Moreover, under Item 101, issuers must disclose information about specific business segments for each of the preceding three fiscal years.[86] Additionally, under Item 101, the business description narrative must describe the business done and intended to be done by the registrant's individual segments (and subsidiaries) by disclosing specific items contained therein, e.g., the principal products produced and services the registrant renders, and the method of distribution of said products and services.[87] Item 10 requires disclosure of financial information about relevant geographic areas, reports filed with the SEC, reports made to security holders, enforceability of liabilities against foreign persons, and smaller reporting companies.[88]

Item 102 sets forth the guidelines for providing a description of the property.[89] A company must state briefly the location and general character of principal plants, mines and materially important physical properties for it and its subsidiaries, as well as identify the segments that use the property, and describe the encumbrances and form of ownership

---

[85] 17 C.F.R. § 229.101(a). A company may have to disclose information going further back than five years if that information is material. *Id.*; *see also* Walzer v. UAL Corp. 351 Fed. Appx. 551 (2d Cir. 2009) (S–K requires disclosure of the nature and results of any bankruptcy or any material pending legal proceedings, corporate directors had no duty to disclose to investors that they had retained counsel to examine the possibility of future bankruptcy).

[86] 17 C.F.R. § 229.101(b). Registrants must be careful when restructuring business operations, as they must disclose any changes in the business segments. For more information on segment reporting, see Segment Reporting, SEC Release No. 7620 (Jan. 5, 1999).

[87] 17 C.F.R. § 229.101(c). Subsection (c) lists a series of 13 items that a registrant must address in the narrative disclosure section. *Id.*

[88] 17 C.F.R. § 229.101(d)–(h).

[89] 17 C.F.R. § 229.102.

for properties not held in fee simple.[90] Moreover, Item 102 provides disclosure requirements for industry-specific companies.[91]

Item 103 sets forth the guidelines for describing legal proceedings.[92] A company must describe briefly any material pending legal proceedings, but not routine litigation incidental to business operations, to which the registrant (or subsidiary) is a party of or a subject to, unless the claim of damages does not exceed 10 percent of the current assets of the registrant and its subsidiaries on a consolidated basis.[93] The 10 percent threshold does not apply to the obligation to report bankruptcy, receivership, or similar proceedings, and material proceedings in which a director, officer or affiliate, and any owner of more than 5 percent of any class of voting securities have a material interest adverse to the registrant.[94] Lastly, a company must disclose any proceedings arising from discharging materials in the environment provided that they are material to the business or financial conditions, involve a claim for damages that exceed 10 percent of the assets, or involve a governmental authority and the proceeding may result in a monetary sanction of greater than $100,000.[95] Disclosure of judicial proceedings, especially those brought or contemplated by governmental authorities, have gained particular importance in light of the recent actions by the Department of Justice and other regulators

[90] 17 C.F.R. § 229.102(1). Note that this requirement does not require detailed descriptions of the physical or legal characteristics of the properties. However, in determining whether to describe a particular property, a registrant should take into account both quantitative and qualitative factors.

[91] 17 C.F.R. § 229.102(3)–(9). These include companies involved in extractive enterprises, oil and gas production, and mining operations; *see also* Modernization of Oil and Gas Reporting, SEC Release No. 78 (Dec. 31, 2008).

[92] 17 C.F.R. § 229.103.

[93] 17 C.F.R. § 229.103. The description must include the name of court or agency in which the proceedings are pending, the date instated, the principal parties, a description of the factual basis on which they are based, and the relief sought. Moreover, a company must disclose proceedings that a governmental authority is contemplating. *Id. See also* Menkes v. Stolt-Nielsen S.A., 2005 WL 3050970 (D.Conn. 2005) (Regulation S-K … mandates the disclosure of "any material pending legal proceedings" and "any such proceedings known to be contemplated by governmental authorities").

[94] 17 C.F.R. § 229.103(4).

[95] 17 C.F.R. § 229.103(5). *Accord* Levine v. NL Industries, Inc., 926 F.2d 199 (2d Cir. 1991), In the Matter of: Attlas Cold Storage, Inc., 2003 WL 22293685, (E.P.A. Aug 12, 2003).

against financial institutions for dubious practices during the sub-prime mortgage crisis.[96]

Part 200—securities of the registrant

Part 200 sets forth guidelines for describing the registrant's securities. Item 201 covers disclosure requirements for the market price of and dividends on common equity and related stockholder matters. Item 201 has specific requirements for information on markets, holders, dividends, securities authorized for issuance under equity compensation plans, and performance graphs. For market information, the registrant must:

1. Identify each principal U.S. market in which each class of common equity is traded, or provide a statement that there is no established public trading market for the class of common equity.[97]
2. State the high and low prices for the equity for each quarter for the two most recent fiscal years and any subsequent interim year for which financial statements are included, if the principal U.S. market is an exchange.[98]
3. If the U.S. market is not an exchange, the range of high and low bid information for the equity for each full quarterly period within the two most recent fiscal years and any subsequent interim year for which financial statements are included, as quoted in an automated quotation system. If no such system is in place, then the registrant must provide the range of reported high and low bid quotations, along with the source of the quotations.[99]
4. Give the same comparable information to the above points for foreign registrants that have identified a principal established foreign trading market for its common equity.[100]

---

[96] *See* Devlin Barrett and Dan Fitzpatrick, J.P. Morgan, U.S. Settle for $13 Billion, Wall St. J., Nov. 19, 2013.

[97] 17 C.F.R. § 229.201(a)(1)(i). Foreign registrants must also identify the principal established foreign public trading markets for each class of common equity.

[98] 17 C.F.R. § 229.201(a)(1)(ii).

[99] 17 C.F.R. § 229.201(a)(1)(iii). In these cases, the registration must include a disclaimer that such over-the-counter market quotations reflect inter-dealer prices, without retail mark-up, mark-down or commission and may not necessarily represent actual transactions. Moreover, where there is an absence of an established public trading market, reference to quotations shall be qualified by appropriate explanation. *Id.*

[100] 17 C.F.R. § 229.201(a)(1)(iv). Foreign issuers must also describe any laws, decrees or regulations in the foreign country that may restrict capital

5. Provide price information as of the latest date prior to the public announcement of a transaction related to a registration statement or proxy information.[101]

On the other hand, if a registrant files the information above in connection with Form S-1 under the 1933 Act or Form 10 under the 1934 Act, and there is no established U.S. public market, the registration must indicate the amount of common equity that:

1. Is subject to outstanding options or warrants to purchase, or securities convertible into, common equity of the registrant;
2. Could be sold pursuant to Rule 144 (17 C.F.R. § 230.144) or that the registrant has agreed to register under the 1933 Act for sale by security holders; or
3. Is being publicly offered by the registrant and the offering of which could have material effect on the market price of the common equity.[102]

When it comes to holders, the registrant must disclose the approximate number of holders of each class of common equity as of the latest practicable date.[103] However, if the information is being presented in a 1933 Act registration statement or 1934 Act proxy statement, the registration must disclose common equity owned by: (i) any person who is the beneficial owner of 5 percent of any class of the registration common security, and (ii) all directors and officers as a group, and the registrant's present commitments to such persons with respect to the issuance of shares of any class of its common equity.[104]

For dividends, the registrant must disclose the frequency and amount of any cash dividends declared on each class of common equity for the two most recent fiscal years and any subsequent interim period for which financial statements are required to be presented, and must give a brief description of restrictions on payments of dividends.[105]

---

movement, and the taxes to which U.S. common equity holders are subject in the foreign country. *Id.*

[101] 17 C.F.R. § 229.201(a)(1)(v).

[102] 17 C.F.R. § 229.201(a)(2)(i)–(iii).

[103] 17 C.F.R. § 229.201(b)(1).

[104] 17 C.F.R. § 229.201(b)(2).

[105] 17 C.F.R. § 229.201(c). For companies that pay no cash dividends, but that have the ability to do so, they should consider the question of their intention to pay cash dividends or provide a statement that no such intention exists. *Id.*

Moreover, Item 201 provides detailed information that must be disclosed for securities authorized for issuance under equity compensation plans.[106]

Lastly, Item 201 requires a line graph comparing the yearly percentage change in cumulative total shareholder return on a class of common stock registered under Section 12 of the 1934 Act with:

1. The cumulative total return of a broad equity market index (assuming reinvestment of dividends), that includes companies whose equity securities trade on the same exchange or are of comparable market cap; and
2. The cumulative total return (assuming reinvestment of dividends) of a published industry or line-of-business index, peer issuers selected in good faith, or issuers with similar market cap.[107]

Item 202 covers the description of registrant's securities.[108] The registrant's disclosure requirements depend on the types of securities, which may include capital stocks, debt securities, warrants and rights, securities other than common equity, American Depositary Receipts. For capital stock, registrants must state the title of the class and:

1. Outline briefly dividend rights, terms of conversion, sinking fund provisions, redemption provisions, voting rights, any classification of the Board of Directors (and its impact on cumulative voting), liquidation rights, preemption rights, liability to further calls or to assessment by the registrant and for liabilities of the registrant imposed on its stockholders under state statutes, any restriction on alienability of the securities to be registered, and any provision discriminating against any existing or prospective holder of such

---

106 17 C.F.R. § 229.201(d). *See also* Disclosure of Equity Compensation Plan Information, SEC Release No. 7944 (Jan. 26, 2001); In re Chicago Bd. Options Exchange, Inc., SEC Release No. 48737 (Oct. 31, 2003) (Item 201(d) requires tabular disclosure concerning equity compensation plans that have been approved by shareholders and equity compensation plans that have not been approved by shareholders).

107 17 C.F.R. § 229.201(e). Item 201 provides specific requirements relating to the preparation of the graph comparison.

108 17 C.F.R. § 229.202.

securities as a result of such security holder owning a substantial amount of securities.[109]

2. Briefly explain whether rights of stockholders may be modified by a vote of a majority or more of outstanding shares, voting as a class.[110]
3. In cases of preferred stock registration, briefly explain restrictions (or lack thereof) on the repurchase or redemption of shares while there is any arrearage in the payment of dividends or sinking fund installments.[111]
4. Include information necessary for investors to understand material limitations or qualifications by the rights of any other authorized security class on rights evidenced by, or the amounts payable with respect to, the shares being registered.[112]
5. Describe briefly or cross-reference to another part of the document any provisions in a charter or by-laws that would affect a change in control of the registrant and that would operate in cases of merger, reorganization, tender offer, sale or transfer of all of the registrant's assets or liquidations.[113]

For debt securities, the registrant must state the title, principal amount offered and, if a series, the total amount authorized and the total amount outstanding as of the most recent practicable date, as well as outline briefly provisions:

1. With respect to maturity, interest, conversion, redemption, amortization, sinking fund, or retirement;
2. With respect to the kind and priority of any lien securing the securities, with a brief identification of relevant collateral;
3. With respect to subordination rights, along with the aggregate amount of outstanding indebtedness that would be senior to such subordinated debt and a limitation on the issuance of additional senior indebtedness (if applicable);

---

[109] 17 C.F.R. § 229.202(a)(1). Registrants do not need to provide this information if disclosure would be immaterial because the financial resources of the registrant or other factors make it improbable that liability under such state statutes would be imposed. *See also* Erath v. Xidex Corp., 1991 WL 338322 (Dist. Ariz. 1991) (finding substantial compliance with Item 202 as to make any omission immaterial).

[110] 17 C.F.R. § 229.202(a)(2).

[111] 17 C.F.R. § 229.202(a)(3).

[112] 17 C.F.R. § 229.202(a)(4).

[113] 17 C.F.R. § 229.202(a)(5).

4. Restricting the declaration of dividends or requiring the maintenance of any asset ratio or the creation of maintenance of reserves;
5. Restricting the incurrence of additional debt or issuance of additional securities and some additional information;
6. On the general type of event that constitutes a default and whether registrant must provide periodic evidence for the absence of default or for compliance with the terms of the indenture;
7. Relating to modification of the terms of the security or the rights of security holders; and
8. Regarding the ability of other classes of securities to materially limit or qualify the rights evidenced.[114]

For warrants and rights, the registrant must disclose the amount of securities called by the warrants and rights, the relevant period, the amount outstanding, provisions for changes to or adjustments in the exercise price, and any other material terms of such rights.[115]

Part 300—financial information

Part 300 sets forth information disclosure requirements on a registrant's financial information.[116] Aside from having to disclose specific financial information, Part 300 is important because it requires management's discussion and analysis ("MD&A") of financial condition and results of operations. Moreover, under Part 300, registrants must disclose changes to accounting and financial disclosure and disagreements with independent accountant reports, disclose controls and procedures, as well as internal controls, the company has regarding financial reporting (a direct result of Enron and WorldCom accounting frauds).

Item 301 sets forth disclosure requirements for select financial data. Registrants must furnish comparative, columnar style financial information for each of the preceding five years (or longer if necessary to make the information not misleading).[117] The financial information must include sales or operating revenues, income (loss) from continuing operations, income (loss) from continuing operations per common share, total assets, long-term obligations and redeemable preferred stock, and

---

[114] 17 C.F.R. § 229.202(b)(1)–(8). Registrants must also provide information on debt securities offered an original issue discount, as well as the name of the trustee, their relationship with registrant.

[115] 17 C.F.R. § 229.202(c).

[116] 17 C.F.R. § 229.300.

[117] 17 C.F.R. § 229.301. Item 301 exempts from its application smaller reporting companies.

cash dividends declared per common share.[118] Item 302 requires disclosure of supplementary financial information for registrants under Sections 12(b) or 12(g) of the 1934 Act.[119] Such information includes net sales, gross profit, income (loss) before extraordinary items and cumulative effect of a change in accounting, per share data based upon such income (loss), net income (loss) and net income (loss) attributable to the registrant.[120] This information shall be provided for each quarter within the two most recent fiscal years and any subsequent interim period, and companies must reconcile information disclosed during a prior quarter that has changed in such a way that it makes it materially misleading.[121] A registrant must also describe the effect of the disposal of a business segment or an unusual/infrequent item.

Item 303 is the most significant provision of Part 300. It contains the management's discussion and analysis of financial condition and results of operations, including information about liquidity, capital resources, results of operations, off-balance sheet arrangements, tabular disclosure of contractual obligations, and any other information necessary to an understating of the registrant's financial condition, changes in financial condition and results of operations.[122]

---

[118] Instruction 2 to Item 301. 17 C.F.R. § 229.301. The information should also touch on other factors that materially affect the comparability of the information reflected in the financial data. *Id.*

[119] 17 C.F.R. § 229.302(a)(5).

[120] 17 C.F.R. § 229.302(a)(1).

[121] 17 C.F.R. § 229.302(a)(2). A registrant must also describe the effect of a segment disposal or an unusual/infrequent item.

[122] 17 C.F.R. § 229.303. For purposes of this section, the term "liquidity" refers to the ability of an enterprise to generate adequate amounts of cash to meet its cash needs for long-term and short-term basis. 17 C.F.R. § 303(a). *See also* Commission Guidance Regarding Management's Discussion and Analysis of Financial Condition and Results of Operations, SEC Release No. 33–8350 (Dec. 19, 2003), and Commission Guidance on Presentation of Liquidity and Capital Resources Disclosures in Management's Discussion and Analysis, SEC Release No. 83 (Sept. 17, 2010). For cases discussing Item 303 disclosure requirements, see Silverstrand Investments v. AMAG Pharmaceuticals, Inc., 707 F.3d 95 (1st Cir. 2013) (complaint's allegations that defendant violated Regulation S-K when it did not disclose 23 material adverse events during its drug trials even though it knew about them were sufficient to survive a motion to dismiss), and Aldridge v. A.T. Cross Corp., 284 F.3d 72 (1st Cir. 2002). *See also* E. I. du Pont d Nemours and Company, SEC No Action Letter (2005) (denying no-action relief to allow company to omit certain information relating to attorney's fees, expect fees, lobbying and public relations/media expense and litigation).

To increase the transparency of the financial statements and to reduce incentives for registrants to shop for accountants, Item 304 sets forth certain disclosure requirements regarding changes in and disagreements with accountants on accounting and financial disclosure.[123] These requirements apply if, during the most recent two fiscal years (or any subsequent interim period), there was a dismissal or resignation of an independent principal accountant who was responsible for auditing the financial statements, or of an independent accountant who audited a significant subsidiary and on whom the principal accountant expressed reliance.[124] If this is the case, the registrant must disclose a series of information, including a statement of whether the accountant resigned, declined to be re-elected or was dismissed; whether there was an adverse opinion, disclaimer of opinion, or qualified opinion, and describe the nature of the foregoing; whether the board of directors (through a committee) recommended or approved the dismissal; whether there were unresolved disagreements regarding accounting principles or practices, disclosure of financial statements, or auditing scope or procedure, which would have caused the accountant to make reference to said disagreements in the report; and whether the former accountant advised the registration of certain inadequacies or deficiencies in the preceding two fiscal years (or subsequent interim period).[125] In addition, registrants must disclose certain information if they engage a new independent accountant, and they must provide the former accountant with a copy of aforementioned disclosures and request that the former accountant issue a

---

[123] 17 C.F.R. § 229.304. For purposes of Item 304, the term "disagreements" shall be interpreted broadly, to include any difference of opinion concerning any matter of accounting principles or practices, financial statement disclosure, or auditing scope or procedure which (if not resolved to the satisfaction of the former accountant) would have caused it to make reference to the subject matter of the disagreement in connection with its report. It is not necessary for there to have been an argument to have had a disagreement, merely a difference of opinion will suffice. *Id. See also* Batchelor v. Deloitte & Touche, LLP, 2009 WL 1255449 (S.D. Fla. 2009), and In the Matter of Citizens Capital Corp., SEC Release No. 67313 (June 29, 2012) (administrative proceeding for failing to disclose, among other things, the resignation of the accountant).

[124] 17 C.F.R. § 229.304(a)(1); *see also* Arthur Andersen LLP, SEC Release No. 2018 (Mar. 18, 2002) (describing Item 304 requirements as affected by the indictment of Arthur Andersen).

[125] 17 C.F.R. § 229.304(a)(1)(i)–(iv).

letter addressed to the SEC stating whether they agree with said disclosures.[126]

Item 305 sets forth quantitative and qualitative disclosure requirements about market risk.[127] An issuer has three alternatives for disclosing quantitative information about market risk. They are:

1. Tabular presentation of information related to market risk sensitive instruments, including fair values of risk sensitive instruments and contract terms sufficient to determine future cash flows from those instruments (categorized by the expected maturity dates);
2. Sensitivity analysis disclosures that express the potential loss in future earnings, fair values, or cash flows of market risk sensitive instruments resulting from one or more selected hypothetical changes in interest rates, foreign currency exchange rates, commodity prices, and other relevant market rates or prices over a selected period of time;[128]
3. Value-at-Risk ("VaR") disclosures that express the potential loss in future earnings, fair values, or cash flows of market risk sensitive instruments over a selected period of time, with a selected likelihood of occurrence, from changes in interest rates, foreign currency exchange rates, commodity prices, and other relevant market rates or prices.[129]

---

[126] *See* 17 C.F.R. § 229.304(2)–(3): *see also* Carnegie Intern. Corp. v. Grant Thornton, LLP, 2006 WL 990960 (Cir. Ct. Md. 2006).

[127] 17 C.F.R. § 229.305; *see also* Fadem v. Ford Motor Co., 352 F.Supp.2d 501 (S.D.N.Y. 2005) (discussing responsibility for disclosing qualitative information about risk exposure); In the Matter of PNC Financial Services Group, Inc., SEC Release No. 8112 (July 18, 2002) (Issuers engaged in transactions with special purpose entities, or in other transactions, particularly where the attainment of a particular financial reporting result is a primary purpose, must be mindful that, even if the transactions comply with GAAP, the issuer is required to evaluate the material accuracy and completeness of the presentation made by its financial statements, as well as its disclosure obligations under the SEC's rules and regulations, including, among other things, the rules and regulations concerning Management's Discussion and Analysis of Financial Condition and Results of Operations and Quantitative and Qualitative Disclosures About Market Risk).

[128] For this alternative, registrants must also provide a description of the model, assumptions, and parameters, which are necessary to understand the disclosures required under the paragraph.

[129] 17 C.F.R. § 229.305(1)(i)–(iii). Each method contains a specific requirement as to quantitative information to be disclosed, and registrants must make sure that they follow the guidance the SEC provides in Item 305 and accompanying instructions.

Registrants must provide specific qualitative information about market risk, including its primary market risk exposures and how they are managed (including a discussion of objectives, general strategies and instruments used to manage exposures), and changes in primary market risk exposures or how those exposures are managed as compared to prior periods.[130]

The last two items of Part 300, Items 307 and 308, require that principal executives and principal financial officers disclose conclusions regarding the registrant's disclosure controls and procedures, and that management provide a report disclosing specific information regarding the registrant's internal control over financial reporting.[131] The management's report must contain statements acknowledging management's responsibility for establishing and maintaining adequate internal controls, and identifying the framework management uses to evaluate the effectiveness of the internal controls, as well as management's assessment of said effectiveness for the most recent fiscal year.[132] Lastly, the registrant must disclose any changes in internal controls over financial reporting that occurred during the last fiscal year.[133]

Part 400—management and certain security holders

Part 400 covers company management and their ownership interest in the company. Specifically, it contains guidelines for directors, executive officers, promoters and control persons, executive compensation, security

---

[130] 17 C.F.R. § 229.305(1)(b). For purposes of this subsection, qualitative information about market risk shall be presented separately for market risk sensitive instruments entered into for trading purposes and those entered into for purposes other than trading. Moreover, for purposes of this subsection, market risk includes rate risk, foreign currency exchange rate risk, commodity price risk, and other relevant market rate or price risks (e.g., equity price risk). *Id. See also* Fadem v. Ford Motor Co., 352 F.Supp.2d 501 (S.D.N.Y. 2005) (disclosure by defendants of the types of risk management products it used was sufficient to satisfy the requirement of Item 305(b)).

[131] *See* 17 C.F.R §§ 229.307 and 229.308.

[132] 17 C.F.R. § 229.308. For additional guidance on management's report, see Commission Guidance Regarding Management's Report on Internal Control Over Financial Reporting Under Section 13(a) or 15(d) of the Securities Exchange Act of 1934, SEC Release No. 33–8810 (June 20, 2007). In the report, management must identify material weaknesses, and it may not offer a conclusion that the internal controls over financial reporting are effective if there is one or more material weaknesses. *Id. See also* In the Matter of China Biotics, Inc., SEC Release No. 70800 (Nov. 4, 2008) (administrative liability for failing to disclose management's assessment of internal controls over financial reporting).

[133] 17 C.F.R. § 229.307(c).

ownership of certain beneficial ownership and management, transactions with related persons, promoters and certain control persons, the code of ethics and corporate governance.

Item 401 applies to directors, executive officers, promoters and control persons.[134] It requires the identification of directors and executive officers, including names, ages, positions/offices, term of office (for directors), and any understandings between directors and other persons regarding their selection as director or executive officer.[135] The registrant must also identify certain significant employees (e.g., employees who will make a significant contribution to the business, like production and sales managers, and research scientists), any family relationship between directors and executive officers, and briefly describe the business background and prior directorships.[136] Lastly, the registrant must disclose certain legal proceedings that are material to the evaluation of ability or integrity of a director or executive officer for the past 10 years.[137]

Item 402 sets forth extensive disclosure requirements for executive compensation.[138] It requires clear, concise and understandable disclosure of all compensation relating to executive officers and directors.[139] Item 402 requires a compensation discussion and analysis for the named executives, including the objective of the compensation program, what it is designed to reward, each element of the compensation and how it is paid, how the amount is determined for each element, how each element

---

[134] 17 C.F.R. § 229.401.

[135] 17 C.F.R. § 229.401(a)–(b).

[136] 17 C.F.R. § 229.401(c)–(e). Disclosure of significant employees is not required for registrants who are subject to periodic requirements under Sections 13(a) and 15(d) of the 1934 Act, or for those who are exempt under Section 12(g)(2)(G) of the 1934 Act.

[137] 17 C.F.R. § 229.401(f).

[138] 17 C.F.R. § 229.402.

[139] Executive officers include principal executive and financial officers and the three most highly paid non-principal executive officers. However, this requirement does not apply if the compensation does not exceed $100,000. 17 C.F.R. § 229.402(a). The information about the directors' compensation must be in tabular format as provided in subsection (k) of Item 402.

The SEC has proposed changes to Item 402 to implement Section 953(b) of the Dodd-Frank Wall Street Reform and Consumer Protection Act, which requires disclosure of the median of the annual total compensation of all employees of an issuer (excluding the chief executive officer), the annual total compensation of that issuer's chief executive officer and the ratio of the median of the annual total compensation of all employees to the annual total compensation of the chief executive officer. Pay Ratio Disclosure, SEC Release No. 9452 (proposed Sept. 18, 2013).

fits in the overall compensation objective and how it affects other elements, and whether and how the registrant has considered the results of the most recent shareholder advisory vote on executive compensation.[140]

Item 403 requires disclosure in tabular form of any person (or group) who is the beneficial owner of more than 5 percent of any class of the registrant's voting securities,[141] as well as the amount for each class of equity security each director and executive officer described in Item 402 beneficially owns.[142] For each of these requirements, the table must show: (i) the title of the class of securities; (ii) the name and address of the beneficial owner (the address is not necessary for directors and executive officers); (iii) the total number of shares beneficially owned; (iv) the nature of the ownership interest; and (v) the percent of the class owned.[143]

Item 404 sets forth disclosure requirements for transactions that exceed $120,000 and in which a related person has a direct or indirect material interest.[144] The registrant must disclose the name of the related person and the basis for the relation, the related person's interest in the transaction, the approximate value of the transaction, the approximate value of the related person's interest, and any other information that is material to investors.[145]

The last two items of Part 400, Items 406 and 407, set forth requirement for the adoption of a code of ethics (defined as written

---

[140] 17 C.F.R. § 229.402(b). Independently of how it is structured, these disclosure requirements are designed to provide to investors material information necessary to an understanding of the registrant's compensation policies and decisions regarding the named executive officers. For a case finding that wrongfully claimed personal expense reimbursement constituted compensation for purposes of Item 402, see S.E.C. v. Kovzan, 807 F.Supp.2d 1024 (D.Kan. 2011); *but see* Andropolis v. Red Robin Gourmet Burgers, Inc., 505 F.Supp.2d 662 (D.Colo. 2007) (improper use of company aircraft for personal use did not constitute executive compensation when company requested to be reimbursed once it found out about the improper use).

[141] 17 C.F.R. § 229.403(a).

[142] 17 C.F.R. § 229.403(b).

[143] 17 C.F.R. § 229.403 (a)–(b).

[144] 17 C.F.R. § 229.404.

[145] 17 C.F.R. § 229.404(a)(1)–(6). In the case of indebtedness, disclosure of the amount involved in the transaction shall include the largest aggregate amount of principal outstanding during the period for which disclosure is provided, the amount thereof outstanding as of the latest practicable date, the amount of principal paid during the periods for which disclosure is provided, the amount of interest paid during the period for which disclosure is provided, and the rate or amount of interest payable on the indebtedness. For an example related party transaction, see S.E.C. v. Das, 2011 WL 4375787 (D.Neb. 2011).

standards reasonably designed to deter wrongdoing), and of a framework for corporate governance, respectively.[146]

Part 500—registration statement and prospectus provisions

Part 500 sets forth the specific mechanics of the registration statement and prospectus, including the cover page, prospectus summary, risk factors and ratio of earnings to fix charges, use of proceeds, determination of offering price, dilution of shares, selling security holders, plan of distribution, interests of named experts and counsel, disclosure of SEC position on indemnification of 1933 Act liabilities, other expenses related to issuance and distribution, and other undertakings.[147]

Item 501 sets forth the guidelines for the forepart of the registration statement and outside front cover page of the prospectus.[148] Generally, it requires the registrant to furnish in plain English an outside front cover page of the prospectus, which cannot be longer than one page, and that provides the registrant's name, title and amount of securities, offering price of the securities,[149] market for the securities (including the exchange name and trading symbol), risk factors, state legend (if required by state law), SEC legend, the name of the lead underwriter and the nature of the underwriting arrangements (e.g., firm commitment, best efforts, etc.), date of prospectus, and the qualifying statements for the prospectus.[150] Item 502 mandates that the inside front or outside back cover pages of the prospectus contain a reasonably detailed table of contents that provides the page numbers of the various sections and subsections, and a statement on the outside back cover advising dealers of their prospectus delivery obligations.[151]

---

[146] *See* 17 C.F.R. §§ 229.406 and 229.407. The registrant must file with the SEC a copy of its code of ethics as an exhibit to its annual report; post the text of such code of ethics on its website and disclose, in its annual report, its Internet address and the fact that it has posted such code of ethics on its website; or undertake in its annual report filed with the SEC to provide to any person without charge, upon request, a copy of such code of ethics and explain the manner in which such request may be made. 17 C.F.R. § 229.406(c). For further information on content of company websites, see Commission Guidance on the Use of Company Web Sites, SEC Release No. 34–58288 (Aug. 1, 2008).

[147] 17 C.F.R. § 229.500 *et seq.*

[148] 17 C.F.R. § 229.501. *See also* Plain English Disclosure, SEC Release No. 1113 (Jan. 29, 1998).

[149] If giving a price to the public is impractical, the registrant must explain the method by which it will determine the price. *Id.* at Instruction 2.

[150] 17 C.F.R. § 229.501(b).

[151] 17 C.F.R. § 229.502.

Pursuant to Item 503, the registrant must provide a prospectus summary in plain English, along with an address and telephone number, and include a discussion of the most significant factors that make the offering speculative or risky in a separate section captioned "Risk Factors."[152] The risk factors described may include lack of operating history, lack of profitable operations, financial position, business or proposed business, or a lack of market for the financial instruments.[153] Item 504 requires registrants to state the principal purpose for which it intends to use the proceeds, or a statement that there are no such plans and provide an alternate reason for the offering.[154] Moreover, pursuant to Item 505, a registrant must describe the various factors considered in determining the offering price for common equity securities for which there is no established market, and the various factors considered in determining the exercise or conversion price for warrants, rights or convertible securities exercisable for common equity.[155]

Item 506 sets forth disclosure requirements for cases when an offering will dilute existing shares for a class of common equity securities.[156] Under Item 507, if the registrant is offering the securities for the account of security holders, it must provide the name of the security holder, indicate the nature of any position, office or material relationship between the seller and registrant over the past three years, as well as state the amount of securities that the holder owns prior to and after the offering, and the amount offered.[157] Pursuant to Item 508, the registrant must identify the principal underwriters, the respective amounts underwritten, any material relationships between the registration and the underwriters, and the nature of the obligation of the underwriter to take

---

[152] 17 C.F.R. § 229.503. The "Risk Factors" section must identify each risk in appropriately captioned subsections, be concise and organized logically, and must immediately follow the summary section (if applicable).

[153] *Id.*

[154] 17 C.F.R. § 229.504. Registrants do not need to provide detailed information, an outline of intended use will suffice. However, registrants must identify other funds that may be needed to achieve a stated objective, disclose that the intended use of the proceeds is to discharge indebtedness, disclose that the proceeds will be used to acquire significant assets not in the ordinary course of business. *Id.*

[155] 17 C.F.R. § 229.505. The registrant must disclose the factors it considered in determining the price also when there is an established market, but there is a disparity between the offering price and the market price.

[156] 17 C.F.R. § 229.506.

[157] 17 C.F.R. § 229.507; *see also* Securities Offering Reform, SEC Release No. 75 (Aug. 3, 2005).

the securities.[158] Moreover, Item 508 requires that the registrant identify new underwriters, outline the plan for distributions not done through underwriting, provide the name of the exchange (if applicable), disclose the underwriters' compensation, whether they have any representatives on the board, underwriters' indemnification, dealers' compensation, identify finders, state whether underwriters will engage in passive market making under Rule 103 of Regulation M, and disclose stabilization transactions.[159]

Item 509 requires disclosure of contingent compensation arrangements between the registrant and named experts (for registration statements), and counsel, underwriters or selling securities holders (for prospectuses) pursuant to which they would receive an ownership interest in the registrant or subsidiaries in exchange for their opinion as to the validity of the securities being offered or other legal matters relating to the registration or offering.[160]

Item 510 requires the following statement to be included the prospectus:

> Insofar as indemnification for liabilities arising under the Securities Act of 1933 may be permitted to directors, officers or persons controlling the registrant pursuant to the foregoing provisions, the registrant has been informed that in the opinion of the Securities and Exchange Commission such indemnification is against public policy as expressed in the Act and is therefore unenforceable.[161]

Items 511 requires disclosure of certain information relating to expenses of issuance and distribution (other than underwriting discounts and commissions).[162] Under Item 512, registrants undertake to disclose certain information upon the occurrence of certain events, including shelf registration pursuant to Rule 415.[163]

Part 600—exhibits

Item 601 of Part 600 is likely the more labor-intensive portion of Regulation S-K. It sets forth a table of exhibits required to be filed with the registration or proxy statements.[164] Item 601 provides specific

---

158 17 C.F.R. § 229.508. Item 508 only requires a brief statement of whether the underwriter is required to take all or part of the securities offered.

159 17 C.F.R. § 229.508(b)–(l): *see also* Passive Market Making, SEC Release No. 6991 (Apr. 8, 1993).

160 17 C.F.R. § 229.509. This requirement only applies if the contingent interest exceeds $50,000.

161 17 C.F.R. § 229.510.

162 17 C.F.R. § 229.511.

163 17 C.F.R. § 229.512.

164 17 C.F.R. § 229.601.

requirements both as to the individual exhibits and the form of presentation. For ease of use, Item 601 requires an index identifying the sequence of the exhibits as they relate to the table of exhibits and stating whether they are incorporated by reference.[165]

Table 3.2 sets forth the specific exhibits that registrants must provide depending on the form they file with the SEC.

Table 3.2 Table of exhibits required under Regulation S-K

Exhibit Table													
	1933 Act Forms								1934 Act Forms				
	S-1	S-3	S-4[a]	S-8	S-11	F-1	F-3	F-4[a]	10	8-K[b]	10-D	10-Q	10-K
Underwriting agreement	X	X	X		X	X	X	X		X			
Plan of acquisition, reorganization, arrangement, liquidation or succession	X	X	X		X	X	X	X	X	X		X	X
Articles of incorporation	X		X		X	X		X	X	X	X	X	X
Bylaws	X		X		X	X		X	X	X	X	X	X
Instruments defining the rights of security holders, including indentures	X	X	X	X	X	X	X	X	X	X	X	X	X
Opinion re legality	X	X	X	X	X	X	X	X					
Correspondence from an independent accountant regarding non-reliance on a previously issued audit report or completed interim review										X			
Opinion re tax matters	X	X	X		X	X	X	X					
Voting trust agreement	X		X		X	X		X	X				X
Material contracts	X		X		X	X		X	X		X	X	X
Statement re computation of per share earnings	X		X		X	X		X	X			X	X
Statements re computation of ratios	X	X	X		X	X		X	X				X

165 17 C.F.R. § 229.601(a)(2). Registrants need only file copies of said exhibits instead of originals, unless Item 601 specifically provides otherwise.

Exhibit Table

	1933 Act Forms								1934 Act Forms				
	S-1	S-3	S-4[a]	S-8	S-11	F-1	F-3	F-4[a]	10	8-K[b]	10-D	10-Q	10-K
Annual report to security holders, Form 10-Q or quarterly report to security holders[c]			X										X
Code of ethics										X			X
Letter re unaudited interim financial information	X	X	X	X	X	X	X	X				X	
Letter re change in certifying accountants[d]	X		X		X				X	X			X
Correspondence on departure of director										X			
Letter re change in accounting principles												X	X
Report furnished to security holders												X	
Other documents or statements to security holders										X			
Subsidiaries of the registrant	X		X		X	X		X	X				X
Published report regarding matters submitted to vote of security holders											X		
Consents of experts and counsel	X	X	X	X	X	X	X	X		X[e]	X[e]	X[e]	X[e]
Power of attorney	X	X	X	X	X	X	X	X	X	X		X	X
Statement of eligibility of trustee	X	X	X			X	X	X					
Invitation for competitive bids	X	X	X			X	X	X					
Rule 13a-14(a)/ 15d-14(a)												X	X
Certifications Rule 13a-14/15d-14 Certifications													X
Section 1350 certifications[f]												X	X
Report on assessment of compliance with servicing criteria for asset-backed issuers													X

Exhibit Table

	1933 Act Forms								1934 Act Forms				
	S-1	S-3	S-4[a]	S-8	S-11	F-1	F-3	F-4[a]	10	8-K[b]	10-D	10-Q	10-K
Attestation report on assessment of compliance with servicing criteria for asset-backed securities													X
Servicer compliance statement													X
Mine safety disclosure exhibit												X	X
Additional exhibits	X	X	X	X	X	X	X	X	X	X	X	X	X
XBRL-related documents									X	X		X	X
Interactive data file	X	X	X		X	X	X	X		X		X	X

Notes: [a] An exhibit need not be provided about a company if: (1) With respect to such company an election has been made under Form S-4 or F-4 to provide information about such company at a level prescribed by Form S-3 or F-3; and (2) the form, the level of which has been elected under Form S-4 or F-4, would not require such company to provide such exhibit if it were registering a primary offering.

[b] A Form 8-K exhibit is required only if relevant to the subject matter reported on the Form 8-K report. For example, if the Form 8-K pertains to the departure of a director, only the exhibit described in paragraph (b)(17) of this section need be filed. A required exhibit may be incorporated by reference from a previous filing.

[c] Where incorporated by reference into the text of the prospectus and delivered to security holders along with the prospectus as permitted by the registration statement; or, in the case of the Form 10-K, where the annual report to security holders is incorporated by reference into the text of the Form 10-K.

[d] If required pursuant to Item 304 of Regulation S-K.

[e] Where the opinion of the expert or counsel has been incorporated by reference into a previously filed Securities Act registration statement.

[f] Pursuant to §§ 240.13a-13(b)(3) and 240.15d-13(b)(3), asset-backed issuers are not required to file reports on Form 10-Q.

Part 700—miscellaneous

Part 700 deals with miscellaneous disclosure requirements for sales of unregistered securities and the use of proceeds from registered securities, indemnification of directors and officers in case of liability, and the purchase of equity securities by the issuer and affiliated purchasers.[166]

166 *See* 17 C.F.R §§ 229.701, 229.702 and 229.703.

Part 800—list of industry guides

Part 800 provides a list of industry specific guides that the 1933 Act and the 1934 Act cover.[167]

Specific Disclosure Requirements—Regulation S-X

Regulation S-X is divided in articles that contain several parts.

Article 1—application of Regulation S-X

As Article 1 explains, Regulation S-X governs the form and content of the financial statements that are required to be filed under the registration statement required under the 1933 Act and 1934 Act, as well as the periodic reports required under Section 13 of the 1934 Act.[168]

Moreover, Regulation S-X covers accountant reports,[169] which are documents in which an independent accountant indicates the scope of the audit they have made, and sets forth the accountant's opinion regarding the financial statements taken as a whole (this may include an assertion that the accountant cannot express an overall opinion, as long as the accountant gives a reason for saying so). The importance of accountant reports comes in the certification. If certified, a registrant is representing

---

[167] *See* 17 C.F.R. §§ 229.801 and 229.802.

[168] The accounting gimmicks that led to some of the biggest scandals since the great depression prompted the radical change in auditing standards. For example, Enron's faulty accounting led to its employees losing some $1.3 billion from their 401(k) accounts, and investors to lose some $61 billion in share value. *See* John Kroger, *Enron, Fraud, and Securities Reform: An Enron Prosecutor's Perspective*, 76 U. Colo. L. Rev. 57 (2005). Enron was able to perpetuate its fraud through systematic misrepresentation of the information contained in its 10-Q and 10-K reports, which included careful manipulation of hard data designed to ensure that the management narrative is accurate. *Id* at 71. *See also* SEC v. KPMG LLP, 412 F.Supp.2d 349 (2006) (on defendant's appeal of SEC order, the court found liability as primary violators for independent auditors for misstatements in audit opinions).

[169] The 1934 Act gave the SEC the power to set accounting standards. The SEC has delegated this power to the Financial Accounting Standards Board ("FASB"), which, in turn, sets the Generally Accepted Accounting Principles ("GAAP"). The role of the FSAB is not without controversy, with it taking center stage with the role that mark-to-market rules played in the most recent financial crisis. *See* Rigers Gjyshi, A History of Mark-to-Market Accounting, in Markham, Gabilondo, and Hazen's Corporate Finance: Debt, Equity, and Derivative Markets and Their Intermediaries (2011).

that it is producing financial statements the contents of which have been certified by an independent accountant.[170]

Article 2—qualifications and reports of accountants

Article 2 of Regulation S-X sets forth the requirements for qualification of accountants. Generally, a certified public accountant must be in good standing and registered under local laws.[171] Moreover, Article 2 mandates that independent accountants must be truly independent, and the SEC will consider all relevant facts and circumstances and will look through from to substance in determining independence. To achieve this, the SEC has imposed restrictions on the financial, employment and business relationship between an accountant and an audit client.[172] These restrictions may apply even when any prior relationship stems from prior provision of non-audit accounting services and companies must check with the SEC before engaging in a relationship that can give the appearance of conflict.[173]

In addition to the independence requirements, an accountant's report must be dated, signed manually, indicate the city and state where issued, and identify each financial statement it covers. The report must state whether the audit followed generally accepted auditing standards and identify those standards that were omitted (if any), must state the accountant's opinion as to the financial statements the report covers, the

---

[170] 17 C.F.R. § 210.1–02.

[171] *See* S.E.C. v. Ramoil Management, Ltd., 2007 WL 3146943 (S.D.N.Y. 2007) (finding that the defendant violated Article 2 by filing a Form 10-KBS without an independent audit signed by a certified public accountant).

[172] 17 C.F.R. § 210.2–01.

[173] *See, e.g.*, Deloitte & Touche LLP, SEC No Action Letter (2006) (providing no-action relief where accounting company sold tax and accounting software to an issuer). *See also* In The Matter of Moore Stephens Wurth Frazer & Torbet LLP and K. Dean Yamagata, CPA, SEC Release No. 3221 (Dec. 20, 2010) (finding liability for accountants who failed to provide accurate audits of corporation's inflated financial statements). In the Matter of Ernst & Young LLP, SEC Release 2580 (Mar. 26, 2007), involved administrative liability for violating auditor independence standards under Article 2 of Regulation S-X. The respondent admitted to violating action concerning violations of auditor independence standards by E&Y. During 2001, E&Y, through one of its National Office partners, compromised its professional independence by assisting one client, AIG, in its development and marketing of an accounting-driven financial product and then advising an audit client, PNC, on the accounting treatment for a version of that product in PNC's financial statements, without E&Y performing a meaningful analysis of the accounting separate from the analysis that the National Office partner had performed.

accounting principles used and the effect of how these principles were applied, identify any exceptions, and contain an attestation report as to the registrant's internal controls over financial reporting related to the financial statements contained in the report.[174]

Article 3—general instructions as to financial statements

Article 3 of Regulation S-X contains guidelines on the balance sheets, statements of income and cash flows to be included in the relevant disclosures. The operating mandate is that these documents must be audited (as specified above). As a preliminary note, Regulation S-X allows filings under the 1933 Act and the 1934 Act to incorporate by reference information disclosed in the prospectus and financial statements filed under the respective acts.[175]

Article 3 requires that for each report, the registrant and its subsidiaries, file consolidated, audited balance sheets for each of the two most recent years (or, for companies in existence for fewer than two years, an audited balance sheet that is from within 135 days for the filing of the registration statement).[176]

Article 3 also requires that for each report, the registrant and its subsidiaries file audited statements of income and cash flows for each of

---

[174] 17 C.F.R. § 210.2–02. In case an accountant who is not the principal accountant prepares the part of the report, and the principal accountant elects to use that part, the separate report must be filed in conjunction with the main report. 17 C.F.R. § 210.2–05.

[175] *See* 17 C.F.R. § 210.3–01. For a case imposing liability for inadequate financial statements, see SEC v. Diversified Growth Corp., 595 F.Supp. 1159 (D.C. Cir. 1984) (annual reports required to be filed by a corporation with SEC were virtually useless for purposes of contempt finding for violating permanent injunction compelling the filings where filings failed to include audited financial statements as required by SEC regulation and there was no showing that corporation fell within exemption clause and that deficiency alone warranted order reducing fines to judgment, regardless of additional deficiencies such as failure to mention lawsuit, inadequate or omitted discussion of properties and failure to have document signed by proper officers and directors).

[176] 17 C.F.R. § 210.3–01. This section allows for use of an interim balance sheet if the filing is made within 45 days of the registrant's end of the fiscal year. *See* Roche Diagnostics Corp. v. Medical Automation Systems, Inc., 646 F.3d 424 (7th Cir. 2011) (Regulation S-X generally requires consolidation if a reporting registrant owns a majority of some other company's stock).

the three fiscal years preceding the date of the most recent audited balance sheet.[177]

The registrant must reconcile any statements of income to reflect business operations for operations that are not reflected in prior SEC filings. Moreover, if a registrant uses unaudited interim financial statements, it must make any such adjustments that management thinks necessary to a fair statement of the results for the interim periods presented.[178]

Moreover, Article 3 provides specific requirements as to how a registrant reports changes in other stockholders' equity on the statements of income,[179] requires financial statements for businesses that the registrant has acquired or plans to acquire,[180] and provides that the financial statements covering a period of nine to twelve months may satisfy the one-year requirements when certain conditions apply.[181] Article 3 also requires separate statements to be filed for subsidiaries not consolidated or for which the registrant owns less than 50 percent of the equity stock,[182] as well as for issuers of guaranteed registered securities and the guarantor of such security.[183] However, Article 3 allows inactive companies to file unaudited financial statements as long as they meet the conditions contained.[184]

---

[177] 17 C.F.R. § 210.3–02. This section also requires the same for the period between the audited balance sheet and any interim balance sheet, though these statements of income and cash flow need not be audited. *Id.*

[178] 17 C.F.R. § 210.3–03. An example of such adjustment would be appropriate estimated provisions for bonus and profit sharing arrangements normally determined or settled at year-end.

[179] 17 C.F.R. § 210.3–04.

[180] 17 C.F.R. § 210.3–05. Acquisitions of a group of related businesses that are probable or that have occurred subsequent to the latest fiscal year end for which audited financial statements of the registrant have been filed should be treated as if they are a single business combination. The required financial statements of related businesses may be presented on a combined basis for any periods they are under common control or management. *Id. See also* SEC v. Prince, 2013 1831841 (D.C. Cir. 2013) (when a public company acquires a significant subsidiary, the financial statements of that subsidiary must be filed with the SEC).

[181] 17 C.F.R. § 210.3–06.

[182] 17 C.F.R. § 210.3–09. Separate financial statements required by this section shall be as of the same dates and for the same periods as the audited consolidated financial statements required to be filed by the other registrant.

[183] 17 C.F.R. § 210.3–10. *See also* Staff Accounting Bulletin No. 53. This rule was in response to the widespread practice whereby a parent company would raise capital through offerings of its own securities that are guaranteed by

Article 3 also governs the age of financial statement. Understandably, the goal is to have financial statements that are current. The age of permitted financial statements depends on the type of issuer and the type of report. Article 3 sets forth the specific requirements, though, as a general matter, financial statements must be as of a date within 135 days of the filing date.[185] If financial statements are stale under Article 3, a registrant must update them with current information on a balance sheet and statements of income and cash flow (though these documents do not have to be audited).[186]

The SEC has the authority to permit a registrant not to file any of the financial statements that Article 3 requires. However, the opposite also holds true, in that the SEC may require a registrant to file additional financial statements if it deems it necessary for the accurate presentation of its financial conditions.[187]

If a registrant is using securities of an affiliate as collateral for a class of securities that are being registered, and those securities equal 20 percent or more of the value of the securities being issued, the registrant must file financial statements of the issuer of securities used as collateral, unless such statement has been filed by the issuer of the collateral securities.[188]

---

one or more of its subsidiaries, or through offerings of securities by a subsidiary that are guaranteed by the parent company. Thus, it stood to reason that investors would want information about the issuer as well as the guarantor on whom the issuer was relying to effectuate the transaction, for a guarantee is only as good as the guarantor. *See* Financial Statements and Periodic Reports for Related Issuers and Guarantors, SEC Release No. 33–7878 (Aug. 4, 2000).

[184] 17 C.F.R. § 210.3–11. *See also* SEC v. Diversified Growth Corp., 595 F.Supp. 1159 (D.C. Cir. 1984), and In the Matter of Citizens Capital Corp., SEC Release No. 67313 (June 29, 2012) (SEC revoked registration statement because of respondent's failure to file audited financial statement, despite respondent's assertion that it was an inactive company under Article 3).

[185] 17 C.F.R. § 210.3–12.

[186] 17 C.F.R. § 210.3–12.

[187] 17 C.F.R. § 210.3–13. *See also* TIAA Real Estate Account, SEC No Action Letter (May 1, 1996) (granting no action relief to registrant where certain precautions were in place and the company represented that any information would be available upon request); In the Matter of Seahawk Deep Ocean Technology, Inc., SEC Release No 35 (May 26, 1993) (finding liability for company's refusal to cooperate with the SEC's request that it file additional financial statements of related businesses).

[188] 17 C.F.R. § 210.3–16. *See also* Financial Statements and Periodic Reports for Related Issuers and Guarantors, SEC Release No. 33–7878 (Aug. 4, 2000).

When it comes to natural persons, Regulation S-X allows for their unaudited balance sheets to be filed within 90 days of the filing, and unaudited statements of income for each of the most recent three fiscal years.[189]

Article 3A—consolidated and combined financial statements

Article 3A governs the presentation of consolidated and combined financial statements.[190] In deciding the method of presentation, the goal is always to provide enough information that will clearly portray the financial position of a registrant and the results of its operations. There is a presumption that consolidated statements are more meaningful than separate statements and that they are necessary for a fair presentation of a complete picture. At the very least, the disclosures these sections require should clearly explain the accounting policies the registrant follows, including the circumstances involved in any departure from the normal practice of consolidating majority-owned subsidiaries and not consolidating entities that are less than majority owned.[191]

Article 4—rules of general application

Article 4 of Regulation S-X provides general rules regarding the form and order of the information that companies must disclose thereunder.[192] Again, the goal is efficient disclosure, and companies must disclose certain minimum material information to make the statements not misleading. To accomplish this goal, Regulation S-X operates under the presumption that if required information is not disclosed, it is misleading. For example, filed financial statements of companies that are not prepared in accordance with GAAP will be presumptively misleading (despite other disclosures).[193] However, a registrant does not have to provide amounts for items that are not material, and they may combine

---

[189] 17 C.F.R. § 210.3–17.

[190] 17 C.F.R. §§ 210.3A-02, 210.3A-03, 210.3A-04 and 210.3A-05.

[191] *Id.*

[192] 17 C.F.R § 210.4–01 *et seq.*

[193] 17 C.F.R. § 210.4–01. Article 4 provides formatting conventions designed to make the presentation of information not misleading. *See generally* SEC v. Caserta, 75 F.Supp.2d 79 (E.D.N.Y. 1999); In The Matter of Medifast, Inc., SEC Release No. 3487 (Sept. 18, 2013).

the amounts of nonmaterial items as well.[194] Moreover, Article 4 prohibits captions for items that are not present, and allows for omission of financial statements that are not required as long as the registrant provides a reason for so doing.[195] Article 4 also requires that a registrant show separately as a deduction from the applicable account or accounts discounts on shares or any unamortized balance thereof.[196]

Lastly, Article 4 sets forth certain items that a registrant must disclose on the face of the filed financial statements with appropriate captions. Those items include (i) principles of consolidation or combination; (ii) assets subject to liens; (iii) defaults); (iv) preferred shares; (v) restrictions that limit the payment of dividends by the registrant; (vi) significant changes in bonds, mortgages and similar debt; (vii) summarized financial information of subsidiaries not consolidated and 50 percent or less owned persons; (viii) income tax expense; (ix) outstanding warrants and rights; (x) related party transactions which affect the financial statement; (xi) repurchase and reverse repurchase agreements; and (xii) accounting policies of certain derivative instruments.[197] It is important to keep in mind that the materiality concept applies to a registrant's failure to follow these guidelines. In *Baron v. Smith*, for example, the court refused to find liability for non-disclosure of a potential default as it did not make the report (Form 10-K, in this case) materially misleading.[198]

---

[194] 17 C.F.R. § 210.4–02; *see* Pavlidis v. New England Patriots Football Club, Inc., 675 F.Supp 688 (Dist. Mass. 1988) (no liability for misleading information where such information was found not to be material).

[195] 17 C.F.R. § 210.4–03. Moreover, if a note covers the same subject matter as the note in another statement, the registrant does not have to file both, but may incorporate the second one by reference. 17 C.F.R. § 210.4–04.

[196] 17 C.F.R. § 210.4–07.

[197] 17 C.F.R. § 210.4–08. These items represent areas that regulators and the investing public view with particular skepticism because they are particularly susceptible to misrepresentation. *See* McUrdy v. SEC, 396 F.3d 1258 (D.C. Cir. 2005) (explaining the inherent skepticism when it comes to related party transactions); *see also* Gordon v. Comm'r, 85 T.C. 309, 326–27, 1985 WL 15384 (1985) (same).

[198] 285 F.Supp2d 96, 104 (2003); *see also* Erath v. Xidex Corp, 1991 WL 338322 (Dist. Ariz. 1991) (omission of the full terms of the Warrant Agreement was neither material nor misleading).

Articles 5, 6, 6A, 7, and 9

Articles 5, 6, 6A, 7, and 9 of Regulation S-X set forth disclosure requirements specific to financial assets filed by commercial and industrial companies, registered investment companies, employee stock purchase, savings and similar plans, insurance companies, and bank holding companies, respectively. A detailed discussion of those articles is beyond the scope of this work.

Article 10—interim financial statements

Article 10 of Regulation S-X provides the rules for interim financial statements. These statements cover periods of less than one year. Generally, registrants may consolidate interim financial statements and they may be unaudited (though companies may provide audited statements if they so choose). Interim balance sheets shall only provide major captions and those captions shall be prominently displayed on the balance sheet or in the notes to the financial statement. Interim statements of income must also include major captions as prescribed elsewhere in Regulation S-X.[199] Moreover, the statement of changes in financial position may be abbreviated, with companies only showing a single figure of funds provided by operations, unless the change exceeds 10 percent of the average of funds for the most recent three years.[200]

More significantly, Article 10 reiterates the need that any interim financial statements contain enough information to make the interim information not misleading. Filing companies, however, may presume that users have access to audited financial statements, and, as such, they do not have to disclose substantially duplicative information, unless there has been a change in the registrant's circumstances, non-disclosure of which would be materially misleading.[201] Article 10 also allows registrants to omit detailed schedules that are otherwise required by Regulation S-X.

---

[199] 17 C.F.R. § 210.10–01. Note that balance sheet captions may be combined with others if they are less than 10 percent of total assets and that has not changed more than 25 percent since the preceding fiscal year. The same rule applies to interim income statements items that constitute less than 15 percent of average net income of the most recent three fiscal years and the change is no more than 20 percent. *Id.*

[200] *Id.*

[201] 17 C.F.R. § 210.10–01(a)(5). Regulation S-X provides the following example: "Disclosures should encompass for example, significant changes since the end of the most recently completed fiscal year in such items as: accounting principles and practices; estimates inherent in the preparation of financial

Article 10 provides additional instructions regarding content. For example, a registrant must provide summarized income statement information for each unconsolidated subsidiary separately.[202] Article 10 also contains specific requirements for earnings per share and dividends declared per share applicable to common stock, and pooling of interests from business combinations.[203] Companies must make pro forma disclosure of the results of operations from material business combinations that occurred during the current fiscal year. The disclosure shall be as of the date of the most recent interim balance sheet as though companies had combined at the beginning of the relevant period.[204] The registrant must disclose the effect on revenue and net income if it disposed of any significant segment of the business.[205] Moreover, the interim financial statement shall reflect any changes in the accounting standards used, along with a letter from the independent accountant explaining the changes if the document filed is Form 10-Q.[206] Lastly, the registrant must disclose any retroactive material adjustment made for a prior period and the effect it has on net income, and any unaudited interim financial statements shall reflect any and all adjustments which management believes are necessary to a fair statement of the results for the interim period.[207]

Subsection (c) of Article 10 covers the periods that interim financial statements cover. For filings on Form 10-Q, the following rules apply:

1. The registrant must provide an interim balance sheet as of the end of the most recent fiscal quarter and preceding fiscal year;
2. Interim statements of income shall be provided for the most recent fiscal quarter, for the period between the end of the preceding fiscal

---

statements; status of long-term contracts; capitalization including significant new borrowings or modification of existing financing arrangements; and the reporting entity resulting from business combinations or dispositions." *Id.*

[202] 17 C.F.R. § 210.10–01(b).

[203] *Id. See also* In the Matter of American Stellar Energy, INC., SEC Release No. 64897 (July 18, 2011) (liability for failing to include a statement of stockholders' equity from the registrant's inception on Form 10-Q).

[204] 17 C.F.R. § 210.10–01(b)(4).

[205] 17 C.F.R. § 210.10–01(b)(5).

[206] 17 C.F.R. § 210.10–01(b)(6). The letter from the independent accountant must be made in the first Form 10-Q after the change occurs, and must state whether the change is to an alternative which the accountant believes is preferable under the circumstances.

[207] *See* SEC v. Snyder, 292 Fed.Appx. 391, 395 (5th Cir. 2008).

year and the end of the most recent fiscal quarter, and for the corresponding periods of the preceding fiscal year; and

3. Interim statements of cash flows shall be provided for the period between the end of the preceding fiscal year and the end of the most recent fiscal quarter, and for the corresponding period of the preceding fiscal year.[208]

Interim financial statements filed along with Form 10-Q must be reviewed by an independent public accountant using professional standards and procedures for conducting such reviews (as established by generally accepted auditing standards), and the registrant must include a report of the accountant on the review.[209] Lastly, the SEC may grant a written request to omit certain financial statements, but the SEC may also send an informal written notice requesting additional information.[210]

Article 11—pro forma financial information

Article 11 of Regulation S-X covers pro forma financial information. Generally speaking, pro forma financial information is designed to provide information about significant registrant events, e.g., year-end earnings and results of operations, without having to adhere to GAAP.

Although pro forma information is intended to provide information about the registrant, there is concern that they are prone to abuse. The SEC has expressed concern that companies use pro forma financial information to give a skewed picture of their financial position.[211] The SEC pointed out that pro forma information is designed to allow

---

208 17 C.F.R. § 210.10–01(c). Note that registrants engaged in seasonal production and sale of a single-crop agricultural commodity may provide interim statements of income and cash flows for the 12-month period ended during the most recent fiscal quarter and for the corresponding preceding period in lieu of the year-to-date statements specified. *Id.*

209 17 C.F.R § 210.10–01(d). *See* In the Matter of Natures Sunshine Products INC., SEC Release No. 59268 (Jan. 21, 2009) (While financial statements in quarterly reports need not be audited, independent accountants must review those statements before filing). *See also* In the Matter of Ernst & Young LLP, SEC Release No. 2580 (Mar. 26, 2007) (liability for violating the requirement that review of interim reports be from an independent public accountant). The SEC did not require interim reviews until 2000, when it changed the rules to reflect the reality that major accounting firms already required audit clients to engage them for interim reviews. Audit Committee Disclosure, 64 Fed. Reg. 73389, 73398 (1999).

210 17 C.F.R. § 210.10–01(e).

211 *See* SEC Release No. 33–8039 (2001).

investors to compare current results with other reporting periods and other companies, and significant departures from GAAP in pro forma statements can make this comparison difficult or misleading.[212] Moreover, the SEC warned that information that is technically true, may be misleading if it omits material components of that information. Thus, the SEC directed registrants to disclose the methodologies and controlling principles used to present significant events, e.g., earnings before EBTA, so the information is not misleading. However, mere deviation from GAAP for information that addresses a limited feature of financial results will not necessarily be misleading if the statement discloses in plain English how the information deviated from the GAAP and the amount of deviation.[213]

With the above in mind, a registrant must provide pro forma financial information when (i) a significant business combination has occurred; (ii) a significant combination of businesses or entities under common control has occurred or is probable; (iii) the registrant will offer registered securities to security holders of business that it is acquiring; (iv) the disposition of significant portions of a business is made; (v) after the acquisition of significant real estate operations or properties are significant;[214] (vi) roll-up transactions; (vii) the registrant has become an independent entity; and (viii) when such information would be material to investors.[215]

Moreover, Article 11 contains specific preparation requirements as to the form and content of pro forma information. Again, the objective is to assist investors in analyzing the future prospects of the registrant by disclosing information on transactions that would affect the registrant's financial positions and results of operations, and adhering to the specific requirements contained in Article 11 ensures the presentation of the information accomplishes this objective.[216]

---

[212] *Id.*

[213] *Id.*

[214] Regulation S-X requires aggregation of acquisition in making a determination of whether an acquisition is significant.

[215] 17 C.F.R. § 210.11–01(a). These requirements do not apply to transactions between a parent company and its totally-held subsidiary. 17 C.F.R. § 210.11–01(e). *See* In Re Conditions for use of Non-GAAP Financial Measures, SEC Release No. 8176 (Jan. 22, 2003). *Accord* SEC v. Melchoir, 1993 WL 89141 (Dist. Utah 1993) (liability for violation of Regulation S-X by failing to include pro forma financial information on probable acquisitions).

[216] 17 C.F.R. § 210.11–02. Article 11 also allows for financial forecasts to be filed in lieu of pro forma condensed statements of income if certain conditions are met. 17 C.F.R. § 210.11–03.

1934 ACT CONTINUOUS DISCLOSURE

Unlike the 1933 Act, the 1934 Act regulates trading in the secondary markets and protects investors by subjecting companies that meet certain conditions to continuous disclosure requirements. While the 1934 Act came after the 1933 Act, it has become the main tool through which investors gain access to material information about public companies. These mandatory disclosures depend on the type of company, but the underlying theme is materiality, i.e., disclosure of information that a reasonable investor would find material in its evaluation of a company's security. Moreover, because large, well-established companies are responsible for issuing most publicly traded securities, the continuous information disclosure provides a vital tool for these companies to communicate with the public. The hook for the 1934 Act is that companies must register any securities that are traded on an exchange. Thus, generally speaking, if a company has to register a security, it must abide by the 1934 Act's disclosure requirements.

Section 12: Registration

Section 12 of the 1934 Act details the registration of securities that are traded on a national securities exchange.[217] Through the registration requirement, the SEC ensures that companies disclose certain information to potential investors. The type of information that a company must disclose is similar to the information that an issuer must disclose during an offering under the 1933 Act. This similarity has given rise to criticism that companies whose securities are most commonly traded have to disclose the same information several times, incurring unnecessary costs in the process.

Section 12(a) of the 1934 Act sets forth the registration requirement.[218] Section 12(a) makes it unlawful for a broker or dealer to trade a security on a national securities exchange unless a registration is effective as to such security for such exchange.

Section 12(b) details the procedure and information that a company must disclose during the registration process.[219] To begin the registration process, a company must file an application with the relevant exchange (along with a duplicate original to the SEC) containing information about

---

217 15 U.S.C. § 78l.

218 15 U.S.C. § 78l(a).

219 15 U.S.C. § 78l(b).

the following: the organization, financial structure, and nature of the business; the terms, position, rights, and privileges of the different classes of securities outstanding; the terms on which their securities are to be, and during the preceding three years have been, offered to the public or otherwise; the directors, officers, and underwriters, and each security holder of record holding more than 10 percent of any class of any equity security of the issuer, their remuneration and their interests in the securities of, and their material contracts with, the issuer and any person directly or indirectly controlling or controlled by, or under direct or indirect common control with, the issuer; the remuneration exceeding $20,000 per annum (excluding directors and officers); bonus and profit-sharing arrangements; management and service contracts; options existing or to be created in respect of their securities; material contracts, not made in the ordinary course of business, which are to be executed in whole or in part at or after the filing of the application or which were made not more than two years before such filing, and every material patent or contract for a material patent right shall be deemed a material contract; balance sheets for not more than the three preceding fiscal years; profit and loss statements the three preceding fiscal years; and any further financial statements which the SEC may deem necessary or appropriate for the protection of investors.[220]

Once filed, the exchange will review and decide whether to approve the application. Normally, the registration application is not an issue as most are filed by large companies well-experienced with the process.

This is only the beginning of the information disclosure process for the purposes of the 1934 Act. That is, the information disclosed in the initial application to the register the securities with an exchange would quickly become stale. Section 13 of the 1934 Act makes up for this.

Section 13: Reports

Section 13 of the 1934 Act provides for continuous disclosures through periodic reports.[221] These periodic reports are supposed to supplement and update information about the company, but they also serve as marketing tool to drum up interest in the company.[222]

---

[220] 15 U.S.C. § 77l(b).

[221] 15 U.S.C. § 78m.

[222] *See* 17 C.F.R. § 240.13a *et seq.* For decisions revoking registration or registered securities for failure to file periodic reports under the 1934 Act, see In The Matter of Acunetx, Inc., SEC Release No. 70710 (Oct. 18, 2013), and In The Matter of Bonanza Once, Inc., SEC Release No. 70690 (Oct. 16, 2013).

The main reports are the quarterly, annual and current reports. These reports are filed on forms the SEC prescribes. Companies must use Form 10-Q for quarterly reports,[223] Form 10-K for annual reports,[224] and Form 8-K to report material events that cannot wait for the quarterly or annual reports.[225]

Form 8-K—reporting material events

Form 8-K sets forth specific information that a company must file therein, the specific events that may trigger the filing requirements and the timing of the filing. Reports on Form 8-K provide material information concerning certain events that have occurred since the annual report on Form 10-K or quarterly report on Form 10-Q.[226]

Generally, a company must file Form 8-K within four days following the day of the triggering event described in sections 1–6 and 9 below, though the SEC may prescribe different filing requirements.[227]

Form 8-K has nine sections, each containing items setting forth specific disclosure requirements. Section 1 covers the registrant's business and operations. The items therein require disclosure of information regarding the entry into, or termination of a material definitive agreement;[228] information on bankruptcy or receivership;[229] and information on shutdowns and patterns of violations in mining operations.

For decisions discussing civil and criminal liability for noncompliance with periodic reporting requirements, see SEC v. Retail Pro, Inc., 673 F.Supp.2d 1108 (S.D. Cal. 2008); SEC v. Sierra Brokerage Services, Inc., et al., 608 F. Supp.2d 923 (S.D. Ohio. 2009); SEC v. IMC International Inc., 384 F.Supp. 889 (N.D. Texas 1974); SEC v. Falstaff Brewing Corporation, 629 F.2d 62 (D.C. Cir. 1980); and United States v. Guterma, 281 F.2d 742 (2d Cir. 1960).

[223] 17 C.F.R. § 240.13a-13.

[224] 17 C.F.R. § 240.13a-1.

[225] 17 C.F.R. § 240.13a-11. Previously, companies had to file semi-annual reports on Form 9-K, but that is no longer the case.

[226] Filers may file Form 8-K voluntarily to report information that may be of interest to investors, independently of whether that information is material for purposes of Form 8-K.

[227] *See* SEC Form 8-K 17 C.F.R. § 249.308. To facilitate disclosure, the SEC allows filings intended as an update to a previously reported event under Form 8-K, to incorporate that information by reference. *Id.*

[228] These agreements are of the type not made in the ordinary course of the company's business, even the contract in question is not uncommon in the industry. Moreover, the reporting requirement does not attach until the actual entry or termination, mere negotiations are not enough.

[229] This prong requires a bankruptcy proceeding that covers all or substantially all of the company's business or assets. The company must disclose

Section 2 covers the registrant's financial information. The items therein require disclosure of information regarding the completion of acquisition or disposition of assets;[230] information on an announcement regarding material non-public information of results of operations or financial conditions for a completed quarter of an annual fiscal period; information on the creation of a direct financial obligation or an obligation under an off-balance sheet arrangement (this includes information on triggering events that give rise to the aforementioned financial obligations); information on the cost associated with the exit or disposal plan that will result in material changes of the company; and information on material impairments to company assets (including impairment to goodwill or those required by accounting rules.

Section 3 covers the registrant's securities and trading markets. The items therein require disclosure of information regarding the notice of delisting or failure to satisfy a continued listing rule or standard, or information on transfer of listing; information on the sale of unregistered equity securities that exceed 1 percent of the particular class of equity securities; and information on material modification to rights of security holders.

Section 4 covers the matters related to accountants and financial statements. The items therein require disclosure of information regarding changes in the company's certifying accountant,[231] and information on the company's decision not to rely on previously filed financial statements or related audit reports because they may contain errors.

Section 5 covers changes in governance and management. The items therein require disclosure of information relating to changes in control of the company (including information on the departure or election of directors, departure or appointment of certain officers and the compensatory arrangements of certain officers); information on amendments to articles of incorporation or bylaws or changes in fiscal year (if such

---

specific information about the proceeding, the governmental authority involved and detail about any plan that may be in effect as part of the bankruptcy.

[230] This requirement applies in cases of significant disposition of assets otherwise than in the ordinary course of business. This requirement does not apply to transactions involving wholly-owned subsidiaries or stock redemption/acquisition from the public.

[231] This change followed a series of accounting scandals including WorldCom and Enron. Companies are required to report this even if the change stems from the refusal of the accountant to accept reappointment. Moreover, this change will result in two Forms 8-K being filed, one to report the dismissal of the old one and one to report the engagement of the new accountant.

information was not disclosed in proxy or information statements); information on temporary suspension of trading under the company's employee benefit plans; information on amendments to the company's code of ethics, or waiver of a provision of the code of ethics; information on changes to shell company status (if applicable); and information on submission of matters to a vote of security holders; information on shareholder director nominations.

In addition to the above information, sections 6 through 9 of Form 8-K cover changes in information regarding asset-backed securities, other events, and financial statements and exhibits.

Form 10-Q—quarterly reports

Companies must file a quarterly report with the SEC on Form 10-Q.[232] Form 10-Q requires disclosure of several areas of a company's business and financial conditions. Form 10-Q contains two parts, each containing several items. A company must file Form 10-Q with the SEC within 45 days after the end of each fiscal quarter.[233] Large accelerated filers and accelerated filers must file it within 40 days. Fortunately, Form 10-Q allows filers to incorporate by reference information previously disclosed to shareholders or to the public provided they include the referenced information as an exhibit to Form 10-Q in accordance with Item 601 of Regulation S-K. Moreover, filers may combine information disclosed to security holders in quarterly reports with their Form 10-Q filing with the SEC provided that the information satisfies the requirements of Form 10-Q and it contains a cross-references sheet to the individual parts of Form 10-Q.

Part I covers substantive requirements and it contains five items. Item 1 contains disclosure requirements for the filer's financial statements. Pursuant to Item 1, a filer must disclose the same information required by Item 10–01 of Regulation S-X, which provides disclosure requirements for interim financial statements, balance sheets, statements of income, and statements of cash flow.[234]

Item 2 requires management's discussion and analysis of the company's financial condition and results of operations. The information

---

232 17 C.F.R. § 249.308a.

233 Companies must file Form 10-Q only for the first three quarters of a fiscal year; Form 10-Q is not required for the last quarter, which is covered in Form 10-K.

234 17 C.F.R. § 210.10–01.

required in Item 2 is the same as the information required in Item 303 of Regulation S-K.[235]

Item 3 requires quantitative and qualitative disclosures about market risk in accordance with Item 305 of Regulation S-K.[236]

Item 4 requires disclosure of company controls and procedures as set forth under Item 307 of Regulation S-K.[237] Item 4T reduced the reporting burden on registrants that are not large accelerated filers or accelerate filers. However this item expired on June 30, 2010.

Part II contains seven items designed to provide additional information that investors may find relevant. However, filers need not provide the information in Part II if it is inapplicable, the answer is negative or the information is provided elsewhere (e.g., Part I).

Item 1 requires disclosure of legal proceedings as required under Item 103 of Regulation S-K,[238] including the date of termination and description of disposition of proceedings terminated prior to the period that the 10-Q report covers.[239]

Item 1A requires filers to set forth any material changes from the risk factors as previously disclosed in Form 10-K.[240]

Item 2 requires disclosure of information for unregistered sales of equity securities and use of proceeds as prescribed in Item 701 of Regulation S-K,[241] information that Item 701(f) of Regulation S-K requires,[242] and information that Item 709 of Regulation S-K requires for any purchase made in the covered quarter.[243]

Item 3 requires disclosure of information on material defaults upon senior securities that have occurred (including those of significant subsidiaries) and that exceed 5 percent of the total assets of the registrant

---

[235] 17 C.F.R. § 229.303.

[236] 17 C.F.R. § 229.305.

[237] 17 C.F.R. § 229.307.

[238] 17 C.F.R. § 229.103.

[239] This requirement only applies to proceedings for the quarter in which it became a reportable event or there has been a material development. Subsequent reports need only reference prior reports.

[240] This item does not apply to smaller reporting companies.

[241] 17 C.F.R. § 229.701. This requirement only applies to the sale of unregistered equity security sold during the relevant quarter, and it does not apply if the registrant reported said sales previously on Form 8-K.

[242] 17 C.F.R. § 229.701(f). This requirement only applies if disclosure is required by Rule 463, which mandates disclosure of the application of all the offering proceeds or disclosure of the termination of the offering.

[243] 17 C.F.R. § 229.703. The registrant must provide disclosures covering repurchases made on a monthly basis.

and its consolidated subsidiaries. However, this requirement is triggered when a default becomes binding under the governing instruments (including the expiration of any grace period).[244] Lastly, Item 3 requires disclosures in case of any material arrearages in dividends payments or any uncured delinquency with respect to any class of certain preferred stock.[245]

Items 4 and 5 set forth requirements for mine safety disclosures and other information. Item 6 requires filers to furnish the exhibits set forth in Item 601 of Regulation S-K.[246] Lastly, the relevant officers must date and sign the report.

Form 10-K—annual reports

Form 10-K, the annual report, is the lengthier and more demanding of the 1934 reports. Companies must file Form 10-K within 60 days of the end of the fiscal year if they are large accelerated filers, 75 days if they are accelerated filers, and 90 days if they are any other registrant. After completing Form 10-K, the filer must submit to the SEC three copies of the report, including financial statements, financial statement schedules, exhibits, and any other required forms, as well as five copies of the report without exhibits. Filers must submit one copy to each exchange on which any class of the filer's securities is registered.

Filers must manually sign at least one copy, with the rest only having a printed signature, and the signature must be from the registrant, principal executive officer or officers, principal financial officer or officers, its controller or principal accounting officer, and by at least a majority of the board of directors.

Importantly, filers may incorporate by reference information disclosed in shareholder annual reports to satisfy the requirements of Parts I and II of Form 10-K provided that the information satisfies the requirements of Form 10-K. Filers may incorporate by reference information disclosed in definitive proxy statements or definitive information statements provided that the filer filed said statements with the SEC within 120 days after the end of the fiscal year.

---

[244] Once the material default event occurs, the registration must identify the indebtedness and state the nature of the default, as well as the amount of the default and the total arrearage (where applicable).

[245] Once the material event occurs, the registrant must give the title of the class and the nature of the arrearage or delinquency.

[246] 17 C.F.R. § 229.601.

Moreover, filers may combine annual reports to security holders with Form 10-K provided that they meet the conditions in Instruction H of Form 10-K.

Form 10-K has four parts.

Part I contains six items. Item 1 requires disclosure of information required in Item 101 of Regulation S-K,[247] however, the discussion of business development need only focus on the current business year.

Item 1A requires disclosure in plain English of risk factors required in Item 503(c) of Regulation S-K.[248] Item 1B requires accelerated filers, large accelerated filers, and WKSIs to disclose unresolved comments from SEC staff received within 180 days before the end of the fiscal year.[249]

Item 2 requires disclosures of information as required in Item 102 of Regulation S-K.[250] Item 3 requires disclosure of legal proceedings as required in Item 103 of Regulation S-K,[251] including the date of termination and description of disposition for proceedings terminated during the fourth quarter of the current fiscal year.

Lastly, Item 4 covers mine safety disclosures.

Part II contains nine items that continue the numbering sequence of Part I. Item 5 requires disclosure of information regarding the market for the registrant's common equity, related stockholder matters and issuer purchases of equity securities. As such, a filer must disclose information required by Items 201, 701, 701(f), 703 for Regulation S-K.[252]

Item 6 requires disclosure of selected financial data as required in Item 301 of Regulation S-K.[253] Item 7 requires the management's discussion and analysis of financial conditions and results of operations as mandated by Item 303 of Regulation S-K.[254] Item 7A requires disclosure of quantitative and qualitative disclosures as required by Item 305 of Regulation S-K.[255]

---

247 17 C.F.R. § 229.101.

248 17 C.F.R. § 229.503(c). Moreover, this requirement does not apply to smaller reporting companies.

249 The information must disclose any material unresolved comments and the position of the SEC on the issue.

250 17 C.F.R. § 229.102.

251 17 C.F.R. § 229.103.

252 17 C.F.R. §§ 229.201, 229.701, 229.701(f), and 229.703.

253 17 C.F.R. § 229.301.

254 17 C.F.R. § 229.303.

255 17 C.F.R. § 229.305.

Item 8 sets forth disclosure requirements for financial statements and supplementary data. Financial statements must meet the requirements of Regulation S-X, and a filer must provide the supplementary financial information required by Item 302 of Regulation S-K.[256]

Item 9 requires disclosure of changes in and disagreements with accountants on accounting and financial disclosures as prescribed in Item 304(b) of Regulation S-K.[257] Item 9A requires disclosure of information provided in Items 307 and 308 of Regulation S-K.[258] Item 9B contains a catch-all provision designed to capture information that filers would have to disclose under Form 8-K for the most recent quarter but did not do so.

Part III contains five parts that continue the numbering sequence of Part II. Item 10 requires information required by Items 401,405, 406 and 407(c)(3), (d)(4) and (d)(5) of Regulation S-K.[259]

Item 11 requires disclosure of information regarding executive compensation as prescribed in Items 402 and 402(e)(4) and (e)(5).[260] Item 12 requires disclosure of information regarding security ownership of certain beneficial owners and management and related stockholder matters as prescribed in Items 201(d) and 403 of Regulation S-K.[261]

Item 13 requires disclosure of information on related-person transactions and director independence as prescribed in Items 404 and 407 of Regulation S-K.[262] Item 14 requires disclosure of principal accounting fees and services, including audit fees, audit-related fees, tax fees and all other fees.

Part IV contains one item that continues the numbering sequence of Part III. Item 15 lists the required exhibits and financial statement schedules. Filers must list all financial statements, financial statements filed under Item 8 of Form 10-K, exhibits that Item 601 of Regulation S-K requires, and the financial statements required by Regulation S-X which are excluded from the annual report to shareholders, including (1)

---

256 17 C.F.R. § 229.302. Filers may include consolidated financial statements under this item. A smaller reporting company may provide the information required under Article 8 of Regulation S-X in lieu of the information that Item 8 requires.

257 17 C.F.R. § 229.304(b).

258 17 C.F.R. §§ 229.307 and 229.308.

259 17 C.F.R. §§ 229.401, 229.405, 229.406 and 229.407(c)(3), (d)(4) and (d)(5).

260 17 C.F.R. §§ 229.402 and 229.407(e)(4)–(5).

261 17 C.F.R. §§ 229.201(d) and 229.403.

262 17 C.F.R. §§ 229.404 and 229.407(a).

separate financial statements of subsidiaries not consolidated and 50 percent or less owned persons; (2) separate financial statements of affiliates whose securities are pledged as collateral; and (3) schedules.

4. Exemptions from 1933 Act registration[1]

Thomas L. Hazen

OVERVIEW OF EXEMPTIONS

Section 5 of the Securities Act of 1933, which contains the basic prohibition against offers and sales without registration, explicitly applies on its face to all offers and all sales of any security. This broadly drafted prohibition is thus presumptively applicable to all securities transactions. However, most transactions that take place on a daily basis are not subject to Section 5's prohibitions and the registration requirements. This is because the 1933 Act provides a number of exemptions from the operation of Section 5 and, hence, from its registration requirements.

There are three statutory bases for exemption from the 1933 Act's registration provisions. Keep in mind that, to a large extent, the exemptions provide only an exemption from the Act's registration requirements and thus do not affect the antifraud provisions. Section 3 of the 1933 Act sets forth various categories of securities that are exempt from registration. Section 4 of the 1933 Act describes a variety of transactions that qualify for an exemption from registration. Section 28 of the 1933 Act gives the SEC broad exemptive rulemaking power beyond that granted by the statutory exemptions in Sections 3 and 4 of the 1933 Act. Notwithstanding the broad exemptive authority granted by Section 28, virtually all of the exemptions are grounded in Section 3 or 4. One must read an exemptive rule under Section 3 or 4 in conjunction with the terms of the statute because, in order to be valid, the rule must fall within the bounds that the statute authorizes. This is not a problem, however, when the SEC exercises its authority under Section 28 as there are no restrictions on either the scope or size of the exemption.

[1] This chapter is adapted from 1 Thomas Lee Hazen, Treatise on the Law of Securities Regulation Chapter 4 (6th ed. 2009)

ESTABLISHING AN EXEMPTION—HARSH CONSEQUENCES OF FAILURE TO DO SO

The person claiming an exemption, which is to be strictly construed, carries the burden of proof. Because of the strict construction and burden of proof, companies must carefully construe and document transactions in order to ensure an exemption will be secured. Many exemptions are easily lost. For example, one nonqualifying offeree or purchaser can destroy the exemption with regard to all investors who purchased securities in the would-be exempt offering.

Another hurdle in establishing a successful exemption from the 1933 Act registration is the integration doctrine. Under the integration doctrine, multiple transactions that in form appear separate may be evaluated as a single series of transactions in order to determine whether an exemption exists for all offers and sales.[2] For example, two transactions that appear to be exempt may be combined and both exemptions destroyed as a consequence of integration. The integration is not limited to successive exempt transactions and can also be used to integrate an exempt transaction with a registered offering.

Once an exemption is destroyed or made unavailable, all offers and sales purportedly made under the failed exemption will be in violation of Section 5 of the 1933 Act, unless the offeror can find some other exemption. Moreover, someone who has purchased a security that has been sold in violation of Section 5 has a one-year right of rescission under Section 12(a)(1) of the 1933 Act.

APPLICABILITY OF STATE SECURITIES LAWS

Until 1996, an exemption from the 1933 Act registration did not affect the need for either an exemption or registration under any applicable state securities laws. However, in 1996, Congress changed this overlapping coverage when it enacted the National Securities Markets Improvement Act of 1996 ("NSMIA"). Section 18(b) of the 1933 Act provides a preemption of, and thus an exemption from, state securities registration

---

[2] As discussed later in this chapter, there are five factors that determine whether integration applies: 1) whether the sales are part of a single plan of financing; 2) whether the sales involve issuance of the same class of securities; 3) whether the sales have been made at or about the same time; 4) whether the same type of consideration is received; and 5) whether the sales are made for the same general purpose.

requirements. The preemption extends to most publicly offered securities which are registered with the SEC and to a number of transactions that are exempt from SEC registration by virtue of Section 3 or 4 of the 1933 Act. Most of the federal exemptions set forth in Section 3 trigger the preemptive provisions. The primary federal exemptions that the 1996 legislation does not preempt are offerings subject to the intrastate exemption in Section 3(a)(11) of the 1933 Act and the Section 3(b) exemptions (most notably, Regulation A and Rules 504 and 505 of Regulation D). Many transactions that are exempt under Section 4 of the 1933 Act also qualify for the federally mandated exemption from state law registration requirements. The discussion that follows tracks through the exemptions in the order that they appear in the statute.

SECURITIES OF GOVERNMENTS, BANKS, INSURANCE COMPANIES, AND QUALIFIED PENSION PLANS—1933 ACT § 3(A)(2)

Section 3(a)(2) of the 1933 Act exempts qualified securities that are either issued or guaranteed by governmental organizations or federal reserve banks. Section 3(a)(2) also provides an exemption from registration for securities of certain insurance companies. Furthermore, Section 3(a)(2) exempts securities issued by state, local, and federal governments, including their subdivisions and administrative bodies. In addition to government securities and bank securities, Section 3(a)(2) exempts certain qualifying employee pension plans from 1933 Act registration when they are set up in the form of a trust or a collective trust maintained by a bank or an insurance company. In order to qualify for the exemption under the terms of the statute, the plan must be a qualified plan under Sections 401 or 402(a)(2) of the Internal Revenue Code.

SHORT TERM COMMERCIAL PAPER—1933 ACT § 3(A)(3)

Section 3(a)(3) of the 1933 Act provides an exemption from registration for notes, drafts, notes of exchange, or bankers' acceptances arising "out of a current transaction" with a maturity at the time of issue of not more than nine months. The nine-month limitation does not include grace periods or any renewal of the security that is limited in the same manner as the original obligation. Short-term commercial paper is thus exempt from 1933 Act registration although it is, nevertheless, subject to the

Act's antifraud provisions. In contrast to the 1933 Act's approach of providing an exemption from registration, short-term commercial paper is expressly excluded from the definition of "security" under Section 3(a)(10) of the 1934 Act, and thus is not subject to the 1934 Act's antifraud provisions.[3]

SECURITIES OF ELEEMOSYNARY ORGANIZATIONS—1933 ACT § 3(A)(4)

Section 3(a)(4) of the 1933 Act exempts from registration securities issued by a not-for-profit issuer that is organized and operated exclusively for religious, educational, benevolent, fraternal, charitable, or reformatory purposes. In order to qualify for Section 3(a)(4)'s exemption for securities of not-for-profit issuers, no part of the issuer's net earnings may inure to the benefit of "any person, private stockholder, or individual." With regard to nonprofit organizations, the availability of this exemption has generally been treated as coextensive with the issuer's federal tax status. Somewhat related to the Section 3(a)(4) exemption is Section 3(a)(13), which was adopted in 1996 to provide an exemption for securities "issued by or any interest or participation in any church plan, company or account" that is excluded from the definition of investment company as a church plan.

SECURITIES OF BUILDING AND LOAN ASSOCIATIONS, FARMERS' COOPERATIVES AND THE LIKE—1933 ACT § 3(A)(5)

Section 3(a)(5) of the 1933 Act provides an exemption from registration for securities issued by savings and loan associations, building and loan associations, cooperative banks, homestead associations, and similar institutions, provided that the issuer is subject to supervision by state or federal governmental authorities. The exemption does not apply, however, where the issuer takes for itself more than 3 percent of the offering's face value in the form of a fee or other remuneration, either at the time of investment or termination. Section 3(a)(5) further exempts securities

---

[3] *But see* Reves v. Ernst & Young, 494 U.S. 56 (1990) (applying the "family resemblance" test in holding that certain demand notes were securities).

issued by farmers' cooperatives and certain corporations that qualify for the federal taxation exemption.

CERTIFICATES ISSUED UNDER THE BANKRUPTCY ACT BY RECEIVERS AND TRUSTEES—1933 ACT § 3(A)(7)

Section 3(a)(7) of the 1933 Act provides an exemption from registration for registration certificates issued by trustees, receivers, or debtors in possession under the Federal Bankruptcy Act, provided that the certificates are issued pursuant to court approval. Even though the exemption may apply to securities sold as part of the original issue, it does not extend to downstream sales, in which case the person selling to secondary recipients of the certificates must register unless some other independent exemption is available. As noted above, the statute expressly requires court approval of the issue in order to render the exemption available. Section 3(a)(7) supplements the exemptions for bankruptcy reorganizations that are included under Section 3(a)(10)'s exemption for securities issued pursuant to certain administratively or judicially approved reorganizations. The Section 3(a)(7) exemption, which applies to trustee certificates, has its counterpart in the Bankruptcy Act (11 U.S.C. § 364(f)), which not only provides an exemption from Section 5 of the 1933 Act, but also from the Trust Indenture Act of 1939, as well as from state and local laws.

Moreover, Section 1145(a) of the Bankruptcy Act exempts from 1933 Act registration securities of the bankrupted if they are 1) offered under a reorganization plan, and 2) exchanged for claims or interests in the debtor. The exemption from 1933 Act registration that the Bankruptcy Act provides does not apply to resales of the securities so issued. However, an exemption for the resales may be secured independently, including, for example, Rule 144 of the 1933 Act, which is discussed later in this chapter. As is the case with other exemptions, it is important to focus on the possibility of downstream resales in connection with the Section 3(a)(7) exemption.

INSURANCE POLICIES AND ANNUITY CONTRACTS—1933 ACT § 3(A)(8)

Section 3(a)(8) of the 1933 Act exempts from 1933 Act registration insurance policies and annuity contracts issued by corporations that are subject to the supervision of a state insurance commissioner, bank commissioner, or agency or officer performing a similar regulatory function. If the insurance or annuity contract does not place upon the issuer a "meaningful mortality risk," the policy cannot be regarded as "life insurance" or an exempt "annuity." Furthermore, simply taking on a "meaningful mortality risk" does not insure the issuer an exemption from registration under Section 3(a)(8) if the annuity or other insurance contract is, in essence, an investment contract. For example, the Section 3(a)(8) exemption does not apply when analyzing a variable annuity under which the entire investment risk rests with the purchaser.[4] As is the case with any question of whether an investment contract exists, the expectations of the policyholder must be viewed in light of an "economic reality" test and the court's inquiry is thus not limited to the policy on its face. Ordinarily, though, a fixed annuity will qualify for Section 3(a)(8)'s exemption because it is a bona fide insurance product and is generally subject to regulation under state law.

SECURITIES EXCHANGED EXCLUSIVELY WITH EXISTING SECURITY HOLDERS—1933 ACT § 3(A)(9)

Section 3(a)(9) of the 1933 Act provides an exemption from 1933 Act registration for securities exchanged that the issuer exchanges exclusively with its existing security holders, provided that no commission or other remuneration is paid for promotional activities in soliciting the exchange. The exemption is not available for securities exchanged in the course of Bankruptcy Act proceedings governed by 11 U.S.C. § 1145. Section 1145 provides its own exemption from state securities laws for securities of a company in bankruptcy proceedings if the securities are 1) offered under a reorganization plan; and 2) exchanged for claims or interests in the debtor. As previously discussed, the Bankruptcy Act exemption is supplemented by Section 3(a)(7) of the 1933 Act. Section 3(a)(9) is limited to exchanges taking place solely between the issuing company and its existing securities holders. The requirement that the exchange be exclusively with existing holders does not, however, mean that all securities holders must be included. It is only required that persons who are not shareholders cannot participate in the exchange in order for the transaction to qualify for the exemption.

---

4 SEC v. Variable Annuity Life Ins. Co., 359 U.S. 65 (1959).

SECURITIES ISSUED IN JUDICIALLY OR ADMINISTRATIVELY APPROVED REORGANIZATIONS—1933 ACT § 3(A)(10)

Section 3(a)(10) of the 1933 Act exempts from registration securities issued in exchange for other securities, where the issuance has been approved by a court or an appropriate administrative body. Section 3(a)(10) is used primarily with respect to securities issued in an exchange pursuant to business combinations and reorganizations that are subject to regulatory approval, securities exchanged pursuant to settlement of litigation, and exchanges of securities in connection with bankruptcy proceedings that are not subject to Chapter 11 of the Federal Bankruptcy Code. The exchange of securities need not be limited solely to securities—it may partly involve cash. In order for the exemption to apply, the administrative or judicial approval must be after a "hearing … at which all persons to whom it is proposed to issue securities … shall have the right to appear." Absent another exemption, all downstream public resales of securities acquired under the exemption must be registered under the 1933 Act.

THE EXEMPTION FOR PURELY INTRASTATE OFFERINGS—1933 ACT § 3(A)(11); 1933 ACT RULE 147

The Statutory Exemption—1933 Act § 3(a)(11)

A company may have a public offering of its securities and avoid the federal registration requirements under the intrastate exemption provided that *all* aspects of the offering, including the company's residence, are within the confines of a single state. Section 3(a)(11) of the 1933 Act exempts "[a]ny security which is part of an issue offered and sold only to persons resident within a single State or Territory, where the issuer of such security is a person resident and doing business within, or, if a corporation, incorporated by and doing business within, such State or Territory." Both the courts and the SEC have narrowly interpreted the scope of the intrastate offering exemption, thus making it a feasible alternative only in relatively few situations.

Although the exemption is dependent upon the premise that all securities which form a part of the offering will come to rest in the hands of local residents, an out-of-state resale that occurs more than nine months after the primary offering to residents may not void the intrastate exemption for the original offering.[5]

The intrastate exemption is more suitable for large states found in the southwest and west rather than in the northeast where metropolitan areas border on other states. One reason for this is that the larger sizes of the states in the southwest and western part of the country make intrastate activities more common than they are in the smaller northeastern states. Also, those states with large metropolitan areas bordering on other states are more perilous locations for an intrastate offering. For example, a corporation located in the heart of New York City may not rely on the intrastate exemption for issuance of stock to a New Jersey resident directly across the river, while an issuer in Amarillo, Texas, may rely on the exemption for sale to a resident of the southernmost tip of Texas.

As discussed below, Rule 147 of the 1933 Act provides a safe harbor for securing the statutory Section 3(a)(11) exemption. Section 3(a)(11) is not a detailed statutory provision and there is relatively scant judicial precedent. From the face of the statute, it is apparent that in order to qualify for a Section 3(a)(11) exemption, all purchasers *and* all offerees of the securities in question must be residents within a single state. Furthermore, the issuer must be a resident of the same state and be doing business there. In the case of a corporation, in addition to the requirement that its principal place of business be within the state, it is also necessary that the state be the corporation's place of incorporation. This last requirement necessarily eliminates the vast number of corporations which, while doing business in one state, select some other jurisdiction, such as Delaware, to be the state of incorporation in order to take advantage of that state's more attractive corporation laws. Section 3(a)(11) does not expressly address whether other business entities such as limited partnerships, limited liability companies, and business trusts must be organized in the state in order to qualify as an issuer under the intrastate exemption. However, the rule of domestic incorporation for corporate issuers should apply by analogy to other forms of doing business. In its safe harbor Rule 147, the SEC expressly extends the requirement of in-state organization to a "limited partnership, trust or other form of business organization."

Even where the above-mentioned statutory requirements appear to have been satisfied, the issuer is still not perfectly safe under the intrastate exemption. For example, it was held that where an offering was

---

[5] Busch v. Carpenter, 598 F.Supp. 519 (D.Utah 1984), aff'd in part, rev'd in part, 827 F.2d 653 (10th Cir.1987).

made only to Minnesota residents and the issuer, a Minnesota corporation with its only office in Minnesota, the fact that the proceeds would be used outside of the state was sufficient in and of itself to make the intrastate exemption unavailable.[6] This decision raises significant questions about the exemption's applicability to any issuer with out-of-state operations, and if the offering proceeds may even be indirectly attributed to that out-of-state portion of the business. This 'use of the proceeds' requirement is not as troubling if it is viewed in terms of the overall business operations, but it seems to be overreaching if it will void the exemption for securities of an issuer who derives substantial income from in-state operations.[7] In contrast, it is clear that where the issuer's income-producing operations are located outside of the state, the intrastate exemption will not be available.

Rule 147's Safe Harbor for Intrastate Offerings

As is the case with SEC policy and court decisions on issuer residence, in order to qualify for the safe harbor offered in Rule 147 of the 1933 Act, both the issuer's place of incorporation or organization and its "principal office" must be located within the same state; if an individual, his or her principal residence must be located within that state. Rule 147 further requires that in order for an issuer to be deemed doing business within the state, it must have derived at least 80 percent of its gross revenues per annum, as well as 80 percent of its assets (including those of its subsidiaries on a consolidated basis), from activities or real property located within the state over the past fiscal year. This 80 percent requirement is not included within the statutory language of Section 3(a)(11), but its appearance in Rule 147 indicates the SEC's position that the statutory concept of "doing business" means something more is

---

[6] SEC v. McDonald Inv. Co., 343 F.Supp. 343 (D. Minn. 1972). *Cf.* 1933 Act Rule 147, 17 C.F.R. § 230.147 (2012) (imposing an 80 percent minimum on the proceeds to be used within the state).

[7] For example, an issuer using the proceeds of the offering to purchase wine outside the state for resale within the state can still satisfy the in-state business requirement. Adventures in Wine, SEC No-Action Letter, 1977 WL 14879, [1976–1977 Transfer Binder] Fed. Sec. L. Rep. (CCH) ¶ 80, 952 (Jan. 14, 1977). Similarly, a local issuer that planned to use 85 percent of the proceeds from an intrastate offering to pay off a loan to an out-of-state bank that was used to finance purchase of an in-state bank dealing primarily with in-state customers was allowed to rely on the exemption. Fina Bancorp., Inc., SEC No-Action Letter, 1987 SEC No-Act. LEXIS 2141, (June 15, 1987).

necessary than just having the state as the location of the principal office and the place of incorporation or organization.

Rule 147 imposes a condition that 80 percent of the net proceeds of the offering be used in the state. Both under the statutory exemption and pursuant to Rule 147, downstream sales of part of an intrastate issue to nonresidents can destroy the availability of the intrastate exemption. An issuer cannot select an in-state resident to operate as a conduit or underwriter and thereby avoid the limitations of the exemption. However, even inadvertent downstream sales to nonresidents, at least those taking place within a reasonably short period after the distribution for which the exemption is claimed, can destroy the exemption for all sales made pursuant to the exemption. Rule 147(e) contains the safe harbor guidelines for limitation on resales, which prohibits all resales to nonresident purchasers within nine months "from the date of the last sale by the issuer of such securities." In such a case, even the resident purchasers will be placed in a position of being able to claim that the securities they purchased were sold in violation of Section 5 of the 1933 Act, thus giving them a right of rescission under Section 12(a)(1) of the 1933 Act. It has long been the SEC's position, however, that once securities sold pursuant to the intrastate exemption have finally come to rest in the hands of residents, subsequent isolated resales to nonresidents will not destroy the prior exemptions. In terms of planning such transactions, the nine-month safe harbor guidelines of Rule 147 provide a good rule of thumb.

Notwithstanding its stringent requirements of residency so far as the issuer is concerned, Rule 147 is much more open with regard to purchasers' and offerees' residence. The test applicable to an individual is "the principal residence," which seems to limit each individual to one state, thus eliminating vacation homes and the like; a similar test has been adopted under Section 3(a)(11). Business entities, including corporations, trusts and partnerships, qualify as resident offerees and purchasers if they have their principal office in the state. There is no requirement that the offeree be incorporated or organized under the laws of that state, although it would have to be so organized in order to qualify as an issuer. Furthermore, Rule 147's "eighty percent revenue and asset" tests do not apply to offerees and purchasers, but apply only to issuers. The Rule also provides that where a corporation, partnership or trust is formed for the purpose of purchasing the securities in question, all of its beneficial owners must be residents. It thus appears that a bona fide *preexisting* entity may qualify as an exempt purchaser although it has nonresident owners.

Another key factor in an intrastate offering and in deciding whether reliance is to be placed upon Rule 147, is the integration doctrine, which telescopes two or more transactions into one. Although originally developed in the context of the intrastate exemption, the integration doctrine applies to other exemptions under the 1933 Act. The integration doctrine is the SEC's counterpart of the IRS' step-transaction analysis under which transactions that appear to be separate in form will be scrutinized closely as to substance in order to determine whether they, in fact, should be treated as two distinct transactions. Specifically, with regard to the intrastate exemption contained in Section 3(a)(11) of the 1933 Act, the question of the exemption's availability arises in the context of determining whether a given security transaction is "part of an issue" within the meaning of the statute. The determination of which transactions constitute an "issue" or "part of an issue" is a matter of federal rather than state law. In determining whether the integration doctrine will apply and whether the transaction is to be considered part of a certain issue, the SEC will consider the following factors: "(1) are the offerings part of a single plan of financing; (2) do the offerings involve issuance of the same class of security; (3) are the offerings made at or about the same time; (4) is the same type of consideration to be received; and (5) are the offerings made for the same general purpose." In its preliminary notes, Rule 147 expressly adopts this five factor test and points out that "any one or more of the... factors may be determinative." It also establishes a six-month safe harbor for avoiding integration with out-of-state sales.

State Registration Requirements

Intrastate transactions that qualify for the Section 3(a)(11) exemption are not exempt from state registration requirements. The entire premise of the intrastate exemption from federal registration is that the states are more appropriate regulators for transactions occurring solely within the borders of a single state. Accordingly, the transactions must be registered under state law unless an exemption can be found.

QUALIFIED EXEMPTIONS FOR SMALL ISSUES; 1933 ACT §§ 3(B), 4(A)(5), RULE 215, LIMITED OFFERINGS—1933 ACT § 3(B)

Section 3(b)(1) of the 1933 Act empowers the SEC to promulgate rules and regulations exempting issues of securities where the aggregate per issue offering price to the public does not exceed $5 million. The only statutory limitation on the creation of the exemption is that the SEC must find "that the enforcement of [the Act] with respect to such securities is not necessary in the public interest and for the protection of investors by reason of the small amount involved or the limited character of public offering." Over the years, Section 3(b)(1) has, to some extent, kept up with inflation. The statutory limit was increased in 1980 to the current $5 million. Congress granted the SEC the authority to effectively raise the limit when it enacted Section 28 of the 1933 Act, which allows the SEC to exempt any person, security, or transaction when it believes that it is in the public interest to do so. Furthermore, in 2012, Congress adopted Section 3(b)(2) that authorizes an exemption for offerings up to $50 million per year, but like Section 3(b)(1), requires SEC rulemaking to implement the exemption.

Section 3(b) in its entirety is dependent upon SEC rules for implementation. The Section 3(b)(1) exemptions include the qualified exemptions for offerings up to $5 million sanctioned by Regulation A and Rule 505 of the 1933 Act, as well as Rule 504 of the 1933 Act's exemption for offerings not exceeding $1 million, each of which is discussed later in this chapter. As of summer 2013, the SEC has not adopted rules to implement Section 3(b)(2)'s $50 million exemption.

Limited Offerings Solely to Accredited Investors—1933 Act § 4(a)(5)

In 1980, Congress enacted Section 4(a)(5) of the 1933 Act to exempt transactions by an issuer involving "accredited investors" where the aggregate amount sold does not exceed the dollar limit of Section 3(b)(1) of the 1933 Act (i.e., $5 million). The only conditions to qualify for the Section 4(a)(5) exemption are that 1) offers are made only to accredited investors; 2) there is no public advertising or solicitation for the offering; and 3) an appropriate notice of reliance on the exemption be filed with the SEC. Section 4(a)(5) is available for sales of securities that have been offered only to "accredited investors" as defined in Section 2(a)(15) of the 1933 Act. The statutory definition of this term expressly includes a number of institutional investors, including banks, insurance companies, and investment companies that are registered under the Investment Company Act of 1940, small business investment companies licensed by the Small Business Administration, and employee benefit plans that are subject to the Employee Retirement Income Security Act ("ERISA").

Rule 215 of the 1933 Act includes in the definition of accredited investor directors, executive officers, and general partners of the issuer, in addition to wealthy individuals (any natural person whose individual net worth, or joint net worth with that person's spouse, at the time of his purchase exceeds $1 million, [and] [a]ny natural person who had an individual income in excess of $200,000 in each of the two most recent years or joint income with that person's spouse in excess of $300,000 in each of those years and has a reasonable expectation of reaching the same income level in the current year). As of July 2010, the net worth computation no longer includes the value of one's personal residence.[8] Section 2(a)(15) of the 1933 Act's concept of an accredited investor is incorporated into Regulation D, which is discussed later in this chapter.

REGULATION A—QUALIFIED EXEMPTION FOR OFFERINGS UP TO $5 MILLION PER YEAR

The oldest, and at one time most widely used of the Section 3(b) exemptions for small issues, is the qualified exemption from registration established pursuant to Regulation A, which is embodied in Rule 251 through 263 of the 1933 Act, and which applies to companies that are not already publicly held. The exemption provided in Regulation A is dependent upon the securities being offered through the use of an offering circular in a manner similar to the use of a prospectus in a registered offering. In order to use the Regulation A exemption, an issuer may not offer securities that exceed an aggregate amount of $5 million in any one year. Additionally, the issuer (and selling shareholders in the case of a secondary distribution) must comply with Regulation A's notification and disclosure requirements, including the offering circular delivery requirements that, in essence, have the same effect as a "mini registration."

The Regulation A disclosure statements contain much of the information that would be included in a full-blown registration statement as Rule 253's provisions for an offering circular are analogous to the Section 5(b) prospectus delivery requirements. Similarly, Rule 255 provides for the use of a preliminary offering circular prior to the date on which the offering becomes qualified for Regulation A sales. As compared with a registered offering, Regulation A has broader provisions for pre-filing gun-jumping sales solicitations. In particular, Rule 254 permits a solicitation of investor interest prior to the use of an offering statement.

---

[8] For decades, the accredited investor threshold for individuals remained $1 million in net worth, $200,000 annual income ($300,000 joint income for a couple), and was not adjusted for inflation. As part of the financial reform legislation in 2010, Congress excluded the principal residence from the net worth calculation and also required the SEC to periodically review the net worth calculation for individuals. *See* Dodd-Frank Wall Street Reform and Consumer Protection Act, Pub. L. No. 111–203, § 413, 124 Stat. 1376, 1577–8 (2010).

This procedure is colloquially referred to as "testing the waters." Regulation A is not simply a safe harbor from 1933 Act registration; it is an exclusive harbor, as there is no self-executing statutory exemption. Accordingly, deviations from the rules' requirements will result in loss of the exemption. Rule 260 provides, however, that trivial deviations from Regulation A do not necessarily result in a loss of the exemption, provided that there has been a good faith attempt to comply and the deviation does not involve "a condition or requirement directly intended to protect the individual or entity" challenging the transaction.

The Regulation A exemption is not available to every issuer. It is not available to public companies subject to the 1934 Act's periodic reporting requirements. Regulation A may be used only by an issuer which is organized under the laws of the United States or Canada and which has its principal place of business in the United States or Canada. The exemption is unavailable for the offer or sale of 1) fractional undivided interests in oil, gas, or mineral rights; or 2) for securities issued by registered investment companies. Additionally, Regulation A may not be used by "development stage" companies, which are those issuers that have no specific business plan. Rule 262 of Regulation A contains so-called "bad boy" provisions which deny the availability of the exemption where the issuer, its predecessors, or any affiliated issuer has been subject to proceedings stemming from violations of the federal securities laws. These bad actor disqualifications also apply to exemptions under Rules 505 and 506 of Regulation D.

SECTION 3(B)(2) AND REGULATION A+

In 2012, the JOBS Act,[9] added Section 3(b)(2) to the 1933 Act to require that the SEC adopt an exemption paralleling Regulation A for offerings up to $50 million per year. The statutory exemption sets forth the minimum conditions for the exemption, but requires SEC rulemaking to fill in the details. The exemption contemplates that a disclosure document in the form of an offering statement be provided to investors. Section 12(a)(2)'s remedy for material misstatements and omissions applies to securities offered under the Section 3(b)(2) exemption. The issuer may test the waters to determine investor interest prior to the filing of the offering statement. Securities issued in a Section 3(b)(2) exemption are not restricted securities and thus are not subject to resale restrictions. The

[9] Jumpstart Our Business Startups Act, Pub. L. No. 112–106, § 401(a)(2), 126 Stat. 306, 324 (2012).

statutory exemption further directs the SEC to require audited financial statements. The statute empowers the SEC to impose other conditions in the public interest, including disqualifying bad actors from using the exemption. A Section 3(b)(2) offering is subject to state blue sky laws unless the securities are listed on a national securities exchange or the securities are offered and sold to a "qualified purchaser" as defined by the SEC. Following a Section 3(b)(2) offering, the company is subject to annual filing of audited financials and such other periodic disclosures as the SEC deems appropriate for the public interest. The details of the Section 3(b)(2) exemption must await SEC rulemaking, which as of summer 2013 has not yet taken place.

THE CROWDFUNDING EXEMPTION

Section 4(a)(6) of the 1933 Act provides an exemption for companies for crowdfunding offerings of up to $1 million during a twelve-month period. The crowdfunding exemption limits the amount of money that a company may raise from an investor and is conditioned on providing investors with certain disclosures that must also be filed with the SEC.[10] The required disclosures include the offering's purpose, the targeted amount to be raised, the deadline for reaching such amount, and the offering price. Risks to investors also must be disclosed, as well as any additional information as the SEC may prescribe. The exemption also expressly requires information about the company, its officers, directors, and major shareholders, in addition to a description of the company's business, business plan, capital structure and financial condition.[11] Audited financial statements are required for offerings over $500,000 and

---

[10] With respect to investors having an annual income or net worth below $100,000, a company may not sell securities to any investor exceeding the greater of either $2,000 or 5 percent of the investor's annual income or net worth within a twelve-month period. For investors over the $100,000 annual income or net worth threshold, the twelve-month investment is capped at 10 percent of the investor's annual income or net worth, but may not exceed $100,000 over the twelve-month period.

[11] The Act also imposes reporting obligations beyond the offering. For companies not subject to the Securities Exchange Act's periodic reporting requirements, crowdfunded companies must file annual reports and provide investors with reports detailing results of operations and financial statements annually. The JOBS Act further directs the SEC to exempt, conditionally or unconditionally, companies relying on the crowdfunding exemption from the 1934 Act's registration and periodic reporting obligations.

for any other thresholds that the SEC may impose by rulemaking. The exemption also requires registration of crowdfunding portals and significantly preempts state law. The only advertising permitted is advertising that directs interested investors to the crowdfunding portal or broker handling the offering. The company may not compensate promoters of the offering unless the compensation is disclosed. The intermediary for a crowdfunding offering must be registered with the SEC either as a broker-dealer or, under the new registration category, as a crowdfunding portal. In addition to SEC registration, the SEC is directed to adopt rules requiring the broker or crowdfunding portal to provide disclosures to investors relating to risks and investor education materials. State blue-sky law registration requirements for public offerings are preempted unless the issuer of the securities has its principal place of business in the state or more than 50 percent of the crowdfunding offering's proceeds are purchasers residing in the state.

RULE 701—EXEMPTION FOR EMPLOYEE COMPENSATION PLANS OF ISSUERS NOT SUBJECT TO EXCHANGE ACT PERIODIC REPORTING REQUIREMENTS

In 1988, the SEC adopted Rule 701 of the 1933 Act under the authority of Section 3(b) of the 1933 Act to exempt from registration employee stock compensation plans up to $5 million annually, provided that the issuer is neither subject to the 1934 Act's periodic reporting requirements nor an investment company which is (or is required to be) registered under the Investment Company Act of 1940. In 1999, the SEC invoked Section 28 of the 1933 Act's general exemptive authority to eliminate the $5 million threshold and made Rule 701 of the 1933 Act available for offerings that do not exceed the greater of $1 million or 15 percent of the issuer's total assets, or 15 percent of the outstanding securities of that class.

The exemption set out in Rule 701 applies to a wide variety of compensation plans. It applies to purchase plans, option plans, bonus plans, stock appreciation rights, profit sharing, thrift, incentive, or similar plans. Rule 701 permits an issuer to offer securities pursuant to a written contract or written compensation plan to its employees, directors, general partners, trustees, officers, consultants, or advisers. The securities can be issued only in return for bona fide services, but not in return for services rendered in connection with a capital raising transaction involving securities. When successive offerings are part of a single plan of financing, ordinarily the SEC will invoke the integration doctrine in order to integrate the multiple transactions into one. Unlike many other exemptions, Rule 701 provides an express exclusion from the integration doctrine. Additionally, securities acquired pursuant to a Rule 701 offering are deemed to be restricted securities within the meaning of Rule 144 of the 1933 Act. The securities may not be resold unless in compliance with the Act's registration requirements or pursuant to an exemption.

EXEMPTION FOR ISSUER TRANSACTIONS NOT INVOLVING A PUBLIC OFFERING ("THE PRIVATE PLACEMENT EXEMPTION")—1933 ACT § 4(A)(2)

Section 4(a)(2) of the 1933 Act exempts "transactions by an issuer not involving any public offering." The exemption for transactions not involving a public offering is limited to issuers and thus cannot be relied upon by persons other than the issuer. However, non-issuers may be able to take advantage of the so-called Section "4(1 1/2)" exemption, which is discussed later in this chapter. Section 4(a)(2)'s exemption for non-public offerings can be used by small firms, as well as by publicly held companies. Public companies issuing securities in unregistered transactions, including those issued under the Section 4(a)(2) exemption, must disclose those transactions in their periodic reports filed with the SEC.

In order to provide more certainty in planning transactions, the SEC adopted the safe harbor rule contained in Rule 506 of the 1933 Act, which is discussed later in this chapter. Compliance with Rule 506 provides an exemption, but according to the SEC, noncompliance does not raise even an inference that the statutory Section 4(a)(2) exemption is unavailable. Because Rule 506 is only a safe harbor rule, and is applicable only to qualifying non-public offerings, the pre-existing judicial and administrative interpretations of the Rule remain an important part of the law today as they are still available to issuers who either choose not to or are unable to comply with each and every provision of Rule 506.

In *SEC v. Ralston Purina Co.*, 346 U.S. 119 (1953), the Supreme Court rejected the defendant's contention that an offering of stock that was limited to its own employees was necessarily exempt as it did not involve a public offering. The defendant, relying on a literal reading of the statute, maintained that an offering to a limited group could not properly be characterized as a public offering. The Court ruled that because the stock being offered was made available to all employees regardless of connection with the issuer and knowledge of the business, the offerees and purchasers represented a sufficiently large and representative slice of the investing public so as to render the exemption unavailable. In discussing the scope of the exemption, the Court announced the guidelines that have continued to form the basis for all private placement exemptions. In the first instance, all offerees must have access to the types of information that would be contained in a full-fledged 1933 Act registration statement. Second, the offerees must be capable of fending for themselves; in more recent cases, this has been interpreted to mean that the offerees must be sufficiently sophisticated to demand and understand the information that is available to them. Both offeree sophistication and access to information must be shown in order for the Section 4(a)(2) exemption to be established. The ability to fend for oneself is thus dependent upon access to information. It has therefore been held that the exemption will not be available, even though the offerees are sufficiently sophisticated, where offerees did not have access to the types of information that would otherwise have to be disclosed in the registration statement. Conversely, the SEC has made it clear that a brochure containing the requisite information by itself is not sufficient, as the nature and sophistication of the offerees is an equally important factor.

The Supreme Court in *Ralston Purina* pointed out that even though the number of purchasers involved will not necessarily be the determinative factor, it is a significant one in considering the scope of the exemption. Accordingly, the fact that there were as many as 500 employee offerees in the *Ralston Purina* case helped tip the balance against finding the Section 4(a)(2) exemption applicable. In addition to the 1) number of offerees, 2) offerees' sophistication, 3) offerees' need for information, and 4) offerees' access to information, the courts will consider the size of the offering, both in terms of the number of securities offered and the aggregate offering price. The number of offerees and size of the offering, as measured by the number of units offered, are significant because the larger the numbers of each, the more difficult it is to control downstream sales that would eventually filter the securities into the hands of the general investing public. As it becomes more likely that the securities sold pursuant to the private placement exemption will filter down to the investing public without a subsequent 1933 Act registration, the less likely it is that the Section 4(a)(2) exemption will be available.

In addition to the foregoing factors, the SEC points out that any "public advertising is inconsistent with a claim of private offering."[12] In light of the ban on public advertising, issuers frequently have to turn to investment bankers and other promoters in order to find an existing pool of potential customers. It is clearly permissible for a brokerage firm that is handling the private placement to contact its customers provided they meet the offering's suitability standard.[13] Where a private placement is not handled by a conduit with a ready list of potential offerees, all activities directed toward contacting the offerees will be closely scrutinized, lest the issuer run afoul of the general solicitation prohibition. In general, where the issuer is unable to prove that there were a limited number of offerees, the uncertainty concerning the number of offerees can preclude reliance on Section 4(a)(2)'s exemption. The use of investment seminars and other promotional meetings have been a significant factor in denying the availability of the exemption for non-public offerings. Investment seminars (or "road shows") that are limited to qualified offerees who have been prescreened presumably would not violate the prohibition of a general solicitation.

A common practice of private placement issuers has been to require all purchasers to sign an "investment letter" attesting to their lack of intent to resell the securities to the public. Although this may still be a necessary precaution, and a requirement under Rule 506, the fact that the issuer requires such investment letters is self-serving and thus will not in and of itself have any probative value as to the applicability of the exemption or the issuer's reasonable efforts to assure that no downstream sales will occur without registration. The Section 4(a)(2) exemption may be denied because of the issuer's failure to demonstrate that all offerees "received both written and oral information concerning [the issuer], that all offerees of its securities had access to any additional information which they might have required or requested, and that all offerees of its securities had personal contacts with the officers of [the issuer]."[14] Although offerees need not have personal contact or a relationship with the issuers in *all* cases, following the lead of the Fifth Circuit Court of Appeals, there have been a number of judicial decisions that have given

---

12 Non-Public Offering Exemption, Exchange Act Release No. 33–4552, 1962 WL 69540, 1 Fed. Sec. L. Rep. (CCH) ¶ 2781 (Nov. 6, 1962).

13 *See* Mary S. Krech Trust v. Lakes Apartments, 642 F.2d 98 (5th Cir. Unit B 1981), *rehearing denied*, 645 F.2d 72 (5th Cir. 1981) (noting that the burden is on the issuer to establish the identity of all offerees and purchasers and to prove their suitability).

14 *See* SEC v. Continental Tobacco Co., 463 F.2d 137 (5th Cir. 1972).

the Section 4(a)(2) exemption a very limited scope, at least with regard to offerees who do not qualify as institutional investors.[15]

A literal reading of a number of cases[16] interpreting the scope of the Section 4(a)(2) exemption leads one to perceive several requirements for private placements not involving institutional investor purchasers, regardless of reliance on the safe harbor provided by Rule 506. As mentioned above, each offeree must have access to the types of information that would be disclosed if the issuer was required to undertake a full-fledged registration under the 1933 Act. This requirement has been held not to have been satisfied if access was not given to each offeree, even though such an offeree without access did not become an eventual purchaser. As one court put it, "[e]ven the offeree-plaintiff's 20–20 vision with respect to the facts underlying the security would not save the exemption if any one of his fellow offerees was blind."[17] Case law further requires that offerees must also be sophisticated, i.e., able to demand and understand the information available to them, with respect to business and financial matters generally. Additionally, an offeree's knowledge of the particular business may be a factor. Knowledgeable investors with generalized investment experience will qualify as purchasers in a non-public offering when the nature of the enterprise does not require that there be a specialized level of sophistication. Questions may be raised as to the propriety of an investor sophistication requirement as a precondition to a Section 4(a)(2) exemption. It is evident that the Supreme Court's primary concern in *Ralston Purina* was that offerees in a non-public offering have access to the types of information that would be available with a registered public offering. However, as discussed directly above, the courts have since required that the offerees possess a certain degree of sophistication. While offeree access to information is a necessary element of any transaction exempted under Section 4(a)(2), it is clearly not sufficient in and of itself. *Ralston Purina* tells us that the offerees, as a class, must somehow represent something more limited and sophisticated than a slice of the general investing public.

---

[15] *See, e.g.,* Doran v. Petroleum Management Corp., 545 F.2d 893 (5th Cir. 1977).

[16] *See, e.g.,* Mary S. Krech Trust v. Lakes Apartments, 642 F.2d 98 (5th Cir. Unit B 1981), *rehearing* denied, 645 F.2d 72 (5th Cir. 1981); Western Federal Corp. v. Erickson, 739 F.2d 1439 (9th Cir. 1984); Doran v. Petroleum Management Corp., 545 F.2d 893 (5th Cir. 1977), appeal after remand, 576 F.2d 91 (5th Cir. 1978).

[17] *See, e.g.,* Doran v. Petroleum Management Corp., 545 F.2d 893, 902 (5th Cir. 1977).

REGULATION D

In Regulation D (Rules 501–508 of the 1933 Act), the SEC adopted a comprehensive scheme for exemptions relating to small issues and small issuers. Regulation D is "designed to simplify and clarify existing exemptions, to expand their availability, and to achieve uniformity between federal and state exemptions."[18] Although embodied in one regulation, it is imperative to keep in mind that Regulation D is not a single integrated exemption, but rather consists of three separate but interrelated exemptions. **Rule 504**, promulgated under Section 3(b), provides an exemption for certain offerings not exceeding $1 million within a twelve-month period. **Rule 505**, which, similarly to Rule 504, is a Section 3(b) exemption, exempts certain offerings not exceeding $5 million within a twelve-month period. The third exemption, **Rule 506**, promulgated under Section 4(a)(2), permits non-public offerings to qualified purchasers without any limitation on dollar amount. While Regulation D contains a number of common definitions and requirements for the three exemptions set forth in Rules 504, 505 and 506, it is best to consider each exemption on its own terms rather than attempting to define a common thread that runs throughout. This is because the three rules are aimed at three different types of transactions.

Definitions

Rule 501 sets forth eight definitions applicable throughout Regulation D. The four most important ones are as follows:

Accredited investor An "accredited investor" as defined in Rule 501(a) of the 1933 Act is any person who in fact comes within, or whom the issuer reasonably believes comes within, any of eight categories of investors at the time securities are sold to the investor. Generally, these categories include wealthy or financially sophisticated investors such as banks, insurance companies, tax-exempt organizations, directors and executive officers of the issuer, and natural persons who have considerable net worth or large annual incomes (any natural person whose individual net worth, or joint net worth with that person's spouse, at the time of his purchase exceeds $1,000,000 [and] [a]ny natural person who

---

[18] Revision of Exemptions from Registration for Transactions Involving Limited Offers and Sales, Exchange. Act Release No. 33–6389, 1982 WL 35662, [1981–1982 Transfer Binder] Fed. Sec. L. Rep. (CCH) ¶ 83,106 (Mar. 8, 1982).

had an individual income in excess of $200,000 in each of the two most recent years, or whose joint income with that person's spouse was in excess of $300,000 in each of those years and has a reasonable expectation of reaching the same income level in the current year). In recent years there has been considerable discussion about raising the benchmark for determining accredited investor status. As part of the Dodd-Frank Wall Street Reform and Consumer Protection Act of 2010, Congress mandated that the SEC reevaluate the accredited investor dollar thresholds and also deleted the value of one's personal residence from the net worth requirement.[19]

Affiliate An "affiliate" is a person who controls, is controlled by, or is under common control with the person with whom he or she is affiliated.[20] This definition captures the same concept that is found in the definition of "control person" under Rule 405 of the 1933 Act, which focuses on the ability to influence management decisions through the use of voting control or otherwise.

Aggregate offering price This term is defined to include all consideration, including non-cash items, received by an issuer for the issuance of its securities. The definition includes a comment regarding how to determine the price of securities sold in whole or in part for non-cash consideration. Determination of the aggregate offering price is important for Rules 504 and 505, which have dollar ceilings of $1 million and $5 million, respectively.

Purchaser representative This term is defined, broadly, to be a person unaffiliated with the issuer who has such knowledge and experience in financial and business matters that he is capable of evaluating the risks and merits of a proposed offering. A purchaser representative can be relied on to qualify purchasers for Rule 506's safe harbor for private placements.

Conditions of Regulation D Offerings

Rule 502 establishes four conditions that are applicable to Regulation D offerings. Those conditions relate to the 1) integration doctrine, 2)

---

19 *See* Dodd-Frank Wall Street Reform and Consumer Protection Act, Pub. L. No. 111–203, § 413, 124 Stat. 1376, 1577–8 (2010).

20 1933 Act Rule 501(b), 17 C.F.R. § 230.501(b) (2012).

information to be supplied to offerees, 3) manner of soliciting purchasers, and 4) limitations on resales.

Integration The first condition sets forth a safe harbor to avoid the integration of more than one exempt offering; it also provides a five-factor test to be considered for offerings that the safe harbor does not protect. Rule 502(a) provides that offers and sales taking place more than six months before the beginning for the Regulation D offering and those taking place more than six months after the completion of the offering will not be integrated into the Regulation D offering. Transactions that are not integrated under either the safe harbor or the five-factor test will not destroy the exemption.

Information requirements The second condition establishes the type of information that an issuer is required to supply to purchasers for an offering exempted by Regulation D. If all of the purchasers are accredited investors as defined in Rule 501, then Rule 502 does not require that any specific information be furnished to them by the issuer. Rule 502(b)(1) provides that the foregoing informational requirements do not apply to offerings of up to $1 million that are made pursuant to Rule 504. In Rule 505 and Rule 506 transactions, any non-accredited offerees must receive the information specified in Rule 502(b). Formerly, the SEC required that if there was at least one unaccredited purchaser, all purchasers (including those who are accredited) had to be provided with the specified information. The SEC has deleted this requirement and replaced it with a *recommendation* that all purchasers be given this information. The amount and format of information depends on the size of the offering and whether the issuer is a reporting company under the 1934 Act.

Absence of general solicitation The third condition of Rule 502 prohibits the offer or sale of securities by a general solicitation or general advertising. However, in 2012, Congress mandated that the SEC permit general solicitation for Rule 506 offerings, so long as the offering is sold only to accredited investors. The rule permitting general advertising in offerings only to accredited investors was adopted in the summer of 2013. The concept of general solicitation is more concerned with the types of potential investors that are contacted rather than the number of potential investors contacted. Thus, for example, a general solicitation may exist even if relatively few potential investors are contacted if those persons contacted do not satisfy the necessary sophistication, wealth or experience requirements for the offering. Similarly, contacting a large number of properly qualified potential investors will not constitute a general solicitation. One of the benchmarks of a general solicitation is contacting potential investors with no previous relationship to the issuer or persons promoting the offering. Accordingly, one way to avoid a general solicitation is to use an underwriter or other promoter who has a ready list of qualified potential investors with whom they have dealt previously. Mass mailings also constitute a general solicitation. The general solicitation provisions apply to both Rule 505 and Rule 506 offerings. The prohibition against general solutions also applies to offerings under Rule 504, unless made in compliance with applicable state laws.

Resale restrictions Fourth, Rule 502(d) sets limits on the resale of securities acquired in a Regulation D transaction. Formerly, these restrictions did not apply to offerings under Rule 504. However, in 1999, the SEC amended Rule 504 to require resale restrictions unless the securities are either 1) registered under state law that requires the filing and distribution of a substantive disclosure document; or 2) offered only to accredited investors under a state law exemption from registration that permits a general solicitation. The resale restrictions apply to both Rule 505 and 506 transactions, as well. Rule 502(d) requires the issuer to take precautions against resales, including issuing appropriate transfer instructions to the transfer agent and placing a legend indicating the transfer restriction on the share certificate.

Filing notice of sales Rule 503 sets forth requirements for maintaining a record of exempt sales. Under Rule 503, the SEC requires an initial filing within fifteen days after the first sale of securities pursuant to a Regulation D offering; subsequent notices of sales are due every six months after the first sale and thirty days after the final sale. Rule 507 does not require the filing of a Form D, as required by Rule 503, as a precondition to the exemption unless the issuer, its affiliates, or predecessor are subject to an order for having failed to comply with the filing requirements.

Insignificant deviations Minor variations from an exemption's requirements will not destroy the availability of the exemption. Rule 508 provides a savings clause for an insignificant failure to comply with a condition of the exemption that is not "directly intended to protect" the investor, provided that the issuer made a good faith and reasonable attempt to comply.

EXEMPTIONS UNDER RULES 504, 505 AND 506

Rule 504—Exemption for Small Issues of $1 Million or Less

Rule 504 provides an exemption from registration for offerings by issuers who are not subject to the 1934 Act reporting requirements, provided the offering does not exceed $1 million in any twelve-month period. Both the ban on general solicitations and the requirement that the securities be restricted that were formerly applicable to all Rule 504 offerings have been eliminated for 1) those offerings made solely to accredited investors; and 2) those offerings where a disclosure document is delivered to purchasers pursuant to state securities law registration requirements, or pursuant to an exemption under applicable state securities laws. Similarly, while there are no longer all-encompassing restrictions on resale of securities purchased in a Rule 504 offering, resale restrictions will apply unless delivery of a disclosure document is required under state law. The Rule 504 exemption is available only to an issuer that is neither an investment company nor subject to the 1934 Act reporting requirements.

Rule 505—Exemption for Limited Offerings Not Exceeding $5 Million

A Rule 505 offering may be made to an unlimited number of "accredited investors" and no more than thirty-five other "purchasers." Unlike the safe harbor for non-public offerings under Rule 506, there is no requirement that the unaccredited purchasers be sophisticated in order to participate in a Rule 505 offering. Furthermore, if an issuer takes reasonable steps to assure that the thirty-five unaccredited investor limit is not exceeded, the presence of an inadvertent extra unaccredited, but otherwise qualified, purchaser should not destroy the exemption. When calculating the number of unaccredited purchasers for the purposes of Rule 505, accredited investors and certain relatives of a purchaser, as well as trusts, estates and corporations in which a purchaser has more than a 50 percent beneficial ownership are not included. Corporations or other business entities will generally be counted as one purchaser, as is each client of an investment adviser or stockbroker. In order to be eligible to take advantage of the Rule 505 exemption the issuer must be neither an investment company nor be subject to any of the "bad boy" disqualification provisions contained in Rule 262(b) and (c) of Regulation A of the 1933 Act. Further, all offers and sales made under Rule 505 must satisfy the terms and conditions of Rules 501 through 503 of Regulation D. Thus, for example, an offering may not be made pursuant to a general solicitation, but instead unaccredited investors must receive the information specified in Rule 502(b), and the securities so issued are subject to resale restrictions.

Rule 506—Safe Harbor for Private Placements

Rule 506 provides an exemption for the offer and sale of securities to no more than thirty-five purchasers; as is the case under the Rule 505 exemption, "accredited investors" are not counted toward that limit. Similarly, the thirty-five purchaser limitation does not include certain relatives of a purchaser, trusts, estates, or corporations in which a purchaser has more than a 50 percent beneficial ownership. Rule 506 places further qualifications on permissible purchasers. Purchasers who are not accredited investors must themselves, or through a purchaser representative, have such knowledge and experience in financial and business matters that the purchaser or qualifying representative is capable of evaluating the merits and risks of the prospective investment. "Purchaser representative" is defined, broadly, as a person unaffiliated with the issuer who has such knowledge and experience in financial and business matters as to be capable of evaluating the risks and merits of a proposed offering. As is the case with transactions exempt under Rule 505, all offers and sales made under Rule 506 must satisfy the terms and conditions of Rules 501 through 503 of Regulation D. Thus, for example, an offering cannot involve a general solicitation, unaccredited investors must receive the information specified in Rule 502(b) of the 1933 Act, and the securities so issued are subject to resale restrictions.

In addition to requiring reconsideration of the accredited investor net worth thresholds, the Dodd-Frank Wall Street Reform and Consumer Protection Act of 2010 mandated that the SEC promulgate rules addressing disqualification of bad actors from the Rule 506 exemption. Congress mandated that the SEC permit general solicitations in Rule 506 offerings. Those rules were adopted in the summer of 2013.

EXEMPTIONS FOR SECONDARY TRANSACTIONS—TRANSACTIONS BY PERSONS OTHER THAN ISSUERS, UNDERWRITERS, AND DEALERS: 1933 ACT § 4(A)(1); UNSOLICITED BROKERS' TRANSACTIONS—1933 ACT § 4(A)(4)

The registration requirements of the 1933 Act are not limited to offerings by the issuer. Secondary transactions—that is, sales by existing shareholders—may also trigger Section 5 registration and prospectus obligations. Because of the proscriptions of Section 5, the burden is on a seller of securities, including existing shareholders, to establish an exemption from registration. Sections 4(a)(1), 4(a)(3), and 4(a)(4) of the 1933 Act provide the most common exemptions available for secondary transactions. Section 4(a)(1) provides a registration exemption for "transactions by any person other than an issuer, underwriter or dealer." Because the private placement exemption of Section 4(a)(2) is limited to issuer transactions, it has no application to the millions of shares that are traded daily on the national exchanges and NASDAQ where, although not involving public offerings, the transactions are not effected by issuers. The Section 4(a)(1) exemption (along with Section 4(a)(3) and 4(a)(4)) helps fill this void. Section 4(a)(1) exempts transactions rather than people and thus may not be available to someone who is not an issuer, underwriter or dealer, but is involved in a transaction with one.[21] However, the mere involvement of a broker in a secondary transaction will not render the exemption unavailable. Furthermore, unsolicited brokers' transactions are exempt under Section 4(a)(4).

Basic Definitions

Issuer By its terms, Section 4(a)(1) exempts all transactions by persons who are not issuers, underwriters or dealers. Section 2(a)(4) of the 1933 Act defines "issuer" to include every person who issues or proposes to issue a security. It has been held that the concept of issuer applies to a corporation acting as a promoter by setting up a number of limited partnerships for syndication.[22] The statutory definition of issuer does not

---

[21] *See* SEC v. Holschuh, 694 F.2d 130, 137–38 (7th Cir. 1982); United States v. Wolfson, 405 F.2d 779 (2d Cir. 1968), *cert. denied*, 394 U.S. 946 (1969).

[22] *See* SEC v. Holschuh, 694 F.2d 130, 138–39 (7th Cir. 1982); SEC v. Murphy, 626 F.2d 633, 644 (9th Cir. 1980).

generally raise any significant problem of judicial interpretation because it is usually easy to identify the issuer for a particular security.

Underwriter The question of who is an underwriter is not nearly as simple as defining "issuer." Section 2(a)(11) of the 1933 Act provides that an "underwriter" is anyone who purchases a security from the issuer with a view toward distribution of the security, as well as anyone who offers to sell securities on behalf of an issuer in connection with a distribution, including anyone involved in any indirect participation in such undertaking or the underwriting of the distribution. The most troubling problems of the definition in operation arise in the context of persons who, although not denominated as underwriters in the generic sense of the term, act as conduits for placing the securities in the hands of members of the investing public. In addition to the general definition of underwriter, Section 2(a)(11) further provides that anyone who sells securities on behalf of a controlling person of the issuer is deemed an underwriter. There are thus three ways to qualify for underwriter status: 1) purchasing from the issuer with a view towards distribution; 2) direct or indirect participation in an underwriting effort; and 3) selling securities on behalf of a control person of the issuer. Underwriter status not only renders the Section 4(a)(1) exemption unavailable, but it also provides the basis for liability for misstatements in connection with a registered offering. The intricacies of the statutory underwriter concept are discussed later in this chapter.

Dealer Section 2(a)(12) of the 1933 Act defines "dealer" to include all people who, for all or part of their time, are in the business of offering, buying, selling, or otherwise dealing or trading in securities issued by others. It does not matter whether such sales activity is direct or indirect, and the statutory definition of dealer further applies whether one is acting as an agent, broker or principal with regard to the securities transactions in question. Because virtually all day-to-day transactions are effected through the means of a registered broker-dealer, the Section 4(a)(1) exemption standing alone would not exempt the transactions from 1933 Act registration. However, as noted above, Section 4(a)(1) must be read in tandem with Section 4(a)(3)'s exemption for most dealers' transactions and Section 4(a)(4)'s exemption for unsolicited brokers' transactions.

1933 Act § 4(a)(4)—Unsolicited Brokers' Transactions

Section 4(a)(4) of the 1933 Act exempts "brokers' transactions executed upon customers' orders on any exchange or in the over-the-counter market, but not the solicitation of such orders." Neither the 1933 Act nor the SEC rules under that Act contain a definition of "broker," but it is clear that the concept cannot be coextensive with that of a "dealer" under Section 2(a)(12). Additional guidance on the meaning of "broker" can be gathered from Section 3(a)(4) of the 1934 Act which defines "broker" generally as anyone engaged in the business of effecting securities transactions for the account of others. The 1934 Act definition of broker comports with the term's generic meaning and thus would seem to be equally applicable to the 1933 Act. As such, brokers form a subcategory of dealers and include anyone who is in the business of effecting securities transactions as an agent for others. Accordingly, persons who only execute transactions on their own behalf or as principals may still be categorized as "dealers," but do not fall within the concept of "broker" as used in the statutory exemption from registration provided in Section 4(a)(4). Although the definition of broker encompasses a wider subset of actors, the Section 4(a)(4) exemption only applies to transactions in which the broker acts as the purchaser's agent, rather than as an agent for someone else such as the issuer or underwriter.

Another significant aspect of the Section 4(a)(4) exemption is that it extends to unsolicited "brokers' *transactions*." Both the courts and SEC have pointed out the distinction in terminology between "transactions" and the concept of a "distribution." The brokers' transaction exemption is inapplicable if the amount of securities sold is so large as to constitute a "distribution"—as compared with the day-to-day "transaction" that the Section 4(a)(4) exemption was designed to cover.[23] The concept of distribution sufficient to confer underwriter status does not depend on a certain percentage of the market float, but rather on the fact that a significant amount of shares are involved.

The Section 4(a)(4) exemption is unavailable to a broker who has reasonable grounds to believe that the customer is a statutory underwriter. Brokers receiving restricted stock have a duty of reasonable inquiry as to whether the customer entering the sell order is a statutory underwriter. A broker or dealer asked to sell a substantial block of securities is obligated to investigate whether the transaction involves a control person or an underwriter; reliance on the customer's assertions alone may not satisfy the obligation of reasonable investigation. The SEC does not have any rules relating specifically to brokers' transactions themselves. However,

---

23 *See, e.g.,* United States v. Wolfson, 405 F.2d 779 (2d Cir. 1968), *cert. denied*, 394 U.S. 946 (1969); In the Matter of Ira Haupt & Co., 23 S.E.C. 589, 1946 WL 24150 (1946).

Rule 144(g) of the 1933 Act's provision relating to brokers' transactions and Rule 144(e)'s safe harbor for the amount of securities sold may give some guidance as to the scope of the Section 4(a)(4) exemption.

Who Is an Underwriter?—1933 Act § 2(a)(11)

As previously noted, Section 2(a)(11) of the 1933 Act sets forth a broad-based statutory definition of "underwriter" which includes 1) persons who acquire securities of the issuer with a view towards distribution; 2) all persons who directly or indirectly participate in the offering, selling, or underwriting process; and 3) persons selling on behalf of a control person of the issuer. The definition's significance goes beyond the Section 4(a)(1) exemption. For example, Section 2(a)(11) also helps determine the scope of the class of persons liable for material misstatements and omissions made in connection with registered offerings under Section 11 of the 1933 Act.

Whether a transaction falls within the Section 4(a)(1) exemption by involving an "underwriter," often boils down to a question of fact as to the would-be underwriter's state of mind in acquiring the security. The essence of underwriter status is established when the securities were acquired from the issuer or control person with intent to resell. In order to be classified as a statutory underwriter, the participant must have been acting on behalf of, or purchasing from, an issuer. In this context, however, the statute provides that a control person is considered to be an issuer. Willfully acting as a conduit for distributing shares is sufficient to create underwriter status, even though the person acting as an underwriter did not intend to act as an underwriter. Underwriter status thus can follow from playing an essential role in the distribution even though the underwriter was not the actual seller. The general approach to underwriter status may be summarized as follows: when one is involved in the selling or purchase of a substantial amount of securities on behalf of or from an issuer (or control person) and the securities are subsequently resold within a short period of time, underwriter status may attach. On the other hand, the mere fact that a dealer sells a large amount of securities will not necessarily create underwriter status. The participant's intent to resell is pivotal in determining whether underwriter status will attach.

The legislative history of Section 2(a)(11) reveals that the congressional intent was to include as underwriters all persons who might operate as conduits for securities being placed into the hands of the investing public. So long as the ultimate purchasers are members of the general public, as opposed to qualified private placement purchasers, the transaction calls for the protection of the 1933 Act's registration provisions. The exemption thus places great emphasis on the ultimate purchasers of the securities, rather than the nature of the person acting as a conduit for the sale of securities to the members of the public.[24] The statutory definition of an underwriter excludes dealers who are members of the selling group.[25] Although certainly involved in the distribution process, those dealers who receive nothing more than their ordinary sales commissions are not classified as Section 2(a)(11) underwriters. The exclusion of transactions in which the only remuneration is "the usual and customary distributors' or sellers' commission" is designed to protect members of the selling group and nonparticipating brokers from being included in the classification of underwriter. Rule 141 of the 1933 Act explains that a dealer's commission includes the normal spread between the offering price and the dealer's cost, whether the dealer was purchasing the security prior to reselling it or acting merely as a broker executing a customer's order.

It is very common for institutional investors, as well as wealthy individuals, to purchase large blocks of both registered and unregistered offerings. When these investors subsequently sell their securities, there frequently is a question as to the necessity for registration under the 1933 Act. The problem is most likely to arise where the initial offering was not registered under the 1933 Act. Downstream sales are dealt with in the safe harbor provided by Rule 144 of the 1933 Act, which requires a one-year holding period (six months for 1934 Act reporting companies) before the securities can be resold under the safe harbor. Rule 144 further imposes limitations on the volume of sales after the one-year period has expired.

Case law developments—inadvertent underwriters

In one of the earliest judicial pronouncements on point, the Second Circuit made it clear that any substantial involvement in the distribution process would confer underwriter status, thus rendering unavailable the Section 4(a)(1) of the 1933 Act exemption. In *SEC v. Chinese Consolidated Benevolent Association*,[26] a not-for-profit association helped solicit

---

[24] *See, e.g.,* In the Matter of Kirby, 2000 WL 1787908 (S.E.C. Initial Dec. Dec. 7, 2000).

[25] The selling group includes dealers who are not subject to underwriting obligations, but who are enlisted by the underwriters to aid in the distribution of securities.

[26] SEC v. Chinese Consolidated Benevolent Association, 120 F.2d 738 (2d Cir. 1941), *cert. denied*, 314 U.S. 618 (1941).

investment in foreign government bonds. The defendants maintained that they were not acting as securities promoters in the traditional sense, and that in promoting a worthy cause they should be exempt from the 1933 Act's coverage. Although their arguments swayed Judge Swan, who wrote a vigorous dissent, the court held that the voluntary association's sales efforts were sufficient participation in the distribution and underwriting process so as to render the defendants "underwriters" within the meaning of Section 2(a)(11). Judge Swan's dissent maintained that a logical extension of the court's opinion would make a newspaper an underwriter if a column or editorial recommends a bond in order to help a struggling government, or merely announces an impending offering. The short answer to Judge Swan's contention is that it is a matter of degree and thus not suitable for a bright-line test. It is most certainly correct that incidental or collateral selling efforts or recommendations should not be sufficient to render someone potentially liable for violations of the 1933 Act. Absent some other exemption, however, when an organization acts as a conduit for the sale of securities, such activity should be sufficient not only to confer jurisdiction, but also to trigger the registration requirements, independently of whether remuneration is received. This method of analysis makes each decision extremely factual, and relatively little firm footing is provided for counselors and corporate planners in relying on the available precedent.

In *SEC v. Guild Films Co.*,[27] the inadvertent underwriters were banks engaging in a foreclosure sale of a substantial block of securities in Guild Films Company; the securities had been held as collateral for loans to a major shareholder of the company. The Second Circuit accepted the SEC's argument that the banks were acting as underwriters under Section 2(a)(11) even though the banks may have accepted the stock as collateral in good faith and had not dealt directly with the corporation that was the issuer of the securities. The court reasoned that "the banks knew that they had been given unregistered stock and that the issuer had specifically forbidden that the stock be sold …" In the court's view, this was sufficient to put the bank in a position in which it must have either held onto the stock, found some other independent exemption, or registered its sales upon foreclosure. The issue was not the bank's culpability in facilitating downstream sale, but rather whether the sales were made in such a manner as to trigger the need for the protection provided by registration. In contrast, when a bona fide pledge is made and there is no

---

[27] SEC v. Guild Films Co., 279 F.2d 485 (2d Cir. 1960), *cert. denied,* 364 U.S. 819 (1960).

substantial likelihood that the pledgee will have to foreclose, it is unlikely that the pledgee will be found to be a statutory underwriter in the event that there is a foreclosure and the securities are sold. Specifically, under Rule 144(d)(4)(D) of the 1933 Act, all securities sold by a bona fide pledgee are deemed to be acquired when they were acquired by the pledgor, and are aggregated with any sales by the pledgor for the purpose of calculating the rule's ceiling on resales.

Investment intent—the holding period

In determining whether a person is a statutory underwriter, one of the key considerations is whether the would-be underwriter had sufficient investment intent at the time of purchase. The issue is raised in the context of whether the securities were purchased with a view toward distribution. One of the primary questions then becomes: how does one determine the seller's original intent at the time the securities were acquired? The period that the securities were held in between the purchase and subsequent sale is a significant factor in determining whether they were originally purchased with the requisite investment intent. A resale closely following the acquisition of the securities is strong circumstantial evidence that an investment intent did not exist. In a leading case, it was held, within the context of a criminal prosecution, that "[t]he passage of two years before the commencement of distribution of any of these shares is an insuperable obstacle to my finding that [defendant] took these shares with a view to distribution thereof, in the absence of any relevant evidence from which I could conclude that he did not take the shares for investment."[28] In 1997, the SEC shortened the holding period for resales of restricted securities under the safe harbor provisions of Rule 144 from two years to one. Rule 144 was subsequently amended to provide that restricted securities of companies subject to the 1934 Act reporting requirements are subject to only a six-month holding period.

The "change in circumstances" exception

In the pre-Rule 144 case law, sales made prior to the expiration of the two-year holding period from the date of acquisition were permitted if the sellers were able to demonstrate that they had sufficient investment intent at the time of the acquisition. As a result, it became common for sellers to claim that although they had the requisite investment intent at the time of purchase, subsequent changes in their personal situations necessitated the resale of the securities. Sellers of securities often took

---

28 United States v. Sherwood, 175 F.Supp. 480, 483 (S.D.N.Y. 1959).

the position that because they had not purchased the securities with a view toward distribution, they should be relieved from the 1933 Act's registration requirements. Although the SEC often refused to issue no-action letters based on this "change of circumstances" defense, it was a position frequently relied upon by planners in permitting transactions without registration and was also acknowledged by the SEC as a legitimate way of avoiding underwriter status. The defense was highly factual and it was difficult to predict when it might be successfully applied. This defense was not available where the changed circumstances were reasonably foreseeable at the time of purchase, nor where the only change was that the issuer failed to meet the investor's expectations of success. Additionally, the availability of the "change in circumstances" defense was directly related to the period of time for which the securities had been held; the shorter the holding period, the more compelling the evidence required.

The "change in circumstances" defense necessarily had to be applied on a case-by-case basis and served to add to the uncertainty in structuring transactions, sometimes resulting in inconsistency. Accordingly, in adopting Rule 144, the SEC purported to rescind the "change in circumstances" defense.[29] There is, however, a question as to the SEC's authority to make such a pronouncement beyond the context of a safe harbor rule. To the extent that the "change in circumstances" defense is a valid interpretation of the Section 2(a)(11) statutory definition of one who purchases with an intent to redistribute, the SEC cannot change the meaning of the statute by administrative fiat. However, if the "change in circumstances defense" was merely an administrative interpretation, rather than a part of the statutory definition, the SEC can effectively eliminate the defense by changing its interpretation. In any event, considering that Rule 144 is not the exclusive method by which an affiliate of the issuer may sell restricted securities in reliance upon an exemption, the "change in circumstances defense" arguably survives even if it is abolished for those relying upon the rule. Further, if the SEC was correct in interpreting the statutory language by applying the "change in circumstances defense," then it cannot change the statute by SEC rule. Nevertheless, the SEC has taken the position that it has been abolished in all cases.

---

[29] *See* Notice of Adoption of Rule 144 Relating to the Definition of the Terms "Underwriter" in Sections 4(a)(1) and 2(11) and "Brokers" Transactions' in Section 4(a)(4) of the Securities Act of 1933, Exchange Act Release No. 33–5223, 1972 WL 121583 (Jan. 11, 1972).

Sales on behalf of control persons

The last sentence of Section 2(a)(11)'s statutory definition of underwriter provides that anyone who sells a security on behalf of a controlling person is an underwriter. Thus, a control person of the company frequently will not be in a position to rely on the Section 4(a)(1) exemption from registration. Although there is no statutory definition of "control," Rule 405 of the 1933 Act defines control as "the possession, direct or indirect, of the power to direct or cause the direction of the management and policies of a person, whether through the ownership of voting securities, by contract, or otherwise." Accordingly, the question of who is a control person is highly factual and is not dependent upon ownership of any specific percentage. For example, any policy-making officer falls within Rule 405's definition and thus would be deemed a control person. The SEC has indicated that in the context of a sizable secondary distribution, the burden of proving the absence of control may be allocated to the person claiming the exemption.

In the leading SEC case *In the Matter of Ira Haupt*, a series of coordinated secondary offerings resulted in a corporation's publicly held shares shifting from 9 percent of those outstanding to 46 percent of those outstanding. The broker/dealer handling such sales on behalf of controlling persons was held to have been a statutory underwriter.[30] The SEC rejected the contention that because the transactions were executed upon the selling customer's orders, they should be exempt under Section 4(a)(4) as unsolicited broker's transactions. The SEC reasoned that such a large infusion of privately held stock into the public market constituted a "distribution," as opposed to the type of day-to-day transaction or "trading" that Section 4(a)(4) was designed to exempt. Thus, it is clear that any large block sales of securities by insiders (i.e., control persons or affiliates) that have not been registered will be subject to the 1933 Act's registration requirements, absent some other independent exemption.

In *United States v. Wolfson*,[31] the Second Circuit alarmed the brokerage industry when it noted that brokers were potentially liable as underwriters for selling a controlling person's securities. The court held that defendant Wolfson, the control person who had siphoned his securities to the public by making sales through a number of brokers, was not exempt because such transactions were through an underwriter as defined in

---

[30] In the Matter of Ira Haupt & Co., 23 S.E.C. 589, 1946 WL 24150 (1946).

[31] United States v. Wolfson, 405 F.2d 779 (2d Cir. 1968), *cert. denied*, 394 U.S. 946 (1969).

Section 2(a)(11). The court noted that Section 4(a)(1) exempts "transactions" and not classes of people. Citing the Section 2(a)(11) definition of underwriter, the court pointed out that the brokers had supplied outlets for the stock of appellants who were "issuers" within Section 2(a)(11)'s definition of that term, even if they were not "issuers" as defined by Section 2(a)(4). Thus, the brokers were "underwriters" within the meaning of Section 2(a)(11), and according to the court, "the stock was sold in 'transactions by underwriters' which are not within the exception of Section 4(a)(1) … ."

A broker is under a duty to be aware of facts surrounding a transaction. "Red flags" that they are participating in a distribution, may lead to a finding that the broker was, in fact, an underwriter. When broker-dealers receive an order to sell a substantial amount of stock, they must investigate to determine if the sale will be in compliance with the securities laws. Underwriter status can thus be found on the basis of knowingly assisting in the sales even without actual intent to act as an underwriter.[32] The Section 4(a)(1) exemption, and hence the definition of underwriter, was not the only issue involved in the *Wolfson* case. The appellants in *Wolfson* also argued that the brokers could not be underwriters because the sales in question fell within the Section 4(a)(4) exemption for brokers' orders executed upon customers' orders on any exchange or in the over-the-counter market. The court agreed that Section 4(a)(4) exempted the brokers for their parts in the transaction, because the brokers had not solicited the orders, and were unaware at the time that the transactions were part of a distribution of securities by the appellants. Wolfson and his associates, on the other hand, were "control persons [who] must find their own exemptions." Otherwise, the court reasoned, appellants would gain from having kept the true facts from the brokers. In a situation in which the broker is *not* an unwitting participant, the size of the total secondary distribution may well preclude the application of Section 4(a)(4) to shield the brokers.

Safe Harbor Exemption for Secondary Transactions—1933 Act Rule 144

As noted above, case law and SEC interpretations of Section 2(a)(11) of the 1933 Act underwriter status, as well as the scope of the exemptions under sections 4(a)(1) and 4(a)(4) of the 1933 Act, have not provided much firm practical guidance to the planners of corporate transactions.

---

32 *See, e.g.*, Geiger v. SEC, 363 F.3d 481 (D.C. Cir. 2004).

There was thus little guidance available to planners of transactions involving the sale of restricted securities, nor for transactions involving the sale of any securities held by control persons. Because many of the questions concerned with the need to register downstream securities sales essentially depend upon the resolution of factual issues, the relevant decisions are frequently confusing and often may even appear to be inconsistent with one another. The resulting uncertainty was widely perceived by the practicing bar and documented by a special report, the "Wheat Report," submitted to the SEC in 1969. In response to this uncertainty and other issues identified in the Wheat Report, the SEC promulgated a number of additional regulations, including Rule 144 of the 1933 Act. Rule 144 operates as a safe harbor and, as such, is not the exclusive method by which an affiliate of the issuer may sell restricted securities in reliance upon an exemption. Rule 144 applies to both the sales of restricted securities by all persons and to the sales of any securities by affiliates of the issuer. As is the case with any safe harbor rule, Rule 144 will not protect a transaction that, although in technical compliance with the rule, is part of a scheme to evade the 1933 Act's registration requirements.

"Restricted securities" are defined in Rule 144 as those securities acquired directly or indirectly from an issuer in a non-public offering, as well as securities subject to the resale restrictions imposed by the exemptions provided in Regulation D. Rule 144's resale restrictions include a one-year holding period for restricted securities, which is reduced to six months for securities of companies subject to the 1934 Act's periodic reporting requirements. Rule 144 is also available with regard to securities issued under Section 3(a)(9)'s exemption for securities issued exclusively in an exchange with existing securities holders. In 1998, securities issued in offshore offerings under Regulation S were added to the list of restricted securities. The SEC has emphasized, however, that persons who offer or sell restricted securities without relying on Rule 144 will have the "substantial burden of proof in establishing that an exemption … is available," and that "brokers … who participate in the transactions do so at their risk."[33]

Compliance with Rule 144 requires dissemination of sufficient current public information concerning the issuer. There are only two ways to satisfy the rule's information requirements. A company that is subject to,

---

[33] Notice of Adoption of Rule 144 Relating to the Definition of the Terms "Underwriter" in Sections 4(a)(1) and 2(11) and "Brokers" Transactions' in Section 4(a)(4) of the Securities Act of 1933, Exchange Act Release No. 33–5223, 1972 WL 121583 (Jan. 11, 1972).

and complies with, the 1934 Act reporting requirements satisfies the rule, provided of course that all reports are accurate and up-to-date. For companies that are not subject to the 1934 Act, issuers must make similar information publicly available in order to qualify for Rule 144—specifically, most of the information required by Rule 15c2–11(a)(4) of the 1934 Act. It is notable that unlike Rule 506 of the 1933 Act's safe harbor exemption for non-public offerings by an issuer, Rule 144 of the 1933 Act's dissemination of information requirements concern information that is publicly available, and does not mandate that this (or any other) information be made specifically available to offerees and purchasers of the restricted securities.

Holding period

In addition to Rule 144's public information requirement, the rule imposes a one-year holding period for resales of restricted securities, which is reduced to six months for securities subject to the 1934 Act's reporting requirements. Rule 144, thus, applies to both affiliates of the issuer as well as non-affiliates who have purchased restricted securities from the issuer (or other seller) and who elect to resell those securities without filing a registration statement. The required one-year/six-month holding period shortened the previous two-year holding period, which was borrowed from the typical holding period that had been established by early decisions. The holding period was meant to aid in determining whether the person purchasing the security from the issuer had an investment intent, as opposed to having purchased the securities with a view towards distribution. In applying the one-year/six-month holding period, any securities obtained by way of stock dividends, splits, recapitalization, or conversions are deemed to have been acquired when the original security was purchased from the issuer.

Securities that have been deposited with a pledgee in the course of a bona fide pledge are deemed to have been acquired by the pledgee on the date that they were originally acquired by the pledgor. However, if there is no recourse against the pledgor, the pledgee's date of acquisition starts the one-year holding period anew. When the securities in question have been purchased with a promissory note or pursuant to an installment contract, the one-year holding period does not begin to run until full payment has been made. Rule 144 of the 1933 Act further provides that securities acquired by gift (from persons other than the issuer) are treated as having been acquired by the donee on the date that the donor acquired them. Additionally, securities acquired from the settlor of a trust or held by a deceased's estate are considered to have been acquired by the trust or estate on the date that they were first acquired by the settlor or the deceased.

Volume limitations

Even beyond the expiration of the one-year/six-month holding period for restricted securities, Rule 144 places limitations on *all sales* of securities by affiliates of the issuer relying on the rule. These restrictions thus apply to affiliates' sales of both restricted and unrestricted securities. Rule 144(e)(1) permits sales by affiliates provided that the aggregate amount sold, combined with all sales of other securities of the same class (whether restricted or not) sold by the affiliate within the preceding three months, does not exceed the volume limits specified in the rule. The rule places a limit of (i) 1 percent of the shares of that class outstanding as shown by the most recent report of the issuer; or (ii) the average weekly reported volume of trading in such securities on national exchanges or reported through the consolidated transaction reporting system, or any automated quotation system of a registered securities association—i.e., NASDAQ. As a result of this provision, a substantial amount of secondary sales may take place following 90 days after an initial public offering, which is when the issuer becomes subject to Section 15(d) of the 1934 Act's periodic reporting requirements. These "dribble out" provisions no longer apply to non-affiliates' sales of restricted securities after the initial one-year holding period has expired. Once the one-year holding period for restricted securities has expired, non-affiliates are free to resell under Rule 144.

Brokers' transactions

Under subsection (f) of Rule 144, all transactions by either affiliates or non-affiliates made in reliance upon the rule must be made in "brokers' transactions" as defined in Section 4(a)(4) of the 1933 Act, or in transactions directly with a market maker.[34] The person selling the security under Rule 144 may not solicit or arrange for solicitations of offers to buy securities in anticipation of the transaction, nor may they make any payment in connection with the offer or sale to any person other than the broker executing the transaction. Rule 144(g) further defines the scope of Section 4(a)(4)'s brokers' transaction exemption for the purposes of the rule: the broker's activity must be limited to the execution of the order or orders to sell as an agent for the person selling.

---

[34] Market makers are broker-dealers who are charged with maintaining an orderly market in the NASDAQ and exchange markets.

In order for Rule 144 to apply, the broker may receive no more than the usual and customary broker's commission as defined by the current market, and may neither solicit nor arrange for customers' orders to buy the securities that would be sold in a transaction.[35]

Notice of sales

In addition to compliance with all of the foregoing requirements, Rule 144(h) requires filing a notice of most Rule 144 sales. Form 144 must be completed whenever the amount of securities sold in reliance on the rule within any three-month period is more than 500 shares, or the aggregate sales price is more than $10,000. As discussed more fully below, in 1990, the SEC adopted Rule 144A of the 1933 Act, which contains an exemption for downstream sales to qualified institutional investors. As is the case with Rule 144, Rule 144A classifies certain offers and sales as not involving a distribution, so that persons participating in such offers and sales are not considered "underwriters."

The § "4(1 1/2)" Exemption for Downstream Sales—1933 Act Rule 144A

As discussed previously, Section 4(a)(1)'s exemption for transactions not involving an issuer, underwriter or dealer, and Section 4(a)(4)'s exemption for unsolicited brokers' transactions both provide avenues to exempt transactions made by persons other than an issuer. In contrast, Section 4(a)(2)'s non-public offering exemption is limited by its terms to "transactions by an issuer" and thus is not available for downstream sales. The rationale underlying the Section 4(a)(2) exemption seems to support a comparable exemption for downstream sales by non-issuers,

---

[35] There are three exceptions to Rule 144(g)'s ban on solicitation for brokers' transactions: 1) the broker may contact other dealers who have indicated interest in the securities within the past sixty days; 2) the broker may make inquiries to other customers who have shown an "unsolicited bona fide interest" in the securities within the past ten business days; and 3) the broker may publish bid and asked quotations in an inter-dealer quotation system "provided that such quotations are incident to the maintenance of a bona fide interdealer market for the security for the broker's own account …" The final prerequisite under subsection (g) is that the broker must make a reasonable inquiry as to whether the person for whose account the securities are being sold is an underwriter or whether the transaction is part of a distribution. Although subsection (g) was adopted solely pursuant to Rule 144, its terms are certainly helpful by way of analogy to anyone planning a transaction in reliance upon a Section 4(a)(4) exemption.

containing the two primary elements of the Section 4(a)(2) exemption: 1) the purchaser's access to current information about the issuer; and 2) the purchaser's ability to evaluate that information.

Consider, for example, a private placement by Issuer Co. where S and B would both qualify as purchasers for a Section 4(a)(2) offering. Assume further that at the time of the offering, S had adequate funds but B did not, and S purchased stock pursuant to Section 4(a)(2). Two months later, S decides to sell its stock and learns that B now has sufficient cash on hand. Because the presumptive one-year holding period has not yet passed, S cannot take advantage of Section 4(a)(1)'s safe harbor Rule 144. Similarly, S cannot be certain that it has satisfied the requirements of the Section 4(a)(1) exemption. Assuming that the issuer is willing to make current information available to B, there would seem no reason to require registration of S's sale to B as the only alternative to waiting until Rule 144's one-year/six-month holding period has elapsed.

In the foregoing example, because the issuer could validly issue shares directly to B as a qualified private placement purchaser, why should S not be able to take advantage of a similar exemption? The answer to this question is that, as noted above, the statutory language of Section 4(a)(2) is limited to transactions by an issuer. It can be argued, however, that Section 4(a)(1) would support such an exemption. In the above example, S clearly is not an issuer or a dealer, so in order to qualify for the exemption, S must be able to demonstrate that she is not an underwriter. As discussed in an earlier Section, an underwriter is someone who assists an issuer during a distribution or someone who has purchased securities from an issuer with the intent to distribute. It would appear that a downstream sale which complies with the requirements of Section 4(a)(2) is not properly classified as a distribution and, as such, the seller is not properly qualified as an underwriter under Section 2(a)(11)'s definition. Accordingly, the proper basis for an exemption for the downstream seller in the foregoing example is Section 4(a)(1), even while the requirements that must be satisfied may be derived from the parameters of the Section 4(a)(2) exemption for issuers. Unfortunately, the SEC no-action letters that have been cited as the basis for the Section 4(1 1/2) exemption do not provide a consistent statement of what is necessary to satisfy the exemption.[36] The Eighth Circuit explained that the Section 4(1 1/2) exemption is merely an application of the Section

---

[36] *See* ABA Committee on Federal Regulation of Securities, The Section "4(1 1/2)" phenomenon: Private Resales of Restricted Securities, 34 Bus. Law. 1961 (1979).

4(a)(1) exemption for transactions not involving an issuer, underwriter or dealer.[37] The court pointed out that the Section 4(a)(1) exemption for private resales depends upon a finding that a distribution has not taken place and that the definition of distribution is coextensive with Section 4(a)(2)'s public offering exemption.

Rule 144A of the 1933 Act permits downstream resales of restricted securities to institutional investors. Rule 144A, like Rule 144, classifies certain offers and sales as not involving a distribution, so that persons participating in such offers and sales are not considered "underwriters" under Section 2(a)(11). Essentially, the exemption covers any sale to a "qualified institutional buyer," or QIB, which is defined as any institution (including insurance companies, investment companies, employee benefit plans, banks, and savings and loan associations) that owns more than $100 million worth of securities of unaffiliated issuers and, in the case of banks and savings and loan associations, has a net worth of at least $25 million. Rule 144A only applies to sales of securities of a class that is not listed on a national securities exchange, nor traded in the NASDAQ system. In order to avoid minimizing or diluting this requirement, the rule specifies that convertible securities do not constitute a separate class of securities unless they are issued with at least a 10 percent conversion premium.

Simultaneously with the adoption of Rule 144A, the SEC approved the NASD's establishment of a screen-based computer and communication system called PORTAL (Private Offerings, Resales and Trading through Automated Linkages) to facilitate secondary trading of Rule 144A securities.

Exemption for Certain Dealers' Transactions—1933 Act § 4(a)(3)

Although dealers' transactions are not exempt from registration by virtue of Section 4(a)(1) of the 1933 Act, many will be exempt as unsolicited brokers' transactions within the meaning of Section 4(a)(4) of the 1933 Act. Section 4(a)(3) exempts additional dealer transactions from the 1933 Act's registration and prospectus delivery requirements. Section 4(a)(3) is probably the most significant of the transaction exemptions in terms of the number of transactions covered. Section 4(a)(3) eliminates the registration and delivery requirements for all dealers' transactions taking place more than forty days, or in some cases ninety days, after the first date on which the security was offered to the public or after the effective

---

37 Ackerberg v. Johnson, 892 F.2d 1328 (8th Cir. 1989).

date of the registration statement, whichever is later. This forty/ninety-day period is known as the "quiet period." Section 4(a)(3)'s exemption applies both to dealers and to underwriters who are no longer acting as underwriters. The forty-day period in Section 4(a)(3) of the 1933 Act does not apply to first-time issuers who have not previously sold securities pursuant to an effective registration statement; for them, the applicable period is ninety, rather than forty, days after the first sale or effective date of the registration statement.

Section 4(a)(3)(C) provides that the exemption for dealer transactions does not apply to sales of securities that are either part or all of an unsold allotment to that dealer. This means that regardless of the amount of time that has elapsed since the start of the offering, any underwriting activity by a dealer will implicate the prospectus delivery requirements. It is notable, however, that once the forty/ninety-day period has expired, a dealer, including an underwriter, no longer acting as such, can take advantage of the exemption even if another dealer has an unsold allotment. Rule 174 of the 1933 Act expands upon the exemption provided in Section 4(a)(3) and thereby provides an additional exemption from the prospectus delivery requirements for certain dealer transactions. Rule 174 dispenses with the delivery requirements during the forty-day period following the first day of the offering, and during the ninety-day period for first time issuers. Rule 174 applies to securities of issuers that, prior to the offering, are subject to the 1934 Act reporting requirements, as well as to foreign issuers whose securities are traded using American Depositary Receipts that have been registered on Form F–6 of the 1933 Act.

Additionally, under Rule 174 the prospectus requirements do not apply to dealers' transactions for all registered offerings that are to be made from "time to time." As a general matter, for issuers that are subject to and current in their 1934 Act periodic reports immediately prior to the public offering, there is no prospectus delivery requirement during the post-effective period for non-participating dealers (which includes participating dealers whose participation has been completed). For first-time issuers (and other issuers who were not subject to and current in their 1934 Act reports immediately prior to the offering) whose securities are listed on a national exchange or NASDAQ, the ninety-day period that otherwise would apply for the prospectus delivery requirements for nonparticipating dealers under Section 4(a)(3) is reduced to twenty-five days.

EXEMPTION FOR CERTAIN OFFSHORE TRANSACTIONS IN SECURITIES OF UNITED STATES ISSUERS—REGULATIONS

With the growing globalization of the securities markets, there have been an increasing number of questions concerning the applicability of the United States securities laws to transactions taking place outside of the United States. To the extent that a United States issuer offers securities exclusively to non-United States citizens in offshore transactions, there is substantial question as to the propriety of requiring registration under the 1933 Act, even though there would be jurisdiction to do so. Regulation S[38] sets forth two safe harbors:

> One safe harbor applies to offers and sales by issuers, securities professionals involved in the distribution process pursuant to contract, their respective affiliates, and persons acting on behalf of any of the foregoing (the "issuer safe harbor"), and the other applies to resales by persons other than the issuer, securities professionals involved in the distribution process pursuant to contract, their respective affiliates (except certain officers and directors), and persons acting on behalf of any of the foregoing (the "resale safe harbor"). An offer, sale or resale of securities that satisfies all conditions of the applicable safe harbor is deemed to be outside the United States within the meaning of the General Statement and thus not subject to the registration requirements of Section 5.[39]

These two safe harbors are premised on two general conditions. First, any offer or sale of securities must be made in an "offshore transaction." This requires that no offers be made to persons in the United States and that either: i) the buyer is (or the seller reasonably believes that the buyer is) offshore at the time of the origination of the buy order; or ii) for the purposes of the issuer safe harbor, the sale is made in, on, or through a physical trading floor of an established foreign securities exchange; or iii) for purposes of the resale safe harbor, the sale is made in, on, or through the facilities of a designated offshore securities market, and the transaction is not pre-arranged with a buyer in the United States. Second, in no event can "directed selling efforts" be made in the United States in connection with an offer or sale of securities made under a safe harbor. "Directed selling efforts" are activities undertaken for the purpose of, or

---

[38] 1933 Act Rules 901 *et seq.*, 17 C.F.R. § 230.901 *et seq.* (2012).

[39] Offshore Offers and Sales, Exchange Act Release No. 33–6863, 1990 WL 311658, [1989–1990 Transfer Binder] Fed. Sec. L. Rep. (CCH) ¶ 84, 524 (Apr. 24, 1990).

that could reasonably be expected to result in, conditioning of the United States market for the securities being offered. Exceptions to the general conditions are made with respect to offers and sales to specified institutions not deemed U.S. persons, notwithstanding their presence in the United States.

Regulation S's safe harbor for issuers has three categories of securities offerings, which are based on various factors including the nationality and reporting status of the issuer and the degree of U.S. market interest in the issuer's securities. The first category consists of securities of foreign issuers with no substantial United States market interest (provided that the securities are offered and sold in offerings that are directed overseas), as well as securities backed by the full faith and credit of a foreign government, and securities issued pursuant to certain employee benefit plans. The second category includes securities of 1934 Act reporting issuers, non-reporting foreign issuers' debt securities, non-reporting foreign issuers' non-participating preferred stock, and asset-backed securities. The third category consists of securities of non-reporting United States issuers and equity offerings by non-reporting foreign issuers with a substantial United States market interest.

THE SEC'S GENERAL EXEMPTIVE AUTHORITY

Until 1996, all exempt securities and transactions had to fit within the guidelines established by Sections 3 and 4 of the 1933 Act. However, that changed when Congress gave the SEC general exemptive authority. Added in 1966, Section 28 of the 1933 Act provides that the SEC may exempt transactions, securities and persons if it is in the public interest and consistent with investor protection. The SEC now has a choice of working within the statutory limitations of the exemptions set forth in Sections 3 and 4, or in expanding those parameters through rulemaking deemed to be in the public interest. Unlike the exemptions set forth in Sections 3 and 4, the exemptive authority established by Section 28 is not constrained by the terms of the securities being offered, the amount of the offering or the nature of the offering. The only meaningful limitation of the SEC's exemptive authority is that it be consistent with investor protection and in furtherance of the public interest. The SEC's exemptive power under Section 28 is limited to rules and regulations. There is a parallel exemptive authority in Section 36 of the 1934 Act, however, the 1934 Act provision is broader than Section 28 of the 1933 Act in that Section 36 of the 1934 Act permits an exemption by order in addition to one granted by a rule or regulation. The SEC has not used this general exemptive authority with great frequency.

INTEGRATION OF TRANSACTIONS

As discussed throughout this chapter, it is necessary to structure transactions carefully in order to assure that they qualify for exemption from the 1933 Act's registration requirements. It is imperative to consider not only each step in a particular offering, but also to be mindful of past and possible future transactions. Whenever there is a series of securities transactions, it may not be sufficient to ensure the exemption for each transaction can stand on its own. In addition to each transaction being able to qualify for an exemption, when viewed as a whole, the series of transactions must not run afoul of the Act's registration provisions and prospectus requirements.

Under the integration doctrine, the SEC will examine multiple offerings to determine whether they should be treated as a single, unitary transaction. Frequently, an issuer will embark on two (or more) separate exempt transactions within a relatively short period. In such a case the SEC may review the transactions with close scrutiny in order to determine whether all offers and sales from the two (or more) securities offerings should be telescoped and integrated into one transaction. When the integration doctrine is employed, it is possible that the two (or more) offerings combined will lose the attributes that entitled them to exemption from registration. The integration doctrine is not limited to multiple exempt transactions; it can also be used to integrate a would-be exempt offering with a registered offering where some of the offers or sales in the registered offering would destroy the availability of the exemption. The integration doctrine is based on highly factual components and, as such, does not provide much bright-line guidance outside of the few safe harbor rules that exist.

Illustrative Examples of Integration

A few examples will help illustrate the ways in which the integration doctrine can operate. Consider an intrastate offering made by a local issuer offered only to residents of the state of incorporation and principal place of business. Assume further that some of the purchasers in the intrastate offering are relatively unsophisticated; the offering would nevertheless qualify for the intrastate exemption. Two weeks later, the issuer offers the same class of stock to several wealthy and sophisticated out-of-state investors in a manner that would satisfy Section 4(a)(2) of the 1933 Act's non-public offering exemption. If the integration doctrine were applied to these transactions, no exemption would be available because the sophisticated out-of-state purchasers would destroy the intrastate exemption while the unsophisticated in-state purchasers would render the non-public offering exemption unavailable.

Similarly, assume that a private placement is followed within two weeks by a registered public offering. If the two transactions are integrated, the private placement sales would be considered part of the registered offering and in violation of Section 5 of the 1933 Act. Although the integration doctrine will not be applied every time two offerings take place within close proximity, the possibility of such application must be taken into account. By taking the possibility of integration into account, transactions can be structured in such a way as to minimize or even eliminate the possibility of the doctrine being applied.

Integration Explained

The integration doctrine first emerged with regard to the intrastate offering exemption (Section 3(a)(11) of the 1933 Act) in the context of determining which transactions constitute "part of an issue" offered in accordance with the intrastate limitations. The "part of an issue" concept (and hence integration) applies to the exemptions in Sections 3(a)(9), 3(a)(10) and 3(b).

The SEC considers five factors to determine whether the integration doctrine should be applied to two or more transactions:

1. Whether the sales are part of a single plan of financing;
2. Whether the sales involve issuance of the same class of securities;
3. Whether the sales have been made at or about the same time;
4. Whether the same type of consideration is received; and
5. Whether the sales are made for the same general purpose.

The SEC has not given any guidance on how these factors should be weighted. Accordingly, it would appear that in a particular case any one or more of the five factors could be determinative. For example, the absence of a prearranged single plan of financing has been held to preclude integration. The decision to integrate transactions is highly factual and absent a safe harbor rule, it is difficult to go beyond generalizations.

5. The underwriting process and secondary distributions

Zachary J. Gubler

INTRODUCTION

Securities underwriters are the midwives of the capital markets, relying on their expertise in valuing and marketing securities, not to mention their deep contacts in the investment world, to help bring a company's securities to market. The federal securities laws acknowledge this institutional reality and leverage it in two distinct ways. First, the laws regulate what underwriters can (or in some cases must) disclose about their clients (whom the law refers to as "issuers") while at the same time relying on underwriters to ensure the accuracy of what issuers disclose about themselves. But the federal securities laws also rely on the underwriter, or at least a particular legal definition of the underwriter, to regulate secondary distributions, or in other words, sales of securities by someone other than the issuer. This chapter discusses these different roles played by the concept of the "underwriter" in the federal securities laws. It also discusses how changes in the law's view of what constitutes underwriting, along with recent institutional developments, has likely contributed to the growth of the market for private (unregistered) securities. This expanding private securities market, the chapter argues, raises a number of issues concerning investor protection and access to the capital markets, both of which may require the consideration of policy reform. Two potential reform avenues are considered, including the recalibration of the rules governing resales and the creation of funds through which retail investors could invest in the market for private (unregistered) securities.

THE UNDERWRITING PROCESS

In its role as a securities underwriter, an investment bank's job is to match up companies in need of capital with investors that are on the lookout for investment opportunities. In this role, the securities underwriter provides its clients with two principal services. First, the investment bank identifies the market for the issuer's securities and assists the issuer in setting the price at which the securities are to be sold to that market. Second, the investment bank assists the issuer in selling those securities to investors. As a practical matter, the investment bank discharges these obligations, at least in the United States,[1] through a process known as "book building." This approach requires the investment bank to gather information from large institutional investors or wealthy individual investors concerning their demand for the security that is up for sale. This information will typically include at a minimum the quantity of shares that the investor would be interested in purchasing, but often will also include the maximum price that the investor would be willing to pay for the security.[2] Armed with this information, the investment bank then constructs a demand function for the security that it uses to determine the price at which the security will be offered to the public.[3] Once the actual offering commences, the investment bank will then sell the securities to those investors that indicated an interest during the book-building process.[4]

In light of its dominant role in the book building process, and given its expertise with respect to valuing securities, the investment bank has substantial discretion in setting the offering price of an issuer's security.

---

1 In other countries, alternative methods, like auctions, are commonly used. There are two principal differences between an auction and the book building process. First, with respect to book building, the pricing and allocation of shares are left to the discretion of the investment bank whereas in an auction, that discretion is replaced with a fixed rule that the shares go to the highest bidder. Second, whereas in the auction context, a bid is binding, the expressions of interest by investors in the book building process do not commit the investors to buy shares at all, let alone at the price indicated. *See, e.g.*, Francesca Cornelli & David Goldreich, *Bookbuilding and Strategic Allocation*, 6 J. Fin. 2337, 2337–38 (2001) (explaining the difference between book building and auctions); Francois Derrien & Kent L. Womack, *Auctions vs. Bookbuilding and the Control of Underpricing in Hot IPO Markets*, 16 Rev. Fin. Studs. 31 (2003) (discussing the use of book building and auctions as a method for pricing IPO shares in France). While auctions are commonly used outside of the United States for selling IPOs, they nevertheless appear to be losing market share relative to the book building process. *See* Ann E. Sherman, *Global Trends in IPO Methods: Book Building Versus Auctions with Endogenous Entry*, 78 J. Fin. Econ. 615 (2005).

2 *See, e.g.*, Francesca Cornelli & David Goldreich, *Bookbuilding and Strategic Allocation*, 6 J. Fin. 2337 (2001).

3 *See id.* at 2337.

4 *See id.* at 2337.

The available data suggest that more often than not, underwriters exercise that discretion by underpricing stock in initial public offerings.[5] For example, in a sample of 6,249 IPOs from 1980 to 2001, the average stock price was found to increase by 18.8 percent in the stock's first day of trading.[6] A number of theories have been advanced to explain this phenomenon. One influential theory is that investment banks underprice IPO shares to compensate the investors who provide price information during the book building process.[7] Otherwise, investors might be hesitant to reveal their true preferences regarding the price of the stock. Of course, investors already have some incentive to reveal their true valuation preferences in this context because if they do not, and instead throw out a low-ball price, they may not end up with any of the IPO shares. Then again, there is also an incentive for an investor not to reveal the highest price at which it would purchase IPO shares, as they want to maximize their return on the investment. The IPO discount, this theory holds, is an attempt to nudge investors to accurately reveal their valuation preferences.

Another theory posits that the underpricing of IPO shares is an attempt by issuers to distinguish themselves from poor quality firms.[8] An increase in the stock price on the first day of trading signals that the firm is of good quality because the poor quality firms could not afford to imitate this strategy. Finally, others argue that the underpricing of IPO shares is a strategy to avoid liability. The federal securities laws provide that a purchaser has the right to sell its stock back to the issuing firm at the

---

[5] *See generally* Alexander Ljungqvist, *IPO Underpricing*, in Handbook of Corporate Finance: Empirical Corporate Finance 375 (B. Espen Eckbo ed., 2007) (noting that the underpricing discount in the United States averaged more than 20 percent in the 1990s); *see also* Jay R. Ritter & Ivo Welch, *A Review of IPO Activity, Pricing and Allocations* 57 J. Fin. 1795, 1802 (2002); Loughran & Ritter, *Why Don't Issuers Get Upset About Leaving Money on the Table in IPOs?*, 15 Rev. Fin. Stud. 413 (2002).

[6] *See* Ritter & Welch, *supra* note 5, at 1802.

[7] *See, e.g.*, L.M. Benveniste & P.A. Spindt, *How investment bankers determine the offer price and allocation of new issues*, 24 J. Fin. Econ. 343 (1989); L.M. Benveniste & W.J. Wilhelm Jr., *A comparative analysis of IPO proceeds under alternative regulatory environments*, 28 J. Fin. Econ. 173 (1990); C. Spatt & S. Srivastava, *Preplay communication, participation restrictions, and efficiency in initial public offerings*, 4 Rev. Fin. Stud. 709 (1991).

[8] R.G. Ibbotson, *Price performance of common stock new issues*, 2 J. Fin. Econ. 235 (1975); F. Allen & G.R. Faulhaber, *Signaling by underpricing in the IPO market*, 23 J. Fin. Econ 303 (1989); I. Welch, *Seasoned offerings, imitation costs, and the underpricing of initial public offerings*. 44 J. Fin. 421 (1989).

offering price in the event of a material misstatement or omission or a failure to comply with the securities laws' disclosure requirements. One way to eliminate this liability risk, or to minimize its magnitude, is to reduce the offering price of the shares.[9]

The underwriter receives a fee in exchange for the pricing and selling services that it provides to the issuer. However, the nature of this underwriting fee depends on the structure of the underwriting process that the issuer and underwriter agree upon. In a "firm commitment underwriting," one or more investment banks agree to purchase the securities from the issuer at a discount from the offering price, with this discount representing the underwriting fee.[10] A firm commitment underwriting shifts the risk of unexpectedly low demand for the offering from the issuer to the underwriters. By contrast, a "best efforts underwriting" places this risk on the issuer, and the only obligation borne by the underwriters is to use their best efforts to sell the securities on behalf of the issuer at the offering price.[11]

The type of underwriting that an issuer decides to undertake depends on a number of different factors, including differences in cost and risk, but one of the less obvious benefits of the firm commitment underwriting is the positive effects that it has on the underwriters' efforts to screen the issuer for quality and the positive signal that this enhanced screening effort sends to the market. Issuers contemplating a public offering of securities face a significant problem involving asymmetrical information. Particularly with respect to initial public offerings, the issuer contemplating a public offering of securities will always have more information about itself than the public does. This is true, despite the mandatory disclosure rules that federal securities laws impose on public companies. One way of overcoming this informational problem is to rely on an agent, like an investment bank, that has significant reputational capital in the market and that can vouch for the issuer's quality. There is a substantial theoretical and empirical literature that supports this understanding of a securities underwriter as a solution to the issuer's information problem.[12] But if this is the case, then one would expect the firm

---

[9] D. Logue, *Premia on unseasoned equity issues, 1965–69*, 25 J. Econ. & Bus. 133 (1973); James C. Spindler, *IPO Liability and Entrepreneurial Response*, 155 U. Pa. L. Rev. 1187 (2007).

[10] In re National Association of Securities Dealers, Inc., Exchange Act Release No. 17,371 (Dec. 12, 1980).

[11] *Id.*

[12] *See, e.g.*, Lily Hua Fang, *Investment Bank Reputation and the Price and Quality of Underwriting Services*, 60 J. Fin. 2729 (2005); Thomas J. Chemmanur

commitment underwriting to enhance the value of securities underwriting as a means of reducing information asymmetries, because the firm commitment underwriting requires the underwriter not simply to use its reputation to market the issuer's stock but rather to use its own capital to purchase the issuer's stock itself. In fact, there is some evidence that this is the case.[13]

The federal securities laws acknowledge, and leverage, the institutional structure within which securities underwriters operate by relying on underwriters to achieve the regulatory goal of accurate disclosure. The law relies on underwriters to accomplish this goal in three ways. First, it imposes certain obligations on underwriters, including regulating what underwriters can and cannot say or write about the issuer during the registration period,[14] and requiring underwriters to deliver the prospectus to purchasers of the issuer's securities.[15] Second, it imposes civil liability on underwriters who fail to "reasonably investigate matters disclosed in the issuer's registration statement and to form a reasonably grounded belief as to their veracity."[16] Finally, the law casts a very broad statutory net in an effort to capture as many entities within the underwriter definition as possible.[17]

In a registered public offering, the Securities Act of 1933[18] ("1933 Act") makes the underwriter a central player in controlling the flow of information about the issuer and the offering to the market. The 1933 Act requires companies making a public offering of securities to register that offering by filing with the SEC a registration statement containing various required disclosures about the issuer and the offering.[19] From the

---

& Paolo Fulghieri, *Investment Bank Reputation, Information Production, and Financial Intermediation*, 49 J. Fin. 57 (1994).

[13] *See* Bae et al., *Determinants of Underwriter Participation in Initial Public Offerings of Common Stock: An Empirical Study*, 26 J. Bus., Fin. & Acct. 595 (1999).

[14] As a legal matter, the registration period begins, at the latest, as soon as an issuer engages an investment bank to serve as its lead underwriter. *See* Thomas Hazen, 1 Treatise on the Law of Securities Regulation (2002).

[15] For an overview of these requirements, see generally Hazen, 1 Treatise on the Law of Securities Regulation 129–98 (2002).

[16] Andrew Tuch, *Multiple Gatekeepers*, 96 Va. L. Rev. 1583 (2010).

[17] *See* Hazen, *supra* note 15, at 429–44.

[18] Securities Act of 1933, Pub. L. No. 73–38, 48 Stat. 74 (1933) (codified as amended at 15 U.S.C. § 77a-aa).

[19] For an overview of the contents of a registration statement, see Chapter 3. *See also* Louis Loss & Joel Seligman, Fundamentals of Securities Regulation 149–208 (2004).

investor's perspective, the most important part of the registration statement is the prospectus, which contains the bulk of the required disclosures, including audited financial statements, a detailed description of the issuer's business, properties, intended use of offering proceeds, litigation, executive compensation and a discussion of trends and developments expected to affect the issuer in the future.[20] The statute requires underwriters, with some exceptions, to deliver the issuer's prospectus to purchasers of the issuer's securities.[21] This prospectus delivery requirement has been relaxed substantially in recent years, so that in most cases, the delivery requirement is satisfied as long as the issuer's registration statement is on file with the SEC and investors can access it.[22] However, even then, sales of securities that take place relatively soon after the commencement of the offering need to be accompanied at the very least by a notice that the sale was made pursuant to a registration statement.[23] The 1933 Act enforces this disclosure requirement by imposing civil liability on anyone who offers or sells a security in violation of the requirement.[24]

The 1933 Act not only relies on underwriters to further the regulatory goal of disclosure but also to ensure its accuracy. It does so primarily through Section 11 of the 1933 Act, which imposes civil liability on the underwriter for material omissions or misstatements anywhere in its client's registration statement.[25] Of course, underwriters are far from perfect monitors and many will fail to uncover material omissions or misstatements in the issuer's registration statement even though they might be engaging in optimal monitoring. For this reason, Section 11 includes a due diligence defense for the underwriter who can show that

---

[20] *See, e.g.*, Form S-1, Registration Statement Under the Securities Act of 1933, Part I, 17 C.F.R. § 239.11 (2005) (specifying the contents of a prospectus).

[21] 15 U.S.C. § 77e(b) (2012).

[22] 17 C.F.R. §§ 230.172, 230.174(d) (2007).

[23] Rule 173 requires the notice of registration where the underwriter is only exempted from the prospectus delivery requirement by virtue of Rule 172's access equals delivery policy but is not exempted from that requirement under Section 4(a)(3) or Rule 174. *See* 17 C.F.R. § 230.173 (2005). Section 4(a)(3) exempts underwriters from the prospectus delivery requirement with respect to sales that take place after 40 days (or 90 days in the case of an IPO) following the offering date. *See* 15 U.S.C. § 77d(b)(3) (2012). Rule 174 reduces this time period to 0 days for 1934 Act reporting companies and 25 days with respect to companies doing an IPO. *See* 17 C.F.R. § 230.173 (2005).

[24] Section 12(a)(1).

[25] 15 U.S.C. § 77k(a) (2012).

"after reasonable investigation, [it had] reasonable ground to believe and did believe … that the statements therein were [not false or misleading]."[26]

Of course, the fact that the federal securities laws require underwriters to help disseminate the issuer's offering disclosure and to ensure that that disclosure is accurate means very little without a sense of how broadly the statute defines the term "underwriter." It suffices to say that the statutory term is quite broad, both in the way it is drafted and in the way courts interpret it. The definition of "underwriter" for purposes of the federal securities laws largely tracks the fact that underwriting, as a practical matter, is divided up between firm commitment and best efforts underwriting. Under the definition, an underwriter includes any person who purchases "from an issuer with a view to … the distribution of any security."[27] This captures firm commitment underwriters because in a firm commitment underwriting, the underwriters actually purchase the securities from an issuer and their goal is to sell them (typically as soon as possible) in the marketplace. The definition however also sweeps within its ambit any person who "offers or sells for an issuer in connection with … the distribution of any security."[28] This captures best effort underwriting where the underwriter does not purchase the security from the issuer but does use its best efforts to sell securities on the issuer's behalf. Furthermore, courts have tended to interpret the term "underwriter" quite broadly as well.[29]

From the perspective of optimal regulatory design, this regulatory structure, in which underwriters are an important means of achieving the goal of accurate disclosure, makes some sense. The underwriter's proximity to investors might suggest that the goal of efficiency will be served by relying on the underwriter as a conduit for the dissemination to the market of information regarding the issuer and the issuer's securities. Additionally, the underwriter's role as a source of reputational bonding for the issuer might once again suggest that the underwriter is the

---

[26] 15 U.S.C. § 77k(b) (2012).

[27] 15 U.S.C. § 77b(11) (2012).

[28] 15 U.S.C. § 77b(11) (2012).

[29] The most well-known case in this regard is the Chinese Consolidated case, where Judge Learned Hand determined that the statutory term includes entities whose activities might benefit an issuer's offering but who does not stand to receive any compensation (pecuniary or otherwise) from the issuer. *See* SEC v. Chinese Consolidated Benevolent Association, 120 F.2d 738 (2d Cir. 1941).

least-cost monitor of the accuracy of the issuer's disclosure.[30] Because the underwriter experiences reputational harm if the issuer or the offering turns out to be of poor quality, the underwriter already has incentives to monitor the issuer, and the federal securities laws simply reinforce these incentives.

However, in assessing the efficiency of this regime, the devil is in the details. After all, the value of the underwriter as an agent for reputational bonding is at its height for initial public offerings (for it is only at that time when the issuer is truly unknown to the market). Yet, the federal securities laws impose roughly the same disclosure requirements and liability standards on underwriters regardless of whether the offering that is being underwritten is an IPO. The issue of underwriter liability has been complicated substantially by the emergence of shelf registration, whereby large, publicly traded issuers who file periodic reports under the Securities Exchange Act of 1934 ("1934 Act")[31] are able to offer and sell securities whenever they wish.[32] Given the extremely compressed time-frame involved in such offerings, underwriters hardly have the time to engage in due diligence of the issuer. In that context, Section 11's underwriter liability provisions do not effectively encourage monitoring and in fact probably do little more than make the underwriter the mandatory insurer of the issuer's offering.[33] Furthermore, it is impossible to assess the desirability of this regime without considering its costs. And it is possible that underwriters simply pass the cost of increased liability risk on to issuers through the underpricing of IPOs.[34]

---

30 The literature on gatekeepers is substantial. *See, e.g.*, Andrew Tuch, *Multiple Gatekeepers*, 96 Va. L. Rev. 1583 (2010); John C. Coffee, Jr., *Gatekeeper Failure and Reform: The Challenge of Fashioning Relevant Reforms*, 84 B.U. L. Rev. 301 (2004); Assaf Hamdani, *Gatekeeper Liability*, 77 S. Cal. L. Rev. 53 (2003); Reinier H. Kraakman, *Gatekeepers: The Anatomy of a Third Party Enforcement Strategy*, 2 J.L. Econ. & Org. 53 (1986); Frank Partnoy, *Barbarians at the Gatekeepers? A Proposal for a Modified Strict Liability Regime*, 79 Wash. U. L.Q. 491 (2001).

31 Securities Exchange Act of 1934, Pub. L. No. 73–291, 48 Stat. 881 (codified at 15 U.S.C. § 78a-pp).

32 *See* 17 C.F.R. § 230.415 (2005); *see also* Hazen, *supra* note 15, at 297–303.

33 *See, e.g.*, Merritt B. Fox, *Civil Liability and Mandatory Disclosure*, 109 Colum. L. Rev. 237 (2009).

34 *See supra* notes 5–9.

THE STATUTORY UNDERWRITER AND SECONDARY DISTRIBUTIONS

In the case of a registered public offering of securities, the legal concept of underwriter is important in determining who has the obligation to deliver the issuer's prospectus to investors and who has an obligation to investigate the issuer's registration statement for material misstatements or omissions. The concept of the statutory underwriter is however of equal (if not greater) importance in the context of a secondary offering, where someone other than the issuer is selling the issuer's securities. This is because, with respect to secondary offerings, the underwriter definition largely determines whether the resale is exempt from the federal securities laws' registration requirements.

Resales of Unregistered Securities

The statutory exemption

Some have described the 1933 Act's registration requirement as both transactional and universal,[35] meaning that every offer or sale of securities must be either registered or exempt from registration. However, with respect to resales of securities, there is no practical means by which the holder (at least a non-controlling shareholder)[36] wishing to conduct a resale could possibly register the securities, because the holder presumably would lack the power to compel the company to complete and file the registration statement. Consequently, the holder who wishes to resell unregistered securities typically must rely on an exemption to registration.

The general exemption is contained in Section 4(a)(1) of the 1933 Act,[37] which exempts from registration "transactions by any person other

---

[35] *See* James D. Cox et al., Securities Regulation: Cases and Materials 337 (2013).

[36] Obviously, the situation is different with respect to a holder who is also a controlling shareholder in the company whose securities the holder wishes to sell. Resales by controlling shareholders are discussed in greater depth below.

[37] *See* 15 U.S.C. § 77d(a)(1) (2012). Sections 4(a)(2) and 4(a)(5) only apply to issuers. *See* 15 U.S.C. §§ 77d(a)(2) & (a)(5) (2012). Section 4(a)(3) to dealers. *See* 15 U.S.C. § 77d(a)(3) (2012). Section 4(a)(4) to brokers involved in a brokers' transaction. *See* 15 U.S.C. § 77d(a)(4) (2012).

than an issuer, underwriter or dealer." By definition, a secondary distribution does not involve the issuer. Nor will it typically involve a dealer.[38] For these reasons, whether a securities holder can rely on Section 4(a)(1) for the resale typically depends on whether the holder is considered an underwriter under the statute. That question, in turn, depends on whether the holder purchased the securities "from an issuer with a view to … the distribution of any security."[39] The courts have determined that whether securities were purchased "from an issuer with a view to" anything, let alone a distribution, depends on whether the holder originally purchased the securities from the issuer with investment intent.[40] And of course, failing proof of such investment intent, the holder wishing to resell unregistered securities can always escape underwriter status by proving that the resale does not involve a distribution.[41]

Investment intent is determined by the "objective criterion of whether securities have come to rest" in the hands of investors.[42] Investment intent is generally established by holding the securities for a sufficiently long period of time prior to the resale. The courts have developed various rules of thumb for evaluating whether investment intent has been met for this purpose. First, a holding period of three years or more is very likely to be dispositive on the issue of investment intent. There is also general agreement that a two-year holding period establishes a presumption in favor of investment intent, in the absence of any evidence to the contrary.[43] Accordingly, anything less than two years would favor a presumption against investment intent. However, one can rebut the

---

[38] The term "dealer" includes "any person who engages either for all or part of his time, directly or indirectly, as agent, broker, or principal, in the business of offering, buying, selling, or otherwise dealing or trading in securities issued by another person." *See* 15 U.S.C. § 77b(a)(12) (2012).

[39] *See* 15 U.S.C. § 77b(a)(11) (2012).

[40] *See, e.g.*, Gilligan, Will & Co. v. SEC, 267 F.2d 461 (2d Cir. 1959); Vohs v. Dickson, 495 F.2d 607, 620–21 (5th Cir. 1974); *see also* Hazen, *supra* note 15, at 437–40.

[41] Prior to the securities having "come to rest," the holder can prove the lack of a distribution by ensuring that the resale is consistent with the issuer's original exemption. After the securities have "come to rest," non-controlling shareholders can typically resell the securities freely; however, controlling shareholders conducting the resale through a broker would have to ensure that the purchasers in its resale were investors who can "fend for themselves." *See infra* notes 43–46.

[42] Ackerberg v. Johnson, 892 F.2d 1328 (8th Cir. 1989).

[43] *See, e.g.*, Hazen, *supra* note 15, at 437–38; Cox et al., *supra* note 35, at 346–47.

presumption against investment intent by showing that the holder originally purchased the securities with an investment purpose but that there was subsequently a change in the holder's circumstances that required her to resell the securities earlier than planned.[44]

Where the securities have not yet come to rest

If the securities have not yet come to rest prior to the holder's resale, then the holder generally can resell the securities as long as it carries out the resale in a manner that is consistent with the exemption that the issuer relied on for its primary offering. In other words, where the securities have not yet come to rest, the holder is entitled to piggyback on the issuer's exemption. This conclusion has support in both the language and structure of the statute. If the securities have not yet come to rest, then they have been purchased "from an issuer with a view to" the resale. Thus, where the securities have not yet come to rest, the only way for the reselling holder to escape the underwriter designation under Section 2(11) is by proving that the resale does not constitute a "distribution." At a very high level of generality, courts have determined that the "distribution" inquiry should focus on "the need of the offerees for the protections afforded by registration."[45] If the securities have not yet come to rest, then the holder's resale is part of the issuer's ongoing offering. Moreover, that offering, by assumption, is exempt from the registration requirement, meaning that Congress or the SEC has made the decision as a policy matter that the purchasers participating in that offering do not need the protections that registration affords. If that is the case, then it should make little difference if the holder turns around and resells securities to a purchaser who could have purchased in the issuer's primary offering consistent with the issuer's exemption.

---

[44] *See, e.g.*, Hazen, *supra* note 15, at 438–40.; Cox et al., *supra* note 35, at 347–48. When it adopted Rule 144, the safe harbor for resales of restricted securities, the SEC disavowed the "change in circumstances" test. *See* Notice of Adoption of Rule 144 Relating to the Definition of the Terms "Underwriter" in Section 4(a)(1) and 2(11) and "Brokers' Transactions" in Section 4(a)(4) of the Securities Act of 1933, Securities Act Rel. No. 33–5223, 1972 WL 18134 (Jan. 11, 1972). However, commentators have questioned whether this disavowal should affect a court's treatment of the change in circumstance defense outside of the context of the safe harbor, since the defense largely flows from an interpretation of the statute itself. *See, e.g.*, Hazen, *supra* note 15, at 439–40.

[45] Securities and Exchange Commission v. Ralston Purina Co., 346 U.S. 119 (1953). Note that this case actually was interpreting Section 4(a)(2). But other courts have said that it's the same question for interpreting the term "distribution." *See, e.g.*, Gilligan, Will & Co. v. SEC, 267 F.2d 461 (2d Cir. 1959).

In addition to the language of the statute, the structure of the statute also supports this approach to resales prior to the securities having come to rest. Recall that the statute is transactional in nature, meaning that the registration requirement, and any relevant exemptions from registration, pertains to a particular transaction. If it is determined that the holder's resale is part of the same transaction as the issuer's exempt offering (because the securities have not yet come to rest), then the resale should benefit from the same exemption as the overall transaction, provided of course that the resale is consistent with the requirements of that exemption.

As an illustration of how this analysis operates in practice, consider the following example. The issuer, a New York corporation, sells stock solely to New York residents in an offering that is exempt from the 1933 Act's registration requirement pursuant to the intrastate offering exemption under Section 3(a)(11).[46] Anne, a New York resident, purchases stock from the issuer in this intrastate offering and then the following week turns around and resells that stock to a New Jersey resident. The securities have not yet come to rest, which means that Anne can resell the stock as long as she does so in a manner that is consistent with the issuer's original exemption. Because the Section 3(a)(11) exemption requires that sales be made only to in-state residents, Anne's resale to the New Jersey resident will violate the exemption. Consequently, she will be deemed an underwriter, and the issuer's transaction as a whole will lose the benefit of the exemption. Of course, if Anne had resold the securities to a New York resident, the resale would be permissible and would not affect the exempt status of the issuer's offering.[47]

---

[46] 17 U.S.C. § 77d. This exemption is motivated largely by federalism concerns: where the issuer, offerees and purchasers in a given offering are all residents of the same state, it is probably preferable that that state's securities authorities regulate the offering instead of their federal counterpart.

[47] Note that where the securities that the holder wishes to resell were acquired in an offering exempt pursuant to Rule 147—the regulatory safe harbor for the Section 3(a)(11) statutory exemption—the SEC applies a nine-month instead of two-year rule of thumb when evaluating whether securities have come to rest. Some commentators have suggested that this makes little sense since the Rule 147 resale provision, in their view, pertains solely to the circumstances under which a resale to a non-resident will destroy the issuer's exemption. *See, e.g.*, Rutheford B. Campbell Jr., *Resales of Securities Under the Securities Act of 1933*, 52 Wash. & Lee L. Rev. 1333, 1352–54 (1995). It does not, in these commentators' view, provide a resale exemption for the holder. However, as previously discussed, the courts and the SEC tend to collapse the question of whether a resale will destroy the issuer's exemption and the question of when a

Where the securities have come to rest—non-controlling shareholders

If a non-controlling shareholder can prove investment intent, then the shareholder can resell the unregistered securities to anyone. After all, if the holder purchases the securities with investment intent, then by definition, the purchase was not made "from an issuer with a view to" their distribution (assuming that the resale even rises to the level of a distribution), and therefore the resale does not make her an underwriter under Section 2(11). Consequently, the holder's resale is exempt under Section 4(a)(1) of the statute because it does not involve an issuer, underwriter or dealer.

Where the securities have come to rest—controlling shareholders

The remaining case to consider is where the holder wishing to resell the securities can prove investment intent, but the holder is a controlling shareholder of the issuer. In that case, the controlling shareholder's resale is permissible if at least one of two things is true: (1) either the controlling shareholder does not use an intermediary to sell securities on their behalf, or (2) the resale does not constitute a "distribution" because it involves only purchasers who can "fend for themselves."

The reason that a resale of securities that have come to rest is treated differently, depending on whether the securities holder is a controlling or non-controlling shareholder, has to do with the special way in which the statute treats controlling shareholders. Under Section 2(11) of the 1933 Act, a controlling shareholder is treated as an "issuer" solely for purposes of the underwriter definition.[48] This is significant because the 1933 Act defines an underwriter not only with respect to those who purchase "from an issuer with a view to … the distribution of any security," but also with respect to those who offer or sell "for an issuer in connection with … the distribution of any security." This means that any broker who sells on

---

holder can resell the securities into the same inquiry, which is whether there is investment intent, or in other words, whether the securities have come to rest. So, it does not seem all that strange to do the same thing in this context. However, these commentators are certainly correct to the extent that they are suggesting that there is something strange about requiring a shorter holding period for proving investment intent with respect to intrastate offerings than other types of exempt transactions.

[48] *See* 15 U.S.C. § 77b(a)(11) ("As used in this paragraph the term 'issuer' shall include, in addition to an issuer, any person directly or indirectly controlling or controlled by the issuer, or any person under direct or indirect common control with the issuer.").

behalf of a controlling shareholder, purchases "for an issuer," and therefore if the sale is viewed as a "distribution," then that broker will be viewed as an underwriter because of the purchase of securities "for an issuer in connection with… [their] distribution." Of course, taken alone, this does not mean that the controlling shareholder himself will be deemed an underwriter as well. However, Section 4(a)(1) exempts transactions, not individuals, and therefore if the controlling shareholder's broker is considered to be an underwriter (because the broker offers or sells securities on the shareholder's behalf), then the *transaction as a whole* falls outside of the Section 4(a)(1) exemption.[49]

Compare this statutory result with the one involving a non-controlling shareholder whose unregistered securities have come to rest. The non-controlling shareholder falls within the underwriter definition only if she lacks investment intent and is carrying out a distribution. Thus, proof of investment intent is sufficient to remove the non-controlling shareholder from the reach of the underwriter definition and therefore the Section 4(a)(1) exemption to registration applies. However, the controlling shareholder falls within the underwriter definition regardless of investment intent if the controlling shareholder is using a broker to sell on their behalf. Once again, this is not because the controlling shareholder is purchasing for an issuer or from an issuer with a view to a distribution, but rather because the broker is doing so with respect to the controlling shareholder, who is treated for that narrow purpose as an issuer.

To illustrate the import of this state of affairs, consider once again the hypothetical shareholder, Anne, who purchased unregistered securities in an offering exempt from registration pursuant to the Section 4(a)(1) intrastate offering exemption. Assume that Anne wishes to resell those securities through a broker after holding them for more than two years. As previously discussed, whether a holder in Anne's position can resell those securities in reliance on the Section 4(a)(1) exemption depends on whether she purchased those securities from an issuer with a view to a distribution. Because Anne has held the securities for more than two years, she will have no problem proving investment intent (meaning that she did not purchase with a view to anything other than an investment), and consequently, the resale transaction will be exempt from registration under Section 4(a)(1). However, this is not true if Anne is instead a controlling shareholder of the issuer. In that case, even if Anne can prove

---

[49] This transactional nature of Section 4(a)(1) has been reinforced by various courts. *See, e.g.*, SEC v. Chinese Consolidated Benevolent Association, 120 F.2d 738 (2d Cir. 1941); United States v. Wolfson, 405 F.2d 779 (2d Cir. 1968).

investment intent, the resale transaction nevertheless falls outside of the exemption's scope because the underwriter definition also captures those who offer or sell "for an issuer in connection with … the distribution of any security," and Anne's broker is clearly selling on her behalf.[50] The result is different in the case of the non-controlling shareholder because a non-controlling shareholder is not treated as an "issuer" for purposes of Section 2(11), and therefore the broker selling on behalf of the non-controlling shareholder is not selling on behalf of an issuer for purposes of that provision.

For the controlling shareholder, therefore, it is not enough to prove investment intent in order to resell unregistered securities. Rather, they must also prove one of two things. First, the controlling shareholder could prove that the resale does not involve a broker selling on their behalf, in which case the statute would treat the controlling shareholder the same as the non-controlling shareholder.[51] Alternatively, the controlling shareholder could prove that even though they used a broker, the resale did not involve a distribution.[52] Recall that courts have interpreted that term to entail an inquiry into whether the purchasers participating in the offering are in need of the protections afforded by registration, or in other words, whether the purchasers of the controlling shareholder's securities can "fend for themselves."[53] Although courts differ somewhat

---

[50] 15 U.S.C. § 77b(a)(11).

[51] This is because the differential treatment of the controlling shareholder turns on whether someone is selling on the controlling shareholder's behalf. *See* 15 U.S.C. § 77b(a)(11) (defining the term "underwriter" to include anyone who "offers or sells for an issuer in connection with … the distribution of any security" and clarifying that the term "issuer" for the purposes of this provision only includes controlling shareholders).

[52] When a controlling shareholder resells unregistered securities that have already come to rest on the basis that the resale does not involve a distribution, this exemption is referred to as a Section 4(1½) exemption. Although this section does not actually appear in the statute, it is the logical result of combining Section 4(a)(1), which exempts "transactions by any person other than issuer, underwriter, or dealer," and Section 4(a)(2), which exempts "transactions not involving a public offering." Under the Section 4(1½) exemption, the controlling shareholder is deemed not to be an underwriter by virtue of the fact that he is not engaged in a distribution (which is the same thing as saying that he is not engaged in a public offering). Thus, the exemption is said to lie somewhere between these two sections. Hence, the Section 4(1½) designation. *See generally* Hazen, *supra* note 15, at 455–66; Cox et al., *supra* note 35, at 384–90.

[53] Securities and Exchange Commission v. Ralston Purina Co. 346 U.S. 119 (1953) (determining that a "transaction not involving any public offering" under Section 4(a)(2) of the 1933 Act is one involving purchasers who can "fend for

on the exact circumstances under which purchasers can fend for themselves, they typically view the inquiry as a function of both the sophistication of the investors and their access to information concerning the issuer and the issuer's securities.[54]

One might ask why the federal securities laws treat controlling and non-controlling shareholders differently with respect to secondary distributions. The answer most likely has to do with control over the issuer and the volume of securities at issue. Controlling shareholders, by definition, have the ability to force the issuer to undertake certain actions, including the registration of securities.[55] Non-controlling shareholders, by contrast, lack this power. For this reason, imposing stricter registration requirements on non-controlling shareholders is likely to result in simply fewer resales by non-controlling shareholders rather than more disclosure. Moreover, resales by controlling shareholders are likely to involve a greater volume of securities than resales by non-controlling shareholders. And, therefore, the difference in the way the law treats resales by the two different types of shareholders may also reflect a decision to focus on the larger transaction where stricter registration requirements will have a greater impact.

The regulatory safe harbor: Rule 144

As should be clear from the prior discussion, the law of resales (and in particular, the law of resales of unregistered securities) is characterized by extraordinary uncertainty. Whether the resale is exempt from registration pursuant to Section 4(a)(1) turns on very detailed, fact-specific inquiries that are likely to be evaluated differently depending on the judge and the jurisdiction. Securities holders wishing to resell their unregistered securities in reliance on the Section 4(a)(1) exemption (or those investors considering whether to invest in unregistered securities in

---

themselves"); Gilligan, Will & Co. v. SEC, 267 F.2d 461 (2d Cir. 1959) (interpreting the term "distribution" in the 1933 Act as an offering involving purchasers who cannot "fend for themselves.").

[54] *See* Cox et al., *supra* note 35, at 267–71.

[55] Of course, whether this is true in practice depends on how one defines the term "control." Curiously, the 1933 Act does not define the term. However, the SEC has defined the term "control" in Rule 405 in terms of the influence that an individual or group has over the company's management and business policies. *See* 17 C.F.R. § 230.405 (2005). It is far from clear that one who exercises control under this definition necessarily has the ability to compel the filing of a registration statement. *See* Rutheford B. Campbell Jr., *Defining Control in Secondary Distributions*, 18 B.C. L. Rev. 37, 40 (1976).

the first place) will consequently react in one of three ways, any of which contributes to less liquidity in the market for unregistered securities.

First, a non-controlling holder might decide to hold onto to the unregistered securities for a longer period of time in the hope of limiting the risk involved in establishing investment intent. Recall that a presumption of investment intent is triggered with respect to a two-year holding period, but this is only a presumption, which may be rebutted by other evidence. By contrast, if the non-controlling holder were to hold onto the securities for three years or more, they would largely eliminate the risk that a court would second-guess the investment intent. Second, a holder (either controlling or non-controlling) might decide to conduct a resale sooner than two years after the issuer's offering, which of course would only be exempt if it were carried out in a manner consistent with the exemption that the issuer relied on for its primary offering. In other words, in that case, the reselling holder would have to limit the universe of purchasers to whom they could sell. Third, the holder may decide to forgo an investment in unregistered securities altogether.

Whether the holder responds to this uncertainty by holding its unregistered securities longer, by constraining the universe of potential purchasers or by not investing at all, the result is the same: greater illiquidity in the market for unregistered securities. For these reasons, the SEC has adopted a series of safe harbors intended to introduce greater certainty and predictability in the law of resales. The most significant safe harbor is Rule 144, which governs resales of "restricted securities" by non-controlling shareholders and resales of restricted or non-restricted securities by controlling shareholders.[56]

Non-controlling shareholders

Rule 144 is a resale safe harbor that applies only to "restricted securities," a defined term that includes, among other things, securities originally acquired from an issuer in a transaction exempt from registration under Section 4(a)(2) or Regulation D.[57] Recall that Section 4(a)(2)

---

[56] Rule 144A is another resale safe harbor, but unlike Rule 144, it applies not to a particular type of security but rather to a particular class of investor, known as "qualified institutional buyers" ("QIBs"), which are basically institutions that in the aggregate invest on a discretionary basis at least $100 million in securities of issuers not affiliated with the institution. Under the safe harbor, resales to QIBS do not involve a distribution, and therefore the reselling holder escapes the underwriter status that would otherwise make the Section 4(a)(1) exemption off limits. *See* 17 C.F.R. § 230.144A (2011).

[57] *See* 17 C.F.R. § 230.144(a)(3) (2011).

is the exemption in the 1933 Act for "transactions not involving a public offering," and Regulation D is typically thought of as the regulatory safe harbor for that statutory exemption.[58] Securities acquired in such "private offerings" are eligible for the Rule 144 resale exemption. Thus, if for example, an issuer sells a significant amount of debt in an offering that does not involve a public offering, perhaps because the purchasers of the debt are wealthy sophisticated individuals who can "fend for themselves" under a Section 4(a)(2) analysis, then subsequent resales of those securities may qualify for the Rule 144 resale exemption, assuming that the other conditions of the rule are met.

Under Rule 144, non-controlling shareholders can resell restricted securities as long as they satisfy the applicable holding period of either six months or one year, depending on whether the issuer of the securities is required to file periodic reports under the 1934 Act and is current in those filings.[59] If the issuer does satisfy those requirements, then the shorter, six-month holding period applies. Otherwise, the longer one-year holding period is used. Importantly, the holding period is measured by reference to the original acquisition of the securities from the issuer or from an affiliate of the issuer, whichever is later.[60] It is not measured by reference to the current holder's acquisition of those securities. To illustrate this point, assume that in Anne's example, the issuer of the securities that Anne wishes to resell is a 1934 Act reporting company that is also current in the filing of those reports. Assume further that Anne holds the securities for two months before reselling them, pursuant to Rule 144A, to a "qualified institutional buyer"[61] ("QIB") who then holds onto the debt for four months and now wants to resell it pursuant to Rule

---

[58] Note that as a technical matter, only Rule 506 of Regulation D was promulgated pursuant to Section 4(a)(2); Rules 504 and 505 being outgrowths of Section 3(b), which is an exemption for offerings under $5 million. However, Regulation D is generally thought of as a safe harbor for non-public offerings, and the relevant statutory exemption for non-public offerings is Section 4(a)(2).

[59] *See* 17 C.F.R. §§ 230.144(b)(1) & (d) (2011).

[60] *See* 17 C.F.R. § 230.144(d) (2011) (providing that in order to the meet the holding period requirement, the relevant amount of time (i.e., six months or one year, as appropriate) "must elapse between the later of the date of the acquisition of the securities from the issuer, or from an affiliate of the issuer, and any resale of such securities in reliance on this section for the account of either the acquirer or any subsequent holder of those securities").

[61] This term is defined in Rule 144A, which provides a safe harbor for resales to these types of investors. *See supra* note 57.

144 to some individual investors.[62] The QIB has only held on to the debt for four months, but the six-month holding period that would apply in this instance (because of the issuer's current status with respect to its 1934 Act filings) is nevertheless satisfied because it has been six months since the securities were originally acquired from the issuer.

The history of Rule 144 is a history of incremental liberalization. When the rule was first adopted in 1972, it permitted a resale of restricted securities after a two-year holding period, but only if the holder satisfied a number of additional requirements: certain information about the issuer had to be publicly available, only a limited number of securities could be sold, the securities had to be sold in "brokers' transactions," and, in some cases, a notice of sale had to be filed with the SEC.[63] Nine years later, in 1981, the SEC adopted Rule 144(k), which provided relief under the rule to non-affiliates who had held the securities for at least three years by eliminating Rule 144's additional requirements, other than the one relating to information disclosure.[64] Two years later, in 1983, the SEC also eliminated the remaining information disclosure requirement, once again only to the extent that the holder was a non-affiliate and had held the securities for at least three years.[65] The next change came in 1997, when the SEC reduced the holding period for purposes of Rule 144(k) from three years to two years and the general holding period, which was still subject to satisfying the additional requirements, from two years to one year.[66] Finally, in 2007, the SEC eliminated all of the additional requirements of Rule 144, at least with respect to non-affiliate holders, and created the two-tiered holding period requirement of six months and one year, the application of which is determined by reference to whether the issuer is a 1934 Act reporting

---

[62] Under Rule 144A, there is no holding requirement, and so the sale of the debt by the wealthy, sophisticated individuals to the QIBs after the two-month holding period does not present a problem.

[63] Notice of Adoption of Rule 144 Relating to the Definition of the Terms "Underwriter" In Sections 4(1) And 2(11) And "Brokers' Transactions" In Section 4(4) Of The Securities Act Of 1933, Adoption Of Form 144, and Rescission of Rules 154 And 155 Under that Act, Release No. 33–5223, 1972 WL 121583 (1972).

[64] *See* Resales of Securities, Securities Act Release No. 6286, 46 Fed. Reg. 12,195 (1981).

[65] Securities; Reporting and Recordkeeping Requirements, Securities Act Release No. 6488, 48 Fed. Reg. 44,770 (1983).

[66] Revision of Holding Period Requirements in Rules 144 and 145, Securities Act Release No. 7390, 62 Fed. Reg. 9242 (1997).

company that is current in its filings.[67] In contrast to its original incarnation, the current version of the rule is therefore quite lax.

Controlling shareholders

Rule 144 also provides a safe harbor for resales by controlling shareholders. But controlling shareholders must satisfy more than just the holding requirement in order to benefit from the safe harbor. They also must satisfy conditions relating to the availability of public information, the volume of securities to be sold and the manner in which the sale is conducted.[68] If these conditions are met, then any broker selling on behalf of the controlling shareholder is deemed not to be an underwriter. And, therefore, consistent with the statutory scheme discussed previously, the entire transaction will be deemed exempt pursuant to Section 4(a)(1) because it is a transaction not involving an underwriter, issuer or dealer.

Resales of Registered Securities

Typically, securities acquired in a registered offering can be resold free of constraints. However, this claim is not as obvious as it might first appear since under the federal securities laws, it is securities transactions, and not the securities themselves, that must be either registered or exempt from registration. And therefore, as a logical matter, the registration of a primary offering only pertains to that offering alone and not to subsequent resales. However, as a practical matter, non-controlling shareholders can resell securities acquired in a registered offering without any constraints. In addition, controlling shareholders can typically resell such securities freely prior to their having come to rest, since such resales would be considered part of the issuer's original offering. However, resales of such securities by controlling shareholders after the securities have come to rest pose the same problem as resales by controlling shareholders more generally.[69] Thus, if a controlling shareholder wishes to resell securities that it acquired in a registered offering after those securities have come to rest, it will typically rely on Rule 144 or avoid a distribution altogether by selling the securities exclusively to purchasers who can "fend for themselves."

---

[67] Revisions to Rules 144 and 145. Securities Act Release No. 33–8869, 72 Fed. Reg. 71,546 (Dec. 17, 2007).

[68] 17 C.F.R. § 230.144(b)(2) (2011).

[69] *See, e.g.*, SEC v. Cavanagh, 1 F. Supp. 2d 337 (S.D.N.Y. 1998); Hazen, *supra* note 15, at 442.

ASSESSING THE SECONDARY SECURITIES MARKETS: EXPANSION GIVING RISE TO ISSUES OF INVESTOR PROTECTION AND ACCESS

As is evident from the preceding discussion, in the United States, there is both a public and private securities market. A company enters the public market, and submits to a mandatory disclosure regime, if it is required to register its securities by filing with the SEC a registration statement containing substantial disclosures about the company, its management and its business. Securities registration under the 1933 Act, in turn, triggers reporting obligations under the 1934 Act, which requires companies to file periodic disclosures on an annual and quarterly basis. However, just as the federal securities laws create a public, regulated market characterized by mandatory disclosure of both offerings and companies, the federal securities laws also create a private, unregulated market free of any mandatory disclosure restraints. Issuers do not have to register securities offerings that they do not make to the public, and as long as the company remains relatively small, it will escape the 1934 Act's periodic reporting requirements.[70]

The main difference between these two markets is their relative liquidity, that is to say the ease with which securities can be bought and sold without much effect on market prices. Securities traded in the private market are typically much less liquid than those traded in the public market are. In fact, the data suggest that securities that trade in the private market trade at a median 35–50 percent discount to the same securities that trade in the public market.[71] Two differences account for the relative illiquidity of the private securities market, one legal and the other structural. The legal explanation has to do with the resale restrictions placed on secondary distributions by virtue of the broad definition of "underwriter" under the 1934 Act. As previously discussed, in order for a holder of unregistered securities to avoid being deemed an underwriter upon resale of those securities (which, recall, is the key inquiry for determining whether the resale is exempt for purposes of

---

[70] This is because there is a separate reporting trigger under the 1934 Act for companies that have not registered an offering with the SEC but are nevertheless significant in size. *See* 15 U.S.C. § 78l(g) (2012). The current registration requirement under Section 12(g) is assets in excess of $10 million and shares of stock "held of record" by more than either 2,000 shareholders generally or 500 non-accredited shareholders in particular. *Id.*

[71] Francis A. Longstaff, *How Much Can Marketability Affect Security Values?*, 50 J. Fin. 1767, 1773 (1995).

Section 4(a)(1) of the 1933 Act), the holder has two options. Prior to the securities coming to rest, the seller could resell them consistently with the issuer's original exemption. Alternatively, the seller could hold them until they have come to rest, which under Rule 144 currently means six months or one year, depending on whether the issuer is a 1934 Act reporting company, at which point the seller would be able to resell them freely. By contrast, there are no resale restrictions for non-controlling holders of registered securities. Thus, the law governing secondary distributions likely accounts for much of the illiquidity in the private securities market.

However, there are also structural differences between these two markets, which may also explain the illiquidity discount applied to securities that trade in the private, unregulated market. Specifically, the private market has traditionally lacked the benefits of developed exchanges, like the New York Stock Exchange or the Nasdaq. Stock exchanges are important because they organize information and they generate information.[72] Stock exchanges organize information by connecting those who demand capital with those who supply capital.[73] By contrast, stock exchanges generate information by allowing parties to track historical stock prices while at the same time providing ready access to current prices.[74] Both of these factors make markets, like the public securities market, more liquid.

However, significant changes are afoot with respect to both the legal and structural barriers to liquidity in the private market. On the legal side, we have already discussed the incremental liberalization of Rule 144. Not only has the SEC omitted all requirements other than the holding period requirement for non-controlling shareholders, but it has also shortened the holding period significantly. Additionally, the SEC created Rule 144A, which allows qualified institutional buyers to trade restricted securities freely without even having to satisfy Rule 144's holding requirement.

Not only are the legal barriers to liquidity in the private markets being chipped away, but the structural ones are falling away as well. This is because of the emergence in recent years of private stock exchanges that provide many of the same liquidity benefits as the NYSE or Nasdaq. These exchanges provide employees of private companies with an ability to sell stock that they have received as compensation for their services.

---

72 *See* Andreas M. Fleckner, *Stock Exchanges at the Crossroads*, 74 Fordham L. Rev. 2541, 2546–47 (2006).

73 *See id.* at 2546.

74 *See id.* at 2547.

They also provide venture capitalists with a potentially "new exist" from the preferred stock that they receive in exchange for their investment in the company. Finally, these exchanges serve not only as trading infrastructure for secondary distributions but for primary offerings as well, as private companies have in recent years completed private placements of stock in reliance on these exchanges.

With the gradual erosion of the legal and structural barriers to liquidity in the private market, that market will increasingly become a closer substitute for its public counterpart.[75] The major benefit of this development is greater choice in accessing capital. The more liquid the private markets become, the more likely issuers will choose to do a private placement over a registered offering. Indeed, the evidence suggests that issuers are increasingly making that choice.[76]

However, what are the costs involved in making our private markets relatively more attractive to issuers, thereby increasing their size and importance? There are primarily two: investor protection and investor access. In other words, does our private securities market provide for adequate protection of investors? Moreover, should we be concerned about capital markets that seem increasingly to be crowding out the retail investor?

---

[75] This may seem odd from a public choice perspective since one would think that the SEC would want to channel folks into the regulated market. But, on the other hand, changes like the liberalization of Rule 144 and the creation of Rule 144A might be due to political pressures on the SEC to make the private market more like the public one. *See* Zachary J. Gubler, *Public Choice and the Private Securities Market*, 91 N.C. L. Rev. 745 (2013).

[76] For example, according to a report prepared for the director of the SEC's Division of Risk, Strategy, and Financial Innovation, the recent trend has been from public to private capital raising. Between 2009 and 2010, for example, public issuances decreased by 11 percent while private issuances increased by 31 percent. *See* Vlad Ivanov & Scott Bauguess, Capital Raising in the U.S.: The Significance of Unregistered Offerings Using the Regulation D Exemption 3 (Feb. 2012) (memorandum to Craig Lewis, Dir., Div. of Risk, Strategy & Fin. Innovation), http://www.sec.gov/info/smallbus/acsec/acsec103111_analysis-reg-d-offering.pdf. In addition, between 2005 and 2007, the amount of equity raised by foreign issuers in the private securities market in the United States, as a percentage of equity raised in the public market, increased more than threefold. *See* Gubler, *supra* note 75, at 765.

Investor Protection in the Expanding Private Securities Market

The question of investor protection arises in the context of both primary offerings and secondary distributions, although the focus here will be mainly on secondary distributions. With respect to investor protection in primary offerings, the question boils down to the merits and demerits of the "accredited investor" criterion under Regulation D, the primary legal driver of the private securities market.[77] Accredited investors are those who meet certain asset or income requirements.[78] As with any bright-line rule, this criterion is both over- and under-inclusive with respect to those investors in need of the protections offered by the federal securities laws. This observation is not new.[79] However, it may be becoming more important in light of a growing private securities market, and for this reason, ideas for policy reform might be in order. To this end, one might consider replacing the accredited investor criterion with a percentage loss criterion, under which anyone could invest up to a certain percentage of their income in private offerings. That way, sophisticated, though non-wealthy, investors who fall below the current income and asset requirements of Regulation D's accredited investor requirement would nevertheless be able to participate directly in the market. In addition, unsophisticated, though wealthy, investors who do meet the current income and asset requirements of the rule would nevertheless be protected from being wiped out financially by an ill-informed investment. Congress adopted this type of percentage loss criterion with respect to the crowdfunding exemption that was included in the JOBS Act of

---

[77] Regulation D offerings dwarf private placements under Section 4(a)(2) and Regulation D offerings themselves are dominated by accredited investors. *See* Ivanov & Bauguess, *supra* note 76, at 3. To be sure, Rules 505 and 506 allow issuers to sell to up to 35 non-accredited investors and Rule 504 imposes no accredited investor requirement. However, in practice, 90 percent of all Regulation D offerings involve no non-accredited investors, while the average and median numbers of non-accredited investors are 0.1 and 0, respectively. *See* Ivanov & Bauguess, *supra* note 76, at 6.

[78] The current requirements for individual investors include an individual net worth, or joint net worth with the investor's spouse, at the time of the purchase in excess of $1 million or an individual income of $200,000 (or joint income with the investor's spouse of $300,000) in each of the two most recent years. *See* 17 C.F.R. § 230.501(a)(5) & (6)(2011).

[79] *See, e.g.*, Stephen Choi, *Regulating Investors Not Issuers: A Market-Based Proposal*, 88 Cal. L. Rev. 279, 310–11 (2000); William K. Sjostrom, Jr., *Carving a New Path to Equity Capital and Share Liquidity*, 50 B.C. L. Rev. 639, 667–68 (2009).

2012,[80] and the SEC could most likely do something similar with respect to Regulation D.[81]

With respect to investor protection in secondary distributions, the question pertains largely to Rule 144, which once again is the principal resale exemption. As already discussed, Rule 144 has undergone significant changes in recent years, and these changes raise important questions about investor protection. With the latest iteration of changes to Rule 144, the SEC eliminated all requirements but the holding requirement. Thus, under the current version of Rule 144, a non-controlling shareholder may sell restricted securities without registration if at least six months (or one year in the case of a non-reporting company) have passed since the primary offering.

For those in favor of liberalizing the private securities market, the best defense of these changes might be to point out that there is also no information disclosure requirement with respect to accredited investors participating in Regulation D offerings, and therefore Rule 144 does not provide its unsophisticated purchasers in resales of restricted securities with any less disclosure than we provide accredited investors in the primary Regulation D offering. Of course, this argument assumes that it is a reasonable policy to treat unsophisticated and sophisticated investors alike with respect to information disclosure, which is an assumption the federal securities laws do not seem to make generally.[82] However, even if one accepts this assumption, the reality is that Rule 144 actually treats unsophisticated purchasers in a resale *worse* than the sophisticated investors who purchase in the primary offering. This is because the purchasers in the primary Regulation D offering have more leverage to persuade the issuer to disclose information than do the purchasers in a subsequent secondary distribution since purchasers in the primary offering can always threaten to walk away from the deal, which would result in the issuer raising less capital. However, this is not the case in a secondary offering, where the sale does not affect the issuer's capital

---

[80] Jumpstart Our Business Startups Act, Pub. L. No. 112–106, 126 Stat. 306 (2012).

[81] The major issue would be whether a percentage loss criterion is consistent with the Supreme Court's interpretation of Section 4(a)(2)'s private placement exemption, upon which Rule 506 of Regulation D is based, that a non-public offering is one where the investors can "fend for themselves."

[82] For example, the Supreme Court has said that the private placement exemption in Section 4(a)(2) has to do with whether investors can "fend for themselves," which is largely about access to information. *See* Securities and Exchange Commission v. Ralston Purina Co. 346 U.S. 119 (1953).

raising efforts and therefore the issuer is more or less agnostic about whether the transaction takes place.[83] Stripped of this leverage, Rule 144 purchasers will generally not be successful in getting the issuer to disclose information in the absence of an information disclosure requirement.[84] Consequently, Rule 144 purchasers will have to rely on whatever information the purchasers in the primary offering were able to persuade the issuer to disclose in connection with that offering. However, because of Rule 144's holding requirement, that information will be stale by the time the Rule 144 resale takes place.

Thus, from an informational perspective, the most recent changes to Rule 144 are probably worse for unsophisticated purchasers of restricted securities in secondary distributions than if the SEC had eliminated the Rule 144 holding requirement altogether, since in that case, at least those unsophisticated purchasers would be able to purchase restricted securities closer to the time of the primary offering when the information disclosed by the issuer is still relatively fresh. However, the SEC could not eliminate the holding period requirement altogether, since that would effectively create an end-run around the registration requirement. In other words, without a holding requirement or an information requirement, Rule 144 would permit a company to make a private placement under Regulation D with the expectation that the accredited investors in the Regulation D offering would then immediately turn around and resell to unsophisticated purchasers in a Rule 144 resale. The resulting transaction would look a lot like a public offering that nevertheless escapes the registration requirement.

In regulating resales of restricted securities, the SEC could take two different approaches consistent with the protection of investors.[85] First, it

---

[83] Of course, liquidity in the secondary market does affect primary offerings but only in an indirect way.

[84] To be sure, the sophisticated investor who purchases restricted securities in the private offering could use its leverage at that time to obtain commitments from the issuer that it will release additional disclosures in the future to ensure a more liquid secondary market. However, in practice this is rarely if ever done.

[85] Of course, this is on the assumption that the market itself will not generate the efficient amount of disclosure, which is a reasonable, but by no means unassailable, assumption. *Compare, e.g.*, John C. Coffee, Jr, *Market Failure and the Economic Case for a Mandatory Disclosure System*, 70 Va. L. Rev. 717, 733–34 (1984) (arguing that mandatory disclosure "reduces wasteful duplication by establishing a central information repository"), *and* Zohar Goshen & Gideon Parchomovsky, *The Essential Role of Securities Regulation*, 55 Duke L. J. 711, 738–40 (2006), *with* Roberta Romano, *The Need for Competition in International Securities Regulation*, 2 Theoretical Inquiries L. 387, 389 (2001), *and*

could allow unsophisticated investors to participate in secondary distributions but require more disclosure for these investors than they do for the sophisticated investors who participate in the primary offering. This is more or less the regime that existed before the most recent changes to Rule 144.[86] Alternatively, the SEC could limit purchases and sales of restricted securities, whether in the primary or secondary market, to sophisticated investors and eliminate any information requirement altogether. However, the current version of Rule 144 tries to have it both ways by allowing unsophisticated investors to participate in the secondary market but without imposing an information disclosure requirement. And the consequence is predictably bad for unsophisticated investors.

Investor Access in the Expanding Private Securities Market

Thus, recent changes to the regulation of secondary distributions raise thorny investor protection issues. But a more general concern surfaces when we take a step back and consider the implications of a growing private securities market: the gradual crowding out of the retail investor from the U.S. securities market. This concern has emerged for two reasons. First, the market for restricted securities does appear to be growing, undoubtedly spurred by the liberalization of Rule 144. Second, despite Rule 144, accredited investors and QIBS appear to dominate this market.[87] Indeed, the private securities exchanges are designed primarily for secondary trading not by unsophisticated investors under Rule 144, but rather by accredited investors among whom resales of restricted securities are permissible prior to the time when such securities have come to rest because such resales are consistent with the issuer's original exemption under Regulation D or Section 4(a)(2). Retail investors, by

---

Roberta Romano, *Empowering Investors: A Market Approach to Securities Regulation*, 107 Yale L. J. 2359, 2361 (1998), *and* Stephen J. Choi & Andrew Guzman, *Portable Reciprocity: Rethinking the International Reach of Securities Regulation*, 71 S. Cal. L. Rev. 903, 916 (1998), *and* Frank H. Easterbrook & Daniel R. Fischel, *Mandatory Disclosure and the Protection of Investors*, 70 Va. L. Rev. 669, 687 (1984), *and* Henry Manne, Insider Trading and the Stock Market (Free Press 1966).

[86] *See supra* notes 63–67 and accompanying text.

[87] For this reason, the investor protection issues identified with respect to Rule 144 are less pressing. But even though the private securities market might be dominated by accredited investors and QIBS, it is not completely closed off to unsophisticated investors who wish to purchase restricted securities in a Rule 144 resale. And with respect to those purchasers, the investor protection issues previously discussed are relevant.

contrast, have a difficult time accessing these markets directly or indirectly: directly, because of the legal and structural barriers,[88] and indirectly, because mutual funds—the primary investment vehicle for retail investors—tend not to invest in the private securities market either.[89]

The retail investor's inability to access the expanding private securities market means that these investors have little access to potentially lucrative (albeit risky) investments.[90] While this has always been the case, it is arguably of greater concern in capital markets where the private market is accounting for an increasingly greater share of capital activity. The deficiency in the principle of equal opportunity demonstrated by the rules regulating primary offerings and resales of restricted securities seems all the more problematic in light of the evidence of dramatically rising wealth and income inequality in the United States.[91] Leveling the playing field in this context seems particularly desirable since it would not require re-distribution from the wealthy to the less wealthy, as is so often the case in debates over whether and how to address economic inequality. But of course, increasing access to the private securities market probably only makes sense to the extent that we can do so while at the same time protecting less sophisticated investors. One approach in this regard might be to relax the rules that prevent mutual funds from investing in restricted securities, thereby permitting less sophisticated investors to gain indirect access to the private securities market through a sophisticated intermediary.[92] The resulting "secondary market funds"[93] would result in greater access to the private securities market and its increasing share of investment opportunities with relatively little loss to investor protection.

CONCLUSION

The role that the underwriter concept plays in the federal securities laws is an essential one. Which individuals and entities the law designates as

---

[88] *See supra* notes 71–74 and accompanying text.

[89] *See* Gubler, *supra* note 75, at 790, 805.

[90] *See* Gubler, *supra* note 75, at 799–801; Usha Rodrigues, *Securities Law's Dirty Little Secret*, 81 Fordham L. Rev. 3389, 3427–29 (2013).

[91] *See, e.g.*, Anthony B. Atkinson, Thomas Piketty & Emmanuel Saez, *Top Incomes in the Long Run of History*, 49 J. Econ. Lit. 3 (2011).

[92] *See* Gubler, *supra* note 75, at 804–06; Rodrigues, *supra* note 90, at 3430–34.

[93] *See* Rodrigues, *supra* note 90, at 3430.

underwriters has important implications for one's obligations and liability exposure in primary offerings and largely determines the permissibility of resales in the secondary markets. For this reason, the SEC's narrowing of the scope of underwriter status (through its liberalization of Rule 144) in recent years has undoubtedly contributed, along with the emergence of private stock exchanges, to the expansion of the market for private (unregulated) securities over that same time period. This expanding private securities market raises questions about whether the law offers adequate protection to investors who currently participate in this market and adequate access to these markets more generally. The policy approaches outlined in this chapter (including recalibrations of Rule 144 and the creation of intermediaries or "secondary market funds" through which retail investors could invest responsibly in these risky, but potentially lucrative opportunities) are potential avenues that policymakers might consider pursuing in addressing these concerns in the future.

6. Secondary markets

Roel C. Campos and Marlon Q. Paz

A NATIONAL MARKET SYSTEM

The secondary market for U.S. securities serves as the centerpiece of the U.S. capital markets. The essence of the "secondary market" was aptly captured in 1974 by Philip A. Loomis, Jr., then Commissioner of the Securities and Exchange Commission ("SEC"), who described it as "… a mechanism by which investors everywhere may have their orders executed in a more efficient way, and hopefully at lower cost and with better prices, and where all the resources of the securities community may be brought to bear to provide fair and orderly markets with depth and liquidity, as well as the benefits of competition."[1] Central to understanding the notion of a secondary market in the United States is that the term defines the process for trading stock after the initial issuance, and does not describe an institution. As former Commissioner Loomis stated, "That, presumably, is why we refer to a central market *system*, not simply to a central market. It is not to be a building located somewhere, nor will it, at least initially, be an organization springing full-blown from the brow of its creators … ."[2] This chapter focuses on the applicable federal regulation of the secondary market for securities in the United States.

The system for trading securities *after* the initial issuance by a company (the secondary market) has evolved considerably in response to periods of stress on the markets and private sector advances. With the Securities Act of 1933 ("1933 Act"), Congress sought to deal with the issuance of securities and the initial registration thereof (the primary market); and, with the Securities Exchange Act of 1934 ("1934 Act"), Congress focused on the trading of securities in the marketplace (the secondary market). The secondary markets today have been shaped by further legislation, agency action, self-regulation, and an ever-evolving

[1] Philip A. Loomis, Jr., Chairman, SEC, "The Central Market System," Speech at the Regional Member Firms' Round Table (May 29, 1974).

[2] Ibid.

market structure that must respond to advances in technology, evolving practices and increased globalization.

PROLOGUE TO THE CURRENT REGULATORY STRUCTURE

Early in its evolution, the secondary markets were the province of stockbrokers who used the shade of a buttonwood tree, street curbs or coffee houses as meeting places for trade and correspondence. Exchanges—groups of people organized for the purpose of engaging in securities transactions—predate the Declaration of Independence, though their organization was then relatively loose. The New York Stock Exchange traces its origins to May 17, 1792, when twenty-four stockbrokers gathered outside 68 Wall Street under a buttonwood tree to sign an agreement that would establish the rules for buying and selling bonds and shares of companies.[3] The agreement came to be known as the "Buttonwood Agreement," because the tree served as the regular meeting place for stockbrokers. While the New York Stock Exchange has been one of the dominant stock exchanges, it has not been the only trading center. Looking back to the 18th Century, many companies found an active market outside of the New York Stock Exchange created by a group of stockbrokers who came to be known as the curbstone brokers because they conducted their auctions in the "curb market," i.e., out in the street. The "curb market" eventually organized as the American Stock Exchange.

In response to the Panic of 1792 and the ensuing legislation, stockbrokers began to form associations and sought control of their own destinies, setting the stage for exchange-based trading. Wall Street had experienced its first major crash during the Panic of 1792,[4] and, in the wake of that crash, New York passed legislation intended to regulate the sale of securities. New York's legislation disallowed open-air, "public outcry" markets. Stockbrokers moved their trade indoors, and, for example, under the Buttonwood Agreement, the signatories pledged to deal primarily among themselves and to honor minimum fixed commission rates. That group of brokers officially formed the New York Stock Exchange on March 8, 1817.

---

[3] *Buttonwood Agreement,* SEC Hist. Soc'y (May 17, 1792) http://sechistorical.org/collection/papers/1790/1792_0517_NYSEButtonwood.pdf.

[4] David J. Cowen, *The First Bank of the United States and the Securities Market Crash of 1792*, 60 J. ECON. HIST. 1041 (2000).

Though organized, stock exchanges were regarded as private clubs and, as such, they were viewed as having the right to govern their own affairs. In 1888, the Court of Appeals of New York characterized the New York Stock Exchange as "a business club, its principal object is the promotion of the convenience of its members, by furnishing facilities which aid them in doing their business, and are therefore of benefit to them."[5] However, the manner in which the exchanges had been conducting business would soon be the subject of public scrutiny.

The period after World War I brought a new era as the public discovered the stock market. During that time, millions upon millions of modestly situated individual investors discovered what they thought was the road to riches (the stock market); and so began a great speculative splurge that led to the crash in 1929. The investigation into the events that led to the stock market crash of 1929, the findings of which are memorialized in the Congressional record, shocked members of Congress and the public alike. The findings detailed mechanisms by which insiders had abused investors through manipulations like "bear raids," "wash sales," and "painting the tape." It had become clear that exchanges had the potential to be the setting of large-scale victimization of the ever-growing individual investors.

In the aftermath of the 1929 crash, it became apparent that securities exchanges had to be more than private clubs. The image of a stock exchange was transformed to a quasi-public institution that should be accountable to the public. Out of this realization, Congress provided for federal regulation, in the form of the Securities Exchange Act of 1934, which provided for the registration of national securities exchanges, forbade certain practices and gave the SEC broad oversight with respect to the exchange activities.

The SEC exercised its new powers with considerable restraint, largely deferring to the industry's self-regulation until the 1970s. In the late 60s and early 70s, the U.S. securities markets saw massive failures of securities firms, agonizing issues in the back rooms of the industry, and the other issues which afflicted the securities markets. During this period, Congress launched the most thorough scrutiny of the securities markets since the investigations that preceded the Securities Act of 1933 and the Securities Exchange Act of 1934. The result of studies into the functioning of the securities markets culminated with the 1975 amendments to

---

5 Belton v. Hatch, 17 N.E. 225, 226 (N.Y. 1888).

the Securities Exchange Act of 1934 ("1975 Acts Amendments"),[6] which firmly planted the idea that the securities markets should move towards a central or national market system.

The "central market system" developed over several years. The SEC's letter of March 10, 1971, transmitting the *Institutional Investor Study* to the Congress[7] contained the seed for the idea, noting that:

> A major goal and ideal of the securities markets and the securities industry has been the creation of a strong central market system for securities of national importance, in which all buying and selling interest in these securities could participate and be represented under a competitive regime.

The concept was further developed with The Martin Report of August 5, 1971 to the New York Stock Exchange, the Commission's Statement of February 2, 1972 on the Future Structure of the Securities Markets, and the Commission's Statement of March 29, 1973 on the Structure of a Central Market System.

In 1975, Congress found that the securities markets are an important national asset that must be preserved and strengthened. Rather than establish a single market, Congress sought to improve on a system of multiple trading centers with new data processing and communications techniques to enable efficient and effective market operations. The fundamental objective of the 1975 Securities Acts Amendments was the creation of an integrated single "National Market System" to unite in one system all trading in covered securities.

MARKET STRUCTURE OVERVIEW

The U.S. secondary market is larger and more complex than at any point in history. Market participants' demand for better services, greater efficiency and better prices, as well as competition among trading venues, has shaped today's market structure. Today, the current market structure is dispersed and complex: it is dispersed in the sense that trading volume, or liquidity, is distributed among many trading centers that compete for order flow in the same stocks; and it is complex in that trading centers offer a wide range of services that are designed to attract different types of market participants with varying trading needs. The

---

[6] Pub. L. 29, 89 Stat. 97 (1975); Section 11A(a) of the Exchange Act, 15 U.S.C. 78k-1(a).

[7] SEC, Institutional Investor Study Report, H.R. Doc. No. 92–64, 92d Cong., 1st Sess. ch. 12 (1971).

secondary market for U.S. securities continues to evolve at a rapid pace. To achieve the goals of the national market system, these trading centers are linked to enable effective trading by market participants.

A "trading center" is defined broadly in Rule 600(b)(78) to include each national securities exchange or national securities association that operates a trading facility, an alternative trading system ("ATS"), an exchange market maker, an over-the-counter ("OTC") market maker, or any other broker or dealer that executes orders internally, whether as principal or agent.

Some trading centers display quotations among the consolidated quotation data that is widely distributed to the public, for example, national securities exchanges and electronic communications networks ("ECNs"). Other trading centers do not display quotation data to the public, for example, dark pools and broker-dealers that execute trades internally. These various types of trading centers—those that display market data and those that do not—are discussed below.

National Securities Exchanges

An exchange is an organization, association or group of persons that (i) brings together the orders of multiple buyers and sellers; and (ii) uses established, non-discretionary methods under which such orders interact with each other, and the buyers and sellers entering such orders agree to the terms of a trade.[8] Unless otherwise exempt, persons that meet the definition under Section 3(a)(1) of the Exchange Act must register as a national securities exchange. Registered national securities exchanges must undertake self-regulatory responsibility for their members and file their proposed rule changes for approval with the SEC.

The national securities exchanges have developed highly automated trading systems that offer extremely high-speed, or "low-latency," order responses and executions.[9] These exchanges typically offer a wide range of order types for trading on their automated systems. Exchanges also

---

[8] *See* Exchange Act Rule 3b-16 (17 C.F.R. § 240.3b-16).

[9] Published average response times at some exchanges, for example, have been reduced to less than 1 millisecond. Many exchanges offer individual data feeds that deliver information concerning their orders and trades directly to customers. To further reduce latency in transmitting market data and order messages, many exchanges also offer co-location services that enable exchange customers to place their servers in close proximity to the exchange's matching engine.

compete for orders by offering attractive transaction prices.[10] Exchanges typically charge a somewhat higher access fee than the amount of their liquidity rebates, and retain the difference as compensation.

Highly automated exchange systems and liquidity rebates have helped establish a business model for a new type of professional liquidity provider that is distinct from the more traditional exchange specialist and OTC market maker. In particular, proprietary trading firms and the proprietary trading desks of multi-service broker-dealers now take advantage of low-latency systems and liquidity rebates by submitting large numbers of non-marketable orders (often cancelling a very high percentage of them), which provide liquidity to the market electronically. These proprietary traders often are labeled high-frequency traders, though the term does not have a settled definition and may encompass a variety of strategies in addition to passive market making.

Electronic Communications Networks

Rule 600(b)(23) of Regulation NMS[11] defines Electronic Communications Networks, or ECNs, as electronic trading systems that automatically match buy and sell orders at specified prices. Participants, typically institutional investors, broker-dealers and market makers, place trades directly with an ECN. In general, ECNs offer trading services (such as displayed and undisplayed order types, maker-taker pricing, and data feeds) that are analogous to those of registered exchanges. ECNs must register with the SEC as broker-dealers and are subject to oversight under Regulation ATS of the Exchange Act.[12] The key characteristic of an ECN is that it provides its best-priced orders for inclusion in the consolidated quotation data, whether voluntarily or as required by Rule 301(b)(3) of Regulation ATS.

ATSs fall within the statutory definition of an exchange, but are exempted if they comply with Regulation ATS. Regulation ATS requires

---

[10] Many exchanges have adopted a "maker-taker" pricing model in an effort to attract liquidity providers. Under this model, non-marketable, resting orders that offer (make) liquidity at a particular price receive a liquidity rebate if they are executed, while incoming orders that execute against (take) the liquidity of resting orders are charged an access fee. Rule 610(c) of Regulation NMS caps the amount of the access fee for executions against the best displayed prices of an exchange.

[11] Regulation NMS, Securities Exchange Act Release No. 51808, 70 Fed. Reg. 37496 (June 9, 2005) ("Regulation NMS Release").

[12] *See* Order Execution Materials, Securities Exchange Act Release No. 37619A, 61 Fed. Reg. 48290 (Sept. 6, 1996) ("Order Handling Rules Release").

ATSs to register as broker-dealers with the SEC, which entails becoming a member of the Financial Industry Regulatory Authority ("FINRA") and fully complying with the broker-dealer regulatory regime. Unlike a registered exchange, an ATS is not required to file proposed rule changes with the SEC or otherwise publicly disclose its trading services and fees. ATSs also do not have any self-regulatory responsibilities, such as market surveillance.

Dark Pools

Dark pools are also ATSs that, in contrast to ECNs, do not provide their best-priced orders for inclusion in the consolidated quotation data. In general, dark pools offer trading services to institutional investors and others that seek to execute large trading interest in a manner that will minimize the movement of prices against the trading interest and thereby reduce trading costs.

Dark pools can vary quite widely in the services they offer their customers. Some dark pools, such as block crossing networks, offer specialized size discovery mechanisms that attempt to bring large buyers and sellers in the same stock together anonymously and to facilitate a trade between them. The average trade size of these block-crossing networks can be as high as 50,000 shares. Most dark pools primarily execute smaller trades that are comparable to the average size of trades in the public markets. The majority of this volume is executed by dark pools that are sponsored by multi-service broker-dealers. Broker-dealers that sponsor dark pools may trade in the sponsored ATS as agents by offering order routing services, as principal or both.

Broker-Dealer Internalization

The other type of undisplayed trading center is a non-ATS broker-dealer that internally executes trades, whether as agent or principal. The internalized executions of broker-dealers, however, primarily reflect liquidity that is not included in the consolidated quotation data. Broker-dealer internalization accordingly should be classified as undisplayed liquidity. There are a large number of broker-dealers that execute trades internally in NMS stocks.[13]

---

[13] NMS stock is any security or class of securities for which transaction reports are collected, processed, and made available pursuant to an effective transaction reporting plan, or an effective national market system plan for reporting transactions in listed options. Rule 600(b)(46) and (47) of Regulation

Broker-dealers that internalize executions generally fall into two categories—OTC market makers and block positioners. An OTC market maker is defined in Regulation NMS as "any dealer that holds itself out as being willing to buy and sell to its customers, or others, in the United States, an NMS stock for its own account on a regular or continuous basis otherwise than on a national securities exchange in amounts of less than block size."[14] To facilitate trades, block positioners often commit their own capital to trade as principal with at least some part of the customer's block order. A block positioner generally means any broker-dealer in the business of executing, as principal or agent, block size trades for its customers. "Block size" is defined in Rule 600(b)(9) as an order of at least 10,000 shares or for a quantity of stock having a market value of at least $200,000.

Broker-dealers that act as OTC market makers and block positioners conduct their business primarily by directly negotiating with customers or with other broker-dealers representing customer orders. OTC market makers, for example, appear to handle a very large percentage of marketable (immediately executable) order flow of individual investors that is routed by retail brokerage firms.

REGULATORY STRUCTURE

In 1975, Congress conceived of a national market system composed of multiple competing trading centers linked through technology. Pursuant to Section 11A of the Exchange Act, Congress directed the SEC to facilitate the establishment of a national market system in accordance with certain findings (e.g., that the national market system is of national importance) and objectives (e.g., fairness, efficiency and transparency). The national market system is premised on promoting fair competition among individual trading centers, while at the same time assuring that all of these trading centers are linked together, through facilities and rules, in a unified system that promotes interaction among the orders of buyers and sellers in a particular NMS stock.

In the 1975 Securities Acts Amendments, Congress granted to the SEC authority to adopt rules that promote:

NMS. 17 C.F.R. § 242.600(b)(46) and (47). Over 200 broker-dealers publish execution quality statistics (Dash 5 Reports) pursuant to Rule 605 of Regulation NMS. 17 C.F.R. § 242.605

[14] Rule 600(b)(52) of Regulation NMS. 17 C.F.R § 600(b)(52).

1. *Efficient Execution.* Economically efficient execution of securities transactions;
2. *Fair Competition.* Fair competition among brokers and dealers, among exchange markets, and between exchange markets and markets other than exchange markets;
3. *Transparency.* The availability to brokers, dealers, and investors of information with respect to quotations and transactions in securities;
4. *Market Access.* The practicability of brokers executing customer orders in the best market; and
5. *Dealer disintermediation.* An opportunity, consistent with efficiency and best execution, for the execution of customer orders without the participation of a dealer.[15]

Congress sought to foster these objectives by the linking of all markets for securities through communication and data processing facilities. As it evolved since 1975, the national market system is comprised of individual trading centers, which are linked together to make their best prices publicly known and accessible; thereby combining the benefits of both market centralization and competition.

The most well known, and most heavily regulated, trading center is the exchange. Under the federal securities laws, an exchange is defined as "any organization, association, or group of persons, … which constitutes, maintains, or provides a market place or facilities for bringing together purchasers and sellers of securities or for otherwise performing with respect to securities the functions commonly performed by a stock exchange as that term is generally understood, and includes the market place and the market facilities maintained by such exchange."[16] A "facility" "when used with respect to an exchange includes its premises, tangible or intangible property whether on the premises or not, any right to the use of such premises or property or any service thereof for the purpose of effecting or reporting a transaction on an exchange … ."[17]

As discussed above, in 1998, the SEC adopted Regulation ATS, which exempted ATSs from registration as exchanges even though they technically fit the definition, opting instead to subject these trading centers to

---

[15] *See* S. Rep. No. 75, 94th Cong., 1st Sess. 8 (1975); H.R. Rep. No. 229, 94th Cong., 1st Sess 92 (1975).

[16] Section 3(a)(1) of the Exchange Act.

[17] Section 3(a)(2) of the Exchange Act.

certain core market-oriented obligations of exchanges and registration as broker-dealers.[18]

With Rule 3b-16 of Regulation ATS, the SEC introduced a fundamental component of the regulatory framework—the definition of an "exchange"—as an interpretation of the statutory definition of "exchange" under Section 3(a)(1) of the Exchange Act.[19]

The SEC's interpretation of "exchange" explicitly excluded (1) systems that merely route orders to other facilities for execution; (2) systems operated by a single registered market maker to display its own bids and offers and the limit orders of its customers, and to execute trades against such orders; and (3) systems that allow persons to enter orders for execution against the bids and offers of a single dealer.

In 2005, the SEC noted that the national market system "needs to be enhanced and modernized, not because it has failed investors, but because it has been so successful in promoting growth, efficiency, innovation, and competition that many of its old rules now are outdated." With that rationale, the SEC adopted the current regulatory framework for a National Market System pursuant to Regulation NMS under the Securities Exchange Act of 1934.[20] Under Regulation NMS, the SEC addressed market data, order protection (trade-through protection), fair market access and subpenny quotes.

Regulation NMS Linkages among the Various Trading Centers

Given that trading activity is widely dispersed across many trading centers, to be unified, the national market system requires that trading centers be sufficiently linked. The primary types of linkages that operate in the current market structure include consolidated market data, order protection and broker routing services.

Market Data

Market data serves an essential linkage function among trading centers by helping assure that the public is aware of the best-displayed prices for a stock, regardless of the trading center within the national market

---

[18] *See* Order Execution Obligations, Securities Exchange Act Release No. 40760, 63 Fed. Reg. 70844 (Dec. 8, 1998).

[19] *See supra* note 8.

[20] *See* Regulation NMS, Securities Exchange Act Release No. 51808, 70 Fed. Reg. 37496 (June 29, 2005).

system. In addition, market participants may monitor the prices at which their orders are executed and assess the quality of the execution.

Congress underscored the importance of systems for collecting and distributing market data in its 1975 design of the national market system, noting that the market data system would "form the heart of the national market system."[21] As envisioned, market participants should have ready access to a reliable source of information that comprehensively and accurately captures price and volume information of any NMS stock at any time during the trading day. This data resource includes pre-trade transparency as well as post-trade transparency: market data provides *consolidated quotation data* (pre-trade transparency), i.e., real-time information on the best-priced quotations at which trades may be executed in the future; and *consolidated trade data* (post-trade transparency), i.e., real-time reports of trades as they are executed. A combination of rules promulgated under the Securities Exchange Act of 1934 and joint industry plans govern the collection and distribution of market data.

With respect to pre-trade transparency, Regulation NMS requires exchange members and certain OTC market makers that exceed a 1 percent trading volume threshold to provide their best-priced quotations to their respective exchanges or FINRA, and these self-regulatory organizations, in turn, are required to make this information available to vendors.[22] Regulation NMS requires exchange specialists and OTC market makers to display certain customer limit orders in their best-priced quotations provided under Rule 602.[23] In addition, Rule 301(b)(3) of Regulation ATS requires an ATS that displays orders to more than one person in the ATS and exceeds a 5 percent trading volume threshold to provide its best-priced orders for inclusion in the quotation data made available under Rule 602.[24]

Note, however, that Regulation NMS explicitly recognizes the ability of customers to control whether their limit orders are displayed to the public.[25] Regulation NMS does not require the display of a customer limit order if the customer does not wish the order to be displayed. Rule 604(b)(2) provides an exception from the limit order display requirement for orders that are placed by customers who expressly request that the order not be displayed. Rule 604(b)(4) provides an exception for all

---

21 H.R. Rep. No. 94–229, 94th Cong., 1st Sess. 93 (1975).

22 *See* Rule 602 of Regulation NMS. 17 C.F.R. § 242.602.

23 *See* Rule 604 of Regulation NMS. 17 C.F.R. § 242.604.

24 *See* Rule 301(b)(3) of Regulation ATS. 17 C.F.R. § 242.301(b)(3).

25 *See* Rule 604 of Regulation NMS. 17 C.F.R. § 242.604.

block size orders unless the customer requests that the order be displayed. However, while customers have the freedom to display or not display depending on their trading objectives, selective display of orders generally is prohibited.[26]

With respect to post-trade transparency, Regulation NMS requires the equity exchanges and FINRA to file a transaction-reporting plan regarding transactions in NMS stock.[27] In turn, members of these self-regulatory organizations ("SROs") are required to comply with the relevant SRO rules for trade reporting. FINRA members must submit a tape report within 30 seconds of trade execution during the hours that the FINRA facility to which the member is reporting is open.[28] Trades executed before the facility opens and after the close of the facility must be reported, but such trades are not subject to the 30-second reporting requirement.[29] FINRA's 30-second reporting requirement applies to transactions in NMS stocks and OTC equity securities, including foreign securities, American Depository Receipts and Canadian issues and non-exchange-listed Direct Participation Program securities by all ATSs that trade NMS stocks, both ECNs and dark pools, and broker-dealers that internalize.[30]

Regulation NMS requires that equity exchanges and FINRA act jointly pursuant to one or more effective national market system plans to disseminate consolidated information on quotations for and transactions in NMS stocks.[31] It also requires that consolidated information for each NMS stock be disseminated through a single plan processor. To comply with these requirements, the equity exchanges and FINRA participate in three joint industry plans ("Joint Industry Plans"). Pursuant to Rule 603(b) of Regulation NMS, three separate networks distribute consolidated market data for NMS stocks: (1) Network A for securities with their primary listing on the NYSE; (2) Network B for securities with their primary listing on exchanges other than the NYSE or NASDAQ; and (3) Network C for securities with their primary listing on NASDAQ.

---

[26] *See, e.g.,* Rule 602(a)(1) of Regulation NMS (17 C.F.R. § 242.602(a)(1) and Rule 301(b)(3) of Regulation ATS (17 C.F.R. § 242.301(b)(3)); Order Executing Obligations, Securities Exchange Act Release No. 37619A, 61 Fed. Reg. 48290, 48307 (Sep. 6, 1996).

[27] *See* Rule 601 of Regulation NMS. 17 C.F.R. § 242.601.

[28] *See* FINRA Rules 6282(a), 6380A(a), 6380B(a) and 6622(a).

[29] *See* FINRA Rules 6282(a), 6380A(a), 6380B(a) and 6622(a).

[30] *See* FINRA Regulatory Notice 10–24 (Apr. 2010).

[31] *See* Rule 603(b) of Regulation NMS. 17 C.F.R. § 242.603(b).

The Networks under the Joint Industry Plans set fees, with SEC approval, for the data. The three Networks collect the applicable fees and, after deduction of network expenses, allocate the remaining revenues to the SROs. Network expenses do not include the costs incurred by SROs to generate market data and provide such data to the Networks.

Many exchanges and ECNs offer individual data feeds directly to customers that include information that is provided to the three Networks for distribution in consolidated data. The individual data feeds of exchanges and ECNs can also include a variety of other types of information, such as "depth-of-book" quotations at prices inferior to their best-priced quotations. Rule 603(a) of Regulation NMS requires all exchanges, ATSs, and other broker-dealers that offer individual data feeds to make the data available on terms that are fair and reasonable, and not unreasonably discriminatory. For example, exchanges, ATSs and other broker-dealers are prohibited from providing their data directly to customers any sooner than they provide their data to the plan processors for the Networks.[32]

Order Protection

The protection against "trade-throughs" provided by Rule 611 of Regulation NMS is another important linkage embedded in the current market structure. A trade-through occurs when one trading center executes an order at a price that is inferior to the price of a protected quotation displayed by another trading center.[33] Shortly after its adoption, Chairman William Donaldson noted that the rule "should promote better outcomes for investor orders, enhanced liquidity and innovation."[34]

The SEC defined a trade-through as the execution of a trade at a price inferior to a protected quotation[35] for an NMS stock. Protection against

---

[32] Regulation NMS Release, 70 Fed. Reg. at 37567 ("… Rule 603(a) prohibits an SRO or broker-dealer from transmitting data to a vendor or user any sooner than it transmits the data to a Network processor.").

[33] Ibid.

[34] William Donaldson, Simple New Rule that Gives Investors Priority, Fin. Times, Apr. 7, 2005; *see also Regulation NMS and Recent Market Developments:* Hearing Before the Senate Comm. on Banking, Housing, and Urban Affairs (May 19, 2005) (testimony of William Donaldson, Chairman, Securities and Exchange Commission), available at http://banking.senate.gov/index.cfm?FuseAction=Hearings.Home.

[35] A protected quotation must be displayed by an automated trading center, must be disseminated in the consolidated quotation data, and must be an automated quotation that is the best bid or best offer of an exchange or FINRA.

trade-throughs is an important linkage among trading centers because it provides a baseline assurance that (1) marketable orders will receive at least the best displayed price, regardless of the particular trading center that executes the order or where the best price is displayed in the national market system; and (2) quotations that are displayed at one trading center will not be bypassed by trades with inferior prices at any trading center in the national market system.

Trade-through protection applies to *all* trading centers, not just those that display protected quotations. Rule 611(a)(1) requires all trading centers to establish, maintain, and enforce written policies and procedures that are reasonably designed to prevent trade-throughs of protected quotations, subject to the exceptions set forth in Rule 611(b).

Regulation NMS promotes linkages among trading centers by encouraging the routing of marketable orders to a trading center that is displaying the best price. Although Rule 611 does not directly require such routing services, competition has led trading centers to offer routing services to their customers.

Broker Routing Services

Brokers play a significant role in linking trading centers together into a unified national market system. Brokers offer advanced technology designed to monitor liquidity at many different trading centers and sophisticated strategies to implement order routing.

A broker's legal duty of best execution, coupled with industry competition to attract customers, supports the linkages among trading centers. The best execution requirement imposes a duty on a broker to obtain the most favorable terms reasonably available when executing a customer order.[36] Brokers implement advanced technology designed to monitor liquidity at many different trading centers and sophisticated strategies to implement order routing. For example, brokers may monitor the execution of orders at both displayed and undisplayed trading centers to assess the availability of trading interest. Using their knowledge of available liquidity, many brokers offer smart order routing technology to access such liquidity.

Regulation NMS supports competition with enhanced transparency of order execution and routing practices. Rule 605 requires trading centers to publish monthly reports of statistics on their order execution quality.

---

[36] *See, e.g.,* Regulation NMS Release, 70 Fed. Reg. at 37537–37538 (discussing duty of best execution).

Rule 606 requires brokers to publish quarterly reports on their routing practices, including the venues to which they route orders for execution.

Of course, price transparency would be meaningless without the ability to access the trading center. Section 6(a)(2) of the Exchange Act promotes fair access by requiring registered exchanges to allow a registered broker-dealer to become a member of the exchange. Contrast this broad access requirement applicable to registered exchanges, for example, with the more limited access requirements that apply to ATSs. Regulation ATS includes two distinct types of access requirements: fair access to services in general in Rule 301(b)(5), and order display and execution access in Rule 301(b)(3). An ATS must meet the general fair access requirement if it exceeds a 5 percent trading volume threshold. An ATS must meet order display and execution access requirements if it displays orders to more than one person in the ATS and exceeds a 5 percent trading volume threshold. If an ATS neither displays orders to more than one person in the ATS nor exceeds a 5 percent trading volume threshold, Regulation ATS does not impose access requirements on the ATS.

Market participants obtain access to the various trading centers through broker-dealers that are members or subscribers of the particular trading center pursuant to the private linkages approach adopted by Regulation NMS.[37] Regulation NMS prohibits an SRO trading facility from imposing unfairly discriminatory terms that would prevent or inhibit any person from obtaining efficient access through an SRO member to the displayed quotations of the SRO trading facility and limits the fees that a trading center can charge for access to its displayed quotations at the best prices.

CONCLUSION

The history of secondary markets in the U.S. is characterized by an ever increasingly fast pace of evolution. This rapid evolution continues to challenge the objectives of the national market system. For example, a secondary market that was primarily manual trading is now primarily automated. Noting the rapid changes in trading technology and practices, in 2010, the SEC took an important step when it published the Market

---

[37] *See* Rule 610 of Regulation NMS. 17 C.F.R. § 242.610.

Structure Concept Release and thereby initiated a comprehensive review of equity market structure.[38]

On May 6, 2010, the secondary market experienced a "flash crash": the prices of many securities experienced an extraordinarily rapid decline and recovery.[39] Major equity indices in both the futures and securities markets plummeted in a matter of minutes before rebounding almost as quickly. What happened? As the SEC explained, the high volatility was sparked by a large sell order in "e-mini" futures on the S&P 500 index by a mutual-fund group (valued at approximately $4.1 billion) as a hedge to an existing equity position. The mutual fund group chose to execute via an automated execution algorithm that was programmed to take account of trading volume, not price or time, and was thus executed unusually rapidly: in 20 minutes, instead of the several hours that would be typical for such an order. This enormous sell pressure was initially absorbed by, among others, high frequency traders, who themselves used automated execution algorithms.

Amid these glitches and the exponential growth of dark pools, SEC Chair Mary Jo White has spoken about a potential overhaul of financial-market oversight, noting that the special regulatory status of U.S. exchanges may not best serve investors or public companies.[40] While many of the themes remain the same, given the rapid pace of evolution in the secondary markets, the applicable regulatory scheme likely will be further refined.

---

[38] *See* Concept Release on Equity Market Structure, Securities Exchange Act Release No. 61358, 75 FR 3594, 3598 (Jan. 21, 2010) ("Market Structure Concept Release").

[39] Findings Regarding the Market Events of May 6, 2010, Report of the Staffs of the CFTC and SEC to the Joint Advisory Committee on Emerging Regulatory Issues, September 30, 2010, available at http://www.sec.gov/news/studies/2010/marketevents-report.pdf.

[40] Mary Jo White, "Focusing on Fundamentals: The Path to Address Equity Market Structure," Security Traders Association 80th Annual Market Structure Conference, Washington, D.C. Oct. 2, 2013.

7. The rise of risk-based regulatory capital: liquidity and solvency standards for financial intermediaries

José Gabilondo

INTRODUCTION

In a capitalist economy, a private firm seeking finance must negotiate with prospective investors in the open market, which establishes standards about the terms on which debt and equity investment will be forthcoming. In addition to these market-financing standards, the capital structure of some financial firms—particularly broker-dealers, federally insured depository institutions, and insurance companies—must satisfy other requirements imposed by federal or state regulators to promote liquidity and solvency. Regulators take a heightened interest in these firms because they serve a public function in providing credit and other financial services. To grasp what regulatory capital rules try to accomplish, the reader must make a conceptual shift to see these financial firms as highly leveraged borrowers, contending with the demands of their own creditors. From this perspective, the financial stability of these firms becomes a matter of public concern.

The first section explains regulatory capital as a corporate finance issue about how capital structure can protect creditors—especially unsecured ones – from unexpected financial losses. The rest of the chapter examines the major features of the regulatory capital regimes that apply to financial intermediaries. The second section starts with depository institutions, i.e., banks. These standards have become the locus of policy debates about risk-based capital. The third section discusses the regulatory capital rules that apply to broker-dealers registered with the U.S. Securities and Exchange Commission ("SEC").[1] Broker-dealers have long been subject to net capital rules that promote the firm's liquidity in order to promote

[1] Futures commission merchants are also subject to regulatory capital. For a comprehensive discussion of their requirements, see Jerry Markham, *The CFTC Net Capital Rule–Should a More Risk-Based Approach be Adopted*, 71 Chicago-Kent L. Rev. 1091 (1996).

orderly self-liquidation. More recently, large broker-dealers have been allowed to adopt a risk-based method—akin to that used in bank capital—for meeting their net capital requirements. The fourth section considers insurance companies, which adhere to risk-based capital standards imposed by state law. The fifth section warns that large, complex financial organizations may find themselves inadvertently subject to bank-style capital rules if deemed "systemically important" by the newly created Financial Stability Oversight Council ("FSOC").

REGULATORY CAPITAL AS A CORPORATE FINANCE PROBLEM

Firms finance their activities by borrowing, issuing equity shares or retaining earnings. Borrowing and share issuance lead to dramatically different claims against the issuer in terms of how it must allocate profit and the extent to which investors can participate in the firm's governance. According to the terms of their contracts, creditors are paid first, receiving what they lent plus interest. To enforce their seniority, creditors can sue for breach. In contrast, the purchasers of a firm's equity own the firm, which gives them a junior but residual interest in a firm: they are paid only after creditors, but they keep the entire residue.

An issuer's balance sheet matches its asset holdings (listed on the left-hand side) with its capital structure (arrayed on the right-hand side). The capital structure arranges the claims of investors in a hierarchy that prioritizes creditor claims and subordinates those of owners. Creditor claims are generally listed in order of descending priority, moving down through hybrid instruments like subordinated or convertible debt, and ending with residual claims like preferred stock and—the sanctum sanctorum of the residual—common stock.

This hierarchy establishes which claim will bear loss when the firm suffers one. For example, when the firm recognizes a loss on an asset, an offsetting deduction must be made on the right-hand side of the balance sheet, because of the accounting identity providing that the assets must equal the sum of equity and liabilities. The liabilities do not bear the asset loss because they are liquidated sums that not do adjust on peril of contract breach. It is the equity that must bear the burden of adjusting to loss in the value of assets. In effect, asset loss makes the balance sheet "shrink up," in that equity shrinks dollar-for-dollar along with the loss. In this sense, equity involves a "first loss" position.

This residual capital cushion may have different names in different legal vehicles, but its function in absorbing loss is the same.[2] Making equity bear loss first helps to protect the interests of creditors—especially unsecured ones—from unanticipated loss. The deeper a firm's capital cushion, the longer it will be able to withstand loss without creditors to unexpected loss.

The firm can also become more leveraged (and suddenly illiquid) without shrinking assets when the issuer takes on new liabilities, especially unexpectedly. Assuming that the asset portfolio stays the same as liabilities increase, the adjustment required by the accounting identity will again happen in the equity account. In effect, the new liabilities are treated like another "first loss" that is borne by the equity account. This time, the balance sheet stays the same size, but it has become more leveraged as in the shrinking asset case in the first example. A recent example is the detonation of contingent liabilities in the AIG Financial Products Unit when its credit default swaps became out-of-the-money.

When courting a lender in the open market, all firms must contend with the loss and leverage dynamics described above. Banks, broker-dealers, and insurance companies must also contend with regulatory requirements about their capital structure. Regulators justify the imposition of these rules in the name of several public interests including protecting customers and other counterparties from the firm's financial instability, promoting stability and integrity in payments and financial services, and shielding the public fisc from clean-up costs when these firms go broke.

As do those demanded by the open market, these requirements address a firm's overall asset-liability structure for similar ends. Both market and regulatory capital rules seek to ensure that the firm will have (i) enough liquidity to meet maturing obligations timely, and (ii) a permanent pool of financial reserves that can absorb unexpected losses without impairing the rights of creditors. So at every moment, broker-dealers, banks and insurance companies are subject to the more exacting of either market or regulatory demands about capital structure (much as U.S. taxpayers are always liable for the higher of their regular income tax liability or that calculated under the alternative minimum tax).

Most of these standards are considered "risk-based" because they attempt to take account of the particular risk of firm's financial structure

---

[2] For example, in a special-purpose vehicle set up to securitize receivables, the account that bears the risk of loss may be called an "excess spread" account or simply a "first loss" position.

rather than using gross balance sheet values. On the asset-side, regulatory capital creates incentives to hold particular assets by influencing the cost of holding them. On the other side of the balance sheet, these rules limit the firm's ability to leverage itself. As a result, these firms have both a conventional balance sheet and what may be thought of as a regulatory balance sheet. From a firm's perspective, one should understand these rules in terms of how they impact a firm's balance sheet at a point in time, e.g., "What will making this loan cost in terms of regulatory capital?" or "What kind of assets can we support by issuing this kind of preferred stock?"

Among financial firms, banks face the most comprehensive regulatory capital rules for two reasons. First, banks are illiquid by design. Banks borrow at short-terms (including on an overnight or demand basis) and then deliberately mismatch their balance sheets by making loans with a longer term, often at fixed rates. This mismatch is no mistake. Rather, it is how banks provide long-term credit on terms that consumers can afford. Profit, not social altruism, drives this mismatch because banks capture a positive net interest spread, since long-term funding rates tend to be higher than short-term interest rates. This mismatch, though, periodically drives some banks—and at times the banking sector as a whole—into liquidity crises.

The second reason is that deposit insurance shifts liquidity and solvency risks from federally insured banks onto the federal government. It is as though the federal government has a residual loss interest (with no offsetting upside). This creates a perverse incentive for bank managers to invest in excessively risky assets when their own capital has declined. In this situation, the owners have little to lose and much to win if the risky investment (funded with taxpayer money) goes well. The severity of bank capital requirements might seem unreasonable (as banks often urge) but the burden must be put in the context of the funding advantages that banks enjoy—cheap deposits and privileged access to central bank liquidity.

Firms try to reduce the cost of complying with regulatory capital, considered a form of "regulatory arbitrage" by its critics. For example, given that many assets are valued at historic cost, a firm can enhance its earnings (which will eventually flow into an equity account) by selling assets with built-in gain and postponing the sale of assets with built-in loss.[3] A more structural form of regulatory arbitrage plays out in financial

---

3 Larry Wall and Pamela Peterson, Banks' Responses to Binding Regulatory Capital Requirements, *Economic Review* 1–17, 8, Federal Reserve Bank of Atlanta (March/April 1996).

conglomerates that operate securities, banking and insurance businesses separately. Faced with a transaction subject to regulatory capital, a conglomerate may have a choice about which of its regulated businesses should be assigned the transaction. Because different business lines are subject to different capital standards, the decision about where to book a deal will tend to consider its regulatory capital implications.

BANKS

Today, the Federal Reserve ("Fed"), the Federal Deposit Insurance Corporation, and the Office of the Comptroller of the Currency (hereinafter "the agencies") subject banks to an expanding regime of regulatory capital, most of them risk-based.[4] To some extent, U.S. banking regulators have always taken risk into account when evaluating whether a bank's capital was sufficient given its loan base.[5] During most of the twentieth century though, regulators tended to make subjective determinations about a particular bank's capital adequacy, often by comparison to peer banks. The Fed had begun experimenting with a more formal risk-based capital approach in the 1950s, but there was no consensus among the agencies about how to apply such a standard.[6]

In the 1980s, U.S. regulators began using bright-line ratios that quantified capital adequacy by comparing assets to equity in order to track how deep the bank's loss-bearing cushion was.[7] These early efforts introduced features—like capital ratios and a hierarchy of loss-bearing capital instruments—that would become permanent parts of the regulatory approach, discussed below.

Institutionalizing Risk-Based Capital

As banks became more active in international markets in the 1980s, regulators concluded that more international coordination was needed to avoid a "race to the bottom" in which international operations would be

---

[4] For an excellent analysis of rationales for regulating bank capital, see Heidi Mandanis Schooner and Michael Taylor, Global Bank Regulation: Principles and Policies 13–45 (2010).

[5] Federal Deposit Insurance Corporation, Basel and the Evolution of Capital Regulation: Moving Forward, Looking Back 1 (Jan. 14, 2003).

[6] Malcolm Alfriend, International Risk-Based Capital Standard: History and Explanation, Economic Review 28–34, Federal Reserve Bank of Richmond (Jan./Feb. 1988).

[7] Federal Deposit Insurance Corporation, *supra* note 5, at 1.

based in the country with the most lax regulations. Moreover, the business of banking was changing as many banks began experimenting with off-balance sheet items like over-the-counter derivatives.[8]

In 1974, a group of major central banks under the auspices of the Basel Committee on Banking Supervision ("BCBS") began working on a risk-based capital standard to apply to internationally active banks.[9] In 1987, the group's first major proposal—the Basel Capital Accord ("Basel I")—proposed a framework that tied the minimum capital of internationally active banks to the estimated risk in their asset portfolios. This proposal would serve as a guideline for implementation by countries through national legislation.

Basel I coincided with efforts in the U.S. to strengthen capital requirements for banks after a series of banking crises in the 1980s. Congress had passed the Federal Deposit Insurance Corporation Improvement Act ("FDICIA"), which imposed risk-based capital standards on all banks, even domestic ones with little international activity. FDICIA established a rating system that classified banks into five different categories based largely on their capital adequacy.[10] In this system, maintaining adequate capital was the only way to avoid administrative penalties, including more examinations, the denial of requests to acquire other banks, requirements to raise capital or suspend dividends, and, in the extreme case, the withdrawal of deposit insurance or the bank's charter.[11] The goal was to look beyond accounting formalisms to more conservatively identify how much real loss-bearing capital a bank had. FDICIA and Basel I worked in tandem to institutionalize risk-based capital for banks.

In effect, the approach involved constructing a regulatory balance sheet by making conservative adjustments to a bank's financial balance sheet and then testing this pro forma balance sheet against capital adequacy standards established by regulators.[12] The first step in building this pro forma balance sheet was to deduct assets that had no actual liquidity, e.g.,

---

[8] Larry Wall and Pamela Peterson, *supra* note 3, at 1–17, 2.

[9] The original members were Belgium, Canada, France, German, Italy, Japan, Luxembourg, the Netherlands, Spain, Sweden, Switzerland, the United Kingdom, and the United States. *See* http://www.bis.org/bcbs/history.htm.

[10] Larry Wall and Pamela Peterson, *supra* note 3, at 1–17, 3.

[11] *Id* at 1–17, 3–4.

[12] This chapter uses several stylized balance sheets to illustrate how regulatory capital requirements apply to banks and broker-dealers. Because the goal is to illustrate general aspects of these requirements, this chapter makes simplifying assumptions about the capital ratios, asset risk-weights, haircuts, and other

goodwill. The right-hand side of the balance sheet would also be adjusted, "shrinking up" as discussed previously.

Some assets—like cash—were deemed so free of risk that a bank could fund them entirely with borrowed money; hence, no equity needed to be assigned to them to bear the risk of unexpected loss. Most assets, however, would require a minimum amount of equity to provision for the risk of unexpected loss. So the next step in constructing the pro forma balance sheet was to identify which asset—or which fraction of gross assets—would have to be financed by some blend of debt-leveraged equity. To this end, Basel I introduced a scheme that assigned different risk-weights to assets based on differences in their relative credit risk: 0 percent, 25 percent, 50 percent, and 100 percent.

These risk-weights determine how much of the asset a bank must fund by some qualifying blend of debt and equity. By implication, the difference between 1 and these risk-weights expressed how much of the asset value can be funded entirely by debt, unbacked by equity. For example, holding $100 in cash exposed a bank to no default risk, so the bank could finance a cash investment entirely with borrowed money. This was accomplished by giving the cash a risk-weight of 0 percent.

A bank could fully debt-finance the first half of the value of an asset assigned a risk-weight of 50 percent, like a residential mortgage, but the remaining half of the asset's value would have to be funded by some qualifying blend of debt and equity.[13] Because an unsecured loan was a riskier investment, the bank would have to allocate more of its loss-bearing capital (equity) to provide for this risk. Banks had to give unsecured loans a 100 percent risk-weight. The weighting to be given particular bank assets has changed over the years—and remains a bone of contention—but the basic mechanism of risk weighting became a permanent part of Basel rules.

The all-in regulatory capital cost of financing reflected both an asset's risk-weight and the amount that could be fully debt-financed. Assuming that a firm had to set aside $8 of equity for every $100 of risk-weighted asset exposure, it would have to finance an asset in the 100 percent bucket (like the unsecured loan in the previous example) by qualifying

requirements. As a result, these calculations do not reflect actual capital requirements for these portfolios.

[13] Although sorting assets into four different risk "buckets" made the capital standard more responsive to a bank's risk, this scheme still let banks game the weighting by letting them pick riskier assets—with a better chance of return—within each risk bucket. Darryl Getter, U.S. Implementation of the Basel Capital Regulatory Framework 3–10, Congressional Research Service (2012).

equity capital up to 8 percent of its value. The rest of its value (92 percent) could be financed by borrowing. An asset in the 50 percent bucket, however, would have an all-in regulatory capital cost of only 4 percent, because the 8 percent capital cost would apply only to half of the asset's value. Hence, 96 percent of its value could be financed by debt. Assuming that debt is cheaper than equity, the first asset would be cheaper to finance.

Not all liability and capital instruments have an equal ability to bear loss, however. To identify the acceptable blend of debt and equity financing, Basel I classified equity and para-equity into Tier 1 core capital and Tier 2 supplementary capital. The most robust forms of capital included common stock and surplus. Preferred stock had less loss-bearing capacity than common with some kinds (like noncumulative perpetual preferred) being more truly residual than others. So Tier 1 capital included the book value of common equity, noncumulative preferred stock, and some minority interests in the equity capital accounts of the bank's consolidated subsidiaries. Tier 2 capital included Tier 1 plus the loan-loss reserve, perpetual preferred stock, subordinated notes, and some hybrid instruments.

Basel I also recognized that off-balance sheet assets and liabilities also impacted a bank's capital adequacy. This is especially true in the case of credit commitments—like a stand-by letter of credit or a credit line—that remain contingent because a counterparty decides whether to issue the asset. For that reason, Basel I also provided a formula for converting off-balance sheet items into on-balance sheet asset equivalents. In effect, the conjunction of the asset weights and the Tier-based capital ratios put in place a schedule of regulatory capital costs by type of asset. Regulators could change the asset weights and the capital thresholds to calibrate the overall system. Once the asset base and the qualifying capital had been determined, the regulatory balance sheet could be tested for compliance with the minimum capital thresholds.

An example in Table 7.1 shows how the regulatory balance sheet is constructed. Imagine a quite modest bank with the following financial balance sheet.

Table 7.1 Bank's financial balance sheet

Assets		Liabilities	
Cash	2,450,000	Demand Deposits	5,000,000
U.S. Treasuries	1,500,000	One year CDs	1,000,000
		Medium-term notes	1,000,000
Residential mortgages	2,000,000	Subordinated debt	2,400,000
Unsecured loans	2,000,000	**Equity**	
Corporate debentures	2,000,000	Noncumulative perpetual preferred stock	200,000
Goodwill	50,000	Common stock	400,000
Total	**10,000,000**	**Total**	**10,000,000**

Several adjustments must be made to construct the regulatory balance sheet consistent with Basel I. Because the purpose of capital is to absorb loss, intangible assets—in this case goodwill—should be deducted so as to arrive at a more realistic estimate of the actual liquidity available to absorb loss. To balance the deduction on the asset-side, the equity account must also be adjusted dollar-for-dollar, because equity bears the first loss arising from reduction in the value of assets. After reducing the value of goodwill from both the asset and common stock accounts, the pro forma balance sheet looks like Table 7.2.

Table 7.2 pro forma regulatory balance sheet #1 – net of goodwill

Assets		Liabilities	
Cash	2,450,000	Demand Deposits	5,000,000
U.S. Treasuries	1,500,000	One year CDs	1,000,000
		Medium-term notes	1,000,000
Residential mortgages	2,000,000	Subordinated debt	2,400,000
Unsecured loans	2,000,000	**Equity**	
Corporate debentures	2,000,000	Noncumulative perpetual preferred stock	200,000
		Common stock	350,000
Total	**9,950,000**	**Total**	**9,950,000**

The next step is to identify which assets need equity funding. These are the only assets to be "booked" and carried on the (pro forma) regulatory balance sheet. For example, the cash and the government securities get a 0 percent risk-weight, hence no portion of their value appears on the regulatory balance sheet. The mortgages receive a risk-weight of 50 percent, which means that one-half of their value is booked on the regulatory balance sheet. The loans and debentures receive a risk-weight of 100 percent, which means that the entire amount of the bank's investment in them must be funded—for regulatory purposes—by a blend of equity and debt. After converting the actual assets into risk-weighted assets, identifying the kind of capital that qualifies as truly loss-bearing (and carrying over the intangible-discounted value of the bank's equity), the construction of the regulatory balance sheet is complete: see Table 7.3.

Table 7.3 Regulatory balance sheet #2 – net of debt-funded assets and liabilities

Assets		Equity	
Residential mortgages	1,000,000	Preferred stock	200,000
Unsecured loans	2,000,000	Common stock	350,000
Corporate debentures	2,000,000		
Total	**5,000,000**	**Total**	**550,000**

Granted, this pro forma exercise is no longer a balance sheet because it ignores liabilities and assets that required no equity funding. Indeed, only half of the bank's gross balance sheet ($5m of $10m) requires any regulatory capital at all. It is this (pro forma) asset balance that is now tested for capital adequacy.

Dividing the qualifying capital by the risk-weighted asset base results in a Tier 1 equity ratio of 11 percent (the sum of the preferred and common). The rest of the risk-weighted asset base (89 percent) is funded with borrowed money. Assuming that the minimum required of Tier 1 equity is 8 percent, the bank substantially exceeds the minimum. Its risk-weighted leverage ratio is about 1:8, i.e., the bank borrows $8 for every $1 of equity.

The outcome is different if we apply market capital standards that look at the bank's gross assets. In that case, the bank's equity base must support a higher asset base, i.e., $10 million rather than $5 million. In terms of gross leverage, the bank's assets would be supported 5.5 percent by tangible equity and 94 percent by borrowed funds. Hence, the gross leverage ratio is closer to 1:19, such that the bank has borrowed $19 for every $1 of equity.

Imagine that some of the bank's borrowers become insolvent such that the bank must write down 20 percent of the value of the unsecured loans, i.e. $400,000.[14] Because common stock bears the first loss (as in the adjustment for goodwill), the value of the common stock must be written down dollar-for-dollar. This loss would deplete the common and run down the preferred by $50,000. The loss-adjusted regulatory balance sheet would then look like Table 7.4.

Table 7.4 Regulatory balance sheet #3 – after write-down of asset and equity

Assets		Equity	
Residential mortgages	1,000,000	Preferred stock	150,000
Unsecured loans	1,600,000	Common stock	0
Corporate debentures	2,000,000		
Total	**4,600,000**	**Total**	**150,000**

Just as debt leverage multiplies a firm's ability to invest in assets, it also amplifies the consequences of loss on these assets. Hence, the consequences of the equity write-down are more serious. As a result of the loan write-off, the bank's Tier 1 ratio now drops to less than 3.3 percent, leaving it in violation of its minimum capital requirement. At this point, the bank can choose between issuing more Tier 1 equity or reducing the amount of its risk-weighted assets subject to minimum equity requirements. Assuming that the bank issues new equity and invests the proceeds entirely in 0 percent weighted assets, e.g., cash, the bank could meet its eight Tier 1 capital by raising as little as $218,000. Insofar as the bank reinvests the proceeds in assets requiring some equity funding, e.g., residential mortgages, more equity capital would be needed to cover the associated marginal equity surcharge on the regulatory balance sheet.

Alternatively, the bank could shrink its risk-weighted asset base. In effect, this strategy asks 'What is the maximum amount in risk-weighted assets that can be supported with $150,000 in Tier 1 capital?' Assuming a minimum Tier 1 ratio of 8 percent, the answer is $1,875,000, suggesting that the bank will have to make substantial reductions of its assets, i.e., $2,725,000.[15]

Its holdings of debentures and loans are more "expensive" than its mortgages because they are risk-weighted at 100 percent, hence the

---

[14] To keep matters simple, this chapter does not include the loan-loss reserve that banks establish as a contra-asset account to absorb expected loss on its credit portfolio.

[15] Solving for x, the equation is 1,875,00 = $.08x.

smallest asset reduction that would return the bank to compliance could be accomplished by converting $2,725,000 of the debentures and loans into cash. Assuming that all of the debentures and some of the loans are sold, the risk-weighted pro forma balance sheet resulting after these adjustments now has a Tier 1 capital ratio of 8 percent and looks like Table 7.5.

Table 7.5 Regulatory balance sheet #4 – assuming conversion of the debentures and some loans into cash

Assets		Equity	
Residential mortgages	1,000,000	Preferred stock	150,000
Unsecured loans	875,000	Common stock	0
Total	**1,875,000**	**Total**	**150,000**

Leaving the regulatory capital calculation, what does the bank's financial balance sheet look like after writing down the equity and selling the loans and debentures, assuming reinvestment of the sale proceeds into cash? See Table 7.6.

Table 7.6 Bank's financial balance sheet – after write-down

Assets		Liabilities	
Cash	5,175,000	Demand Deposits	5,000,000
U.S. Treasuries	1,500,000	One year CDs	1,000,000
		Medium-term notes	1,000,000
Residential mortgages	2,000,000	Subordinated debt	2,400,000
Unsecured loans	875,000	**Equity**	
		Noncumulative perpetual preferred stock	200,000
Goodwill	50,000	Common stock	0
Total	**9,600,000**	**Total**	**9,600,000**

Rather than reinvesting the asset-sales into cash, the bank could also have chosen to use the $2,725,000 to redeem its subordinated debt and $225,000 of its medium-term notes, becoming a smaller, dramatically less-leveraged institution, as in Table 7.7. Because the Tier 1 ratio is calculated only on the basis of risk-adjusted assets and Tier 1 capital, this smaller less leveraged entity would have the same Tier 1 ratio, although its gross leverage ratio would be lower, as suggested in Table 7.7.

Table 7.7 Bank's financial balance sheet – assuming debt repayment rather than holding cash

Assets		Liabilities	
Cash	2,450,000	Demand Deposits	5,000,000
U.S. Treasuries	1,500,000	One year CDs	1,000,000
		Medium-term notes	675,000
Residential mortgages	2,000,000		
Unsecured loans	875,000	**Equity**	
		Noncumulative perpetual preferred stock	200,000
Goodwill	50,000	Common stock	0
Total	**6,875,000**	**Total**	**6,875,000**

Self-Evaluation of Capital Adequacy: Basel II and Internal Models

The business of banking kept changing after the adoption of Basel I as yield-hungry banks increased their derivatives activities and began substituting riskier loans for low-risk securities.[16] Not surprisingly, modifications to the first Basel proposal were proposed in 2004 as the Capital Adequacy Framework ("Basel II").[17] Notably, it gave banks substantial discretion in picking how their regulatory capital would be calculated.[18]

The process of letting banks evaluate their own capital adequacy had begun in 1996, when regulators let banks use proprietary risk models to estimate the market risk in their asset portfolios. Basel II would expand this discretion by letting banks choose between calculating their capital requirements under a modified version of Basel I or using their own internal statistical models. Banks that used their own models could

---

[16] Federal Deposit Insurance Corporation, *supra* note 5, at 4. *See generally* Heidi Mandanis Schooner and Michael Taylor, *supra* note 4, at 147–64.

[17] Although Basel II expected to become effective in the United States in 2008, the agencies granted waivers from compliance for certain aspects of Basel II due to the financial crisis.

[18] Basel II also took account of "operational risk," an umbrella category for contingencies not related to credit or market risk but that could, nonetheless, impact a bank's solvency.

choose between using statistical assumptions provided by regulators or developing their own assumptions, known as the "advanced approach."[19]

Large banks welcomed the discretion, which often let them save on regulatory capital costs.[20] For example, under Basel I, a bank would have to hold capital of $8 to support an AAA-rated loan of $100. The cost for that loan would be lower under any of the Basel II options, dropping to $1.81 under the standard approach, $1.41 under the internal ratings model approach, and somewhere between $.037 and $4.45 for the advanced approach. At the same time, though, riskier loans tended to require a higher capital charge. For example, under Basel I, a $100 B-rated loan would require $8 of capital (the same as the AAA loan). Under Basel II, the equity cost would rise to $12.21 in the standard approach, $18.53 in the internal ratings model, and between $3.97 and $41.65 under the advanced model approach.

Regulators modified Basel II in 2009 in response to the 2007 financial crisis to better track the credit risk in the securities traded by banks. Known as Basel II.5, these revisions attempted to limit a kind of regulatory arbitrage made possible by accounting differences in how a firm recorded its investments in debt securities.[21] If a firm intended to hold the debt security to maturity, it could be booked at its historic cost, ignoring ongoing fluctuation of the market price. However, if a firm intended to sell a security rather than hold it to maturity, it would have to mark the value of the security to market, increasing the volatility of its gross earnings. Hence, banks could strategically assign securities with unrealized built-in gain to their trading book—that way boosting the bank's asset value—and relegate securities with built-in loss to the banking book.

Capital After the Crisis

The financial crisis that began in 2007 cast a harsh spotlight on regulatory capital requirements, in part because they did not obviate the need for large-scale public bailouts of illiquid and insolvent banks.

---

[19] In the basic and more conservative approach, the bank would estimate the probability of a default on its assets and the regulators would provide the expected loss given default, the bank's exposure at default, and the maturity at exposure. Using the advanced approach, the bank would use its own values rather than those of the regulator.

[20] The following estimates of regulatory capital costs appear in the Federal Deposit Insurance Corporation, *supra* note 5, at 2.

[21] Darryl Getter, *supra* note 13, at 3–4.

Consequently, the Dodd-Frank Act of 2010 ("Dodd-Frank") sought to raise minimum regulatory capital requirements and to extend them to previously unregulated firms that participated in the credit market.[22] Released in 2010, Basel III also raised capital requirements, gave regulators more options to address the capital impact of financial cycles, and enhanced requirements about liquidity.[23] The final contours of the new capital requirements will not be known until federal agencies issue regulations, but the discussion below outlines the major features of the capital changes envisioned by Dodd-Frank and Basel III.

New charges and standards

Much of what Basel III does is refine the existing tools and standards, including the definition of capital and the ratios. For example, Tier 1 capital is now divided into two categories: Common Equity Tier 1 ("CET1") and total Tier 1. CET1 is the most residual layer of the bank's capital, where the first losses and short-term volatility will be absorbed.[24] Total Tier 1 is the sum of CETI plus some adjustments. In addition to raising risk-based capital requirements, Basel III establishes a leverage ratio, calculated by dividing the bank's Tier 1 capital by an expanded asset base not just the bank's risk-weighted assets. Set at a minimum of 3 percent, this leverage ratio is not required of all banks; rather, regulators impose it on banks selectively.

Basel III also adds new "charges" designed to mitigate financial cycles—a capital conservation buffer and a counter-cyclical buffer. The capital conservation buffer prohibits banks from making certain distributions to their owners or paying discretionary bonuses unless the bank has an adequate capital buffer in excess of its minimum capital requirements. Supervisors also retain discretion to modify capital charges in order to make requirements more counter-cyclical, i.e., greater as a credit bubble inflates but smaller after it bursts.

---

[22] Dodd-Frank also prohibits the use of trust-preferred securities as Tier 1, although this ban is phased in and subject to grandfather to avoid shocking the capital structure of banks that relied on them.

[23] The Fed approved some of the Basel III rules in July 2013 and said that more would be forthcoming. *See* http://www.federalreserve.gov/newsevents/press/bcreg/20130702a.htm.

[24] CET1 is calculated like tangible net equity for private firms because it is the sum of common stock, related surplus, and retained earnings minus a variety of charges (including goodwill, other intangibles, securitization gain on sale, and fair value changes in the bank's financial liabilities) that remove residual assets of dubious liquidity. By imposing more stringent criteria it is hoped that banks will be better able to absorb unexpected losses.

Dodd-Frank requires bank holding companies and other financial companies to assess their capital adequacy through statistical stress tests that posit how their liquidity and solvency would fare under adverse market conditions. Also, the Fed must now conduct an annual stress test of large bank holding companies and certain entities designed by the FSOC, to determine whether these entities have sufficient capital to absorb losses resulting from negative market conditions.[25]

However, legal uncertainty remains about what the new capital minimums are because Dodd-Frank defines them in terms of "generally applicable" risk-based capital and leverage requirements in effect when the statute was passed, which includes Basel I and features of Basel II.[26] Because regulatory capital rules were already changing during this period, identifying the precise contours of this standard may be difficult. Moreover, Dodd-Frank directs prudential regulators to use regulatory capital to mitigate systemic risk, a notion that continues to evolve. As a result, regulators will have to become more specific about the capital standards to which financial firms are expected to adhere.

Liquidity and funding

The financial crisis revealed that markets could treat solvent but illiquid firms as though they were insolvent. Regulators responded by paying more attention to a firm's funding liquidity. To that end, Basel III imposes two new requirements designed to promote a bank's funding stability—a Liquidity Coverage Ratio and a Net Stable Funding Ratio.

Designed to promote the bank's short-term stability, the Liquidity Coverage Ratio requires the bank to have enough liquid assets on-hand to honor its obligations for 30 days, even in crisis conditions in which the bank would be locked out of its funding markets. Cash, deposits at central banks, and some sovereign obligations would qualify as conforming assets, as would others of sufficient credit quality, liquidity or transferability. In general, when determining which of the bank's assets count as liquid, its holdings of liabilities issued by commercial banks, investment firms, financial holding companies, insurance companies or liabilities issued by a parent or subsidiary of the bank would not count.

---

[25] In November 2012, the Fed conducted a systematic stress test of capital for 18 bank holding companies, including several with large trading and mark-to-market exposures. Styled as the Comprehensive Capital Analysis and Review, it also incorporated stress-testing requirements mandated by the Dodd-Frank Act. *See* http://www.federalreserve.gov/bankinforeg/stress-tests/dodd-frank-act-stress-testing.html.

[26] Darryl Getter, *supra* note 13, at 3–5.

The Net Stable Funding Ratio promotes funding stability over a longer-term horizon, i.e., one year. It classifies the sources of a bank's financing in terms of its permanence and callability. All of a bank's Tier 1 and 2 capital plus preferred stock with a maturity of over one year counts as stable funding dollar for dollar. Other forms of funding common to banks are discounted based on the risk that they may not be refinanced upon maturity. In effect, this ratio imposes a maturity tax on funding by reducing the compliance value of longer-term funding.

BROKER-DEALER REGULATORY CAPITAL

The SEC imposes regulatory capital rules on registered broker-dealers. The primary goal of these rules is to ensure that broker-dealers hold enough liquid assets to make good on their obligations to customers and other creditors in the case of liquidation. Although bank regulators have now increased their surveillance of liquidity, the net capital rule has long recognized the crucial link between the market liquidity of a firm's assets and the firm's own liquidity. Recently, the SEC has let some large broker-dealers demonstrate their capital adequacy by using internal statistical models, similar to those approved by Basel II. Most broker-dealers calculate their minimum capital using the traditional approach, but the largest broker-dealers use this alternative internal models approach.

The Net Capital Rule

In the late 1960s, several broker-dealers became insolvent, producing losses to their customers. As a result, Congress directed the SEC to adopt a rule to protect customers from loss by promoting minimum capital levels at registered broker-dealers. Congress also established the Securities Investor Protection Corporation ("SIPC") to provide limited indemnification to investors for losses in their accounts at insolvent broker-dealers.[27]

In response, the SEC implemented a revised regulatory capital standard—the uniform net capital rule.[28] The goal of the rule was to allow a broker-dealer that was no longer a going concern to honor its duties to customers and other creditors in the case of self-liquidation. A customer might still have recourse to funds through SIPC, but the net

---

[27] Michael Jamroz, The Net Capital Rule, 47 Bus. Law. 863, 864–65 (1991).

[28] 17 C.F.R. § 240.15c3–1—Net capital requirements for brokers or dealers.

capital rule was designed to promote orderly self-liquidation rather than a SIPC liquidation, which would involve limited recovery and delays.

Like the regulatory capital process for a bank, the net capital calculation generates a pro forma balance sheet and then tests it for capital adequacy. The process involves two steps. First, the firm's actual net capital is calculated, by calculating the tentative net capital and then finalizing it with asset haircuts. Second, the firm's net capital requirement is calculated using either a leverage ratio or a method based on the firm's customer assets.

The calculation of the actual net capital starts by determining the firm's equity according to Generally Accepted Accounting Principles ("GAAP"). This involves marking to market the firm's securities positions and recognizing unrealized gains and losses. Then some adjustments are made to GAAP equity to conform the balance sheet to the net capital rule. As in the bank case, goodwill and other liquid assets are deducted from the balance sheet. Unlike the bank case, some of the broker-dealer's subordinated debt is also counted as qualifying capital because it can absorb unexpected loss.[29] This part of the calculation generates tentative net capital.

Important adjustments are then made to the broker-dealer's assets to finalize the net capital calculation. The valuation of an asset as part of a going concern is predicated on the notion that the broker-dealer would have some discretion in selling it, such that the assumed price is as favorable as the seller can obtain. In contrast, the net capital rule adopts the perspective of liquidation in which the broker-dealer is forced to sell assets without the luxury of waiting for the best possible price. To estimate a liquidation price for assets that reflects this price risk, the net capital rule applies discounts ("haircuts") to assets intended to reflect what they would fetch if sold in haste. This approach results in conservative pricing of a broker-dealer's assets.

Once this regulatory balance sheet has been calculated, there are two alternative methods of meeting the firm's minimum net capital requirement: (i) a basic method that measures the adequacy of net capital against a set of the firm's unsecured liabilities, and (ii) an alternative method that compares net capital to assets generated from the firm's

---

[29] To qualify as net capital, the subordinated debt must have a term of at least one year and be fully subordinated to other creditors, including customers of the broker-dealer. For purposes of this exercise, assume that all of the subordinated debt will count in the net capital calculation.

dealings with customers. According to the basic method, the broker-dealer must hold at least $1 of capital for every $15 of its uncollateralized debt. This requirement directly limits the broker-dealer's ability to leverage itself. The second method lets the broker-dealer calculate its minimum net capital as a minimum percentage of the firm's obligations to its customers. Any net liquidity above this minimum requirement is considered excess net capital.

To understand a simple version of the net capital calculation, consider the following stylized broker-dealer balance sheet in Table 7.8.[30]

Table 7.8 Broker-dealer's financial balance sheet

Assets		**Liabilities**	
		Aggregate indebtedness	
Cash	3,000,000	• Customer payables	5,000,000
U.S. Treasuries	3,500,000	• Two month commercial paper	1,000,000
Customer receivables (unsecured)	500,000	• Medium-term notes	1,000,000
Corporate equities	1,000,000	Subordinated debt	2,500,000
Unsecured loans	500,000	**Equity**	
		Noncumulative perpetual preferred stock	100,000
Goodwill	1,500,000	Common stock	400,000
Total	**10,000,000**	**Total**	**10,000,000**

To identify only the liquid assets available to honor the firm's obligations, the goodwill, unsecured customer receivables, and unsecured loans are all deducted on the theory that they have no ready market in which they could be converted to cash. Based on this balance sheet, the size of this adjustment will eliminate all of the firm's equity. Since net capital includes qualifying subordinated debt, however, the subordinated debt can bear the rest of the adjustment. The resulting balance sheet in Table 7.9 indicates a tentative net capital of $500,000.

30 The net capital rule establishes different requirements based on the type of business that a broker-dealer maintains. Because these requirements are quite intricate, this example presents an elemental version of the calculation.

Table 7.9 Broker-dealer's tentative net capital – net illiquid assets

Assets		Liabilities	
		Aggregate indebtedness	
Cash	3,000,000	• Customer payables	5,000,000
U.S. Treasuries	3,500,000	• Two month commercial paper	1,000,000
		• Medium-term notes	1,000,000
Corporate equities	1,000,000	Subordinated debt	500,000
		Equity	
		Noncumulative perpetual preferred stock	0
		Common stock	0
Total	**7,500,000**	**Total**	**7,500,000**

Since the net capital calculation assumes a forced liquidation in which assets would have to be sold quickly, some of the assets must be haircut. The cash is not haircut. Although some government securities may be subject to haircuts, assume for purposes of this problem that the U.S. Treasuries are short-term securities deemed to be risk-free, such that the only assets that must be haircut are the equity securities. For simplicity of calculation, assume that they are haircut by 20 percent, i.e., $200,000. Since the subordinated debt account has become the first loss position (once the write-down for goodwill has burned through the common and preferred equity), it too must be reduced by $200,000. This is the resulting balance sheet at Table 7.10.

Table 7.10 Broker-dealer's net capital—net illiquid assets and asset haircut

Assets		Liabilities	
		Aggregate indebtedness	
Cash	3,000,000	• Customer payables	5,000,000
U.S. Treasuries	3,500,000	• Two month commercial paper	1,000,000
		• Medium-term notes	1,000,000
Corporate equities	800,000	Subordinated debt	300,000
		Equity	
		Noncumulative perpetual preferred stock	0
		Common stock	0
Total	**7,300,000**	**Total**	**7,300,000**

Now the broker-dealer must calculate its net capital requirements and compare them against its actual net capital. As noted above, the broker-dealer may choose between two methods. Under the first method, the firm must hold the greater of $250,000 or $1 of net capital for every $15 of aggregate indebtedness. The firm's remaining subordinated debt—$300,000—does exceed $250,000. Assuming that all of its liabilities (not the subordinated debt) count as aggregate indebtedness, the broker-dealer's relevant debts equal $7,000,000. To qualify under the first method, the firm's net capital would have to be at least $470,000, which exceeds the firm's remaining subordinated debt of $300,000.

A second method—which often results in a lower minimum net capital—lets the broker-dealer calculate its minimum net capital as the greater of $250,000 or 2 percent of its customer receivables. Two percent of its customer receivables of $500,000 is only $10,000. Because the firm's subordinated debt exceeds the $250,000 floor, the firm's net capital is sufficient to meet its net capital requirements.

A broker-dealer must perform these regulatory capital computations daily and notify the SEC if it is at risk of not meeting its minimum net capital requirements. A broker-dealer must also file quarterly reports of financial condition and an annual report, with audited financial statements. As measured by the few broker-dealers that have undergone SIPC liquidation since it was adopted, the net capital rule has been relatively successful in promoting financial integrity.

Internal Models Approach

In 2004, the SEC amended the net capital rule to let qualifying broker-dealers demonstrate their minimum net capital with internal risk-management models that used statistical methods to forecast loss. This was attractive to broker-dealers that belonged to large financial conglomerates.[31] Many of these conglomerates already had sophisticated risk-management systems designed to comply with their banking regulators, so an argument was made that net capital compliance for broker-dealers that belonged to such conglomerates could be based on internal models like those approved for banks in Basel II.

---

[31] The idea for it came out of an experiment by six large securities firms that used their own models to calculate the amount of portfolio risk they faced in their over-the-counter derivatives portfolios. General Accounting Office, RISK BASED CAPITAL Regulatory and Industry Approaches to Capital and Risk 7, 14, GGD-98–153 (1998).

The internal models method gave broker-dealers more flexibility in maintaining capital adequacy by reducing the deductions that would otherwise have to be taken to reflect the market and credit risks in their portfolios. As a result, these firms could reduce their minimum net capital and then upstream excess capital to their holding company. Nevertheless, broker-dealers using the alternative approach must hold a tentative net capital of at least $1 billion.[32] They must also hold net capital of at least $500 million.

Firms using the internal models method would no longer have to use the SEC's asset haircuts, but they would have to provide information about their risk models. The broker-dealer's holding company also had to agree to provide the SEC regularly with comprehensive information about the financial condition of the broker-dealer, the holding company and its affiliates.

While attractive to the firm, this relaxation of capital constraints is viewed by many as having contributed to the financial crisis of 2007. Since then, some broker-dealers that had used this alternative converted to bank holding companies, thereby becoming subject to the prudential oversight of the Fed.[33]

INSURANCE COMPANIES

Insurance companies in the U.S. follow risk-based capital standards developed by the National Association of Insurance Commissioners ("NAIC") and imposed by individual states.

State Regulation

As of yet, little research demonstrates that insurance companies present systemic risks to the financial sector.[34] The federal government does not indemnify policyholders for losses incurred when insurance companies

---

[32] The requirements to qualify for this method are found in Appendix E to 17 C.F.R. § 240.15c3–1.

[33] Five broker-dealers participated in the program: Goldman Sachs, Merrill Lynch, Bear Stearns, Lehman Brothers, and Morgan Stanley. Lehman Brothers has since declared bankruptcy. Bear Stearns was acquired by J.P. Morgan, a bank. Goldman Sachs and Morgan Stanley have moved their operations to be under the Fed as their principal regulator.

[34] Mary Weiss, Systemic Risk and the U.S. Insurance Sector 2; Richard Herring and Til Schuermann, Capital Regulation for Position Risk in Banks, Securities Firms, and Insurance Companies in Hal Scott (ed.), Capital Adequacy

become insolvent. Insurance is largely regulated by states, which have a commissioner or director to monitor the conditions under which insurance can be offered. Individual states operate guaranty funds to cover some shortfalls in insurance coverage, but the recovery provided by these funds is often limited.[35] When an insurance company fails, any resulting loss tends to be borne by policyholders, other creditors and shareholders.

As a result, there has been no federal prudential oversight of insurance companies, although they must conform to state standards about capital adequacy. This type of state regulation of insurance capital involves (i) guidelines on how an insurance company should establish its minimum net capital based on its business lines and (ii) statutes that give state regulators the authority to take actions against an insurance company if it becomes financially impaired.

NAIC has also developed the Risk-Based Capital ("RBC") for Insurers Model Act ("Model Act"), which has been adopted by all states (except Texas) and the District of Columbia. Used as an accreditation standard by the NAIC, the Model Act defines regulatory capital by incorporating by reference the level of "statutory capital" that insurance companies must hold under state law. State law also exposes reinsurers to similar capital standards.[36] While depository institutions follow GAAP, insurance companies follow statutory accounting principles that tend to be more actuarially conservative than GAAP.

In addition to these state-level constraints, large insurance companies now face the risk of being classified as "systemically important financial institutions," which would make them subject to prudential oversight by the Fed. Also, if an insurance company owns a savings and loan, then it becomes a "savings and loan holding company" ("SLHC") now subject to regulation by the Fed under the terms of Dodd-Frank. Until now, insurance companies that were also SLHCs did not have to comply with formal regulatory capital requirements, but the Fed may change that. In particular, the Fed may require these insurance companies to use GAAP (which the Fed requires bank holding companies to use) rather than the more conservative statutory accounting principles that insurance companies use.

Beyond Basel: Banking, Securities, and Insurance, 17 (Oxford, 2005). The AIG Financial Products Unit was not part of AIG's regular insurance operations.

[35] Weiss, *id.* at 8.

[36] Scott Harrington, Capital Adequacy in Insurance and Reinsurance in Hal Scott (ed.), Capital Adequacy Beyond Basel: Banking, Securities, and Insurance, 110 (Oxford, 2005).

Determining Minimum Risk-Based Capital Requirements

Insurers face the risk that the ultimate cost of paying claims will exceed the amounts set aside to fund those claims.[37] An insurer undertakes to pay claims on the occurrence of certain loss events. The insurer pre-funds the costs of settling these claims by charging customers premiums. It reduces its net risk by diversifying through pooling many such contracts and by transferring risk to a reinsurer. The risk-based framework used in this business identifies five general kinds of risk that insurance companies face—asset, interest, underwriting, and business risk.

Asset risk refers to the potential that the company's assets (including fixed income securities, equity shares and real estate) will lose value. Interest rate risk refers to the generic potential for loss due to changes in levels of the interest rate. Underwriting risk refers to the possibility that the firm has made mistakes when calculating the potential for loss on its core business. Mistakes can include errors in forecasting mortality or casualty.[38] Such mistakes may be expressed in underestimating the reserves or the price of premiums for coverage. Eventually these mistakes would be reflected in a balance sheet liability called the policyholders' fund, which reflects the aggregate value of the company's duty to pay claims.[39] Similar to underwriting risk, business risk refers to unexpected fluctuations in premium income, annuity costs and other liabilities.

Some of these same risks are common to other financial firms.[40] However, the liabilities that an insurer takes on—in the form of promises to honor claims—may stretch out over a long period. As a result, insurance companies often remain relatively liquid because they have time to adjust to unexpected losses or liquidity events. For this reason, assuming liquidation values—as the net capital rule does for broker-dealers—makes little sense in an insurance context.

The risk profile of any particular insurer will depend on the kind of business that it conducts. To respond to the particular risk profiles of these different lines of insurance, NAIC has developed separate quantitative formulas that establish minimum net capital requirements for life insurance, property and casualty insurance, and health insurance. For example, life insurers face less risk because morbidity and mortality can

---

[37] *Id.* at 88.

[38] General Accounting Office, *supra* note 31, at 10.

[39] Richard Herring and Til Schuermann, *supra* note 34, at 28.

[40] As with banks and broker-dealers, market risk also becomes relevant because if the insurance company's assets underperform that will also compromise its ability to make good on its promises. *Id.* at 17.

be estimated with a relatively high degree of actuarial accuracy.[41] In contrast, property and casualty insurers face the risk of unexpected losses. Capital standards for nonlife insurers provision for asset, credit, underwriting, and off-balance sheet risks.[42] Those for life insurers plan for asset, underwriting, interest rate, and business risks.[43]

In the 1990s, NAIC began using internal statistical models to estimate risk-based capital for life insurance activities.[44] In the NAIC framework, the insurer must calculate its risk-based capital both based on its own internal assumptions as well as with NAIC-mandated assumptions. State regulators tend to rely on a firm's own testing of its model rather than submitting models to a centralized review.[45] Because these models are intended to capture risks that escape measurement in the standard risk-based formulas, the use of internal models has often tended to increase an insurance company's minimum capital, i.e., the opposite of what happened for broker-dealers.[46] At present, the use of internal models has not become the norm for other kinds of insurance businesses.

SYSTEMICALLY IMPORTANT FINANCIAL INSTITUTIONS

The last financial crisis showed that unregulated financial firms—like AIG's Financial Products Group—could negatively impact the financial system as much and often more than could regulated firms. In response, Dodd-Frank gave the FSOC the power to identify firms whose potential systemic impact would justify the imposition of risk-based capital and leverage requirements.[47]

Statutory Classification

Dodd-Frank provides a two-step process in which a firm must first be deemed a "nonbank financial company," and then further classified as a systemically important nonbank financial institution ("SIFI"). Status as a

---

[41] Harrington, *supra* note 36, at 101.

[42] *Id.*

[43] *Id.*

[44] Therese Vaughn, The Implications of Solvency II for U.S. Insurance Regulation 7, (Feb. 2009) 2009-PB-03.

[45] *Id.*

[46] *Id.*

[47] Section 113 of Dodd-Frank Act.

nonbank financial company depends on quantitative criteria to evaluate whether a company is predominantly engaged in financial activities. A firm is predominantly engaged in financial activities if (i) 85 percent of its gross revenues come from ownership of depository institutions or the conduct of financial activities, or (ii) 85 percent of its assets are financial or related to its ownership of depository institutions. These thresholds cast a wide net that brings in various asset managers (pension funds, mutual funds, investment funds, special-purpose vehicles), hedge funds, private equity funds, sovereign wealth funds, and insurance and reinsurance entities.

The second step—becoming a SIFI—depends on whether the nonbank financial company may expose the U.S. economy to financial instability by virtue of (i) financial distress at the company, or (ii) the nature, scope, size, scale, concentration, or interconnectedness, of the company's activities. To flesh out this standard, the FSOC has published a rule that establishes a three-part process—including appeal rights—to determine whether a nonbank financial company is a SIFI.

First, any nonbank financial company will be subject to an initial screening if it has more than $50 billion in consolidated assets and one of five other factors that target high leverage, liquidity risk and derivatives activities. For U.S. companies, these thresholds are applied to global assets, liabilities and operations of the company and its subsidiaries. For foreign companies, only United States assets, liabilities and operations of the foreign nonbank financial company and its subsidiaries count. Next, the FSOC will analyze companies captured in this initial screening based on a six-category framework to determine the company's exposure to financial distress and its potential impact on the broader economy. Companies found to pose risk enter the final stage of the process, at which point, the FSOC will request information—including confidential business information—from the company. The FSOC then makes its final determination.

On June 3, 2013, the FSOC issued its first proposed determinations of nonbank financial companies to be designated as SIFIs. Three companies had been under consideration—AIG, Prudential Insurance and GE Capital. Both AIG and Prudential Insurance were deemed SIFIs, suggesting that insurance business models may be at particular risk for this regulatory status.[48] Prudential Insurance is appealing the decision,

---

[48] The Fed also regulates AIG as a savings and loan holding company because AIG owns a thrift, AIG Federal Savings Bank.

becoming the first insurance company likely to adjudicate the question of whether insurance companies pose systemic risks to the financial sector.

Capital Standards

A firm deemed to be a SIFI becomes subject to prudential oversight by the Fed of its capital structure similar to that imposed on banks. The Fed has statutory authority to exempt a SIFI from risk-based capital and leverage requirements. To date, the Fed has suggested that prudential standards for a SIFI could be tailored to an individual firm or to a business line. SIFIs will likely be subject to several capital and liquidity requirements akin to those currently applicable to banks and bank holding companies. If so, the SIFI would have to provide the Fed with quarterly reports about its capital adequacy, develop a contingency funding plan explaining how the company would fund itself during extreme liquidity events, and provide an annual capital plan addressing capital adequacy under financial stress. The SIFI may also have to hold a liquidity buffer along the lines of the net liquidity coverage ratio introduced by Basel III.

Complying with some of these requirements may require a firm to develop new risk-management processes. For example, in order to determine whether it complies with the limit on counterparty exposure, a firm must add up all positions with the counterparty. Whether a SIFI might also enjoy privileged access to central bank liquidity like that enjoyed by banks remains to be seen given that its systemic relevance may help to justify access to emergency stabilizing liquidity.

8. Investment adviser regulation

Wulf A. Kaal[*]

The Investment Advisers Act of 1940[1] ("IAA") regulates investment advisers that manage funds through custodial accounts or investment companies and disseminate advice through newsletters and other publications. Non-exempt investment advisers are required to register with the SEC,[2] file periodic reports[3] and subject themselves to periodic examinations.[4] Investment advisers cannot engage in fraudulent practices and make material misrepresentations when rendering investment advice.[5] Investment advisers who are exempt from registration are still subject to the IAA's antifraud provision,[6] which applies to negligent misstatements and misstatements made with the intent to defraud.

The IAA also regulates contracts between investment advisers and their clients. Because contingent fee arrangements could lead to inappropriate risk taking by investment advisers, contingent fee arrangements between investment advisers and their clients are prohibited.[7] Instead, investment adviser fees are based on the total value of the managed fund(s) at pre-specified times. Since 1985, however, certain qualifying large advisory contracts are exempt from the general prohibition of contingent fee arrangements. Moreover, to protect investors against changes in the character or quality of advisory services, the IAA prohibits the assignment of contracts with clients unless the client consents.[8] Should investment advisers violate the securities laws, the SEC has the authority to impose sanctions on registered and unregistered

* The author would like to thank research librarians Ann Bateson, Valerie Aggerbeck and Megan McNevin for their support.

1 Investment Advisers Act of 1940, ch. 686, tit. II, 54 Stat. 847 (codified as amended at 15 U.S.C. §§ 80b-1–80b-20 (2012)).

2 15 U.S.C. § 80b-3 (2012).

3 *Id.* § 80b-4.

4 *Id.* § 80b-4(b)(6).

5 *Id.* § 80b-6.

6 *Id.*

7 15 U.S.C. § 80b-5(a)(1) (2012).

8 *Id.* § 80b-5(a)(2).

investment advisers.[9] Sanctions may include limiting the adviser's activities, imposing a bar order, as well as suspending or censuring the adviser.

DEFINITIONS

A basic precept of securities law is the definition of a security. Providing investment advice and being considered an investment adviser under the IAA requires that a person renders advice with regard to a security. The investment adviser and the client have to deal with a security in order for the definition of investment adviser under the IAA to apply. Securities have traditionally been defined broadly.[10]

Assuming that the parties are dealing with a security, the IAA defines an "investment adviser" as "any person who, for compensation, engages in the business of advising others, either directly or through publications or writings, as to the value of securities or as to the advisability of investing in, purchasing, or selling securities, or who, for compensation and as part of a regular business, issues or promulgates analyses or reports concerning securities … ."[11]

Several factors determine if a person's rendering of investment advice falls within the definition of investment adviser. Generally speaking, a person must be in the business of rendering advice, and the more individualized his or her advice is, the more likely the person is to be classified as an investment adviser. Several factors can determine if a person is in the business of providing investment advice. These factors include: (i) holding oneself out as an investment adviser or as someone who provides investment advice; and (ii) receiving separate or additional compensation. While providing investment advice without compensation makes the person less likely to provide investment advice as an investment adviser under the IAA's definition, the SEC is broadly construing the meaning of compensation for advisory services. Finally, the frequency of rendering investment advice helps define whether a person is an investment adviser. Providing investment advice occasionally or rarely and in a non-periodic fashion makes it less likely for a person to be considered an investment adviser.

Persons who are not covered by the "investment adviser" definition are excluded and not subject to regulation under the IAA. The IAA excludes

---

[9] *Id.* § 80b-3(e).

[10] SEC v. W. J. Howey Co., 328 U.S. 293, 298–99 (1946).

[11] 15 U.S.C. § 80b-2(a)(11).

banks, lawyers, accountants, engineers, and teachers from the definition if these persons are providing investment advice incidental to their professions.[12] Advisers who render advice solely with respect to United States government securities are also excluded from the definition of investment adviser.[13]

Perhaps the most important exclusion, however, is the exclusion for broker dealers. A broker dealer holding him or herself out as a financial planner alone does not trigger IAA registration obligations.[14] A broker dealer who provides investment advisory services that are "solely incidental to the conduct of his business as a broker or dealer" is also exempt from the IAA definition of broker dealer, provided the broker dealer does not receive "special compensation."[15] The burden of proof is on the plaintiff to show that the broker dealer received special compensation and that the investment advice was more than incidental to the brokerage activities.[16] A broker dealer cannot be classified as an investment adviser without proof of special compensation.

ADVISER CATEGORIES

When it passed the Dodd-Frank Act,[17] Congress recognized that not all hedge fund advisers pose the same systemic risks and therefore require the same level of oversight. Congress therefore created different hedge fund adviser categories in Title IV of the Dodd-Frank Act.[18] Categorizing hedge fund advisers by size, Title IV and SEC forms suggest that the

---

[12] *Id.* § 80b-2(a)(11)(A), (B).

[13] *Id.* § 80b-2(a)(11)(E).

[14] Applicability of the Investment Advisers Act to Financial Planners, Pension Consultants, and Other Persons Who Provide Investment Advisory Services As a Component of Other Financial Services, Investment Advisers Act Release No. 1092, 39 SEC Docket 494 (Oct. 8, 1987) (superseding Applicability of the Investment Advisers Act to Financial Planners, Pension Consultants, and Other Persons Who Provide Investment Advisory Services As an Integral Component of Other Financially Related Services, Investment Advisers Act Release No. 770, 23 SEC Docket 556 (Aug. 13, 1981)).

[15] 15 U.S.C. § 80b-2(a)(11)(C).

[16] SEC v. Kenton Capital, Ltd., 69 F. Supp. 2d 1, 13 (D. D.C. 1998).

[17] Dodd-Frank Wall Street Reform and Consumer Protection Act, Pub. L. No. 111–203, 124 Stat. 1376 (2010) (codified in scattered sections of U.S.C. tits. 7, 12, 15, 18, 22, 31, 42 (2012)).

[18] *Id.* tit. IV, §§ 402, 403, 407, 408, 410 (codified at 15 U.S.C. §§ 80b-2(a), 80b-3(b), 80b-3, 80b-3, 80b- 3a(a)); *see also* Exemptions for Advisers to Venture Capital Funds, Private Fund Advisers with Less than $150 Million in Assets

larger the hedge fund advisers, as measured by their assets under management ("AUM"), the higher the possible systemic threat the respective fund poses. Accordingly, the disclosure requirements increase with the AUM size of hedge fund advisers.

Investment advisers with between $25 and $100 million AUM are defined as mid-sized investment advisers.[19] Under Title IV, state authorities are responsible for mid-sized investment advisers.[20] While mid-sized advisers are not required to register with the SEC, they may still be required to register with the state agency in the state of their principal place of business.[21] Should a particular state not provide sufficient regulation, the SEC will oversee the mid-sized investment adviser.[22]

Investment advisers having more than $150 million regulatory assets under management ("RAUM") are defined as large private fund advisers and are required to register with the SEC.[23] The registration of large private fund advisers increases the availability of data and may help protect against systemic risk. Large private fund advisers are required to file Form PF with the SEC. Additional filing requirements apply to investment advisers that substantially exceed the general RAUM requirement of $150 million.

REGISTRATION

The financial crisis of 2007–08 precipitated a renewed emphasis on regulatory oversight of the global hedge fund industry.[24] Congress enacted the Private Fund Investment Advisers Registration Act of 2010 in

---

Under Management, and Foreign Private Advisers, Investment Advisers Act Release No. 3222, 101 SEC Docket 1649 (June 22, 2011).

[19] Dodd-Frank Act § 410 (codified at 15 U.S.C. § 80b–3a(a)); *see also* Rules Implementing Amendments to the Investment Advisers Act of 1940, Investment Advisers Act Release No. 3221, 101 SEC Docket 1467, 37–40 (June 22, 2011) [hereinafter IAA Release No. 3221].

[20] Dodd–Frank Act § 410 (codified at 15 U.S.C. § 80b–3a(a)).

[21] *Id.*; *see also* IAA Release No. 3221, *supra* note 19, at 8–9.

[22] IAA Release No. 3221, *supra* note 19, at 8–9.

[23] 17 C.F.R. § 275.204(b)-1 (requiring private fund advisers to file Form PF with the SEC periodically).

[24] Dodd-Frank Act §§ 401–416 (incorporating the Private Fund Investment Advisers Registration Act (PFIARA) in Title IV); *Proposal for a Directive of the European Parliament and of the Council on Alternative Investment Fund Managers and Amending Directives 2004/39/EC and 2009/ … /EC*, COM (2009) 207 final (Apr. 30, 2009); *Alternative Investments*, EUROPEAN COMMISSION,

Title IV of the Dodd-Frank Act ("PFIARA Act" or "Title IV").[25] Title IV amends the IAA and establishes rules and regulations for the registration of private funds with the SEC. The SEC has rulemaking authority to implement the provisions in Title IV. All non-exempt investment advisers are required to register with the SEC by filing Form ADV.[26]

Several adviser categories are excluded from mandatory investment adviser registration. Until the enactment of Title IV in the Dodd-Frank Act of 2010, most hedge fund advisers were not subject to IAA registration requirements. Advisers with fewer than 15 clients who did not hold themselves out as advisers either to the public or to investment companies were exempt.[27] Most hedge fund advisers set up their operations and legal structure to comply with the former exemption so as to avoid registration and supervision by the SEC.[28] In 2010, however, Congress repealed the exemption by enacting Title IV of the Dodd-Frank Act and substituted instead an exemption for foreign private advisers.[29] Foreign private advisers qualify for the foreign private adviser exemption if they have fewer than 15 clients and investors in the U.S., do not have a place of business in the U.S., do not hold themselves out to the U.S. public as an investment adviser, and do not attribute more than $25 million AUM solely to U.S. clients and investors.[30]

The threshold registration requirement for private fund advisers under Title IV of the Dodd-Frank Act requires a majority of hedge fund advisers who had previously relied on the fewer than 15 clients exemption[31] to register with the SEC. Under Title IV, investment advisers that

---

http://ec.europa.eu/internal_market/investment/alternative_investments_en.htm (last visited Sept. 17, 2013).

[25] Dodd–Frank Act §§ 401–416; *see also* Wulf A. Kaal, *Hedge Fund Regulation via Basel III*, 44 VAND. J. TRANSNAT'L L. 389 (2011) (stating that prior to the enactment of Title IV, the SEC had attempted to increase regulatory oversight of the hedge fund industry on several occasions).

[26] 15 U.S.C. § 80b-3(c) (2012); SEC, Form ADV Part 1A, Uniform Application for Investment Adviser Registration and Report by Exempt Reporting Advisers, *available at* http://www.sec.gov/about/forms/formadv-part1a.pdf [hereinafter Form ADV, Part 1A].

[27] Former Investment Advisers Act § 203(b)(3) (codified at 15 U.S.C. § 80b-3(b)(3)) (2006) was repealed by the Dodd-Frank Act § 403.

[28] *See* Kaal, *supra* note 25.

[29] Dodd-Frank Act §§ 402(a), 403 (codified at 15 U.S.C. §§ 80b-2(a)(30), 80b-3(b)(3)).

[30] Dodd-Frank Act § 402(a) (codified at 15 U.S.C. § 80b-2(a)(30)).

[31] Former Investment Advisers Act § 203(b)(3) (codified at 15 U.S.C. § 80b-3(b)(3) (2006) was repealed by the Dodd-Frank Act § 403.

advise one or more private funds and manage more than $150 million AUM are required to register with the SEC.[32] Private fund advisers with less than $150 million AUM are exempt from registration.[33]

Advisers that do not provide advice with regard to exchange-listed securities and whose clients are residents of the adviser's principal place of business are exempt as local advisers.[34] Similarly, advisers with less than $25 million AUM that do not advise registered investment companies are subject to the exclusive regulatory jurisdiction of the states.[35] Advisers that only have insurance companies as clients,[36] advisers with less than $100 million AUM who provide advice to clients on investments other than private funds,[37] and venture capital fund advisers[38] are also excluded.

A person or entity that is exempt from registration as an investment adviser may still be subject to regulation under the IAA, but is not required to comply with certain provisions. Exempt persons or entities are still subject to the IAA's antifraud provisions,[39] which apply to misstatements made with the intent to defraud and negligent misstatements.

DISCLOSURE

The registration of investment advisers facilitates the collection of data and enhanced disclosure by hedge fund managers. The Dodd-Frank Act increased the disclosure requirements for registered investment advisers to address concerns over systemic risk.[40] Registered investment advisers must maintain records and any other information the SEC and the Financial Stability Oversight Council ("FSOC") may deem necessary.[41]

---

[32] 17 C.F.R. § 275.204(b)-1 (2013) (requiring private fund advisers to file Form PF with the SEC periodically).

[33] Dodd-Frank Act § 408 (codified at 15 U.S.C. § 80b-3(m)).

[34] 15 U.S.C. § 80b-3(b)(1) (2012).

[35] *Id.* § 80b-3a. Since the enactment of Investment Advisers Act § 203A, Pub. L. No. 104–290 § 303, 110 Stat. 3410, 3437 (1996) took effect in 1997, the exemption has proven more important to advisers than the local adviser exemption in § 80b-3(b)(1) (2012).

[36] *Id.* § 80b-3(b)(2).

[37] Dodd-Frank Act § 410 (codified at 15 U.S.C. § 80b-3a(a)).

[38] *Id.* § 407 (codified at 15 U.S.C. 80b-3(l)).

[39] 15 U.S.C. § 80b-6.

[40] Dodd-Frank Act § 404 (codified at 15 U.S.C. § 80b-4(b)(3)(H)) .

[41] *Id.* (codified at 15 U.S.C. § 80b-4(b)(1)(A)).

They are also required to maintain records and must provide reports with respect to, among others: trading and investment positions, the amount of AUM, trading practices, valuation policies, side letters, the use of leverage, and counterparty credit risk exposures.[42]

Investment advisers registering with the SEC are required to file Form ADV, which is also used for registration with state securities authorities. Part 1 of Form ADV requires disclosure of investment advisers' ownership, affiliations, clients, employees, business practices, and disciplinary events.[43] Part 2 of Form ADV requires investment advisers to provide a narrative brochure in plain English to prospective advisory customers. The brochure should contain the information set forth in Form ADV Part 2.[44] As the primary disclosure document for investment advisers' clients, the brochure must describe the business and educational background of the adviser's managers and key advisory personnel, the adviser's fee schedule, the types of advisory services offered, conflicts of interest, and disciplinary information.[45] Registered investment advisers must file annual reports with the SEC using Form ADV-S.

Generally speaking, the information in an investment adviser's registration statement is available to the public. Advisers must maintain certain records and make them available to the SEC for periodic inspection. The records subject to SEC inspection include accounting statements such as income statements, balance sheets and a journal of all accounts. Other records the SEC may inspect include advertisements sent to more than ten customers, records of all securities transactions, records pertaining to investment advice or order execution, as well as any notices.

The SEC amended Form ADV after the enactment of the mandatory registration requirements under Title IV of the Dodd-Frank Act. Investment advisers were required to file the amended Form ADV by March 30, 2012.[46] Both registered investment advisers and exempt reporting advisers are required to file reports with the SEC pertaining to the private funds they manage.[47] The version of Form ADV that was in effect on March 30, 2012, increased the mandated disclosures by adding several

---

42 *Id.* (codified at 15 U.S.C. § 80b-4(b)(3)(H)).

43 Form ADV Part 1A, *supra* note 26.

44 17 C.F.R. § 275.204–3 (2013).

45 SEC, Form ADV Part 2, Uniform Requirements for the Investment Adviser *Brochure* and *Brochure Supplements*, *available at* http://www.sec.gov/about/forms/formadv-part2.pdf. [hereinafter Form ADV Part 2].

46 17 C.F.R. 275.203A-5(b) (2013); *see also* IAA Release No. 3221, *supra* note 19, at 93.

47 Form ADV Part 1A, *supra* note 26, Item 2.B.

disclosure items, including the number of employees[48] registered as representatives of broker dealers, employees performing advisory functions, employees registered with state authorities as investment adviser representatives, employees working as insurance agents,[49] and non-employees soliciting advisory clients on the adviser's behalf.[50] Advisers must also disclose the fund's investment strategy, its gross asset value, the percentage of AUM attributable to each client type,[51] the fund's structure and ownership, the fund's use of consultants and other gatekeepers, and the scope of services provided.[52] Finally, Form ADV requires disclosure of clients' assets in custody and the number of persons who are acting as qualified custodians for clients in connection with advisory services.[53] To prevent fraud or mistakes, any irregularities must be disclosed in Form ADV.[54] Investment advisers must also indicate the total number of clients' cash, bank accounts or securities subject to adviser or related person custody and the total U.S. dollar amount held in custody.

To avoid potential conflicts of interest between different types of businesses and services, investment advisers must disclose compensation given or received for client referrals,[55] related persons status of brokers and dealers,[56] and soft dollar benefits, i.e., research or other products and services received in connection with client transactions.[57] Investment advisers also have to disclose their transactions[58] and any services provided other than investment advice to advisory clients,[59] including the types of business activity,[60] and if one of those businesses is primary to the adviser.[61]

---

48 *Id.* Item 5.A.

49 *Id.* Item 5.B.

50 *Id.* Item 5.

51 Form ADV Part 1A, *supra* note 26.

52 *Id.* Item 5.G.

53 *Id.* Item 9.D.

54 *Id.* Item 9.C.

55 *Id.* Items 8.H, 8.I, 8.C.(3); Items 8.E, 8.D; Items 8.F, 8.G.(2); s*ee also* IAA Release No. 3221, *supra* note 19, at 77.

56 Form ADV Part 1A*, supra* note 26, Items 8.D, 8.F.

57 *Id.* Item 8.G.

58 *Id.* Item 8.A; *see also* IAA Release No. 3221, *supra* note 19, at 77–78.

59 Form ADV Part 1A, Item 6.B.(3) (asking the adviser to describe other products and services).

60 *Id.* Item 6.A.

61 *Id.* Item 6.B.(1), (2).

Information about voting on portfolio securities must be available to advisory clients; this requires registered investment advisers to adopt proxy policies and procedures[62] and inform advisory clients about advisers' proxy voting policies and procedures. Upon request, investment advisers must provide clients with a copy of the proxy voting policies and procedures, including information regarding how advisory clients may obtain information about the adviser's proxy voting. Similarly, managers of investment companies must disclose their voting of portfolio securities.

In addition to the registration and disclosure requirements included in Form ADV, Title IV of the Dodd-Frank Act also increased the periodic reporting requirements for registered investment advisers.[63] Form PF was enacted in October 2011[64] to improve investigations and examinations by the SEC and the Commodity Futures Trading Commission ("CFTC") and to facilitate the FSOC's[65] monitoring of systemic risk in U.S. financial markets.[66] Unlike Form ADV, Form PF filings are confidential and not publicly available.

Investment advisers, commodity pool operators, and commodity trading advisers that manage at least $150 million AUM and are registered with the SEC must file Form PF periodically. Private funds with less than $150 million AUM, however, are not required to file Form PF. The frequency of Form PF filings is dictated by the size of the investment adviser's RAUM. Large private fund advisers, defined as investment advisers with at least $1.5 billion RAUM attributable to hedge funds,[67]

---

[62] 17 C.F.R. § 275.206(4)-6 (2013).

[63] Dodd-Frank Act, Pub. L. No. 111–203, § 404, 124 Stat. 1376, 1571 (2010) (codified at 15 U.S.C. § 80b-4).

[64] 17 C.F.R. § 275.204(b)-1 (2013).

[65] Dodd-Frank Act § 112(d)(1) (codified at 12 U.S.C. § 5322(d)(1)) (authorizing the FSOC to collect information to support its functions).

[66] Dodd-Frank Act § 112(a)(1) (codified at 12 U.S.C. § 5322(a)(1)). ("The purposes of the Council are – (A) to identify risks to the financial stability of the United States that could arise from the material financial distress or failure, or ongoing activities, of large, interconnected bank holding companies or nonbank financial companies, or that could arise outside the financial services marketplace; (B) to promote market discipline, by eliminating expectations on the part of shareholders, creditors, and counterparties of such companies that the Government will shield them from losses in the event of failure; and (C) to respond to emerging threats to the stability of the United States financial system").

[67] SEC, Form PF, Reporting Form for Investment Advisers to Private Funds and Certain Commodity Pool Operators and Commodity Trading Advisors,

must update Form PF filings on a quarterly basis.[68] Investment advisers with less than $1.5 billion RAUM only have to file Form PF on an annual basis.[69] The quarterly reporting for large private fund advisers is intended to provide the FSOC with timely data to identify emerging trends in systemic risk.

Form PF disclosures are unprecedented in the private fund industry and require disclosures pertaining to the investment adviser, the funds it manages, and individual investors.[70] Other significant Form PF disclosures include risks metrics, credit exposure, positions, the investment adviser's strategies, performance and changes in performance, the products used by the investment adviser, and financing information, among others.[71]

Form PF also requires certain disclosures pertaining to the funds managed by the investment adviser. More specifically, Form PF requires investment advisers to list the Net Asset Value ("NAV") by hedge fund strategy.[72] The reporting fund's greatest net counterparty credit exposure is another important disclosure item for investment advisers.[73] This includes disclosure of information pertaining to the dollar amount owed to each creditor and the name of the creditor,[74] collateral and credit support,[75] and the effect of changes in market factors on the long and short components of the portfolio as a percentage of NAV.[76] Form PF also mandates the disclosure of the percentage of the reporting fund's NAV managed by using computer-driven trading algorithms.[77]

To help the SEC understand the liquidity of the reporting fund's portfolios, Form PF requires the investment adviser to disclose the reporting fund's positions and how long it would take to liquidate them.[78] Similarly, to enable the SEC to understand the exposure of the advised

---

General Instructions, instruction 3, sec. 2a, *available at* http://www.sec.gov/about/forms/formpf.pdf [hereinafter Form PF].

68 *Id.* instruction 9 ("[Large hedge fund advisers] must file a quarterly update that updates the answers to all Items in this Form PF relating to the hedge funds … .")

69 *Id.* instruction 1.

70 Form PF, *supra* note 67, secs. 1a, 2; 17 C.F.R. § 279.9 (2013).

71 Form PF, *supra* note 67, secs. 1b, 1c, 2a, 2b, 3, 4.

72 *Id.* sec. 1c, item B.20.

73 *Id.* sec. 1c, items B.22–23.

74 *Id.* sec. 2b, item D.47.

75 *Id.* sec. 2b, item B.36.

76 *Id.* sec. 2b, item C.42.

77 *Id.* sec. 1c, item B.21.

78 *Id.* sec. 2b, item B.32.

hedge funds and their assets, Form PF requires disclosure of the investment adviser's exposure of long and short positions[79] and the value of turnover by asset class.[80] Form PF requires investment advisers to disclose the reporting fund's restrictions of investor redemptions and withdrawals[81] and investors' liquidity, measured by time period and percentage of NAV locked.[82] Moreover, disclosures are required for the aggregate value of all derivative positions for each advised fund[83] and the value of the advised funds' borrowings and the types of creditors.[84] Finally, Form PF mandates the disclosure of clearing mechanisms.[85]

BLUE SKY LAWS

In 1996, with the enactment of the National Securities Markets Improvement Act ("NSMIA"), Congress decided that the SEC should regulate larger investment advisers while states would oversee smaller investment advisers. The distinction between larger and smaller investment advisers manifests itself in the NSMIA's threshold requirement of $25 million in AUM for state regulation. The Dodd-Frank Act mandates state oversight for investment advisers with up to $100 million AUM. However, should the $100 million AUM threshold result in an adviser's registration with 15 or more states, the adviser is allowed to register directly with the SEC.[86] Investment advisers that manage less than $25 million AUM can register with the SEC if they otherwise would have to be registered in 15 or more states.[87] Newly formed investment advisers qualify for federal registration if they reasonably expect to satisfy the 30-state test within 90 days of registering with the SEC. Regardless of the amount of AUM, investment advisers that provide investment advice exclusively through the Internet may register with the SEC.[88] Investment advisers that are

---

79 *Id.* sec. 1c, items B.22–23, 30.

80 *Id.* sec. 1c, item B.27.

81 *Id.* sec. 2b, item E.49.

82 *Id.* sec. 2b, item E.50.

83 *Id.* sec. 2b, item D.45.

84 *Id.* sec. 2b, item D.43.

85 *Id.* sec. 1c, item A.24.

86 15 U.S.C. § 80b-3a(a)(2)(A) (2012) (as amended by the Dodd-Frank Act, Pub. L. No. 111–203, § 410, 124 Stat. 1376, 1576) (2010).

87 17 C.F.R. § 275.203A-2 (2013).

88 *Id.* at § 275.203A-2(e).

exempt from federal registration may still be subject to disclosure and recordkeeping requirements.[89]

QUALIFIED CLIENTS

The Dodd-Frank Act also changed the IAA with regard to qualified client standards. The SEC has the authority to exempt any person or transaction from IAA requirements pertaining to investment advisory contracts with clients, provided the SEC determines that the person does not require the protections of the IAA. The Dodd-Frank Act added an inflation-based adjustment to the qualified client standard for exemption under the IAA.[90] If the SEC uses a net asset threshold or any other dollar-amount test to determine the qualified client standard for exemption under the IAA, the SEC is required to adjust the dollar-amount test for the effects of inflation within one year after enactment and every five years thereafter.[91]

Because persons who meet the net-worth test by virtue of including the value of their primary residence are less likely to be able to bear the risk of performance fee arrangements, the SEC excludes the value of a person's primary residence and related debts from the net-worth test.[92] The SEC reasoned that the value of a residence is only limitedly connected to a person's experience in finance and investments and the risks of performance fee arrangements. SEC estimates suggest that with the exclusion of the primary residence from the net-worth test, roughly 1.3 million households were excluded from qualifying under the revised net-worth test.[93] The net-worth test also excludes the amount of a person's debt secured by his or her primary residence, provided the value of the debt is not greater than the primary residence's market value.[94] If the debt exceeds the value of the primary residence, it can be included as a liability in the net-worth calculation.

---

[89] Dodd-Frank Act § 408 (codified at 15 U.S.C. § 80b-3(m)(2)) (giving the SEC authority to require even exempted advisers to keep records and make reports as it deems necessary).

[90] Dodd-Frank Act § 418 (codified at 15 U.S.C. § 80b-5(e)).

[91] *Id.*

[92] 17 C.F.R. § 275.205–3 (2013); Investment Adviser Performance Compensation, Investment Advisers Act Release No. 3372, 103 SEC Docket 172, 3 (Feb. 15, 2012) [hereinafter IAA Release No. 3372].

[93] IAA Release No. 3372, *supra* note 92, at 9.

[94] 17 C.F.R. § 275.205–3(d)(1)(A)(2).

CUSTODY OF CLIENT ASSETS

Custody of client assets plays an important role in protecting the clients of investment advisers. The SEC adopted rules to increase the standards for custodial accounts in 2009, before the enactment of the Dodd-Frank Act.[95] In 2010, in an effort to address concerns over theft and to lower clients' exposure to the risks of Ponzi schemes, the Dodd-Frank Act amended the IAA, heightening custodial practices by requiring safeguards for client assets and the use of independent accountants to verify assets.[96] The custodian requirements under the Dodd-Frank Act curtail investment advisers' ability to pay existing investors with the funds invested by new investors. Custodians can accept client instructions to buy or sell securities but cannot remit the sales proceeds to the investment adviser or to third parties.

INTERNET RELATED UPDATES

Providing investment advice in the age of the Internet presents regulatory challenges. Unregistered persons who provide investment advice via Internet chat rooms and websites may be required to register as an investment adviser with the SEC. Registration is not required if the person provides impersonal investment advice.[97] The SEC has provided guidance on how to avoid registration requirements under the IAA when providing advice via the Internet.[98] For instance, the provider of a bulletin board is exempt from registration if he or she provides a mere "passive" electronic bulletin board by posting information about securities on the Internet. In order to remain exempt from registration as an investment adviser under the IAA, the provider of a "passive" electronic bulletin board cannot give advice regarding the merits of any particular

---

[95] Custody of Funds or Securities of Clients by Investment Advisers, Investment Advisers Act Release No. 2968, 97 SEC Docket 1849 (Dec. 30, 2009) (amending 17 C.F.R. § 275.206(4)-2).

[96] Dodd-Frank Act, Pub. L. No. 111–203, § 411, 124 Stat. 1376, 1577 (2010) (codified at 15 U.S.C. § 80b-18b) (2012).

[97] SEC v. Park, 99 F. Supp. 2d 889, 898 (N.D. Ill 2000); Lowe v. SEC, 472 U.S. 181, 207–8 (1985).

[98] Angel Capital Electronic Network, SEC No-Action Letter, 1996 WL 636094 (Oct. 25, 1996); Internet Capital Corp., SEC No-Action Letter, 1998 WL 9357 (Jan. 13, 1998); Progressive Technology Inc., SEC No-Action Letter, 2000 WL 1508655 (Oct. 11, 2000).

trade and he or she cannot be involved in the purchase of securities or sale negotiations.

PROHIBITED PRACTICES

The IAA prohibits fraudulent, deceptive, or manipulative acts or practices,[99] as defined in SEC rules,[100] as well as any conduct that "operates as a fraud or deceit upon any client or prospective client."[101] Fraudulent practices include, among others, undisclosed conflicts of interest, excessive trading, splitting fees with unregistered persons, misleading advertising,[102] and scalping.

Investment advisers cannot commingle clients' funds and are required to keep accurate records and separate accounts. Investment advisers who are holding securities or funds must hold them in custodial accounts on behalf of the clients. Independent public accountants can inspect and certify these custodial accounts. Similarly, because investment advisers are subject to a duty to obtain the best execution for customer orders,[103] investment advisers ought to periodically evaluate the executions on behalf of their clients.

Mandatory ethics codes, disclosures and client consents can curtail fraudulent practices. An investment adviser must disclose and obtain a client's consent before acting as a principal in a transaction with a client.[104] Investment advisers are required to supervise their personnel as well as to adopt and enforce codes of ethics for supervised staff.[105] If the investment adviser's code of ethics has been violated, the adviser must report the incident to the SEC. The ethics code must include a provision that mandates reporting of any code violation to designated persons.

Reacting to several scandals in the mutual fund industry, and in an effort to curb violations of the IAA, the SEC has mandated the

---

99 15 U.S.C. § 80b-6(4).

100 17 C.F.R. pt. 275.

101 15 U.S.C. § 80b-6(2).

102 17 C.F.R. § 275.206(4)-1.

103 *See, e.g.*, Portfolio Advisory Servs., Investment Advisers Act Release No. 2038, 77 SEC Docket 2759 (June 20, 2002), *available at* http://www.sec.gov/litigation/admin/ia-2038.htm; Duties of Brokers, Dealers, and Investment Advisors, Investment Advisers Act Release No. 3558, Exchange Act Release No. 69013, 2013 WL 771910 (Mar. 1, 2013); Securities; Brokerage and Research Services, Exchange Act Release No. 23170, 51 Fed. Reg. 16004 (Apr. 23, 1986).

104 15 U.S.C. § 80b-6(3).

105 *Id.* § 275.204a-1.

implementation of written policies and procedures for investment advisers,[106] among other compliance measures. Registered investment advisers must designate a chief compliance officer. The chief compliance officer should have sufficient knowledge of IAA obligations and adequate authority to develop and enforce appropriate policies and procedures. These policies and procedures, at a minimum, should address the following investment management processes: (i) creation and maintenance of required records; (ii) valuation of client assets; (iii) assessment of fees; (iv) safeguarding of client assets; (v) business continuity plans; (vii) allocation of investment opportunities; (viii) assessment and compliance with clients' investment objectives and restrictions; (ix) best execution and soft dollar arrangements, among other trading arrangements; (x) proprietary trading of the investment adviser and personal trading activities of its employees; (xi) marketing services; and (xii) safeguards for client privacy protection. To ensure the adequacy and effectiveness of their policies, registered investment advisers must review their policies and procedures annually.

The enforcement of a violation of prohibited transactions under the IAA is limited. In *Transamerica Mortgage Advisors, Inc. v. Lewis*,[107] the Supreme Court determined that a violation of the IAA's prohibited transactions provision[108] does not allow for implied private rights of action. Accordingly, the enforcement of the IAA's prohibited transactions provision is relegated to injunctive relief, administrative sanctions and criminal prosecution.

FEES

The IAA restricts fee arrangements in advisory contracts.[109] It also prohibits performance-based compensation if the adviser's fee is linked to the performance of the client's account.[110] The IAA does, however, allow investment advisers to tie their compensation to the average value of the client's assets.[111]

---

106 *Id.* § 275.206(4)-7.
107 Transamerica Mortg. Advisors, Inc. v. Lewis, 444 U.S. 11 (1979).
108 *Id.* at 24.
109 15 U.S.C. § 80b-5 (2012).
110 *Id.* § 80b-5(a)(1).
111 *Id.* § 80b-5(b)(1).

The SEC limits the referral fees that investment advisers pay to third parties.[112] Advisers may pay referral fees provided the referral fee recipients are bona fide persons under securities laws, the fees have been disclosed to the investment adviser's clients, and the fees are paid in accordance with a written agreement.[113] Similarly, client referrals in exchange for an increased share of an investment adviser's advisory and order execution business have to be disclosed to the investment adviser's clients, especially if such arrangements are more expensive in comparison with other custody/brokerage options and could interfere with the investments adviser's best execution of client orders.

---

[112] 17 C.F.R. § 275.206(4)-3 (2013).

[113] *Id.*

9. Corporate governance and the regulation of mergers and acquisitions

Jerry W. Markham and Rigers Gjyshi

CORPORATE GOVERNANCE

Introduction

The first part of the chapter addresses provisions in state and federal securities laws that regulate corporate governance. This includes restrictions on boards of directors and executive managers. The second part addresses requirements in state and federal securities laws governing mergers and acquisitions of corporations. It focuses on a discussion of the Williams Act, which is the federal law (along with applicable SEC regulations) that regulates corporate takeovers through tender offers.

Corporate Governance—Background and History

An important element of stock market regulation involves "corporate governance," a term used for describing management structures and procedures that intended to assure that managers do not abuse their positions. Corporate governance is a broad term that encompasses everything involving the management of a corporation from director elections and meetings to the preparation of financial statements.[1] As this chapter describes, corporate governance is carried out by statute, rules and case law at both the state and federal levels. Managers may also

---

[1] Investopedia defines corporate governance as follows: "The system of rules, practices and processes by which a company is directed and controlled. Corporate governance essentially involves balancing the interests of the many stakeholders in a company—these include its shareholders, management, customers, suppliers, financiers, government and the community. Since corporate governance also provides the framework for attaining a company's objectives, it encompasses practically every sphere of management, from action plans and internal controls to performance measurement and corporate disclosure." http://www.investopedia.com/terms/c/corporategovernance.asp., accessed on June 11, 2013.

employ "best practices," which are not required by statute but are deemed desirable.[2]

Corporate governance has a long history that can be traced back to the trading companies of the sixteenth century. The East India Co., for example, was governed by stockholder's meetings and by a "court of directors." Adam Smith raised concerns with the governance of such corporations in 1776, noting that company directors "being the managers rather of other people's money than their own, it cannot well be expected, that they should watch over it with the same anxious vigilance with which the partners in a private copartnery frequently watch over their own," and that "negligence and profusion, therefore, must prevail, more or less, in the management of the affairs of such a company.[3]

In England, and elsewhere, the government did not much interfere in corporate affairs of those early corporations. However, after the Great South Sea Bubble in 1720,[4] Parliament passed a "bubble act" that required a Crown charter in order for a business to gain corporate status.[5] The bubble act was imposed on the American colonies in 1740, raising issues over what government body had power to issue charters, i.e., the Royal governor or the legislative assemblies.[6] The result was that there were few business corporations in the colonies. Rather, most charters were issued to schools, such as Harvard and Yale, and to public projects, like fountain societies. However, the American Revolution freed the new states of these charter restrictions and many corporations were formed and flourished, especially banks.[7]

---

[2] *See* Brehm v. Eisner (In re Walt Disney Co. Derivative Litig.), 906 A.2d 27 (Del. Sup. 2006) (describing best practices and their legal status).

[3] Adam Smith, An Inquiry Into the Nature and Causes of the Wealth of Nations 800 (1776).

[4] *See* I Jerry W. Markham, A Financial History of the United States, From Christopher Columbus to the Robber Barons (1492–1900) 97–99 (2002) (describing that bubble).

[5] Essay: *Investor Power & Liquidity: Corporations, Capital Markets and the Industrialization of America*, 5 J. Small & Emerging Bus. L. 345, 360–362 (2001).

[6] *See* Correspondence: *The Nature of Litigation in Early New England*, 111 Yale L.J. 1881, 1887 (2002) (describing that event).

[7] I Jerry W. Markham, A Financial History of the United States, From Christopher Columbus to the Robber Barons (1492–1900) 105–107 (2002).

State Corporate Law Statutes

Historically, corporate governance issues was left to the states until the 1930s when the federal securities laws were enacted.[8] The states initially exercised that power through a requirement that allowed corporations to operate only through a charter granted by the state's legislature. Those charters were sometimes difficult to obtain and usually limited the powers of the corporation that could be used to carry out its carefully defined business.[9] Those charters were restrictive, limiting the activities of the corporation and even its size.[10] That system led to much corruption and also limited the growth of business. As a result, the states switched to general incorporation laws that allowed anyone to freely obtain a corporate charter from the state's Secretary of State, and corporations were given the power to engage in any lawful business, freeing them of the restrictions found in the earlier legislative charters.[11]

A competition arose among the states to attract corporate charters, which were a popular source of tax revenue. New Jersey won that competition, initially, through a lenient corporate law that, among other things, allowed corporations to own other corporations. However, then Governor Woodrow Wilson achieved a repeal of that legislation.[12] Delaware took over as the leader in corporate charters through a pledge to make its laws as favorable as possible for corporations.[13]

---

[8] There are exceptions to that rule. For example, the federal government has itself chartered various corporations, starting with Alexander Hamilton's Bank of the United States. *See* McCulloch v. Maryland, 17 U.S. 316 (1819). More recently, Fannie Mae and Freddie Mac were given federal corporate charters and sold stock to their shareholders, but they are now wards of the federal government.

[9] Acts outside the corporate charter were considered to be *ultra vires* and void. *See* Wiswall v. Greenville and Raleigh Plank Road Co., 56 N.C. 183 (Sup. 1857).

[10] For a description of those limitations, see Louis K. Liggett Co. v. Lee, 288 U.S. 517, 548–557 (1933) (Brandeis J., dissenting).

[11] *See* Susan Pace Hamill, *From Special Privilege to General Utility: A Continuation of Willard Hurst's Study of Corporations*, 49 Am. U. L. Rev. 81 (1999) (describing that history).

[12] H.C.F. Bell, Woodrow Wilson and the People 91 (1945).

[13] Thomas Lee Hazen & Jerry W. Markham, Corporations and Other Business Organizations, Cases and Materials, 10–11 (3d ed. 2009).

As a result, many large corporations chose to charter in Delaware even though their principal place of business was located elsewhere.[14] Moreover, even though a corporation might be operating in several states the law of the state of incorporation would generally govern the application of those activities.[15] Consequently, the choice of state law for incorporation was, and is, important, at least to large corporations.

Many large and small companies, nevertheless, charter in the state where they are located. A competing uniform corporate statute, the Model Business Corporation Act and its subsequent revision ("RMBCA"), was created to offer a uniform statute that would compete with the Delaware corporate law. Numerous states have adopted the RMBCA.[16] The RMBCA tracks the Delaware Act in many ways. However, the experience and competency of the Delaware courts on corporate governance issues drives much of the jurisprudence under both statutes.

The classic model of corporate governance under the Delaware statute, the RMBCA and other statutory schemes was that a board of directors elected by the shareholders would set company policy.[17] The board also selects the officers who will run the day-to-day operations of the corporation. This structure separates control from ownership.[18] This means that the directors will control the operations of the corporation, rather than its owners, i.e., the stockholders. Directors thus have a special status. They are supposed to operate independently of the shareholders, even though the shareholders elect them and own the company.

The state corporation statutes further regulate many aspects of corporate governance, such as notice requirements for corporate board

---

[14] Delaware continues to attract large corporations as the place for obtaining their charters, *Id.* at 11.

[15] The "internal affairs doctrine" is: "[A] conflict of laws principle which recognizes that only one State should have the authority to regulate a corporation's internal affairs—matters peculiar to the relationships among or between the corporation and its current officers, directors, and shareholders—because otherwise a corporation could be faced with conflicting demands." Atherton v. FDIC, 519 U.S. 213, 224 (1997) (citation omitted).

[16] *See* James D. Cox & Thomas Lee Hazen, Cox & Hazen on Corporations § 2.02 (2d ed. 2003) (describing development of the RMBCA).

[17] *See* Charlestown Boot & Shoe Co. v. Dunsmore, 60 N.H. 85 (1880) (describing this structure).

[18] This separation of ownership and control has long raised concerns that managers will manage for their own benefit, rather than for the benefit of shareholders. *See* Adolf Berle & Gardiner Means, The Modern Corporation and Private Property (1932) (making the argument for the possibility of such abuse).

meetings, quorum requirements for those meetings, provisions for voting by shareholders and shareholder meetings. The theme in these housekeeping provisions is to seek corporate decisions by collegial action at a duly called meeting where matters to be voted on can be openly discussed in order to reach a more informed decision than would be expected from a decision taken by a single executive.

These state corporate statutes often operate by default, allowing their requirements to be varied to some extent by the corporate charter or by-laws. For example, the statute may allow a higher quorum requirement to be set by the by-laws, but may restrict how much the statutory quorum requirement can be reduced in the by-laws.[19] These statutes also usually allow action to be taken without an actual meeting if there is unanimity on the matter. Each of these variations is intended to further the goal of collegial decision-making. For example, a meeting is not required where there is unanimity because the body as a whole has collegially agreed to the decision.[20]

Another governance mechanism regulated by the state of incorporation is that of proxy votes by shareholders. This is the equivalent of an absentee ballot in a political contest. Among other things, state laws will govern the timing of proxy votes, the assignment of a proxy and their fairness.[21] There have been a number of cases in the Delaware courts that have considered whether proxy voting was conducted properly. In one case, for example, plaintiffs claimed that the head of Hewlett-Packard improperly suborned proxies from one of the company's bank trust department, but the Delaware Supreme Court rejected that claim.[22]

Fiduciary Duties

The states also impose fiduciary duties on officers and directors that may or may not be found in the corporate law statute. This is an equitable concept that has been strongly endorsed by the chancery courts of Delaware, which hear cases under the Delaware corporate statute. Other state courts have followed the lead of the Delaware courts in imposing these fiduciary duties.

The concept of fiduciary duties was borrowed from the law of trusts and estates and imposes special obligations on trustees who manage the money of others. Often, that management is for the benefit of persons

---

19 *See* Delaware General Corporation Law § 141.
20 *See* RMBCA § 8.21.
21 *See* RMBCA § 7.22.
22 Hewlett v. Hewlett-Packard Co., 2002 WL 818091 (Del. Ch. 2002).

who are incapable of managing their own affairs, such as minors, or who are not financially sophisticated. Fiduciary duties basically require the trustee to avoid undue risks in managing the funds of others.

The fiduciary relationship imposes special duties and obligations on a trustee that are not found in arms-length contractual relationships.[23] The concept of a trust relationship is, however, an imperfect model for corporate managers who, to be sure are managing other peoples' money, but they are also working for a limited liability company that has risk taking as its goal, sometimes even extreme risks.

In recognition of the difference in management goals between a trust and a corporation, the Delaware courts have crafted what it calls the "business judgment rule." That rule posits that, as long as fiduciary duties are not breached, the courts will not second-guess the business judgment of the officers and directors of a corporation, even if their decisions turn out badly.[24] Still, the scope of the fiduciary duties owed by officers and directors under state law is uncertain.

One fiduciary duty imposed on officers and directors is that of "loyalty." This means that an officer or director should not have a conflict of interest with the corporation. The duty of loyalty also means that an officer or director should not compete with, or seize an opportunity from, the corporation, except under certain permitted conditions.[25]

The imposition of such a duty on its face does not appear controversial, but a closer inspection reveals an inherent conflict of interest that the duty of loyalty fails to address, i.e., the terms of the officers' compensation. The board of directors sets the terms of the officers' compensation, not the shareholders. The board of directors usually is effectively controlled by the officers even though its members are elected by the shareholders. This control is achieved because the chief executive officer ("CEO") will effectively control the selection of the director nominated for election. The result has been large, sometimes incredibly large, pay packets given out to the top officers of public companies.[26]

---

[23] Jerry W. Markham, *Fiduciary Duties Under the Commodity Exchange Act*, 68 Notre Dame L. Rev. 199, 210 (1992).

[24] *See* In re Caremark International, Inc. Derivative Litigation, 698 A.2d 959, 967–968 (Del. Ch. 1996) (describing the business judgment rule).

[25] *See* Guth v. Loft, Inc., 5 A.2d 503 (Del. 1939) (breach of the duty of loyalty).

[26] *See* Jerry W. Markham, *Regulating Excessive Executive Compensation—Why Bother?*, 2 Md. J. of Bus. & Tech. L 277, 284–287, 304 (2007) (describing concerns over those payments).

The courts, for the most part, have refused to hold that excessive compensation paid to executives breaches a fiduciary duty.[27] The Supreme Court did hold during the Great Depression that, at some point, excessive corporate compensation could constitute a waste of corporate assets in breach of the manager's fiduciary duties.[28] However, the court offered no guidelines on how such a determination could be made. The case was settled on remand with few changes, and a state court threw out a companion case because the court had no means of determining whether the compensation was excessive.

More recently, a lawsuit brought by shareholders of the Walt Disney Co. claimed a breach of fiduciary duties when the Disney board of directors authorized an incredible $130 million severance package for a Disney executive, Michael Ovitz. Although Ovitz had served only fourteen unproductive months at Disney before being fired, the Delaware Supreme Court could find no breach of fiduciary duty.[29]

Another fiduciary duty is that of "care," which means that directors should fully inform themselves before taking a corporate decision. However, after some overreaching by the Delaware Supreme Court,[30] the Delaware legislature enacted legislation that allows shareholders to waive this duty, but not the duty of loyalty.[31] Most Delaware corporations adopted such waivers. Several other states also allowed duty of care waivers.[32]

Still another fiduciary duty that has crept into Delaware law is that of "good faith," which is yet, still ill defined. Plaintiffs have tried to use this amorphous concept as a work around where there is a waiver of the duty of care. The Delaware Supreme Court has given mixed signals on whether that effort will be successful.[33]

---

27 *Id.* at 280–284.

28 Rogers v. Hill, 289 U.S. 582 (1933).

29 Brehm v. Eisner (In re Walt Disney Co. Derivative Litig.), 906 A.2d 27 (Del. Sup. 2006).

30 Smith v. Van Gorkom, 488 A.2d 858 (Del. 1985).

31 *See* Delaware General Corporation Law § 1o2(b)(7).

32 Thomas Lee Hazen & Jerry W. Markham, Corporations and Other Business Organizations, Cases and Materials, 293–294 (3d ed. 2009).

33 Emerald Partners v. Berlin, 787 A.2d 85 (Del. 2001).

Limited Liability Companies

This classic model of corporate governance has given way in recent years to the limited liability company ("LLC"), which essentially is an incorporated partnership with limited liability.[34] An LLC need not operate through a board of directors. Instead, the owners are allowed to structure their governance mechanism in any way they deem appropriate through an "operating agreement," which functions much like a general partnership agreement, but allows limited liability for the LLC's owners.[35] Still, the decision-making members of the LLC may owe some fiduciary duties to other participants.[36]

Muddling this picture further are limited partnerships that have a general partner that actively manages the business, but also have limited partners that are passive investors.[37] The limited partners have limited liability, but the general partner does not.[38] This form of organization is much preferred by hedge funds that do not want their passive investors to have any say in management.

The Securities Act of 1933

The federal securities laws seek to influence corporate governance in several ways. Principal among them is the concept of "full disclosure."[39] This concept posits that full disclosure of all material information will shame officers and directors into not engaging in activities that might be

---

[34] *See* Elf Atochem North America, Inc. v. Jaffari, 727 A.2d 286 (Del. 1999) (describing the development of the Revised Uniform Limited Partnership Act and the introduction of LLC's).

[35] *See* Liberman v. Wyoming.com LLC, 11 P.3d 353 (Wyo. 2000) (describing role of operating agreements).

[36] *See* Carson v. Lynch Multimedia Corp., 123 F.Supp.2d 1254 (D. Kan. 2000) (fiduciary duties apply even though LLC operating agreement did not provide for such duties).

[37] *See* James D. Cox & Thomas Lee Hazen, Cox & Hazen on Corporations § 1.09 (2d ed. 2003) (describing operations of limited partnerships).

[38] The general partner can effectively achieve limited liability by incorporating itself and acting as a general partner only in that corporate capacity. Frigidaire Sales Corp. v. Union Properties, Inc., 562 P.2d 244 (Wash. 1977).

[39] The Investment Company Act, however, broadly regulates the corporate governance and structure of investment companies. 15 U.S.C. § 80a-1 *et seq.*

inimical to the interests of shareholders.[40] Full disclosure begins with an initial public offering ("IPO") that is governed by the terms of the 1933 Act.[41] As Chapter 3 details, the issuer of the IPO must file a registration statement with the SEC disclosing all material information about the company and the shares being sold.[42] This will include financial statements, such as a balance sheet and income statement for present and prior years.[43]

Officers and directors signing the registration statement (and underwriters that do not use due diligence in vetting the registration statement) may be held personally liable for false information contained in the registration statement and prospectus.[44] There are, however, a number of defenses that may be raised in response to such claims. For example, officers and directors may rely on experts to prepare portions of the registration statement, including accountants.[45] However, that reliance will not be recognized if the officer, director or underwriter was aware that the accounting report was inaccurate.[46]

The registration statement must be audited by a certified public accountant ("CPA"), which may be held liable if the audit is conducted incorrectly.[47] This audit requirement requires management to conduct its corporate governance in a manner that assures accountability to shareholders. This means detailed records of all material transactions must be maintained and all losses and profits must be fully disclosed before the offering.

Financial Reporting Under the Securities and Exchange Act of 1934

After the IPO, the now public company must continue to make timely public disclosures of its finances. As described in Chapter 3, that requirement is imposed by SEC rules adopted under the 1934 Act.[48]

---

40 Supreme Court Justice Louis D. Brandeis famously stated that "[p]ublicity is justly commended as a remedy for social and industrial diseases. Sunlight is said to be the best of disinfectants; electric light the most efficient policeman."

41 15 U.S.C. § 77a *et seq*.

42 15 U.S.C. § 77e.

43 *See* Jones v. Securities and Exchange Commission, 298 U.S. 1. (1936) (describing registration process).

44 15 U.S.C. §§ 77k & 77l.

45 In re Software Toolworks Inc. v. PaineWebber Inc., 50 F.3d 625 (9th Cir. 1994).

46 Escott v. BarChris, Construction Corp., 283 F.Supp. 643 (S.D.N.Y. 1968).

47 Gustafson v. Alloyd Co., 513 U.S. 561, 581 (1995).

48 15 U.S.C. § 78 m.

Issuers are required to file quarterly financial reports on SEC Form 10-Q,[49] an annual audited financial report on SEC Form 10-K,[50] and a report on special events as they occur on SEC Form 8-K.[51] Liability will lie for officers and directors signing these reports. Indeed, after a series of accounting scandals at the Enron Corp. and others, Congress included in the Sarbanes-Oxley Act of 2002 a provision that requires the chief executive officer and chief financial officer to sign and attest that their company's financial reports are accurate. Those signers will be held liable if that statement is false.[52] Another controversial provision in the Sarbanes-Oxley Act requires an attestation that the company's internal systems and controls are sufficient to assure accurate financial reports. The issuer's auditor must also opine on their effectiveness.[53]

Among other things that must be included, in addition to financial statements, is management discussion and analysis ("MDA"), which is a statement from the senior manager of the issuer describing that person's views on the company's operation over the prior year, unusual events affecting the company and its prospects for the future.[54]

Compensation Disclosures

The federal securities laws seek to curb excessive officer compensation by requiring full disclosure of the total compensation of top officers, including prerequisites ("perks"). This disclosure starts with the IPO registration statement and carries over into the periodic reports required by SEC rules under the 1934 Act. In 1992, the SEC substantially increased its executive compensation disclosure requirements and it did so again in 2006.[55] Among other things, management's Management

---

49 17 C.F.R. § 240.13a-13.

50 17 C.F.R. § 240.13a-1.

51 17 C.F.R. § 240.13a-11.

52 *See* Jerry W. Markham, A Financial History of Modern U.S. Corporate Scandals: From Enron to Reform 455–56 (2005) (describing this provision).

53 *See* Horizon Asset Mgmt. v. H&R Block, Inc., 580 F.3d 755, 765–766 (8th Cir. 2009) (describing this requirement).

54 Slayton v. Am. Express Co., 604 F.3d 758, 767 (2d Cir. 2010).

55 *See* Jerry W. Markham, A Financial History of the United States, From Enron Era Scandals to the Subprime Crisis (2004–2006) 101–103 (2011) (describing those changes).

Compensation and Discussion Analysis must describe the structure and objectives of the company's compensation programs.[56]

The Dodd-Frank Wall Street Reform and Consumer Protection Act of 2010 ("Dodd-Frank") also requires disclosure of the payments made to managers and an analysis of how executive compensation relates to the performance of the company.[57] Transactions that are used by management to hedge their company stock against a decline must also be disclosed.[58]

It was thought that such disclosures would embarrass executives from seeking compensation that might be deemed excessive in the press. In fact, those disclosures had the opposite effect. Rather than be embarrassed, executives competed with each other for even higher compensation packages. They used disclosures by competitors to leverage their boards into exceeding the competitor's payouts, and the competitor then used the disclosure to demand a further increase, and so on.[59]

Full disclosure and executive compensation also collided over the use of stock options to reward executives. Stock options were thought by corporate governance advocates as a means of aligning management interests with those of shareholders because an increase in the share price would benefit shareholders and the stock options would give management a strong incentive to increase that price. Management of most public companies responded with alacrity to this proposal. Congress assisted in this effort through a provision in the Omnibus Revenue Reconciliation Act of 1993,[60] which limited the deductibility of corporate salaries (non-incentive pay) to $1 million, but placed no such limits on incentive pay in the form of stock options.

A chairman of the SEC later admitted this change in the tax laws "deserves pride of place in the Museum of Unintended Consequences." Instead of a ceiling, the $1 million tax deduction limitation became the corporate executive's "minimum wage." Moreover, rather than curbing

---

[56] *See* Jerry W. Markham, *Regulating Excessive Executive Compensation—Why Bother?*, 2 Md. J. of Bus. & Tech. L. 277, 284–287, 304 (2007) (describing these disclosure requirements and their ineffectiveness).

[57] Dodd-Frank Act § 953.

[58] Dodd-Frank Act § 955.

[59] *See* Jerry W. Markham, *The Politics of Executive Compensation*, 38, 41 Regulation (Cato Institute, Spring 2011).

[60] Pub. L. No. 103–66, 107 Stat. 312.

executive pay, options bestowed incredible amounts of wealth on executives as the stock market boomed in the 1990s.[61] In addition, management was given a strong incentive to cook the books of the company in order to keep the stock price up so that they could make massive profits from their options. This led to numerous accounting scandals at the Enron Corp., WorldCom, Inc. and others, where executives received hundreds of millions of dollars in options-based compensation.[62] The congressional response to the Enron era scandals was the Sarbanes-Oxley Act of 2002, which imposed further full disclosure requirements, including the attestation requirement described previously in this chapter. Companies were also given the right to claw back the pay of executives engaging in accounting manipulations.[63]

Proxy Rules

Another corporate governance reform in the federal securities laws involves the use of SEC proxy rules. The 1934 Act allows the SEC to adopt rules governing the proxy procedures for publicly owned companies.[64] SEC Rule 14a-8 that was adopted under that authority requires public companies to submit proposals from shareholders for inclusion in the annual proxy vote, provided that the proposal does not fall within an area improper for shareholder voting. Even small shareholders may submit such proposals.[65]

Matters that violate state law are among the issues that may be excluded from a proxy vote on a shareholder proposal. This exception allows management to exclude proposals requiring specific action by the company's board of directors. This is because under state law, management decisions rest with the board of directors, and not with shareholders.[66] Among other things, this exemption has been used to exclude shareholder proposals seeking to require their approval of executive

---

[61] Jerry W. Markham, *Regulating Excessive Executive Compensation—Why Bother?*, 2 Md. J. of Bus. & Tech. L. 277, 294 (2007).

[62] *See* Jerry W. Markham, A Financial History of Modern U.S. Corporate Scandals: From Enron to Reform (2005).

[63] Pub. L. No. 107–204, 116 Stat. 745 (2002).

[64] 15 U.S.C. § 78n.

[65] 17 C.F.R. § 240.14a-8.

[66] CA, Inc. v. AFSCME Employees Pension Plan, 953 A.2d 227 (Del. Sup. 2008).

compensation. This is because state laws vest the board of directors with discretion to set executive pay, rather than shareholders.[67]

Activist shareholders found a way to work around this limitation through proposals that sought only an "advisory" vote on executive compensation. Such proposals do not violate state law because they merely inform the board of the shareholders' views on their compensation and are not binding on the board.[68] The Dodd-Frank Act now requires such votes at least every three years.[69] Although such "say-on-pay" votes are becoming more frequent, the results have generally been supportive of management.[70]

Another effort to effect corporate reform through the proxy process involves votes on the structure of the board of directors. Although there appears to be no proof supporting such a theory, corporate governance advocates seek to require that the role of the CEO and the chairman of the board of directors be separated.[71] The CEO prefers both roles because it allows for better control of the board of directors. Corporate advocates desire a weaker CEO and a chairman that might be more receptive to shareholder activists.

The SEC requires a description of company governance structure in proxy materials, including an explanation of why a company believes that the roles of the CEO and chair should be combined.[72] The SEC has also required companies to include shareholder proposals seeking a non-binding vote on whether the role of the chair and CEO should be split. However, most such votes fail, including the one mounted at JPMorgan Chase in June 2013, where the bank's strong-willed executive, Jamie Dimon, was able to keep both roles.[73]

---

[67] Jerry W. Markham, *Regulating Excessive Executive Compensation—Why Bother?,* 2 Md. J. of Bus. & Tech. L. 277, 332 (2007).

[68] *Id.*

[69] Dodd-Frank Act § 951. *See also* 17 C.F.R. § 240.14a-21.

[70] John K. Wilson & Joshua A. Agen, *Say on Pay Best Practices for 2012*, http://m.foley.com/files/Publication/24555eaf-c1a2–4d41–8086-bec2a82aacad/Presentation/PublicationAttachment/1dc649bc-c983-4330-ba58-bef546e60130/TheCorporateBoardMarch-April%202012.pdf (accessed on June 15, 2013).

[71] Jerry W. Markham, A Financial History of the United States, From Enron Era Scandals to the Subprime Crisis (2004–2006) 124–125 (2011).

[72] Proxy Disclosure Enhancements, Securities and Exchange Commission Final Rule, adopted Dec. 16, 2009, effective Feb. 28, 2010 http://www.sec.gov/rules/final/2009/33–9089-secg.htm (accessed on June 15, 2013).

[73] Nick Summers, *Jamie Dimon Wins Big In JPMorgan Shareholder Vote*, http://www.businessweek.com/articles/2013–05–21/jamie-dimon-wins-big-in-jpmorgan-shareholder-vote (accessed on June 12, 2013).

The SEC adopted rules that required the chairman of mutual fund boards to be independent from the chief executive officer after a number of scandals involving abusive mutual trading practices were uncovered.[74] However, the District of Columbia Circuit Court of Appeals set that rule aside because the SEC had not given adequate consideration to such a requirement.[75]

Corporate reformers also seek representation on the board of directors of public companies. Historically, nominations for election to corporate boards were made through nominating committees controlled by the corporation's executives. The SEC requires disclosures to the shareholders on the nominating process and the role of the nominating committee.[76]

Shareholders could engage in a proxy fight in order to elect their own representatives, but such contests are enormously expensive and management is likely to prevail in any event. In order to avoid that expense and difficulty, corporate reformers sought a change in the SEC proxy rules that would require companies to include dissident nominations in proxy votes at the company's expense.[77]

The SEC agreed to make this action available and the authority to impose that requirement was confirmed by the Dodd-Frank Act, and by a change in Delaware law. The SEC rule change providing proxy access right for board nominations was limited to shareholders holding at least 3 percent of the company's stock for at least three years. Only large institutional traders, like state employee pension funds, will meet that criteria. In any event, the District of Columbia Circuit Court of Appeals set the rule aside because of inadequate consideration by the SEC before its adoption.[78]

This new rule was coupled with a successful effort by corporate reformers to convince the SEC to require institutional investors to disclose their proxy vote policies and to adopt policies that would assure their proxy votes are in the best interest of their clients. Many of those

---

[74] *See* Jerry W. Markham, *Mutual Fund Scandals—A Comparative Analysis of the Role of Corporate Governance in the Regulation of Collective Investments*, 3 Hastings Bus. L. J. 67, 95–96 (2006) (describing those rules).

[75] Chamber of Commerce of the United States v. SEC, 443 F.3d 890, 909 (D.C. Cir. 2006).

[76] James Hamilton, Anne M. Sherry & Ted Trautmann, Responsibilities of Corporate Officers and Directors Under Federal Securities Law ¶106 (2012).

[77] American Federation of State, County & Municipal Employees Pension Plan v. American International Group, Inc., 462 F.3d 121 (2d Cir. 2006).

[78] Business Roundtable v. SEC, 647 F.3d 1144 (D.C. Cir. 2011).

institutions, like mutual funds and bank trust departments, have no interest in managing the companies in which they invest. Therefore, in order to satisfy the SEC rule, these institutions often delegated their proxy votes to the discretion of a group of corporate governance firms that specialize in corporate political correctness.[79]

Corporate governance advocates also convinced the SEC to approve a change in stock exchange rules that prohibits broker-dealers from voting the shares of their non-objecting customers in board elections. Previously, because retail investors rarely voted their own proxies, their broker-dealers were allowed to act as the customers' proxy. The broker-dealers cast the vote of non-objecting shareholders in board elections for management-supported nominees.[80] However, this rule change has now stopped those votes.

Independent Directors

Corporate governance advocates have long sought majority representation of independent directors on boards, i.e., directors who are not employees of the company. Following the Enron era scandals, the exchanges required that at least 50 percent of listed companies be outside directors.[81] The Sarbanes-Oxley Act also requires that all of the members of the audit committee must be independent directors.[82] The Dodd-Frank Act extended that requirement to compensation committees that set executive pay.[83]

Other Restrictions

The Sarbanes-Oxley Act imposed an additional corporate governance standard in the form of a requirement that outside legal counsel to public companies "report up the ladder" if they observe illegal behavior.[84] This means that the outside legal counsel must report such conduct to a supervisor and if not corrected then to the next supervisory level, up to

---

79 Jerry W. Markham, A Financial History of the United States, From Enron Era Scandals to the Subprime Crisis (2004–2006) 123–124 (2011).

80 *Id.* at 124.

81 Thomas Lee Hazen & Jerry W. Markham, Corporations and Other Business Organizations, Cases and Materials 229 (3d ed. 2009).

82 Sarbanes-Oxley Act § 301.

83 Dodd-Frank Act § 952.

84 15 U.S.C. § 7245.

the CEO and principal in-house counsel and, if not satisfied that the conduct will be corrected, to the board of directors.[85]

Sarbanes-Oxley also prohibited loans by an issuer to its officers and directors.[86] That provision was added after it was discovered that massive loans had been made to executives Enron and WorldCom using their stock-based compensation as security.[87]

Insider Trading

Another effort to regulate corporate governance involved the SEC's campaign against insider trading. Congress did not include a broad prohibition against insider trading when it enacted the 1934 Act. Rather, it adopted only a limited restriction in Section 16 of that statute,[88] which required officers, directors and persons holding more than 10 percent of the issuer's stock, to report their transactions in the company's stock, and those persons were prohibited from making short sales in the issuer's stock. The statute further required forfeiture of short-term profits by these insiders, i.e., profits made by such persons within a six-month period from a buy-and-sell or sell-and-buy transaction in their company's stock.[89]

The SEC also places restrictions on the sale by insiders of their company's stock in order to assure that they are not engaged in underwriting. Such "restricted" stock can be sold after a specified holding period and in amounts tied to the volume of trading in the stock. SEC Rule 144 governs these sales.[90]

Otherwise, absent other fraud, those "insider" traders were free to trade on inside information under Section 16(b). In 1961, however, the SEC created what was then a novel crime of trading on insider information beyond that set forth in Section 16(b).[91] This was based on a claim that insiders were breaching their fiduciary duties in engaging in such conduct in violation of the antifraud provision in the 1934 Act.[92]

---

85 17 C.F.R. § 205.1 *et seq.*

86 Sarbanes-Oxley § 402.

87 *See* Jerry W. Markham, A Financial History of Modern U.S. Corporate Scandals: From Enron to Reform 101–102, 336–337 (2005).

88 15 U.S.C. § 78p.

89 *See, e.g.*, Smolowe v. Delendo Corp., 136 F.2d 231 (2d Cir. 1943) (describing the computation of such profits).

90 17 C.F.R. § 230.144.

91 In re Cady Roberts & Co., 40 S.E.C. 907 (1961).

92 15 U.S.C. § 78j.

Although the Supreme Court later rejected any broad imposition of fiduciary duties under that provision,[93] it agreed partially with the SEC that insider trading is fraudulent because of the fiduciary duties of insiders.[94]

These broader insider trading cases dominate SEC enforcement efforts. There are exceptions to that prohibition, however, that allow some trading by an insider. For example, an insider can trade in their company's stock when they have a plan in place for future purchases or sales.[95]

The SEC has also adopted Regulation FD to require that the executives of issuing companies not make selective disclosures of nonpublic information.[96] This means that company disclosures must be made to the market as a whole. Such disclosures are often carried out by conference calls that financial analysts can freely join. The executives making such announcements are given some safe harbor treatment for forward-looking statements and predictions.[97] Even if those predictions prove wrong, the executive making them is not liable provided that the speaker "bespoke" caution, i.e., warned that the prediction was just an opinion and might not come to pass.[98]

Conclusions on Corporate Governance

Corporate governance has become a principal concern of management as more and more limitations are placed on how managers manage. The amount of disclosures that must be made to shareholders continues to increase as well. After each era of scandal (as in the case of the failure of the Enron Corp.) and after each financial crisis more regulation is added (the Dodd-Frank Act being the most recent example).

---

93 Santa Fe Industries, Inc. v. Green, 430 U.S. 462 (1977).
94 United States v. O'Hagan, 521 U.S. 642, 667–677 (1997).
95 17 C.F.R. § 240.10b5–1.
96 17 C.F.R. §§ 243.100–243.103.
97 17 C.F.R. § 230.175 and 17 C.F.R. § 240.3b-6.
98 In re Donald J. Trump, 7 F.3d 357 (3d Cir. 1993).

REGULATION OF MERGERS AND ACQUISITIONS

Introduction

In 1969, Congress enacted the Williams Act,[99] which amended the 1934 Act to bring regulation of tender offers under federal jurisdiction.[100] Sections 13(e), 13(d), 14(d) and 14(e) are the main sections under the 1934 Act that regulate tender offers. Further, the SEC has issued several regulations (each containing individual rules) designed to implement the requirements of those sections. Under Section 14(d), any person or group of persons intending to make a tender offer or an invitation for tenders that would result in that person or group of persons owning directly or indirectly more than 5 percent of a class of securities, must file a statement with the SEC disclosing certain information. Section 14(d) only applies to classes of equity securities registered under Section 12 of the 1934 Act, or which are exempt from registration under the exemptions for insurance companies or for a closed-end investment company registered under the Investment Company Act of 1940.

Section 14(e) contains provisions that regulate prohibited activities—activities that are endemic to securities transactions—during the tender offer process. Section 13(d) contains provisions regulating the type of information that companies must disclose and the manner of such disclosure. Additionally, Section 13(e) gives the SEC authority to regulate issuer tender offers.

Ultimately, the goal of the Williams Act is to protect shareholders from tender offer abuses by imposing disclosure requirements on the bidder, regulating the tender offer process so similarly situated shareholders are

---

[99] P.L. 90–439 (July 29, 1969) Securities Exchange Act of 1934, § 14(d)(1, 6), as amended, 15 U.S.C. § 78n(d)(1, 6).

[100] Congress adopted Section 14(d) in 1968 "in response to the growing use of cash tender offers as a means of achieving corporate takeovers … which … removed a substantial number of corporate control contests from the reach of existing disclosure requirements of the federal securities laws." Piper v. Chris-Craft Industries, 430 U.S. 1, 22, 97 S.Ct. 926, 939, 51 L.Ed.2d 124 (1977). *See also* S.Rep. No. 550, 90th Cong., 1st Sess., 2–4 (1967); H.R.Rep. No. 1711, 90th Cong., 2d Sess., 2–4 (1968) U.S.Code Cong. & Admin.News 1968, 2811; 114 Cong.Rec. 21483–21484 (July 15, 1968) (Comments of Representatives Springer and Whalen); 113 Cong.Rec. 854–855 (Jan. 18, 1967) (Comments of Senator Williams); *id.* at 24664 (Aug. 30, 1967) (Comments of Senator Williams); *id.* at 24666 (Comments of Senator Javits).

afforded equal opportunities and by regulating the activities of actors involved in the process.[101]

States have their own regulations that apply to tender offers and defenses to such offers. However, the Williams Act is the main player in the area and state regulations that are in conflict with the Williams Act will be preempted.[102]

Definitions

Person or group of persons

Rule 13d-3(a) defines a "person or group of persons" as a "person who, directly or indirectly, through any contract, arrangement, understanding, relationship, or otherwise has or shares (1) voting power, which includes the power to vote, or to direct the voting of, such security; or (2) investment power, which includes the power to dispose, or to direct the disposition of, such security.[103] Moreover, under Section 13(d)(3), the term "person" includes a partnership, limited partnership, syndicate, or other group.[104] Thus, a person for purposes of the Williams Act, would include a group of people or entities recognized as persons under the laws of the United States. Generally, courts will look at the surrounding facts to determine whether there is a common effort toward the transaction, but determining whether there is a common effort to engage in a tender offer presents its own challenges.

To hammer in the purpose behind the concept of group ownership, Rule 13d-5 mandates that when determining ownership of shares by a person or group of persons, one must consider all equity securities that each person beneficially owns.[105] In *Wellman v. Dickinson*, the court found that for purposes of the Williams Act, the "[t]ouchstone of 'group' [...] is that the members combined in furtherance of a common objective,

---

[101] *See* Bath Industries, Inc. v. Blot, 427 F.2d 87 (1970) ("... legislative history convinces us that the overriding purpose of Congress in enacting this legislation was to protect the individual investor when substantial shareholders or management undertake to acquire shares in a corporation for the purpose of solidifying their own position in a contest over how or by whom the corporation should be managed").

[102] *See* Edgar v. MITE Corp. 457 U.S. 624 (1982).

[103] 17 C.F.R. § 240.13d-3(a). *See also* CSX Corp. v. Children's Inv. Fund management (UK) LLP, 654 F.3d 276 (2d Cir. 2011).

[104] 17 C.F.R. § 240.13d-3(d).

[105] 17 C.F.R. § 240.13d-5.

but concerted action of the members of the group need not be expressly memorialized in writing."[106]

Tender offer

Before the disclosure requirements of the Williams Act kick in, one must determine whether there has been a tender offer, i.e., a solicitation for tendering of registered equity securities for cash, and if there was, did the person or group of persons make the necessary disclosures?

Fittingly, the Williams Act does not define the term "tender offer," in part because of the complexity of the task.[107] Instead, that term is defined through judicial and regulatory precedents developed since the enactment of the Williams Act. Aside from the straightforward solicitation to tender registered equity shares for cash at a premium above market, there are cases where determining whether there has been a tender offer is challenging. Courts use three tests.

Williams Eight-Factor Test The SEC has championed, and some courts have adopted, an eight-factor test to determine whether there has been a tender offer. These factors are disjunctive, meaning that not all have to be present and their relative weight depends on the circumstances of a particular transaction. Courts applying the *Williams* test look at the following:

1. Active and widespread solicitation of public shareholders for the shares of an issuer
2. Solicitation made for a substantial percentage of the issuer's stock
3. Offer to purchase made at a premium over the prevailing market price
4. Terms of the offer are firm rather than negotiable
5. Offer contingent on the tender of a fixed number of shares, often subject to a fixed maximum number to be purchased
6. Offer open only for a limited period of time
7. Offeree subjected to pressure to sell his stock
8. Public announcements of a purchasing program concerning the

[106] 682 F.2d 355, 363 (2d Cir. 1982). *See also* Bath Industries, Inc. v. Blot, 427 F.2d 97 (7th Cir. 1970), citing House Rep. No. 1711, 90th Cong., 2d Sess., July 12, 1968, pp. 8–9.

[107] Tender Offers, SEC Release No. 34–12676 (Aug. 2, 1976).

> target company precede or accompany rapid accumulation of large amounts of the target company's securities.[108]

Courts have used the *Williams* test as a flexible tool to reach the goal of the Williams Act. For example, in *In re General Motors Class E Stock Buyout Securities Litigation*, the court applied the *Wellman* factors to hold that a corporation's offer to purchase shares in a subsidiary from subsidiary's founder and three high-ranking employees was not a tender offer. The court placed particular emphasis on the subsidiary shareholders' status as sophisticated investors and the parties' attorneys negotiated the offer, instead of the pressure that a shareholder usually faces in a tender offer.[109]

However, the holding in *SEC v. Carter Hawley Hale Stores, Inc.*,[110] is one of the better known cases associated with the *Wellman* test. The court held the eight factors found in the *Wellman* case applied to tender offers.[111] Though not all eight factors need to be present, the court found there was no tender offer when only two of the factors were present.[112]

Totality of Circumstances Test As the name suggest, this test takes a more pragmatic approach to make the same determination as the courts using the *Wellman* factors. That is, the court looks at whether the circumstances are such that unless a bidder files the pre-acquisition disclosures required under the Williams Act, there will be a substantial risk that shareholders will lack the information needed to judge the cash offer.[113]

In *Hanson Trust PLC v. SCM Corp.*, the court applied that principle to find that negotiation of five private purchases did not qualify as a tender offer because there were only five sellers, who were highly sophisticated professionals, the sellers were not "pressured" to sell, there was no active

---

108 Wellman v. Dickinson, 475 F.Supp. 783, 823–824 (S.D.N.Y. 1979), aff'd on other grounds, 682 F.2d 355 (2d Cir.1982), *cert. denied*, 460 U.S. 1069 (1983); *see also* SEC v. Carter Hawley Hale Stores, Inc., C.D.Cal.1984, 587 F.Supp. 1248, aff'd 760 F.2d 945 (1985).

109 D.Del.1988, 694 F.Supp. 1119, 1130 (1988).

110 C.D.Cal.1984, 587 F.Supp. 1248, affirmed 760 F.2d 945.

111 SEC v. Carter Hawley Hale Store, Inc., 587 F.Supp. 587 (E.D.N.Y. 1984).

112 *Id.*

113 Hanson Trust PLC v. SCM Corp., 774 F.2d 47, 58 (2d Cir. 1985). *See also* S.E.C. v. Ralston Purina Co., 346 U.S. 119 (1953) (The applicability of Section 14(d) should turn on whether the holders of the target securities need the protection that the Williams Act affords or whether they are able to fend for themselves).

or widespread advance publicity or public solicitation, the offering price was not at a premium above the market price, there was no set time limit during which to tender the shares, and the share purchases were not contingent on the purchase of a minimum number of outstanding shares. The *Hanson* decision is of particular interest because the buyer in that case made the required filings to make a tender offer, but the target company implemented what is commonly referred to as a poisonous pill, which led the buyer to withdraw its offer and proceed with the private purchases. The key, again, was the fact that the sellers were sophisticated entities looking to take advantage of what they perceived was a favorable price.[114]

Two-Step Test Another test, one that has not gained much traction, is a two-step test that looks whether there was a public announcement of acquisition followed by rapid purchase of securities.[115] Although this analytical framework works well in straightforward tender offer cases, it is limited when it comes to determining the existence of a tender offer in more nuanced cases.

Beneficial ownership

Under Rule 13d-3, a person or group of persons will have beneficial ownership if such person directly or indirectly has voting (including power to direct the voting) or investment power over such security (including the power to control the disposition of said security), or has the right to acquire such security within sixty days by exercising options, warrants, rights, or conversion privileges.[116] Rule 13d-3 exempts certain entities and types of ownership from its requirement to avoid certain otherwise unintended consequences of the Williams Act. For example, Rule 13d-3 specifically excludes from its applications cases where

---

[114] 774 F.2d 47 (2d Cir. 1985). *See also* Chromalloy American Corp. v. Sun Chemical Corp., 483 F.Supp. 116 (E.D.Mo. 1980) (There was no tender offer where corporations' lengthy history of purchases was conducted almost entirely on open market, and one purchase made off the exchange involved a normal block purchase transaction which involved no solicitation of shares, no premiums offered, no time limit, and there was no minimum purchase contingency). The SEC proposed a rule that would have instituted a "cooling off" period, for non-issuer tender offers, but it was never adopted. *See* Regulation of Takeovers and Security Holder Communications, Release No. 33–7607 (proposed Nov. 3, 1998). The Hanson court also discussed so-called defacto tender offer. *See* Hanson Trust PLC v. SCM Corp, 774 F.2d at 59–60.

[115] S-G Sec., Inc. v. Fuqua Inv. Co., 466 F.Supp. 1114 (D.C.Mass. 1978).

[116] 17 C.F.R. § 240.13d-3.

exchange members have the power to vote on routine matters and certain lenders in regards to pledged securities.[117] Pursuant to SEC guidance, determining whether there is beneficial ownership goes beyond form. The crux of the determination is whether there is actual control. Thus, mere possession of the legal right to vote will not attribute beneficial ownership if another person has the power to direct the voting.[118] Lastly, Rule 13d-4 affords parties further protection by allowing them to include a statement with any filing that the filing does not constitute an admission of beneficial ownership.[119]

More than 5 percent of securities

Rule 13d-3(c) states that independently of the form of ownership, the securities of the same class shall be aggregated in determining the number of shares the person (or group of persons) beneficially owns for the purposes of calculating whether the 5 percent threshold is met.[120]

Disclosure Requirements

Once there is a tender offer, a bidder must satisfy the disclosure requirements under Sections 14(d), 13(d), 13(e) and SEC regulations implementing those sections, as well as follow the procedural rules under Section 14(e). Responding to complaints about the onerous (and often duplicative) burden of complying with the relevant sections and regulations, the SEC streamlined the required disclosures by adopting Regulation M-A,[121] which incorporates the disclosure requirements for issuer and third-party tender offers, tender offer recommendation statements and going-private transactions.[122] Schedule TO, which is a part of Regulation M-A, for example, will satisfy disclosure requirements for issuer and third-party tender offers, thus avoiding the duplicative task of

---

[117] 17 C.F.R. § 240.13d-3(d).

[118] Securities and Exchange Commission (S.E.C.) Adoption of Beneficial Ownership Disclosure Requirements, SEC Act Release No. 13291 (Feb. 24, 1977). *See also* Calvary Holdings, Inc., v. Chandler, 948 F.2d 59 (1st Cir. 1991) (Recognizing that the focus is on who can actually vote the shares not who is the record owner).

[119] 17 C.F.R. § 240.13d-4.

[120] 17 C.F.R. § 240.13d-3(c).

[121] 17 C.F.R. § 229.1000—Mergers and Acquisitions ("Regulation M-A").

[122] *See* Regulation of Takeovers and Security Holder Communications, SEC Release No. 34–42055 (Oct. 22, 1999).

filing a separate schedule for each transaction.[123] The idea was to adopt the same integrated disclosure system used for proxy and registration statements for tender offers.

Required Disclosures under Section 13(d)—Schedule 13D and Schedule 13G

Section 13(d) of the Williams Act requires bidders disclose certain information if there is a tender offer (as described above) that will result in the bidder owning more than 5 percent of the target's voting class securities that are registered under Section 12 of the 1934 Act.[124] To implement Section 13(d), the SEC adopted a number of rules located in Regulation 13D.[125] Rule 13d-1 requires that in case of a tender offer, the person (or group of persons) carrying it out disclose the information contained in Schedule 13D.[126] Also known as the "beneficial ownership report,"[127] Schedule 13D requires disclosure of personal information about the security and issuer, the identity and background of the bidders, the source and amount of remuneration that the bidders are using, the purpose behind the transaction, whether the bidders have any additional ownership interests in the target company, contracts arrangements and understanding or relationships regarding the securities, and certain materials to be filed as exhibits.[128] The bidders must file Schedule 13D with the issuer of the securities, national exchanges on which the security may be traded, and the SEC through its EDGAR online system within ten days of the acquisition date.

Pursuant to Rule 13d-2, filers of Schedule 13D or 13G must file an amendment if any material change of the facts contained in those schedules occurs.[129] For purposes of changes in ownership, anything beyond 1 percent will constitute a material change that requires reporting.

---

123 *See id.* Schedule TO replaced Schedules 13E-4 and 14D-1 by coordinating the disclosure requirements in issuer and third-party tender offers, especially in two-tiered transactions that may have both components. The information disclosed pursuant to Schedule TO is mandatory and will become publicly available (unless confidential treatment is available), but there are no retention requirements associated with Schedule TO. *Id.*

124 15 U.S.C. § 77m(d).

125 17 C.F.R. § 240.13d-1 *et seq.*

126 17 C.F.R. § 240.13d-1.

127 http://www.sec.gov/answers/sched13.htm (accessed on Aug. 3, 2013).

128 17 C.F.R. § 240.13d-101.

129 17 C.F.R. § 240.13d-102.

Changes below 1 percent may trigger reporting requirements if other circumstances dictate so.[130]

Bidders that own between 5 percent and 20 percent of a class of shares may file Schedule 13G,[131] which is simpler and less burdensome than Schedule 13D. However, filers of Schedule 13G are representing that they intend to act as passive investors and that they will not engage in activist shareholder activities.[132] The purpose behind Schedule 13G is to avoid encumbering the functions of entities that act as intermediaries, like broker-dealers, banks, insurance companies, and investment companies registered under Section 8 of the 1934 Act.[133] Schedule 13G must be filed within forty-five days of the last day of the calendar year in which the bidder became the beneficial owner. However, if the purchase resulted in an aggregate ownership of more than 10 percent of a class, Schedule 13G is due within ten days of the last day of the month in which the transaction took place.[134]

Bidders who have filed Schedule 13G and decide to engage in activities associated with activist shareholders must file Schedule 13D with the SEC within ten days of the date that the bidder holds the securities with a purpose or effect of changing or influencing control of the issuer.[135] The same holds true for investors that become passive shareholders, who may file Schedule 13G to signal that they are no longer subject to Schedule 13D.[136]

Lastly, Rule 13d-1 permits multiple associated filers to use one common form if each person would be eligible to file individually, each person is responsible for the accuracy and timeliness of the part of Schedule 13D that pertains to them, and the joint filing contains an attestation by each person concerning the information provided.[137] Once complete, the bidder must send copies of Schedules 13D and 13G to the issuer of the securities and to each of the national exchanges where the security may be traded.[138]

---

[130] 17 C.F.R. § 240.13d-2.
[131] 17 C.F.R. § 240.13d-102.
[132] 17 C.F.R. § 240.13d-1.
[133] 17 C.F.R. § 240.13d-1(b)-(c).
[134] 17 C.F.R. § 240.13d-1(b).
[135] 17 C.F.R. § 240.13d-1(e).
[136] 17 C.F.R. § 240.13d-1(h).
[137] 17 C.F.R. § 240.13d-1(k).
[138] 17 C.F.R. § 240.13d-7.

Required Disclosures under Section 14(d)—Regulation 14D

Section 14(d) of the Williams Act makes it illegal for anyone to purchase more than 5 percent of class of securities registered under Section 12 of the 1934 Act, for securities of an insurance company not exempt from registration under Section 12(g)(2)(G) of the 1934 Act, or for securities of a closed-end investment company registered under the Investment Company Act of 1940, unless they disclose relevant information at the time of the tender offer.[139] To implement Section 14(d), the SEC adopted a series of rules contained in Regulation 14D.[140]

Rule 14d-2 covers the commencement of a tender offer.[141] For there to be a commencement, the bidders must publish, send or give the means to tender to the security holders at 12:01 a.m. of the day of the offer.[142] However, a prior communication will not constitute commencement if it does not include a means to tender, and the bidders have included said communications under Schedule TO with the SEC before or on the date of the communication.[143] Pre-commencement communications usually include public announcements of the bidders' interest in the shares. Although these announcements can be oral or written, written ones must contain a "prominent legend in clear, plain language" telling the shareholders to read the tender offer statement, which they can get free from the SEC's website. The SEC defines as a public announcement any communication (written or oral) that "is reasonably designed to, or has the effect of, informing the public or security holders [...] of the offer."[144] The offer commencement date is important because it triggers certain other filing requirements that Rules 14d-4 and 14d-5 mandate.

Once a bidder announces the offer for tender, Rule 14d-3 requires the bidder to file Schedule TO with the SEC "as soon as practicable" on the same day as the commencement.[145] Additionally, Rule 14d-3 requires that a bidder deliver a copy of Schedule TO (along with any applicable

---

139 15 U.S.C. § 78n(d)(1).

140 17 C.F.R. §§ 240.14d–1 through 240.14d–101. The application of Regulations 14D and 14E depends on whether the tender offer is subject to Section 14(d)(1) of the 1934 Act. If the tender offer is subject to Section 14(d)(1), both regulations apply. *See* Tender Offers, SEC Release No 6158 (Nov. 29, 1979).

141 17 C.F.R. § 240.14d-2. *See also* Edgar v. MITE Corp., 457 U.S. 624 (1982).

142 17 C.F.R. § 240.14d-2(a). "Means to tender" include the transmittal form or a statement regarding how such form may be obtained.

143 17 C.F.R. § 240.14d-2(b).

144 17 C.F.R. § 240.14d-2(b)(5).

145 17 C.F.R. § 240.14d-3(a)(1).

exhibits) to the subject company and any other bidder who may have filed Schedule TO for the same class of securities.[146]

In addition, the bidder must give phone notice, as well as mail a copy of Schedule TO, to each national securities exchange on which the securities are registered and listed for trading and the NASD (assuming the class of securities is authorized for question in the Nasdaq interdealer quotation system).[147]

A bidder must file amendments to Schedule TO to report any "material changes" in the information contained therein, and to report the results of the tender offer.[148] Lastly, subsection (c) of Rule 14d-3 allows a bidder to file an amendment that only discloses the number of shares tendered or an extension of the "tender-by" deadline promptly after making the announcement.[149]

Rule 14d-4 governs the dissemination of tender offers to security holders.[150] Pursuant to this rule, the bidder must publish, send or give disclosure of the offer to the holders of securities.[151] The form of dissemination pursuant to that rule depends on the consideration the bidder is offering, for example, cash for securities or securities for securities. If the offer is for cash,[152] the bidder may satisfy the dissemination rules through a long-form publication of the tender offer in a newspaper or newspapers.[153] For summary publications, the bidder will satisfy the Rule 14d-4's requirements by publishing a summary advertisement of the tender offer in a newspaper or newspapers, and mailing or furnishing with reasonable promptness the tender offer materials to the security holders who may request them.[154] Lastly, if a bidder is using stockholder lists or security position listings, it must comply with the long-form publication procedures above.

There are different dissemination rules for cases in which the bidder offers securities registered under the 1933 Act as consideration for the

---

[146] 17 C.F.R. § 240.14d-3(a)(2).

[147] 17 C.F.R. § 240.14d-3(a)(3).

[148] 17 C.F.R. § 240.14d-3(b). The bidder must follow the same procedure for notifying the issuer and relevant SROs as under subsection 240(a)(2) and (3).

[149] 17 C.F.R. § 240.14d-3(c).

[150] 17 C.F.R. § 240.14d-4.

[151] "Adequate publication" is a fluid term, especially considering the demise of the print media, but publication in all the editions of a daily newspaper with a national circulation will suffice. 17 C.F.R. § 240.14d-4(c).

[152] The rule states groups cash and securities exempt from registration under Section 3 of the Securities Act of 1933. 17 C.F.R. § 240.14d-4.

[153] 17 C.F.R. § 240.14d(a)(1).

[154] 17 C.F.R. § 240.14d-4(a)(2).

tender offer. In these cases, there must be a registration statement for these securities, and the bidder must deliver a preliminary prospectus to the holders of the securities.[155] If the bidder sends the prospectus by mail, it may mail it by the day the offer commences. In addition, the preliminary prospectus must not omit certain information and the registration statement for the securities given as consideration must become effective prior to the tender.[156]

Lastly, the bidder must disseminate any material changes to the offer through means "reasonably designed" to inform the security holders of said changes. However, if the material changes are in connection to an offer involving a preliminary prospectus (that is, the consideration was in the form of registered securities), the offer must remain open from the date of the dissemination of the material changes until (i) five business days if there is a material change other than price or share levels, (ii) ten business days if there are changes to price, share levels, the dealer's soliciting fee (or other similarly significant change), (iii) ten business days for a prospectus supplement included as post-effective amendment, and (iv) twenty business days for revised prospectus if the initial prospectus was materially deficient.[157]

If the bidder requests from the issuer a stockholder list or security position listings, the issuer company must respond in accordance with the guidelines in Rule 14d-5.[158] After receiving the request, the issuer will take prompt steps to notify transfer agents or other relevant parties who will assist in preparing the lists, and the issuer shall ascertain that any existing lists are not prepared earlier than ten business days before the date of the request.[159] Subsection (a)(3) of the rule allows the issuer to elect whether to distribute the tender offer materials to the relevant shareholders on behalf of the bidder or to provide the lists that the bidder

---

[155] 17 C.F.R. § 240.14d-4(b).

[156] 17 C.F.R. § 240.14d-4(b). *See also* 17 C.F.R. § 230.430 (Prospectus for use prior to effective date), 17 C.F.R. § 230.430A (Prospectus in a registration statement at the time of effectiveness), and 17 C.F.R. § 230.162 (Submission of tenders in registered exchange offers).

[157] 17 C.F.R. § 240.14d-4(d).

[158] 17 C.F.R. § 240.14d-5. The bidder's request must identify the bidder, the title of the class of the relevant securities, a statement that the bidder is requesting the information for the purposes of disseminating a tender offer, a statement that the bidder is aware the of the information contained in paragraph (f) for Rule 14d-5, a statement whether the bidder elects that the issuer disseminate material changes to the offer, and the name, address and phone number of the bidder's contact information. *See* 17 C.F.R. 240.14d-5(e).

[159] 17 C.F.R. § 240.14d-5(a)(1)-(2).

has requested. Once made, however, the election is irrevocable, and the issuer must orally notify the bidder of its election within two business days, and must confirm the notice in writing.[160] If the issuer elects to distribute the materials, it must use its best efforts to distribute by mail the bidder's tender offer materials to the persons on the stockholder lists or on the securities positions listings.[161] If the issuer instead elects to provide the shareholder contact information through the stock list and security positions listings, it must provide said lists within three business days of the bidder's request.[162] Lastly, Rule 14d-5 shields issuers from liability arising from its actions in the process of complying with the requirements of this rule, it requires bidders to take steps to facilitate the issuer's role, as well as providing guidelines on calculating reimbursements for expenses incurred in the process.[163]

Rule 14d-6 governs the information that an issuer must provide to shareholders on the commencement date under the long-form or summary publications discussed above.[164] The long-form publication must effectively contain all the information that Schedule TO requires.[165] If the issuer is able to use a summary publication, it must disclose the information required by Rule 14d-6(d)(2).[166]

Rule 14d-7 implements the requirement of Section 14(d)(5) of the Act, and allows any person who has deposited securities in connection with a tender offer to withdraw them during the time the tender offer remains open so long as the person withdrawing provides timely notice of withdrawal.[167] The bidder, however, does not have to offer withdrawal rights during a subsequent offering period and the bidder may require

---

[160] 17 C.F.R. § 240.14d-5(a)(4). This notification will also indicate (i) the approximate amount of shares involved with the bidder's request, and (ii) the cost involved with mailing the tender offer materials, if the issuer elects to distribute the materials on behalf the of bidder.

[161] 17 C.F.R. § 240.14d-5(b). The issuer must also inform the bidder orally and in writing of the commencement of the mailing, only send materials related to the offer and distribute any material amendments that the bidder submits.

[162] 17 C.F.R. § 240.14–5(c).

[163] 17 C.F.R. § 240.14d-5(d)–(g).

[164] 17 C.F.R. § 240.14d-6.

[165] 17 C.F.R. § 240–14d-6(d)(1). This section excludes the exhibits that would normally accompany Schedule TO.

[166] 17 C.F.R. § 240.14d-6(d)(2). Summary advertisements may not include a transmittal letter, which is a letter furnished to security holders for transmission of securities sought in the tender offer.

[167] 17 C.F.R. § 240.14d-7.

that any notice of withdrawal contain a certain minimum amount of information.[168]

Rule 14d-8 mandates that if an offer for tender is for less than the entire class, the bidder must accept all shares tendered, and if the shares tendered exceed those sought by the bidder, the bidder must prorate the shares it buys.[169]

Often, a party other than the bidder may want to make a statement in connection with the tender offer. This party may be the subject company or an affiliate, or an unaffiliated third party. Rule 14d-9 governs non-bidder communications.[170] Pursuant to that rule, such communications must be accompanied by a filing with the SEC of a Tender Offer Solicitation/Recommendation Statement on Schedule 14D-9, and the filer must deliver said statement to the bidder and give telephonic notice to relevant exchanges and the NASD (if applicable).[171]

Rule 14d-10 is one of the more controversial rules in Regulation 14D. Also known as the "All Holders Rule," it requires a bidder to make invitations for tender open to all security holders of the class of securities in question, and the consideration paid to any security holder is the highest paid to any holder who has tendered the securities.[172] However, the bidder is free to offer more than one type of compensation if the holders are "afforded an equal right" to choose among the compensations.[173] Rule 14d-10 was a controversial rule when the SEC enacted it; there was significant industry push back and the SEC has amended the rule as part of an effort to appease industry lobbying and to reflect operational realities.[174] However, courts have made it clear that the SEC was within its Williams Act mandate when it enacted it.[175]

---

[168] *Id. See also* Macfadden Holdings, Inc. v. JB Acquisition Corp., 802 F.2d 62 (2d Cir. 1986) (reversing lower court holding rescinding tender offer purchase on the basis of misrepresentation of the date the offer expired).

[169] 17 C.F.R. § 240.14d-8.

[170] 17 C.F.R. § 240.14d-9.

[171] *Id.*

[172] 17 C.F.R. § 240.14d-10(a).

[173] 17 C.F.R. § 240.14d-10(c).

[174] *See, e.g.,* Amendments to the Tender Offer Best-Price Rules, SEC Release No. 54684 (Nov. 1, 2006).

[175] Polaroid Corp. v. Disney, 862 F.2d 987 (3d Cir. 1988). The same restrictions apply to issuer tender offers under Rule 13e-4(f)(8).

Purchase of Securities by Issuer (Going Private Transaction)

Rule 13e-1 and its companions govern cases when the issuer purchases its own shares as part of a self-initiated tender or after a third party has announced a tender offer. The issuer may engage such purchases for a variety of reasons, for example, to fend off an unwelcomed tender offer or to reduce the amount of outstanding shares of the issuer. In either case, an issuer faces certain procedural and substantive obstacles before they may engage in the offer.

Rule 13e-1, for example, prohibits an issuer from buying its own equity securities during the duration of a third-party tender offer subject to Regulation 14D (assuming proper notice by the other bidder), unless the issuer files a statement with the SEC containing the title and number of securities, the names or classes of persons from whom the issuer will purchase the securities, the name of any exchange through which the purchase will take place, the purpose of the purchase, state whether the issuer will retire, hold or dispose the securities,[176] and the source[177] and amount of funds used to carry out the purchase.[178] The information that the issuer must report pursuant to this rule does not need to be disseminated to the security holders, and the issuer will satisfy Rule 13e-1 if it meets the filing requirements contained in Rule 13e-4 below.[179]

Rule 13e-3 covers going private transactions by the issuer or its affiliated persons. If an issuer is subject to Rule 13e-3, it must disclose the information required in Schedule 13E-3. Schedule 13E-3 disclosure only attaches if an issuer or its affiliates engage in specified transactions involving (1) any class of equity security of the issuer that is subject to Sections 12(g) or 15(d) of the 1934 Act to be held of record by less than 300 persons, or (2) any class of equity securities of the issuer which is either listed on a national securities exchange or authorized to be quoted in an inter-dealer quotation. This schedule requires detailed information addressing whether the filing persons believe the transaction is fair to

---

[176] If the issuer intends to dispose of the securities, it must disclose how it intends to do so.

[177] If the issuer borrows the means used for the purchase, it must describe the terms of the transaction.

[178] 17 C.F.R. § 240.13e-1. The issuer must also pay a fee equal to 1/50 of 1 percent of the value of the securities to be acquired (17 C.F.R. § 240.0–11(b). *Id.*

[179] *See* Regulation of Takeovers and Security Holder Communications, SEC Release No. 34–42055 (Oct. 22, 1999).

unaffiliated security holders and why, and the bidder or affiliated persons must disseminate it to the shareholders.[180]

Rule 13e-4 governs tender offers for equity securities[181] that the issuer of the securities carries out.[182] The information that an issuer must disclose to the SEC pursuant to that rule is set forth in Schedule TO, which replaced old Schedule 13E-4.[183] Pursuant to Rule 13e-4, the issuer must disclose certain information to the SEC and the shareholders as soon as practicable on the day of commencement of the offer.[184] As far as the SEC goes, the issuer must file all written communications the issuer (or affiliate) has made relating to the tender offer, Schedule TO (including exhibits), amendments to Schedule TO reflecting material changes to previously filed information, and a final amendment to Schedule TO reporting the results of the tender offer.[185]

In addition to the SEC filings, the issuer must disclose certain information to the security holders, including the information required by Item 1 of Schedule TO, a fair and adequate summary of the rest of information that Schedule TO requires (except for Item 12 (Exhibits) and any material changes to previously disclosed information.[186] If the issuer (or affiliate) disseminates the tender offer by summary publication, the summary publication may not contain a transmittal letter and must disclose the identity of the issuer making the offer, the information in Item 1004[187] and Item 1006[188] of Regulation M-A, the means of obtaining the information in the preceding sentence as well as a statement that said information is incorporated by reference.[189]

Additionally, Rule 13e-4 also sets forth the requirements for tender offers to be deemed published, sent or given to the security holders.[190] If

---

[180] 240 C.F.R. § 240.13e-3. *See also* Regulation of Takeovers and Security Holder Communications, SEC Release No. 34–42055.

[181] Rule 13e-4 applies to equity securities registered under Section 12 of the Exchange Act, or to issuers who must file periodic reports to Section 15(d) of the 1934 Act, or closed-end investment companies registered under the 1940 Act.

[182] 17 C.F.R. § 240.13e-4.

[183] *Id.*

[184] 17 C.F.R. § 240.13e-4(b)(1).

[185] 17 C.F.R. § 240.13e-4(c).

[186] 17 C.F.R. § 240.13e-4(d)(1)–(2).

[187] 17 C.F.R. § 229.1004.

[188] 17 C.F.R. § 229.1006.

[189] 17 C.F.R. § 240.13e-4(d)(3).

[190] 17 C.F.R. § 240.13e-4(e).

the tender offer consideration is only cash,[191] the issuer must disseminate the offer by long-form publication through a newspaper (or newspapers) on the commencement date, by using a stockholder list to mail said materials, or by contacting each participant in the most recent security position listings of any clearing agency.[192] If the tender offer is not subject to Rule 13e-3 (going private transactions), the issuer may disseminate the above information through summary publication in a newspaper and by sending copies of the long-form information to any security holder that requests them.[193]

If the tender offer consideration consists of securities registered under the 1933 Act and a registration statement has been filed, the issuer must transmit a prospectus, including a letter of transmittal to the security holders.[194] Subsection (f) of Rule 13e-4 mandates that the offer must remain open for at least twenty consecutive business days, and if there is a change in percentage of the class being sought or the consideration offered, at least ten days from the date said change is published.[195] In addition, security holders may withdraw their tender at any point during the period the offer remains open, and within forty business days if the issuer has not accepted the securities for payment.[196]

If more shareholders tender more shares than originally sought, the buyer must prorate the shares it accepts pursuant to the tender offer.[197] Also, if the issuer increases the consideration, such increase will apply to all holders who tender their offers or accepted payments,[198] and the

---

[191] This also includes securities exempt from registration under Section 3 of the 1933 Act (15 U.S.C. § 77c).

[192] 17 C.F.R. § 240.13e-4(e)(1)(i)–(ii). If the issuer exercises the last option, it must provide sufficient numbers of disclosure statements as well as reimburse the participants for expenses incurred in connection with the transaction.

[193] 17 C.F.R. § 240.13e-4(e)(1)(iii).

[194] 17 C.F.R. § 240.13e-4(e)(2). The prospectus must contain all the information required by Section 10(a) of the Securities Act of 1933 (15 U.S.C. 77j(a)). Additionally, subsection (e)(2) of this rule contains specific requirements if the issuer uses a preliminary prospectus.

[195] 17 C.F.R. § 240.13e-4(f)(1). This requirement, however, does not apply if the increase in the shares sought does not exceed 2 percent.

[196] 17 C.F.R. § 240.13e-4(f)(2).

[197] 17 C.F.R. § 240.13e-4(f)(3). This requirement does not apply in cases where the securities tendered are less than 100 shares and the holder is tendering all of their shares, or in cases where the tenderor elects to have either all or none or at least a minimum amount or none accepted. *Id.*

[198] 17 C.F.R. § 240.13e-4(f)(4).

issuer shall promptly pay the consideration or return the shares promptly after termination or withdrawal.[199]

Subsection (f)(6) of Rule 13e-4 bars a bidder (or affiliate) from purchasing securities of the same class as those in the tender offer for at least ten days after the tender offer termination date.[200] Similarly to restrictions placed on bidders as discussed above under Rule 14d-10, issuers must offer the same price to all holders and the invitation to tender must be open to all holders.[201] The type of consideration offered, however, does not have to be the same for all holders as long as they have the right to choose between the available methods of consideration.[202]

Lastly, Rule 13e-4 exempts from its extensive disclosure requirements for issuer tender offers that involve (1) calls or redemptions of securities in accordance with the governing instrument, (2) securities representing a fraction interest in a share, (3) statutory purchases of dissenting security holders, (4) tender offers subject to Section 14(d) of the Williams Act, (5) offers to purchase from security holders who own an aggregate of not more than a specified number of shares that is less than one hundred (with some exceptions), (6) an offer made only to effect a rescission offer, (7) offers by closed-end management investment companies to repurchase equity securities pursuant to 17 C.F.R. § 270.23c-3, and (8) certain cross-border transactions.[203] Subsection (j) contains a prohibition on fraudulent, deceptive or manipulative acts in connection with an issuer tender offer.[204]

---

[199] 17 C.F.R. § 240.13e-4(f)(5).

[200] 17 C.F.R. § 240.13e-4(f)(6). These two waiting periods must be calculated concurrently and not consecutively. 17 C.F.R. § 240.13e-4(f)(7).

[201] 17 C.F.R. § 240.13e-4(f)(8). However, an issuer is excused from this subsection if applicable state blue-sky laws prohibit them from offering to purchase shares from certain members of a class. 17 C.F.R. § 240.13e-4(f)(9).

[202] 17 C.F.R. § 240.13e-4(f)(10). *See also* In re Digital Island Securities Litigation, 357 F.3d 322 (3d Cir. 2004) (Where plaintiff argues that "best price rule" has been violated by transaction executed prior to tender offer, plaintiff necessarily alleges that tender offeror has fraudulently devised scheme to circumvent rule, and therefore must comply with fraud particularity pleading requirements of federal civil procedure rules and Private Securities Litigation Reform Act).

[203] 17 C.F.R. § 240.13e-4(h)(1)–(8).

[204] 17 C.F.R. § 240.13e-4(j).

Prohibited conduct—Regulation 14E

Section 14(e) of the Williams Act is the antifraud provision that covers tender offers, and it prohibits fraudulent, deceptive and manipulative acts if carried out in connection with a tender offer. It applies to all tender offers, regardless of size and regardless of whether the securities involved are registered under the 1934 Act. However, the Supreme Court has made clear that Section 14(e) prohibits manipulative practices only if there has been at least some deception in the form of a material misrepresentation/omission.[205] To implement Section 14(e), the SEC adopted Regulation 14E, which contains a number of rules that set forth certain procedural safeguards.[206] It is worth noting, that in addition to the antifraud provisions of Section 14(e), the antifraud provision of Section 10(b) of the 1934 Act and Rule 10b-5 also apply.[207]

Once a tender offer commences, Rule 14e-1 requires that a tender offer be open for at least twenty business days, that it remain open for ten business days following a change in the offer price or the amount of securities a bidder is seeking, and that the bidder promptly pay (or return) for the securities when the offer period expires.[208]

Rule 14e-2 requires that the target company state its position about the offer within ten business days after the offer begins.[209] Pursuant to that rule, the target must issue a statement that it (1) recommends acceptance or rejection of the bidder's tender offer; (2) expresses no opinion and is remaining neutral toward the bidder's tender offer; or (3) is unable to take a position with respect to the bidder's tender offer. Such statement shall also include the reason(s) for the position (including the inability to take a position) disclosed therein.[210]

Rule 14e-3 is the anti-tipping provision of Regulation 14E.[211] It prohibits persons in possession of material information relating to a tender offer for which a person has taken substantial steps to commence

---

[205] Schreiber v. Burlington Northern, Inc., 472 U.S. 1 (1985).

[206] 17 C.F.R. § 240.14e-1 e*t seq.*

[207] 15 U.S.C. § 78j; 17 C.F.R. § 240.10b-5.

[208] 17 C.F.R. § 14e-1(a)-(c). An issuer may extend the offer by period through a public announcement in a newspaper, and it does not have to give individual notice to tendering shareholders. *But see* CTS Corp. v. Dynamics Corp. of America, 481 U.S. 69 (1987) (state law that required certain types of tender offers to have a longer open period was not preempted by the Williams Act).

[209] 17 C.F.R. § 14e-2.

[210] *Id.*

[211] 17 C.F.R. § 14e-3.

(or has commenced), to disclose that information to other persons if it is reasonably foreseeable that the disclosure will result in a violation of this rule.[212]

Following along the prohibition in Rule 14e-3, Rule 14e-4 prohibits short tenders during partial tender offers—defined as invitations to tender for less than all of the securities subject to the offer—in order to avoid or reduce the risk of pro rata acceptance in such offers. Pursuant to Rule 14e-4, a person may tender shares into a partial tender offer only if the person has a net long position in the applicable security (or an equivalent security) equal to or greater than the amount tendered into the partial tender offer both at the time of tender and at the end of the proration period.[213]

Rule 14e-5 prohibits covered persons from directly, indirectly or through other arraignments from buying securities that are the target of a tender offer during the offer period (commencement to expiration).[214] Rule 14e-5 contains a number of exceptions to this prohibition that reflect regulatory accommodations of business realities.[215]

Rule 14e-7 prohibits certain tender offer transactions in connection with roll-up transactions to complement Rule 14e-6.[216] Moreover, Rule 14e-8 prohibits any person to announce publicly that the person plans to

---

212 *See also* U.S. v. O'Hagan, 521 U.S. 642 (1997) (recognizing the SEC's authority to promulgate rule proscribing transactions in securities on basis of material, nonpublic information in context of tender offers, and upholding a guilty finding on purchaser of securities who acted based on insider nonpublic information received as an employee of the law firm involved in the tender offer).

213 17 C.F.R. § 14e-4. *See also* Commission Guidance on the Application of Certain Provisions of the Securities Act of 1933, The Securities Exchange Act of 1934, and Rules Thereunder to Trading In Security Futures Products, SEC Release No. 8107, 2002 WL 1357820, *15 (June 21, 2002). A "net long position" in a subject security equals the excess, if any, of such person's "long position" over a person's "short position." The calculation of the net long position must be done both at the time of tender and at the end of the proration period, or period during which securities are accepted by lot, including any extension thereof. *Id.*

214 17 C.F.R. § 240.14e-5. The term "covered person" includes (i) the bidder and its affiliates; (ii) the bidder's dealer-manager and its affiliates; (iii) any advisor to any of the persons specified in (i) and (ii), whose compensation is dependent on the completion of the offer; and (iv) any person in concert with the aforementioned persons in connection with any purchase or arrangement to purchase any subject securities or any related securities. *Id.*

215 *Id.*

216 17 C.F.R. § 240.14e-7. This rule was designed to complement rule Section 14(h) of the 1934 Act (15 U.S.C. 78n(h)).

make a tender offer that has not yet been commenced.[217] This prohibition, however, only applies if the person (a) is making the announcement without the intention to commence the offer within a reasonable time and actually complete the offer; (b) intends, directly or indirectly, for the announcement to manipulate the market price of the stock of the bidder or subject company; or (c) does not have the reasonable belief that the person will have the means to purchase securities to complete the offer.[218]

Changes of directors or officers to facilitate tender offers—Rule 14f-1

Rule 14f-1 covers cases in which bidders attempt to facilitate tender offers by offering incentives to the directors or officers of the target company.[219] Note that Rule 14f-1 does not prohibit incentives, but the bidder must disclose to the SEC and target shareholders certain information within ten days if any persons are to be elected or designated as directors of the issuer, otherwise than at a meeting of security holders, if the persons so elected or designated will constitute a majority of the directors of the issuer.

Mini Tender Offers

Smaller offers to tender shares that do not result in the offeror owning more than 5 percent of a class of equity securities are not subject to Sections 14(d), 13(e) and 13(d) discussed above. However, Section 14(e) applies to all offers, including offers that do not exceed the 5 percent threshold. Thus, bidders of so-called mini tender offers must abide by the limitations contained in Section 14(e) of the Williams Act.[220]

Hart-Scott-Rodino Act

The Hart-Scott-Rodino Act established the federal premerger notification program intended to provide the Federal Trade Commission and the Department of Justice with information about large mergers and acquisitions by requiring the parties to certain transactions to submit premerger notification to the aforementioned regulators. Specifically, parties to these types of mergers must submit a "Notification and Report Form for

---

[217] 17 C.F.R. § 240.14e-8.

[218] *Id.*

[219] 17 C.F.R. § 240.14f-1.

[220] *See* Commission Guidance on Mini-Tender Offers and Limited Partnership Tender Offers, SEC Release No. 34–43069 (July 31, 2000).

Certain Mergers and Acquisitions," with information about each company and their business. The Hart-Scott-Rodino Act prevents companies from closing on the deal until the waiting period as passed or until the government grants an early termination of the waiting period.[221]

[221] Federal Trade Commission, Hart-Scott-Rodino, Premerger Notification Program, http://www.ftc.gov/bc/hsr/ (accessed on Aug. 13, 2013).

10. The Sarbanes-Oxley Act of 2002: a regulatory hodge-podge arising from highly visible financial fraud

*Joan MacLeod Heminway**

In November 2001, a single business combination transaction held the attention of many in the legal and financial world: the Enron Corp./ Dynegy Inc. merger. The transaction represented a stunning reversal for former Wall Street and media darling Enron, a firm whose stock had tumbled in the market as the firm revealed reduced earnings followed by restatements of its publicly reported historical financial statements. The merger with Dynegy was widely seen as a rescue of Enron, and none too soon. In fact, it turned out to be too late. By the end of November, the deal was scuttled when Dynegy got cold feet amid continuing revelations of significant financial misstatements and allegations of management misconduct at Enron.

> Dynegy Inc. scrapped its proposed $9 billion merger with Enron Corp. Wednesday, a move that leaves what had been one of the nation's biggest and most influential companies teetering on the edge of bankruptcy ...
>
> Enron's woes started after regulators began an investigation of transactions with a partnership created by its former chief financial officer, Andrew Fastow, that resulted in a $1.2 billion reduction in the value of investors' holdings.
>
> It became increasingly clear, as Dynegy sought to renegotiate the merger, that Enron's complex and often indecipherable finances were becoming a sticking point, sources close to the negotiations told Reuters ... [1]

---

* Work on this chapter has been supported by research funding from The University of Tennessee College of Law. The author acknowledges with gratitude the contributions of Michael Craig Grubbs (The University of Tennessee College of Law, J.D. 2014) to this chapter.

[1] *Dynegy Scraps Enron Deal*, CNNMoney, Nov. 28, 2001: 5:27 p.m. ET, *available at* http://money.cnn.com/2001/11/28/companies/enron/.

The announcement of the termination of the Enron/Dynegy transaction marked the beginning of the end in a number of respects: the end of Enron as the world knew it and, with it, over the course of a number of years, the end of light-touch financial regulation in the United States. The financial accounting comeuppances of Tyco International Ltd., WorldCom Inc., and others followed in the coming months. By the end of July 2002 the U.S. Congress, feeling compelled to act, had passed the Sarbanes-Oxley Act of 2002 ("Sarbanes-Oxley"),[2] and the President had signed it into law. As a result, the landscape of U.S. securities regulation was markedly, and perhaps permanently, changed. Subsequent regulatory initiatives over the next ten years—including principally the Dodd-Frank Wall Street Reform and Consumer Protection Act,[3] signed into law in 2010 ("Dodd-Frank"), and the Jumpstart Our Business Startups Act,[4] which became law in 2012 (the "JOBS Act")—would institute further changes of a similar nature as the system of securities regulation in the United States struggled to respond to (first) the global financial crisis and (later) a perceived post-crisis need to revive the U.S. economy by promoting activity in public and private securities markets. It all started, however, with the enactment of Sarbanes-Oxley.

OVERVIEW

U.S. federal securities regulation exists as a means of encouraging capital formation in businesses through the promotion of two core values: investor protection and the maintenance of fair securities trading markets. These policy objectives often operate in a state of symbiosis. There are occasions, however, where investor and market interests may not be consonant with each other as means of promoting business capital formation. The regulatory tools used to effectuate the policies underlying federal securities regulation in the United States have an impact on the overall policy mix.

A Change in the Mix of Regulatory Tools

Prior to Sarbanes-Oxley, federal securities regulation used two primary methods of regulation to accomplish federal securities regulation's policy objectives: the mandatory regulation of disclosure through required

---

2 Pub. L. No. 107–204, 116 Stat. 745 (2002) [hereinafter Sarbanes-Oxley].
3 Pub. L. No. 111–203, 124 Stat. 1376 (2010) [hereinafter Dodd-Frank].
4 Pub. L. No. 112–106, 126 Stat. 306 (2012) [hereinafter JOBS Act].

transactional and periodic public filings and the prevention of fraud and misstatements through liability provisions (which, among other things, foster accurate and complete public disclosures). In the pre-Sarbanes-Oxley era, little use was made of substantive regulation—a third regulatory tool consisting of legal directives defining both permitted participants in securities transactions and related activities and the ways (place, timing, manner) in which those transactions and activities may be undertaken. Sarbanes-Oxley changed the mix of regulation to favor more heavily substantive rules in the overall regulatory mix. The information in this chapter illustrates how Congress used these three key tools of securities regulation—mandatory disclosure, fraud and misstatement liability, and substantive regulation—as well as other aspects of its legislative power to respond to the financial fraud of the late 20th and early 21st centuries.

Federal Regulation of Corporate Governance

The substantive regulation in Sarbanes-Oxley included a significant number of federal corporate governance initiatives applicable to public and reporting companies.[5] This is an extraordinary part of Sarbanes-Oxley—an aspect of the legislation that separated it from prior federal securities regulation efforts and heralded a new era of federal incursions into public company corporate governance (including through provisions in Dodd-Frank and SEC regulatory efforts under both Sarbanes-Oxley and Dodd-Frank). Most see Sarbanes-Oxley as a true watershed in this respect. Prior to Sarbanes-Oxley, the overwhelming majority of corporate governance rules for public and reporting companies, like those for their privately held, non-reporting brethren, were state corporate law rules.

---

[5] Sarbanes-Oxley focuses its attention almost exclusively on public companies (entities with a class of securities registered under Section 12(b) or Section 12(g) of the Securities Exchange Act of 1934, as amended (the "1934 Act")) and reporting companies (entities that file periodic reports under Section 13(a) or 15(d) of the 1934 Act). *See* 15 U.S.C. §§ 78l(b) & (g), 78m(a), 78o(d) (2012). These securities issuers, often referred to as registrants, are subject to the periodic and transactional (e.g., proxy solicitation, tender offer, going private transaction) reporting requirements included in Sections 13 and 14 of the 1934 Act. *See id.* §§ 78m & 78n.

Disclosure as an Instrument of Behavioral Change

Mandatory disclosure is most often associated with fostering informed decision-making (by shareholders and investors, in the securities regulation context). Information is power and moves markets (a connection supported by economic theory, including the well-known efficient capital markets hypothesis). So, Congress employs mandatory disclosure regulation in Sarbanes-Oxley to empower investors to protect themselves and to promote market integrity by ensuring that standardized information is widely available to market participants.

However, Congress also uses mandatory disclosure rules in Sarbanes-Oxley to encourage desired behaviors consistent with the promotion of capital formation, investor protection and fair securities markets. By requiring that issuers disclose the existence and nature of certain important programs and policies, for example, Sarbanes-Oxley incentivizes a firm to have those programs and policies, to tailor those programs and policies to the firm's unique structures and operations, and to conform the contents of those programs and policies to applicable best practices. This effect of mandatory disclosure has made it a tool of choice for addressing public company issues that extend well beyond the core subject matter of federal securities regulation. For example, proponents of social and environmental change may become advocates for mandatory disclosure regulation that guides public companies to engage in more socially or environmentally responsible behaviors. The popularity of mandatory disclosure for the comprehensive regulation of public company behaviors has both devotees and detractors. Regardless, this expanded use of mandatory disclosure gives securities regulation a more central role in broad-spectrum business regulation in the United States.

Extensive Use of Congressionally Mandated Studies

Sarbanes-Oxley also signaled a new regulatory epoch in its inclusion of numerous studies and post-study reports on unresolved regulatory questions.[6] These legislatively mandated studies and reports typically are required to be completed within specified statutory time limits set forth in the legislation. Although the resort to mandatory studies and reports is arguably a responsible approach to important federal legislation in the

---

[6] Although these required studies are sprinkled throughout Sarbanes-Oxley, it seems important to note that the entirety of Title VII of the Act is devoted to studies and reports. *See* Sarbanes-Oxley §§ 701–05.

absence of a clear regulatory path (and given, in the case of Sarbanes-Oxley, Congress's relative lack of expertise in securities regulation), the required completion of multiple studies and reports under statutorily imposed deadlines (especially when considered together with compelled agency rulemaking, also under statutorily defined deadlines) taxes limited agency resources. The weight of congressionally mandated regulatory activity at the federal agency level increased significantly, at least in the area of federal securities regulation, starting with Sarbanes-Oxley. For example, Congress also relied on these study and reporting provisions in Dodd-Frank and the JOBS Act to handle unsettled regulatory matters relating to those legislative projects.

A Multifaceted, Multidimensional, Disjointed Legislative Response

At its most basic level, Sarbanes-Oxley can be divided into two major parts. The first part—the overwhelming majority of the legislation—focuses on public financial and accounting-related matters central to the auditing process (including the regulation of the supervision of public company auditors, public company auditor independence, and the structure and function of the public company audit committee). The remainder of Sarbanes-Oxley, however, comprises a veritable potpourri of legal provisions geared to providing or encouraging better disclosure transparency and curbing (through, among other things, mandatory disclosure, new offenses and penalties, substantive regulation, and other methods) behaviors associated with the financial frauds at Enron, Tyco, WorldCom and other public companies. A quick look at the individual provisions in Sarbanes-Oxley, when mapped to the conduct associated with the financial frauds that immediately preceded Sarbanes-Oxley's passage, reveals that many of the provisions in the Act are direct responses to individual elements of that conduct. The descriptions in this chapter note some of these responsive pieces of the statute.

Interestingly, even some of these apparently responsive provisions in Sarbanes-Oxley were not new when Congress took up consideration of Sarbanes-Oxley. A number of provisions in the act had been languishing in the U.S. Congress (some pieces for more than one congressional session) but were revived and re-packaged together in a single bill once Congress felt pressure to react to the revelations of financial fraud in 2001 and early 2002. By dusting off these pre-existing provisions, Congress was able to proceed rapidly once it determined to take action.

The entirety of Sarbanes-Oxley moved from action in the Senate Banking Committee to final passage in a matter of about six weeks.[7]

The Nature of this Chapter

This chapter describes and characterizes the key provisions in Sarbanes-Oxley and the attendant agency regulations—most, but not all, of which were promulgated by the U.S. Securities and Exchange Commission ("SEC"). The text also notes important catalysts and effects of the depicted provisions, as relevant. These descriptions, characterizations, catalysts and effects illustrate the themes described in this overview.

It is important to note that some of the provisions in Sarbanes-Oxley have been litigated or refined over the years. Litigation involving provisions in Sarbanes-Oxley offers us some additional insights. Refinements of Sarbanes-Oxley's mandates were included in, among other legislation, Dodd-Frank and the JOBS Act. Where relevant to the statutory and regulatory information presented, the chapter also portrays these related legal actions and rule enhancements.

REGULATING THE SUPERVISION OF PUBLIC COMPANY AUDITORS

Perhaps the most well-known and controversial aspect of Sarbanes-Oxley was its establishment of the Public Company Accounting Oversight Board, or PCAOB (also known fondly as "peekaboo," a play on its initials). The PCAOB is a quasi-public body charged with supervising the accounting profession's activities in auditing public companies. Prior to the enactment of Sarbanes-Oxley, the accounting profession was essentially self-regulated. This self-regulatory system was widely criticized in the wake of the financial fraud that led to the adoption of Sarbanes-Oxley.

The Nature and Structure of the PCAOB

The PCAOB was established under Section 101 of Sarbanes-Oxley with the following simple words:

---

[7] *See generally* R. William Ide, *Post-Enron Corporate Governance Opportunities: Creating a Culture of Greater Board Collaboration and Oversight*, 54 MERCER L. REV. 829, 830–31 (2003) (describing the legislative environment in the months preceding the passage of Sarbanes-Oxley).

> There is established the Public Company Accounting Oversight Board, to oversee the audit of public companies that are subject to the securities laws, and related matters, in order to protect the interests of investors and further the public interest in the preparation of informative, accurate, and independent audit reports for companies the securities of which are sold to, and held by and for, public investors. The Board shall be a body corporate, operate as a nonprofit corporation, and have succession until dissolved by an Act of Congress.[8]

The statute goes on to clarify that the PCAOB is not a federal agency, but, rather, a non-profit corporation under the law of the District of Columbia.[9] Only Congress can dissolve the PCAOB,[10] but the SEC has supervisory authority over it (including the express statutory power, in the public interest, for the protection of investors, and in accordance with the purposes of the Securities Exchange Act of 1934, as amended (the "1934 Act"), and the federal securities laws generally, to modify the PCAOB's responsibilities and reprimand its members).[11] The SEC approves all of the PCAOB's rulemaking and amendments and reviews (and may alter) the PCAOB's final dispositions of disciplinary actions against accounting firms.[12] Moreover, the SEC has enforcement authority with respect to violations of the rules governing the PCAOB.[13] The PCAOB's operations are funded through annual fees levied against issuers, subject to certain limitations.[14]

The five PCAOB members must be

> appointed from among prominent individuals of integrity and reputation who have a demonstrated commitment to the interests of investors and the public, and an understanding of the responsibilities for and nature of the financial disclosures required of issuers under the securities laws and the obligations of accountants with respect to the preparation and issuance of audit reports with respect to such disclosures.[15]

---

[8] Sarbanes-Oxley § 101(a) (codified at 15 U.S.C. § 7211(a)).

[9] *See id.* § 101(b) (codified at 15 U.S.C. § 7211(b)) ("The Board shall not be an agency or establishment of the United States Government, and, except as otherwise provided in this Act, shall be subject to, and have all the powers conferred upon a nonprofit corporation by, the District of Columbia Nonprofit Corporation Act.").

[10] *See id.* § 101(a) (codified at 15 U.S.C. § 7211(a)).

[11] *See id.* § 107 (codified at 15 U.S.C. § 7217).

[12] *Id.*

[13] *See id.* § 3(b)(1) (codified at 15 U.S.C. § 7202(b)(1)).

[14] *Id.* § 109 (codified at 15 U.S.C. § 7219).

[15] *See id.* § 101(e)(1) (codified at 15 U.S.C. § 7211(e)(1)).

Two members are required to be certified public accountants;[16] but if one of those members is the chair, that member "may not have been a practicing certified public accountant for at least five years prior to his or her appointment."[17] The term of each PCAOB member is five years, and no member of the PCAOB may serve more than two terms.[18]

The Function of the PCAOB

All accounting firms auditing public company financial statements are required by Sarbanes-Oxley to register with the PCAOB.[19] The PCAOB is charged with establishing and altering

> auditing and related attestation standards, … quality control standards, and … ethics standards to be used by registered public accounting firms in the preparation and issuance of audit reports, as required by this Act or the rules of the Commission, or as may be necessary or appropriate in the public interest or for the protection of investors.[20]

The PCAOB also conducts periodic compliance inspections of all public accounting firms.[21]

Constitutional Questions about the PCAOB's Authority

The PCAOB, established under the express provisions of the Sarbanes-Oxley Act as a non-governmental body, was structured and given broad authority to regulate public accountants in the manner of a governmental actor. In the first few years after the passage of Sarbanes-Oxley, scholars and other commentators began to question the PCAOB's equivocal private-public status.[22] These questions included a federal constitutional

---

16 *See id.* § 101(e)(2) (codified at 15 U.S.C. § 7211(e)(2)).

17 *Id.*

18 *Id.* § 101(e)(5)(A) & (B) (codified at 15 U.S.C. § 7211(e)(5)(A) & (B)).

19 *See id.* § 102 (codified at 15 U.S.C. § 7212).

20 *Id.* § 103(a)(1) (codified at 15 U.S.C. § 7213(a)(1)).

21 *See id.* § 104 (codified at 15 U.S.C. § 7214).

22 *See, e.g.*, Kimberly Brown, *Presidential Control of the Elite "Non-Agency,"* 88 N.C.L. REV. 71, 76 (2009) ("If Congress and the Supreme Court are to continue down the path of creating and endorsing structural novelties with substantial governmental powers, they should first have in mind some notion of where the outermost constitutional boundary for such entities lies."); Donna M. Nagy, *Playing Peekaboo with Constitutional Law: The PCAOB and its Public-Private Status*, 80 NOTRE DAME L. REV. 975, 980 (2005) ("Congress's creation of the PCAOB raises core constitutional questions about whether its actions

issue raised by a prominent legal scholar: whether the PCAOB is a public entity under the U.S. Constitution and, therefore, subject to constitutional restrictions inapplicable to private entities.[23]

Eventually, constitutional questions involving the PCAOB's structure and operation were addressed in high-profile litigation. In *Free Enterprise Fund v. PCAOB*,[24] the U.S. Supreme Court assessed the constitutionality of the PCAOB in light of the constitutional role of the executive branch to ensure faithful execution of U.S. law, including through the activities of officers in the executive branch. Specifically, the Court reviewed the constitutionality of Sarbanes-Oxley's provision for the removal of PCAOB members. Sarbanes-Oxley provides that the SEC can remove members of the PCAOB only for cause.[25] In and of itself, this provision is not unusual—or, as the Court finds, constitutionally problematic.[26]

However, when viewed in light of the President's limited power to remove members of the SEC, created by Congress as an independent federal agency,[27] the constitutional validity of Sarbanes-Oxley's PCAOB for-cause removal provision takes on a different character.

> The question is whether these separate layers of protection may be combined. May the President be restricted in his ability to remove a principal officer, who is in turn restricted in his ability to remove an inferior officer, even though that inferior officer determines the policy and enforces the laws of the United States?

---

constitute "state action" for purposes of the rights and protections secured by the U.S. Constitution."); Donna M. Nagy, *Is the PCAOB a "Heavily Controlled Component" of the SEC?: An Essential Question In The Constitutional Controversy*, 71 U. PITT. L. REV. 361 (2010) (concluding that the structure of the PCAOB violates the Appointments Clause and the separation of powers doctrine); David H. Roberts, *Too Close for Comfort: The Potential Dilemma Facing the Securities and Exchange Commission and the Public Company Accounting Oversight Board*, 28 PACE L. REV. 495, 496 (2008) ("An unintended consequence of the creation of dual authority in the SEC and the … PCAOB … to oversee public accountants is that an enforcement action by one of these parties may preclude or severely limit an enforcement action by the other.").

[23] *See* Nagy, *supra* note 22, at 1036, 1040, 1044–50.

[24] 130 S. Ct. 3138 (2010).

[25] Sarbanes-Oxley § 101(e)(6).

[26] 130 S. Ct. at 3147 ("[I]n *United States v. Perkins* … and *Morrison v. Olson* … , the Court sustained … restrictions on the power of principal executive officers—themselves responsible to the President—to remove their own inferiors.").

[27] *See* Humphrey's Executor v. United States, 295 U.S. 602 (1935).

> We hold that such multilevel protection from removal is contrary to Article II's vesting of the executive power in the President. The President cannot "take Care that the Laws be faithfully executed" if he cannot oversee the faithfulness of the officers who execute them. Here the President cannot remove an officer who enjoys more than one level of good-cause protection, even if the President determines that the officer is neglecting his duties or discharging them improperly. That judgment is instead committed to another officer, who may or may not agree with the President's determination, and whom the President cannot remove simply because that officer disagrees with him. This contravenes the President's "constitutional obligation to ensure the faithful execution of the laws."[28]

Although the Court determined that the removal provision was unconstitutional, it did not strike down the existence of the PCAOB itself; rather, the Court found the defective provision to be severable from the remainder of the Sarbanes-Oxley provisions establishing and providing for the PCAOB.[29] The PCAOB also survived three other challenges under the Appointments Clause in the *Free Enterprise Fund* case.[30]

REGULATING AUDITOR INDEPENDENCE

Public company auditors are certification intermediaries.[31] They provide audit services and render audit reports to business firms for consumption by their management and their actual and prospective owners—their shareholders and investors. Acting in this role, auditors must, among other things, avoid conflicts of interest that could taint their judgment.

Accounting self-regulation of auditor conflicting interests was largely seen as a failure that contributed to the financial fraud revealed in the

---

28 130 S. Ct. at 3147.

29 *Id.* at 3161.

30 *Id.* at 3162–64.

31 Although this is not a standardized term of art, "certification intermediary" is descriptive. Commentators have used it before to refer to non-governmental third parties that provide evaluation and monitoring services that supply a certification or verification function for participants in securities markets. *See* Stephen Choi, *Market Lessons for Gatekeepers*, 92 NW. U.L. REV. 916, 918 (1998) (describing certification intermediaries as those who "screen for product quality and certify value to purchasers in the market"); Joan MacLeod Heminway, *The New Intermediary on the Block: Funding Portals under the Crowdfund Act*, 13 U.C. DAVIS BUS. L.J. 177, 184 (2013) (describing certification intermediaries as "a specific type of information intermediary that also serves as a reputational intermediary" and referencing other scholarship that identifies this role).

new millennium. It was widely hypothesized that public company auditors would have been (and could be) better gatekeepers in screening out financial fraud if they did not have direct or indirect relationships with their audit clients and the clients' management personnel outside the audit process. Accordingly, in Sarbanes-Oxley, Congress focused specific attention on limiting and eliminating potential conflicts of interest commonly present in public company audit engagements.

> One of the purposes of … Sarbanes-Oxley … was to address … financial intermediary conflicts of interest. For example, Sarbanes-Oxley (i) makes it unlawful for statutory auditors for registered companies to provide a wide range of non-auditing services to its clients, [and] (ii) prohibits an auditing firm from auditing a registered firm whose CEO, controller, CFO, Chief Accounting Officer, or person in an equivalent position had been employed by the auditing firm during the one-year period preceding the audit … .[32]

These and other related provisions in Sarbanes-Oxley are important enough to warrant a brief description.

Provision of Non-Audit Services

Certain provisions in Sarbanes-Oxley address the provision of non-audit services at the firm level. For example, Sarbanes-Oxley prohibits a registered public accounting firm from performing any non-audit services for an issuer while auditing that issuer.[33] An exemplar list of non-audit services is included in the statute.[34] In addition, Sarbanes-Oxley mandates audit committee preapproval of non-audit services (subject to an exception for *de minimis* services)[35] and the disclosure to investors of any non-audit services provided by the auditor and approved by the audit committee.[36]

---

[32] John L. Orcutt, *Improving the Efficiency of the Angel Finance Market: A Proposal to Expand the Intermediary Role of Finders in the Private Capital Raising Setting*, 37 Ariz. St. L.J. 861, 896–97 (2005) (footnotes omitted).

[33] *See* Sarbanes-Oxley § 201(a) (codified at 5 U.S.C. 78j–1(g)).

[34] *See id.*

[35] *See id.* (codified at 5 U.S.C. 78j–1(h)); Sarbanes-Oxley § 202 (codified at 5 U.S.C. 78j–1(i)).

[36] *See id.* § 202 (codified at 15 U.S.C. 78j–1(i)).

Other Auditor Relationships

Although some observers had advocated the codification of a mandatory rotation system for public company audit firms, Sarbanes-Oxley calls for a "study and review of the potential effects of requiring the mandatory rotation of registered public accounting firms" and mandates a report to the Committee on Banking, Housing, and Urban Affairs of the Senate and the Committee on Financial Services of the House of Representatives on that study and review.[37] Instead, provisions in Sarbanes-Oxley addressing auditor independence outside the non-audit services context focus more intently on the status and potential relationships among individuals engaged in performing audit services and approving audit reports. For instance, once a lead, coordinating or reviewing audit partner has worked with an audit client for five years, the firm is prohibited from providing audit services for that client.[38] This forces audit firms to rotate the partner with primary responsibility for the audit or lose the audit client. In addition, Sarbanes-Oxley prohibits any registered public accounting firm from performing auditing services for an issuer if the chief executive, chief financial, chief accounting officer, controller, or like individual employed by a potential audit client was employed by the public accounting firm and participated in the audit for that issuer within the preceding year.[39] Finally, Sarbanes-Oxley prohibits a public company director or officer, as provided in SEC rules, from taking any action "to fraudulently influence, coerce, manipulate or mislead any public or certified accountant engaged in the performance of an audit of the financial statements of that issuer for the purpose of rendering such financial statements seriously misleading."[40]

REGULATING THE STRUCTURE AND FUNCTION OF PUBLIC COMPANY AUDIT COMMITTEES

The audit committee—a standing committee of the board of directors of each public company issuer—is a critical gatekeeper for audit services and financial disclosures. Weaknesses in this monitoring system were, like auditor conflicting interests, branded as possible causes contributing to the public company financial fraud that immediately preceded the

---

[37] *Id.* § 207 (codified at 15 U.S.C. § 7232).
[38] *See id.* § 203 (codified at 15 U.S.C. 78j–1(j)).
[39] *See id.* § 206 (codified at 15 U.S.C. 78j–1(l)).
[40] *See id.* § 303(a) (codified at 15 U.S.C. § 7242).

passage of Sarbanes-Oxley. As a result, Congress took action in Sarbanes-Oxley to strengthen the role and standardize the activities of the public company audit committee. Sarbanes-Oxley requires the SEC to engage in rulemaking that compels the national securities exchanges and national securities associations to prohibit the listing of any security of an issuer that fails to comply with the Sarbanes-Oxley rules governing audit committees.[41]

This portion of Sarbanes-Oxley is one among many that reach into a regulatory area previously reserved almost exclusively to state law. Board committees are authorized, and the permitted scope of their authority is determined, in state corporate statutes.[42] By defining the structure and function of the audit committees of public companies, Congress enacted federal corporate governance regulation that layers requirements onto state corporate governance rules.

Sarbanes-Oxley provides that members of audit committees of public companies be members of the company's board of directors and be independent.[43] Independence requirements demand that each

> member of an audit committee of an issuer… not, other than in his or her capacity as a member of the audit committee, the board of directors, or any other board committee—(i) accept any consulting, advisory, or other compensatory fee from the issuer; or (ii) be an affiliated person of the issuer or any subsidiary thereof.[44]

The independence of audit committee members was deemed to be important as a means of better enabling objective thought and action in connection with the reporting of the issuer's financial condition and results of operations—thought and action that is untainted by conflicting interests or management influence.[45]

Sarbanes-Oxley did not stop at defining the *composition* of a public company's audit committee, however. Congress also defined the *role* of the public company audit committee in the act.

---

41 *See id.* § 301 (codified at 15 U.S.C. 78j-1(m)(1)(A)).

42 *See, e.g.*, 8 DEL. C. § 141(c); TENN. CODE ANN. § 48–18–206.

43 *See* Sarbanes-Oxley § 301 (codified at 15 U.S.C. 78j-1(m)(3)(A)).

44 *Id.* (codified at 15 U.S.C. 78j-1(m)(3)(B)). The statute also empowers the SEC to exempt certain relationships from the independence requirement. *See id.* (codified at 15 U.S.C. 78j-1(m)(3)(C)).

45 *See generally* Robert A. Prentice & David B. Spence, *Sarbanes-Oxley as Quack Corporate Governance: How Wise is the Received Wisdom?*, 95 GEO. L.J. 1843, 1871–79 (2007) (describing the basis for and merits of the audit committee provisions in Sarbanes-Oxley, including the independence provision).

> The audit committee of each issuer, in its capacity as a committee of the board of directors, shall be directly responsible for the appointment, compensation, and oversight of the work of any registered public accounting firm employed by that issuer (including resolution of disagreements between management and the auditor regarding financial reporting) for the purpose of preparing or issuing an audit report or related work, and each such registered public accounting firm shall report directly to the audit committee.[46]

The audit committee also is charged under Sarbanes-Oxley with establishing complaint procedures for "accounting, internal accounting controls, or auditing matters"[47] and procedures for "the confidential, anonymous submission by employees of the issuer of concerns regarding questionable accounting or auditing matters."[48] Congress provided support for the audit committee's work through statutory authority to retain advisers and through mandates of appropriate funding.[49]

REGULATING PUBLIC COMPANY DISCLOSURES

The audit-related provisions in Sarbanes-Oxley constitute a significant portion of the Act. They are undoubtedly important as a matter of audit policy and have made significant changes in audit practice. Much of the remainder of Sarbanes-Oxley consists of mandatory disclosure rules—provisions requiring the disclosure of designated information, most of which (given Sarbanes-Oxley's genesis in revelations of financial fraud) concerns matters of financial importance to public company issuers. In some respects, the disclosure-related provisions in Sarbanes-Oxley are little more than clarifications of disclosure rules and practices applicable to public companies *before* the enactment of Sarbanes-Oxley. Moreover, some of the other disclosure-related provisions in Sarbanes-Oxley, while new, are arguably unnecessary for other reasons. Nevertheless, Congress believed (or hoped) that Sarbanes-Oxley's clarifications and additions to the disclosure rules would better guide responsible management behavior (or at least facilitate public or private enforcement against wrongdoers).

The disclosure-related requirements in Sarbanes-Oxley are supported by new required administrative process. Specifically, Sarbanes-Oxley

---

[46] Sarbanes-Oxley § 301 (codified at 15 U.S.C. 78j-1(m)(2)).
[47] *Id.* § 301 (codified at 15 U.S.C. 78j-1(m)(4)(A)).
[48] *Id.* § 301 (codified at 15 U.S.C. 78j-1(m)(4)(B)).
[49] *Id.* § 301 (codified at 15 U.S.C. 78j-1(m)(5) & (6)).

dictates the timing of SEC reviews of public company disclosures.[50] Congress also indicated the criteria that the SEC should be attentive to in establishing a review schedule.[51] The listed criteria focus principally on attributes of the issuer (e.g., issuers with material restatements in their financial results, issuers with significant relative stock price volatility, issuers with a relatively high market capitalization, "emerging companies with disparities in price to earning ratios," and issuers with operations that have significant affects on an important part of the economy), but Congress also authorized the SEC to consider other relevant factors in determining the schedule for its reviews.[52] Congress required, however, that a particular reporting issuer's disclosure be reviewed at least once every three years.[53]

A cursory review of even a selected set of the significant mandatory disclosure and disclosure-based requirements in Sarbanes-Oxley illustrates the diverse nature of the legislation well. The assorted rules cover a wide range of subject matters and represent a number of different approaches to effectuating disclosure policy. Despite the fact that many of the provisions are of questionable necessity, they have (or promise to have), individually and in the aggregate, far-reaching effects on the regulatory system and, in at least some cases, corporate behavior.

CEO and CFO Certifications

Among the more highly publicized disclosure-related provisions in Sarbanes-Oxley is the requirement that the SEC adopt rules mandating the certification, by an issuer's key executives, of information in the issuer's SEC filings. Sarbanes-Oxley requires that the chief executive and chief financial officer of each public issuer certify that they have reviewed the financial statements included in the issuer's periodic reports, as well as the accuracy and completeness of those financial statements, the financial statements' fair presentation of the financial condition and results of operations of the issuer, and certain matters regarding the internal controls of the issuer.[54] Although an issuer's chief executive and chief financial officer were required to individually sign periodic reports

---

[50] *See id.* § 408(a) (codified at 15 U.S.C. § 7266(a)) (mandating, as a general matter, SEC review of disclosures made by reporting issuers "on a regular and systematic basis for the protection of investors.").

[51] *See id.* § 408(b) (codified at 15 U.S.C. § 7266(b)).

[52] *See id.*

[53] *See id.* § 408(c) (codified at 15 U.S.C. § 7266(c)).

[54] *See id.* § 302(a) (codified at 15 U.S.C. § 7241(a)).

prior to the enactment of Sarbanes-Oxley, the personal accountability and responsibility of chief executive officers and chief financial officers under the Sarbanes-Oxley certification requirements arguably are clearer and more comprehensive than the signature requirement that predated Sarbanes-Oxley.[55] As a compliance incentive, Congress provided for criminal penalties for officers who fail to comply with the Sarbanes-Oxley financial statement certification requirements.[56]

Accuracy and Completeness of Financial Statements

Given that Sarbanes-Oxley was the product of faulty financial statements owing in part to deficiencies in the reporting of off-balance sheet transactions, it is not surprising that Congress focused some attention in Sarbanes-Oxley on shoring up disclosure rules relating to financial statements in general and off-balance sheet transactions specifically. Sarbanes-Oxley provides that reports containing an issuer's financial statements must "reflect all material correcting adjustments that have been identified by a registered public accounting firm in accordance with generally accepted accounting principles" and SEC rules and regulations.[57] Sarbanes-Oxley also requires the SEC to

> issue final rules providing that each annual and quarterly financial report required to be filed with the Commission shall disclose all material off-balance sheet transactions, arrangements, obligations (including contingent obligations), and other relationships of the issuer with unconsolidated entities or other persons, that may have a material current or future effect on financial condition, changes in financial condition, results of operations, liquidity, capital expenditures, capital resources, or significant components of revenues or expenses.[58]

Other financial statement disclosure provisions in Sarbanes-Oxley include a required SEC study and report on the extent and disclosure of off-balance sheet transactions and required SEC rulemaking on the

---

[55] *See generally* Lisa M. Fairfax, *Form Over Substance?: Officer Certification and the Promise of Enhanced Personal Accountability under the Sarbanes-Oxley Act*, 55 RUTGERS L. REV. 1, (2002) (analyzing the officer certification requirements under Sarbanes-Oxley); *see also* Betty Joan Thurber, *Behavioral Science Analysis of Sarbanes-Oxley's Certification Requirements—The Right Kind of Deterrence?*, 7 TRANSACTIONS: TENN. J. BUS. L. 123 (2005).

[56] *See* Sarbanes-Oxley § 906 (codified at 18 U.S.C. § 1350).

[57] *Id.* § 401(a) (codified at 15 U.S.C. § 78m(i)).

[58] *Id.* (codified at 15 U.S.C. § 78m(j)).

reporting of pro forma financial information.[59] The SEC's rulemaking in this area enhanced disclosures in the Management's Discussion and Analysis of Financial Condition and Results of Operations ("MD&A") portions of SEC statements and reports[60] and in general reporting and recordkeeping requirements.[61]

Transactions Involving Management and Principal Stockholders

Sarbanes-Oxley also amended the reporting provisions in Section 16(a) of the 1934 Act[62] (associated with the short-swing profit liability provision in Section 16(b) of the 1934 Act[63]). These reporting provisions require directors, officers and beneficial owners of more than 10 percent of a registered class of equity security to report ownership of and transactions in the issuer's equity securities, subject to certain exceptions.[64] Sarbanes-Oxley shortened the filing deadlines for the statements that comply with these reporting requirements,[65] increasing the prompt public availability of accurate and complete information about these trading transactions. In addition, Congress provided in Sarbanes-Oxley for electronic filings of the required statements and mandated that the SEC and each public company issuer make the filings available electronically on their respective websites within one day.[66]

Internal Controls

The structures and processes that firms have in place to ensure the accuracy and completeness of their reported financial statements are referred to as internal controls.[67] The failure of adequate internal controls

---

59 *See id.* §§ 401(b) & (c) (codified at 15 U.S.C. § 7261(b) & (c)).

60 *See* 17 C.F.R. § 228.303 (2013).

61 *See id.* § 244.102.

62 15 U.S.C. § 78p(a) (2012).

63 *Id.* § 78p(b). Under this provision in the 1934 Act, directors, officers, and beneficial owners of more than 10 percent of an issuer's registered equity securities may be compelled to disgorge any deemed profit from the matched purchase and sale of any of those securities within in six-month period. *Id.*

64 *Id.* § 78p(a).

65 *See* Sarbanes-Oxley § 403 (codified at 15 U.S.C. § 78p(a)(2)(C)).

66 *See id.* (codified at 15 U.S.C. § 78p(a)(4)).

67 This definition is a general one. The concept of an internal control has different meanings for different people in different contexts. *See generally* Management's Report on Internal Control Over Financial Reporting and Certification of Disclosure in Exchange Act Periodic Reports, Exchange Act Release

is also among the often-listed contributing causes of financial fraud at Enron and elsewhere. Sarbanes-Oxley requires the SEC to adopt rules providing for the inclusion of an internal control report in each annual report.[68] This internal control report articulates "the responsibility of management for establishing and maintaining an adequate internal control structure and procedures for financial reporting" and assesses the effectiveness of these internal controls.[69] Under Sarbanes-Oxley, the issuer's auditor must attest to and report on management's assessment of the effectiveness of its internal controls.[70]

From the beginning, the SEC's rules for internal control reports, which were codified in a new integrated disclosure rule in Regulations S-B and S-K,[71] engendered significant negative commentary, especially as applied to smaller public company issuers, because compliance costs were deemed to be unacceptably high.[72] More than ten years after the enactment of Sarbanes-Oxley, the controversy about the efficacy of this provision persists. As part of the Dodd-Frank Act, Congress formally exempted non-accelerated filers (issuers with a public float less than $75 million) from the internal controls reporting requirements[73] and commissioned studies by the SEC and the Comptroller General of the United States[74] in an attempt to better ascertain the benefits and burdens of the internal controls mandates in Sarbanes-Oxley. The JOBS Act further reduces the number of issuers subject to internal controls reporting by exempting emerging growth companies from auditor attestation requirements for five years after going public and by reducing the number of firms that may become public companies because of the dollar value of their total assets and the aggregate number of record owners of a class of their equity securities.[75] These congressional retrenchments regarding internal controls disclosures have occurred despite evidence that internal

---

No. 47986 (June 5, 2003) (noting and explaining, in Part II.A. that "that internal control is a broad concept.").

68 *Id.* § 404(a) (codified at 15 U.S.C. § 7262(a)).

69 *Id.*

70 *Id.* § 404(b) (codified at 15 U.S.C. § 7262(b)).

71 *See* 17 C.F.R. § 228.308 (2013); *id.* § 229.308.

72 *See* Robert Prentice, *Sarbanes-Oxley: The Evidence Regarding the Impact of SOX 404*, 29 Cardozo L. Rev. 703 725–32 (2007) (noting and assessing the validity of this criticism).

73 Dodd-Frank § 989G(a) (codified at 15 U.S.C. § 7262(c)).

74 *Id.* §§ 989G(b) (providing for the SEC study) & 989I (providing for the Comptroller General study).

75 *See* JOBS Act §§ 103 (amending 15 U.S.C. § 7262(b)) & 501 (codified at 15 U.S.C. § 78l(g)(1)(A)); *see also* James D. Cox, *Strengthening Financial*

controls assessment and reporting would have positive effects on the financial reporting of the exempted firms.[76]

Code of Ethics for Senior Financial Officers

Sarbanes-Oxley also requires the SEC to adopt rules compelling public companies to disclose, in their periodic reports under Sections 13(a) or 15(d) of the 1934 Act (e.g., Forms 10-K and 10-Q), whether they have adopted a code of ethics for senior financial officers (and if not, why not).[77] Congress also required the SEC to mandate *immediate* disclosure, in a current report on Form 8-K or by electronic means, of any change to, or waiver of, the code of ethics.[78] Congress defined its conception of a code of ethics in the statute as comprising three emphases: "(1) honest and ethical conduct, including the ethical handling of actual or apparent conflicts of interest between personal and professional relationships; (2) full, fair, accurate, timely, and understandable disclosure in the periodic reports required to be filed by the issuer; and (3) compliance with applicable governmental rules and regulations."[79] The SEC adopted rules that both implement and broaden the ethics code requirements set forth in Sarbanes-Oxley.[80]

Undoubtedly, the code of ethics disclosure requirement in Sarbanes-Oxley has informational value that may help protect investors and promote market integrity. However, it also encourages public companies to adopt and maintain compliance programs that have an ethical component (because non-disclosure of a code of ethics or disclosure of a waiver signals that the firm may be engaged in unethical activities).[81] As a result, this aspect of Sarbanes-Oxley's disclosure mandates has a substantive regulation aspect to it—one that borders on federal corporate governance rulemaking in that it comes close to mandating action by an issuer's board of directors.[82] The plan and waiver disclosure requirements

---

Reporting: An Essay on Expanding the Auditor's Opinion Letter, 81 GEO. WASH. L. REV. 1036, 1039–40 (2013).

[76] *See, e.g.*, Cox, *supra* note 75, at 1040 (noting and citing to studies to this effect).

[77] *See* Sarbanes-Oxley § 406(a) (codified at 15 U.S.C. § 7264(a)).

[78] *See id.* § 406(b) (codified at 15 U.S.C. § 7264(b)).

[79] *See id.* § 406(c) (codified at 15 U.S.C. § 7264(c)).

[80] *See* Disclosure Required by Sections 406 and 407 of the Sarbanes-Oxley Act of 2002, Exchange Act Release No. (Jan. 23. 2003).

[81] *See, e.g.*, Usha Rodrigues & Mike Stegemoller, *Placebo Ethics: A Study In Securities Disclosure Arbitrage*, 96 VA. L. REV. 1, 15 (2010).

[82] *See id.* at 16.

can be traced directly back to the Enron affair, in which the board of directors of Enron waived a board policy that would have prevented related-party transactions entered into by Enron's chief financial officer as part of Enron's financial fraud.[83]

Compliance programs are incentivized in various ways at the federal and state levels, including through federal sentencing guidelines and regulatory initiatives applicable to firms in specific industries, as well as through compliance with and the enforcement of director and officer fiduciary duties. Sarbanes-Oxley adds to these incentives through its ethics code and waiver disclosure mandate.[84] This is a laudatory objective. However, the code of ethics disclosure mandate may have unintended consequences in that it may encourage registrants to water down their codes of ethics to minimize the prospect that waivers would have to be disclosed.[85]

Disclosure of Audit Committee Financial Expert

Sarbanes-Oxley also calls upon the SEC to require public company issuers to disclose in their periodic reports whether the audit committee includes at least one financial expert, and if not, why not.[86] Although Congress stopped short of defining the concept of a "financial expert" in the statute, it offers substantial guidance to the SEC in engaging that task by requiring the SEC to consider specific attributes of audit committee members, including:

> whether a person has, through education and experience as a public accountant or auditor or a principal financial officer, comptroller, or principal accounting officer of an issuer, or from a position involving the performance of similar functions—
>
> (1) an understanding of generally accepted accounting principles and financial statements;
> (2) experience in—
>   (A) the preparation or auditing of financial statements of generally comparable issuers; and

---

[83] *See id.* at 14–15.

[84] *See id.* at 16 (noting that "the law's ethics requirement was couched, somewhat awkwardly, as a disclosure mandate.").

[85] *See id.* at 19.

[86] *See* Sarbanes-Oxley § 407(a) (codified at 15 U.S.C. § 7264(a)).

(B) the application of such principles in connection with the accounting for estimates, accruals, and reserves;

(3) experience with internal accounting controls; and

(4) an understanding of audit committee functions.[87]

The SEC's rulemaking (together with that of the major national stock exchanges) clarifies, enhances and modifies Congress's disclosure rule.[88] Resulting rules adopted by the New York Stock Exchange and NASDAQ further provide that all members of audit committees must be financially literate.[89]

Again, while Sarbanes-Oxley's financial expert disclosure requirement unquestionably has informative value, it also encourages specific corporate conduct in public companies—namely, the inclusion of a financial expert on their audit committees.

> Although Sarbanes-Oxley inserted Section 407 in the section entitled "Enhanced Financial Disclosures," with other provisions aimed at financial disclosures, the effect of the section is to require each public company audit committee to have at least one financial expert, because most public companies would not wish to disclose that they did not have a financial expert. In addition, the section, together with the SEC's, NYSE's, and Nasdaq's subsequent rules, has the effect of determining at least one person who is qualified to sit on the board of a public company.[90]

As such, the financial expert disclosure requirement is, in effect, a substantive federal corporate governance initiative (albeit a precatory one).

Real-Time Issuer Disclosures

Sarbanes-Oxley requires reporting issuers to disclose to the public "on a rapid and current basis … , in plain English," any material financial or operating information required to be disclosed by the SEC.[91] This real-time disclosure rule has the purpose, even if not the actual effect, of better informing the market of significant corporate developments as they

---

[87] *Id.* § 407(b) (codified at 15 U.S.C. § 7264(b)).

[88] *See, e.g.*, Lyman P.Q. Johnson & Mark A. Sides, *Corporate Governance and the Sarbanes-Oxley Act: The Sarbanes-Oxley Act and Fiduciary Duties*, 30 WM. MITCHELL L. REV. 1149, 1175–77 (2004).

[89] *See* NASD and NYSE Rulemaking: Relating to Corporate Governance, Exchange Act Release No. 48745 (Nov. 4, 2003).

[90] Johnson & Sides, *supra* note 8, at 1175.

[91] Sarbanes-Oxley § 409 (codified at 15 U.S.C. § 78m(l)).

occur as a means of avoiding the occurrence and market effects of financial fraud seen in the pre-Sarbanes-Oxley era. Though often overlooked by commentators, this provision has the capacity to accomplish something quite striking in the overall scheme of U.S. securities regulation: continuous disclosure. Prior to the adoption of Sarbanes-Oxley, the U.S. mandatory disclosure system was explicitly and clearly a regime built around periodic (annual and quarterly) and event-based (triggered by the nature of the transaction or other event), rather than continuous, disclosure.

Under the authority of Sarbanes-Oxley's "rapid and current" disclosure rule, the SEC adopted changes to the current report on Form 8-K that significantly expanded its required use and accelerated the timing for required filings.[92] Specifically, in these post-Sarbanes-Oxley amendments to the Form 8-K requirements, the SEC added new triggering events that require the filing of a Form 8-K and shortened the Form 8-K filing deadlines from fifteen days to four days for most purposes. The combined effect of the congressional and SEC rulemaking was a significant increase in the number and frequency of Form 8-K filings. The efficacy of these additional filings in creating a more well-informed, efficient public trading market for securities is, however, unclear.[93]

REGULATING FRAUD, MISSTATEMENTS AND SIMILAR MISCONDUCT

Although they are a relatively minor part of the Act, a number of provisions in Sarbanes-Oxley modify or fill gaps in the web of federal securities law liability provisions prohibiting fraud, misstatements and other misconduct. These provisions cover both criminal and civil enforcement activities and are located in Titles VII, IX and XI of Sarbanes-Oxley. As is true for the disclosure-related regulation in Sarbanes-Oxley, the misconduct regulation in the Act includes disparate provisions impacting many kinds of conduct.

---

[92] *See* Additional Form 8-K Disclosure Requirements and Acceleration of Filing Date, Exchange Act Release No. 49424A (Aug. 4, 2004).

[93] *See, e.g.*, Jennifer B. Lawrence & Jackson W. Prentice, *The SEC Form 8-K: Full Disclosure or Fully Diluted? The Quest for Improved Financial Market Transparency*, 41 WAKE FOREST L. REV. 913, 936 (2006) ("[O]ur results leave open the question of whether the expansion of 8-K filing requirements has increased the quality of financial disclosures or diluted an already saturated labyrinth of investor information.").

New Crimes and Criminal Penalties

Congress defined new criminal offenses in Sarbanes-Oxley in the hopes of better deterring and punishing corporate malfeasance. For example, as earlier noted, Sarbanes-Oxley criminalizes knowingly noncompliant certifications of periodic reports by an issuer's chief executive officer and chief financial officer.[94] Congress also inserted a new criminal attempt and conspiracy provision in Sarbanes-Oxley.[95]

In addition, Sarbanes-Oxley specifies and penalizes certain obstructions of justice, including:

1. The knowing alteration, destruction, mutilation, concealment, cover-up, falsification, or false recording or documentation of information "with the intent to impede, obstruct, or influence the investigation or proper administration of any matter within the jurisdiction of any department or agency of the United States or any case filed under title 11, or in relation to or contemplation of any such matter or case;[96] and
2. The knowing or willful destruction of public company audit records.[97]

These new offenses are a direct reaction to the destruction of Enron's audit records by its auditor, Arthur Andersen LLP, on the eve of civil litigation and government investigations (after the firm became aware those legal and administrative actions were forthcoming). Arthur Andersen was successfully prosecuted for obstruction of justice in the aftermath of the Enron affair, but Congress enacted new obstruction of justice offenses and penalties in any case. (Admittedly, Sarbanes-Oxley was enacted before the Arthur Andersen prosecution had fully devolved.)

Sarbanes-Oxley also includes criminal penalties for particular types of securities fraud. Specifically, Congress included in Sarbanes-Oxley fines and imprisonment (not exceeding twenty-five years) for defrauding any person in connection with any security of a public company or a reporting company and for obtaining money or property in connection with the purchase or sale of any security of a public or reporting

---

[94] *See* Sarbanes-Oxley § 906(a) (codified at 18 U.S.C. § 1350(c)).
[95] *See id.* § 902(a) (codified at 18 U.S.C.. § 1349).
[96] *See id.* § 802 (codified at 18 U.S.C. § 1519).
[97] *See id.* (codified at 18 U.S.C. § 1520).

company "by means of false or fraudulent pretenses, representations, or promises."[98]

The rationale behind the adoption of the new offenses is quite general (and a bit muddled).

> According to the Judiciary Committee, Congress enacted the Securities Fraud Statute for three primary reasons. First, the Enron debacle and subsequent escalation of corporate scandals revealed significant gaps in federal securities and criminal fraud laws. ... Second, Congress sought to give federal prosecutors an elastic statute that would enable them to prosecute yet unforeseen securities fraud schemes ... . Third, Congress sought to deter securities fraud more effectively.[99]

The net effect of these provisions is to give federal prosecutors a new enforcement tool carrying significant penalties that may deter potential violators.

Sarbanes-Oxley also increases penalties for specific crimes. For instance, Congress increased maximum prison sentences from five to twenty years for mail and wire fraud.[100] Congress also increased fines and prison sentences for certain violations of the Employee Retirement Income Security Act of 1974, as amended.[101] Perhaps most importantly, Congress significantly boosted maximum fines and prison terms for general criminal violations under the 1934 Act.[102]

Provisions in the Act requiring the U.S. Sentencing Commission to review (and, as appropriate, promulgate or amend) federal sentencing guidelines support the prosecution of existing crimes and the new crimes and criminal penalties introduced in Sarbanes-Oxley.[103] First, Congress asked the U.S. Sentencing Commission to take a look at the sentencing guidelines applicable to securities and accounting fraud and related offenses.[104] Second, Congress focused the U.S. Sentencing Commission on a review of the sentencing guidelines applicable to obstruction of

---

98 *See id.* § 807 (codified at 18 U.S.C. § 1348).

99 Luke A.E. Pazicky, Note: *A New Arrow in the Quiver of Federal Securities Fraud Prosecutors: Section 807 of the Sarbanes-Oxley Act Of 2002 (18 U.S.C. § 1348)*, 81 WASH. U. LAW Q. 801, 804–09 (2003) (footnotes omitted).

100 *See* Sarbanes-Oxley § 903 (amending 18 U.S.C. §§ 1341 & 1343).

101 *See id.* § 904 (amending 29 U.S.C. § 1131).

102 *See id.* § 1106 (amending 15 U.S.C. § 78ff(a)).

103 *See id.* §§ 805(a) & 1104.

104 *See id.* § 1104.

justice and certain types of criminal fraud (e.g., falsification of records).[105]

In Sarbanes-Oxley, Congress requested or required a review of the sentencing guidelines in order to generally ensure appropriate, effective responses to organizational criminal misconduct. However, Congress also had specific objectives in mind. These objectives included a variety of factors relevant to deterrence and punishment based on base offense levels and enhancements.[106] The U.S. Sentencing Commission undertook a review and adopted several related amendments to the sentencing guidelines.[107]

Civil Enforcement Actions

A few key provisions in Sarbanes-Oxley contend with civil actions and remedies for financial fraud. Most importantly, Congress lengthened the statute of limitations applicable to "a claim of fraud, deceit, manipulation or contrivance in contravention of a regulatory requirement concerning the securities laws."[108] Actions seeking to vindicate those types of claims may, under the rule enacted in Sarbanes-Oxley, be brought until two years after the discovery of the facts constituting the violation or five years after the violation, whichever occurs earlier.[109] Congress expressly disclaimed the creation of any new private rights of action in Sarbanes-Oxley.[110]

REGULATING THE SUBSTANCE OF PUBLIC COMPANY ACTIVITIES

Sarbanes-Oxley's substantive regulation provisions are among the most simple and direct rules in the act. They also are among the most controversial aspects of the legislation, for many observers, because of their extensive reach into corporate operations and governance. In sum,

---

105 *See id.* § 805(a).

106 *See id.* § 805(a) & 1104.

107 *See* Frank O. Bowman, III, *Pour encourager les autres? The Curious History and Distressing Implications of the Criminal Provisions of the Sarbanes-Oxley Act and the Sentencing Guidelines Amendments That Followed*, 1 OHIO ST. J. CRIM. L. 373, 411–35 (2004); *see also* Pamela H. Bucy, "*Carrots and Sticks": Post-Enron Regulatory Initiatives*, 8 BUFF. CRIM. L. R. 277, 299–304 (2004).

108 *See* Sarbanes-Oxley § 804(a) (amending 28 U.S.C. § 1658).

109 *See id.*

110 *See id.* § 804(c).

Sarbanes-Oxley proscribes public companies from making personal loans to senior management, provides for chief executive officer and chief financial officer compensation clawbacks and prohibits trading in public company securities by senior management of public companies during pension fund blackout periods.

Prohibition on Personal Loans to Directors and Executives

Sarbanes-Oxley expressly prohibits public companies from extending credit (including by making personal loans) to their directors and executive officers, subject to certain limitations.[111] This provision in Sarbanes-Oxley is a reaction to loans and financial comingling that occurred at public companies that engaged in financial fraud.[112] Nevertheless, to many, a flat-out prohibition on director and executive officer loans seems like a draconian response—a patronizing federal usurpation of what had been a matter wholly within the power of the board of directors of corporate issuers under state corporate law.[113]

Adding insult to injury, the loan prohibition provision has been hard to interpret in application. For example, it has not been entirely clear that indemnification advances can be paid to directors or officers.[114] The SEC has been stingy in offering guidance on the application of the loan prohibition provision.

Executive Compensation Clawbacks and Asset Freezes

Sarbanes-Oxley imposes direct financial penalties on key executive officers by providing for compensation clawbacks under certain circumstances. After revelation of the financial frauds at Enron, Tyco, WorldCom, et al., commentary focused around the incentive compensation earned by key executives based on the inflated results of operations

---

111 *See id.* § 402 (codified at 15 U.S.C. § 78m(k)).

112 *See* Miriam A. Cherry, *Whistling in the Dark? Corporate Fraud, Whistleblowers, and the Implications of the Sarbanes-Oxley Act for Employment Law*, 79 WASH. L. REV. 1029, 1060–61 (2004).

113 *See* William B. Chandler III & Leo E. Strine, Jr., *Views From the Bench: The New Federalism of the American Corporate Governance System: Preliminary Reflections of Two Residents of One Small State*, 152 U. PA. L. REV. 953, 971–72 (2003); Johnson & Sides, *supra* note 88, at 1177–78.

114 *See* Cynthia Bulan, *A Small Question in the Big Statute: Does Section 402 of Sarbanes-Oxley Prohibit Defense Advancements?*, 39 CREIGHTON L. REV. 357, 363–82; Chandler & Strine, *supra* note 113, at 972.

reported by these public companies.[115] Specifically, the Act requires a public company issuer's chief executive officer and chief financial officer to reimburse the issuer for bonuses, incentive or equity-based compensation, and any profits received by the executives from the sale of the issuer's securities in the twelve months following "an accounting restatement due to the material noncompliance of the issuer, as a result of misconduct, with any financial reporting requirement under the securities laws."[116] The SEC has the authority to exempt people from compliance with the rule "as it seems necessary and appropriate."[117] The compensation clawback provision is supplemented by a provision that permits the SEC to freeze an issuer's assets during the course of a lawful investigation to prevent it from paying amounts (including compensation amounts) to wrongdoers in cases involving "possible violations of the Federal securities laws by an issuer of publicly traded securities or any of its directors, officers, partners, controlling persons, agents, or employees."[118]

Interpretive questions in these provisions abound. For instance, "misconduct" is not defined in the clawback statute or in any SEC regulation. Especially when combined with the notion of "material noncompliance" (which incorporates the broad, uncertain standard-based definition of materiality applicable elsewhere under the federal securities laws), the operation of the clawback provision in specific circumstances may be unclear. Courts have begun to construe the clawback provision, determining (among other things) that personal misconduct by the chief executive officer or chief financial officer is not a prerequisite to effectuating a clawback.[119] However, many interpretive questions remain unresolved.

Nevertheless, Congress pressed forward with a further clawback provision in Dodd-Frank. Under Dodd-Frank, each public company with securities listed on a national securities exchange must implement,

---

[115] *See* Michael C. Macchiarola, *In the Shadow of the Omnipresent Claw: In Response to Professors Cherry & Wong*, 95 MINN. L. REV. HEADNOTES 1, 11 (2010).

[116] *See* Sarbanes-Oxley § 304(a) (codified at 15 U.S.C. § 7243(a)).

[117] *Id.* § 304(b) (codified at 15 U.S.C. § 7243(b)).

[118] *Id.* § 1103(c) (codified at 15 U.S.C. § 78u-3(c)).

[119] *See* SEC v. Baker, 2012 U.S. Dist. LEXIS 161784, at *12–14 (W.D. Tex. Nov. 13, 2012); United States SEC v. Geswein, 2011 U.S. Dist. LEXIS 111906, at *70 (N.D. Ohio Aug. 5, 2011); SEC v. Microtune, Inc., 783 F. Supp. 2d 867, 886–87 (N.D. Tex. 2011); SEC v. Jenkins, 718 F. Supp. 2d 1070, 1074–79 (D. Ariz. 2010).

sustain and disclose a clawback policy. That policy must provide for the recovery of incentive compensation "based on financial information required to be reported under the securities laws" from current and former executive officers "in the event that the issuer is required to prepare an accounting restatement due to the material noncompliance of the issuer with any financial reporting requirement under the securities laws."[120] As a means of incentivizing and enforcing compliance with the clawback rule, Congress required the SEC to engage in rulemaking to ensure that the national securities exchanges and national securities associations forbid the listing of any security of an issuer that does not comply with the requirements of this section.[121] Like the Sarbanes-Oxley clawback provision, the Dodd-Frank clawback rule raises numerous as-yet unanswered interpretive questions as applied in specific cases.

Prohibition on Director and Executive Securities Trading During Blackouts

Sarbanes-Oxley prohibits directors and executive officers of an issuer from acquiring or disposing of any of the issuer's equity securities during any pension plan blackout period if the equity security was acquired in connection with the director's or executive officer's service or employment with the issuer and in his or her capacity as a director or executive officer of the issuer.[122] This provision acts as an insider trading prophylactic—a way of preventing directors and executive officers from benefitting especially from inside information. For purposes of this provision in Sarbanes-Oxley, a "blackout period" is any

> period of more than 3 consecutive business days during which the ability of not fewer than 50 percent of the participants or beneficiaries under all individual account plans maintained by the issuer to purchase, sell, or otherwise acquire or transfer an interest in any equity of such issuer held in such an individual account plan is temporarily suspended by the issuer or by a fiduciary of the plan.[123]

In the Sarbanes-Oxley blackout provision, Congress directs the SEC to prescribe certain exclusions from the operation of the rule.[124]

---

120 Dodd-Frank § 954 (codified at 15 U.S.C. § 78j-4(b)).
121 *See id.* (codified at 15 U.S.C. § 78j-4(a)).
122 *See* Sarbanes-Oxley § 306(a)(1) (codified at 15 U.S.C. § 7244(a)(1)).
123 *See id.* § 306(a)(4)(A) (codified at 15 U.S.C. § 7244(a)(4)(A)).
124 *See id.* § 306(a)(4) (B) (codified at 15 U.S.C. § 7244(a)(4)(B)).

Sarbanes-Oxley also includes notice provisions and statutory remedies relating to the blackout period trading prohibition. The issuer is responsible for giving timely notice of each blackout period to the SEC and to directors and executive officers subject to the rule.[125] Plan administrators also have notice obligations.[126] The issuer or a security holder acting on its behalf can recover the profits from any director or executive officer trading transaction that violates the statutory prohibition.[127]

REGULATING OTHER MATTERS

Although in passing Sarbanes-Oxley Congress used its legislative power to engage in the regulation of disclosures, fraud and other similar misconduct, and substantive matters impacting corporate governance and operations, Congress also took action in Sarbanes-Oxley to regulate other matters in other ways—all centered on curbing financial fraud and restoring investor confidence in the national securities markets (if not corporate America). These further measures touch on participants in business activities that are not typically regulated through securities regulation and corporate law. As a result, these additional Sarbanes-Oxley provisions alter and implicate areas of law and regulation outside securities and corporate law.

Employee Whistleblowing

For example, Sarbanes-Oxley promoted employee reporting of financial fraud by enacting a whistleblower protection rule.[128] This rule is more a matter of employment law than securities regulation or corporate law. In fact, the Department of Labor regulates procedures and conduct under this part of Sarbanes-Oxley.[129]

Specifically, Sarbanes-Oxley prohibits public company and reporting issuers, as well as their officers, employees, contractors, subcontractors, and agents from taking adverse employment action or discriminating against any employee who lawfully provides information "or otherwise assist[s] in an investigation regarding any conduct which the employee reasonably believes constitutes a violation of" specified provisions in the

---

125 *See id.* § 306(a)(6) (codified at 15 U.S.C. § 7244(a)(6)).
126 *See id.* § 306(b) (codified at 29 U.S.C. 1021(i)).
127 *See id.* § 306(a)(2) (codified at 15 U.S.C. § 7244(a)(2)).
128 *See id.* § 806(a) (codified at 18 U.S.C. § 1514A).
129 *See* 29 C.F.R. §§ 1980.100–115 (2013).

federal securities laws.[130] Whistleblowers may bring an action for reinstatement, back pay, or compensatory damages for violating the rule by filing a complaint with the Secretary of Labor or,

> if the Secretary has not issued a final decision within 180 days of the filing of the complaint and there is no showing that such delay is due to the bad faith of the claimant, bringing an action at law or equity for de novo review in the appropriate district court of the United States, which shall have jurisdiction over such an action without regard to the amount in controversy.[131]

The whistleblower provision addresses concerns that an employee, who may have exposure to evidence of financial fraud in the employee's day-to-day employment, has few incentives to report that evidence and has good reason to refrain from reporting it (e.g., a justified fear of retaliation from those who have the power to fire or demote the employee, discriminate against the employee in awarding promotions or other employment benefits, or take other adverse employment action). Among those who helped bring Enron's massive fraud to light was an Enron Vice President, Sherron Watkins, who was publicly heralded as a whistleblower and (among other things) named as one of *Time Magazine*'s persons of the year for 2002 as a result of her role.[132] This provides an important frame for the whistleblower protections in Sarbanes-Oxley.

Attorney Conduct

Sarbanes-Oxley also compelled the SEC to promulgate rules establishing professional conduct standards "for attorneys appearing and practicing before the Commission in any way in the representation of issuers."[133] Congress specifically required the SEC to adopt a rule

> requiring an attorney to report evidence of a material violation of securities law or breach of fiduciary duty or similar violation by the company or any agent thereof, to the chief legal counsel or the chief executive officer of the company (or the equivalent thereof); and … if the counsel or officer does not appropriately respond to the evidence (adopting, as necessary, appropriate remedial measures or sanctions with respect to the violation), requiring the

---

[130] *See* Sarbanes-Oxley § 806(a) (codified at 18 U.S.C. § 1514A).

[131] *See id.*

[132] Richard Lacayo & Amanda Ripley, *Persons of The Year 2002: The Whistleblowers*, TIME MAGAZINE, Dec. 30, 2002, *available at* http://content.time.com/time/magazine/article/0,9171,1003998,00.html (subscription required).

[133] Sarbanes-Oxley § 307 (codified at 15 U.S.C. § 7245).

> attorney to report the evidence to the audit committee of the board of directors of the issuer or to another committee of the board of directors comprised solely of directors not employed directly or indirectly by the issuer, or to the board of directors.

The notion of reporting evidence of a material violation "up the ladder" raised significant concerns among lawyers and others—some arguing that the statute did not go far enough (and advocating reporting "out" as well as "up"), and some noting pernicious effects—collateral damage—that may result from the lawyer's obligation to report up the ladder (e.g., that an organizational client's officers and employees may be more hesitant to be forthcoming with legal counsel for fear that counsel might be required to report revelations).[134] After significant debate, however, the SEC adopted rules of attorney conduct applicable to counsel appearing and practicing before the SEC.[135]

An important foundational aspect of the rules for corporate legal counsel is the breadth of the concept of "appearing and practicing before the Commission," which can be triggered by simply advising a client whether a document must be filed with the SEC.[136] Lawyers generally understand that they need to be attentive to state professional responsibility rules, but they may be unaware of their need to comply with far-reaching, specialized federal rules of professional conduct like those promulgated by the SEC under Sarbanes-Oxley. The SEC's attorney conduct rules therefore represent a possible trap for the unwary.

As required by Congress in Sarbanes-Oxley, the crux of the SEC's rules of professional conduct is the requirement that an attorney report evidence of a material violation up the ladder of corporate management.[137] The up-the-ladder reporting requirement preserves attorney-client confidentiality by keeping the reporting within the issuer-client. However, the SEC rules also *allow* attorneys to make limited disclosures of confidential information to the SEC "without the issuer's consent" to prevent or rectify a material violation by the issuer.[138] The interaction of

---

134 *See, e.g.*, Roger C. Cramton & Susan P. Koniak, *Legal and Ethical Duties of Lawyers after Sarbanes-Oxley*, 49 VILL. L. REV. 725 (2004) (identifying and analyzing these and other concerns).

135 *See* 17 C.F.R. § 205 (2013).

136 *See id.* § 205.2(a)(1)(iv).

137 *See id.* §§ 205.3(b)(1), (3) & (4).

138 *Id.* § 205.3(d)(2).

the SEC's reporting requirements with state rules of professional responsibility has created some hand wringing among attorneys and bar associations.[139]

Discharge of Debts in Bankruptcy

In a move to prevent wrongdoers from eliminating their malfeasance-related obligations by legal fiat, Congress reached into federal bankruptcy law in Sarbanes-Oxley. Sarbanes-Oxley amended existing federal bankruptcy law provisions to prevent the bankruptcy discharge of judgment debts resulting from the violation of federal securities laws or the commission of "common law fraud, deceit or manipulation in connection with the purchase or sale of any security."[140] This incorporation of other laws into the federal bankruptcy process affects not only the determinations of the bankruptcy court but also potentially the incentives for reorganizing a firm under federal bankruptcy law.

> To the extent that these and other changes in federal law have the effect of making management and related lawyer misconduct a violation of federal securities laws, the effect is to widen the scope of the 523(a)(19) exception to discharge. Concomitantly, bankruptcy protection is weakened for managers and lawyers who are held liable for breaching fiduciary duties. The risk of this liability is increasing when the firm files bankruptcy, and the net effect may be that 523(a)(19) indirectly works to discourage management and the firm's lawyers from taking the firm into Chapter 11.[141]

It is not clear that Congress took this and other possible attendant effects of the bankruptcy discharge rule into account in its legislative rulemaking.

---

[139] *See, e.g.*, Corporations Committee of the Business Law Section of the California State Bar, *Conflicting Currents: The Obligation to Maintain Inviolate Client Confidences and the New SEC Attorney Conduct Rules*, 32 PEPP. L. REV. 89, 106–08 (2004) (describing the SEC's interactions with the Washington State Bar Association and related commentary); Cramton & Koniak, *supra* note 134, at 799–810 (same).

[140] *See* Sarbanes-Oxley § 803 (amending 11 U.S.C. § 523(a)).

[141] Steve H. Nickles, *Behavioral Effect of New Bankruptcy Law on Management and Lawyers: Collage of Recent Statutes and Cases Discouraging Chapter 11 Bankruptcy*, 59 ARK. L. REV. 329, 428 (2006).

SEC Enforcement Authority Modifications

Congress also included provisions in Sarbanes-Oxley authorizing and amending the SEC's administrative authority consistent with the Act's policy objectives, prescriptions and proscriptions. For example, Congress gave the SEC express statutory authority to prohibit, in cease and desist proceedings, any person who has violated securities laws from serving as a director or officer of a public or reporting company if that person is unfit to serve.[142] In connection with these so-called director and officer bars, Sarbanes-Oxley also lowered the unfitness standard from the prior "substantial unfitness" touchstone to "unfitness."[143] In addition, Congress authorized the SEC to provide equitable relief in administrative actions.[144] These provisions afford the SEC a broader scope of enforcement authority.

CONCLUSION

Enacted in the wake of significant public revelations of financial fraud in the early part of the new millennium, Sarbanes-Oxley is a landmark piece of federal securities regulation. SEC rulemaking under Sarbanes-Oxley—which is part of a fluid administrative and regulatory process—also breaks significant new ground. Decisional law—criminal and civil; public and private—provides (and will continue to provide) interpretive wisdom that supplements and fills gaps in the legislative and regulatory rulemaking in and under Sarbanes-Oxley.

Has Sarbanes-Oxley served its intended purpose? The jury is still out and may never return with a verdict. No doubt, academic and industry studies will continue to analyze the effects of Sarbanes-Oxley's numerous rules, and the Dodd-Frank and JOBS Act rules that build on many of the initiatives in Sarbanes-Oxley. But the results of these studies are not likely to be conclusive, especially in light of continuing modifications to the regulatory framework.

---

[142] *See* Sarbanes-Oxley § 1105 (amending 15 U.S.C. 77h–1 & 15 U.S.C. 78u–3).

[143] *See id.* § 305(a) (amending 15 U.S.C. 77t(e) & 15 U.S.C. 78u(d)(2)); *see also* Jayne W. Barnard, *Rule 10b-5 and the "Unfitness" Question*, 47 ARIZ. L. REV. 9 (2005).

[144] *See* Sarbanes-Oxley § 305(b) (amending 15 U.S.C. 78u(d)).

What can be said about Sarbanes-Oxley is that it represents the beginning of a number of important, interrelated, ongoing trends in securities regulation in the United States. It exemplifies, for example:

1. a more prevalent legislative focus on substantive regulation (in addition to the continued traditional regulation of mandatory disclosures, fraud, and other misconduct);
2. greater federal regulation of corporate governance for public and reporting companies as an overlay to state corporate governance rules;
3. more awareness, if not consideration and use, of the behavioral (as well as informational) effects of disclosure regulation;
4. more significant and extensive use of congressionally mandated studies and reports as an adjunct or precursor to rulemaking; and
5. larger legislative projects that include diverse components and subcomponents, rather than more focused legislation offering a comprehensive regulatory scheme.

These themes also can be seen in Congress's subsequent enactment of Dodd-Frank and the JOBS Act and appear likely to have a lasting effect on the federal regulation of securities.

11. Regulation of derivative instruments

Jerry W. Markham

INTRODUCTION

This chapter will focus on the regulation of derivative instruments by the Commodity Futures Trading Commission ("CFTC") under the Commodity Exchange Act of 1936 ("CEA")[1] and the Securities and Exchange Commission ("SEC") under the federal securities laws.[2] This chapter will describe and define the various derivative instruments that are subject to regulation under those regulatory schemes.

This chapter also describes various aspects of the regulation of derivative instruments and compares the regulatory schemes of the CFTC and SEC. The jurisdiction of those two agencies is increasingly overlapping, but their regulatory structures have significant differences in providing customer protection and in the regulation of industry participants. This chapter will further describe amendments to the CEA by the Dodd-Frank Wall Street Reform and Consumer Protection Act of 2010 ("Dodd-Frank Act").[3] The Dodd-Frank Act broadly regulated over-the-counter instruments such as swaps that had previously been unregulated. Dodd-Frank divided regulatory jurisdiction over those instruments between the SEC and CFTC.

DERIVATIVE CONTRACTS DEFINED

Cash and Forward Contracts

A derivative contract has been defined as one "whose value depends (or 'derives' from) the value of an underlying asset, reference rate, or index."[4] The most popular derivative contracts are futures, options and swaps, but there are many other forms of derivatives that combine some

---

1 7 U.S.C. § 1 *et seq.*

2 *See*, *e.g.*, Securities Exchange Act of 1934, 15 U.S.C. § 78a *et seq.*

3 Pub. L. No. 111–203.

4 Group of Thirty, Derivatives: Practices and Principles 2 (July 1993).

or all of the elements of those basic derivative instruments. At one point, there were more than 1,200 different financial derivative products being offered to institutional traders. They included such things as inverse floaters, caps, floors, ceilings, collars, swaptions, embedded options, credit default swaps, synthetic indexing, synthetic stocks and synthetic collateralized debt obligations.[5]

The key to understanding derivative contracts is gaining an understanding of their essential building blocks. At the base of any derivative is the variously called "cash," "spot" or "actual" commodity or financial instrument that underlies the derivative contract. The cash transaction involves the actual purchase and immediate delivery of a commodity, which may be an agricultural product or a financial instrument such as the value of a stock index.[6]

A simplistic example of a cash transaction is found in the purchase of a pair of sneakers at a shoe store. The person buying the sneakers is engaging in a spot market transaction because delivery is immediate. Payment need not be immediate, the cash market purchase could be made on credit, but delivery is nearly always immediate or nearly immediate.

The next building block in understanding derivatives is the "forward" contract, which is sometimes called a "deferred delivery" contract.[7] Here, the commodity is actually being purchased, but the forward contract differs from the spot contract because delivery of the commodity under the forward contract is deferred until some agreed-upon time in the future. For example, you are building a house that will not be completed for some months, but you want to purchase furniture for the house so that it can be furnished immediately upon completion. In order to do that, you enter into a forward contract with a furniture store that calls for delivery upon the expected completion date of the house. Payment terms may vary under forward contracts. The furniture could be paid for in advance of delivery or payment could be deferred until the furniture is delivered, or at some other time as agreed to by the parties.

---

[5] *See* Jerry W. Markham, *"Confederate Bonds," "General Custer," and the Regulation of Derivative Financial Instruments*, 25 Seton Hall L. Rev. 2, n. 4 (1994) (referencing these instruments).

[6] *See* Jerry W. Markham, The History of Commodity Futures Trading and Its Regulation 201–202 (1986) (describing cash contracts).

[7] *See id.* at 202–203 (describing forward contracts).

Commodity Futures Contracts

A commodity futures contract is a derivative contract that evolved from the cash and forward contract. Historically, commodity futures contracts were traded on agricultural products, but today most commodity futures contracts involve some type of financial instrument.[8]

A futures contract is an obligation on the part of the purchaser (the "long") to buy a stated amount of a commodity. Delivery is to be made by the "long" trader at a future date and location specified by the rules of the commodity exchange on which the futures contract is traded. The seller (the "short") in this arrangement incurs a reciprocal obligation to deliver the commodity at the specified date and agreed-upon price.[9]

Commodity futures contracts are standardized (i.e., they have the same delivery dates and specifications for the quantity and quality of the commodity). The only term that is not standardized is the price of the commodity, which is negotiated through an exchange trading floor or now more frequently through an electronic trading system managed by an exchange. Standardizing the terms of exchange traded futures and options make them interchangeable, and thereby allow a secondary market for their trading.

Standardization also allows the holders of futures contracts to liquidate their long or short positions simply by entering an offsetting short or long position. The result of the offsetting trades is that the parties will keep just the profits or pay the losses determined by the difference between the price set by the initial contract and the price set by the liquidating contract. This allows a trader to exit the market and take a profit or loss from price changes without making or taking delivery of the underlying commodity. Because of this liquidation process, delivery occurs only on a very small percentage of futures and options contracts, and some contracts allow only cash settlement of the price differences.

Commodity futures contracts must be traded on an exchange ("board of trade") that is registered under the CEA as a "designated contract market" ("DCM"). That registration imposes a requirement of self-regulation on the contract market, which means that it must require that its members comply with contact market rules, CEA requirements and CFTC rules. Commodity futures contracts must be "cleared" by a

---

[8] Peter Farmery & Keith Walmsley (eds.), United States Securities and Investments Regulation Ch. 8 (1992) (describing this transformation from agricultural to financial derivative instruments).

[9] *See* Jerry W. Markham, The History of Commodity Futures Trading and Its Regulation, 203–206 (1986) (describing futures contracts).

clearinghouse, which guarantees performance on those contracts in the event of a default by either party to a futures contract. To carry out that purpose, the clearinghouse is interceded as the buyer to every seller and the seller to every buyer of the futures contracts traded on a registered contract market. These clearinghouses are registered with the CFTC as "Derivatives Clearing Organizations" ("DCOs").[10]

A person trading commodity contracts on a contract market must utilize the services of a futures commission merchant ("FCM") or an introducing broker ("IB"), which are required to register as such with the CFTC.[11] The FCM or IB will act as the customers' brokers. A registered IB may solicit customer orders but is not allowed to handle customer funds. A FCM is allowed to solicit customer orders and to handle customer funds. The FCM will also often be a "clearing member," which means that it is allowed to trade on, and carry customer accounts with, a contract market and its DCO.

Certain other persons are also required to register with the CFTC under the CEA, including retail foreign exchange dealers (which act as specially regulated brokers in foreign currency trading), floor brokers (customer representatives on the floors of commodity exchanges), commodity pool operators (the commodity industry's version of a mutual fund), commodity trading advisers (persons providing advice to clients on the projected values of commodities), and associated persons of such entities (i.e., employees of registrants).[12]

Customers trading commodity futures are required by contract market rules to "post" margin to protect the contract market's clearinghouse and the FCM from a default by the customer. Margin posted by a commodities futures customer thus constitutes a good faith deposit of money to help ensure that the customer will perform its obligations. In the first instance, "initial" margin is required to be posted for each contract when it is initially executed. This amount is expressed as a small portion of the notional value of the futures contract. Initial margin is computed by exchange created algorithms that are based on an assessment of the potential amount that a commodity price might change before the FCM is able to liquidate the account of a defaulting customer. The minimum amount of initial margin that must be posted by a customer is set by

---

10 *See id.* at 204 (describing this regulatory structure).

11 *See* Jerry W. Markham, *"Confederate Bonds," "General Custer," and the Regulation of Derivative Financial Instruments*, 25 Seton Hall L. Rev. 1, 14 (1994) (describing these registration requirements).

12 17 C.F.R. § 166.5.

exchange rules, but FCMs may require more than those minimums to be posted by customers when deemed necessary for the FCM's protection.

In addition to initial margin, "variation" margin payments are required to be posted by customers when their account value drops below an exchange set "maintenance margin" level. Variation margin is an additional deposit of money required to reflect losses incurred by a customer from adverse price changes on open commodity futures positions. Variation margin requirements are computed through a "mark to market" system. That is, the market value of the commodity is computed daily or more frequently to determine if its value has changed. The purchaser or seller experiencing a loss is required to post an additional amount equivalent to that loss, often called a "margin call." Conversely, if a customer is experiencing a gain, that amount is credited to the customer's account.[13]

Commodity futures contracts may be used for speculation or for hedging. A speculator is trying to achieve a profit through favorable price changes in the commodity underlying the futures contract.[14] This activity is judged by some to be gambling, but speculators perform the useful function of price discovery, and they provide liquidity in the market for hedgers. In any event, the low margin requirements for futures contracts, typically less than 5 percent of the notional value of the contract, provides great leverage, making these contracts attractive for speculation.

A hedger is a party that is seeking to protect itself from a price risk. For example, a party owning a portfolio of indexed stocks needs to protect itself from an expected temporary decline in their value through a hedge, say a correlated S&P 500 stock index futures contract. By selling the futures contract short, the portfolio manager will be protected in the event of a market decline because the profit from the futures contract will offset the decline in the value of the actual portfolio. If, instead, prices increase, the portfolio value would be increased. However, that increase will be offset by the loss on the futures contract. In both instances, however, the portfolio manager maintained the existing value of the portfolio.

This hedging concept can be applied to a large range of risks associated with exposure to changes in commodity prices. A farmer can hedge against the risk that the crop he just planted will experience a drop

---

[13] *See* Jerry W. Markham, *Federal Regulation of Margin in the Commodity Futures Industry—History and Theory*, 64 Temple L. Rev. 59 (1991). (describing these margin requirements).

[14] *See* Merrill Lynch, Pierce, Fenner & Smith Inc. v. Curran, 456 U.S. 353, 358–359 (1982) (describing hedging and speculation in futures contracts).

in price before harvest. An airline company can hedge against the risk of increased fuel prices. Exposures to foreign currency risk can be hedged, and risks associated with interest rate changes can also be protected through such trading.

Options Contracts

Another form of derivative contract is the "option."[15] The option contract gives the purchaser the right, but not the obligation, to either buy something or to sell something at a specified price. The buyer pays a "premium" for that right. For example, an "American" "call option" could give the purchaser the right to buy ("call") a specified number of stock shares from the seller of the option at a specified price ("the strike price") at any time during the life of the option, that is, at any time up to its expiration date. The purchaser of the option will pay a "premium" to the seller of the option for accepting the contractual obligation to deliver the stock in the event that it is called by the purchaser. Conversely, an American "put" option gives the purchaser the right to sell or "put" a specified number of stock shares to the seller of the option at a specified strike price at any time until the expiration date of the option. A premium is also paid for that right by the purchaser.

To illustrate, Party A buys a call option from Party B covering 100 shares of the stock of the ABC Corp., which is presently trading at $99 per share. The option gives Party A the right to purchase those shares from Party B at any time during the next three months at $100 per share. Party A pays a premium of say $500 for that right. Say after 30 days, the price of the shares of the ABC Corp. rose to $110 per share. Party A could then "exercise" the option and purchase the shares from the seller of the option for $100 each. The shares could then be sold in the market at $110 per share, giving the option purchaser a profit of $500 (i.e., $1,000 profit on the difference in the share prices less the $500 premium payment). A purchaser of a put option could make a profit in a similar manner if the stock price declined.

Like futures contracts, the terms of commodity options traded on an exchange are standardized. Exchange traded options are also generally liquidated by offset rather than through the exercise of the option and the delivery of the underlying commodity. Exchange traded securities options are cleared and guaranteed by the Options Clearing Corporation

---

[15] *See* Jerry W. Markham, The History of Commodity Futures Trading and Its Regulation 193 (1986) (describing option contracts).

("OCC"). That clearinghouse acts in much the same way as a clearinghouse in the futures industry. Indeed, the OCC was modeled after those clearinghouses. Commodity options may also be traded on futures exchanges and cleared by the exchanges' clearinghouses.

Options contracts include so-called "American" options, which are exercisable at any time during the life of the option. A "European option" can be exercised only at the end of its life. A "Bermuda option" can be exercised only on predetermined dates, which typically occur monthly. There are also numerous other variations of exercise or payoff arrangements under option structures such as barrier options, best-of-two options, down-and-out options, deferred stop or deferred start options, lateral options, look back options and exploding options.[16]

Swaps

A swap contract involves an exchange of cash flows or values between the parties to the swap contract. For example, in a "plain vanilla" swap one party might exchange a floating interest rate on a notional amount of a loan for a fixed interest rate with the counterparty to the swap.[17] More complex swaps may swap the value of an asset in exchange for a flow of cash payments and there are many other exotic combinations that are used as a part of a swap agreement.

A particularly popular swap is the credit default swap. A credit default swap involves, for example, an arrangement whereby a swap dealer agrees to pay the value of a credit instrument should it default. In exchange for that obligation, the party receiving this credit protection agrees to make periodic payments to the credit swap dealer in much the same form as an insurance payment.[18] The growth of the credit default swaps market was phenomenal. Although it was estimated that 80 percent of the credit default swap market was speculative in nature,[19] credit default swaps also performed a hedging function. Among other things,

---

[16] *See* Jerry W. Markham, *"Confederate Bonds," "General Custer," and the Regulation of Derivative Financial Instruments*, 25 Seton Hall L. Rev. 1, 2, n. 4 (1994) (describing the history behind this allocation of regulation).

[17] *See* Thrifty Oil Co. v. Bank of Am. Nat'l Trust & Sav. Ass'n, 322 F.3d 1039, 1042–1043 (9th Cir. 2002) and Procter & Gamble Co. v. Bankers Trust Co., 925 F. Supp. 1270 (S.D. Ohio 1996) (describing swap transactions).

[18] *See* Jerry W. Markham, A Financial History of the United States From the Subprime Crisis to the Great Recession (2006–2009) 406 (2011) (defining credit default swaps).

[19] *See* Arthur D. Postal, *Credit Default Swaps Belong Under Supervision of States*, P&C Nat'l Underwriter, Feb. 23, 2009, http://www.property-casualty.com/

they were used to enhance the creditworthiness of subprime mortgage securitizations that were bundled into collateralized debt obligations ("CDOs").[20]

Historically, swaps traded in the then unregulated over-the-counter market or on non-regulated exchanges. The International Swaps & Derivatives Association ("ISDA") has provided standardized documentation for most swaps. This was done through a master agreement pursuant to which individual transactions are confirmed by separate confirmation statements.[21]

Unfortunately, credit default swaps received a large part of the blame for causing the Financial Crisis of 2008.[22] This led to the passage of provisions in the Dodd-Frank Act that now require most swaps to be traded on regulated exchanges and cleared by regulated clearinghouses. Jurisdiction over regulated swap contracts was divided between the SEC and CFTC. The SEC now has jurisdiction over security-based swaps, while CFTC has jurisdiction over commodity-based swaps. Those two agencies share joint jurisdiction where a swap contract has elements of contracts regulated by each agency.[23] As a result of this legislation, some swaps trading facilities are converting their swap contracts to futures contracts, which is being called the "futurization" of swaps.

REGULATORY HISTORY

Background of the CEA

Derivative contracts were virtually unregulated until the 1920s when legislation was enacted to govern the trading of my futures contracts on

---

Issues/2009/7/Pages/Credit-Default-Swaps-Belong-Under-Supervision-Of-States.aspx (last visited Nov. 12, 2009).

[20] *See* UBS AG, Shareholder Report on UBS's Write-Downs § 4.22 (2008) (describing the role of credit default swaps in subprime CDO securitizations).

[21] *See* Wachovia Bank, N.A. v. VCG Special Opportunities Master Fund, Ltd., 661 F.3d 164, 167 (2d Cir. 2011), cert. denied, – U.S. – (2012) (describing ISDA swap documentation).

[22] Jerry W. Markham, *Glass Steagall vs. Gramm-Leach-Bliley—A Test Match for the Bankers*, 12 U. Penn. L. & Bus. J. 1081 (2010) (describing those concerns).

[23] *See* Jerry W. Markham, A Financial History of the United States From the Subprime Crisis to the Great Recession (2006–2009) 743–744 (2011) (describing this allocation of jurisdiction).

organized exchanges.[24] Concerns had been expressed for decades over abuses in commodity futures and options trading, particularly large-scale manipulations of agricultural commodity prices.[25] Nevertheless, Congress was reluctant to act until after concerns over abuses in the trading of those instruments arose in the wake of World War I. The Futures Trading Act of 1921[26] was passed to limit futures trading in grain to boards of trade designated as "contract markets" by the Secretary of Agriculture. However, in *Hill v. Wallace*,[27] the Supreme Court held that the Futures Trading Act of 1921 was an unconstitutional exercise of the taxing power of Congress. The Supreme Court also held in *Trusler v. Crooks*,[28] that a provision in the Futures Trading Act that sought to tax trading in options on grain out of existence was unconstitutional.

One day after the Supreme Court's decision *Hill v. Wallace*,[29] a blatant manipulation of the wheat futures market occurred.[30] Congress responded to that market disruption by repackaging the Futures Trading Act[31] into the Grain Futures Act of 1922.[32] In order to pass constitutional muster, the Grain Futures Act was based on the commerce power of Congress under the Constitution. The Supreme Court upheld the Grain Futures Act under that power in *Chicago Board of Trade v. Olsen*.[33]

This legislation proved to be unsuccessful. There were a number of market manipulations through the use of commodity futures contracts during the 1920s and into the 1930s.[34] In addition, a number of abuses occurred in stock options trading during the 1930s that raised congressional concerns.[35] As a result of those problems, derivatives regulation

---

[24] *See* Jerry W. Markham, The History of Commodity Futures Trading and Its Regulation 3–16 (1986) (describing that history).

[25] *See* Jerry W. Markham, Law Enforcement and The History of Financial Market Manipulation (2013) (describing those manipulations).

[26] 42 Stat. 187 (1921).

[27] Hill v. Wallace, 259 U.S. 44 (1922).

[28] Trusler v. Crooks, 269 U.S. 475 (1926).

[29] Hill v. Wallace, 259 U.S. 44 (1922).

[30] H.R. Rep. No. 1095, 67th Cong., 2d Sess. 2 (1922).

[31] 42 Stat. 187 (1921).

[32] 42 Stat. 998 (1922).

[33] Chicago Board of Trade v. Olsen, 262 U.S. 1 (1923).

[34] *See* Jerry W. Markham, *The Manipulation of Commodity Futures Prices—The Unprosecutable Crime*, 8 Yale J. on Reg. 281, 303–311 (1991) (describing those abuses).

[35] *See* Jerry W. Markham & David J. Gilberg, *Stock and Commodity Options—Two Regulatory Approaches and Their Conflicts*, 47 Albany L. Rev. 741, 747 (1983) (describing those concerns).

became a part of Franklin D. Roosevelt's "New Deal" that led to the regulation of both the securities and commodity futures markets.

The CEA is Enacted

The Grain Futures Act was replaced in 1936 by the Commodity Exchange Act of 1936 ("CEA").[36] The CEA sought to strengthen regulation over the FCMs, and floor brokers on the commodity futures exchanges were required by the CEA to register with the government.[37] Fraud and manipulation were prohibited by the CEA, and the government was authorized to set position limits on the amount of trading that could be conducted by speculators.[38]

The CEA also extended regulatory jurisdiction over some previously unregulated futures trading on other commodities, i.e., cotton, rice, mill feeds, butter, eggs, and potatoes. Wool tops, fats and oils, cottonseed meal, cottonseed, peanuts, soybeans, and soybean meal were added to that list in 1938.[39] Options trading on these "regulated" commodities was prohibited.[40]

The CEA was administered by the Commodity Exchange Commission, which was comprised of the secretaries of agriculture and commerce and the attorney general. The secretary of agriculture was given day-to-day regulatory authority over the commodity futures markets, and he created a small bureau, the Commodity Exchange Authority, to carry out those functions under the CEA.[41]

The Commodity Exchange Authority was a small and little noticed agency until inflation in the 1970s and concerns over market abuses, gave rise to new legislation in 1974. That statute created the CFTC and expanded regulation, indeed giving the CFTC exclusive jurisdiction, over all commodity futures and options trading, including such trading on financial instruments.[42]

---

[36] 7 U.S.C. § 1 *et seq.*

[37] *See* II Jerry W. Markham, A Financial History of the United States, From J. P. Morgan to the Institutional Investor (1900–1970) 222–223 (2002) (describing this legislation).

[38] *See* Jerry W. Markham, The History of Commodity Futures Trading and Its Regulation 27 (1986) (describing these requirements).

[39] 52 Stat. 205 (1938).

[40] *See* Jerry W. Markham, The History of Commodity Futures Trading and Its Regulation 27–28 (1986) (describing this limitation).

[41] *Id.*

[42] Commodity Futures Trading Commission Act of 1974, 88 Stat. 1389.

CFTC ORGANIZATIONAL STRUCTURE

The Commission

The CFTC is composed of five commissioners appointed by the President, with the advice and consent of the Senate. These commissioners serve staggered five-year terms. No more than three of the commissioners may be from the same political party. One of their number is designated by the President to be the agency's chairman.[43] The CFTC commissioners meet periodically as a body to decide matters that are the subject of commission orders or other agency action. Many CFTC meetings are public, but enforcement matters are not subject to public attendance.

The CFTC Staff Divisions

The CFTC's staff carries out many of the day-to-day activities of the agency. The staff is organized into various divisions and offices. The Division of Clearing and Risk oversees DCOs. The Division of Market Oversight oversees the commodity exchanges and seeks to assure that those exchanges are meeting their core regulatory principles. This division also conducts market surveillance for disruptive trading activity, and it reviews new exchange applications and new products.

The CFTC's Swap Dealers and Intermediary Oversight Division oversees registration and compliance by intermediaries and self-regulatory organizations. It is also responsible for monitoring compliance with regulations addressing business conduct standards, capital adequacy and margin requirements for swap dealers.[44]

The CFTC's Division of Enforcement investigates and prosecutes violations. The CFTC may authorize it to issue subpoenas and compel the production of documents and deposition testimony. This subpoena power is not self-enforcing. Rather, in the event of a refusal to comply with the subpoena, the CFTC's Division of Enforcement must, with the permission of the CFTC, seek the assistance of a Federal District Court to compel production of documents or testimony.[45]

---

[43] *CFTC Organization*, available at http://www.cftc.gov/About/CFTC Organization/index.htm (accessed on Feb. 24, 2013).

[44] *Id.*

[45] 7 U.S.C. § 15. *See* Jerry W. Markham, 13A Commodities Regulation: Fraud, Manipulation & Other Claims Ch. 22 (2012) (summarizing cases involving investigations by the CFTC's Division of Enforcement).

Once an investigation is concluded, the Division of Enforcement may recommend to the CFTC that it authorize the institution of an administrative proceeding before a CFTC administrative law judge or judgment officer. The CFTC may impose monetary penalties against persons violating the statute, of up to $1 million in the case of a person found to have manipulated commodity prices or triple the monetary gain to the person, whichever is greater. Restitution may also be ordered for the benefit of persons injured by violations. A respondent may appeal a CFTC hearing officer's orders, first to the CFTC and from there to a Court of Appeals.[46]

Alternatively, the CFTC may authorize its Division of Enforcement to bring an injunctive action in federal court. If violations are found, and if it is determined that there is a likelihood of future violations, the federal district court may enter an order enjoining the defendant from such future violations. Civil penalties may also be assessed against defendants in the amount of $100,000 or triple the monetary gain of the defendants, whichever is greater. In addition, the CFTC may seek ancillary relief in the form of an order requiring a defendant to make restitution to injured customers and to disgorge the profits made from illegal activity.[47]

CFTC Offices

The CFTC also has several "offices," in addition to its divisions. They include the Office of the Chief Economist, which provides economic support and economic advice to the CFTC. The Office of Data and Technology provides technology and data management support for the CFTC. The Office of the Executive Director is responsible for the allocation of the CFTC's resources and is the overall staff manager for the agency.

The Office of General Counsel acts as the CFTC's own lawyer. It represents the agency in appellate, bankruptcy and other litigation, including actions brought against the CFTC. The CFTC's Office of the Inspector General acts as the agency's own internal watchdog. The Office of International Affairs is responsible for providing guidance to the CFTC with respect to international issues. The globalization of the

---

[46] 7 U.S.C.§ 9. *See also* Jerry W. Markham, 13A Commodities Regulation: Fraud, Manipulation & Other Claims Ch. 22 (2012) (summarizing cases involving these disciplinary proceedings).

[47] 7 U.S.C. § 13a-1. *See also* Jerry W. Markham, 13A Commodities Regulation: Fraud, Manipulation & Other Claims Ch. 25 (2012) (summarizing cases involving these injunctive proceedings).

commodity markets has increased the importance of this office. The Office of Legislative Affairs, and the Office of Public Affairs also provide support services to the CFTC.[48]

CFTC REGULATORY POWERS

The CFTC was given expanded regulatory powers when it was created. New classes of market participants were subject to regulation, including commodity trading advisers and commodity pool operators. Their associated persons were also subject to registration requirements. CFTC registration requirements require a FBI background review of applicants, which allows the exclusion of unfit persons from the industry, including persons previously convicted of financial crimes.[49]

Market Regulation

Upon its creation, the CFTC was given expanded jurisdiction over the operations of contract markets.[50] Congress subsequently amended the CEA several times to further expand the CFTC's powers. A new industry self-regulatory body was also later created, the National Futures Association ("NFA"), which is similar in nature to FINRA that is the self-regulator in the securities industry (these entities are sometimes referred to as self-regulatory organizations ("SROs"). Most recently, as described below, Congress, through the Dodd-Frank Act, expanded the CFTC's jurisdiction into the commodity swap market.

The NFA is responsible for much of the self-regulation carried out under the umbrella of the CEA, but the exchanges still maintain an SRO role. The SRO concept is based on a belief that if the industry acts to prevent violations, it will be unnecessary for the government to interfere with the market and will lessen the cost of regulation to taxpayers. Unfortunately, SROs have not always been effective in discovering and

---

[48] *CFTC Organization*, available at http://www.cftc.gov/About/CFTCOrganization/index.htm (visited Feb. 24, 2013).

[49] *See* Jerry W. Markham, 13A Commodities Regulation: Fraud, Manipulation & Other Claims Ch. 24 (2012) (summarizing cases involving the denial of registration under the CEA).

[50] *See* Jerry W. Markham, The History of Commodity Futures Trading and Its Regulation 65–72 (1986) (describing this legislation).

deterring violations.[51] Nevertheless, they form the core of regulation in the futures industry. Their rules govern nearly every facet of the operations of a FCM or IB. Among other things, the SROs will inspect registrants' operations to measure compliance with minimum capital requirements and proper treatment of customer segregated funds and sales practices. Sanctions may be imposed for compliance failures.

Regulation of FCMs

CFTC rules also broadly regulate FCMs and other registrants. FCMs are subject to periodic reporting requirements and provisions that require maintenance of certain records, which allows the CFTC to review their operations. These records must be maintained for a period of five years and are subject to inspection by the CFTC at any time.[52] CFTC rules, for example, require FCMs to maintain complete records of all transactions relating to their business of dealing in futures, commodity options and cash commodities. Those records include filled, unfilled and canceled orders, journals, ledgers, canceled checks, confirmations and customer purchase, and sale statements. Records must be maintained that show all charges and credits to customer accounts, including deposits, withdrawals, transfers, and credits.[53] In addition, a record must be kept of all securities and property received from customers for the purpose of margining trades.[54]

FCM customers must be provided with monthly statements that show their open positions and the prices at which they were acquired, their net unrealized profit or loss on open contracts marked to the market and any customer funds maintained in the account belonging to the customer. FCM customers must also be provided with a confirmation statement promptly after the execution of an order.[55]

FCMs are also subject to CFTC financial reporting requirements. Among other things, financial reports on CFTC Form 1-FR must be filed by FCMs monthly, and an annual financial report certified by a CPA must be filed with the CFTC.[56] CFTC rules require CPAs to audit these

---

[51] *See* Jerry W. Markham & Daniel J. Harty, *For Whom the Bell Tolls: The Demise of Exchange Trading Floors and the Growth of ECNs*, 33 J. Corp. L. 865 (2008) (describing concerns over self-regulation).

[52] 17 C.F.R. § 1.31.

[53] 17 C.F.R. § 1.35.

[54] 17 C.F.R. § 1.36.

[55] 17 C.F.R. § 1.33.

[56] 17 C.F.R. § 1.10.

annual financial statements in accordance with generally accepted auditing standards.[57] A CPA may be sanctioned by the CFTC if it fails to conduct a proper audit.[58]

Custody of Customer Funds

Customers often have excess margin funds ("excess funds") in their commodity futures accounts that are not needed to margin their open commodity futures contracts. That excess arises for many reasons, such as the closing of futures trading positions, which frees up the funds that were used to margin those positions. A favorable gain from an open trading position can also create excess funds. FCMs are required to hold those customer excess margin funds in a specially marked segregated account.[59] This provision was intended to require that customer funds be held in a trust account.[60]

The Bankruptcy Reform Act of 1978[61] and Part 190 of the CFTC's regulations[62] promulgated under that statute give customer funds held in CEA segregated accounts priority over the claims of general creditors of the FCM. Customers of broker-dealers registered with the SEC under the Securities Exchange Act of 1934 are covered by an account insurance scheme that provides up to $500,000 in insurance in the event of a broker-dealer's bankruptcy that results in a shortage of customer funds. No such insurance is available under the CEA for FCM customers.

CFTC's rules governing customer segregated accounts seek to assure that (1) customer funds are separately accounted for by the FCM; (2) customer funds are not commingled with the FCM's own funds, except that an FCM may keep excess funds of its own in a segregated account to cover any short-term imbalances; (3) customer funds must be held for the benefit of customers only; (4) customer funds must be available to the customer (and the FCM when held by a custodian) immediately upon demand; (5) customer funds must be calculated so as to prevent the use

---

[57] 17 C.F.R. § 1.16.

[58] *See, e.g.*, In re Deloitte & Touche, LLP, 1996 WL 547883 (C.F.T.C.) (auditing firm sanctioned by consent for failing to audit using generally accepted auditing standards).

[59] *See* 7 U.S.C. § 6d.

[60] H.R. Rep. No. 1637, 73d Cong., 2d 6 (1934).

[61] Pub. L. No. 95–598, 92 Stat. 2549 (1978).

[62] 17 C.F.R. § 190.01 et seq.

of one customer's funds to margin another customer's position; and (6) customer funds may not be used to secure a loan of the FCM.[63]

CFTC rules require that any bank receiving commodity customer funds must provide a written acknowledgement that the bank was informed that "the customer funds deposited therein are those of commodity or option customers and are being held in accordance with the provisions of the [Commodity Exchange] Act … ." and CFTC rules.[64] CFTC rules prohibit the commingling of customer funds with those of the FCM or any other person, except that customer funds may be commingled with those of other customers.[65] CFTC rules also allow FCMs to keep their own funds in customer-segregated accounts to serve as a cushion in the event of an unexpected shortfall.[66]

An FCM may invest the customer funds held in segregation in securities specified in CFTC rules, which include obligations of the U.S. government or of the states.[67] CFTC rules allow FCMs to keep for themselves the interest or other return from such investments.[68]

FCMs are required to compute on a daily basis the total amount of customer funds held and required to be held in segregated accounts and the amount of the FCM's residual interest in those funds.[69] CFTC rules require the FCM to notify the CFTC if funds and securities on deposit in segregated accounts are less than the requirement.[70]

Historically, losses in customer funds held in CEA segregated accounts as a result of FCM failures have been limited. However, in recent years several large FCMs failed, causing concerns over the treatment of customer funds held in those entities.[71] Refco, Inc. failed in 2005 as the

---

[63] *See* CFTC Interpretative Letter No. 88–14, Comm. Fut. L. Rep. (CCH) ¶24,295 (Aug. 1, 1988) (describing these requirements).

[64] 17 C.F.R. § 1.20.

[65] 17 C.F.R. § 1.20.

[66] 17 C.F.R. § 1.23.

[67] 17 C.F.R. § 1.25. CFTC Rule 1.26 (17 C.F.R. § 1.26) requires such investments to be held in segregated accounts.

[68] 17 C.F.R. § 1.29.

[69] 17 C.F.R. § 1.32.

[70] 17 C.F.R. § 1.12(h).

[71] Capital Management Select Fund v. Bennett, 680 F.3d. 214, 223 (2d Cir. 2012); In re: Sentinel Management Group Inc., Debtor, 2008 Bankr. LEXIS 3488 (Bkrptcy N.D. Ill. 2008); *Trustee's Preliminary Investigation Report and Recommendations*, In re Lehman Brothers Inc., Case No. 08–01420 (JMP) SIPA (S.D.N.Y. Aug. 25, 2010); *MF Global Staff Report Prepared for Rep. Randy Neugebauer, Chairman Subcommittee on Oversight and Investigations, Committee on Financial Services*, U.S. House of Rep., 112th Cong. (Nov. 15, 2012);

result of a massive fraud by its officers and the misuse of hundreds of millions of dollars of customer funds held at a foreign affiliate.[72] In 2007, Sentinel Management Group Inc. ("Sentinel") failed after it had used several hundred million dollars of customer assets to leverage the firm's trading position.[73]

A shortage of some $1.2 billion in customer funds was discovered after MF Global Inc. declared bankruptcy in October 2011.[74] That highly publicized failure was followed by a giant fraud at the Peregrine Financial Group, where the firm's owner simply looted nearly $215 million in customer funds held in custody.[75] These failures occurred and resulted in customer losses or delays in receiving their funds even though those funds were supposed to have been maintained in strict custody.

The CFTC allowed FCMs to set aside only partial amounts of excess margin funds held for U.S. customers trading on foreign exchanges.[76] However, the collapse of MF Global resulted in a shortfall of almost $1 billion in those accounts and that alternative calculation is no longer permitted. In the wake of that and other failures, the CFTC has sought to tighten its segregation requirements.[77]

Capital Requirements

Another significant regulatory effort by the CFTC involves the imposition of capital requirements on FCMs and introducing brokers.[78] The CFTC has described the purposes of this rule as follows:

Ann Saphir, *Peregrine Trustee Plans Return of $123 Million Client Funds* (Reuters, Sept. 6,2012) (available at http://www.reuters.com/article/2012/09/06/us-peregrine-bankruptcy-distribution-idUSBRE88512D20120906 (visited on Dec. 23, 2012). (describing those failures).

[72] *See generally Refco, Rotten Yet Robust*, The Economist Oct. 20, 2005) (describing this failure).

[73] *See* In re: Sentinel Management Group, Inc., 689 F.3d 855 (7th Cir. 2012) (describing this failure).

[74] Report of the Trustee's Investigation and Recommendations, In re Mf Global Inc., at pp. 95–98, Case No. 11–2790 (MG) (S.D.N.Y. June 4, 2012).

[75] Jacob Bunge, *Global Finance: Peregrine Accounts To Be Transferred To Vision Financial*, Wall St. J., Oct. 8, 2012 at c3.

[76] 17 C.F.R. § 30.02.

[77] *See Enhancing Protections Afforded Customers and Customer Funds Held by Futures Commission Merchants and Derivatives Clearing Organizations*, 77 Fed. Reg. 67866, 67869 (C.F.T.C. Nov. 14, 2012) (describe those proposals).

[78] 17 C.F.R. § 1.17. An introducing broker does not accept customer funds. Rather, it maintains those funds with a FCM. 17 C.F.R. § 1.3(mm).

> First, it ensures that a firm has made a sufficient financial commitment to doing business and that it has an adequate inclination to operate as a responsible business. Second, the capital requirement promotes a firm's stability and enhances its ability to perform as an agent to its customers. Finally, and most importantly, the minimum adjusted net capital requirement promotes a firm's financial integrity and coupled with margin, protects against firm insolvencies.[79]

The CFTC's net capital rule allows for alternative computations. For example, an FCM could choose the greater of $1 million; an amount equal to 8 percent of the total risk margin requirement for positions carried by the FCM in customer accounts and noncustomer accounts; or, for registered securities broker-dealers the amount of capital required by the SEC. The NFA is also authorized to impose even higher capital requirements.[80] Capital rules are also being imposed on the newly regulated swap dealers.

Customer Protection Rules

The CFTC has adopted customer protection rules. One of these rules imposes a supervision requirement on CEA registrants.[81] This requirement has two aspects. First, the registrant must have in place a system reasonably designed to prevent and detect violations of the CEA and CFTC rules. Second, the registrant must diligently apply those supervisory requirements.[82]

Unlike the SEC, the CFTC has not adopted a suitability requirement for futures and options. In the securities industry, broker-dealers must evaluate their customers' suitability for any security that is recommended by the firm or its associated persons.[83] The CFTC rejected such an

---

79 19 Sec. Reg. & L. Rep. (BNA) 1152, 1155 (July 31, 1987).

80 17 C.F.R. § 1.17.

81 17 C.F.R. § 166.3. *See also* 7 U.S.C. § 12a(3)(C) (statutory supervision requirement).

82 *See, e.g.*, In the Matter of Cadent Financial Services, LLC, Comm. Fut. L. Rep. (CCH) ¶31,972 (C.F.T.C. 2011) (consent order describing those requirements). *See also* Jerry W. Markham, 13 Commodities Regulation: Fraud, Manipulation & Other Claims Ch. 6 (2012) (summarizing CFTC supervision cases).

83 *See* Jerry W. Markham & Thomas Lee Hazen, 23A Broker Dealer Operations Under Securities and Commodities Law: Financial Responsibilities, Credit Regulation, and Customer Protection Ch. 10 (2012) (describing SEC suitability requirements).

approach.[84] Instead CFTC rules, require FCMs to provide customers with a risk disclosure statement, which they must sign and thereby acknowledge their understanding of the risks associated with commodity futures and commodity options trading.[85] Nevertheless, FCMs are subject to a NFA rule that requires them to "know their customers."[86] This know-your-customer requirement was long used in the securities industry to protect brokers from the failures by their customers, but it evolved into the existing SEC suitability standard. The CFTC has also adopted know-your-customer and a suitability requirement for swaps after passage of the Dodd-Frank Act in 2010.

Fraud Prohibition

The CEA prohibits fraud in connection with regulated commodity option or commodity futures trading.[87] The CFTC has imposed a scienter requirement under this provision which requires a showing that the defendant acted recklessly with a mental state embracing an intent to deceive, manipulate or defraud.[88]

The CFTC has brought numerous cases involving misrepresentations such as unrealistic predictions of profits that customers should expect to make.[89] The CFTC has also attacked misrepresentations concerning the expertise of traders, success of trading programs, and downplaying risks associated with trading futures and options. High-pressure "boiler room" sales operations have also been attacked.[90]

---

[84] *See, e.g.*, Hannay v. First Commodity Corp., Comm. Fut. L. Rep. (CCH) ¶32,250 (C.F.T.C. 1986) (consent order describing those requirements). *See also* Jerry W. Markham, 13 Commodities Regulation: Fraud, Manipulation & Other Claims Ch. 10 (2012) (summarizing CFTC cases rejecting suitability requirements).

[85] 17 C.F.R. § 1.55. *See also* Jerry W. Markham, 13 Commodities Regulation: Fraud, Manipulation & Other Claims Ch. 9 (2012) (summarizing CFTC cases involving failure to provide risk disclosure statements).

[86] NFA Compliance Rule 2–30 (1985).

[87] 7 U.S.C. § 6b.

[88] *See, e.g.*, In the Matter of Haveman, Comm. Fut. L. Rep. (CCH) ¶31,948 (C.F.T.C. 2011) (consent order describing that requirement). *See also* Jerry W. Markham, 13 Commodities Regulation: Fraud, Manipulation & Other Claims Ch. 3 (2012) (summarizing cases considering this scienter requirement).

[89] *See* Jerry W. Markham, 13 Commodities Regulation: Fraud, Manipulation & Other Claims Ch. 7 (2012) (describing those cases).

[90] *Id.* at Ch. 8 (describing those cases).

Another CFTC customer protection rule requires that FCMs obtain authorization from customers before trading in the customer's account.[91] The CFTC has rendered numerous decisions on unauthorized trading claims under the CEA.[92] FCMs try to protect themselves from such claims by taping the order entry process for non-electronically traded orders and by requiring customers to make prompt complaints of any unauthorized trades.

The CFTC has also determined that excessively trading ("churning") a customer's account that is controlled by an FCM or its associated persons is fraudulent.[93] This concept of churning was borrowed from the securities industry. However, the test for churning in the two industries is different. This is because many securities investors adopt a long-term buy-and-hold strategy that results in only infrequent trading. In contrast, speculators who trade derivative conduct tracks tend to trade more frequently than the typical securities investor. Another distinguishing factor is that options and futures are only relatively short term in duration, while stocks and bonds may exist for long investment periods.

Interestingly, the CEA does not prohibit insider trading, a charge that is the centerpiece of the SEC's enforcement program.[94] Rather, the CEA only prohibits insider trading by members of the CFTC or its staff or the staff or directors of a SRO.[95] The CFTC has also asserted that persons who misappropriate information may be charged with fraud if that information is used for trading.[96]

---

[91] 17 C.F.R. § 166.2.

[92] *See* Jerry W. Markham, 13 Commodities Regulation: Fraud, Manipulation & Other Claims Ch. 12 (2012) (describing those cases).

[93] *Id.* at Ch. 11 (describing those cases).

[94] *See* 7 U.S.C. § 6b (stating that disclosure of nonpublic information is not required unless the failure to disclose would mislead another person to whom disclosures had been made). *See also* CFTC, *A Study of the Nature, Extent and Effects of Futures Trading by Persons Possessing Material, Nonpublic Information*, submitted to the Committee on Agriculture of the House of Representatives and the Committee on Agriculture, Nutrition and Forestry of the Senate Pursuant to Sec. 23(b) of the Commodity Exchange Act, as amended (Sept. 1984) (CFTC study rejecting application of an insider trading probation under the CEA).

[95] 7 U.S.C. § 6c and § 13(e).

[96] CFTC v. Kelly, Comm. Fut. L. Rep. (CCH) ¶27,465 (S.D.N.Y. 1998) (consent order involving misappropriation of information that was used for trading).

Manipulation and Abusive Trading Practices

The CEA prohibits manipulation of commodity prices. Such claims have, however, historically been difficult to prove.[97] Four elements were required to establish a manipulation claim. They are:

1. The existence of an "artificial price";
2. The ability to cause the artificial price;
3. A showing that the party in fact caused the artificial price; and
4. An intent to create the artificial price.[98]

Commodity price manipulations may involve a "corner" where the manipulator buys up all available supplies of a commodity in order to dictate prices to would-be purchasers who need the commodity in their operations. A lesser form of the corner is the "squeeze." In such operations, the manipulator gains control of a substantial portion of the available supplies for a particular commodity, but not all. This creates a shortage for other purchasers and the manipulator is able to "squeeze" prices higher because of the reduction in supply created by his operations.

Corners and squeezes are "market power" manipulations that generally require substantial resources to carry out. Smaller traders can manipulate prices through various fraudulent practices. For example, false reports and rumors may be used to manipulate illiquid markets.

The Dodd-Frank Act sought to expand the powers of the CFTC to attack commodity price manipulations by including a provision in the CEA that tracks the anti-fraud and anti-manipulation language in Section 10(b) of the Securities Exchange Act of 1934.[99] Section 753 of the Dodd-Frank Act thus prohibits any "manipulative or deceptive device or contrivance" in violation of CFTC rules adopted within one year of the enactment of that legislation.[100] This "fraud based"[101] provision was

---

[97] *See* Jerry W. Markham, *The Manipulation of Commodity Futures Prices—The Unprosecutable Crime*, 8 Yale J. on Reg. 281 (1991) (describing that difficulty).

[98] *See, e.g.*, In re Indiana Farm Bureau Coop. Association, 1982 CFTC LEXIS 25 (C.F.T.C.) (describing those elements).

[99] 15 U.S.C. § 78j.

[100] Dodd-Frank §§ 753, *codified* at 7 U.S.C. 9(c). This limitation set a deadline of July 21, 2011 for those rules. *Id.*

[101] 156 Cong. Rec. S5902 (July 15, 2010) (remarks of Sen. Reed).

intended to create "a strong bright line" as to what constitutes manipulation.[102] The new Section 10(b) language will be interpreted in the same manner as it is under the 1934 Act since it was borrowed from that provision.[103]

The Commodity Exchange Act additionally prohibits "false or misleading or knowingly inaccurate reports concerning crop or market information or conditions that affect or tend to affect the price of any commodity in interstate commerce … ."[104] The CFTC has brought numerous cases and reached settlements involving hundreds of millions of dollars in penalties over charges of false price reports designed to manipulate energy prices or to present a false appearance in the market.[105]

Section 753 in Dodd-Frank also added a "special provision" for manipulation by "false reporting." That provision establishes a "good faith mistake" exception to this prohibition. This would include mistakenly transmitting, in good faith, false, misleading or inaccurate information to a price reporting service.

Dodd-Frank also left the CFTC's pre-existing anti-manipulation authority intact. The CFTC can now proceed under the new Dodd-Frank authority or its pre-existing powers against persons believed to be engaged in manipulative activities. The CFTC has adopted rules implementing both of those approaches.[106]

The Commodity Exchange Act of 1936 further proscribes a number of trading practices that are deemed to be fraudulent, such as wash trades, fictitious transactions and bucketing.[107] The latter involves a bet against a customer by a trader by not executing the order and hoping to keep the profits from the losses paid by the customer.[108]

Section 747 of the Dodd-Frank Act amended the CEA[109] by expanding its prohibitions to include other "disruptive" trading such as "spoofing,"

---

[102] 156 Cong. Rec. S3348 (May 6, 2010) (remarks of Sen. Cantwell).

[103] A familiar canon of statutory construction holds that where language is borrowed by the legislature from one statute it should generally be given the same meaning in both statutes. 2A Sutherland, Statutory Construction § 52.02 (N. Singer 4th ed. 1984).

[104] 7 U.S.C. § 13(a)(2).

[105] *See* Jerry W. Markham, Law Enforcement and the History of Financial Market Manipulation § 6:3 (2013) (describing those cases).

[106] 17 C.F.R. § 180.1 & § 180.2.

[107] 7 U.S.C. § 6c.

[108] *See* 13 Jerry W. Markham, Commodities Regulation: Fraud, Manipulation and Other Claims Ch. 14 (2012) (describing cases addressing these issues).

[109] 7 U.S.C. § 6c.

which involves bidding or offering with the intent to cancel the bid or offer before execution. Another prohibition was directed at violating existing bids and offers of other traders. In addition, under Section 747, the CFTC now has the authority to prohibit "any other trading practice that is disruptive of fair and equitable trading."

Forums Available for Customers Damaged by CEA Violations

The CEA provides three alternative forums for assessing liability and imposing damages in favor of persons injured by violations of that statute or CFTC rules. They are a private right of action in federal court, arbitration and reparations proceedings before the CFTC. Each of these forums have their individual advantages and disadvantages, and are each subject to separate restrictions and availability.

A private right of action is available in federal court under the CEA if certain conditions are met.[110] That statutory provision was added after the Supreme Court ruled that there was a broad implied private right of action under the CEA.[111] The CEA was amended in 1982 to narrow the scope of such actions, and it imposed a two-year statute of limitations. That amendment also limited relief only to persons injured through the receipt of trading advice or where they were damaged through their trading of regulated derivative contracts.[112]

Arbitration is another forum for the resolution of customer disputes arising under the CEA. These arbitration proceedings are carried out by the NFA and are available as an alternative dispute resolution forum for customers who are injured by violations committed by NFA members. However, such arbitration must be voluntary on the part of the customer.[113] Consequently, in order for a pre-dispute arbitration agreement to be binding it must be entered into voluntarily.[114]

A customer injured by a CEA registrant's violation of the CEA or CFTC rules, may alternatively seek damages through a CFTC "reparations" proceeding. The CEA thus allows the CFTC to award reparations

---

[110] 7 U.S.C. § 25.

[111] Merrill Lynch, Pierce, Fenner & Smith Inc. v. Curran, 456 U.S. 353, 358–359 1982).

[112] *See* Jerry W. Markham, 13A Commodities Regulation: Fraud, Manipulation & Other Claims Ch. 21 (2012) (describing those limitations).

[113] 7 U.S.C. § 21(b)(10).

[114] 17 C.F.R. § 166.5. *See* Jerry W. Markham, 13A Commodities Regulation: Fraud, Manipulation & Other Claims Ch. 19 (2012) (describing this limitation).

in the form of actual damages and punitive damages in an amount not more than twice the amount of actual damages.[115]

The CFTC has adopted rules which govern reparations proceedings. Among other things, those rules govern the pleadings and discovery by the parties. The CFTC's rules also create three forms of reparations proceedings, which vary in formality according to the size of the claim.[116] A CFTC hearing officer will conduct these proceedings and determine whether violations have occurred.[117] The decision of those hearing officers maybe appealed to the CFTC and from there to a Court of Appeals.[118]

CTA and CPO Regulation

The legislation creating the CFTC also regulated commodity pool operators ("CPOs") and commodity trading advisers ("CTAs"). The CPO is the analogue to the mutual funds in the securities industry that are regulated by the SEC. The Dodd-Frank Act required hedge funds and other commodity pools trading in securities on behalf of customers to register with the SEC as a trading adviser under the Investment Advisers Act of 1940 ("1940 Act").[119] In addition, the offering of investments in a CPO will be treated as a security and is subject to SEC registration requirements, unless an exemption is available.[120]

The counterparts to the securities investment advisers, which are regulated under the 1940 Act, are the CTAs, which are regulated under the CEA. The CFTC has adopted rules governing the operations of both CPOs and CTAs.

The CFTC requires CPOs to provide their investors with a brochure, which, among other things, must contain a risk disclosure statement describing the risk of trading the instruments used by the CPO to obtain profits. The risk disclosure statement must also describe the fees that may

---

115 7 U.S.C. § 18.

116 17 C.F.R. Part 12, Subpart C.

117 *See generally* Jerry W. Markham, 13A Commodities Regulation: Fraud, Manipulation & Other Claims Ch. 20 (2012) (describing issues arising in CFTC reparations proceedings).

118 7 U.S.C. § 18.

119 *Private Fund Investment Advisers Registration Act of 2010*, contained in Title IV of Dodd-Frank.

120 *See generally* Jerry W. Markham, *Mutual Fund Scandals—A Comparative Analysis of the Role of Corporate Governance in the Regulation of Collective Investments*, 3 Hastings Bus. L. J. 67, 99–121 (2006) (describing the background for the regulation of hedge funds by the SEC and CFTC).

be charged by the CPO to investors and any restrictions on the withdrawal of funds by investors. The brochure must further describe the background of the CPO and its CTA.[121] CPOs are also required to provide investors with their past investment performance information,[122] and the CFTC imposes extensive recordkeeping requirements on CPOs.[123]

There is an antifraud provision in the CEA that is applicable to CTAs and CPOs.[124] Some of the abuses associated with commodity pools have included Ponzi schemes, failing to disclose that claimed trading successes from a commodity pool's investment program were hypothetical rather than actual trading results, failure to disclose losses, misrepresentations of profits, conversion of funds, failure to provide proper risk disclosures, and misrepresentations concerning trading experience and success.[125] The CFTC also frequently brings cases against persons acting as unregistered CTAs.[126]

The CTA antifraud provisions in the CEA are often interpreted in the same manner as the antifraud provisions in the 1940 Act. However, the Seventh Circuit has held that the registration provisions in the CEA are broader than those in the 1940 Act in that the former would require even impersonal advisers providing advice through newsletters to register.[127] Nevertheless, the Court held that the CFTC could bring an action for fraud against unregistered CTAs.[128]

The CFTC has a set of rules for CTAs. Among other things, CTAs are required to provide a risk disclosure document to their clients.[129] CTAs must also make disclosures of their prior investment performance.[130] CFTC rules make that provision applicable to CTAs even if they are not required to be registered with the CFTC.[131] The CFTC also imposes advertising restrictions on CPOs and CTAs that, among other things,

---

[121] 17 C.F.R. § 4.24.

[122] 17 C.F.R. § 4.25.

[123] 17 C.F.R. § 4.23.

[124] 7 U.S.C. § 6o.

[125] *See* 13 Jerry W. Markham, Commodities Regulation: Fraud, Manipulation and Other Claims § 17A:2 (2012) (describing these cases).

[126] *Id.*

[127] *Compare*, Lowe v. SEC, 472 U.S. 181 (1985) (The 1940 Act registration requirements did not apply to advisers rendering impersonal advice through a newsletter).

[128] Commodity Trend Service, Inc. v. CFTC, 233 F.3d 981 (7th Cir. 2000).

[129] 17 C.F.R. § 4.34.

[130] 17 C.F.R. § 4.35.

[131] 17 C.F.R. § 4.15.

impose restrictions on the use of testimonials and hypothetical trading results.[132]

JURISDICTIONAL BATTLES

The SEC did not exercise its jurisdiction over stock options trading under Section 9 of the 1934 Act[133] until the 1970s, when options began trading on security exchanges.[134] The Chicago Board Options Exchange, Inc. ("CBOE") was the first of these exchanges. It began trading in 1973 and was soon followed by other exchanges.

The SEC adopted a rule that required those exchanges to act as SROs.[135] The creation of the CBOE signaled that derivative contracts would no longer be restricted to the commodity markets that were regulated under the CEA.

The creation and rapid growth of new financially based commodity futures contracts resulted in several clashes between the SEC and CFTC over which agency had jurisdiction over those instruments. The SEC did not fare well in fighting these battles in the Seventh Circuit Court of Appeals, which sits in Chicago, the home of the largest contract markets.[136]

The two agencies did reach an agreement in 1981 over how to divide their jurisdiction. This agreement was referred to as the Shad-Johnson Accord, being so named in reference to the chairmen of the two agencies who negotiated this demarche. That agreement was included in the Futures Trading Act of 1982.[137]

Under that statute, regulation of options contracts was divided between the CFTC and SEC.[138] The SEC is responsible for the regulation of options traded on securities exchanges or on options on securities traded in the over-the-counter market. The SEC also has jurisdiction over

---

[132] 17 C.F.R. § 4.41.

[133] 15 U.S.C. § 78i.

[134] 17 C.F.R. § 240.9b-1.

[135] *See* Jerry W. Markham & David J. Gilberg, *Stock and Commodity Options—Two Regulatory Approaches and Their Conflicts*, 47 Albany L. Rev. 741, 747–748 (1983) (describing the development of these exchanges).

[136] Board of Trade of the City of Chicago v. SEC, 677 F.2d 1137 (7th Cir. 1982), vacated as moot, 459 U.S. 1026 (1982).

[137] Pub. L. No. 97–444, 96 Stat. 2294.

[138] *See* Jerry W. Markham & David J. Gilberg, *Stock and Commodity Options—Two Regulatory Approaches and Their Conflicts*, 47 Albany L. Rev. 741 (1983) (describing stock and commodity options).

options traded on stock indexes, while the CFTC has jurisdiction over futures on stock indexes. The CFTC also regulates options on commodity futures contracts, which entitle the purchaser to exercise the option and obtain a futures contract on an underlying commodity. The SEC was given limited veto authority on futures trading on narrow-based indexes that might be subject to manipulation, a power that the SEC subsequently sought to abuse.[139] As a result of subsequent legislation, the CFTC and SEC were given shared jurisdiction over futures traded on a single stock.[140]

Unfortunately, the Shad-Johnson Accord did not end disputes between the SEC and CFTC.[141] Another concern that continued after the creation of the CFTC was whether OTC derivatives, such as swaps, should be subject to CFTC oversight. It was unclear whether swaps were a form of futures contract that was subject to regulation under the CEA.[142] If such regulation had been applied, the swaps market could not have developed because futures contracts could only be traded on regulated exchanges known as "contract markets," which would have been impractical at the time for swaps.[143]

The CFTC issued a policy statement in 1989, which declared that OTC swaps were not subject to the exchange-trading requirement. The CFTC set several restrictions on this interpretation, including requirements that the swaps not be exchange-traded or cleared by a clearinghouse, that their terms not be standardized or subject to offset and that only commercial entities could be counterparties to the swaps.[144] There were

---

[139] Board of Trade of the City of Chicago v. SEC, 187 F.3d 713 (7th Cir. 1999).

[140] *See* Jerry W. Markham, *Super-Regulator: A Comparative Analysis of Securities and Derivatives Regulation in the United States, Great Britain & Japan*, 28 Brooklyn J. Int'l L. 319, 356–360 (2003) (describing the background of this allocation of jurisdiction).

[141] *See, e.g.*, Chicago Mercantile Exchange v. SEC, 883 F.2d 537 (7th Cir. 1989) and Board of Trade of the City of Chicago v. SEC, 713 (7th Cir. 1999) (rejecting SEC jurisdictional claims over futures products).

[142] *See* Mark D. Young and William L. Stein, *Swap Transactions Under the Commodity Exchange Act: Is Congressional Action Needed*? 76 Geo. L. J. 1917 (1988) (discussing the need to resolve regulatory uncertainty over the swaps market).

[143] *See* Jerry W. Markham, "*Confederate Bonds,*" "*General Custer,*" *and the Regulation of Derivative Financial Instruments*, 25 Seton Hall L. Rev. 1 (1994) (describing concerns over swaps regulation).

[144] *Statement Concerning Swap Transactions*, 54 Fed. Reg. 30694 (July 21, 1989).

concerns, however, over whether that interpretation was binding on the courts, since the CFTC had no exemptive authority to limit its jurisdiction under the CEA jurisdiction.[145]

In order to provide regulatory certainty for the OTC energy and swaps markets, Congress included a provision in the Futures Trading Practices Act of 1992 that allowed the CFTC to exempt OTC derivatives from regulation when the parties were institutional traders.[146] The CFTC thereafter adopted exemptions for swaps and OTC energy derivatives.[147] That energy market exemption applied to institutional trading in contracts for the purchase and sale of crude oil, condensates, natural gas, natural gas liquids or their derivatives when used primarily as an energy source.[148]

The swaps market then grew rapidly. Thereafter, Congress directed the Presidential Working Group on Financial Markets ("PWG") to conduct a study of the OTC derivatives market and make recommendations on whether it should be regulated.[149] The PWG's recommendations were followed by the enactment of the Commodity Futures Modernization Act of 2000 ("CFMA").[150] The CFMA exempted OTC instruments from regulation where the parties to the transactions were sophisticated counterparties. The exempted institutions included banks, investment bankers, pension funds, large businesses, and high net worth individuals.[151]

---

[145] *See* Jerry W. Markham, *Merging the SEC and CFTC—A Clash of Cultures*, 78 U. Cinn. L. Rev. 537, 575 (2009) (discussing that uncertainty).

[146] Pub. L. No. 102–546, 106 Stat. 3590.

[147] *See* William T. Maitland & Jerry W. Markham, *CFTC Rules to Provide Legal Certainty for OTC Products*, Fut. Indust. Mag., Nov/Dec., 1992, at 20 (describing that action).

[148] CFTC, *Exemption for Certain Contracts Involving Energy Products*, 58 Fed. Reg. 21286 (Apr 20, 1993).

[149] *See* Report of the President's Working Group on Financial Markets, Over-the-Counter Derivatives Market and the Commodity Exchange Act (1999), available at http://www.treas.gov/press/releases/reports/otcact.pdf.

[150] Commodity Futures Modernization Act of 2000, Pub. L. No. 106–544, 114 Stat. 2763 (2000).

[151] "The primary justifications for recommending exclusion for such transactions were a determination that most OTC financial derivatives were not susceptible to manipulation and that the counterparties in such transactions do not need the same protections as smaller, unsophisticated market participants who rely on intermediaries to conduct their transactions." U.S. Department of the Treasury, Blueprint for a Modernized Financial Regulatory Structure 47 (2008).

The CFMA authorized the SEC to apply the anti-fraud provisions of Section 10(b) of the 1934 Act to security-based swaps, but other SEC regulation was prohibited.[152] The CFMA also created an exemption and exclusions from most regulation for electronic trading facilities used by institutional traders. These facilities were called "exempt commercial markets" ("ECMs").[153] The ECM exclusion was often referred to as the "Enron loophole." This was because it was inserted into the CFMA at the last minute through the lobbying efforts of the Enron Corp., which was seeking to protect its popular electronic trading platform, EnronOnline, from regulation.[154]

Much criticism arose over the Enron loophole, which allowed the Intercontinental Exchange Inc. ("ICE") in Atlanta Georgia to become a major unregulated market for trading swaps. As a result of concerns over such trading, the CFTC Reauthorization Act of 2008[155] expanded the CFTC's regulatory authority over the ECMs that were operating under the Enron Loophole. The new Act created a new regulatory category for ECMs that trade "significant price discovery contracts" ("SPDCs").[156]

The CFTC Reauthorization Act of 2008 failed to close the Enron Loophole for OTC credit default swaps, but that oversight was corrected under the Dodd-Frank Act.[157] The Dodd Frank Act, which was signed into law on July 21, 2010, regulated the previously unregulated swaps market.[158] Most swaps will now be exchange-traded and cleared through a regulated central counterparty.[159]

---

[152] *See* CSX Corp. v. Children's Inv. Fund Mgmt. (UK) LLP, 654 F.3d 276,288–290 (2d Cir. 2008) (Winter J. concurring and describing limited jurisdiction of SEC for security-based swaps under CFMA).

[153] *See Hearing Before the CFTC to Examine Trading on Regulated Exchanges and Exempt Commercial Markets*, 110th Cong. 1 (2007) (statement of Terry S. Arbit, CFTC General Counsel).

[154] Eric Lipton, *Gramm and the Enron Loophole*, N.Y. Times, Nov. 17, 2008.

[155] The CFTC Reauthorization Act of 2008 was enacted as Title XIII of the Food, Conservation, and Energy Act of 2008 on June 18, 2008 Pub. L. No. 110–246 (2008).

[156] *See* Jerry W. Markham, A Financial History of the U.S. From Enron Era Scandals to The Subprime Crisis (2004–2006) 210–211 (2011) (describing this legislation).

[157] Pub. L. No. 111–203, 124 Stat. 1376 (2010).

[158] *See* Kristin N. Johnson, *Things Fall Apart: Regulating The Credit Default Swap Commons*, 82 U. Colo. L. Rev. 167 (2011) (describing that legislation).

[159] Dodd-Frank §§ 762 & 763.

Dodd-Frank also allowed regulators to impose capital and margin requirements on swap dealers and major swap participants,[160] but not end-users.[161] It requires standardized swaps to be cleared through a central counterparty/clearinghouse.[162]

The Dodd-Frank Act amended the federal securities laws, and repealed a residue of the Enron Loophole, in order to authorize the SEC substantively to regulate securities-based swaps and security-based swap dealers.[163] Dodd-Frank gave the SEC exclusive jurisdiction over security-based swaps, while the CFTC was given jurisdiction over other swaps, and joint jurisdiction was declared for the SEC and CFTC over mixed swaps.[164]

To delineate the regulatory roles of the SEC and CFTC over swaps, Dodd-Frank defines the term "swap"[165] and then defines smaller subsets of that—the "securities-based swap" (i.e., a swap on a narrow-based index of securities or on the single issuer) and the "mixed swap" (basically any other swap that has a financial basis such as interest rates, currencies, quantitative measures or the occurrence of an associated with a potential financial, economic or commercial event.[166]

Dodd-Frank sought to regulate swaps in much the same manner as futures contracts. ICE and others began transforming their swap transactions into futures because there was no longer a regulatory arbitrage that made swaps more attractive.[167]

The SEC and CFTC began the process of implementing this new authority through several rule proposals. Among other things, those agencies jointly defined the terms commodity-based and security-based swaps that would be subject to their new regulatory authority under Dodd-Frank.[168]

---

[160] Dodd-Frank §§ 747 & 753.

[161] Dodd-Frank §§ 731 & 764.

[162] Dodd-Frank §§ 723. Commercial entities were exempted from the clearinghouse requirement. Dodd-Frank § 723.

[163] Dodd-Frank § 762.

[164] Dodd-Frank § 712.

[165] Dodd-Frank § 721.

[166] Dodd-Frank § 761.

[167] *See generally CFTC Staff to Host Public Roundtable to Discuss the "Futurization of Swaps*," available, at http://www.cftc.gov/PressRoom/Events/opaevent_cftcstaff013113 (accessed on Feb. 19, 2013) (discussing this issue).

[168] 77 Fed. Reg. 48208 (Aug. 13, 2012).

OVERLAPPING JURISDICTION

The trading of commodity futures contracts on a single stock was prohibited until 2000, when the CFMA authorized such trading. That legislation granted the CFTC jurisdiction where the option on a single stock is traded on a contract market, while the SEC has jurisdiction where the option on a single stock is traded on a regulated securities market. Under that legislation, securities futures customers could elect to have their securities futures transactions traded either in an SEC regulated account held at an SEC regulated broker-dealer or, alternatively, in a CEA regulated account held with an FCM.[169]

The Dodd-Frank Act and other legislation created more overlapping jurisdiction between the SEC and the CFTC. As described above, the SEC and CFTC jointly regulate single stock futures. In addition, they now jointly regulate swaps that have elements of both futures and securities. As described above in more detail, the two agencies share jurisdiction over commodity pool operators that trade securities and derivatives products.

Overlapping jurisdiction was also given to other agencies through earlier legislation. Following concerns over the manipulation of commodity prices in the energy sector after the turn-of-the-century, Congress granted anti-manipulation authority to FERC and to the FTC.[170] The Energy Policy Act of 2005 ("EP Act")[171] gave FERC power to attack the manipulation of energy prices. That legislation also added civil penalty authority.[172] In enacting this provision, Congress borrowed anti-manipulation language in Section 10(b) of the 1934 Act.[173]

This new grant of authority soon led to a jurisdictional battle between the CFTC and FERC over whether FERC could apply its new anti-manipulation authority to commodity trading that was historically under

---

[169] *See* 7 U.S.C. § 2(1)(D) and 17 C.F.R. § 41.41 (implementing and describing the dual regulation of these products).

[170] *See* Jerry W. Markham, Law Enforcement and The History of Financial Market Manipulation Ch. 6 (2013) (describing the background for that legislation).

[171] Pub. L. No. 109–58, § 1283, 119 Stat. 594 (2005).

[172] 15 U.S.C. §§ 717t-1 & 3414(b)(6); 16 U.S.C. §§ 823b, 825o-1, & 1824(e).

[173] *Compare* 15 U.S.C. § 78j(b), *with*, 16 U.S.C. § 824v(a). *See generally* Catherine Krupka & Athena Velie, *There's a New Sheriff in Town: Energy Derivatives and FERC*, Fut. Indust. Mag. 19 (July–August 2007) (discussing this legislation).

the regulatory umbrella of the CFTC.[174] The District of Columbia Court of Appeals ruled that FERC did not have jurisdiction to bring such an action.[175]

Concerns over high gasoline prices in the wake of Hurricane Katrina led Congress to add additional anti-manipulation powers. In 2007, Congress added the Federal Trade Commission ("FTC") to the list of agencies tasked with attacking commodity price manipulations. The Energy Independence and Security Act ("EISA Act") contained provisions that gave the FTC new authority to police "market manipulation" and "false reporting" in the petroleum industry.[176] This new anti-manipulation authority was also modeled after the one found in the 1934 Act.

CONCLUSION

The derivatives and securities markets have been converging over the last several decades, but they are still governed by two different regulators under separate regulatory schemes that are increasingly overlapping. This division of labor is costly and raises complicated jurisdictional problems and uncertainty for market participants.

---

[174] *U.S. Regulators Square Off on Who can Sanction Trader*, Reuters, Feb. 7, 2013, available at http://www.reuters.com/article/2013/02/06/usa-ferc-hunter-idUSL1N0B69HH20130206 (visited on Feb. 7, 2013).

[175] Hunter v. FERC, 2013 U.S. App. LEXIS 5167 (D.C. Cir. 2013).

[176] Pub. L. 110–140, 121 Stat. 1492, Title VIII, Subtitle B, *codified at* 42 U.S.C. §§ 17301–17305. *See* Malyshev, Panhuys and Dorn, *FTC Joins Others Agencies in Policing Oil Industry "Market Manipulation" and "False Reporting*," 4 Fut. & Derv. L. Rep. 1 (2008) (discussing this legislation).

12. An overview of compliance-related issues in broker-dealer regulation

James Fanto

INTRODUCTION

Broker-dealers are an important part of the economy for, together with other financial intermediaries, they help channel the savings of millions of investors into businesses of the United States and, to some extent, of the rest of the world. They also help create and maintain markets for securities that enable investors to obtain liquidity for their investments. Broker-dealers are thus highly regulated because of their economic importance. In the United States, they are subject to a complex system of federal, state and industry-based regulation. As will be discussed further below, when a person or firm decides to go into business as a broker-dealer, it must register with the Securities and Exchange Commission ("SEC"), and it must become a member of the Financial Industry Regulatory Authority ("FINRA"),[1] a self-regulatory organization ("SRO") that is itself under the SEC's authority, and comply with the SEC's and FINRA's detailed rules. In addition, if the broker-dealer intends to do business on one or more of the nation's stock exchanges (which also are SROs), it must become a member of them and comply with their rules. Finally, the broker-dealer must register with and be subject to the rules of the securities commissions of those states in which it intends to conduct its business.

Broker-dealers engage in numerous securities activities, such as brokerage for individual and institutional customers, market making and other market support activities and acting as exchange specialists and clearing agents. They serve as investment bankers, which generally

[1] FINRA is the successor of the regulatory arm of the former National Association of Securities Dealers ("NASD") and Member Regulation of the New York Stock Exchange ("NYSE"). It is in the process of establishing one set of rules for all of its members from the former NASD Rules and the NYSE Rules. Under the United States system of securities regulation, the securities industry regulates itself through member organizations, like FINRA and the NYSE, under SEC oversight.

means they engage in underwriting and otherwise placing securities with investors, providing mergers and acquisitions advice and in acting as merchant bankers, which involves buying, restructuring and then selling companies. Broker-dealers provide investment advice and financial planning, which makes them like investment advisers, and offer investment products and trading strategies to protect institutions and wealthy investors against market risks and, through arbitrage, to take advantage of market mispricing, which makes them similar to hedge funds. They also trade securities for their own account, which is known as proprietary trading.

Although broker-dealers offer their clients all kinds of financial products, they are regulated as such because they buy and sell "securities," a term defined in the Securities Exchange Act of 1934 ("Exchange Act") to include not only standard examples of securities as stocks, bonds or debentures, but also more exotic types of financial instruments, including participations in a profit-sharing agreement, options to buy or sell a security, investment contracts, voting trust certificates and, most recently, security-based swaps.[2] For definitional purposes, a broker is a person engaged in the business of effecting securities transactions for others, which is the classic agent, whereas a dealer is a person engaged in the regular business of buying and selling securities for its own account.[3] As discussed further below, the Exchange Act requires all brokers and dealers that are not natural persons, or who are natural persons not associated with a broker or dealer that is a firm, to register as a broker-dealer with the SEC, subject to a number of exceptions.[4]

Like many other types of financial firms, such as banks and insurance companies, there are different kinds of broker-dealers. There are approximately 4,300 broker-dealer firms,[5] which fall into four rough categories: (1) the approximately 200 large firms, which historically were NYSE

---

[2] Exchange Act § 3(a)(1), 15 U.S.C. § 78c(a)(1).

[3] *See* Exchange Act §§ 3(a)(4), (5), 15 U.S.C. §§ 78c(a)(4), (5).

[4] Exchange Act §§ 3(a)(12), 15(a), 15 U.S.C. § 78c(a)(12), § 78*o*(a). "Associated person" is defined in § 3(a)(18) of the Exchange Act to include the following: "any partner, officer, director, or branch manager of such broker or dealer (or any person occupying a similar status or performing similar functions), any person directly or indirectly controlling, controlled by, or under common control with such broker or dealer, or any employee of such broker or dealer … ." 15 U.S.C. § 78c(a)(18). This definition sweeps within it all those who engage in the securities business in a broker-dealer, as well as controlling persons, but excludes clerical and ministerial employees.

[5] According to FINRA statistics, which are the most recent, as of April 2013, there are 4,251 member firms, with 162,066 branch offices and 629,807

members, which have most of the customer assets and most of the industry's revenues and which are often in large financial groups;[6] (2) mid-sized, full-line firms, which are generally regional; (3) discount brokerage firms; and (4) smaller firms, sometimes with only few brokers or registered representatives.[7] Although the largest firms are only approximately 4 percent of all broker-dealers in 2011, they accounted for 62 percent of all revenues and 87 percent of all assets of them.[8] At the end of that same year, broker-dealers employed approximately 804,300 persons in the United States, about 21 percent of whom worked in New York City.[9]

It is not possible in one chapter to discuss comprehensively the detailed regulation of broker-dealers in the United States. Accordingly, the remaining sections in this chapter will focus on several key areas of this regulation, in particular (1) the registration requirements, (2) the registration process, (3) recordkeeping, reporting and regulatory examinations, (4) supervision, and (5) compensation. The discussion of each of these issues will suggest how extensive is this regulation and will highlight current topics of interest in them. All of these areas are related to the important compliance function in broker-dealers, which is designed to help ensure that the firm and its employees comply with applicable laws and regulations.

REGISTRATION REQUIREMENTS

Under the Exchange Act,[10] no firm, whether organized as a corporation, partnership or other business form, may conduct or solicit securities

---

registered representatives (those qualified to do securities business). *See* FINRA Statistics, http://www.finra.org/Newsroom/Statistics/ (accessed May 31, 2013).

[6] *See* Securities Industry and Financial Markets Association (SIFMA), *2012 Fact Book* 28–34 (2012) (reporting data on former NYSE-regulated firms).

[7] *See* SIFMA, *Fact Book 2009* 43 (2009) (discussing the kinds of broker-dealers). SIFMA also provides a map of the location of broker-dealers in the United States, which shows that they are concentrated in urban areas, with a significant percentage in the New York City area. *See* SIFMA, *BrokerDealer Heatmap*, Table 1.1 (as of Jan. 31, 2013).

[8] *See* SIFMA, *2012 Fact Book* 28.

[9] *See* SIFMA, *2012 Fact Book* 6. Approximately one-third of employees works in the tri-state area of Connecticut, New Jersey and New York. *See* SIFMA, *U.S. Securities Industry Employment Report: Fourth Quarter 2012* 2 (2012).

[10] Exchange Act § 15(a), 15 U.S.C. § 78*o*(a)(1).

transactions unless it is registered with the SEC, and no individual may do the same without registering as a broker-dealer or being "associated" with a firm that is registered. An associated person of a broker-dealer is thus not required to register with the SEC, but may be subject to the registration requirements of FINRA and of any other SRO of which the broker-dealer is a member. The registration requirements ensure that all persons engaged in the securities business will either be subject to the numerous regulations applicable to broker-dealers or be supervised by a registered broker-dealer.

The Exchange Act defines broker as "any person engaged in the business of effecting transactions in securities for the account of others"[11] and dealer as "any person engaged in the business of buying and selling securities (not including security-based swaps, other than security-based swaps with or for persons that are not eligible contract participants) for such person's own account through a broker or otherwise."[12] Since almost all firms act as both a broker and a dealer, they are generally referred to as broker-dealers.

The above definitions of "broker" and "dealer" both require that the person be "engaged in the business" of securities transactions, a term that the Exchange Act does not define. The critical test here is whether a person's transaction business is regular, as opposed to involving an isolated occurrence.[13] Regularity is often established by the history of the person's participation (or future willingness to participate) in securities transactions, even if this represents only a small part of a person's business. Several factors determine whether a person is in the business of engaging in securities transactions. The most significant include receiving transaction-based compensation, advertising for clients, taking custody of investors' funds and securities, giving advice to them, actively soliciting them and negotiating the sale of securities to them.[14] Indeed, the receipt

---

[11] Exchange Act § 3(a)(4)(A), 15 U.S.C.§ 78c(a)(4)(A).

[12] Exchange Act § 3(a)(5)(A), 15 U.S.C. § 78c(a)(5)(A). Section 761 of the Dodd-Frank Wall Street Reform and Consumer Protection Act of 2010 (Dodd-Frank) added the parenthetical on security-based swaps because the Act brought swaps within regulation. "Security" is defined in Exchange Act § 3(a)(10), 15 U.S.C. § 78c(a)(10).

[13] *See* Massachusetts Fin. Services, Inc. v. Securities Investor Protection Corp., 411 F. Supp. 411, 415 (D. Mass. 1976), aff'd, 545 F.2d 754 (1st Cir.), cert. denied, 431 U.S. 904 (1977) (referring to the "regularity of participation in securities transactions").

[14] The SEC provides an online guide to broker-dealer registration and in it lists these and other factors that must be considered as to whether a person is acting as a broker or dealer. *See* SEC Division of Trading and Markets, *Guide to*

of commissions or other transaction-related compensation is considered the key factor in determining whether registration as a broker or dealer is required.

The importance of transaction-based compensation for determining whether one is a broker-dealer is exemplified by the SEC's views on "finders," who help to bring together two parties who wish to engage in a securities transaction. The question on whether a finder should register as a broker should turn on how closely tied are the finder's activities to the transaction and thus should focus on the traditional broker-dealer factors mentioned above. However, the SEC staff is particularly likely to require registration of a finder if the finder's compensation for its services is transaction-based.[15] The SEC is also likely to require registration where a finder, rather than simply bringing together the parties, is involved in the negotiations with one or both of the parties that are necessary to effect the transaction or where he or she advises one of them. The SEC will seek enforcement against persons who, like finders, should have been registered as broker-dealers. Yet it often adds the charge of failure to register when it is pursuing a more serious abuse relating to securities, such as that a person offered unregistered securities in a Ponzi or other dubious investment scheme.[16]

The recent Jumpstart Our Business Startups ("JOBS") Act[17] introduces two new categories of intermediaries that are like broker-dealers, but that need not register as such. New Section 4(b) of the Securities Act of 1933 ("Securities Act")[18] requires the SEC to modify its regulation of private offerings under Rule 506 of Regulation D to permit general solicitation and general advertising, provided that all purchasers in the offering are accredited investors. New Section 4(b)(1) of that Act provides that those supplying an offering platform, due diligence services and standard

---

Broker-Dealer Registration 4 (Apr. 2008) http://www.sec.gov/divisions/marketreg/bdguide.htm (accessed May 8, 2013).

[15] Courts occasionally resist the SEC's contention that broker-dealer registration turns primarily on transaction-based compensation. *See, e.g.*, SEC v. Kramer, 778 F.Supp.2d 1320, 1334 (M.D. Fla. 2011) (stating that under the correct approach, "an array of factors determine the presence of broker activity"). The SEC has appealed this decision.

[16] *See, e.g.*, SEC v. Mowen, Fed. Sec. L. Rep. ¶ 96,914 (D. Utah 11 June 2012) (summary judgment against person who assisted in the sale of unregistered securities); SEC v. Gagnon, Fed. Sec. L. Rep. ¶ 96,773 (E.D. Mich. Mar. 22, 2012) (person operates a website where numerous unregistered offerings are conducted).

[17] Pub. L. No. 112–106, 126 Stat. 306 (Apr. 5, 2012).

[18] 15 U.S.C. § 77d(b).

documents for investment in these offerings will not be subject to broker-dealer registration solely because of the provision of these services.[19] To qualify for this exemption, this new form of intermediary and any associated person (1) must receive no compensation in connection with the purchase or sale of any security in the offering, (2) must not have possession of customer securities or funds in connection with the purchase or sale of any security in the offering, and (3) must not be subject to a statutory disqualification.[20] This exemption is designed for "platforms" or systems that bring together, and facilitate transactions between, issuers and investors in private offerings.

The JOBS Act also added a new "crowdfunding" exemption, Section 4(a)(6) of the Securities Act, which basically provides that, during any 12-month period, a company can raise $1 million through securities transactions pursuant to this exemption (together with amounts raised under other existing exemptions).[21] There are limits on the amount of the company's securities that can be sold to an investor, depending upon the investor's annual income or net worth. The exemption is available only if the offering is conducted through a broker or a "funding portal" and if the company complies with certain requirements as to disclosure and the manner of offering. A funding portal is defined in a new Section 3(a)(80) of the Exchange Act.[22] Exchange Act Section 3(h) directs the SEC to exempt registered funding portals from broker-dealer registration so long

---

[19] 15 U.S.C. § 77d(b)(1).

[20] 15 U.S.C. § 77d(b)(2).

[21] 15 U.S.C. § 77d(a)(6). "Crowdfunding" refers to a process of raising capital from dispersed investors over the Internet.

[22] 15 U.S.C. § 78c(a)(80), which provides:

FUNDING PORTAL.—The term "funding portal" means any person acting as an intermediary in a transaction involving the offer or sale of securities for the account of others, solely pursuant to Section 4(6) of the Securities Act of 1933 (15 U.S.C. 77d(6)), that does not—

(A) offer investment advice or recommendations;

(B) solicit purchases, sales, or offers to buy the securities offered or displayed on its website or portal;

(C) compensate employees, agents, or other persons for such solicitation or based on the sale of securities displayed or referenced on its website or portal;

(D) hold, manage, possess, or otherwise handle investor funds or securities; or

(E) engage in such other activities as the Commission, by rule, determines appropriate.

This is in fact the second § 3(a)(80) of the Exchange Act.

as they remain subject to the SEC's examination, enforcement and other rule-making authority, they become FINRA members and they comply with whatever other SEC requirements are imposed upon them.[23] FINRA can apply to them only rules specifically designed for these portals. The portals must satisfy detailed statutory standards of conduct when they participate in a crowdfunding offering.[24] Neither the SEC nor FINRA has yet issued any rules for the registration of the portals or regarding their conduct.

There is an important exclusion from the definition of broker-dealer for banks engaging in both broker and dealer activity. Section 3(a)(5)(C) of the Exchange Act exempts a bank from being a dealer if it conducts certain traditional bank dealer activities, such as dealing in banking products like government securities.[25] Similarly, Section 3(a)(4)(B) of this Act excludes from the broker definition a bank doing one of a laundry list of traditional bank brokerage activities.[26] These amendments, enacted by the Gramm-Leach-Bliley Act of 1999, refined the longstanding exclusion of banks from the broker and dealer definitions. After much back and forth between the SEC and bank regulators over the exact meaning of the exclusions, they jointly came to an agreement about them in Regulation R.[27] While the SEC always desired to have jurisdiction over banks when they were acting as broker-dealers, bank regulators were able to prevail in their view that banks had always performed certain broker-dealer activities under bank regulator oversight.

As for significant exemptions from broker-dealer registration, Section 15(a) of the Exchange Act does not require registration of broker-dealers "whose business is exclusively intrastate and who do not make use of any facility of a national securities exchange,"[28] an exemption that is narrowly construed. There is no statutory exemption for foreign broker-dealers that essentially operate outside the United States and have minimal contacts with US investors. The assumption is that, if a US person seeks out a foreign broker-dealer to effect a transaction overseas, the SEC will assert no jurisdiction over that broker-dealer. The SEC codified in Exchange Act Rule 15a-6 this assumption, as well as exemptions that its staff had granted in no-action letters for some US

23 15 U.S.C. § 78c(h).
24 15 U.S.C. § 77d-1.
25 15 U.S.C. § 78c(a)(5)(C).
26 15 U.S.C. § 78c(a)(4)(B).
27 17 C.F.R. pt. 247 (2012).
28 15 U.S.C. § 78*o*(a)(1).

activities by foreign broker-dealers.[29] This rule exempts foreign broker-dealers from registration in various circumstances: (1) a US investor seeks out a foreign broker-dealer outside the United States and initiates transactions in foreign securities markets entirely of its own accord; (2) a foreign broker-dealer furnishes research reports to "major U.S. institutional investors" (certain kinds of institutional investors with investment assets of more than $100 million) presumably on foreign securities and effects transactions on securities discussed in these research reports with or for these customers, but only through a US registered broker-dealer (a "chaperone"); (3) a foreign broker-dealer solicits purchases or sales of any security by either a US institutional investor or a major US institutional investor, but again any resulting transaction must be effected through the US chaperone; and (4) a foreign broker-dealer solicits, and effects, securities transactions with certain enumerated groups (e.g., foreign person temporarily in the United States with whom the foreign broker-dealer has a pre-existing relationship). The SEC has proposed to loosen this rule, essentially to allow foreign broker-dealers that are adequately regulated in their home jurisdiction to effect transactions in foreign securities, without a US chaperone, for certain wealthy US investors, but this proposal has languished.[30]

It should also be noted that a company buying and selling its own securities is generally not a broker or a dealer. It is not a broker because it generally sells its securities for itself, not for others, and it is not a dealer because it is not engaged in the business of both buying and selling securities for its own account (it is just selling its securities). Indeed, the typical situation involves a company that is attempting to raise capital on its own, without the assistance of market professionals. However, if a company employee assists it in selling or purchasing the company's securities, particularly as part of a securities offering, the employee would generally have to register as a broker-dealer, absent an exemption. Exchange Act Rule 3a4–1 sets forth a non-exclusive "safe harbor" with limited circumstances when an associated person of an issuer, which means officers, directors, employees, etc., shall not be deemed to be a broker "solely by reason of his participation in the sale of the securities of such issuer … ."[31]

---

[29] 17 C.F.R. § 240.15a-6 (2012).

[30] *See* Exemption of Certain Foreign Brokers or Dealers, Exchange Act Release No. 58,047, 73 Fed. Reg. 39,182 (July 8, 2008).

[31] 17 C.F.R. § 240.3a4–1 (2012). A current related area of concern is the potential broker status of individuals, often associated with investment advisers, who help raise investments in funds managed by these advisers.

The SEC is authorized to deny registration as a broker-dealer to a firm, and to bar a person from association with a broker-dealer, if the firm or person falls within any of the enumerated statutory grounds for disqualification.[32] To take this action the SEC must find, after giving the applicant notice and an opportunity for a hearing, that the denial or bar is "in the public interest."[33] The SEC has considerable discretion in determining whether an applicant should be disqualified.

THE REGISTRATION PROCESS AND ITS IMPLICATIONS

Under the Exchange Act, a broker-dealer registers by filing with the SEC an application for registration.[34] The SEC requires that a broker-dealer file the Uniform Application for Broker-Dealer Registration ("Form BD").[35] The Form, together with its Schedules and Reporting Pages, requires detailed information about the applicant's legal status and organization, its affiliates and parties performing services for it, any events that may give rise to a statutory disqualification of the applicant or any of its affiliates, the businesses that it engages in or proposes to engage in (other than those that account or would account for less than 1 percent of its revenues) and a list of its proposed branches. The Form BD must be filed with the computerized database, the Central Registration Depositary of FINRA ("CRD"),[36] which processes and maintains applications for the SEC, state securities regulators, and other SROs and

---

[32] Exchange Act § 15(b)(4), 15 U.S.C. § 78*o*(b)(4), sets forth the grounds for suspending or revoking a broker-dealer's registration (including, among others, material misstatements in an application for registration, conviction of certain crimes, and willful violation of securities law). Section 15(b)(1) of the Exchange Act provides that the SEC may deny registration to an applicant if the applicant would be subject to suspension or revocation if it were already registered. 15 U.S.C. § 78*o*(b)(1). Similarly, Exchange Act § 15(b)(6), 15 U.S.C. § 78*o*(b)(6), provides that certain of these grounds are also a basis for barring persons from association with a broker-dealer.

[33] 15 U.S.C. §§ 78*o*(b)(4) & (b)(6).

[34] 15 U.S.C. § 78*o*(b)(1).

[35] *See* 17 C.F.R. § 240.15b1–1(a) (2012). The form is available on the SEC's website, http://www.sec.gov/about/forms/secforms.htm#bdreg (accessed May 8, 2013).

[36] The Web CRD is operated by FINRA, but the database is jointly owned by the North American Securities Administrators Association ("NASAA"), an organization of state securities commissions, and FINRA.

which allows broker-dealers and associated persons to update information electronically. By statute, the SEC, which receives a broker-dealer's Form BD electronically from the CRD, must either grant registration or institute proceedings to determine whether the application should be denied, within 45 days of the filing of a completed application.[37] In practice, however, the SEC's review of a broker-dealer application is usually perfunctory and the SEC will normally permit the applicant to be registered, subject to the applicant's acceptance by FINRA as a member. A broker-dealer must "promptly" amend any application for registration on Form BD to maintain the accuracy of its information.[38]

A broker-dealer may not engage in its securities business until it has been accepted as a member of an SRO,[39] which today means FINRA. Since the SEC allows FINRA to perform the task of reviewing applicants' qualifications, FINRA makes the initial determination as to whether a firm is permitted to become a broker-dealer, subject to the SEC's power under Section 19(d) of the Exchange Act to review SRO actions denying membership, either on its own motion or on application by the aggrieved person.[40] FINRA's website provides detailed information on, and the forms required for, membership.[41] Essentially, the applicant for FINRA membership must file its application, primarily electronically through FINRA's CRD, with FINRA's Regulatory Review and Disclosure Department. The application consists of FINRA's Form NMA, the applicant's signed and notarized paper Form BD, including its applicable schedules, a FINRA-approved fingerprint card and a Form U4 (to be discussed below) for each associated person of the prospective broker-dealer and other FINRA forms and fees. The application demands, among other things, comprehensive information about the applicant, including a detailed business plan, its associated and control persons, its history of securities law and related violations, servicing agreements with third parties, its recordkeeping system and its supervisory and other controls. An applicant can appeal a denial of admission through FINRA's appeal process and ultimately to the SEC. Additionally, a broker-dealer that becomes a member must seek FINRA approval for, among other

---

37 *See* 15 U.S.C. § 78*o*(b)(1).

38 17 C.F.R. § 240.15b3–1 (2012).

39 15 U.S.C. § 78*o*(b)(8).

40 15 U.S.C. § 78s(d)(2).

41 This is available on FINRA's website, www.finra.org/Industry/Compliance (accessed May 14, 2013), under the Registration section, with a link to the part entitled "Member Application Program (Firms)" and then a further link entitled "How to Become a Member."

things, significant ownership changes, acquisitions or changes in its business operations.[42]

A broker-dealer must consider whether it needs to register in the state or states where it will be conducting business. Most states allow the Form BD to count as a registration and to have it submitted to their state securities regulators through the CRD. Every registered broker-dealer is automatically registered with the Securities Investor Protection Corporation, which provides protection for customer losses in certain cases, unless several exceptions apply.[43] A registered broker-dealer may also withdraw from registration by written notice to the SEC upon the terms and conditions as the SEC shall determine.[44] Pursuant to Exchange Act Rule 15b6–1, a withdrawing broker-dealer must file a Uniform Request for Broker-Dealer Withdrawal ("Form BDW") with the CRD.[45] The broker-dealer can withdraw fully from all registration, or partially, and must explain such matters as when it ceased doing business, whether it owes money to any customer or other broker-dealer, as well as arrangements for paying them, whether it is the subject of any investment-related investigation, consumer complaint, or private litigation and who will maintain its books and records. The SEC may delay the effective date of the withdrawal (normally 60 days after filing) and retains the power to discipline the broker-dealer, which is not allowed to withdraw in order to escape punishment or to avoid its obligations to customers and others.

As for individuals, they must register with the SEC as broker-dealers, but only if they are "not associated with" any registered broker-dealer. Most people working as brokers are thus exempted from SEC registration as a broker-dealer because they work for a registered firm. A registered broker-dealer may not effect transactions in securities unless all of its associated natural persons "meet such standards of training, experience, competence, and such other qualification" as the SEC may provide.[46] The SEC has in fact delegated the registration and qualification of associated persons to the SROs by providing that a broker-dealer cannot effect a securities transaction unless its associated persons are "registered and approved" in accordance with SRO rules.[47] Associated persons, whether they are employees or independent contractors, are required to be registered, generally with FINRA. In addition, as a registered securities

---

42 *See* FINRA Rule 1160.
43 *See* 15 U.S.C. § 78ccc(a)(2)(A).
44 *See* 15 U.S.C. § 78*o*(b)(5).
45 *See* 17 C.F.R. § 240.15b6–1(a) (2012).
46 *See* Exchange Act § 15(b)(7), 15 U.S.C. § 78*o*(b)(7).
47 *See* 17 C.F.R. § 240.15b7–1 (2012).

association under the Exchange Act, FINRA is allowed to require that an associated person meet its "standards of training, experience, and competence" and to "examine and verify the qualifications" of an associated person of its member firms.[48] FINRA thus sets standards and qualifications for membership of associated persons and excludes those individuals subject to a disqualification. FINRA rules also establish categories of individuals who must be registered if they are to be associated with a member firm, in particular (1) principals and (2) representatives and assistant representatives.

Under FINRA regulation, "principals" include a sole proprietor, officer, partner, manager of an office with supervisory jurisdiction, or corporate director, each of whom is "actively engaged in the management of the member's investment banking or securities business, including supervision, solicitation, conduct of business, or the training of persons associated with the member for any of these functions."[49] FINRA divides principals into categories on the basis of their responsibilities or the kinds of investment products that they oversee. A principal may register as a "general securities principal," which qualifies him or her to supervise investment banking or securities business with respect to corporate securities, direct participation programs and investment company products/variable contracts.[50] An individual may also register as one of the categories of "limited principal" with more targeted or defined supervisory responsibilities (e.g., principal for financial and operations, a "FINOP"). For registration, principals and limited principals in each category must pass a qualification examination that is tailored to the particular responsibilities or kinds of investments relevant to the registration category. Similarly, registered representatives (i.e., those other than principals engaged in investment banking or securities business, as well as related support tasks) are divided into categories (including limited representatives) with different qualification examinations, with the broadest category being the general securities representative, who can be

---

[48] *See* Exchange Act § 15A(g)(3)(A) & (B), 15 U.S.C. § 78*o*-3(g)(3)(A) & (B).

[49] NASD Rule 1021(b). Again, since FINRA is now consolidating its rules, some of them still maintain the former NASD label.

[50] *See* NASD Rule 1022(a).

involved in the solicitation, purchase and/or sale of all securities products.[51] There are also several categories other than principal and representative, as well as exemptions from registration, with the most significant exemption being for clerical and ministerial employees.[52]

Just as a broker-dealer has to complete its Form BD and FINRA Form NMA for registration, an associated person, independently of whether the person is a principal, representative or a person in some other category, has the Uniform Application for Securities Industry Registration or Transfer ("Form U4"). The broker-dealer must file the Form for an individual, through the CRD, when it first applies for FINRA membership or when a new principal or employee becomes associated with the firm. The Form U4 asks for detailed information from the person in question, including the kind of FINRA registrations and the state registrations that the person is applying for, any professional designation, residences for the past five years, employment information, other business activity and information that might disqualify the person from registration (e.g., past securities law violations), which might require fuller discussion and disclosure. The associated person must keep the Form U4 current and allow SROs and regulators to share information about the applicant. The broker-dealer certifies that the person is qualified to engage in the designated securities business, that it has communicated with the person's employer(s) for the last three years and that it has verified the accuracy of the information on the Form. Broker-dealers are required by FINRA rule to conduct background checks on their employees,[53] as well as to have them fingerprinted and to submit the fingerprint card with the Form U4.[54] When an employee resigns or is terminated, the broker-dealer must file with the CRD a Uniform Termination Notice for Securities Industry Registration ("Form U5"). As in the case of a broker-dealer, an individual who is denied registration by FINRA may appeal this denial through the FINRA appellate process, with review by the SEC. A broker-dealer employee may also have to be registered, and be properly qualified, in any state where the employee conducts any securities business.[55]

There are numerous consequences of registration for a broker-dealer and for an associated person, several of which will be discussed in other

---

51 *See* NASD Rule 1032(a).

52 *See* NASD Rule 1060(a)(1).

53 *See* NASD Rule 3010(e).

54 *See* FINRA Rule 1010(d).

55 There is a Uniform Securities Agent State Law Examination (Series 63) used for qualification by many states.

sections of this chapter. But an important one should be noted here. The CRD contains a great deal of information about every firm and associated person and stores "customer dispute information," which is available to member firms and regulators. More importantly, every member of the public has access to certain information from broker-dealer and associated person CRD records through the FINRA BrokerCheck system.[56] This system includes information about criminal actions, customer complaints (including, in certain circumstances, unsettled as well as settled customer complaints) and regulatory discipline. The information remains on the system long after the individual has left the industry and, in some cases, permanently. It is not easy for a firm or a broker to have this information "expunged" or removed (it requires a court order or a court confirmation of an arbitral decision).[57] In addition, an associated person must undergo continuing education in regulatory matters (generally, every three years), which can be supplied inside or outside the firm (the "Regulatory Element"). And the broker-dealer has to develop its own additional education program (known as a "Firm Element") for certain of its personnel, chiefly those who have contact with customers. In sum, the consequences of registration for an individual as an associated person are significant.

THE SIGNIFICANCE OF RECORDKEEPING, REPORTING AND EXAMINATIONS

This section briefly reviews the recordkeeping and reporting requirements of broker-dealers. These requirements give FINRA and the SEC a convenient way of monitoring broker-dealers and their employees for their compliance with applicable laws and regulations. Without adequate records and reports, regulators would have no ready way of conducting this surveillance or investigating an allegation of misconduct in, or a customer complaint involving, a broker-dealer or broker. This is why both the SEC and FINRA treat violations of the recordkeeping and reporting requirements harshly on their own account, even in the absence of a substantive violation. The section concludes by looking at a related subject, SEC and FINRA examinations of broker-dealers, which are based upon records and reports and complement the firm's own surveillance.

---

[56] *See* FINRA Rule 8312.
[57] *See* FINRA Rule 2080.

Section 17(a) of the Exchange Act authorizes the SEC to adopt rules prescribing recordkeeping requirements for all broker-dealers,[58] with records "mean[ing] accounts, correspondence, memorandums, tapes, discs, papers, books, and other documents or transcribed information of any type, whether expressed in ordinary or machine language."[59] The SEC thus adopted Exchange Act Rule 17a-3, which specifies the records to be kept, and Exchange Act Rule 17a-4, which prescribes the periods of time during which a broker-dealer must retain these records and the conditions of storage.[60] FINRA requires its members to comply with the SEC's recordkeeping and retention rules.[61] A broker-dealer can keep its records in electronic form (and many of them do only this) so long as the records comply with the requirements of Rule 17a-4(f), including that the records are not erasable.[62]

The actual recordkeeping and retention rules are too detailed other than to be very broadly summarized in this section. To give a flavor of the required records, a broker-dealer must keep, in hard or electronic form generally for six years, such records as follows: (1) "blotters," which are daily records of purchases and sales of securities, receipts and deliveries of securities, and receipts and deliveries of cash; (2) detailed ledgers carrying all kinds of financial data, including for transactions affecting customer accounts and assets (e.g., securities borrowed and loaned, its holding of each security); (3) trading records, including order tickets with detailed information on the order for the customer or for itself; (4) extensive records about customer accounts with information collected about the customer (without which the broker-dealer could not satisfy many of its legal obligations, like suitability); (5) option records; (6) employee records (facilitated through recordkeeping on the CRD), including as to written (or electronic) customer complaints about a particular broker; (7) lost or stolen securities (which must be reported to the SEC and the FBI);[63] (8) any internal trading system that it operates;

---

58 *See* Exchange Act § 17(a), 15 U.S.C. § 78q(a).

59 *See* Exchange Act § 3(a)(37), 15 U.S.C. § 78c(a)(37).

60 *See* 17 C.F.R. §§ 240.17a-3, 17a-4 (2012).

61 *See* FINRA Rule 4511. This Rule also requires a broker-dealer to preserve all books and records for six years, unless a specific FINRA or SEC rule provides otherwise.

62 *See* 17 C.F.R. § 240.17a-4(f) (2012).

63 Section 929W of Dodd-Frank added a new Exchange Act § 17A(g), 15 U.S.C. § 78q-1(g), which, among other things, required the SEC to amend Exchange Act Rule 17Ad-17, 17 C.F.R. § 240.17Ad-17, to extend that Rule's requirement to search for "lost securityholders" to broker-dealers (it had formerly

(9) compliance with rules about advertising to customers; (10) a list of responsible persons who, in each office, understand the records kept there; and (11) all business-related external and internal communications (i.e., written and email). This list could go on and on.

A "hot" topic in recordkeeping in recent years involves brokers' use of instant messaging and social media like Facebook and Twitter. The simple reality is that all customer communications in electronic form must be recorded so that they can be supervised and monitored, and so that there is a record of any securities law or other violation. FINRA has had to weigh in repeatedly to remind broker-dealers of their responsibilities in this area.[64] Most recently, FINRA issued guidance on the use by registered representatives and firms of social media sites (e.g., Facebook) and blogs, cautioning firms that, above all, they had to be able to maintain records of any communications made by their personnel on the sites.[65] FINRA emphasized that broker-dealers are not required to prohibit associated persons from engaging in business communications on personal communication devices, such as an iPad, or on particular social media applications, but they must be able to record all such communications. Indeed, recordkeeping and retention of email and other electronic communications or blog posts has been a ground for discipline of broker-dealers and their associated persons in almost countless proceedings in recent years, in both large and small firms.[66]

The reporting requirements of broker-dealers are similarly voluminous, and thus only a few of them can be mentioned here. Like broker-dealer

---

applied just to transfer agents). The SEC just finalized that rule amendment. *See* Lost Securityholders and Unresponsive Payees, Exchange Act Release No. 68,668, 78 Fed. Reg. 4768 (Jan. 23, 2013).

64 *See* FINRA, *Supervision of Electronic Communications*, Regulatory Notice 07–59 (Dec. 2007).

65 FINRA, *Social Media Web Sites*, Regulatory Notice No. 10–06 (Jan. 2010). *See also* FINRA, *Social Media Websites and the Use of Personal Devices for Business Communications*, Regulatory Notice No. 11–39 (Aug. 2011). Indeed, the SEC's Office of Compliance Inspections and Examinations ("OCIE") released observations and guidance about investment adviser use of social media, many of which equally apply to broker-dealers. *See* OCIE, *Investment Adviser Use of Social Media*, National Examination Risk Alert, Vol. II, Issue 1 (Jan. 4, 2012).

66 *See, e.g.*, In re Citigroup Global Markets Inc., FINRA Acceptance, Waiver and Consent No. 2010021823 (Dec. 2, 2011) (firm is fined $750,000 for instituting a new email retention system without adequate testing, so that a defective server failed to send emails of approximately 3,000 associated persons to a journaling-based server, which would resend them to an archive).

records, broker-dealer reports, many of which can be filed electronically, allow the SEC and FINRA to monitor the firm and to have additional information to examine if an investigation is warranted. Rule 17a-5 requires every registered broker-dealer to file with the SRO designated as its examining authority (this generally means FINRA) a uniform report on Form X-17A-5, known as the FOCUS Report.[67] The frequency (monthly vs. quarterly) and nature of the filing depend upon the broker-dealer's status as a "carrying" (i.e., one who holds customer accounts and assets) or "introducing" firm (one who delegates these tasks to a carrying firm). The content of the Form deals with the financial condition and operational capacity of the broker-dealer, particularly its capital position.[68] In addition, with a few exceptions, a broker-dealer must file, on a calendar or fiscal year basis, an annual financial statement, which has been audited by an independent public accountant in accordance with generally accepted auditing standards, within 60 days after the date of the financial statements.[69] In addition, a carrying broker-dealer must send annual financial information to its customers.[70] There are also a number of special reports that a broker-dealer is required to file that are

---

[67] *See* 17 C.F.R. § 240.17a-5(a) (2012). FOCUS is an acronym for the Financial and Operational Combined Uniform Single report.

[68] Under FINRA Rule 4524, FINRA may require its members to file additional schedules and reports to supplement the FOCUS Report. The SEC is proposing to have a broker-dealer file, as part of its quarterly FOCUS Report, a new Form Custody. *See* Broker-Dealer Reports, Exchange Act Release No. 64,676, 76 Fed. Reg. 37,572, 37,603 (June 27, 2011) (proposed Rule 17a-5(a)(5)). The goal here is to enhance the SEC's and FINRA's oversight of the custody function of broker-dealers, particularly in light of the numerous recent scandals involving the loss of customer assets.

[69] *See* 17 C.F.R. § 240.17a-5(d)(1)(i) & (5) (2012). Section 982 of the Dodd-Frank amended the Sarbanes-Oxley Act of 2002, which, among other things, enhanced the auditing of public companies, to now include broker-dealers within Sarbanes-Oxley's auditing requirements and to make their auditing (and the auditing firms conducting broker-dealer audits) expressly subject to the oversight and direction of the Public Company Accounting Oversight Board. The SEC is also proposing to modify Rule 17a-5(d) to include new annual reports, in addition to the annual audit and its related financial statements. *See* Broker-Dealer Reports, Exchange Act Release No. 64,676, 76 Fed. Reg. 37,572 (June 27, 2011). These would include a Compliance Report by a carrying broker-dealer about its compliance with financial responsibility rules relating to reserve requirements and its safeguarding of customer assets, which would be audited, and an Exemption Report by a non-carrying broker-dealer concerning its exemption from these rules.

[70] *See* 17 C.F.R. § 240.17a-5(c) (2012).

designed to give an early warning of a problem in its financial condition. Finally, a broker-dealer must report to FINRA, within 30 calendar days after it knows or should have known of them, certain disciplinary and litigation-related information about itself and any associated person.[71]

Recordkeeping and reporting, in turn, facilitate SEC and FINRA examinations, which are provided for in the Exchange Act. Under Section 17(b)(1) of the Exchange Act, the records of any registered broker-dealer are subject to "such reasonable, periodic, special, or other examinations" by the SEC as it deems appropriate.[72] Moreover, under Section 19(g)(1) of that Act, every SRO, like FINRA, shall enforce compliance with SEC rules and its own rules by its members, unless the SEC relieves it of that obligation.[73] In addition, under Exchange Act Rule 15b2–2, each SRO must conduct examinations of newly registered broker-dealers, within six months of their registration for compliance with financial responsibility rules and within 12 months for overall compliance.[74] Examinations are one way for FINRA to accomplish this task.

The SEC's Office of Compliance Inspections and Examinations ("OCIE"), which was founded in 1995 to consolidate the examination activities of the different SEC divisions, oversees and conducts the examinations of broker-dealers. OCIE supervisors in Washington establish policies and procedures for broker-dealer examinations, which the staff in the SEC field offices conducts, generally as to broker-dealers in their jurisdiction. However, FINRA is the "front-line" examiner of broker-dealers. The OCIE thus conducts no annual examination of a broker-dealer and its examinations are generally targeted and based upon its perception of a particular risk or problem in a broker-dealer or class of broker-dealers. Accordingly, SEC examinations tend to be "cause" examinations, which are initiated for a reason, such as an investor complaint, or a "surveillance" or "risk" examination, which is triggered by the OCIE's broker-dealer program's identification of a troubling issue in a broker-dealer. Alternatively and more broadly, the examinations can be "sweeps" and "mini-sweeps," which are examinations into an industry-wide issue (or, for mini-sweeps, an issue only in a number of firms) conducted by OCIE staff, sometimes with the help of FINRA and state securities regulators, throughout many broker-dealers. There is no time here to review OCIE examination procedure, other than to say that

---

[71] *See* FINRA Rule 4530.
[72] *See* 15 U.S.C. § 78q(b)(1).
[73] *See* 15 U.S.C. § 78s(g)(1).
[74] *See* 17 C.F.R. § 240.15b2–2 (2012).

its review of a broker-dealer will be extensive, both offsite (reviewing records and reports beforehand) and onsite (with interviews of personnel, checks of internal controls and compliance procedures). The examination may result in a deficiency letter setting forth problems that need correction or, in the worst case, a referral to the SEC's Enforcement Division.

The quality of SEC examinations was cast into doubt by the Bernard Madoff scandal. The SEC's Inspector General conducted a study of the history of the SEC staff's dealings with Madoff and his firm, particularly the SEC examinations. He concluded that, despite numerous and credible warnings about Madoff's activities, the SEC never conducted an adequate examination of Madoff's firm.[75] The Inspector General's report thus raised serious questions about the quality of SEC examinations of broker-dealers and the competency of OCIE and its examiners. In light of this scandal, the OCIE committed to improving the examination process, particularly by increasing examiners' expertise and even by drawing into OCIE service individuals who are experienced in complex financial products. Moreover, as an implicit criticism of OCIE and its lack of specialized examiners, Section 965 of Dodd-Frank directed the SEC's Division of Trading and Markets (responsible for the oversight of broker-dealers) to have its own staff of examiners who perform compliance examinations and report to its Director.[76]

FINRA conducts regular compliance examinations of its members, generally every four years (although every two years for clearing or carrying firms).[77] In addition, FINRA has instituted a risk-based examination focus, which assigns a yearly risk profile to each firm on the basis of the data on the firm in FINRA's possession. Those firms presenting the greatest risk profile receive a special examination for that year, and this risk-based focus even influences the regular compliance examinations. Moreover, like the SEC (and even with the SEC), FINRA conducts "sweep" examinations on particular issues, which are often designed to gather information about them.[78] Also like SEC examiners, FINRA examiners consult records and reports offsite before coming into a broker-dealer, often to focus on particular issues in the form of concern

---

[75] *See* SEC Office of Investigations, *Investigation of Failure of the SEC to Uncover Bernard Madoff's Ponzi Scheme—Public Version* (Rep. No. OIG-509, Aug. 31, 2009).

[76] It adds a new Section 4(h)(1) of the Exchange Act, 15 U.S.C. § 78d(h)(1).

[77] *See* FINRA Rule 8210(a).

[78] *See, e.g.*, FINRA, Targeted Examination Letter: Spread-Based Structured Products (Nov. 2011) (requesting information on how these products were sold, from the period January 1, 2011 through August 31, 2011).

to FINRA.[79] And the examination can have results similar to those of an SEC examination (deficiency letter up to an enforcement referral).

State securities authorities may conduct examinations of broker-dealers, or their branch offices, within their jurisdiction as well.[80] Their focus is generally on consumer-oriented issues, including the sales practices of broker-dealers in local offices. As noted above, they may also conduct sweep examinations with the SEC and FINRA.

THE OVERRIDING IMPORTANCE OF SUPERVISION

The duty of broker-dealers to supervise their business and employees is one of the most important areas of SEC and FINRA regulation. Section 15(b)(4)(D) of the Exchange Act empowers the SEC to discipline a broker-dealer for, among other things, the willful violation of, or the inability to comply with, the federal securities laws or their regulations by the broker-dealer or by any person associated with the broker-dealer.[81] Thus, if an employee of a broker-dealer willfully violates the securities laws or regulations, the broker-dealer would be subject to SEC discipline under this provision, which could include suspension of its registration for up to 12 months or the death sentence of revocation of registration. More particularly, under Section 15(b)(4)(E), a broker-dealer can be subject to sanctions if, among other things, it, or an associated person, willfully aids or abets a federal securities law or rule violation or "failed reasonably to supervise, with a view to preventing" the violation, another person who committed the violation.[82] Thus, this provision makes the broker-dealer explicitly liable for its own, and its associated persons, supervisory violations. Furthermore, Section 15(b)(6) provides for SEC discipline of the associated person himself or herself who, among other things, willfully aids and abets a violation of the federal securities laws or who commits a supervisory violation.[83] Under this latter section, the

---

[79] Each year, FINRA identifies its examination priorities. *See, e.g.*, Letter from Daniel M. Sibears, Executive Vice President, FINRA Member Regulation Programs, Regulatory and Examination Priorities (Jan. 11, 2013).

[80] NASAA, the organization of state securities regulators, regularly publishes results of state examinations and areas of concern in broker-dealers. *See* http://www.nasaa.org (accessed May 9, 2013).

[81] *See* 15 U.S.C. § 78*o*(b)(4)(D).

[82] 15 U.S.C. § 78*o*(b)(4)(E).

[83] 15 U.S.C. § 78*o*(b)(6). This section imposes the supervisory obligation through a cross-reference to Section 15(b)(4)(E).

SEC can discipline branch managers and other supervisors in a broker-dealer for their failure to supervise employees under their authority.

Section 15(b)(4)(E) provides both the firm and, through Section 15(b)(6), firm supervisors with a defense to a charge of supervisory liability. It states that no person "shall be deemed to have failed reasonably to supervise any other person" if, first, there were "established procedures and a system for applying" them, "which would reasonably be expected to prevent and to detect, insofar as practicable," any securities law violations by the supervised person.[84] It further stipulates that the supervisor has "reasonably" to discharge the duties under the procedures and system "without reasonable cause to believe" that these procedures and system were not being complied with.[85] This means that, to evoke this statutory defense, a firm has to have well drafted supervisory procedures for ensuring that the firm and all its employees comply with securities laws and regulations as well as a system, which means the resources and responsible people, to implement these procedures. Moreover, the firm and its supervisors have in fact to demonstrate that they fulfilled their responsibilities under these procedures and system and, therefore, that the procedures and system were not simply "window dressing." This latter point requires that they monitor employees for legal compliance and follow up on any problem or potential problem (known in the trade as a "red flag") that surfaces in a firm, which could suggest a legal violation and thus potentially a supervisory one.

FINRA also has detailed supervisory rules. The Exchange Act requires SROs to enforce among their members compliance with federal securities laws and regulations, as well as their own rules, and to have rules designed to "prevent fraudulent and manipulative acts and practices, [and] to promote just and equitable principles of trade."[86] FINRA requires each of its members to have "a system to supervise the activities of each registered representative, registered principal, and other associated person that is reasonably designed to achieve compliance" with securities laws and regulations, and FINRA rules.[87] Among other things,

---

[84] 15 U.S.C. § 78*o*(b)(4)(E)(i).

[85] 15 U.S.C. § 78*o*(b)(4)(E)(ii).

[86] *See* Exchange Act § 15A(b)(2) & (6), 15 U.S.C. § 78*o*-3(b)(2) & (6) (for securities associations); Exchange Act § 6(b)(1) & (5), 15 U.S.C. § 78f(b)(1) & (5) (for exchanges). The SEC reviews the rules in connection with the registration of an association or an exchange, as well as ongoing proposed rule changes or ones initiated by the SEC. *See* Exchange Act § 19(a)-(c), 15 U.S.C. § 78s(a)–(c).

[87] *See* NASD Rule 3010(a).

the system requires a broker-dealer to have written procedures for the supervision ("written supervisory procedures" or "WSPs") of each of its securities businesses and associated persons, to designate supervisors for each regulated business, to have annual compliance reviews for each registered representative and principal, to have internal inspections of all offices, to have a principal review the transactions and correspondence with the public of registered representatives relating to their securities business and to investigate the character and qualifications of any associated person.[88] In other words, while the duty of supervision under the Exchange Act is general, the SRO supervisory requirements are both general and detailed. Since SRO rules govern each securities business activity and generally dictate how it is to be conducted in accordance with the law, nearly every SRO rule has supervisory implications.

NASD Rule 3012 also requires that a firm have one or more principals who set up supervisory controls to test its supervisory system on a yearly basis in order to assess its compliance effectiveness and to identify the need for additional WSPs.[89] Under the rule, the responsible principal or principals establish the controls, conduct the testing, create additional WSPs to respond to weaknesses revealed by the testing and annually report to a broker-dealer's senior management about the above.[90] At a minimum, the controls must cover (1) customer account activity conducted by branch office managers and other supervisors, (2) customer account activity, such as the transmittal of funds or securities, address changes, changes of investment objectives, and (3) heightened supervision of certain "producing managers" who generate a significant portion of the revenue of a particular business unit.[91] Even more specifically for oversight of supervisory systems, FINRA Rule 3130 requires a firm to appoint at least one chief compliance officer ("CCO").[92] Moreover, under this rule, a firm's chief executive officer ("CEO") must certify annually that there are "in place processes to establish, maintain, review, test and modify written compliance policies and written supervisory procedures reasonably designed to achieve compliance with" SRO rules and federal securities laws and regulations and that the CEO has had "one or more meeting" with the CCO in the

---

[88] *See* NASD Rule 3010(a)–(e).
[89] *See* NASD Rule 3012(a)(1).
[90] *See* NASD Rule 3012(a)(1).
[91] *See* NASD Rule 3012(a)(2).
[92] *See* FINRA Rule 3130(a).

preceding 12 months to discuss the processes.[93] In addition, nearly every significant FINRA rule has either a supervisory element or else FINRA provides guidance on how a firm's supervisory system must incorporate the rule.

Broker-dealers thus have detailed supervisory systems, with the comprehensiveness of the systems depending upon how extensive is the business of a particular broker-dealer. As a result, the firms also have a compliance function, which can range in size to a CCO in smaller firms, who might also be involved in business, to a compliance department in larger firms that reflects in its own organization the complexity of the firm and its business. Compliance is closely associated with, and essentially makes possible, supervision in the broker-dealer because, as noted above, the purpose of supervision is to ensure that a firm and its employees comply with the federal securities laws and regulations, other applicable laws and SRO rules and industry standards. A major job of compliance officers is thus to produce, and to keep current, the WSPs that FINRA mandates.[94] The WSPs dictate how firm employees should conduct a particular business activity so as to comply with laws and regulations and how the activity should be supervised and monitored. They thus specify, in a step-by-step way, how a broker conducts an activity, how recording or reporting relating to the activity is done, how the designated supervisor oversees the broker conducting the activity, how additional monitoring occurs by compliance staff, often through the review of transaction records, how problems might emerge and what the broker, supervisor, compliance officer and/or another person should do in response to those problems.

This reference to compliance raises a particular issue about the relationship between supervision and compliance that has come to the foreground in recent years.[95] Supervision generally refers to the power of

---

[93] *See* FINRA Rule 3130(b). The Rule provides a model certification for the CEO. *See* FINRA Rule 3130(c).

[94] *See* Securities Industry Ass'n: Legal & Compliance Division, *White Paper on the Role of Compliance* 4 (Oct. 2005); SIFMA, *The Evolving Role of Compliance* 21 (Mar. 2013).

[95] The issue discussed below was raised in a case involving an SEC disciplinary action of a general counsel who was also the CCO of a broker-dealer. *See* In re Theodore W. Urban, SEC Initial Decision Release No. 402 (Sept. 8, 2010). In that case, Urban attempted to take action against a rogue broker, who engaged in numerous legal violations, including unauthorized trading in client accounts and doing trades for a stock manipulator. Urban urged that the broker be dismissed, but he was overruled by the head of retail sales who agreed to supervise the broker personally. The broker ultimately left the firm in

one person over another in a firm's chain of command, which includes, as discussed above, the obligation to ensure that the supervised employee complies with securities laws and regulations.[96] It is often typified by the ability of the supervisor to control the actions of an employee, such as the ability to dismiss an employee. Compliance officers in a broker-dealer are not, without more, part of the supervisory structure and are thus not supervisors. Rather, they make effective supervision possible. They prepare the WSPs to direct how employees must conduct themselves to satisfy their legal and regulatory obligations and how supervisors should perform their supervision; they monitor that the procedures are, in fact, followed and they investigate potential violations. If a violation is found, compliance officers do not make disciplinary decisions, but refer the matter to the appropriate supervisor.[97]

---

the wake of numerous customer problems that resulted in a significant financial outlay by the broker-dealer. Urban was charged with a supervisory violation. The administrative law judge ruled that Urban was in fact a supervisor, but that he had fulfilled his supervisory responsibilities. At the urging of the Enforcement Division, the SEC declined to affirm summarily the judge's ruling, stating, among other things, that it needed to consider whether it was enough for Urban to report problems to the supervisor of the broker or whether it should have escalated the matter to the firm's chief executive officer and its board of directors. *See* In re Theodore W. Urban, SEC Admin. Proc. File No. 3–13655 (Dec. 7, 2010). Eventually, the SEC dismissed the proceedings because, with three members recusing themselves, the other two split on the decision. *See* In re Theodore W. Urban, SEC Admin. Proc. File No. 3–13655 (Jan. 26, 2012). The case raised concern among practitioners that compliance officers were being inappropriately pulled into the supervisory structure of a firm. *See, e.g.*, David C. Prince, 'NSCP Files Amicus Brief with SEC in Theodore W. Urban Case', NSCP Currents 1 (Nov./Dec. 2010) (discussing position of the National Society of Compliance Professionals on this case).

[96] In one important SEC decision on this subject, In re John H. Gutfreund, et al., Exchange Act Release No. 31,554, 52 S.E.C. Docket 2849, 1992 WL 362753, *15 (Dec. 3, 1992), the SEC made the following observation in the context of discussing the supervisory responsibilities of legal and compliance officers:

> Employees of brokerage firms who have legal or compliance responsibilities do not become "supervisors" for purposes of Sections 15(b)(4)(E) and 15(b)(6) solely because they occupy those positions. Rather, determining if a particular person is a "supervisor" depends on whether, under the facts and circumstances of a particular case, that person has a requisite degree of responsibility, ability or authority to affect the conduct of the employee whose behavior is at issue.

[97] The SEC has held that, once a compliance or legal officer has a sufficient position of influence within a firm, he or she may have the responsibility, with

As noted above, supervisory status comes with being able to affect the conduct of an employee, often typified by the ability to hire and fire him or her, although one could be a supervisor without this power. Customarily, there is a hierarchy of supervisors in a typical broker-dealer. Supervisory status generally is given to branch managers and other brokerage-firm employees in a firm's chain of command, such as regional managers and financial officers, who have "line" responsibility over an employee. Moreover, the CEO is responsible for ensuring that the firm establishes a proper system of supervision and for delegating supervisory functions to firm personnel. If he or she fails to set up a proper system or to make proper delegation, the CEO has total supervisory liability.

A supervisor must act reasonably under the circumstances, which generally means, at the very least, following the supervisory tasks as set forth in the WSPs. In particular, a supervisor must respond reasonably when confronted by any sign that a registered representative under the supervisor's supervision may be engaging in improper activity (again, the "red flag"). Reasonable action here is also usually set forth in the WSPs, and it clearly means checking up on the employee, including contacting any customers involved, and not taking at face value the employee's explanation of the problem. Although in certain cases a supervisor may delegate supervisory responsibilities, such as when he or she uses a subordinate to review written and electronic correspondence of brokers, the supervisor remains ultimately responsible for the supervision. Similarly, neither a broker-dealer nor an individual supervisor can escape the supervisory or other regulatory requirements by "outsourcing," i.e., contracting with third parties to perform activities and functions. Outsourcing typically occurs in smaller firms, which do not have the compliance staff or technological resources to do certain tasks, including certain supervisory tasks. FINRA has reminded firms that supervisory responsibility continues for the firm or supervisor even if the task in question has been delegated to a third party.[98]

SEC and FINRA enforcement actions charging firms and individuals with failure to supervise are numerous. Indeed, a cynical observer of

---

other supervisors, for taking appropriate action in response to misconduct. This action could include, in extreme circumstances such as when the main supervisors do not adequately respond to the misconduct, escalating the matter to the board of directors, resigning or reporting the problem to regulatory authorities. *See* In re John H. Gutfreund, et al., Exchange Act Release No. 31,554, 52 S.E.C. Docket 2849, 1992 WL 362753, *16 (Dec. 3, 1992).

[98] *See* FINRA, *Third-Party Service Providers*, Regulatory Notice No. 11–14 (Mar. 2011) (setting forth proposed rule 3190).

these actions could contend that every time a securities law violation occurs in a firm, the SEC or FINRA will assume that someone should have prevented it from occurring, which means that there must be a supervisory violation. Whether this observation is in fact true, supervisory violations generally appear in certain kinds of cases. First, occasionally a firm simply fails to have WSPs for a given business activity, sometimes because it has recently expanded into the activity without the adequate control structure.[99] This kind of supervisory violation may be detected in an examination of the firm. Second, a firm or supervisor may fail to follow the steps set out in the WSPs, whether they concern the monitoring of a particular activity or the response to a particular indication of a problem.[100] In a way, this is the worst, and most damning, offense because all the supervisor had to do was to follow the steps set out in the WSPs. Third, and finally, a supervisory violation occurs when the firm or the supervisor fails to investigate a matter or a broker when alerted to by "red flags."[101]

BASICS OF THE REGULATION OF BROKER-DEALER COMPENSATION

As a final issue, this section briefly reviews the basic compensation structure for broker-dealers. Broker-dealers customarily act as agents for their customers and are compensated by a commission consisting of a small percentage of the amount involved in the transaction. For the most part, brokerage firms negotiate commissions with institutional customers and establish commission schedules for retail customers.

There are basic problems with this system, even if a broker does not cause the customer to engage in blatantly excessive trades (known as "churning"). Under the commission system, a broker can increase his or

---

[99] *See* In re Citigroup Global Markets, Inc., FINRA Letter of Acceptance, Waiver and Consent No. 2008012808101 (May 22, 2012) (faulting firm for lacking procedures for underwriting of mortgage-backed securities and for the appropriate pricing of collateralized debt obligations); In re Feltl & Co. Inc., Exchange Act Release No. 65,838 (Nov. 28, 2011) (firm has few WSPs devoted to growing investment advisory business).

[100] *See, e.g.*, In re TD Ameritrade, Exchange Act Release No. 63829 (Feb. 3, 2011) (no follow through on supervisory procedures relating to the sale of a particular mutual fund).

[101] *See, e.g.*, In re Hector Gallardo, Exchange Act Release No. 65,658 (Oct. 31, 2011) (supervisor fails to monitor representative's emails, which would have revealed fraudulent promises representative was making to customers).

her compensation by encouraging customers to trade frequently and thus to generate commissions for the broker and for the firm. Yet frequent trading may be inappropriate for the customer whose interests may be best served by buying, and then holding, securities that appreciate in value over time, or a stock or bond with a good dividend or interest yield. Moreover, under the commission schedules of most firms, the commission—and the payout to individual brokers—varies according to the kind of security being sold and the price at which it is sold. In general, the commissions are higher for lower-priced securities, which tend to be less liquid and more speculative, than for higher-priced securities, which tend to be more liquid and safer. Furthermore, brokerage firms often allow their salespersons to retain a larger percentage of the commission on securities that the firm particularly wants to sell.[102]

The problems of the commission system have been somewhat remedied by industry developments. Discount and online brokerage firms provide transaction services at low commission rates, but no "full service" help to investors. Another development had been the "wrap" account where, for a set fee based on assets in the account, a broker-dealer would execute transactions and steer a client towards particular investments. This latter structure ultimately proved to be legally untenable, for the compensation structure which was tied to advisory services put broker-dealers over the investment adviser line.[103] As a result of this decision, broker-dealers now generally offer customers the alternatives of the standard brokerage account, where the customer pays commissions, or an enhanced fee-based account where the customer receives the services of a registered investment adviser (a good portion of the larger broker-dealers are dually-registered as broker-dealers and investment

---

[102] For an example of brokers' maximizing their commissions, at the expense of clients, see In re Jefferies & Co., Inc., FINRA Letter of Acceptance, Waiver and Consent No. 2008013863701 (Apr. 14, 2011). There, two brokers who worked with institutional clients bought auction-rate securities for "discretionary clients" (i.e., those who had orally (but not in writing) given the brokers discretion over their accounts). However, they failed to disclose to the clients (1) that they purchased new issue auction-rate securities only because the brokers received a higher commission on them than on already issued auction-rate securities, which even had a higher yield, and (2) that they arranged purchases of auction-rate securities from the brokers' other clients so as to maximize their commission income (i.e., commissions were paid by both clients), again when other, better yielding securities were available, but not from other clients.

[103] *See* Financial Planning Association v. SEC, 482 F.3d 481 (D.C. Cir. 2007) (striking down the SEC rule allowing broker-dealers to offer this form of wrap accounts).

advisers, and their employees offering advisory services are appropriately qualified as advisers).

This compensation issue points to the two regulatory schemes for investment professionals who deal with retail customers and raises the issue of the partial harmonization of these regulations, at least when these kinds of customers are involved. In Section 913 of Dodd-Frank, Congress directed the SEC to conduct a study to see if, among other things, the standards of care of broker-dealers, investment advisers, and their associated persons, when they were providing personalized investment advice about securities to retail customers, were effective or had legal or regulatory gaps, and to address them if necessary. The SEC staff issued the study and recommended the adoption of a uniform fiduciary standard to act in a customer's best interests for broker-dealers and investment advisers when they provide personalized investment advice to retail customers.[104] The SEC has so far taken no action on this issue, but recently asked for more information from market participants on the various possibilities of harmonizing the standard of care.[105] An issuance of the uniform standard may come soon.

There is additional regulation of compensation of broker-dealers in the over-the-counter market, where they act as dealers with respect to transactions with customers. In these transactions, they receive a mark-up from their purchase price, which is charged to the customer, or they impose a mark-down when they purchase from a customer. The SEC regulates mark-ups (and mark-downs) under the antifraud provisions of the federal securities laws, particularly Exchange Act Rule 10b-5,[106] pursuant to several theories (e.g., that a broker-dealer must deal fairly with a customer and charging an excessive, undisclosed mark-up is a fraudulent violation of that duty). More specifically, FINRA has a longstanding "Mark-up Policy" that is based upon FINRA Rule 2010, which requires members to "observe high standards of commercial honor and just and equitable principles of trade,"[107] and upon NASD Rule 2440, which states that a broker-dealer must charge fair mark-ups and commissions.[108] This policy applies to all transactions on exchanges or in the OTC market (i.e., to mark-ups, mark-downs and commissions). FINRA

---

[104] *See* SEC Staff, *Study on Investment Advisers and Broker-Dealers* (Jan. 2011).

[105] *See* Duties of Brokers, Dealers, and Investment Advisers, Exchange Act Release No. 69,013 (Mar. 1, 2013).

[106] *See* 17 C.F.R. § 240.10b-5 (2012).

[107] *See* FINRA Rule 2010.

[108] *See* NASD Rule 2440.

provides a guideline that mark-ups and mark-downs should not exceed 5 percent, although the fair mark-up for certain kinds of securities, such as debt and municipal securities, would be less, and mark-downs tend to be less than mark-ups in general. In interpretive material, FINRA provides additional guidance about mark-ups and mark-downs and lists seven factors for determining whether a mark-up, mark-down or commission is excessive: (1) kind of security involved, (2) availability of security in the market, (3) price of the security, (4) amount of money involved in the transaction, (5) disclosure to customer, (6) pattern of mark-ups or mark-downs and (7) nature of the broker-dealer's business.[109]

FINRA's regulation on compensation applies to both broker-dealers and their associated persons. It is the subject of regular disciplinary actions.[110] And, as in all matters, a broker-dealer may be disciplined for failing to conduct supervision to see that the rules regarding compensation are enforced.[111]

CONCLUSION

This chapter surveyed the regulation of broker-dealers, a significant financial intermediary in the US capital markets. It focused particularly on compliance issues that are important in the day-to-day life of broker-dealers and that indicate the extent of SEC and FINRA regulation of these firms and the individuals associated with them. Accordingly, it reviewed the definitions of "broker" and "dealer" and the kinds of persons falling within these categories, as well as several significant

---

[109] *See* NASD Rule 2440, IM-2440–1(b). As part of its rule consolidation process, FINRA is proposing to combine and amend the mark-up rules. *See* FINRA, *Markups, Commissions and Fees*, Regulatory Notice No. 11–08 (Feb. 2011) (setting forth a new FINRA Rule 2121).

[110] One of the most significant recent FINRA enforcement cases dealing with debt mark-ups is FINRA v. David Lerner Associates, Inc. & William Mason, FINRA Disciplinary Proceeding No. 20050007427 (Apr. 4, 2012) (involving improper mark-ups of municipal bonds and CMOs; requiring payment of over $2 million in fines, as well as restitution to customers).

[111] *See, e.g.*, In re Detwiler, Fenton & Co., FINRA Letter of Acceptance, Waiver and Consent No. 200901630060 (Dec. 20, 2011) (among other things, pointing out that the firm had no procedures whereby a supervisor could determine the amount of mark-ups, except manually, and that the firm principals did not use exception reports provided by the clearing firm which showed when representatives had overridden commission schedules).

exceptions. It then surveyed the registration requirements for broker-dealers and associated persons, which showed the "gatekeeping" done by the SEC and particularly FINRA as to this industry. The chapter next discussed the important topic of recordkeeping, reporting and examinations, which some might regard as a necessary evil but which is a foundation to regulation. Without them, no regulation could occur, for there are few other ways for the SEC or FINRA to check on a broker-dealer's compliance with laws and regulations. Equally as important was the next topic, supervision, for broker-dealer regulation depends upon the firm regulating itself and its associated persons, which is achieved by imposing a supervision obligation upon all broker-dealers and any supervisors. Finally, no chapter would be complete without a reference to the basic regulation of broker-dealer compensation. This topic had the virtue of also pointing to a transformation in the industry as a significant portion of broker-dealers are dually registered and offer investment advisory services, in addition to brokerage.

Admittedly, this chapter could give only a general survey of the topics covered and must omit many others that are important in US broker-dealer regulation. A full treatment of this regulation would demand a treatise.[112] Yet several of the omitted topics are referred to in other chapters of this book. In any event, this part of the financial industry is consolidating, and will no doubt continue to consolidate, and there are ongoing transformations of it. However, its regulatory model, as outlined above, is likely to endure and indeed is being used for other financial intermediaries.[113]

---

[112] The author is a co-author of one such work. *See* 1 & 2 Norman S. Poser & James A. Fanto, Broker-Dealer Law and Regulation (4th ed. 2007 & Supp. 2013).

[113] The example that comes to mind is the new regulation of swap dealers. Congress in Dodd-Frank and the SEC in its regulations used the existing model of compliance as it brought previously unregulated financial participants under regulation. For instance, a significant part of that legislation involved the regulation of the swap markets and major participants in them, which regulation is divided between the Commodity Futures Trading Commission and the SEC, depending upon the nature of the underlying asset that is the subject of the swap. *See* title VII of Dodd-Frank, 124 Stat. 1658–1802 (Sections 721–774). Swap dealers are now regulated in a manner that parallels, and is modeled on, that of broker-dealers.

13. Fraud, manipulation and other prohibited practices

Jerry W. Markham

INTRODUCTION

The federal securities laws seek to prohibit fraud manipulation and other abuses associated with securities transactions. The most prominent of these prohibitions is found in Section 10(b) of the Securities Exchange Act of 1934 (the "34 Act")[1] and Rule 10b-5 promulgated thereunder by the Securities Exchange Commission ("SEC").[2] There are, however, additional anti-fraud provisions in others of the so-called federal securities laws, including the Securities Act 1933 (the "33 Act")[3] and the Investment Advisers Act of 1940 (the "1940 Act").[4] This chapter will focus principally upon Section 10(b) of the 34 Act, but it will also more briefly describe the anti-fraud provisions in the 33 and 1940 Acts.

SECTION 10(B) OF THE 34 ACT

Section 10(b) of the 34 Act states that:

> It shall be unlawful for any person, directly or indirectly, by the use of any means or instrumentality of interstate commerce or of the mails, or of any facility of any national securities exchange—
>
> .... (b) To use or employ, in connection with the purchase or sale of any security registered on a national securities exchange or any security not so registered, or any securities-based swap agreement any manipulative or deceptive device or contrivance in contravention of such rules and regulations as the Commission may prescribe as necessary or appropriate in the public interest or for the protection of investors.[5]

---

1 15 U.S.C. § 78j(b).
2 17 C.F.R. § 240.10b-5.
3 15 U.S.C. § 77q.
4 15 U.S.C. § 80b-6.
5 15 U.S.C. § 78j(b).

SEC Rule 10b-5 adopted under that statute states that:

> It shall be unlawful for any person, directly or indirectly, by the use of any means or instrumentality of interstate commerce, or of the mails or of any facility of any national securities exchange,
>
> (a) To employ any device, scheme, or artifice to defraud,
> (b) To make any untrue statement of a material fact or to omit to state a material fact necessary in order to make the statements made, in the light of the circumstances under which they were made, not misleading, or
> (c) To engage in any act, practice, or course of business which operates or would operate as a fraud or deceit upon any person, in connection with the purchase or sale of any security.[6]

Rule 10b-5 was adopted in 1942 to fill a gap in the coverage of the anti-fraud provisions of Section 17 of the 33 Act,[7] which applied only to sellers, and not to buyers of securities.[8] The reach of Rule 10b-5 was extended in 1946 by a federal district court, which held that there was an implied private right of action under Section 10(b) of the 34 Act.[9] That decision would lead in future years to a litigation explosion in securities litigation, with Rule 10b-5 being cited in some 15,000 federal court decisions. As "Justice Rehnquist would write several years later in reference to Rule 10b-5, 'we deal with a judicial oak which has grown from little more than a legislative acorn.'"[10]

The courts initially read Rule 10b-5 liberally. As noted by Professor Thomas L. Hazen:

> In the 1960s and early 1970s, many federal appellate courts and district courts developed expansive interpretations of Rule 10b-5 (and other antifraud provisions of the securities laws). They applied it to impose liability for negligent as well as deliberate misrepresentations, for breaches of fiduciary duty by corporate management, and for failure by directors, underwriters, accountants and lawyers to prevent wrongdoing by others. In private actions for damages, the courts were willing to imply a private right of action in

---

6 17 C.F.R. § 240.10b-5.

7 15 U.S.C. § 77q.

8 Blue Chip Stamps v. Manor Drug Stores, 421 U.S. 723, 767 (1975) (describing the origin of that rule); In the Matter of Cady, Roberts & Co., 40 S.E.C. 907 (1961).

9 Kardon v. National Gypsum Co., 69 F. Supp. 512 (E.D. Pa. 1946).

10 Morrison v. National Australian l. Bank Ltd., 561 U.S. – , – (2010) (concurring opinion of Stevens and Ginsburg, quoting Rehnquist J., citations omitted).

> anyone whose losses were even remotely connected with the alleged wrongdoing, or even in someone who had suffered no loss if her suit would help to encourage compliance with the law. The Supreme Court aided and abetted this development, giving an expansive reading to the terms "fraud" and "purchase or sale" and to the "connection" that had to be found between them.[11]

The Supreme Court's jurisprudence on Rule 10b-5 began to change in the 1970s. As Professor Hazen also notes, "a new conservative majority on the Supreme Court sharply reversed this trend, in a series of decisions giving a narrow reading to the terms of Rule 10b-5 and other antifraud provisions … ."[12]

Among other things, the Supreme Court required a showing that a defendant accused of violating the rule be shown to have acted with scienter.[13] The courts have interpreted this requirement to require a showing that the defendant acted with some form of "recklessness."[14] In another case, the Supreme Court held that Rule 10b-5 applies only to deceptive conduct that is fraudulent in some form.[15]

The Supreme Court further held that "Section 10(b) does not punish all deceptive conduct, but only deceptive conduct 'in connection with the purchase or sale of any security registered on a national securities exchange or any security not so registered.'"[16] This meant that a person who was dissuaded from purchasing securities by fraudulent information would have no claim or right of action under Rule 10b-5 because they were not a purchaser or seller of the security.

The Supreme Court imposed a "materiality" requirement on Rule 10b-5, which requires a showing that there was a substantial likelihood

---

[11] Thomas L. Hazen, *The Jurisprudence of SEC Rule 10b-5, Securities Law for Nonsecurities Lawyers*, San Diego, CA (July 28–29, 2005), http://files.ali-aba.org/thumbs/datastorage/skoobesruoc/pdf/Cl001-ch36_thumb.pdf (visited July 6, 2011).

[12] Thomas L. Hazen, *The Jurisprudence of SEC Rule 10b-5, Securities Law for Nonsecurities Lawyers*, San Diego, CA (July 28–29, 2005), http://files.ali-aba.org/thumbs/datastorage/skoobesruoc/pdf/Cl001-ch36_thumb.pdf (visited July 6, 2011).

[13] Ernst & Ernst v. Hochfelder, 425 U.S. 185 (1976).

[14] *See, e.g.*, Thompson v. RelationServe Media, Inc., 610 F.3d 628, 634 (11th Cir. 2010); Lormand v. US Unwired, Inc., 565 F.3d 228, 251 (5th Cir. 2009); South Cherry St., LLC v. Hennessee Group LLC, 573 F.3d 98, 109–110 (2d Cir. 2009).

[15] Santa Fe v. Green, 430 U.S. 462 (1977).

[16] Morrison v. National Australia Bank Ltd., 561 U.S. – , – (2010) (citing Blue Chip Stamps v. Manor Drug Stores, 421 U.S. 723 (1975).

that a reasonable shareholder would consider information important in deciding how to make an investment decision. The materiality element excludes information of "dubious significance" and seeks not to set too low a standard that "might bring an overabundance of information within its reach."[17]

Another element required to prove a Rule 10b-5 claim is reliance upon the misrepresentation or omission. "Reliance by the plaintiff upon the defendant's deceptive acts is an essential element of the § 10(b) private cause of action."[18] The Supreme Court has further limited Section 10(b) of the 34 Act and Rule 10b-5 by imposing causation requirements in private actions. The Supreme Court held that plaintiffs must plead and prove "proximate causation and economic loss" in order to prove a violation.[19]

Another blow was dealt to Rule 10b-5 plaintiffs by the Supreme Court in a decision that rejected aiding and abetting liability in private rights of action.[20] This meant that many deep pocket defendants, such as banks and law firms, would not be subjected to secondary liability for the acts of others. This further meant that, in a private action under Rule 10b-5, "the conduct of a secondary actor must … satisfy each of the elements or preconditions for § 10(b) liability, … [including] reliance upon a material misrepresentation or omission by the defendant."[21]

The Supreme Court also limited the extraterritorial application of Rule 10b-5, excluding claims that had extraterritorial application.[22] However, the Dodd-Frank Wall Street Reform and Consumer Protection Act of 2010 ("Dodd-Frank") amended both the 34 and 33 Acts to extend the SEC's jurisdiction to "(1) conduct within the United States that constitutes significant steps in furtherance of a violation, even if the securities transaction occurs outside the United States and involves only foreign investors; or (2) conduct occurring outside the United States that has a

---

[17] Basic Inc. v. Levinson, 485 U.S. 224, 231 (1988).

[18] Stoneridge Inv. Partners, LLC v. Scientific-Atlanta, Inc., 552 U.S. 148, 159 (2008) (citation omitted). *Accord* Erica P. John Fund, Inc. v. Halliburton Co., – U.S. – , – (2011).

[19] Dura Pharmaceuticals, Inc. v. Broudo, 544 U.S. 336, 346 (2005).

[20] Central Bank of Denver v. First Interstate Bank of Denver, 511 U.S. 164 (1994); Janus Capital Group, Inc. v. First Derivative Traders, 564 U.S. – (2011).

[21] Stoneridge Investment Partners, LLC v. Scientific-Atlanta, Inc., 552 U.S. 148, 158 (2008).

[22] Morrison v. National Australia Bank Ltd., 561 U.S. – (2010).

foreseeable substantial effect within the United States."[23] This new legislative foreign jurisdiction standard will apply to SEC actions in the future and the prior more limited standard set by the Supreme Court will continue to apply to private rights of action, at least until Congress takes some additional action.[24]

The Private Securities Litigation Reform Act of 1995 ("PSLRA") imposed restrictions on class actions under the federal securities laws that have had some effects on Rule 10b-5 cases.[25] It heightened the burden for pleading a claim under Rule 10b-5 for private plaintiffs. The PSLRA requires, among other things, particularized pleadings that evidence the basis of a fraud claim. As the Supreme Court has noted, the PSLRA requires that "securities fraud complaints 'specify' each misleading statement; that they set forth the facts 'on which [a] belief' that a statement is misleading was 'formed'; and that they 'state with particularity facts giving rise to a strong inference that the defendant acted with the required state of mind.'"[26]

The complaint must establish a "strong inference" of scienter as a condition for bringing a class action under Rule 10b-5. The Supreme Court has held that, in order to qualify as a strong inference of scienter, there must be pleaded facts that are "more than merely plausible or reasonable—it must be cogent and at least as compelling as any opposing inference of non-fraudulent intent."[27]

The PSLRA addressed causation required in private actions under Rule 10b-5. The PSLRA now requires plaintiffs to prove that the act or omission of the defendant alleged to violate Rule 10b-5 "caused the loss for which the plaintiff seeks to recover damages."[28] The PSLRA also created special standards for proving damages in a Rule 10b-5 class action involving fraud or manipulation. The purpose of this provision is to prevent "windfall" damages arising from market fluctuations unrelated

---

[23] Dodd-Frank Act § 929P (amending 15 U.S.C. § 77v(a) and 15 U.S.C. § 78aa). *See also* 15 U.S.C. § 80b-14 (amending the Investment Advisers Act of 1940 by adding the same language).

[24] *See* Richard W. Painter, *The Dodd-Frank Extraterritorial Provision: Was it Effective, Needed or Sufficient?* 1 HARV. BUS. L. REV. 195 (2011) (discussing the effects of Section 929P of Dodd-Frank on Rule 10b-5 claims).

[25] Pub. L. No. 104–67, 109 Stat. 737 (1995).

[26] Dura Pharms., Inc. v. Broudo, 544 U.S. 336, 345–346 (2005).

[27] Tellabs, Inc., v. Makor Issues & Rights, Ltd., 551 U.S. 308, 314 (2007).

[28] 15 U.S.C. § 78u-4(b)(4).

to the fraud, "thereby limiting damages to those losses caused by the fraud and not by other market conditions."[29]

Class action lawyers sought to avoid the restrictions in the PSLRA by filing their cases in state courts. Congress responded to that evasion with the Securities Litigation Uniform Standards Act of 1998 ("SLUSA").[30] That legislation preempted state class actions with more than fifty class members involving publicly traded securities that raise claims of state securities laws or common law fraud.[31] Congress acted again in 2005 to limit class action abuses with the Class Action Fairness Act ("CAFA"),[32] which conferred original federal jurisdiction over class actions with at least 100 claimants, with at least some diversity and an aggregate amount in controversy of at least $5 million.[33]

SECTION 17(A) OF THE 33 ACT

The 33 Act governs public offerings of stock either in an initial public offering or in a secondary offering, while the 34 Act governs trading in those securities after their initial issuance. The 33 Act requires the filing of a registration statement with the SEC that must disclose all material facts about the issuer and the securities being issued.[34] The securities being issued may be reviewed by the SEC's staff for completeness and accuracy. An offering may be halted if deficiencies are found. The distribution process is also tightly regulated under SEC Regulation M, which governs stabilizing transactions by an underwriter during the offering.[35]

---

[29] THOMAS L. HAZEN & JERRY W. MARKHAM, CORPORATIONS AND OTHER BUSINESS ORGANIZATIONS, CASES AND MATERIALS 782 (3d unabridged ed. 2009), citing and quoting PSLRA Conference Report.

[30] 15 U.S.C. § 78bb(f)(1)(A).

[31] *See* Merrill Lynch, Pierce, Fenner & Smith Inc. v. Dabit, 547 U.S. 71 (2006) (describing that statute).

[32] Pub. L. No. 109–2, 119 Stat. 4 (2005) codified at 28 U.S.C. §§ 1332(d), 1453 & 1711–1715.

[33] *See* Stephen J. Shapiro, *Applying the Jurisdictional Provisions of the Class Action Fairness Act of 2005: In* Search of A Sensible Judicial Approach, 59 BAYLOR L. REV. 77, 80 (2007) (describing that statute).

[34] 15 U.S.C. § 77e.

[35] 17 C.F.R. Part 242. *See* 23A JERRY W. MARKHAM & THOMAS LEE HAZEN, BROKER-DEALER OPERATIONS UNDER SECURITIES AND COMMODITY LAWS § 9:13 (2012) (describing those requirements and application of this regulation).

Sections 11 and 12 of the 33 Act also contain provisions that impose liability on officers, directors, underwriters and others where a prospectus for the securities being issued is false or misleading. Much stock is issued under exemptions to the registration requirement in the 33 Act, as where the offering is made to "accredited" wealthy or sophisticated investors. In such cases Sections 11 and 12 of the 33 Act will not be available.

There are also a number of defenses available for claims brought under Sections 11 and 12 of the 33 Act. For example, an underwriter who uses "due diligence" in investigating the issuer before the registration statement will be protected from liability for undiscovered misstatements or omissions. Officers and directors of the issuer may escape liability for portions of the prospectus that have been "expertised" by a professional such as an accountant or engineer.[36]

There are also several restrictions on damages and permitted defenses under Sections 11 and 12 that make these claims difficult to prove.[37] However, the Supreme Court has held that an implied private right of action could be brought under Section 10(b) of the 34 Act, even if the activities at issue were subject to the express private rights under the 33 Act. Consequently, claims that would otherwise be brought under the more difficult to prove provisions of the 33 Act are instead, brought under the 34 Act.

The 33 Act does contain a separate antifraud prohibition that applies to such sales. Section 17(a) of the 33 Act makes it unlawful for any person offering or selling securities:

(1) to employ any device, scheme, or artifice to defraud, or
(2) to obtain money or property by means of any untrue statement of a material fact or any omission to state a material fact necessary in order to make the statements made, in light of the circumstances under which they were made, not misleading; or
(3) to engage in any transaction, practice, or course of business which operates or would operate as a fraud or deceit upon the purchaser.[38]

The courts have held that there is no private right of action implied in Section 17(a) of the 33 Act.[39] The statute is also by its term limited to

---

36 15 U.S.C. §§ 77k & 77l.

37 *See id.*

38 15 U.S.C. § 77q(a).

39 *See*, *e.g.*, Sears v. Likens, 912 F.2d 889, 893 (7th Cir. 1990); Newcome v. Esrey, 862 F.2d 1099, 1102 (4th Cir. 1988); Finkel v. The Stratton Corp. 962 F.2d 169, 175, (2d Cir. 1992).

fraud by persons offering or selling securities, rather than those buying securities.[40] As noted, in adopting Rule 10b-5 in 1942, the SEC issued a press release, which stated that the new Rule 10b-5 sought to close "a loophole in the protections against fraud administered by the Commission by prohibiting individuals or companies from buying securities if they engage in fraud in their purchase."[41]

The Supreme Court has considered whether the provisions of Section 17(a)(1), (2) and (3) of the 33 Act impose a scienter requirement.[42] Like Rule 10b-5,[43] Section 17(a)(1) of the 33 Act proscribes employment of any "device," "scheme," or "artifice to defraud."[44] However, neither Rule 10b-5 nor Section 17(a) of the 33 Act contain the "any manipulative or deceptive device or contrivance" language on which Section 10(b) of the 34 Act is premised. Conversely, Section 10(b) of the 34 Act does not contain the "device," "scheme," or "artifice to defraud" language found in Rule 10b-5 and Section 17(a)(1) of the 33 Act. The Court held that certain provisions in Section 17(a)(2) and (3) of the 33 Act did not contain language that would evidence that Congress intended a specific intent requirement.[45]

The securities that are subject to the 33 Act registration requirements have been broadly construed by the courts to include everything from orange groves to vacuum cleaners.[46] There are, however, a number of exemptions and exceptions that allow many securities distributions to avoid registration. Nevertheless, the anti-fraud provisions of both the 33 Act and the 34 Act will remain applicable to those offerings.

SECTION 206 OF THE 1940 ACT

Section 206 of the 1940 Act provides in pertinent part that:

---

[40] *See generally* United States v. Naftalin, 441 U.S. 768, 778 (1979) (Section 17(a) of the 33 Act "was intended to cover any fraudulent scheme in an offer or sale of securities, whether in the course of an initial distribution or in the course of ordinary market trading").

[41] SEC Release No. 3230 (May 21, 1942).

[42] Aaron v. SEC, 446 U.S. 680 (1980).

[43] 17 C.F.R. § 240.10b-5.

[44] 15 U.S.C. § 77q(a).

[45] 446 U.S. at 696.

[46] *See* I THOMAS LEE HAZEN, TREATISE ON THE LAW OF SECURITIES REGULATION § 16[1] (describing those decisions).

It shall be unlawful for any investment adviser, by use of the mails or any means or instrumentality of interstate commerce, directly or indirectly–

(1) to employ any device, scheme, or artifice to defraud any client or prospective client;
(2) to engage in any transaction, practice, or course of business which operates as a fraud or deceit upon any client or prospective client;
(3) ....
(4) to engage in any act, practice, or course of business which is fraudulent, deceptive, or manipulative.... .[47]

The Supreme Court held that intent to deceive was not required to establish a violation of Section 206(2) of the 1940 Act.[48] The Supreme Court concluded that this language "quite plainly focuses upon the *effect* of particular conduct on members of the investing public, rather than upon the culpability of the person responsible."[49] However, the Supreme Court also held that there is no private right of action available under Section 206 of the 1940 Act.[50]

The SEC has adopted various rules under this anti-fraud provision. Those rules include restrictions on advertisements,[51] requirements regarding the custody of customer funds,[52] restrictions on cash payments for client solicitations[53] and other disclosure requirements.[54]

ACCOUNTING FRAUD

A matter of concern over fraudulent activities in the securities markets has been the manipulation of the financial statements of publicly traded companies. This is not a new phenomenon but became the subject of much scrutiny after the Enron Corp. failed in 2001. Thereafter, several

---

47 15 U.S.C. § 80b-6.

48 SEC v. Capital Gains Research Bureau Inc., 375 U.S. 353 (1963).

49 Aaron v. SEC, 446 U.S. 680, 697 (1980) (emphasis supplied by the Court).

50 Transamerica Mortgage Advisors Inc. v. Lewis, 444 U.S. 11, 15–16 (1979).

51 17 C.F.R. § 275.206(4)-1.

52 17 C.F.R. § 275.206(4)-2.

53 17 C.F.R. § 275.206(4)-3.

54 17 C.F.R. § 275.206(4)-4.

other large companies reported that they too had falsified their financial statements, including WorldCom and Tyco International Ltd.[55]

These accounting frauds involved sometimes complicated schemes whereby earnings were inflated in order to meet the expectations of financial analysts. The failure to meet those expectations would almost inevitably result in a drop in the price of the company's stock. This decline in price would prevent the executives of the company from profiting from their stock options, which was the principal basis of their compensation. Enron executives, for example, had massively manipulated the company's financial statements in order to pump up the stock price and thereby provide profits to company executives who were holding large amounts of options on Enron stock.

Accounting failures at several other public companies, raised concerns in Congress that auditing standards needed to be strengthened. This led to the inclusion of a provision in the Sarbanes-Oxley Act of 2003 that created a new Public Company Accounting Oversight Board ("PCAOB"), which was tasked with the responsibility of overseeing the auditing standards of public accounting firms.[56] That legislation also required company executives to certify the accuracy of their company's financial statements and the adequacy of internal accounting controls.

INSIDER TRADING

The courts had ruled that insider trading was permitted under common law when conducted on an exchange. The leading case so holding was decided in 1933, just when Congress was considering the creation of the 34 Act.[57]

Congress did not include a broad prohibition against insider trading when it enacted the 34 Act. Rather, it adopted only a limited restriction in Section 16(b) of the 34 Act,[58] requiring forfeiture of short-term profits by officers, directors and large shareholders, i.e., profits made by such persons within a six-month period from a buy and sell or sell and buy

---

[55] *See* Jerry W. Markham, A Financial History of Modern U.S. Corporate Scandals, From Enron to Reform (2006) (describing these scandals).

[56] *Id.* at 451–452.

[57] Goodwin v. Agassiz, 186 N.E. 659 (Sup. Mass. 1933). Disclosure of insider information could be required in face-to-face transactions involving "special facts." Strong v. Repide, 213 U.S. 419 (1909).

[58] 15 U.S.C. § 78p.

transaction in their company's stock.[59] Otherwise, absent other fraud, those traders were free to trade on inside information.

In 1961, however, the SEC created what was then a novel crime of trading on insider information beyond that set forth in Section 16(b) of the 34 Act. That was accomplished by a liberal reading of Section 10(b) of the 34 Act that was announced in an administrative proceeding order that was settled by consent.[60] The SEC asserted in that case that Section 10(b) created a duty to disclose inside (nonpublic) information before trading, even on an exchange, or refrain from trading if disclosure is not made. The SEC decreed in that case that it was unlawful to trade where any person has access to information that was not generally known to the marketplace. The SEC was of the view that all investors were to have equal access to material information.

The Second Circuit Court of Appeals subsequently adopted the SEC's insider trading theory of equal access to information.[61] However, the Supreme Court rejected that theory, holding that there is no requirement for equal access to information.[62] The Supreme Court stated "[a] duty to disclose under Section 10(b) does not arise from the mere possession of nonpublic market information."[63] Such a duty to disclose would arise only where there existed a fiduciary relationship between the trader and the source of the information. This meant that an investor having no fiduciary relationship could trade upon nonpublic market information. "Moreover, neither the Congress nor the Commission ever has adopted a parity-of-information rule. Instead, the problems caused by misuse of market information have been addressed by detailed and sophisticated regulation that recognizes when use of market information may not harm operation of the securities markets."[64]

The Supreme Court did later recognize two forms of prohibited insider trading under Section 10(b) of the 34 Act. One such form was the so-called "classical" insider-trading theory under which an officer, director or other insider trades on the basis of their company's nonpublic information. This theory was deemed appropriate because officers and directors are under a fiduciary duty not to use that information in such a

---

59 *See, e.g.*, Smolowe v. Delendo Corp., 136 F.2d 231 (2d Cir. 1943) (describing the computation of such profits).

60 In the Matter of Cady, Roberts & Co., 40 S.E.C. 907 (1961).

61 SEC v. Texas Gulf Sulphur Co., 401 F.2d 833 (2d Cir. 1968), *cert. denied sub nom.*, Coates v. SEC, 394 U.S. 976 (1969).

62 Chiarella v. United States, 445 U.S. 222 (1980).

63 445 U.S. at 235.

64 445 U.S. at 233.

manner. A second form of prohibited insider trading is where information is misappropriated by someone for use in their own trading.[65]

The Supreme Court has also addressed circumstances under which a person who is "tipped" with inside information may be liable even though they are not themselves an insider. Such liability may attach where the "tippor" is breaching a fiduciary duty in order to make some profit or gain some advantage.[66]

The SEC has sought to expand the reach of this "tippee" liability by adopting a rule that bars trading on non-public information given in confidence to relatives and others. The rule treats the use of such information by those persons to be a misappropriation.[67] SEC Rule 14e-3 also prohibits any person who is in possession of material nonpublic information relating to a tender offer from trading on such information.[68]

In another area, a SEC rule allows persons in possession of inside information to trade as long as they do not use that information to form the basis for the trades. This rule led many executives to have in place written plans for the sale of their company's stock in order to show that they do not use nonpublic information in their sales.[69]

The SEC may seek a civil penalty of up to three times the amount of profits of the inside trader.[70] The 34 Act also contains whistleblower incentives for those who tip the SEC on insider trading.[71] Persons trading on inside information may also be subject to criminal prosecution under the 34 Act with fines of up to $1 million for individuals. Prosecution may also be brought under mail and wire fraud statutes.[72] The 34 Act also makes an insider trader liable to persons who were contemporaneously trading the security. Criminal prosecutions for insider trading also often include charges of mail and wire fraud.

---

65 *See* United States v. O'Hagan, 521 U.S. 642, 667–677 (1997) (describing these forms of insider trading).

66 *See* Dirks v. SEC, 463 U.S. 646 (1983) (describing instances where a "tippee" may be held liable for trading on information received from a classical insider).

67 17 C.F.R. § 240.10b-5–2.

68 17 C.F.R. § 240.14e-3.

69 17 C.F.R. § 240.10b-5–1.

70 15 U.S.C. § 78u-1.

71 15 U.S.C. § 78u-6.

72 *See, e.g.*, Carpenter v. U.S. 484 U.S. 19 (1987) (prosecution under mail fraud statute).

Insider trading cases are the centerpiece of the SEC's enforcement program. The agency frequently brings high-profile cases against well-known individuals, and it often refers such cases to the Department of Justice for criminal proceedings.

The SEC and FINRA maintain surveillance over the markets and look for suspicious trading activities around events that move the price of a company's stock. The SEC also receives information on insider trading from confidential informants who are cooperating with the government in order to reduce their sentences or to avoid liability for their own criminal conduct. In addition, the SEC has enforcement powers that allow it to subpoena documents and compel testimony of witnesses.

The approach taken by the SEC for insider trading should be contrasted with that of the Commodity Futures Trading Commission ("CFTC"). In enacting the legislation that created the CFTC, Congress considered various insider trading prohibitions for possible inclusion into the Commodity Exchange Act of 1936 ("CEA").[73] However, the amending legislation that was eventually enacted only prohibited CFTC commissioners or employees from trading futures contracts or tipping others on nonpublic information.[74]

In a 1984 study ordered by Congress in the Futures Trading Act of 1982,[75] the CFTC decided that it would not adopt the SEC's broad prohibition on trading on the basis of nonpublic information in the futures markets. The CFTC noted that many commodity market participants, particularly hedgers, had unequal access to market moving information that was proprietary to their businesses. In 2008, Congress added a proviso to Section 4b of the CEA, which states that the antifraud provision in the Commodity Exchange Act does not require disclosure of "nonpublic information that may be material to the market price, rate, or level of the commodity or transaction, except as necessary to make any statement made to the other person in or in connection with the transaction not misleading in any material respect."[76] The CFTC did

---

[73] CFTC, *A Study of the Nature, Extent and Effects of Futures Trading by Persons Possessing Material, Nonpublic Information*, submitted to the Committee on Agriculture of the House of Representatives and the Committee on Agriculture, Nutrition and Forestry of the Senate pursuant to Sec. 23(b) of the Commodity Exchange Act, as amended, at App.I-B (Sept. 1984).

[74] 7 U.S.C. § 13(d) & (e).

[75] 96 Stat. 2294, § 236 (1982).

[76] 7 U.S.C. § 6b(b).

adopt a misappropriation theory for imposing liability for trading on stolen information.[77]

MANIPULATION CLAIMS

Statutory Prohibitions

Section 9 of the 34 Act prohibits the manipulation of security prices.[78] Section 9 was designed "to prevent rigging of the market and to permit operation of the natural law of supply and demand."[79] It sought to prohibit the creation of a price "mirage" rather than the reflection of a genuine demand.[80] The prohibitions in Section 9(a)(2) include the following:

1. wash sales involving no change in beneficial ownership that are effected "for or the purpose of creating a false or misleading appearance of active trading… , or a false or misleading appearance with respect to the market for any such security."[81]
2. securities transactions effected for the "purpose of creating actual or apparent active trading in such security, or raising or depressing the price of such security, for the purpose of inducing the purchase or sale of such security by others."[82]
3. the inducement of the purchase or sale of a security "by the circulation or dissemination in the ordinary course of business of information to the effect that the price of any such security will or is likely to rise or fall because of market operations of any one or more persons conducted for the purpose of raising or depressing the price of such security."[83]

---

[77] CFTC v. Kelly, COMM. FUT. L. REP. (CCH) ¶27,465 (S.D.N.Y. 1998).

[78] 48 Stat. at 889. *See generally* Lewis D. Lowenfels, *Sections 9(A)(1) And 9(A)(2) Of The Securities Exchange Act Of 1934: An Analysis Of Two Important Anti-Manipulative Provisions Under The Federal Securities Laws*, 85 NW. U. L. REV 698 (1991) (describing this statute).

[79] United States v. Stein, 456 F.2d 844, 850 (2d Cir. 1972), *cert. denied*, 408 U.S. 922 (1973).

[80] United States v. Stein, 456 F.2d 844, 850 (2d Cir. 1969), citing S. Rep. No. 1455, 73d Cong. 2d Sess. 54 (1934).

[81] 15 U.S.C. § 78i(a)(1).

[82] 15 U.S.C. § 78i(a)(2).

[83] 15 U.S.C. § 78i(a)(3).

4. to make, for the purpose of inducing the purchase or sale of a security or a security-based swap agreement, "any statement which was at the time and in the light of the circumstances under which it was made, false or misleading with respect to any material fact, and which he knew or had reasonable ground to believe was so false or misleading."[84]
5. for consideration received directly or indirectly from a person offering or selling a security, circulating or disseminating "information to the effect that the price of any such security will or is likely to rise or fall because of the market operations of any one or more persons conducted for the purpose of raising or depressing the price of such security."[85]
6. to effect alone or with one or more persons "any series of transactions for the purchase and/or sale of any security other than a government security for the purpose of pegging, fixing, or stabilizing the price of such security in contravention of such rules and regulations as the Commission may prescribe...."[86]

Section 10(b) of the 34 Act also authorizes the SEC "to prohibit or regulate the use of any other manipulative or deceptive practices which it finds detrimental to the interests of investors."[87] Section 10(b) contains no definition of what the term manipulation means, but the Supreme Court has held that the term was intended by Congress to refer "generally to practices, such as wash sales, matched orders, or rigged prices, that are intended to mislead investors by artificially affecting market activity," citing Section 9 of the 34 Act.[88]

The Supreme Court also noted that Section 10(b) was a "general prohibition of practices deemed by the SEC to be 'manipulative'—in this technical sense of artificially affecting market activity in order to mislead investors ... "[89]

Pump-and-Dump Schemes

Numerous manipulative schemes have been carried out over the Internet by pumping up the value of an illiquid stock through false or misleading

---

84 15 U.S.C. § 78i(a)(4).
85 15 U.S.C. § 78i(a)(5).
86 15 U.S.C. § 78i(a)(6).
87 15 U.S.C. § 78j(b).
88 Santa Fe v. Green, 430 U.S. 462, 476 (1977).
89 430 U.S. at 476–477.

claims. These frauds took many forms but generally involved the buying up of a large number of shares of the stock of a particular company by the promoter of the scheme. The price of that stock was then pumped up by the promoter through a fraudulent sales campaign, which falsely touted the prospects of the company, which often were non-existent.[90] The manipulator would then dump the previously purchased stock into the market at the inflated price.

Such "pump-and-dump" schemes can produce large profits for the manipulator. These pump-and-dump operations involved such characters as Tokyo Joe's Societe Anonyme, Corp., which charged Internet subscribers up to $2,400 per year for Tokyo Joe's stock tips. The company collected over $1.1 million in fees.[91]

The SEC created a "cyber force" of some 200 lawyers to prosecute the perpetrators of these schemes. In one case, a group of Georgetown law students, and one of their mothers, created a website touting stocks that had some 9,000 subscribers. The students made $350,000 from trading in four stocks promoted on their website. In another case, a seventeen-year-old high school student defrauded over 1,000 investors through an Internet pump-and-dump scheme.[92]

Rigged Trades

Rigged trading manipulations are also carried out for a number of reasons. For example, a trader might want to "paint the tape" in order to set the daily closing or settlement price of a stock at a lower or higher level. One reason for such a manipulation is that the trader is seeking to set the price for a related position. For example, a trader may have entered into an options contract on an exchange. By manipulating the stock underlying the option, the trader can boost profits on his options contract.

There is some confusion in the courts over whether "open market" trades can constitute manipulation. An open market trade is a bona fide

---

90 *See* Joseph I. Goldstein, Sarah B. Ackerson & Laura A. Novack, An Overview of Market Manipulation: Legal and Practical Aspects, at pp. 28–37, Conference on Market Manipulation: Law, Economics, and Public Policy sponsored by the Center for Study of Futures and Options Markets and the American Bar Association, Washington, DC (Nov. 8–9, 1990) (describing the elements of such "hype-and-dump manipulations").

91 SEC v. Park, 99 F. Supp.2d 889 (N.D. Ill. 2000).

92 JERRY W. MARKHAM, A FINANCIAL HISTORY OF MODERN U.S. CORPORATE SCANDALS, FROM ENRON TO REFORM 25, 27 (2005).

transaction that is conducted with manipulative intent. An open market transaction "involves real parties and real economic risk," while a closed market trade is a non bona fide transaction, say a wash trade.[93]

Short Sales

There has also historically been much controversy over whether "short" sales are manipulative in pushing down stock prices artificially. These trades involve the sale of stock that the seller does not own. The seller borrows the stock that is being sold short, hoping that the price of the stock will decline. In the event of a price decline, the short seller can purchase the stock at the lower price, deliver it back to the lender and profit on the difference between the purchase and sale price. Conversely, of course, the short seller will experience a loss if prices increase because he will have to purchase the stock at a higher price that he had sold for less.

Short sales are not inherently manipulative and are even considered by many economists to be useful in assuring better price discovery and market efficiency. Short sales may also be used to hedge against price declines on a stock owned by the trader. Nevertheless, there is much concern that short sales are abusive when they seek to depress the market by continually selling down at lower prices.

A debate inevitably arises during market downturns over whether the short seller is simply following the market or whether the short sales drive or intensify the decline. The SEC adopted a short sale "tick test" after a market decline in 1937,[94] which it abandoned just in time for the Financial Crisis in 2008.[95] The latter event led to claims by financial services firms that their stock was facing unwarranted attacks from short sellers. Those protesting included Lehman Brothers, Bear Stearns and AIG.[96] Jamie Dimon, the JPMorgan CEO, claimed that this short selling

---

[93] David L. Kornblau, Allison Lurton & Jonathan M. Sperling, *Market Manipulation and Algorithmic Trading: The Next Wave of Regulatory Enforcement*, 44 SEC. REG. & L. RE. (BNA) 369, 370 (Feb. 20, 2012). *See Markowski v. SEC*, 274 F.3d 525 (D.C. Cir. 2001), *cert. denied*, 537 U.S. 819 (2002) (holding that open-market trades could be manipulative if engaged in with the intent to create an artificial price).

[94] 17 C.F.R. § 240.10a-1.

[95] *Regulation SHO and Rule 10a-1*, 72 Fed. Reg. 36348 (July 3, 2007).

[96] JERRY W. MARKHAM, A FINANCIAL HISTORY OF THE U.S. FROM THE SUBPRIME CRISIS TO THE GREAT RECESSION (2006–2009) 511 (2011).

was "even worse than insider trading," and that it was a "deliberate and malicious destruction of value and people's lives."[97]

On September 18, 2008, the SEC imposed a temporary ban on short selling in the stocks of 799 financial services firms. The SEC believed that "unbridled" short selling was contributing to the recent, sudden price declines in the securities of financial institutions "unrelated to true price valuation."[98] That ban was widely criticized as being ineffective and even harmful. Nevertheless, after the Financial Crisis, the SEC adopted a new short sale price test restriction, which halts shorts sales for the day when a stock's price declines by 10 percent.[99] The SEC also adopted an "interim final temporary rule" requiring hedge funds and other large institutional investors to disclose their short positions on a daily basis.[100]

Section 417 of the Dodd-Frank Act also required the SEC to conduct a study on short selling and directed the SEC to consider creating a pilot program in which public companies would agree to have their trades marked "short," "market-maker short," "buy," "buy to cover," or "long." Those trades would then be reported in real time in the pilot program. The SEC sought comments on that study and pilot program in May 2011, but took no immediate action.[101]

The SEC received thousands of complaints about "naked" short sales during the Financial Crisis. These were short traders who sold without having first located securities for borrowing to cover their short position.[102] The SEC attacked "naked shorts" in enforcement actions.[103]

---

97 Jenny Anderson, *S.E.C. Unveils Measures to Limit Short Selling*, N.Y. TIMES, July 16, 2008, at C1.

98 *SEC Halts Short Selling of Financial Stocks to Protect Investors and Markets*, SEC News Digest, available at http://www.sec.gov/news/digest/2008/dig091908.htm.

99 *Amendments to Regulation SHO,* 2010 WL 675942 (Feb. 26, 2010). Germany, France, Spain, Italy, Belgium and the European Union also imposed short sale restrictions after the crisis. Nina Mehta, *Shorting Bans Do Little to Help Europe Banks, Instinet Says.*, Bloomberg, available at http://www.bloomberg.com/news/2011–10–03/short-sale-bans-doing-little-to-help-europe-banks-instine-says.html (accessed on Mar. 23, 2012).

100 *Disclosure of Short Sales and Short Positions by Institutional Investment Managers*, 73 Fed. Reg. 61678 (Oct. 17, 2008).

101 *Short Sale Reporting Study Required by Dodd-Frank Act Section 417(a)(2)*, 76 Fed. Reg. 26787 (May 9, 2011).

102 *See generally* Kevin A. Crisp, *Giving Investors Short Shrift: How Short Sale Constraints Decrease Market Efficiency and a Modest Proposal for Letting More Shorts Go Naked*, 8 J. BUS. & SEC. L.135 (2008).

Short sales can also be abused when they are coupled with false rumors that are intended to depress prices so that the short can buy in at a lower more profitable price. Manipulative short sale practices also evidence the fact that traders may try to manipulate market prices both up and down.

MARGIN REQUIREMENTS

The 34 Act authorizes the Federal Reserve Board ("Fed") to set margin limits on the amount of funds that investors can borrow in order to purchase stock.[104] Regulation T, which was adopted by the Fed under that authority, imposes a 50 percent margin requirement on most publicly traded stocks. Exchange rules may also require additional margin to be posted when a margined stock drops in value.[105]

An abuse associated with margin requirements is "free riding." Free riding occurs when a customer purchases a security but does not have the ability to pay for it. The customer hopes that the security will increase in price so that it can be made and a profit gained before settlement is required for the security. The sale of the profitable stock provides the funds to pay for the stock. If the stock drops in price, the investor simply walks away from the trade.[106] The SEC has sanctioned numerous broker-dealers for allowing free riding to occur.[107]

Another problem with margin occurred with respect to trading by so-called "day traders" who engage in large volumes of quick in-and-out trades in order to capture profits. These day traders raised concerns

---

[103] Jerry W. Markham, A Financial History of the U.S. From the Subprime Crisis to the Great Recession (2006–2009) 511–512 (2011). *See generally* Alexis B. Stokes, *In Pursuit of the Naked Short*, 5 N.Y.U. J. L. & Bus. 1 (2009).

[104] 15 U.S.C. § 78g.

[105] *See* 23A Jerry W. Markham & Thomas Lee Hazen, Broker-Dealer Operations Under Securities and Commodity Laws Ch. 8 (2012) (describing those requirements).

[106] *See* 57 Fed. Reg. 37,109 (Aug. 18, 1992) (describing free riding).

[107] *See* 23 Jerry W. Markham & Thomas Lee Hazen, Broker-Dealer Operations Under Securities and Commodity Laws § 8:4 (2012) (describing those cases).

because they were not required to post margin on their trades if they were not carried overnight.[108]

FINRA required "pattern day traders" to maintain minimum equity of $25,000 on any day that the customer day trades and imposed other leverage restrictions.[109] A pattern day trader "includes any margin customer that day trades (buys then sells or sells short then buys the same security on the same day) four or more times in five business days, provided the number of day trades are more than 6 percent of the customer's total trading activity for that same five-day period."[110]

BROKER-DEALER FRAUD

Shingle Theory

Broker-dealers are intensely regulated by the SEC. That regulation includes an array of recordkeeping requirements, financial reports, and minimum net capital requirements.[111] The SEC has also identified various practices that are associated with fraudulent broker-dealer operations. The SEC has also developed a "shingle theory," which posits that broker-dealers are professionals who hold out their shingle to the public as such. In hanging out that shingle, the broker-dealer is making an implied representation that the public may seek and receive professional advice from the broker-dealer.

The SEC and FINRA also impose a duty on broker-dealers to diligently supervise their employees. An SEC commissioner compared self-regulation in the securities industry to be a "pyramid, with the SEC at the top, FINRA in the middle and the brokerage firms providing the

---

108 *See* 23A Jerry W. Markham & Thomas L. Hazen, Broker-Dealer Operations Under Securities and Commodities Law § 8:11 (2012) (describing this concern).

109 *See* Jerry W. Markham & Thomas L. Hazen, Broker-Dealer Operations Under Securities and Commodities Law § 8:11 (2012) (describing these restrictions).

110 FINRA, *Day Trading Margin Requirements: Know the Rules*, available at http://www.finra.org/investors/smartinvesting/advancedinvesting/daytrading/p005906 (accessed on Mar. 22, 2013).

111 *See* 23 Jerry W. Markham & Thomas Lee Hazen, Broker-Dealer Operations Under Securities and Commodity Laws Chs 4 & 5 (2012) (describing those requirements).

base through their own self-supervision."[112] This supervision requirement is twofold. First, the broker-dealer must have in place a system of procedures designed to detect and discover abuses. Second, the broker-dealer must have reasonably enforced those procedures.[113]

Cases involving failure to supervise claims frequently focus on flaws in a supervisory system that allowed violations to go undetected. Other cases look for "red flags" that should have alerted a supervisor to misconduct but were ignored. Unfortunately, this latter analysis is subject to the benefit of 20–20 hindsight that was not available to the supervisor at the time.[114]

Financial service firms are also required to have anti-money laundering programs in place as a part of their supervisory structure. The Insider Trading and Securities Fraud Enforcement Act of 1988 further requires broker-dealers to have special supervisory procedures in place to prevent the abuse of inside information.[115] The SEC is also requiring broker-dealers to set up anti-identity theft programs.

Fair Dealing and Suitability

The SEC imposes a further duty of "fair dealing" on broker-dealers. In that regard, it has been noted that:

> An important aspect of a broker-dealer's duty of fair dealing is a suitability obligation, which generally requires a broker dealer to make recommendations that are consistent with the interest of its customer. Broker-dealers are also required under certain circumstances, such as when making a recommendation, to disclose material conflicts of interest to their customers, in some cases at the time of the completion of the transaction. The federal securities laws and FINRA rules restrict broker-dealers from participating in certain transactions that may present particularly acute potential conflicts of interest.[116]

Under this doctrine, a broker-dealer may not recommend an investment that is not suitable for a customer. Security recommendations by a

---

[112] John H. Walsh, *Right the First Time: Regulation, Quality and Preventive Compliance in the Securities Industry*, 1997 COLUM. BUS. L. REV. 165, 166–167.

[113] *See* 23A JERRY W. MARKHAM & THOMAS LEE HAZEN, BROKER-DEALER OPERATIONS UNDER SECURITIES AND COMMODITY LAWS Ch. 11 (2012) (describing those cases).

[114] *Id.*

[115] 15 U.S.C. § 78*o*(g).

[116] Staff of the U.S. Securities and Exchange Commission, *Study on Investment Advisors and Broker-Dealers* iv (Jan. 2011).

broker-dealer must be based on the particular needs and investment objectives of individual customers. This means that broker dealer recommendations must be based on the interests of individual customers and not on the amount of compensation that the broker-dealer receives from the recommended trade.[117] Special suitability requirements are imposed by the SEC on broker-dealers selling low priced "penny stocks."[118]

This suitability requirement has also been incorporated into the rulebook of FINRA. FINRA has described this rule as follows:

> FINRA Rule 2111 requires, in part, that a broker-dealer or associated person "have a reasonable basis to believe that a recommended transaction or investment strategy involving a security or securities is suitable for the customer, based on the information obtained through the reasonable diligence of the [firm] or associated person to ascertain the customer's investment profile." In general, a customer's investment profile would include the customer's age, other investments, financial situation and needs, tax status, investment objectives, investment experience, investment time horizon, liquidity needs and risk tolerance. The rule also explicitly covers recommended investment strategies involving securities, including recommendations to "hold" securities. The rule, moreover, identifies the three main suitability obligations: reasonable-basis, customer-specific, and quantitative suitability. Finally, the rule provides a modified institutional-customer exemption.[119]

Special suitability requirements have been imposed on particular securities products, such as variable life insurance and variable annuities.[120] Low priced speculative "penny stocks" are subject to special suitability requirements adopted under the Penny Stock Reform Act of 1990.[121] There has also been much debate over whether the suitability requirement

---

[117] *See* Jerry W. Markham & Thomas Lee Hazen, Broker-Dealer Operations Under Securities and Commodity Laws § 10:1 *et seq.* (2012) (describing the suitability requirement).

[118] 17 C.F.R. § 240.15g-9.

[119] FINRA, *Frequently Asked Questions FINRA Rule 2111 (Suitability)*, available at ww.finra.org/web/idcplg?IdcService=GET_FILE...1 (accessed on Mar. 12, 2013).

[120] *See* Jerry W. Markham & Thomas Lee Hazen, Broker-Dealer Operations Under Securities and Commodity Law § 10:12.50 (describing this requirement).

[121] *See* Jerry W. Markham & Thomas Lee Hazen, Broker-Dealer Operations Under Securities and Commodity Law § 10:8 (describing this requirement).

should apply to institutional investors that have the wherewithal to conduct their own investigation of their suitability for securities products.[122]

The CFTC declined to adopt a suitability requirement for the futures commission merchants ("FCMs") that it supervises. Instead, it opted for a requirement that customers be given a risk disclosure statement that advises customers to consider whether they are suitable for trading in commodity futures and commodity options.[123] The CFTC has asserted that FCMs and their associated persons must have a reasonable basis in fact for making trading representations to customers.[124]

In order to allow trading on single stock futures contracts, Congress required the National Futures Association ("NFA") to conform its rules to those in the securities industry. Pursuant to that directive, the NFA adopted a "know-your-customer" rule that requires FCMs to obtain information about their customers so that appropriate risk disclosures may be made.[125]

Reasonable Basis in Fact

Related to the suitability concept is the requirement that broker-dealers have a reasonable basis in fact for their securities recommendations to customers.[126] This requires broker-dealers to conduct a reasonable investigation of securities before they are recommended. Unreasonable profit claims are also prohibited.[127] The SEC has stated that, in making

---

[122] *Compare* Jerry W. Markham, *Protecting the Institutional Investor—Jungle Predator or Shorn Lamb?*, 12 YALE J. ON REG. 345 (1995), *with*, Donald C. Langevoort, *Selling Hope, Selling Risk: Some Lessons for Law from Behavioral Economics About Stockbrokers and Sophisticated Customers*, 84 CALIF. L. REV. 627 (1996); Norman S. Poser, *Liability of Broker-Dealers for Unsuitable Recommendations to Institutional Investors*, 2001 BRIGHAM YOUNG U.L. REV. 1493 (2001).

[123] *Id.* at § 10:14 *et seq.* (describing the CFTC's decision not to adopt a suitability requirement).

[124] *Id.* at § 10:21.

[125] NFA Rule 2–30.

[126] *See* JERRY W. MARKHAM & THOMAS LEE HAZEN, BROKER-DEALER OPERATIONS UNDER SECURITIES AND COMMODITY LAW § 10:14 (describing this requirement).

[127] *See* JERRY W. MARKHAM & THOMAS LEE HAZEN, BROKER-DEALER OPERATIONS UNDER SECURITIES AND COMMODITY LAW § 10:13 (describing this requirement).

recommendations to customers, broker-dealers and their associated persons are also making an implied representation that they have a reasonable basis in fact for the recommendation and for any representations, opinions or predictions on the value of a security. In order to meet this duty, broker-dealers and their associated persons must conduct a reasonable investigation of that security, and the broker have a reasonable basis for its recommendation.[128]

The SEC also believes that predictions of specific and substantial increases in the price of a speculative security of an unseasoned company are fraudulent per se and cannot be justified on any grounds.[129]

Best Execution

The SEC has held that broker-dealers have a duty of "best execution,"[130] which if not met will constitute fraud in a violation of the federal securities laws. The duty of best execution requires a broker-dealer to seek the most favorable terms available under the circumstances for the orders of its customers whether acting as a broker-dealer, agent or as a principal.[131] The SEC has further ruled that the routine execution of customer orders at the national best bid and offer ("NBBO") for actively

---

[128] Mihara v. Dean Witter & Co., Inc., 619 F.2d 814 (9th Cir. 1980); In the Matter of Goodman, SEC Release Notice, Release No. 34–43889, 2001WL 62607 (S.E.C. Release No. 2001).

[129] In re Merrill Lynch, Pierce, Fenner & Smith Inc., Sec. Exch. Act Release No. 14149 at ns. 18–19 (Nov. 9, 1977).

[130] The SEC has stated that:

In accepting orders and routing them to a market center for execution, brokers act as agents for their customers and owe them a duty of best execution. The duty is derived from common law agency principles and fiduciary obligations. It is incorporated both in self-regulatory organization rules and, through judicial and Commission decisions, in the antifraud provisions of the federal securities laws. The duty requires a broker to seek the most favorable terms reasonably available under the circumstances for a customer's transaction.

Commission's Request for Comment on Market Fragmentation, 65 Fed. Reg. 10577, 10584 (Feb. 28, 2000) (footnote omitted). For a discussion of the best execution obligation, see Francis J. Facciolo, *A Broker's Duty of Best Execution in the Nineteenth and Early Twentieth Centuries*, 26 PACE L. REV 155 (2005); and David A. Lipton, *Best Execution: The National Market System's Missing Ingredient*, 57 NOTRE DAME L. REV. 449 (1982).

[131] SEC Division of Market Regulation, *Guide to Broker-Dealer Registration* (Aug. 2004).

traded securities when better prices are available is a violation of the duty of best execution.[132]

Churning

"Churning" is a fraudulent activity that a broker-dealer may use to increase compensation. This practice involves excessive trading in a customer's account in order to generate commissions. In order to prove this violation, it must be shown that the broker controlled the customer's account and that the trading in the account conducted by the broker was excessive in light of the customer's trading goals.[133] If the account is not controlled by a broker liability will not lie for churning, but a suitability claim may be brought if improper recommendations were made.

Damages for churning are limited to the amount of commissions and fees that are found to be excessive. Consequently, such claims are often coupled with suitability or other violations in order to recover damages from investment losses.

Courts often use a "turnover ratio" that examines how many times that the funds in the account have been turned over by the broker. Churning will generally be found where the turnover ratio exceeds 6.0.[134]

Unauthorized Trading

Broker-dealers are prohibited from engaging in unauthorized trading in a customer's account. This means that broker-dealers and their associated persons may not enter orders for customer accounts without their authorization.

Broker-dealers have a duty to execute customer orders completely and promptly.[135] Broker-dealers often seek to defend these claims on the grounds that the customer was given notice of the trade through a confirmation statement but failed to object to the trade in a timely

---

[132] *In the Matter of Geman*, 2001 WL 124847 (S.E.C.), *aff'd*, *Geman v. SEC*, 334 F.3d . 1183 (10th Cir. 2003). Similarly, the Third Circuit held in *Newton v. Merrill Lynch, Pierce, Fenner & Smith*, 135 F.3d 266, 268 (3d Cir. 1998) that investors could recover damages for failure to price improve through private on-line services like SelectNet and Instinet.

[133] *See, e.g.*, Costello v. Oppenheimer & Co., 711 F.2d 1361 (7th Cir. 1983) (describing the elements of churning).

[134] Jerry W. Markham & Thomas Lee Hazen, Broker-Dealer Operations Under Securities and Commodity Law § 10:25 (2012).

[135] *Id.* at § 10:26.

manner. This, it is claimed, is an effort by the customer to keep the trade if it is successful and deny the trade if it results in a loss.[136]

MARKUPS, MARKDOWNS AND COMMISSIONS

It had been a long-standing securities practice for exchanges to set the rate of commissions charged by their broker-dealer members to customers. However, that practice was eliminated in 1975 at the direction of the SEC.[137] Commissions are now freely negotiable between a broker and its customers, but their amount must be disclosed to the customer through a confirmation statement, which must also disclose whether the broker-dealer is acting as an agent or dealer.[138] FINRA rules also require that commissions be fair and reasonable.[139]

When acting as a dealer, i.e., the firm is selling to or buying from the customer for the dealer's own account, the dealer may not excessively markup the securities when sold to the customer or excessively mark them down when buying from the customer. This liability rests on the belief that a broker-dealer is making an implied representation that securities bought from or sold to customers are reasonably related to prices charged in an open and competitive market.

Markups or markdowns in excess of 5 percent for equity securities will generally be viewed as excessive. Even smaller markups or markdowns may be considered excessive for bonds and other fixed rate instruments where the risk of loss is lower.[140]

FIDUCIARY DUTIES

Courts impose a range of fiduciary and other duties on broker-dealers that vary in scope based on the amount of control exercised by the

---

[136] Unauthorized trading is also prohibited under the Commodity Exchange Act of 1936. *Id.* at § 10:26.50. The CFTC has also adopted a rule prohibiting unauthorized trading for customer accounts. 17 C.F.R. § 166.2.

[137] *See* III JERRY W. MARKHAM, A FINANCIAL HISTORY OF THE UNITED STATES, FROM THE AGE OF DERIVATIVES TO THE NEW MILLENNIUM (1970–2001) 29–30 (2002) (describing this history).

[138] 17 C.F.R. § 240.10b-10.

[139] FINRA Rule 2440.

[140] *See* JERRY W. MARKHAM & THOMAS LEE HAZEN, BROKER-DEALER OPERATIONS UNDER SECURITIES AND COMMODITY LAW § 10:23 (2012) (describing these limitations).

broker-dealer over the customer's account. Those duties are minimal for non-discretionary accounts and quite broad for discretionary accounts managed by a broker-dealer.[141] A non-discretionary account is one in which the customer originates the orders. In a discretionary account, the broker has been given discretionary authority by the customer to enter orders without first seeking the permission of the customer.

To the extent a broker-dealer is handling only non-discretionary accounts, the courts see no need to impose anything other than the most basic duties, for example, refraining from engaging in unauthorized trades.[142] One court summarized the case law on broker-dealer duties for a non-discretionary account as imposing the following duties:

1. the duty to recommend a stock only after studying it sufficiently to become informed as to its nature, price and financial prognosis;
2. the duty to carry out the customer's orders promptly in a manner best suited to serve the customer's interest;
3. the duty to inform the customer of the risks involved in purchasing or selling a particular security;
4. the duty to refràin from self-dealing or refusing to disclose any personal interest a broker may have in a particular recommended security;
5. the duty not to misrepresent any fact material to the transaction; and
6. the duty to transact business only after receiving prior authorization from the customer.[143]

In contrast, where discretion is exercised over trading in a customer's account by a broker-dealer, a broad range of fiduciary duties is imposed. The same court described the broader and additional duties imposed in a discretionary account as follows:

1. the duty to manage the account in a manner directly comporting with the needs and objectives of the customer as stated in the

[141] *Compare* SEC v. Capital Gains Research Bureau, Inc., 375 U.S. 180 (1963) (investment advisers' fiduciary duties), *with* Leib v. Merrill Lynch, Pierce, Fenner & Smith Inc., 461 F. Supp. 951 (E.D. Mich. 1978), *aff'd*, 647 F.2d 165 (6th Cir. 1981) (broker-dealer fiduciary duties) and de Kwiatkowski v. Bear Stearns, 306 F.3d 1293 (2d Cir. 2002) (broker-dealer fiduciary duties).

[142] de Kwiatkowski v. Bear Stearns, 306 F.3d 1293 (2d Cir. 2002).

[143] Leib v. Merrill Lynch, Pierce, Fenner & Smith Inc., 461 F. Supp. 951, 953 (E.D. Mich. 1978), *aff'd*, 647 F.2d 165 (6th Cir. 1981).

authorization papers or as apparent from the customer's investment and trading history;

2. the duty to keep informed regarding the changes in the market which affect his customer's interest and act responsibly to protect those interests;
3. the duty to keep his customer informed as to each completed transaction; and
4. the duty to explain forthrightly the practical impact and potential risks of the course of dealing in which the broker is engaged.[144]

MISUSE OF CUSTOMER FUNDS

The failure over the last several years of several large financial services firms, some with funds held for commodity and securities customers, have raised concerns over whether customer funds held in custody at those institutions were properly protected. Lehman Brothers failed during the Financial Crisis in 2008. It was the largest bankruptcy in U.S. history and resulted in extensive litigation over rights to customer funds held in custody. Shortly after the Lehman failure, Bernie Madoff confessed to running a massive Ponzi scheme, which became the largest fraud ever. Only a few months later, U.S. authorities charged that R. Allen Stanford had been running another giant Ponzi scheme out of Antigua that involved $7 billion in customer funds.[145]

After the failure of numerous brokerage firms at the end of the 1960s,[146] Congress enacted the Securities Investor Protection Act of 1970 ("SIPA"), which directed the SEC to adopt rules designed to protect customer funds in the custody of registered broker-dealers.[147] In response to that direction, the SEC adopted Rule 15c3–3 to require broker-dealers

---

[144] 461 F. Supp. at 953–954.

[145] Clifford Krauss, *Jury Convicts Stanford in $7 Billion Ponzi Fraud*, N.Y. TIMES, Mar. 7, 2012, at B1.

[146] *See* HURD BARUCH, WALL STREET SECURITY RISK (1971) (criticizing these practices).

[147] SIPA also created an insurance scheme that provided account insurance of up to $100,000 per customer (later increased to $500,000, including $100,000 of customer cash) for losses caused by their broker-dealer's insolvency—it does not insure against investment losses. That insurance fund is administered by the Securities Investor Protection Corporation ("SIPC"), a private non-profit corporation that is funded by assessments on broker-dealers. *See* Holmes v. Securities Investor Protection Corp., 503 U.S. 258, 261–262 (1992) (describing SIPC insurance).

to account for customer funds and securities and hold them in specially designated accounts.[148] This requirement "was designed to assure that customers' funds (as well as securities) held by broker-dealers are protected against broker-dealer misuse or insolvency."[149] SEC Rule 15c3–3 is generally referred to as the SEC's "Customer Protection Rule."[150]

The Customer Protection Rule includes a requirement that broker-dealers maintain special accounts "in the nature of a trust fund through which a broker-dealer must effectuate all transactions with regard to all 'funds carried for the account of any customer' … ."[151] Rule 15c3–3 requires that broker-dealers maintain at a bank a "'Special Reserve Bank Account for the Exclusive Benefit of Customers' ('Reserve Bank Account') and deposit in this account its reserve requirement as computed in accordance with the Formula for Determination of Reserve Requirement For Brokers and Dealers ('Reserve Formula') … ."[152]

The SEC has also created custody requirements for customer funds held by investment advisers. SEC Rule 206(4)-2 imposes those custody requirements.[153] That rule was intended to "enhance the protections afforded to advisory clients' assets, harmonize the rule with current custodial practices, and clarify circumstances under which advisers have custody."[154] Rule 204(4)-2 was designed to require "an investment adviser who has custody of funds or securities of any client to maintain them in such a way that they will be insulated from and not be jeopardized by financial reverses, including insolvency, of the investment adviser."[155]

---

[148] 17 C.F.R. § 240.15c3–3.

[149] SEC, *Customer Protection Rule*, Securities Exchange Act Release No. 34–21865, 1985 SEC LEXIS 2502 (Mar. 19, 1985).

[150] SEC, *Customer Protection Rule*, Securities Exchange Act Release No. 34–21865, 1985 SEC LEXIS 2502 (Mar. 19, 1985).

[151] SEC, *Proposal To Adopt Rules 15c3–3 and 15c3–4 Under the Securities Exchange Act …* , Securities Exchange Act Release No. 34–9388, 1971 SEC LEXIS 231 (Nov. 8, 1971).

[152] SEC, *Customer Protection Rule*, Securities Exchange Act Release No. 34–21865, 1985 SEC LEXIS 2502 (Mar. 19, 1985).

[153] 17 C.F.R. § 275.206(4)-2.

[154] 68 Fed. Reg. 56692 (Oct. 1, 2003).

[155] 27 Fed. Reg. 2149 (Mar. 16, 1962).

FINANCIAL ANALYSTS SCANDALS

Another Enron era scandal involved the financial analysts employed by financial services firms to make recommendations for security purchases to the firms' customers. This service presented some potential conflicts of interest because the firm might be tempted to have their analysts hype a stock that the firm was trading or underwriting or to engage in other such misconduct. The brokerage firms put supervisory procedures in place to prevent such abuses. However, it was discovered that several financial analysts, including Henry Blodget at Merrill Lynch, had been promoting particular investments as good investments when their internal emails were highly disparaging of those same investments.

Some analysts were also working with their investment banking divisions by touting the securities of investment banking clients and received remuneration for doing so. Several firms that employed those financial analysts reached a global settlement agreement with state regulators and with the SEC in which they agreed to stop those practices and to pay penalties totaling over $1.4 billion.[156]

The SEC also enacted Regulation FD in order to prohibit employees of public companies from selectively disclosing information to favored financial analysts. Previously, financial analysts that followed particular public companies would meet periodically with management in order to gain a better "feel" for the companies' operations and prospects. Regulation FD, however, curbed those contacts and required management when disseminating information on their companies to conduct conference calls that any and all analysts could join if they wished.

Regulation FD was adopted after the Supreme Court ruled that selective disclosure to financial analysts did not constitute prohibited insider trading, even where the analyst acted on the information.[157] That rule, unfortunately, limited the ability of financial analysts to analyze anything other than the public filings of the companies they follow.

UNDERWRITING SCANDALS

Still another Enron era scandal involved underwriting abuses in the "hot" issues being offered by companies making public offerings of their stock.

---

[156] *See* JERRY W. MARKHAM, A FINANCIAL HISTORY OF MODERN U.S. CORPORATE SCANDALS, FROM ENRON TO REFORM 405–420 (2006) (describing these scandals and the settlement).

[157] Dirks v. SEC, 463 U.S. 646 (1983).

A hot issue is one that trades up quickly above its offering price and usually involves the initial public offering by a company.

Access to a hot issue distribution is a valuable asset and underwriters were found to have allocated hot issues stock to executives at client firms in order to gain business, a practice known as "spinning." In other cases, hot issue shares were allocated to clients with an agreement that the recipient would buy additional shares at higher prices in the after market in order to gain further support for the stock's price.[158]

MUTUAL FUND ISSUES

A number of issues involving fraud have arisen in the context of mutual fund sales. The Investment Company Act of 1940 governs the operations of mutual funds and other investment companies.[159]

Sales Loads

Mutual funds are often sold in classes that charge differing commissions, "sales loads." Some classes are front-end loaded, while others are back-end loaded and some charge no-loads. In a front-end sales load the investors pays the commission when the fund shares are purchased. In a back-end or deferred sales load the commission is paid when the mutual fund shares are redeemed. A no-load fund does not charge a commission as such, but may still charge purchase fees, redemption fees, exchange fees, and account fees. FINRA rules govern the amount of the loads that may be charged on mutual fund shares.[160]

Breakpoints

The loads on mutual funds may be reduced based on the amount of the investment. Many mutual funds thus create "breakpoints" that will reduce the sales load at various investment amounts, the larger investment being

---

[158] *See* Jerry W. Markham, A Financial History of Modern U.S. Corporate Scandals, From Enron to Reform 410–412 (2006) (describing these practices).

[159] 15 U.S.C. § 80a-1 *et seq.*

[160] *See* Jerry W. Markham & Thomas Lee Hazen, Broker-Dealer Operations Under Securities and Commodity Law § 10:24 (2012) (describing these loads).

given reduced loads. The SEC has prohibited broker-dealers that distribute mutual funds from breaking up individual investments into smaller amounts in order to avoid the reduced sales load that they would otherwise be entitled to under the breakpoint schedule. Broker-dealers must provide customers with a breakpoint schedule in order to assure that they are informed of the varying charges and the savings they may achieve from a larger investment.[161]

Switching

Another prohibited practice for mutual fund sales called "switching" occurs where the broker-dealer switches from one mutual fund to another in order to generate additional sales loads. Customers are required to sign a form authorizing a switch from one mutual fund to another in order to help deter this practice.[162]

The SEC has also imposed sanctions where broker-dealers were given inducements to give preference for one mutual fund over that of another in making customer recommendations. The SEC has brought cases charging that broker-dealers were given lavish entertainment by mutual fund sponsors in order to induce the broker-dealers to give preference in recommending the sponsor's fund over that of others.[163]

Late Trading and Market Timing

In 2003, New York Attorney General Eliot Spitzer filed several actions against mutual funds and others who had engaged in the abusive practices of mutual fund market timing and late trading. The SEC also brought several actions challenging these activities as constituting fraud. The SEC and Spitzer were not always successful in the prosecution of those claims.[164]

Late trading occurs when a purchase or redemption of a mutual fund share is made after 4:00 p.m., which is the time at which the net asset value ("NAV") of the mutual funds is computed for the purpose of pricing the fund's shares for the next trading day. The late entry of a

---

[161] *Id.*

[162] *Id.*

[163] *Id.*

[164] *See* Jerry W. Markham, *Mutual Fund Scandals—A Comparative Analysis of the Role of Corporate Governance in the Regulation of Collective Investments*, 3 HASTINGS BUS. L. J. 67 (2006) (describing those actions).

trade allows the trader to take advantage of favorable market developments that occur after the NAV is set at 4:00 p.m. For example, a trader could buy cheap mutual fund shares where the market has advanced over the NAV set at 4:00 p.m.[165]

Market timing involves a trader taking advantage of stale prices used to set NAV. This activity may not always be fraudulent. Nevertheless, Spitzer asserted that such trading was unfair to other mutual fund holders and that it diluted their holdings.[166] Market timing is also disliked by mutual funds because it requires them to keep excess liquidity on hand to meet redemptions and increases fund costs.

Investment Advisers

Concern over fraud may arise under the 1940 Act, which as described above, contains an antifraud provision applicable to securities investment advisers. In recent years, the SEC has encountered concerns with hedge fund managers. The SEC passed a rule requiring them to register as investment advisers, but that rule was stricken by the D.C. Circuit.[167] However, a provision was added to the Dodd-Frank Wall Street Reform and Consumer Protection Act of 2010 to require such registration for most hedge funds.[168] It is uncertain how much protection this requirement will provide since Bernie Madoff was registered as an investment adviser with the SEC while he was carrying out his fraud.

Another concern with investment advisers has been "soft dollar" practices. Soft dollars involve arrangements in which an investment adviser uses commission dollars generated by its transactions with a broker dealer for customers to pay for research services or expenses. These payments are permitted by the 34 Act, but fraud may be charged where the charges are misrepresented.[169]

---

165 *Id.* at 89.

166 *Id.* at 89–90.

167 Goldstein v. SEC, 451 F.3d 873 (D.C. Cir. 2006). Among those registering under that provision was the operations of Bernie Madoff. He was supposedly conducting billions of dollars of trades through his hedge fund with an affiliated broker-dealer. Despite several SEC staff inspections, no claim was made that he should register his hedge fund as a broker-dealer. *See* JERRY W. MARKHAM, A FINANCIAL HISTORY OF THE U.S. FROM THE SUBPRIME CRISIS TO THE GREAT RECESSION (2006–2009) 609–613 (2011) (describing that event).

168 15 U.S.C. §§ 80b-2 & 3.

169 *See* JERRY W. MARKHAM & THOMAS LEE HAZEN, BROKER-DEALER OPERATIONS UNDER SECURITIES AND COMMODITY LAW § 6:14 (2012) (describing these abuses).

Section 913 of the Dodd-Frank Act amended the 34 Act to allow the SEC to impose the same fiduciary duties on broker-dealers in dealing with customers that investment advisers owe to their customers. Section 913 of the Dodd-Frank Act also directed the SEC to conduct a study regarding the effectiveness of current rules regulating broker-dealers and investment advisers and public perception of their respective duties to clients.

The SEC staff conducted that study and recommended the creation of a uniform fiduciary standard for investment advisers and broker-dealers when providing investment advice about securities to retail customers. This recommendation would heighten the fiduciary duties of broker-dealers to a level comparable to that of investment advisers. The staff further recommended that the regulatory structure for broker-dealers and investment advisers be harmonized.[170]

CONCLUSION

The federal securities laws contain a broad array of antifraud and anti-manipulation measures for the protection of the public. However, each has complicated requirements for proving fraud and damages.

---

170 *SEC Staff Study on Investment Advisers and Broker-Dealers* (Jan. 2011).

14. The past, present and future of securities arbitration between customers and brokerage firms

Barbara Black

INTRODUCTION

The Financial Industry Regulatory Authority ("FINRA")[1] is, for all practical purposes, the sole arbitration forum for resolving disputes between broker-dealers, associated persons and their customers. FINRA requires arbitration of disputes between customers and broker-dealer firms and associated persons at the request of the customer.[2] The dispute must arise in connection with the business activities of the member or the associated person (except disputes involving the insurance business activities of a member that is also an insurance company). FINRA Rule 12100(i) defines a customer to exclude a broker or a dealer. Recent litigation has provided more content to the definition.[3] In addition, a

---

[1] Until mid-2007, the National Association of Securities Dealers ("NASD") and the New York Stock Exchange ("NYSE") ran separate arbitration forums that handled a combined 99 percent of all securities arbitrations in the country. On July 30, 2007, NASD and NYSE Regulation, including their respective arbitration forums, consolidated and formed FINRA. *See* Press Release, FINRA, NASD and NYSE Member Regulation Combine to Form the Financial Industry Regulatory Authority (July 30, 2007), *available at* http://www.finra.org/Newsroom/NewsReleases/2007/P036329. This chapter will, in most instances, refer to the regulator by its name at the time of the event being discussed. When referring to the regulator generally or over an extended period of time, it will be referred to as FINRA.

[2] FINRA Arbitration Rule 12200. FINRA's Code of Arbitration Procedure is available at FINRA's website, at http://finra.complinet.com/en/display/display_main.html?rbid=2403&element_id=4096.

[3] *See* Raymond James Fin. Serv., Inc. v. Cary, 709 F.3d 382 (4th Cir. 2013) (defining customer as "an entity that is 'not a broker or dealer, who purchases commodities or services from a FINRA member in the course of the member's business activities,' namely, 'the activities of investment banking and the securities business'"); Wachovia Bank, Nat. Ass'n. v. VCG Special Opportunities Master Fund, LTD., 661 F.3d 164 (2d Cir. 2011) (holding that hedge fund was

written agreement can require arbitration of customers' disputes.[4] Although some securities firms included predispute arbitration agreements ("PDAAs") in customers' brokerage agreements at least since the 1950s,[5] modern securities arbitration began with the 1987 U.S. Supreme Court opinion, *Shearson/American Express Inc. v. McMahon*,[6] which held that brokerage firms could enforce PDAAs and require customers to arbitrate their claims arising under federal securities law.[7] Since that pivotal decision, virtually all broker-dealers require their customers to execute PDAAs.

FINRA has hearing locations in every state, the District of Columbia, Puerto Rico, and London. From 2002 through 2012, the number of arbitration cases filed in its forum ranged from a high of 8945 (2003) to a low of 3238 (2007).[8] From 2008 through 2012, the percentage and number of cases that resulted in an award where claimants were awarded damages ranged from 42 percent (199 cases) in 2008 to 47 percent (415 cases) in 2010.[9]

Over the years FINRA, and its predecessors the National Association of Securities Dealers ("NASD") and NASD-Dispute Resolution ("NASD-DR"), have amended the arbitration rules to provide fair procedures and to reduce the influence of the securities industry. In addition, the Securities and Exchange Commission ("SEC") must approve FINRA's arbitration rules upon a finding that the rules are consistent with the requirements of the Securities Exchange Act of 1934 ("1934 Act") and its rules.[10] FINRA has worked hard to increase investor confidence in the arbitration process, although doubts persist because of its mandatory nature.

---

not a customer because it did not have a brokerage agreement with the firm and it acknowledged that it received no advice, recommendations or services from the firm).

[4] FINRA Rule 12200.

[5] Wilko v. Swan, 346 U.S. 427 (1953) (holding that a PDAA was not enforceable with respect to claims under Securities Act of 1933).

[6] 482 U.S. 220 (1987).

[7] *McMahon*'s holding technically applied only to claims under the Securities Exchange Act. Two years later, the Court extended its holding to claims under the Securities Act of 1933 in Rodriguez de Quijas v. Shearson/Am. Express Inc., 490 U.S. 477 (1989).

[8] FINRA, Arbitration Cases Filed, at http://www.finra.org/ArbitrationAndMediation/FINRADisputeResolution/AdditionalResources/Statistics/.

[9] *Id.*

[10] SEA § 19(b)(2)(C), 15 U.S.C. § 78s(b)(2)(C).

PRE-*McMAHON* ARBITRATION

Prior to the 1987 *McMahon* decision, some brokerage firms included PDAAs requiring customers to arbitrate their disputes before one or more of the forums of the self-regulatory organizations ("SROs")—NASD, NYSE, Amex. The PDAAs, however, were enforceable only with respect to state law claims. The Supreme Court held, in *Wilko v. Swan*,[11] that firms could not enforce PDAAs with respect to claims arising under the Securities Act of 1933 ("1933 Act"), because arbitration was inadequate to enforce the substantive rights created by the statute. The *Wilko* Court specifically noted aspects of the arbitration process that it thought could lessen the 1933 Act's substantive protections: arbitration proceedings were not suited for cases requiring "subjective findings on the purpose and knowledge of an alleged violator"; arbitrators must make legal determinations "without judicial instruction on the law"; an arbitration award "may be made without explanation of [the arbitrator's] reasons and without a complete record of their proceedings"; the "power to vacate an [arbitration] award is limited"; and "interpretations of the law by the arbitrators in contrast to manifest disregard are not subject, in the federal courts, to judicial review for error in interpretation."[12] Accordingly, the Court concluded arbitration would deny investors advantageous judicial remedies in violation of Section 14 of the 1933 Act,[13] which declares void any waivers of compliance with provisions of the 1933 Act. The SEC, in turn, prohibited brokerage firms from attempting to require arbitration of federal securities laws.[14] As a result, when a customer who had signed a PDAA asserted claims against a broker-dealer under both federal securities and state laws, the broker-dealer could compel arbitration only of the state law claims, resulting in inefficient bifurcated proceedings.[15]

---

[11] 346 U.S. 427 (1953).

[12] *Id.* at 435–37.

[13] 15 U.S.C. § 77n.

[14] Former SEC Rule 15c2–2, 17 C.F.R. § 240.15c2–2, codified the SEC's view that PDAAs purporting to bind customers to arbitration of all future disputes is "a misleading statement of customers' rights under the federal securities laws." Exch. Act Rel. No. 20397 (Nov. 18, 1983).

[15] Dean Witter Reynolds, Inc. v. Byrd, 470 U.S. 213 (1985). Because Dean Witter assumed that the claim under the 1934 Act was not subject to the PDAA and could only be resolved in federal court, it sought to compel arbitration only of the state law claims. Although the firm and amici curiae representing the securities industry urged the Supreme Court to resolve the applicability of *Wilko*

In 1977, the SEC asserted a need for a nationwide investor dispute resolution system to resolve expeditiously small claims; it noted that investors with large claims apparently found litigation a feasible method of seeking redress.[16] As a result the Securities Industry Conference on Arbitration ("SICA")[17] was organized, consisting of representatives of the SROs, the public, and the Securities Industry Association ("SIA").[18] SICA developed a Uniform Code of Arbitration that SROs adopted in 1979–1980.[19] While each SRO had to approve changes in its procedural rules and submit the changes to the SEC for approval, and while the SROs did not always adopt all the SICA proposals, for many years the NYSE and NASD versions of the Uniform Code remained generally the same.

Procedures The arbitration procedures in effect at the NASD were very informal.[20] The provisions on discovery were aspirational: "prior to the first hearing session, the parties shall cooperate in the voluntary exchange of such documents and information as will serve to expedite the arbitration."[21] Moreover, the Code instructed that "the parties shall produce witnesses and present proofs to the fullest extent possible without resort to the issuance of the subpoena process,"[22] although the arbitrators and any counsel of record had the power of the subpoena process as provided by applicable law.[23] The only provisions relating to

---

to claims under the SEA, the Court declined to do so because the issue was not properly before it.

[16] *See* Implementation of an Investor Dispute Resolution System, Exch. Act Rel. No. 34–13470, 12 SEC Docket 186 (Apr. 26, 1977).

[17] *See* Constantine N. Katsoris, *SICA: The First Twenty Years*, 23 FORDHAM URB. L.J. 483, 488–90 (1996) (setting forth the background on the creation of SICA).

[18] The successor to the SIA is the Securities Industry and Financial Markets Association ("SIFMA"), the principal trade organization of securities firms in the United States and Canada. *See* http://www.sifma.com.

[19] *See* In re NASD, Order Approving Proposed Rule Change, Exch. Act Rel. No. 34–16860, 20 SEC Docket 233 (May 30, 1980).

[20] *See* Deborah Masucci & Edward W. Morris, Jr., *Securities Arbitration at Self-Regulatory Organizations: Administration and Procedure*, in SECURITIES ARBITRATION 1988, at 309, 399 (PLI Corp. Law & Practice Course, Handbook Series No. 601, 1988). The NASD's Code of Arbitration Procedure in effect in July 1987 is set forth as Exhibit 24; Part III governs customers' disputes with broker-dealers.

[21] Nat'l Assoc. of Securities Dealers, Code of Arbitration Procedure § 32(b).

[22] *Id.* § 32(a).

[23] *Id.*

the hearing set forth what was not required: arbitrators were not bound by rules of evidence governing the admissibility of evidence,[24] and no record of the proceeding was required, unless requested by the arbitrators or a party.[25]

Selection of arbitrators The NASD arbitration staff selected the panel of arbitrators from the pool of qualified arbitrators.[26] When the amount in controversy did not exceed $500,000, the panel generally consisted of three arbitrators, one of whom was an industry (or non-public) arbitrator.[27] When the amount in controversy was $500,000 or more, the panel consisted of five arbitrators, at least a majority of whom shall not be from the industry.[28] Each party had the right to one preemptory challenge.[29] All arbitrators were required to be neutral.[30]

THE *McMAHON* DECISION

In its 1987 opinion, *Shearson/American Express Inc. v. McMahon*,[31] the Supreme Court held that PDAAs were legally binding and did not violate Section 29(a) of the 1934 Act, which invalidates "any condition, stipulation, or provision binding any person to waive compliance" with any provision of the statute.[32] Thirty-six years after *Wilko v. Swan*, the Court looked at the current SRO arbitration process and concluded that it provided an adequate means of enforcing the statutory provisions.[33] The Court noted that it had recently recognized, in opinions enforcing arbitration clauses in other areas of the law,[34] that arbitration panels can

---

24 *Id.* § 34.

25 *Id.* § 37.

26 *Id.* §§ 4, 20.

27 *Id.* § 19(a).

28 *Id.* § 19(b).

29 *Id.* § 22.

30 Self-Regulatory Organizations; Order Approving Proposed Rule Changes by the New York Stock Exchange, Inc., National Association of Securities Dealers, Inc., and the American Stock Exchange, Inc. Relating to the Arbitration Process and the Use of Predispute Arbitration Clauses, Exch. Act Rel. 34–26805, 54 Fed. Reg. 21144 (May 10, 1989).

31 482 U.S. 220 (1987).

32 15 U.S.C. § 78cc(a).

33 482 U.S. at 231.

34 *See, e.g.* Mitsubishi Motors Corp. v. Soler Chrysler-Plymouth, Inc., 473 U.S. 614 (1985) (upholding the arbitrability of federal antitrust claims).

handle factual and legal complexities without judicial instruction and supervision and that the streamlined procedures did not curtail claimants' substantive rights.[35] Thus, in rejecting McMahon's contention that the arbitration process could not fairly vindicate his federal statutory rights, the Court stated that "[b]y agreeing to arbitrate a statutory claim, a party does not forgo the substantive rights afforded by the statute; it only submits to their resolution in an arbitral, rather than a judicial, forum."[36]

In support of this conclusion, the Court observed: "there is no reason to assume at the outset that arbitrators will not follow the law; although judicial scrutiny of arbitration awards necessarily is limited, such review is sufficient to ensure that arbitrators comply with the requirements of the statute."[37] While in *Wilko* the lack of meaningful judicial review (other than for "manifest disregard" of the law[38]) supported its view that arbitration could not preserve investors' rights under the law, in *McMahon* the limited amount of judicial review provided assurance that investors could be protected.

Crucial to the Supreme Court's opinion was the assumption that arbitrators must and do apply the law, at least with respect to federal statutory claims.[39] In at least some states, however, unless the parties agree otherwise, arbitrators are not bound by the law and need not apply substantive principles of law when deciding disputes. Rather, these states acknowledge that an arbitrator "may do justice as he sees it, applying his own sense of law and equity to the facts as he finds them to be and making an award reflecting the spirit rather than the letter of the agreement [to arbitrate] … ."[40]

McMahon thus marked a change in the Court's view of arbitration from distrust to acceptance of the process. Moreover, in the specific area of securities arbitration, the Court pointed to changes in the SEC's regulatory authority since *Wilko*, principally SEC oversight over the SRO arbitration forums, that would ensure that the process adequately vindicated the rights of individual customers.[41] Indeed, it may well be that the

---

35 482 U.S. at 229–30.

36 *Id.* (quoting Mitsubishi, 473 U.S. at 628).

37 482 U.S. at 232.

38 *See supra* note 12 and accompanying text.

39 In fact, this assumption has been widely challenged since the *McMahon* opinion. *See* Barbara Black & Jill I. Gross, *Making It Up As They Go Along: The Role of Law in Securities Arbitration,* 23 CARDOZO L. REV. 991 (2002).

40 Silverman v. Cooper, 61 N.Y.2d 299, 308 (1984); *accord* Schnurmacher Holding, Inc. v. Noriega, 542 So.2d 1327, 1328 (Fla. 1989).

41 482 U.S. at 238; *Rodriguez,* 490 U.S. at 483.

Court had come to believe that characteristics (principally, informality and limited judicial review) that previously made arbitration deficient because it was not the functional equivalent of a judicial proceeding had become virtues that made arbitration an attractive alternative. The decision thus marked the perfect alignment of two strong Supreme Court policies: support for arbitration and antipathy toward investors' securities fraud claims in federal courts.[42]

POST-*McMAHON* REFORMS: THE DEBATE OVER THE MODEL OF SRO SECURITIES ARBITRATION

Brokerage firms had achieved a major victory in *McMahon*. Although the SEC assumed that arbitration would not become the exclusive forum for resolution of customers' complaints,[43] in fact, as a result of the decision, the use of PDAAs became virtually universal, and arbitration of customers' disputes became mandatory. The question arose: Could investors have confidence in the impartiality and independence of arbitration forums sponsored by the securities industry? It became increasingly important that the SRO forums provide a fair process in which investors could have confidence.

Immediately following *McMahon*, the SEC and SICA engaged in a debate over the model of SRO securities arbitration. Should it retain the traditional characteristics of arbitration, with informal procedures where arbitrators are not strictly bound to apply the law, or should it more closely resemble a judicial proceeding, with formal procedures where the arbitrators are expected to apply the law? How should arbitrators be selected, and what are the appropriate qualifications and training for arbitrators? How should public and industry arbitrators be defined?

---

42 *See, e.g.,* Santa Fe Industries v. Green, 430 U.S. 462 (1977); Ernst & Ernst v. Hochfelder, 425 U.S. 185 (1976); Blue Chip Stamps v. Manor Drug Stores, 421 U.S. 723 (1975), all of which refer to the vexatious nature of securities fraud litigation.

43 An SEC survey showed that in 1989 only 39 percent of cash accounts required a PDAA. "The continuation of such investor access to brokerage services without having to sign a PDAA is a significant factor in the Commission's evaluation of this matter." Self-Regulatory Organizations; Order Approving Proposed Rule Changes by the New York Stock Exchange, Inc., National Association of Securities Dealers, Inc., and the American Stock Exchange, Inc. Relating to the Arbitration Process and the Use of Predispute Arbitration Clauses, Exch. Act Rel. 34–26805, 54 Fed. Reg. 21144 (May 10, 1989).

Should the practice of including an industry arbitrator on all panels be continued?

SEC staff recommendations Soon after *McMahon*, SEC staff sent a list of recommended changes to the arbitration procedures to SICA.[44] In the exchange between the SEC staff and SICA culminating in changes in the SRO arbitration rules approved by the SEC in 1989, the competing visions of securities arbitration were delineated. The SEC staff contemplated a process that was more judicial than the SICA (and SRO) vision: arbitration would involve a hearing where the parties presented evidence obtained through a discovery process, and arbitrators would apply the law to arrive at a decision. The SEC endorsed the continued use of mixed public/industry panels, but indicated that "[t]he absence of clear guidelines for qualifying public arbitrators … and the inclusion in the pool of public arbitrators of persons with clear affiliations with the securities industry is a source of great concern."[45] It recommended tightening the definition of public arbitrator to include only individuals "who are not so connected with the industry that it may hinder their ability to make independent judgments with respect to specific industry practices."[46]

Specific recommendations included:[47]

- Discovery procedures should be expanded to resolve discovery disputes prior to the hearing;[48]
- Pre-hearing and preliminary conferences should be held in complex cases;[49]

---

[44] Letter from Richard G. Ketchum, Director of Division of Market Regulation, SEC, to SICA members, in Mark D. Fitterman, Catherine McGuire, & Robert A. Love, *SEC Initiatives for Changes in SRO Arbitration Rules*, SECURITIES ARBITRATION 1988, at 257, 279 app. A (PLI Corp. Law & Practice Course, Handbook Series No. 601, 1988).

[45] Self-Regulatory Organizations; Order Approving Proposed Rule Changes by the New York Stock Exchange, Inc., National Association of Securities Dealers, Inc., and the American Stock Exchange, Inc. Relating to the Arbitration Process and the Use of Predispute Arbitration Clauses, Exch. Act Rel. 34–26805, 54 Fed. Reg. 21144 (May 10, 1989).

[46] *Id.*

[47] In addition to those discussed in the text, many of the recommendations related to expanding the pool of arbitrators who are not affiliated with the securities industry and other issues relating to arbitrator selection and qualification.

[48] Fitterman *et al., supra* note 44, at 287.

[49] *Id.*

- Arbitrators should be trained in the relevant state and securities law;[50]
- A record of the proceedings should be preserved for judicial review of awards, using what the SEC staff referred to as the "developing 'manifest disregard' standard;"[51]
- Arbitrators should include in the awards a summary of legal issues resolved in a dispute and indicate whether the arbitrators concur or dissent from the award;[52]
- Awards should be made publicly available, so that investors can check the track record of arbitrators and the public can evaluate the system;[53]
- Special guidelines for administration of large and complex cases are needed, and parties could ask for opinions, so that a body of precedent could be created.[54]

SICA's response In its response,[55] SICA expressed its vision of the post-*McMahon* arbitration process. It agreed with the need for a discovery rule, a pre-hearing conference in large and complex cases, and preservation of a record.[56] It also agreed that the definition of public arbitrator should be tightened. With respect to other recommendations, it showed less enthusiasm. SICA acknowledged generally the importance of training arbitrators, but did not directly address the SEC staff's recommendations that arbitrators receive instruction in the law.[57]

With respect to awards, SICA believed that the SEC's concerns could be addressed by maintaining a list of cases, the general subject matter of each case, the amount of the claim and award, the names of the arbitrators and a notation if the claim was dismissed on jurisdictional grounds. This list would delete the names of parties and would only be available to parties in pending cases and their counsel.[58] In the view of SICA, this information "will serve little utility and may mislead parties

[50] *Id.* at 282.
[51] *Id.* at 286.
[52] *Id.*
[53] *Id.*
[54] *Id.* at 290.
[55] *Id.* at 293 (letter set forth as Appendix B).
[56] *Id.* at 298–99.
[57] The letter merely commented, in response to a specific suggestion of a periodic newsletter about developments in arbitration, that this should be left to the discretion of the individual SROs. *Id.* at 296.
[58] *Id.* at 298.

regarding an arbitrator's track record,"[59] and it was "not reasonable to conclude that awards written in the manner [SEC staff] suggest could capture the decision making process of a panel."[60]

With respect to the recommendation for written opinions in large cases, SICA was blunt: "any rule which purports to require written opinions… could very well hinder, rather than enhance, the administration of arbitration proceedings."[61] It expressed concern that this would decrease the willingness of arbitrators to participate, and might interfere with parties' expectations that arbitration proceedings were confidential.

Post-McMahon arbitration rules In 1989, the SEC approved significant changes in SRO arbitration rules,[62] while making it clear that it continued to have concerns about the process. The agency implied that its views on the fairness of arbitration might change if SRO arbitration became, *de facto*, the exclusive forum for investors.[63] It signaled that it awaited further changes, noting that SICA was still considering its recommendations regarding the training of arbitrators, the evaluation of arbitrators' performance, and additional procedures for large and complex cases. The SEC stressed the need for development of judicial precedent in cases involving novel legal theories or challenging established industry practices.[64] To the SEC, it was also important that the process have greater transparency so that the public could understand the arbitration process, in contrast to the SROs' traditional view of arbitration as a confidential matter between the parties.

Procedures

(a) Discovery A discovery process would allow parties to obtain information and documents in sufficient time to prepare for a hearing.[65]

---

[59] *Id.* at 299.

[60] *Id.*

[61] *Id.* at 303.

[62] Self-Regulatory Organizations; Order Approving Proposed Rule Changes by the New York Stock Exchange, Inc., National Association of Securities Dealers, Inc., and the American Stock Exchange, Inc. Relating to the Arbitration Process and the Use of Predispute Arbitration Clauses, Exch. Act Rel. 34–26805, 54 Fed. Reg. 21144 (May 10, 1989).

[63] *Id.*

[64] *Id.*

[65] Nat'l Assoc. of Securities Dealers, Code of Arbitration Procedure § 32. The Code reflecting the 1989 rule changes is set forth as Exhibit 20 to Deborah Masucci & Edward W. Morris, Jr., *Arbitration at the National Association of*

Arbitrators would be involved in the discovery process through a pre-hearing conference between the parties and the arbitrators, and at least one arbitrator would participate in settling discovery disputes. Limited use of depositions was also authorized.

(b) Record of hearing A verbatim record of a hearing must be kept, either by stenographic reporter or tape recording,[66] for judicial review of the proceedings.

(c) Awards Both the contents and the public availability of arbitration awards were expanded;[67] arbitrators were not required to set forth reasons for their decisions. The SEC indicated that this might be an issue that it would revisit, and it stated that it expected SICA to consider making opinions a requirement in large and complex cases.

Classification of Arbitrators

(a) Non-public (industry) arbitrator The definition of non-public, or industry, arbitrator included anyone who was associated with a member of an SRO, broker, dealer, government securities broker, government securities dealer, municipal securities dealer. It also included anyone retired from the securities industry. A former associated individual could be classified as a public arbitrator after three years, if the individual had gone on to other work and was not retired from the securities industry.[68]

(b) Professionals Attorneys, accountants and other professionals who devoted at least 20 percent of their professional work effort to securities industry clients within the past two years were classified as industry arbitrators.[69]

Securities Dealers and the New York Stock Exchange, SECURITIES ARBITRATION 1989, at 437, 530 (PLI Corp. Law & Practice Course, Handbook Series No. 650, 1989).

[66] Nat'l Assoc. of Securities Dealers, Code of Arbitration Procedure § 37.

[67] *Id.* § 41.

[68] *Id.* § 19 (the NYSE had tighter definitions).

[69] *Id.* In addition, the rules excluded from service as either a public or industry arbitrator persons who are spouses or other members of a household of an associated person.

The SEC noted that these changes regarding the classification of arbitrators were "very significant to the continued success of SRO arbitration"[70] and "reflect a reasonable judgment in striking a necessary balance in obtaining impartial and qualified arbitrators, and take appropriate account of the need to avoid arbitrarily limiting the pool of knowledgeable public arbitrators."[71]

Predispute Arbitration Agreements

In 1989 the SEC also approved a new rule designed to improve disclosure to customers and to prescribe the content of the PDAA.[72] This rule mandated disclosure of certain information about the arbitration process and prohibited certain conditions that were inconsistent with SRO arbitration. It also set forth formatting requirements to make the required disclosures more visible and readable. Broker-dealers were required to place immediately before the PDAA introductory language that would inform customers that they were waiving their right to seek remedies in court, that arbitration was final, that discovery was generally more limited than in court proceedings, that the award was not required to contain factual findings and legal reasoning, and that the arbitration panel typically would include a minority of arbitrators associated with the securities industry.[73] In addition, the disclosure language must be highlighted in several ways.[74] SRO members were prohibited from having agreements with customers that limited or contradicted the rules of any SRO or limited the ability of a party to file any claim in arbitration or limit the ability of the arbitrators to make any award.[75]

In approving the rule, the SEC identified two principal benefits to investors. First, the disclosure provisions "address many of the concerns regarding customer notice and choice that have been considered over recent years" and the language "should promote more knowledgeable

---

70 Self-Regulatory Organizations; Order Approving Proposed Rule Changes by the New York Stock Exchange, Inc., National Association of Securities Dealers, Inc., and the American Stock Exchange, Inc. Relating to the Arbitration Process and the Use of Predispute Arbitration Clauses, Exch. Act Rel. 34–26805, 54 Fed. Reg. 21144 (May 10, 1989).

71 *Id.*

72 *Id.*

73 Article III, Section 21, NASD's Rules of Fair Practice.

74 *Id.*

75 *Id.*

acquiescence or rejection by customers of arbitration provisions."[76] Second, the prohibition against inconsistent conditions was necessary because "agreements cannot be used to curtail any rights that a party may otherwise have had in a judicial forum."[77] The SEC approved the latter provision because it made clear that that the use of arbitration forum could not curtail rights that a party would have in a judicial forum, such as punitive damages and attorney's fees, to the extent available under state law.[78] Similarly, terms purporting to shorten an applicable statute of limitations, restrict the situs of an arbitration hearing contrary to SRO rules, or limit SRO forums otherwise available to parties were not permitted.

In short, the SEC concluded that the new rule "appropriately balance[s] the need to strengthen investor confidence in the arbitration systems at the SROs … with the need to maintain arbitration as a form of dispute resolution that provides for equitable and efficient administration of justice."[79]

Conclusion This comparison of the pre- and post-*McMahon* Codes demonstrates that the changes made the process more like litigation (discovery, pre-hearing conference, publication of awards, requirement of a hearing record). Standards for classifying public arbitrators were tightened, because of concerns about the impartiality of arbitrators with industry ties. Highlighted disclosures about the inclusion of a PDAA in customers' agreements and the characteristics of arbitration were adopted to inform investors. Finally, broker-dealers were prohibited from including contractual provisions that would take away rights customers would have in court, as well as terms that would take away protections under the SRO rules. In contrast, the SROs did not adopt standards that relate to training arbitrators in the applicable law or requiring arbitrators to state the applicable law, despite SEC recommendations.

---

[76] Self-Regulatory Organizations; Order Approving Proposed Rule Changes by the New York Stock Exchange, Inc., National Association of Securities Dealers, Inc., and the American Stock Exchange, Inc. Relating to the Arbitration Process and the Use of Predispute Arbitration Clauses, Exch. Act Rel. 34–26805, 54 Fed. Reg. 21154 (May 10, 1989). At this time, the SEC believed that customers opening cash accounts could find a broker that did not require a PDAA.

[77] *Id.*

[78] *Id.*

[79] *Id.* at 21155.

ASSESSING THE FORUM: THE RUDER REPORT

Introduction The NASD Board of Governors appointed an Arbitration Policy Task Force in 1994 to study its arbitration forum and make recommendations for reform. The Task Force's 1996 report, known as the "Ruder Report" after its Chairman, former SEC Chairman David S. Ruder, greatly influenced the future direction of securities arbitration.[80] The Ruder Report concluded that the securities industry should be permitted to continue to use PDAAs because "even with its flaws, securities arbitration is clearly preferable to civil litigation."[81] Consistent with this view, it did not propose a radical overhaul of the arbitration forum, but instead proposed changes that would retain the traditional advantages of speed, informality and reduced costs and yet meet the demand for increased professionalism.[82] It also expressed concern that "the increasingly litigious nature of securities arbitration has gradually eroded the advantages of SRO arbitration."[83]

Recommendations The Ruder Report set forth a number of recommendations to improve the efficiency of the process, including:

- "Automatic production of essential documents should be required for all parties, and arbitrators should play a much greater role in directing discovery and resolving discovery disputes."[84]
- "Arbitrator selection, quality, training, and performance should be improved by various means, including adoption of a list selection method, earlier appointment of arbitrators, enhancement of arbitrator training, and increased compensation."[85] The Ruder Report noted that parties had little opportunity to participate in the choice of arbitrators. For a three person panel, the NASD arbitration staff selected two public members (one of whom was appointed Chair) and one industry member. Each party generally could exercise only

---

[80] SECURITIES ARBITRATION REFORM: REPORT OF THE ARBITRATION POLICY TASK FORCE TO THE BOARD OF GOVERNORS NATIONAL ASSOCIATION OF SECURITIES DEALERS, INC. (1996).

[81] *Id.* at 17–18.

[82] *See, e.g.*, *id.* at 88 (discussing the need for a more professional corps of arbitrators).

[83] *Id.* at 7.

[84] *Id.* at 2, 82–86.

[85] *Id.* at 2, 88–113.

one preemptory challenge; thereafter, a party could challenge an arbitrator only for cause, a difficult standard to meet.[86]

Implementation of these proposals is discussed later in this chapter.[87]

In addition, the Ruder Report recommended the expansion of a voluntary mediation program to prove a more informal alternative to arbitration.[88] It also recommended a prohibition against brokerage firms raising issues of procedural arbitrability in judicial proceedings before entry of an arbitration award.[89]

The Ruder Report assumed, but did not closely examine the question, that arbitrators should apply the law; this is made clear in its recommendation that arbitrators should receive more training in substantive law.[90] Its most explicit statement to this effect is found in a note: "Although we recognize that arbitration generally is considered to be an equitable forum, we believe that arbitrators should consider applicable statutory and common law with respect to all matters as to which they must make decisions in the arbitration forum. …"[91]

Punitive damages At the time of the Ruder Report the award by arbitration panels of punitive damages was a hotly debated issue. In its 1995 opinion, *Mastrobuono v. Shearson Lehman Hutton, Inc.*,[92] the Supreme Court held that a choice-of-law provision specifying New York law (which at that time did not permit arbitrators to award punitive damages) contained in a standard-form customer's agreement did not preclude an arbitral award of punitive damages. *Mastrobuono* did not, however, in the view of the Ruder Report, "resolve the policy issue of whether punitive damages *should* be available in securities arbitrations."[93] Investors asserted that they should have the same right to recover punitive damages in arbitration as they did in court, and the SEC agreed with

---

86 *Id.* at 93–94.

87 *See infra* notes 104–129 and accompanying text.

88 Ruder Report at 47. NASD adopted a separate Code of Mediation Procedure effective Jan. 30, 2006; the current version is posted on its website, http://:finra.complinet.com:/en:/:display/:display_main.html?rbid=2403&element_id=4293. FINRA encourages parties to use non-binding mediation as an alternative to arbitration.

89 Ruder Report at 2, 32–33.

90 *Id.* at 108–10.

91 *Id.* at 31, note 51.

92 514 U.S. 52 (1995).

93 Ruder Report at 40 (emphasis added).

them.[94] Brokers, on the other hand, asserted that punitive damages were inappropriate in arbitration because procedural safeguards and the right of appeal were limited.[95] The Ruder Report's recommendations on punitive damages illustrate its ambivalence over the issue. It recommended that investors be able to recover punitive damages in arbitration in situations where courts in the relevant state would award them (even if the relevant state did not recognize the authority of arbitrators to award punitive damages), but also recommended a cap on the amount of punitive damages awarded in arbitration.[96] NASD proposed a rule capping punitive damages that it subsequently withdrew.[97] FINRA takes the position that the Supreme Court's limits on punitive damages deal with the issue.

The eligibility rule FINRA first adopted an eligibility rule in 1968 that barred stale claims from the forum claims. FINRA Rule 12206(a) provides that "[no] claim shall be eligible for submission to arbitration under the Code where six years have elapsed from the occurrence or event giving rise to the claim." FINRA's eligibility rule operates independently of any applicable statute of limitations (although whether statutes of limitations apply to arbitration claims varies from state to state and is often not clear). Dismissal of a claim under Rule 12206 does not prohibit a party from pursuing the claim in court, and by filing a motion to dismiss under the eligibility rule, the moving party agrees that if the panel dismisses a claim under Rule 12206, the non-moving party may

[94] *Supra* note 78 and accompanying text. Article III, § 21(f) of NASD's Rules of Fair Practice was not before the Court in *Mastrobuono*, since the customer's agreement was entered into prior to its effective date.

[95] The Supreme Court has held that there are due process limitations on the award of punitive damages; *see* Cooper Indus., Inc. v. Leatherman Tool Group, Inc., 532 U.S. 424 (2001). Circuit courts have split on whether due process limitations are applicable in securities arbitration. *Compare* Glennon v. Dean Witter, 83 F.3d 132 (6th Cir. 1996) (assuming due process concerns are applicable), *with* Davis v. Prudential Securities, Inc., 59 F.3d 1186 (11th Cir. 1995) (asserting due process concerns are not applicable).

[96] Ruder Report at 36–45.

[97] Self-Regulatory Organizations; Notice of Filing of Amendments Nos 3 and 4 to a Proposed rule Change by the National Association of Securities Dealers, Inc., Relating to NASD Rule 3110(f) Governing Use of Predispute Arbitration Agreements with Customers, Exch. Act Rel. No. 34–48444, 80 S.E.C. Docket 2917 (Sept. 4, 2003).

withdraw any remaining related claims without prejudice and may pursue all claims in court.[98]

The Ruder Report noted that the eligibility rule had deleterious unintended consequences. Brokerage firms went to court, seeking to enjoin arbitrations based on the eligibility rule, which led to extended collateral litigation. This created confusion about the rule's application and contributed to the erosion of investor confidence in the SRO arbitration forum.[99] In the view of the Ruder Report, a preferable approach to stale claims would be to direct arbitrators to decide statute of limitations issues based on applicable law.

The Supreme Court largely solved the problem of collateral litigation by holding, in *Howsam v. Dean Witter Reynolds, Inc.*,[100] that the applicability of the eligibility rule was a procedural question that did not present a "question of arbitrability"[101] and therefore was presumptively a matter for the arbitrator to decide, not a judge.[102] While the Court decided a narrow procedural issue, its opinion made an important point: that NASD arbitrators should decide those issues for which they have greater expertise than judges in interpreting the forum's own rules. More broadly, the Court indicated its confidence in the arbitration process. Rule 12206(a) reinforces the Supreme Court's holding by expressly providing that the panel will resolve any questions regarding the eligibility of claims.

KEY REFORMS IN RESPONSE TO THE RUDER REPORT

From 1997 to 2007, NASD filed more than 65 proposed rule changes with the SEC dealing with various aspects of its securities arbitration process.[103] This section addresses the regulatory response to two key

---

[98] FINRA Rule 12206(b). The Rule also sets forth the procedure for making a motion to dismiss under the eligibility rule.

[99] Ruder Report at 23.

[100] 537 U.S. 79 (2002).

[101] Questions of arbitrability are presented when there is a question whether the party is bound by an agreement to arbitrate, *id.* at 84. *See also* Barbara Black, *Securities Arbitration Is Not Supposed To Be So Complicated: Arbitrability, the Eligibility Rule, and Whose Law Decides,* 30 SEC. REG. L.J. 134, 137–40 (2002).

[102] 537 U.S. 79 (2002) at 85.

[103] Jill I. Gross, McMahon *Turns Twenty: The Regulation of Fairness in Securities Arbitration*, 76 U. CIN. L. REV. 493, 514 (2008).

issues identified in the Ruder Report: the discovery process and the selection, classification and training of arbitrators.

The Discovery Guide In 1999 the SEC approved the NASD's Discovery Guide, a consensus document developed over a two-year period to address the Ruder Report's recommendations to improve the exchange of information in arbitration proceedings.[104] Participants in the process included members of SICA, members of the SIA, directors of the Public Interest Arbitration Bar Association, industry representatives, and counsel for both claimants and industry. As described in the SEC release:

> NASD Regulation proposes to create a Discovery Guide to streamline the discovery process in NASD arbitrations involving customers. The Discovery Guide, which contains Document Production Lists, provides parties to an arbitration proceeding guidance on which documents they should exchange without arbitrator or NASD Regulation staff intervention. Further, the Discovery Guide provides arbitrators with guidance in determining which documents should be produced by customers and member firms or associated persons in customer arbitrations.
>
> The Discovery Guide, which includes the Document Production Lists, is intended to function as a guide for parties and arbitrators in the discovery process. It is not intended to bind arbitrators or parties in a particular case. Further, nothing in the Discovery Guide precludes parties from voluntarily agreeing to an exchange of documents in a manner or scope different from that set forth in the Discovery Guide or Document Production Lists. In addition, any party can make a motion objecting to the production of particular documents included on the applicable Document Production List(s) in any arbitration proceeding. Likewise, any party can request that additional documents, not included on any of the Document Production Lists, be produced. However, if an arbitrator directs compliance with the Discovery Guide in connection with ordering the production of documents, the order, like any other document production order, is binding on the parties.[105]

The Discovery Guide, as approved in 1999, included fourteen Document Production Lists. The first two lists set forth documents that were presumptively discoverable in all customer cases. The other lists set forth additional presumptively discoverable documents tailored with respect to the alleged misconduct. The Discovery Guide also provides guidance on

---

[104] Self-Regulatory Organizations; Order Granting Approval to Proposed Rule Change by the National Association of Securities Dealers, Inc. Creating a Discovery Guide for Use in NASD Arbitrations, Exch. Act Rel. No. 34–41833, 70 S.E.C. Docket 1139 (Sept. 2, 1999).

[105] *Id.*

other issues such as confidential treatment of documents, depositions and sanctions.

In 2011 the SEC approved amendments to the Discovery Guide and observed that the revisions were the product of "over six years of consultation by FINRA with its constituents."[106] The amendments included consolidation of the fourteen-document production lists into two, in response to suggestions from advocates for claimants to eliminate the twelve lists for specific claims since claimants are not required to plead causes of action.[107]

The Discovery Guide was a welcome and largely uncontroversial improvement to the NASD arbitration process. While over the years there have been numerous complaints about abuse of the discovery process, FINRA has issued Notices to Members to remind them that it monitors compliance with discovery orders and has brought disciplinary proceedings against brokerage firms for failures to comply.[108]

Arbitrator selection, classification and training Since *McMahon,* FINRA has grappled with the related issues of arbitrator selection, classification and training. In particular, investor advocates wanted customers to have the ability to select their own arbitrators and to select a panel consisting wholly of public arbitrators. Twenty-four years later, investors can do just that.

Arbitrator Selection

(a) The Neutral List Selection System ("NLSS") Investor representatives had long advocated for a role in the selection of the arbitrators who would decide their cases. In 1998 NASD responded by proposing new procedures for the selection of arbitrators.[109] The NLSS allowed the

---

[106] Self-Regulatory Organizations; Financial Industry Regulatory Authority, Inc.; Notice of Filing of Amendment No. 1 and Order Granting Accelerated Approval of a Proposed Rule Change, as Modified by Amendment No. 1, Relating to Amendments to the Discovery Guide and Rules 12506 and 12508 of the Code of Arbitration Procedure for Customer Disputes. Exch. Act Rel. No. 34–64166, 100 S.E.C. Docket 2909 (Apr. 1, 2011).

[107] *Id.*

[108] *See, e.g.,* NASD Fines Citigroup, Merrill Lynch and Morgan Stanley a Total of $750,000 for Failing to Comply with Discovery Obligations in Arbitrations (July 19, 2004), http://www.finra.org/newsroom/newsreleases/2004/p009925.

[109] Self-Regulatory Organizations; Order Granting Approval to Proposed Rule Change and Notice of Filing and Order Granting Accelerated Approval to

parties to rank arbitrators from lists generated through an automated process.[110] The SEC approved the proposal because it believed "that allowing parties greater input into the selection of the arbitrators to hear their cases will help ensure a more fair and neutral arbitration process."[111] In cases heard by a three-person arbitration panel,[112] parties received two lists of arbitrators, one for public arbitrators, one for industry arbitrators, along with background information on each arbitrator and a list of arbitration awards signed by the arbitrator. Parties could strike any and all names on the lists and rank the remaining ones. NASD then appointed the two highest-ranking public arbitrators and the highest-ranking industry arbitrator. In the event the panel could not be filled from the consolidated lists, NASD filled the panel with arbitrators from another computer-generated list, whom the parties could challenge for cause. As originally adopted, the pubic arbitrator who received the highest ranking was appointed chairperson. In 2007, as part of the extensive Code revision,[113] the selection process was changed to provide for a separate list of chairperson-qualified arbitrators.[114]

(b) The All Public Panel Option After adoption of the NLSS, many investor advocates continued to have suspicions about the fairness and

---

Amendment Nos 3 and 4 to Proposed Rule Change by the National Association of Securities Dealers, Inc., Relating to the Selection of Arbitrators in Arbitrations Involving Public Customers, Exch. Act No. 34–40555, 63 Fed. R.eg 56670 (Oct. 22, 1998).

110 Effective 2005, the method of generating the arbitrator lists was changed from rotational to random, Self-Regulatory Organizations; Order Approving Proposed Rule Change and Amendment No. 1 Thereto by National Association of Securities Dealers, Inc. Relating to the Random Selection of Arbitrators by the Neutral List Selection System, Exch. Act No. 34–51339 (Mar. 9, 2005).

111 Self-Regulatory Organizations; Order Granting Approval to Proposed Rule Change and Notice of Filing and Order Granting Accelerated Approval to Amendment Nos 3 and 4 to Proposed Rule Change by the National Association of Securities Dealers, Inc., Relating to the Selection of Arbitrators in Arbitrations Involving Public Customers, Exch. Act No. 34–40555, 63 Fed. Reg. 56670 (Oct. 22, 1998).

112 Under the current rule, a three-person panel hears arbitrations of claims of more than $100,000, as well as claims that do not specify an amount and do not request money damages. Claims that are $50,000 or less are heard by one arbitrator. Claims that are more than $50,000 but not more than $100,000 are heard by one arbitrator, unless the parties agree to three. FINRA Rule 12401. In arbitrations heard by one person, the arbitrator is a public arbitrator.

113 *See infra* note 130 and accompanying text.

114 *See infra* notes 124–25 and accompanying text.

neutrality of the SRO arbitration forums because of the mandatory presence of a non-public, or industry, arbitrator on each three-person arbitration panel. A 2008 survey of users of the NASD and NYSE arbitration forums found that (1) investors have a far more negative perception of securities arbitration than all other participants, and (2) investors have a strong negative perception of the bias of arbitrators.[115] Industry representatives denied there was any evidence of a pro-industry bias and argued that the presence of an industry arbitrator provided expertise that benefitted both parties.[116] After years of resisting pressure to eliminate the requirement of a mandatory industry arbitrator, in 2008 FINRA took steps to move in that direction by launching a voluntary pilot program with a number of brokerage firms that allowed eligible claimants to select all public panels. FINRA cited the positive reaction from participants in the pilot program as a motivating factor for its October 2010 proposed rule change to give customers the option to choose an arbitration panel consisting entirely of public arbitrators.[117]

As approved by the SEC in early 2011,[118] customers can choose between two panel selection options: the Majority Public Panel, which retains the current panel composition method, or the Optional All Public Panel, which allows any party to select an all public panel. Customers must affirmatively elect the Optional All Public Panel procedures early in the process, otherwise, FINRA applies the procedures for the Majority Public Panel option. Under the Majority Public Panel option, the parties select their panel by striking names from three lists (public arbitrator, chairperson, and non-public arbitrator), each containing ten arbitrators,

---

[115] Jill I. Gross & Barbara Black, *When Perception Changes Reality: An Empirical Study of Investors' Views of the Fairness of Securities Arbitration,* 2008 J. DISPUTE RESOLUTION 349.

[116] Sec. Indus. & Fin. Mkts. Ass'n,, *White Paper on Arbitration in the Securities Industry* 35 (Oct. 2007), *available at* http://www.sifma.org/issues/item.aspx?id=21334.

[117] Self-Regulatory Organizations; Financial Industry Regulatory Authority, Inc.; Notice of Filing of Proposed Rule Change Relating to Amendments to the Panel Composition Rule, and Related Rules, of the Code of Arbitration Procedure for Customer Disputes, Exch. Act No. 34–63250, 75 Fed. Reg. 69481, 69482 (Nov. 12, 2010).

[118] Self-Regulatory Organizations; Financial Industry Regulatory Authority, Inc.; Notice of Filing of Amendment No. 1 and Order Granting Accelerated Approval of a Proposed Rule Change Relating to Amendments to the Panel Composition Rule, and Related Rules, of the Code of Arbitration Procedure for Customer Disputes, Exch. Act No. 34–63799, 100 S.E.C. Docket 1148 (Jan. 31, 2011).

and then ranking the remaining arbitrators. Each party may strike up to four names from each list, and FINRA appoints the panel from among the names remaining on the lists that the parties return. The process for striking non-public arbitrators, however, is different under the Optional All Public Panel approach. Instead of limiting strikes to four non-public arbitrators, each party can strike all ten names and thus guarantee that no non-public arbitrator would be appointed to the panel. Instead, FINRA appoints the next highest-ranked public arbitrator to complete the panel.

Providing investors with the option of an all-public arbitrator panel was a welcome, and long overdue, improvement. In 2012, the first complete year that the all public panel option was in effect, all public panels awarded damages in 49 percent of cases, while majority public panels awarded damages in 33 percent.[119] In 2013 FINRA proposed a rule change that would no longer require customers to elect a panel selection method. Instead, parties in all customer cases with three arbitrators would receive three lists of arbitrators (chair-qualified, public and non-public). Any party could select an all public panel by striking all non-public arbitrators from the list.[120]

Classification of Arbitrators

Investors' advocates have, over the years, raised concerns that they do not perceive certain arbitrators on FINRA's public arbitrator roster as public because of their background or experience. FINRA has frequently amended the definition of public and non-public (industry) arbitrators to exclude individuals with significant ties to the securities industry from serving as public arbitrators.[121]

The definition of non-public arbitrator in effect in 2013[122] means:

---

[119] There were 99 cases decided by all public panels, and 111 cases by majority public panels. http://www.finra.org/ArbitrationAndMediation/FINRADisputeResolution/AdditionalResources/Statistics/

[120] Self-Regulatory Organizations; Financial Industry Regulatory Authority, Inc.; Notice of Filing of Proposed Rule Change Relating to Amendments to the Code of Arbitration Procedure for Customer Disputes Concerning Panel Composition. Exch. Act Rel. No. 34–69762, 78 Fed. Reg. 37269 (June 20, 2013).

[121] *See, e.g.,* Self-Regulatory Organizations; National Association of Securities Dealers, Inc.; Order Granting Approval to a Proposed Rule Change Relating to Arbitrator Classification and Disclosure in NASD Arbitrations, Exch. Act Rel. 34–49573, 71 Fed. Reg. 21871 (Apr. 22, 2004) (modifying definitions of public and non-public arbitrator in response to recommendations in Perino Report, in order to provide additional assurance to investors that process is neutral and fair).

[122] FINRA Rule 12100(p).

- Anyone who is currently, or was within the past five years, associated with a broker-dealer or registered under the Commodity Exchange Act, a member of a commodities exchange or a registered futures association, or associated with a member or firm registered under the Commodity Exchange Act;
- Anyone who is retired from, or spent a substantial part of his career engaged in, any of the business activities listed above;
- Any professional (including attorneys and accountants) who has devoted at least 20 percent of his professional work in the last two years to clients who are engaged in the business activities listed above;
- An employee of a bank or other financial institution who effects transactions in securities and commodities futures or options, or monitors the compliance of employees engaged in these activities.

Conversely, the definition of public arbitrator in effect as of July 1, 2013,[123] means anyone who is *not*:

- Engaged in the conduct or activities described above (i.e., securities and commodities options and futures) or was engaged in those activities for a total of twenty years;
- An investment adviser or associated with a mutual fund or hedge fund;
- A professional whose firm derived at least 10 percent of its annual revenue in the past two years from clients in the securities and commodities future industry;
- A professional whose firm derived at least $50,000 in annual revenue in the past two years from services rendered to respondents in customer disputes concerning investment accounts or transactions;
- An employee of an affiliate of a securities firm;
- A director or officer of an affiliate of a securities firm.

In addition, spouses and immediate family members are generally excluded from the definition of public arbitrator. Anyone whom FINRA would not designate as a public arbitrator because of an above-listed affiliation will not be designated as a public arbitrator for two calendar years after ending the affiliation.

---

[123] FINRA Rule 12100(u).

Qualifications for Chairperson

In the 2007 Code revision FINRA created a chairperson roster and established eligibility requirements for service as a chairperson.[124] Previously, parties could agree to select any of the three arbitrators as the chairperson, or, failing agreement, staff would select the highest-ranked public arbitrator. Because of the increased responsibilities placed on chairpersons to manage the arbitration process, FINRA determined that they should meet certain standards of qualifications, experience and training. In essence, this was a watered-down effort to create a more professional corps of arbitrators.

In customer disputes, chairpersons must be public arbitrators. In addition, arbitrators are eligible for the chairperson roster if they have completed FINRA's chairperson training[125] and

- Have a law degree, are a member of a bar, and have served as an arbitrator through award in at least two SRO arbitrations in which hearings were held; or
- Have served as an arbitrator through award on at least three SRO arbitrations in which hearings were held.

Arbitrator Training

Since *McMahon*, securities arbitration has increasingly become a quasi-judicial process, with frequently contentious disputes over discovery requests and motions. More claims are filed, sometimes based on novel legal theories, and larger awards are issued, sometimes with substantial punitive damages. Arbitrators' responsibilities have increased, as have the parties' expectations that arbitrators can handle these responsibilities.

Since 1993, FINRA has required all new arbitrators to receive mandatory arbitration training.[126] The Ruder Report found that "the overall

---

[124] FINRA Rule 12400(b), (c).

[125] Chairperson training is an online course that requires approximately nine hours of study time and can be completed over a period of thirty days, http://www.finra.org/ArbitrationAndMediation/Arbitrators/Training/AdvancedTraining/P124939.

[126] The Basic Arbitrator Training Program consists of an online basic arbitrator training course, an online expungement training course and a live video or onsite classroom training session, http://www.finra.org/ArbitrationAndMediation/Arbitrators/BecomeanArbitrator/WhattoExpect/index.htm

performance of NASD arbitrators is not as high as it could be"[127] and called for enhanced arbitrator training, particularly for chairpersons, and increased compensation for arbitrators. Since then FINRA has worked to improve the training of arbitrators, from the basic arbitrator and chairperson training programs to a series of subject-specific online modules.[128] There is general recognition of the need for more training, but uncertainty about how to accomplish this in a manner that is both effective and efficient from the perspectives of both cost and time. Moreover, the premise of an arbitration panel consisting of lay decision-makers who receive nominal consideration for hearing disputes on an occasional basis goes largely unchallenged.[129]

OTHER IMPORTANT REFORMS

The 2007 revision of the arbitration code The SEC's "plain English" initiative was the impetus for NASD's project to rewrite the arbitration rules to make them more "user-friendly," and in 2003 NASD filed with the SEC a completely revised arbitration code for customer claims.[130] The project evolved from this modest goal to include a complete reorganization of the arbitration code, codification of some current arbitration practices, and a few significant substantive changes, such as the creation of the chair-qualified public arbitrator classification.[131] Although NASD resisted efforts to convert the project into a vehicle for major reforms, the numerous comments filed with the SEC in the course of the extended rulemaking served to set the agenda for future reforms, including the all public panel option.[132] The SEC approved the new arbitration code in 2007.[133]

---

[127] Ruder Report at 108.

[128] Described at http://www.finra.org/ArbitrationAndMediation/Arbitrators/Training/

[129] Barbara Black, *Do We Expect Too Much from NASD Arbitrators?* SECURITIES ARBITRATION COMMENTATOR 1 (vol. 2004, no. 7).

[130] Self-Regulatory Organizations; National Association of Securities Dealers, Inc.; Notice of Filing of Proposed Rule Change and Amendment Nos 1, 2, 3, and 4 Thereto To Amend NASD Arbitration Rules for Customer Disputes, Exch. Act Rel. No. 34–51856, 70 Fed. Reg. 36442 (June 23, 2005).

[131] *See supra* notes 124–25 and accompanying text.

[132] *See supra* note 116 and accompanying text.

[133] Self-Regulatory Organizations; National Association of Securities Dealers, Inc.; Order Approving Proposed Rule Change and Amendments 1, 2, 3, and 4 To Amend NASD Arbitration Rules for Customer Disputes and Notice of

The new code for the first time explicitly recognized motion practice. Although NASD acknowledged the concern, expressed in the Ruder Report and by other commentators, about the increasing use of motions in arbitration, it opted to accept the reality of motion practice as part of the arbitration process and added a rule that established procedures and deadlines for making, responding to, and deciding motions.[134] NASD's proposed rule to authorize dispositive motions before a hearing on the merits was especially controversial. In the face of numerous critical comments NASD withdrew the dispositive motions proposed rule; it was revised, reproposed and adopted, as described below.

Dispositive motions Dispositive motions, or motions to dismiss claims prior to a hearing on the merits, were for many years one of the most controversial issues. Customers and their representatives firmly believed that they had a right to present their claims before an arbitration panel, particularly since arbitration practice does not require claimants to state a legal claim and arbitrators have considerable discretion about whether to apply the law in deciding the dispute. Therefore, they asserted, motions to dismiss for failure to state a legal claim were not appropriate in the arbitration forum. Respondents and their representatives, in contrast, believed strongly that there needed to be an expeditious process for dismissing frivolous claims. The "plain English" revision of the Code, as originally filed with the SEC in 2003,[135] included a rule that would have allowed arbitration panels to grant dispositive motions in extraordinary circumstances. Because it soon became clear that this was a contentious issue, NASD withdrew the proposed rule from the code revision, and refiled it separately in 2006, but subsequently withdrew it because of criticisms that it did not provide effective guidance on the handling of dispositive motions. FINRA redrafted the proposed rule to provide specific procedures to govern dispositive motions and filed it with the SEC in 2007.[136] FINRA stated that the rule was necessary because of

---

Filing and Order Granting Accelerated Approval of Amendments 5, 6, and 7 Thereto; Order Approving Proposed Rule Change and Amendments 1, 2, 3, and 4 To Amend NASD Arbitration Rules for Industry Disputes and Notice of Filing and Order Granting Accelerated Approval of Amendments 5, 6, and 7 Thereto, Exch. Act Rel. No. 34–55158, 72 Fed. Reg. 4574 (Jan. 31, 2007).

[134] FINRA Rule 12503.

[135] *See supra* note 130 and accompanying text.

[136] Self-Regulatory Organizations; Financial Industry Regulatory Authority, Inc.; Notice of Filing of Proposed Rule Change and Amendment No. 1 Relating to Amendments to the Code of Arbitration Procedure for Customer Disputes and

> concerns raised by investors' counsel, SEC staff and other constituent groups about abusive and duplicative filing of dispositive motions. Specifically, FINRA received complaints that parties (typically respondent firms) were filing dispositive motions routinely and repetitively in an apparent effort to delay scheduled hearing sessions on the merits, increase investors' costs, and intimidate less sophisticated parties. In some cases, if parties did not receive a favorable ruling on a dispositive motion filed at a particular stage in an arbitration proceeding, they would refile the same or similar dispositive motion at a later time, which often served only to increase investors' costs and delay the hearing and the issuance of the award. Moreover, FINRA learned through various constituent and focus groups that some respondents' attorneys were being counseled by their firms that an acceptable and useful tactic was to file multiple dispositive motions at various stages of an arbitration proceeding.[137]

The final rule[138] begins with a policy statement: motions to dismiss a claim prior to the conclusion of a party's case in chief are "discouraged in arbitration."[139] The rule goes on to set forth the procedure for making such motions to dismiss. They must be made in writing, separately from the answer, and after the answer is filed.[140] The rule sets forth filing deadlines to prevent a moving party from filing a motion shortly before a hearing as a surprise and delaying tactic.[141] The full panel must decide a motion to dismiss,[142] and a panel cannot decide a motion to dismiss prior to the conclusion of a party's case in chief unless the panel holds a

---

the Code of Arbitration Procedure for Industry Disputes To Address Motions To Dismiss and To Amend the Eligibility Rule Related to Dismissals, Exch. Act Rel. No. 34–57497, 73 Fed. Reg. 15019 (Mar. 20, 2008).

[137] *Id.* at 15021. The release approving the rule cites a Securities Arbitration Commentator study showing that the number of motions to dismiss filed in customer cases had begun to increase over a two-year period starting in 2004, a finding FINRA called "alarming," Self-Regulatory Organizations; Financial Industry Regulatory Authority, Inc.; Order Approving Proposed Rule Change, as Modified by Amendment No. 1 Thereto, Relating to Amendments to the Code of Arbitration Procedure for Customer Disputes and the Code of Arbitration Procedure for Industry Disputes To Address Motions To Dismiss and To Amend the Eligibility Rule Related to Dismissals, Exch. Act Rel. No. 34–57497, 74 Fed. Reg. 731, 739 (Jan. 7, 2009). In 2007 FINRA began tracking motions to dismiss filed in the forum and found that the number of motions to dismiss may be declining, perhaps because of its focus on this issue. *Id.* at 740.

[138] Rel. 12504.

[139] *Id.* (a)(1).

[140] *Id.* (a)(2).

[141] *Id.* (a)(3).

[142] *Id.* (a)(4).

recorded in-person or telephonic conference.[143] The panel can only grant motions to dismiss prior to the conclusion of a party's case in chief upon the following grounds: (1) the non-moving party previously released the claim in writing, or (2) the moving party was not associated with the accounts, securities or conduct at issue.[144] A motion to dismiss can only be granted upon a unanimous, explained written decision.[145] A party is prohibited from refiling a denied motion to dismiss without specific permission from the panel.[146] The rule also requires arbitrators to award fees associated with denied motions to dismiss against the party filing the motion[147] and to award fees and costs associated with frivolously filed motions to the prevailing party.[148] If the panel determines that a party filed a motion in bad faith, it may also impose sanctions.[149]

Expungement The Central Registration Depository ("CRD"®) is the securities industry's online registration and licensing database.[150] NASD operates the CRD system pursuant to policies developed jointly with the North American Securities Administrators Association ("NASAA"). Information in the CRD is obtained through forms that brokerage firms, associated persons and regulators complete as part of the securities industry registration and licensing process. The CRD includes information about criminal matters, regulatory disciplinary actions, civil judicial actions, and information relating to customer disputes, such as customer complaints, arbitration claims, and arbitration awards. Through BrokerCheck® investors can research the professional backgrounds of brokerage firms and associated persons.[151]

There has long been a tension between the importance of accurate historical information and the harm that can result to an associated person if a customer's complaint is unfounded. Since the inception of the CRD system in 1981, NASD generally honored court-ordered expungements, and until January 1999 it honored arbitrator-ordered expungements contained in final awards. NASAA and some states, however, took the position that information in the CRD system was a record of any state

---

143 *Id.* (a)(5).
144 *Id.* (a)(6).
145 *Id.* (a)(7).
146 *Id.* (a)(8).
147 FINRA Rule 12504(a)(9).
148 FINRA Rule 12504(a)(10).
149 FINRA Rule 12504(a)(11).
150 http://www.finra.org/industry/compliance/registration/crd/.
151 http://www.finra.org/Investors/ToolsCalculators/BrokerCheck/.

that used the information in making licensing decisions, and that state laws did not permit expungement without an explicit court order. In January 1999, NASD announced a moratorium on arbitrator-ordered expungements unless the award was confirmed by a court of competent jurisdiction and undertook to establish clear standards for expungement.

In 2002, NASD filed a proposed rule change with the SEC to establish procedures for expunging customer dispute information from the CRD system.[152] NASD acknowledged:

> the need to balance three competing interests: (1) the interests of NASD, the states, and other regulators in retaining broad access to customer dispute information to fulfill their regulatory responsibilities and investor protection obligations; (2) the interests of the brokerage community and others in a fair process that recognizes their stake in protecting their reputations and permits expungement from the CRD system when appropriate; and (3) the interests of investors in having access to accurate and meaningful information about brokers with whom they conduct, or may conduct, business.[153]

Indeed, while there was general agreement about the need for a rule establishing procedures and criteria for expungement, there was considerable debate over both the procedures and the criteria. NASAA took the position that only "factually impossible" claims should be expunged, while representatives of the brokerage community urged that it was unfair to require associated persons to institute a cumbersome procedure to remove from their record unfounded allegations by disgruntled customers. The final product was necessarily a product of compromise.

The rule[154] requires all directives to expunge customer dispute information from the CRD system to be confirmed by or ordered by a court of competent jurisdiction and requires the brokerage firm or associated person to name NASD as a party in any judicial proceeding seeking confirmation of an arbitration award containing expungement relief. NASD may, however, waive the requirement to name it as a party if it determines that the requested expungement relief is based on affirmative judicial or arbitral findings that (1) the claim, allegation or information is factually impossible or clearly erroneous, (2) the associated person was

---

[152] Self-Regulatory Organizations; Notice of Filing of Proposed Rule Change and Amendment No. 1 Thereto by the National Association of Securities Dealers, Inc. Relating to Proposed Rule 2130 Concerning the Expungement of Customer Dispute Information From the Central Registration Depository System, Exch. Act Rel. No. 34–47435, 68 Fed. Reg. 11435 (Mar. 10, 2003).

[153] *Id.* at 11437.

[154] FINRA Rule 2080.

not involved in the alleged investment-related sales practice violation, forgery, theft, misappropriation or conversion of funds, or (3) the claim, allegation, or information is false.[155] In addition, NASD has sole discretion "under extraordinary circumstances" to waive the requirement if the expungement request is meritorious and expungement would not have a material adverse effect on investor protection, the integrity of the CRD system, or regulatory requirements.[156] In approving the rule, the SEC stated that it was "clearly an improvement over the current expungement system in which there are no parameters placed on expungements being incorporated into arbitration awards."[157]

By 2008, FINRA became aware that some arbitrators were approving expungement requests that were part of a negotiated settlement without inquiring into the terms of the settlement.[158] Accordingly, FINRA proposed, and the SEC approved, procedures that arbitrators must follow in granting expungement requests. Specifically, the panel must (i) hold a recorded hearing session by telephone or in person regarding the appropriateness of expungement, even if a claimant did not request a hearing on the merits; (ii) for cases involving settlements, review the settlement documents to examine the amount paid to any party and any other terms and conditions of the settlement that might raise concerns about the associated person's involvement in the alleged misconduct before awarding expungement; (iii) indicate in the arbitration award which of the grounds for expungement in Rule 2130 serves as the basis for the expungement order and provide a brief written explanation of the reason(s) for its finding that one or more grounds for expungement

---

[155] *Id.* (b)(1).

[156] *Id.* (b)(2).

[157] Self-Regulatory Organizations; National Association of Securities Dealers, Inc; Order Granting Approval of Proposed Rule Change and Amendment No. 1, Thereto, and Notice of Filing and Order Granting Accelerated Approval to Amendment No. 2, Thereto, Relating to Proposed NASD Rule 2130 Concerning the Expungement of Customer Dispute Information From the Central Registration Depository System, Exch. Act Rel. No. 34–48933, 68 Fed. Reg. 74667, 74672 (Dec. 24, 2003).

[158] Self-Regulatory Organizations; Financial Industry Regulatory Authority, Inc.; Order Approving a Proposed Rule Change Amending the Codes of Arbitration Procedure To Establish Procedures for Arbitrators To Follow When Considering Requests for Expungement Relief, Exch. Act Rel. No. 34–48933, 73 Fed. Reg. 66086, 66087 (Nov. 6, 2008).

exists; and (iv) assess forum fees for hearing sessions in which the sole topic is the determination of the appropriateness of expungement against the parties requesting expungement.[159]

In the public comment period, some commenters questioned whether it was appropriate to give the responsibility of expungement to arbitrators rather than regulators, given the importance of the CRD system in providing information to investors. FINRA asserted that these comments were beyond the scope of the rulemaking process, but the SEC, in approving the rule, stated its expectation that expungement would be an "extraordinary remedy."[160] Moreover, "[b]ecause of the central role that arbitrators have in the expungement process, the Commission believes that it is critical for arbitrators to be well-informed regarding FINRA's rules governing expungement."[161] FINRA, in turn, requires all arbitrators to take an online expungement training course.[162] The SEC also urged FINRA that "[g]iven the importance of CRD for regulators and to customers … to monitor how this rule is applied by arbitrators to assure that it is achieving its goals, and to propose additional changes, if needed."[163]

Reasoned awards Awards must be in writing and are publicly available. They must contain certain bare-bones information, including the names of the parties, a summary of the issues, the damages and other relief requested and the damages and other relief granted.[164] Although the award "may contain a rationale underlying the award,"[165] this is not the usual practice. A common complaint among parties, particularly customers, who are dissatisfied with the outcome of arbitration, is the absence of any explanation. Yet arbitrators are not judges, and requiring them to write decisions is counter to an informal, expedited process. In addition, the presence of an explanation may increase the possibility of judicial review of the arbitration award, which is also contrary to the understanding that, except in rare cases, such as arbitrator misconduct,

---

159 FINRA Rule 12805.

160 73 Fed. Reg. at 66089.

161 73 Fed. Reg. at 66090.

162 http://www.finra.org/ArbitrationAndMediation/Arbitrators/Training/RequiredBasicArbitratorTraining/P124905.

163 73 Fed. Reg. at 66090.

164 FINRA Rule 12904(e).

165 *Id.* (f).

arbitration awards are final and non-reviewable.[166] *Hardy v. Walsh Manning Securities, LLC*[167] illustrates the danger. The arbitration panel stated in its award that both the firm and the CEO were "jointly and severally liable … based on the principles of respondeat superior." The district court confirmed the award, even though employees cannot be held liable under respondeat superior, because it found evidence in the record of the CEO's personal involvement in the wrongdoing. The Second Circuit, however, vacated the award as to the CEO and directed a remand to the arbitration panel for clarification of the grounds for imposing liability on the CEO.

FINRA first tackled this issue in 2005, when NASD filed a proposed rule change with the SEC to require arbitrators to provide explained decisions upon the request of customers, in order to increase investor confidence in the fairness of the arbitration process.[168] The proposed rule received many critical comments, including brokerage representatives' complaints about its "one-sided nature." In addition, many commenters, both from the industry and investors' advocates, feared that explained decisions would result in more motions to vacate. FINRA withdrew the proposed rule in 2008 and subsequently filed a revised proposed rule, which the SEC approved in 2009.[169]

FINRA took pains to distinguish the reproposed rule from its earlier version: all parties must request an explained decision, the request must be made sufficiently in advance of the hearing to provide notice to the arbitration panel, and only the chairperson was responsible for preparing the explained decision. In addition, FINRA emphasized that it was a "fact-based award stating general reasons:"

> FINRA believes that requiring only fact-based reasons in explained decisions will reduce the potential for misstatements in an award, thereby decreasing the possibility of a subsequent vacatur, modification or remand of an award and ensuring the continued finality of a FINRA award. FINRA believes the proposed rule change would provide the parties with the information they

---

[166] *See generally* Barbara Black & Jill Gross, *The Explained Award of Damocles: Protection or Peril in Securities Arbitration,* 34 SEC. REG. L. J. 17 (2006).

[167] 341 F.3d 126 (2d Cir. 2003).

[168] Black & Gross, *supra* note 166, at 19.

[169] Self-Regulatory Organizations; Financial Industry Regulatory Authority, Inc.; Order Approving Proposed Rule Change Relating to Amendments to the Codes of Arbitration Procedure To Require Arbitrators To Provide an Explained Decision Upon the Joint Request of the Parties. Exch. Act Rel. No. 34–48933, 74 Fed. Reg. 6928 (Feb. 11, 2009).

> want while simultaneously maintaining the expediency, flexibility, and finality of arbitration.[170]

The final rule requires the chairperson to provide "an explained decision," described as a "fact-based award stating general reason(s) for the arbitrators' decision," which need not include legal authorities or damages calculations, if all parties jointly request it no later than the time for the prehearing exchange of documents and witness lists (generally twenty days before the first scheduled hearing date).[171] Arbitrators maintain the discretion to write an explained decision in other instances.[172]

The SEC approved the new rule, but expressed doubt about whether it would, in fact, promote investors' perceptions of fairness, particularly since the industry party could thwart a customer's desire for an explanation. Nevertheless, it concluded that the rule represented "a reasonable compromise between the status quo, whereby the Codes offer parties no formal means of requesting an explained decision, and the original proposal, whereby claimants alone would have the right to request an explained decision."[173] The SEC requested FINRA to gather statistics on the number of joint requests for explained decisions made in the first year the rule was in effect and to report on "any anecdotal evidence it receives during this one-year period that may shed light on how often parties are unable to agree to request an explained decision."[174] In fact, the rule appears to have made little impact. Joint requests for explained awards have not become common; FINRA arbitration data shows only fifteen joint requests since 2009.

Representation of parties in the FINRA forum Prior to 2007, the arbitration code did not address who could represent parties in the FINRA forum. FINRA's consistent practice is to permit parties to represent themselves or to be represented by an attorney. Two issues relating to the unauthorized practice of law, however, had surfaced that created uncertainty and controversy. First, non-attorney representatives ("NARs"), who are generally former associated persons, held themselves out as qualified to represent investors in securities arbitration. Second, attorneys licensed in one jurisdiction represented parties in an arbitration conducted in

---

170 74 Fed. Reg. at 6929.

171 FINRA Rule 12904(g)(2).

172 The honorarium to the chairperson, however, is paid only when the parties have jointly requested an explained decision pursuant to Rule 12904(g).

173 74 Fed. Reg. at 6931.

174 *Id.*

another jurisdiction. In 2005, NASD filed a proposed rule change to address the second issue, but, in response to comments that expressed concern over NARs, NASD withdrew the proposed rule and filed a new proposed rule to address this issue as well. The SEC approved new Rule 12208 in 2007.[175]

The rule codifies customary practice that parties may represent themselves.[176] It also defers to applicable state law on issues of unauthorized practice of law. Thus, parties may be represented in any proceeding by an attorney licensed to practice law and in good standing in a U.S. jurisdiction, unless prohibited by state law. Similarly, NARs may represent parties in the FINRA forum unless prohibited by state law. FINRA, however, bars individuals from representing parties in the FINRA forum if they are suspended or barred from the securities industry in any capacity or are suspended from the practice of law or disbarred.[177] While acknowledging that NARs may provide a service to small claims investors, who otherwise would not be able to obtain representation, FINRA took the position that NARs should not be persons who have been found by a regulatory body to be unfit to represent clients or to conduct securities business with the public.

Small claims The special problems of investors with small claims, who cannot obtain legal representation, is worthy of some special attention. The arbitration process is too complicated for pro se claimants, and the simplified arbitration process for claims not exceeding $50,000, where one arbitrator decides the dispute on submitted papers without a hearing,[178] is an unsatisfactory alternative for two reasons. First, many pro se investors may not be capable of composing a document that both sets forth in an orderly fashion the relevant sequence of events and makes a persuasive argument for imposing liability on the broker. Second, most disputes involve issues of credibility, which the arbitrator has no way to assess on paper submissions. While the customer can request a hearing, a claimant confronts the same difficulties in fashioning an effective oral

---

175 Self-Regulatory Organizations; National Association of Securities Dealers, Inc. (n/k/a Financial Industry Regulatory Authority, Inc.); Order Approving Proposed Rule Change as Modified by Amendment Nos 1 and 2 Thereto Relating to Representation of Parties in Arbitration and Mediation, Exch. Act Rel. No. 34–56540, 72 Fed. Reg. 56410 (Oct. 3, 2007).

176 In addition, consistent with customary practice, family members or friends can assist pro se investors.

177 FINRA Rule 12208(c).

178 FINRA Rule 12800.

presentation. I have previously recommended that either the SEC or FINRA should establish a "small claims" arbitration forum, where a trained, professional arbitrator would hold one hearing session where he would allow the customer and the brokerage firm or associated person to tell their side of the story and present their evidence. While the customer could, if she chose, be represented by an attorney, the firm cannot be represented by counsel, but would send a representative.[179] While creating additional expense for the regulator, a small claims forum could help to instill greater investor confidence in the arbitration process by affording small claims investors a meaningful opportunity to present their case in person.

Law school arbitration clinics have been established to provide assistance to small claims investors.[180] While these clinics provide a valuable service, they are few in number, and each can represent only a small number of investors. In addition, law school clinics are expensive for law schools to operate, although FINRA Investor Education Foundation has provided grants to law schools to defray initial costs. Hence, law school clinics cannot solve the problem of small claims investors who cannot obtain legal representation.

JUDICIAL REVIEW OF ARBITRATION AWARDS

Arbitration is a binding resolution of the parties' dispute. To that end, Section 10(a) of the Federal Arbitration Act[181] sets forth very limited grounds, based on arbitrator misconduct, for vacating an arbitrator award:

1. Where the award was procured by corruption, fraud, or undue means;
2. Where there was evident partiality or corruption in the arbitrators, or either of them;
3. Where the arbitrators were guilty of misconduct in refusing to postpone the hearing, upon sufficient cause shown, or in refusing to hear evidence pertinent and material to the controversy; or of any

---

179 Barbara Black, *Is Securities Arbitration Fair to Investors?*, 25 PACE L. REV. 1, 13–14 (2004).

180 A list of the law school clinics is available at the FINRA website, http://www.finra.org/arbitrationandmediation/finradisputeresolution/optionsforinvestors/findanattorney/.

181 9 U.S.C. § 10(a). In addition, 9 U.S.C. § 11 sets forth limited grounds for correcting an award.

other misbehavior by which the rights of any party have been prejudiced; or

4. Where the arbitrators exceeded their powers, or so imperfectly executed them that a mutual, final, and definite award upon the subject matter submitted was not made.

In addition, the Supreme Court has several times referred to a non-statutory standard of "manifest disregard of the law." The Court first referred to this standard in *Wilko v. Swan*[182] and relied on it in *Shearson/American Express Inc. v. McMahon*[183] as providing some assurance that investors' statutory rights would be upheld. Another Supreme Court opinion, *First Options of Chicago v. Kaplan*,[184] also refers to the manifest disregard standard as applicable to securities arbitration awards, without explanation. The Court, however, called into question the existence of a non-statutory "manifest disregard" standard in *Hall Street Associates, LLC v. Mattel, Inc.*[185] Subsequently, in *Stolt-Nielsen SA v. AnimalFeeds International Corp.*,[186] it declined to decide

> whether "manifest disregard" survived *Hall Street Associates* as an independent ground for review or as a judicial gloss on the enumerated grounds for vacatur set forth at 9 U.S.C. § 10. AnimalFeeds characterizes that standard as requiring a showing that the arbitrators knew of the relevant [legal] principle, appreciated that this principle controlled the outcome of the disputed issue, and nonetheless willfully flouted the governing law by refusing to apply it. Assuming, *arguendo,* that such a standard applies, we find it satisfied.[187]

The Circuit Courts have split on the issue.[188]

Indeed, as previously discussed,[189] there is uncertainty over whether arbitrators have to apply the law. In the traditional model of arbitration, arbitrators were expected to do equity, and a compromise might be the

---

182 *See supra* note 12 and accompanying text.

183 *See supra* note 37 and accompanying text.

184 514 U.S. § 938, 942 (1995).

185 552 U.S. § 576 (2008).

186 559 U.S. § 662 (2010).

187 *Id.* at 1763, note 3.

188 *See, e.g.,* Wachovia Sec. LLC v. Brand, 671 F.3d 472, 481 note 7 (4th Cir. 2012) (summarizing the cases). *See* Jill I. Gross, *Hall Street Blues: The Uncertain Future of the Manifest Disregard*, 37 SEC. REG. L.J. 232 (2009) (arguing that unclear dicta in Hall Street should not collide with strong policy reasons to provide a narrow exception to finality rule, to impose accountability on arbitrators).

189 *See supra* note 40 and accompanying text.

best result. Under New York law, for example, unless the parties agree otherwise, arbitrators are not bound by the law.[190] From the investors' perspective, the great advantage of the FINRA equitable model of arbitration is that arbitrators may be able to find a remedy for investors that is not supported by the law. Because of the difficulties of proving federal securities fraud, with its scienter requirement, and because brokerage firms generally have exculpatory language in the customers' agreements, customers are frequently better off in an equitable forum.

If arbitrators do not give reasons for their awards, it is difficult for a party challenging an award to establish manifest disregard, since a court has to posit that there is no scenario under which the award could be upheld. If, however, the practice of explained awards becomes more common, it is likely that courts would examine those reasons and conduct a review on the merits.[191]

THE FUTURE OF SECURITIES ARBITRATION

Perceptions of fairness Ever since *Shearson/American Express, Inc. v. McMahon*, there has been ongoing debate over the fairness of SRO securities arbitration. Many investors perceive the FINRA arbitration forum as unfair, and journalists frequently report negatively on the securities arbitration process. In contrast, academics who have studied the forum give it high marks for meeting most generally recognized standards of fairness.[192] Despite FINRA's ongoing efforts to improve the arbitration process, the FINRA arbitration forum continues to be plagued with suspicions about whether the process treats investors fairly. These suspicions are unlikely to go away, given the mandatory nature of arbitration and the fact that arbitrations are conducted in an industry-sponsored forum.

In 2002, California and FINRA were engaged in litigation over the state's attempt to impose its conflict disclosure standards on arbitrators in

---

190 Silverman v. Cooper, 61 N.Y.2d 299, 308 (1984).

191 *See supra* note 167 and accompanying text.

192 Barbara Black, *Is Securities Arbitration Fair to Investors?*, 25 PACE L. REV. 1, 3–12 (2004) (discussing the author's view that securities arbitration is a fairer process than many consumer/employee arbitration processes); Jill Gross, McMahon *Turns Twenty: The Regulation of Fairness in Securities Arbitration,* 76 U. CIN. L. REV. 493, 518 (2008) (expressing the author's belief that current regulation of securities arbitration ensures that it is fair to investors and concluding that SEC oversight sufficiently regulates the fairness of securities arbitration).

FINRA securities arbitrations.[193] The SEC filed an *amicus curiae* brief in support of FINRA's position that federal regulation preempted state standards and also requested that Professor Michael A. Perino assess the adequacy of the current SRO arbitrator disclosure requirements. In his report, Professor Perino concluded that the disclosure rules appeared to be adequate. He also observed that any "lingering perceptions of pro-industry bias" related to "panel composition, not the presence of undisclosed arbitrator conflicts."[194] Because of "lingering concerns about pro-industry bias" and the insufficient amount of empirical evidence addressing investors' perceptions of the securities arbitration process, Professor Perino recommended that the "SROs sponsor additional independent studies to further evaluate the impartiality of the SRO arbitration process."[195]

In response to this recommendation, NASD asked SICA to conduct a study of participants' perceptions of the fairness of securities arbitration. Professors Jill Gross and Barbara Black conducted this survey, which was completed in 2008. The primary findings were that (1) investors have a far more negative perception of securities arbitration than all other participants, (2) investors have a strong negative perception of the bias of arbitrators, and (3) investors lack knowledge of the securities arbitration process. The authors recommended further reforms, including the elimination of the industry arbitrator requirement and further public deliberation on the value of the explained award. FINRA subsequently implemented both of these recommendations, as discussed previously in this chapter.[196]

In the aftermath of the financial crisis, both Congress and the Executive Branch have called for further study of securities arbitration, particularly as it affects retail investors. In 2009, Congress considered, but did not pass, legislation to invalidate PDAAs in employment and consumer arbitration and expressly included securities arbitration within

---

[193] *See* NASD Dispute Resolution v. Judicial Council of California, 488 F.3d 1065 (9th Cir. 2007) (dismissing appeal because of mootness and vacating district court's judgment); *see also* Credit Suisse First Boston v. Grunwald, 400 F.3d 1119 (9th Cir. 2005) (holding that federal securities law preempted the California standards in the context of SROs); Jevne v. Superior Court, 35 Cal. 4th 935 (2005) (to same effect).

[194] *See* Michael Perino, *Report to the Securities and Exchange Commission Regarding Arbitrator Conflict Disclosure Requirements in NASD and NYSE Securities Arbitration* at 3 (Nov. 4, 2002), available at http://www.sec.gov/pdf/arbconflict.pdf.

[195] *Id.*

[196] *See supra* notes 115–19, 168–74 and accompanying text.

the definition.[197] The 2009 Treasury white paper on financial regulatory reform[198] recommended an SEC study of the issue as well as an amendment of the federal securities laws to give the SEC authority to prohibit PDAAs in brokerage and investment advisory contracts with retail investors. Section 921 of the Dodd-Frank Wall Street Reform and Consumer Protection Act gives the SEC the authority to prohibit, or to impose conditions or limitations on the use of, "agreements that require customers or clients … to arbitrate *any future dispute between them arising under the Federal securities laws, the rules and regulations thereunder, or the rule of a self-regulatory organization* if it finds that such prohibition, imposition of conditions, or limitations are in the public interest and for the protection of investors."[199] Section 921 is solely enabling and does not require the SEC to take any action. By its terms, the statutory language imposes a significant limitation on the SEC's authority to prohibit the use of PDAAs; its authority does not extend to future disputes arising under state law. If the SEC chose to exercise its authority to ban PDAAs, it could not prevent brokerage firms from continuing to use them to require arbitration of state law claims which, because of the difficulties in proving federal claims, are the basis of many investors' claims. Although investor advocates have urged the SEC to act, the agency's lack of full authority to prohibit the use of PDAAs may act as a powerful disincentive.

Debate over the fairness of the arbitration process has heated up as the result of the 2011 decision by the brokerage firm Charles Schwab & Co to amend its customer agreement to provide that customers could not bring judicial class actions to vindicate any rights it may have against the brokerage firm.[200] Instead, the agreement provides that a Schwab customer's exclusive remedy is individual arbitration in the FINRA forum, even if the amounts of the individual claims make arbitration economically infeasible. The Schwab class action waiver is a clear violation of

---

[197] *See* Jill Gross, *The End of Mandatory Securities Arbitration?*, 30 PACE L. REV. 1174, 1177–78 (2010).

[198] U.S. DEPT OF TREASURY, FINANCIAL REGULATORY REFORM, A NEW FOUNDATION: REBUILDING FINANCIAL SUPERVISION AND REGULATION (2009), available at http://www.financialstability.gov/docs/regs/FinalReport_web.pdf.

[199] Dodd-Frank Act, Pub. L. No. 111–203, § 921(a), 124 Stat. 1376, 1841 (2010).

[200] *See* Barbara Black & Jill I. Gross, *Investor Protection Meets the Federal Arbitration Act*, 1 STANFORD J. COMPLEX LITIG. 1 (2012).

FINRA rules that bar their inclusion in customers' agreements.[201] Both FINRA and the SEC have consistently stated that customers that have claims against a brokerage firm suitable for class action treatment are permitted to institute a class action in court, and that a brokerage firm cannot enforce a PDAA against a member of the class so long as the class action appears viable.[202] In February 2013 a FINRA hearing panel held that the FINRA rule was unenforceable because it conflicted with the Federal Arbitration Act.[203] In April 2014, however, FINRA's Board of Governors reversed the Hearing Panel on this critical point, finding that the FAA did not preclude FINRA's enforcement of its rules.[204] The Board began its decision by noting that "[f]or over twenty years, FINRA has been in the forefront of establishing rules under which securities industry arbitrations take place"; that "[t]here can be little doubt that Congress and the federal courts have repeatedly scrutinized the FINRA rules that govern securities arbitration"; and that "Schwab's misconduct in this case demonstrates its attempted piecemeal erosion of FINRA's well-established arbitration rules."[205]

The Board relied on Supreme Court precedent that the FAA's mandate is not absolute, but can be overridden by a "contrary Congressional command."[206] In the case of SRO securities arbitration, the Exchange Act contains Congress's command that the SEC approve FINRA's arbitration rules, upon a determination that they are consistent with the legislative purpose. Specifically, Exchange Act § 15A empowers FINRA to regulate broker-dealers, including their dispute resolution processes with customers, subject to SEC oversight. Indeed, in the past 20 years, the SEC has approved dozens of FINRA's arbitration rules after public notice and comment. "Therefore, the Exchange Act gives the SEC the authority to approve FINRA rules that govern arbitration in FINRA's forum and that regulate the content of predispute arbitration agreements."[207]

> The SEC is implementing Congress's plan by evaluating and approving SRO rule proposals that govern the conduct of the securities industry, including the

---

[201] FINRA Rules 12204, 2268(d), (f).

[202] Black & Gross, *supra* note 200, at 27–28.

[203] Dept. of Enforcement v. Charles Schwab & Co., Inc. (FINRA OHO Feb. 21, 2013).

[204] Dept. of Enforcement v. Charles Schwab & Co., Inc. (FINRA Bd. of Governors Apr. 24, 2014).

[205] Id. at 3.

[206] Id. at 18.

[207] Id. at 19.

> rules that govern what FINRA firms can include in their predispute agreements with their customers.[208]

Finally, because FINRA rules have the force and effect of a federal regulation for the purpose of resolving federal conflicts of law, those rules can override the FAA when the latter would produce conflicting guidance in an area that is addressed by the securities laws.[209] As the Board explained:

> The Supreme Court's holdings that federal antitrust laws are impliedly repealed when they conflict with securities laws support the conclusion that the Exchange Act, effectuated through FINRA rules, overrides the FAA here. First, the SEC, through its oversight of the FINRA arbitration forum and its review of FINRA rules, has consistently exercised its authority to oversee the arbitration process. Second, the Schwab dispute represents a direct conflict between the FAA, which mandates enforcement of arbitration agreements according to their terms, and FINRA rules, which require broker dealers to preserve judicial class actions for investors. Third, FINRA's arbitration rules for customer disputes with FINRA firms and associated persons address a critical aspect of investor protection under the Exchange Act, namely in what forum a customer class action will be litigated. In reconciling the conflict between FINRA arbitration rules that prohibit use of a predispute arbitration agreement to eliminate judicial class actions and the FAA's enforcement of class action waivers, we find – based on the SEC's approval orders – that FINRA's rules are in furtherance of the Exchange Act's protection of investors. This core aspect of the Exchange Act prevails over the FAA.[210]

Schwab settled with FINRA by paying a $500,000 fine and agreeing to notify its customers that the class action waiver was no longer in effect.[211]

The Schwab decision was a significant victory for retail investors. If the Hearing Panel's decision had been upheld on appeal, it was expected that other brokerage firms would also adopt class action waivers in their PDAAs. As a result, customers with small claims that could be aggregated in a judicial class action would be relegated to individual arbitrations in the FINRA forum, even if the amounts of the individual claims made arbitration economically infeasible. Although this result would be exactly the opposite of consistent FINRA and SEC policy, such an outcome would have exacerbated investors' concerns about mandatory securities arbitration and would have provided ammunition to investor

---

[208] Id. at 20–21.
[209] Id. at 21.
[210] Id. at 22.
[211] http://www.finra.org/Newsroom/NewsReleases/2014/P493587

advocates who have long argued that it is unfair. Because Schwab chose to settle with FINRA, however, there remains the lingering doubt about whether a federal appellate court, or ultimately the U.S. Supreme Court, would agree with FINRA's legal analysis.

Should arbitration be mandatory? With the elimination of the requirement of an industry arbitrator on every three-person panel, the principal argument of unfairness rests on arbitration's mandatory nature. Why should not investors have a choice between judicial and arbitration forums, ask investor advocates.

As an initial matter, it is a puzzle that virtually all brokerage firms include PDAAs in their customers' agreements and that there is no competition among firms on this contract term. In the entire universe of investors, there may well be some who want a choice between litigation and arbitration and would be willing to pay for it. If so, one expects that some firms would offer to drop the PDAA in exchange for higher commissions. Why has this not happened? Behavioral economics provides insight into this puzzle.[212] Even though investors likely know about PDAAs, rational ignorance, over-optimism, and the status quo bias help explain why the PDAA is likely not a salient term, at least at the time of the initial contract. Thus, behavioral economics may explain why investors, at least when they first enter into a brokerage relationship, do not negotiate over the PDAA. Behavioral economics does not entirely provide an answer, however, particularly with respect to investors who have suffered a bad arbitration experience and may be motivated to find (and pay for) a broker that does not require a PDAA. Brokerage firms may be unwilling to drop PDAAs because of their significant investment in the FINRA process or because they have achieved significant savings through FINRA arbitration. Moreover, brokerage firms likely do not see "you can sue us" as an attractive ad campaign.[213]

What would happen if Congress or the CFPB prohibited PDAAs? The outcome would not necessarily be as favorable to the customer as some investor advocates believe. Critics of mandatory securities arbitration frequently assert that, if the FINRA arbitration forum is perceived as fair,

---

[212] *See* Barbara Black, *Can Behavioral Economics Inform our Understanding of Securities Arbitration?,* 12 TRANSACTIONS THE TENNESSEE J. OF BUS. L. 107 (2011).

[213] If Charles Schwab had prevailed and was permitted to enforce its class action waiver, and if other brokerage firms did not adopt a similar waiver, we would have had the opportunity for a natural experiment on whether firms choose to compete on this basis.

PDAAs are not necessary because the parties will agree post-dispute to arbitrate; conversely, if the forum is not perceived as fair, investors should not be forced to arbitrate. While this argument is superficially plausible, it does not hold up upon analysis, because it fails to take into account that after the dispute has arisen, the parties will have strategic considerations to favor one forum over the other. Consider, for example, two investors A and B. A, a sympathetic plaintiff with a large claim based on blatant broker fraud, will want to litigate her claim before a sympathetic jury, while B, with a small claim based on the broker's breach of the FINRA suitability rule, will want to arbitrate her claim. The broker's strategic choice is exactly the opposite; it will not want A's claim to go to court, with the attendant risk of high liability and unfavorable publicity, while it is to its advantage if B is forced to bring her claim in court, because the costs of litigation, as well as the lack of strong legal basis for the claim (at least in some states), make a judicial proceeding infeasible. Studies of employment arbitration confirm that post-dispute arbitration agreements are rare.[214]

If Congress prohibited PDAAs, so long as FINRA Rule 12200[215] remains in effect, customers would have a choice of arbitrating or litigating their disputes. Accordingly, investors whose claims would likely fare better in arbitration, like investor B, would invoke their right to pursue arbitration. As a result, the FINRA forum could be transformed to a small claims forum. FINRA's revised mission would be to maintain a securities arbitration forum for small investors and small claims, which was, in fact, the SEC's original vision of SRO securities arbitration. Moreover, we can expect the industry will mount opposition to Rule 12200 and assert that it is unfair to give investors the choice of litigation or arbitration while not giving the same choice to the industry. SIFMA has previously stated that eliminating PDAAs would give investors "an unfair strategic advantage."[216] FINRA, in contrast, has asserted that Rule 12200 is an integral part of investor protection if mandatory securities arbitration is abolished.[217] Accordingly, we can expect that if mandatory securities arbitration is abolished, Rule 12200 will be the next battle.

214 Black, *supra* note 212, at 118–120.

215 *See supra* note 2 and accompanying text.

216 SIFMA, White Paper on Arbitration in the Securities Industry 3 (Oct. 2007), http://www.sifma.org/issues/item.aspx?id=21334.

217 *See* Linda Fienberg, President, FINRA Dispute Resolution, SEC Investor Advisory Committee: Open Meeting (May 17, 2010), http://www.sec.gov/news/otherwebcasts/2010/iacmeeting051710.shtml.

How compelling is FINRA's argument that Rule 12200 is necessary for investor protection? FINRA's argument in support of Rule 12200 is that the consequence of not allowing investors and firms to agree, pre-dispute, to arbitrate their claims is that, post-dispute, some investors will, as a practical matter, be foreclosed from maintaining their claims. Accordingly, Rule 12200 is necessary for protection of at least investors with small damages claims. In addition, since investor confidence is essential to maintaining strong capital markets, the anger that could result if small investors had no realistic remedy for losses caused by broker misconduct could negatively impact the markets. Accordingly, a strong argument can be made for the continued existence of Rule 12200 based on market realities and the policy judgment that retail investor confidence is important for maintaining the capital markets. In its *Schwab* decision, however, FINRA's Board of Governors stated that the Supreme Court's opinion in *American Express Co. v. Italian Colors Restaurant* foreclosed the argument that class actions were necessary for effective vindication of the rights of small claims plaintiffs.[218] An industry challenge to Rule 12200 would test the extent of FINRA's power and commitment to protect investors and maintain investor confidence in the capital markets.

Are arbitrators up to the task? A final question is whether the quasi-judicial process constructed after *McMahon* can function effectively without a corps of full-time professional arbitrators. Arbitrators are not required to have legal training, and, unlike judges, do not have law clerks to assist them. As they are assigned individual cases and work on a piecemeal basis at below-market rates, they have neither the resources nor much incentive to devote time to caseload management. FINRA has constructed an elaborate structure on a shaky foundation; despite all their good intentions, many arbitrators may not be up to the increased responsibilities FINRA expects from them.[219]

CONCLUSION

This chapter has recounted the evolution of the FINRA arbitration forum as a consequence of *Shearson/American Express v. McMahon* and increasing recognition that investor confidence requires a fair alternative to litigation. As PDAAs have become universal, the forum has adopted a

---

218 Opinion at 24, note 27.

219 Barbara Black, *Do We Expect Too Much from NASD Arbitrators?*, SEC. ARB. COMMMENTATOR 1 (vol. 2004, No. 7).

comprehensive set of procedural rules, with some sacrifice of its original virtues of informality, efficiency and speed. With the all-public panel options, customers have less reason to complain about industry bias.

This history also shows that brokerage firms, which long campaigned for mandatory securities arbitration, have not hesitated to expend their considerable resources to create an arbitration forum that served their purposes, sometimes with little regard for maintaining investor confidence in the forum. Charles Schwab is only the most recent example. Indeed, the securities industry should breathe a sigh of relief over Schwab's defeat. If the firm had been permitted to enforce its class action waiver, detractors of mandatory securities arbitration would certainly have put pressure on Congress and the SEC to eliminate mandatory arbitration of cutomers' disputes.

15. Private rights of action under U.S. securities laws: key differences between litigation and arbitration of securities disputes, limited right of action against investment advisers, and the uncertain future of class litigation

Leslie A. Blau, Mark Liston, and Peter Evans

INTRODUCTION

When a customer wants to bring claims against securities broker-dealers or their salespersons for violations of the law or the rules of self-regulatory organizations, it is important to bear in mind the differences between arbitration and litigation of such disputes. If one has a choice of forum (in most cases, the agreement between the customer and the dealer will mandate arbitration), these differences may be crucial when deciding whether to bring the claims in court or in FINRA arbitration.

With respect to investment advisers (who are not FINRA members and therefore not subject to mandatory FINRA arbitration), violations of the Investment Adviser Act may give rise to a private right of action for rescission. However, there are limitations on who may be liable for such violations, and money damages are unavailable.

Finally, class actions in the courts have long been an important vehicle for vindicating claims based on violations of securities laws. But recent developments within FINRA and the U.S. Supreme Court now threaten their existence.

RULES RELATING TO SUITABILITY AND SUPERVISION

Prior to 2007, there were two dominant self-regulatory organizations with jurisdiction over almost all brokers and brokerage firms: the National Association of Securities Dealers ("NASD") and the New York Stock

Exchange ("NYSE").[1] The Financial Industry Regulatory Authority ("FINRA") was created on July 30, 2007, when the NASD and NYSE merged their regulatory, compliance and arbitration functions.

The NASD and NYSE each had arbitration functions and compliance rules, and each had rules relating to suitability and supervision, as FINRA has now. Those rules prohibit brokerage firms and their salespersons/registered representatives, as well as persons associated with those firms, from recommending unsuitable investments. Those rules also require brokerage firms to supervise such persons.

"Know Your Customer" and "Suitability" Rules

Before FINRA existed, it was a violation of NASD Rule 2310 and NYSE Rule 405 for a brokerage firm or salespersons (now known as "associated persons" and then known as "registered representatives")[2] to recommend an unsuitable investment. It is still prohibited today, under FINRA Rule 2111.[3]

---

[1] A broker was required to register with an SRO, such as the NASD or NYSE. If a broker only does business on one national securities exchange and meets other conditions, it may only have to be a member of that exchange. As a result, some brokers were subject to the jurisdiction of other exchanges such as the American Stock Exchange ("AMEX"), the Chicago Board Options Exchange ("CBOE") or the Philadelphia Stock Exchange ("PHLX"). However, any broker effecting transactions on multiple exchanges was required to be a member of the NASD.

[2] FINRA Rule 1011(b) defines "Associated Persons" as:

> (1) a natural person registered under NASD Rules; or (2) a sole proprietor, or any partner, officer, director, branch manager of the Applicant, or any person occupying a similar status or performing similar functions; (3) any company, government or political subdivision or agency or instrumentality of a government controlled by or controlling the Applicant; (4) any employee of the Applicant, except any person whose functions are solely clerical or ministerial; (5) any person directly or indirectly controlling the Applicant whether or not such person is registered or exempt from registration under the FINRA By-Laws or NASD Rules; (6) any person engaged in investment banking or securities business controlled directly or indirectly by the Applicant whether such person is registered or exempt from registration under the FINRA By-Laws or NASD Rules; or (7) any person who will be or is anticipated to be a person described in (1) through (6) above.

[3] *See also* FINRA Regulatory Notice 12–55, issued on December 10, 2012, http://finra.org/Industry/Regulation/Notices/2012/P197436 (accessed on Dec. 5, 2013).

A brokerage firm or an associated person cannot escape the duty to recommend only suitable investments by claiming that they did not know their customer, because FINRA Rule 2090 contains a "Know Your Customer" requirement, a requirement which also appeared as NYSE Rule 405.[4]

Duty to supervise

Before FINRA existed, brokerage firms had a duty to supervise their salespersons under NASD Rules 3110 and 3112. The NYSE also had rules setting out supervisory requirements: Rule 342 (Offices-Approval, Supervision and Control), Rule 343 (Office-Sole Tenancy and House), Rule 351(e) (Reporting Requirements), Rule 354 (Reports to Control Persons), and NYSE Rule 401 (Business Conduct). FINRA has two rules, Rule 3110 (Supervision) and Rule 3120 (Supervisory Control System), with similar requirements.[5]

NO PRIVATE RIGHT OF ACTION IN COURT FOR VIOLATION OF RULES RELATING TO SUITABILITY AND SUPERVISION

A lawyer representing an investor suing a brokerage firm or a salesperson for violating one of the above-mentioned rules, or any other FINRA rule for that matter, faces an uphill battle. But, that was not always the case. For years, courts were willing to find an implied private right of action under NASD or exchange rules.[6] Generally, the only requirement before

---

[4] For a discussion of the relationship between FINRA "Know Your Customer" and "Suitability" rules and the NASD and NYSE rules on which the rules are based, see FINRA Regulatory Notice 11–02 (Jan. 2011) http://www.finra.org/web/groups/industry/@ip/@reg/@notice/documents/notices/p122778.pdf (accessed on Dec. 5, 2013). The SEC routinely enforces these rules. *See* In the Matter of the Application of Dane S. Faber, Admin. Proc. File No. 3–11156 (Feb. 10, 2004); In the Matter of Dale E. Frey, Roger A. Rawlings & William C. Piontek, Admin. Proc. File No. 3–10310 (Feb. 5, 2003).

[5] The SEC routinely enforces these rules. *See* In the Matter of the Application of Gordon Kerr, Admin. Proc. File No. 3–10133 (Oct. 5, 2000); In the Matter of the Application of Joseph G. Chiuli, Admin. Proc. File No. 3–9776 (Jan. 28, 2000); In the Matter of the Application of Gordon Kerr, Admin. Proc. File No. 3–10133 (Oct. 5, 2000).

[6] *See, e.g.*, Buttrey v. Merrill Lynch, Pierce, Fenner & Smith, Inc., 410 F.2d 135 (7th Cir. 1969) (private right of action implied in NYSE rules).

a court would imply a private right of action was that the rule must have been intended to protect the public.[7] However, after the Supreme Court decided the duo of *Touche Ross & Co. v. Redington*[8] and *Transamerica Mortgage Advisors, Inc. v. Lewis*,[9] courts limited the instances in which private rights of action could be implied. As a result, the previously implied right of action for violation of NASD or exchange rules was no longer available.[10]

Today, it is widely accepted that no private right of action exists for violations of FINRA rules or those of its predecessors. In *Mill Bridge V, Inc. v. Benton*, the court discussed in length the lack of a private right of action under exchange rules.[11] There, the plaintiff sought rescission of its contract under Section 29(b) of the Securities Exchange Act ("Exchange Act")[12] based on the broker's violation of PHLX Exchange Rule

---

[7] *See, e.g.*, SEC v. First Sec. Co. of Chi., 463 F.2d 981, 988 (7th Cir. 1972) (violation of NASD rule provides a basis for private damages actions where the rule violated protects the public); Avern Trust v. Clarke, 415 F.2d 1238, 1242 (7th Cir. 1969) (same); Neill v. David A. Noyes & Co., 416 F. Supp. 78, 81 (N.D. Ill. 1976) (same).

[8] 442 U.S. 560 (1979).

[9] 444 U.S. 11 (1979).

[10] *See* Jablon v. Dean Witter & Co., 614 F.2d 677 (9th Cir. 1980); Jaksich v. Thomson McKinnon Sec., Inc., 582 F. Supp. 485, 489–500 (S.D.N.Y. 1984) (no private right of action for violating NASD or NYSE rules because no such right is supported by the legislative history).

[11] No. 08–2806, 2009 WL 4639641, *11–12 (E.D. Pa. Dec. 3, 2009) (citing Walck v. Am. Stock Exch., Inc., 687 F.2d 778 (3d Cir. 1982) ("[plaintiff] overlooks the reality that *the Exchanges and not Congress promulgated the rules*; and we perceive no basis for an inference that the Exchanges in their quasi-legislative capacity intended to subject themselves to damages for non-enforcement." (alteration and emphasis original)); Carapico v. Phila. Stock Exch., No. CIV. A. 93–3066, 1994 WL 50294 (E.D. Pa. Feb. 14, 1994), *aff'd* 43 F.3d 1460 (3d Cir. 1994); In re Farmers Grp. Stock Ops. Litig., No. CIV. A. 88–4994, 1989 WL 73245 (E.D. Pa. Jul. 5, 1989); Ferreri v. Mainardi, 690 F. Supp. 411, 413 (E.D. Pa. 1988)).

[12] Section 29(b) provides:

> Every contract made in violation of any provision of this title or of any rule or regulation thereunder, and every contract (including any contract for listing a security on an exchange) heretofore or hereafter made, the performance of which involves the violation of, or the continuance of any relationship or practice in violation of, any provision of this title or any rule or regulation thereunder, shall be void (1) as regards the rights of any person who, in violation of any such provision, rule, or regulation, shall have made or engaged in the performance of any such contract, and (2) as regards the rights of any person who, not being a party to such contract, shall have acquired any

708.[13] However, Section 29(b) only allows a party to rescind its contract when there has been a violation of another substantive provision of the Exchange Act.[14] And, because an exchange rule violation does not constitute a violation of the Exchange Act, i.e., it does not give rise to an independent cause of action, such a violation is insufficient to state a claim for relief under Section 29(b).[15]

A similar result was reached in *Fernea v. Merrill Lynch Pierce Fenner & Smith, Inc.*[16] In *Fernea*, the court rejected the rationale of *Buttrey*, in which the court upheld a private right of action, and held that no right of action exists for violations of NASD and NYSE rules.[17] Instead, it relied on *Transamerica* and its progeny for the premise that because "Congress specifically provided for private causes of action for violations of some securities rules, yet did not provide a cause of action for violations of NASD and NYSE rules … Congress did not intend to create a private right of action [for such violations]."[18] And, because there was no congressional intent, no private right of action could be implied.

---

right thereunder with actual knowledge of the facts by reason of which the making or performance of such contract was in violation of any such provision, rule, or regulation: Provided, (A) That no contract shall be void by reason of this subsection because of any violation of any rule or regulation prescribed pursuant to paragraph (3) of subsection (c) of section 15, and (B) that no contract shall be deemed to be void by reason of this subsection in any action maintained in reliance upon this subsection, by any person to or for whom any broker or dealer sells, or from or for whom any broker or dealer purchases, a security in violation of any rule or regulation prescribed pursuant to paragraph (1) or (2) of subsection (c) of section 15, unless such action is brought within one year after the discovery that such sale or purchase involves such violation and within three years after such violation. The Commission may, in a rule or regulation prescribed pursuant to such paragraph (2) of such section 15(c), designate such rule or regulation, or portion thereof, as a rule or regulation, or portion thereof, a contract in violation of which shall not be void by reason of this subsection.

13 Rule 708. Acts Detrimental to the Interest or Welfare of the Exchange: A member, member organization, or person associated with or employed by a member or member organization shall not engage in acts detrimental to the interest or welfare of the Exchange.

14 Mill Bridge, 2009 WL 4639641, at *12.

15 *Id.*

16 No. 03–0900566-CV, 2011 WL 2769838 (Tex. App. Ct. Jul. 12, 2011).

17 *See id.* at *3–5.

18 *Id.* at *5; *see also* Landow v. Wachovia Sec., LLC, No. 12-CV-3277 (SJF)(AKT), 2013 WL 4432383 (E.D.N.Y. Aug. 12, 2013) (cause of action

FINRA Rule Violations Framed as Breach of Contract Claims

Despite court decisions denying such rights, plaintiffs have attempted to create a private right of action through a breach of contract claim premised on the incorporation of exchange rules into customer agreements. In *Appert v. Morgan Stanley Dean Witter, Inc.*,[19] the plaintiff argued that her account agreement and trade confirmation slips imposed a contractual duty on the broker to follow NASD rules and, since the broker did not follow those rules, plaintiff had a valid breach of contract claim.[20] The broker argued plaintiff was attempting to plead around the established rule that there is no longer an implied right of action for violations of exchange rules,[21] to which the plaintiff responded that the rules were incorporated into her account agreement.[22] However, the Northern District of Illinois refused to allow the contract claim to move forward, holding that the account agreement merely indicates "[p]laintiff's accounts and transactions are generally governed by such regulations."[23]

The *Appert* court gave significant weight to dicta in *Kurz v. Fidelity Management & Research Co.*, which rejected the contention that a plaintiff may bring a breach of contract claim for violating exchange rules allegedly incorporated into the customer agreement.[24] The court examined the facts in *Kurz* and concluded that even if the *Kurt* plaintiffs could have produced language similar to that in Appert's contract, they would not be able to couch exchange rule violations as a state law breach of contract claim.[25] As a result, the court dismissed plaintiff's breach of contract claim on the grounds that no private right of action exists for exchange rule violations; though, the court did leave open the possibility of such an action being successful if the contract contained "language expressly binding defendant to an obligation."[26]

---

alleging violation of NASD and NYSE rules dismissed for failure to state a claim for which relief may be granted because there is no private right of action).

19 No. 08-CV-7130, 2009 WL 3764120 (N.D. Ill. Nov. 6, 2009).

20 *Id.* at *1.

21 *Id.* at *2 (citing Spicer v. Chi. Bd. of Options Exch., Inc., 977 F.2d 255 (7th Cir. 1992)).

22 Appert, 2009 WL 3764120, at *2.

23 *Id.* at *4.

24 556 F.3d 639, 641–42 (7th Cir. 2009).

25 Appert, 2009 WL 3764120, at *3.

26 *Id.* at *4.

In reaching this conclusion, the *Appert* court also relied on *Gurfein v. Ameritrade*,[27] in which plaintiffs brought nearly identical claims to those in *Appert*. In *Gurfein*, the court held that the language referencing exchange rules were "notice provisions" meant to inform customers that the agreement was governed by the rules, not to impose additional obligations on the broker.[28] The *Gurfein* court premised its decision on earlier Second Circuit cases in which the court decided not to recognize an implied right of action for violation of exchange rules and its unwillingness to allow plaintiffs to plead around this rule.[29]

The Supreme Court of Nebraska also encountered this issue and addressed it in the same manner. In *Knights of Columbus Council 3152 v. KFS BD, Inc.*,[30] former customers of the broker brought claims based on its failure to abide by NASD rules incorporated into their contracts. The court first acknowledged that "no private right of action exists for violations of rules promulgated by a securities exchange or a self-regulatory organization."[31] Then, the court refused to allow plaintiffs to create a private right of action through a breach of contract claim where no such right exists.[32] The court further held that:

> a contract's implied incorporation of rules and regulations that govern a broker-dealer's dealings with an investor will not support a private cause of action when the rules and regulations themselves provide no private cause of action.[33]

Thus, in accord with *Appert* and *Gurfein*, the Nebraska Supreme Court dismissed the breach of contract claims.

---

27 312 Fed. Appx. 410 (2d Cir. 2009).

28 *Id.* at 413–14.

29 *Id.* at 414 ("[Plaintiff] is precluded from creating a private cause of action for violations of these rules and regulations by fashioning her claim as one for breach of contract based on violations of rules and regulations impliedly incorporated into the agreement.").

30 791 N.W.2d 317 (Neb. 2010).

31 *Id.* at 326.

32 *Id.* at 325 ("federal courts do not permit a common-law breach of contract claim against NASD or a securities exchange for violating or failing to enforce its own rules").

33 *Id.* at 326.

PRIVATE REMEDIES AVAILABLE BASED ON FINRA RULE VIOLATIONS

The absence of a private right of action under FINRA rules does not mean a plaintiff cannot recover when a broker violates the rules. Recovery is available, but it requires the plaintiff to consider either the forum in which it seeks recovery or the manner in which it pleads its claims.

FINRA Arbitrators Routinely Award Damages for Violation of Its Rules

While the courts refuse to allow a private claim for FINRA rule violations, a plaintiff may seek recovery via arbitration. And, while a lawyer who sues a broker in FINRA arbitration for violating FINRA rules may be confronted with an argument that he has no private right of action, that argument is without merit. In an unpublished opinion from the New York Supreme Court, an NASD member sought to vacate an arbitration award in favor of its investor and for violating two NASD rules.[34] The broker argued that "the arbitrator ignored the rule of law that an alleged violation of a self-regulatory organization rule does not provide an investor with a private right of action."[35] But, the court found that:

> [t]he cases cited by the petition denied private rights of action in federal court based on violation of self-regulatory organization rules. The petitioner has not cited any case law for the proposition that a private right of action based on the violation of self-regulatory organization rules cannot be brought in arbitration. Accordingly, it is ordered that the petition is denied and the proceeding is dismissed.[36]

Therefore, an investor may be able to recover for a FINRA rule violation in arbitration, even though a court would dismiss such a claim.

In fact, each year, FINRA arbitration panels hear thousands of cases involving claims of failure to supervise and recommending unsuitable investments. From 2009 to 2013, there were more than 24,000 arbitration

---

[34] Marc Bennett Freeman v. Damian Arahill, No. 111119/01 (N.Y. Sup. Ct. Oct. 18, 2001).

[35] *Id.*

[36] *Id.*

cases filed, as indicated by Table 15.1.[37] Out of those cases, almost 8,500 included claims of brokers recommending unsuitable investments as prohibited by FINRA Rule 2111 and previously prohibited by NASD Rule 2310 and NYSE Rule 405, discussed above. Additionally, more than 10,000 cases included claims of failure to supervise as prohibited by FINRA Rules 3110 and 3120 and previously prohibited by NASD Rules 3110 and 3112 and NYSE Rules 342, 343, 351(e), 354 and 401, discussed above. These statistics lead to the conclusion that the *Freeman* case discussed above is not an exception and that FINRA arbitration panels routinely hear cases alleging claims that would otherwise be dismissed by a state or federal court.

Table 15.1 Claims Submitted to FINRA Arbitration from 2009–13

	Total Arbitration Cases Filed	Unsuitability Cases	Failure to Supervise Cases
2009	7,137	2,473	2,691
2010	5,680	1,974	2,372
2011	4,729	1,619	2,007
2012	4,299	1,354	1,657
2013*	3,156	1,049	1,241

Note: * Statistics represent claims filed in 2013 at the time of publication (Oct. 2013).

There is also a policy rationale in support of a FINRA panel's right to hear claims for failure to supervise or for recommending unsuitable investments. Like FINRA, several other organizations regulate their members by imposing a set of rules or laws. In baseball, the players are subject to the rules of Major League Baseball. These rules are enforced through arbitration, not in court. Likewise, churches and synagogues have their own rules, and these rules are enforced by canonical and rabbinical tribunals. Some canonical or rabbinical principles are quite different from the rules that courts apply. Courts are not in business to enforce these rules—it would be ludicrous to claim there is any private right of action in a state or federal court for violations of such rules—but courts do confirm the decisions of such tribunals when the parties agree the tribunal may hear their dispute. FINRA arbitration is no different.

[37] Statistics taken from FINRA website http://www.finra.org/ArbitrationAndMediation/FINRADisputeResolution/AdditionalResources/Statistics/index.htm.

Negligence Claims Based on FINRA Rule Violations

Investors who prefer to seek recovery in court for a rule violation are not necessarily precluded from doing so by the lack of a private right of action. While courts frown upon plaintiffs attempting to couch rule violations as breach of contract claims, as discussed above, courts have repeatedly allowed the same violations to serve as evidence of other traditional common law causes of action, such as negligence. Not long after the Supreme Court eliminated the private right of action under NASD rules, courts began to allow plaintiffs to use rule violations to support other causes of action despite objections that those claims were just an attempt to plead around the new rule eliminating the private right of action.[38]

In *Miley v. Oppenheimer & Co.*, the investor brought claims of churning against the broker and cited to the NASD and NYSE rules regulating such behavior. The trial instructed the jury that conduct violating the "Know Your Customer" and "Suitability" rules was one of six factors the jury could consider when assessing the broker's conduct.[39] On appeal, the Fifth Circuit held it was proper for the court to instruct the jury as it did, stating that the NASD and NYSE rules were "excellent tools," along with other factors, to assess the reasonableness of the broker's conduct and to assess whether there was excessive trading of a customer's account.[40]

Similarly, in *Merrill Lynch, Pierce Fenner & Smith v. Cheng*, the plaintiff sued for negligence and based its claim on an alleged violation of the NASD's "Suitability Rule."[41] The court acknowledged that there was no private right of action for violations of the rule, but held the stockbroker may be liable for negligence.[42] The court noted that a claim

---

[38] Miley v. Oppenheimer & Co., 637 F.2d 318 (5th Cir. 1981); *see also* Merrill Lynch, Pierce Fenner & Smith v. Cheng, 697 F. Supp. 1224 (D.D.C. 1988).

[39] Miley, 637 F.2d at 333 ("[Judge] Mahon told the jury that they could consider six factors: (1) the nature and objectives of the account; (2) the turnover rate; (3) in-and-out-trading; (4) the holding period of the respective securities; (5) the broker's profit; and (6) *observance of the Know-Your-Customer and Suitability rules*.") (emphasis added) (alteration original).

[40] *Id.* ("these NYSE and NASD rules are excellent tools against which to assess *in part* the reasonableness or excessiveness of a broker's handling of an investor's account" (emphasis original)) (citing Mihara v. Dean Witter & Co., Inc., 619 F.2d 814, 824 (9th Cir. 1980)).

[41] Cheng, 697 F. Supp. at 1227.

[42] *Id.*

for negligence based on a rule violation does not improperly circumvent the prohibition of a private right of action for such a violation.[43] This is because a violation does not automatically result in negligence; it is simply indicative of the relevant standard of care.[44]

The theory that, even if no private right of action exists, FINRA rules establish the relevant standard of care continues to carry weight today.[45] Very recently, in *Remington v. Newbridge Securities Corp.,* the Southern District of Florida allowed a claim to proceed under this theory.[46] In *Remington*, the plaintiff claimed negligence for the broker's failure to act in the best interests of its customers.[47] In support of its claim, the plaintiff cited FINRA Rule 2430, which it claimed established the proper standard of care.[48] The court agreed and held that even though there is no private cause of action for violation of FINRA rules, the claim was proper because evidence of the rule violation will not automatically result in a finding of negligence.[49] The rule is merely indicative of the standard of care.[50] This is identical to theory accepted by the courts in *Miley*, *Cheng* and even earlier cases, and it reaffirms the relevance that a FINRA rule violation can have to claims brought in court.

So, while an investor who walks into court spouting claims of rule violations will almost surely be turned away, he is not forced to sit idly by while his broker runs amuck. There are at least two avenues through which an investor may seek recovery. First, a FINRA arbitration panel will allow private actions for FINRA rule violations even if courts do not. Second, if the investor did not sign forms committing to arbitration and if the investor prefers to pursue the claims in court, the investor is still able to do so under traditional common law causes of action, citing FINRA rules as evidence of the proper standard of care.

---

43 *Id.*

44 *Id.* (citing Nelson v. Hench, 428 F. Supp. 411, 420 (D. Minn. 1977)).

45 *See, e.g.* Fernea, 2011 WL 2769838; Javitch v. First Montauk Fin. Corp., 279 F. Supp. 2d 931, 938 (N.D. Ohio 2003) (even if no private right of action for NASD rule violations, the rules reflect the standard of care for the industry) (citing Miley, 637 F.2d 318, 333 (5th Cir. 1981); U.S. v. Bloom, 450 F. Supp. 323 (E.D. Pa. 1978); Lange v. H. Hentz & Co., 418 F. Supp. 1376 (N.D. Tex. 1976); Stevenson v. Rochdale Inv. Mgmt., Inc., 2000 WL 1278479 (N.D. Tex. 2000)).

46 *See* Remington v. Newbridge Sec. Corp., No. 13–60384-CIV, 2013 WL 2444719 (S.D. Fla. June 5, 2013).

47 *Id.* at *5.

48 *Id.*

49 *Id.* at *6.

50 *Id.*

LIMITED PRIVATE RIGHT OF ACTION UNDER SECTION 215 OF THE INVESTMENT ADVISERS ACT

While the private right of action for violations of exchange rules is virtually non-existent in state and federal courts after *Transamerica*, the Supreme Court in *Transamerica* did establish an implied private right of action under Section 215 of the Investment Adviser Act ("IAA"). Section 215(b) provides that "[e]very contract made in violation of any provision of [the IAA] and every contract heretofore or hereafter made, the performance of which involves the violation of … any provision of this subchapter … shall be void."[51]

In *Transamerica*, the plaintiff brought three claims under the IAA, but the trial court dismissed all of them on the theory that the IAA provides no express private right of action.[52] The court of appeals reversed and the Supreme Court granted certiorari to clarify the issue.[53] Despite the lack of any statutory language creating a private right of action, the Supreme Court concluded such a right was implied. The Court started its analysis by acknowledging that Section 215 was "intended to benefit… the parties to advisory contract."[54] And, that the lack of an express private right of action does not preclude a finding that Congress implicitly intended to include such an action through "the language or structure of the statute, or in the circumstances of its enactment."[55]

Turning to the language of Section 215, the Court further held that "[b]y declaring certain contracts void, § 215 by its terms necessarily contemplates that the issue of voidness under its criteria may be litigated

---

51 (b) Rights affected by invalidity
(1) Every contract made in violation of any provision of this subchapter and every contract heretofore or hereafter made, the performance of which involves the violation of, or the continuance of any relationship or practice in violation of any provision of this subchapter, or any rule, regulation, or order thereunder, shall be void as regards the rights of any person who, in violation of any such provision, rule, regulation, or order, shall have made or engaged in the performance of any such contract, and
(2) as regards the rights of any person who, not being a party to such contract, shall have acquired any right thereunder with actual knowledge of the facts by reason of which the making or performance of such contract was in violation of any such provision. 15 U.S.C. § 80b-15.

52 444 U.S. at 14.

53 *Id.*

54 *Id.* at 17.

55 *Id.* at 18.

somewhere."[56] And, "[a] person with the power to avoid a contract ordinarily may resort to a court to have the contract rescinded and to obtain restitution of consideration paid."[57] Thus, the private right of action under Section 215 of the IAA was born.

However, in the same discussion, the Court held that no private cause of action exists under Section 206 of the IAA because that section only proscribes certain conduct; it does not create or alter any liabilities.[58] Section 206 provides a list of prohibited transactions by investment advisers meant to protect investors from fraudulent and deceptive practices.[59] And, because "Congress expressly provided both judicial and administrative means for enforcing compliance with § 206, … it is highly improbable that 'Congress absentmindedly forgot to mention an intended private action.'"[60]

---

56 *Id.*

57 *Id.*

58 *Id.* at 19.

59 It shall be unlawful for any investment adviser by use of the mails or any means or instrumentality of interstate commerce, directly or indirectly—to employ any device, scheme, or artifice to defraud any client or prospective client;

> (2) to engage in any transaction, practice, or course of business which operates as a fraud or deceit upon any client or prospective client;
> (3) acting as principal for his own account, knowingly to sell any security to or purchase any security from a client, or acting as broker for a person other than such client, knowingly to effect any sale or purchase of any security for the account of such client, without disclosing to such client in writing before the completion of such transaction the capacity in which he is acting and obtaining the consent of the client to such transaction. The prohibitions of this paragraph shall not apply to any transaction with a customer of a broker or dealer if such broker or dealer is not acting as an investment adviser in relation to such transaction; or
> (4) to engage in any act, practice, or course of business which is fraudulent, deceptive, or manipulative. The Commission shall, for the purposes of this paragraph (4) by rules and regulations define, and prescribe means reasonably designed to prevent, such acts, practices, and courses of business as are fraudulent, deceptive, or manipulative. 15 U.S.C. § 80b-6.

60 Transamerica, 444 U.S. at 20 (citation omitted) (Section 206 violations may be enforced by (1) fine or imprisonment; (2) civil action by the SEC; and (3) administrative sanctions).

Only Parties to an Investment Adviser Contract May Bring a Claim Under Section 215

Following *Transamerica*, several courts clarified the requirements for a party to sue under Section 215. Specifically, only those parties who are subject to an investment adviser contract can utilize the implied private right of action.[61]

In *Frank Russell Co. v. Wellington Management Co.*, a broker, Arnold Schneider, left Wellington Management Co. to start his own firm. After Schneider's departure, several Wellington clients, including Frank Russell Co., transferred several of their accounts to Schneider's new firm.[62] Russell was a client of Wellington at the time, having entrusted more than $1 billion to Wellington's care.[63] As part of its relationship with Wellington, Russell entered into several contracts with Wellington that gave Russell the right to terminate the relationship without notice.[64]

Prior to Schneider's departure from Wellington, Russell assured Schneider it would follow him to his new firm.[65] After Schneider's partnership with Wellington was terminated, Russell terminated its contracts with Wellington and moved its investments to Schneider's firm.[66] Wellington then sued Schneider for violating his non-compete agreement.[67] Later, Russell filed suit against Wellington to enjoin Wellington from enforcing the non-compete agreement.[68] Russell's argument was that "it [was] entitled to enjoin Wellington from enforcing the non-compete agreement because such enforcement [would] cause Wellington to breach its fiduciary duties … under the Investment Advisers Act."[69]

In reviewing Russell's claims, the Third Circuit began by acknowledging the private right of action implicitly included in Section 215.[70] It went on to state that "[i]f Russell seeks to void its contract with

---

61 *See* Frank Russell Co. v. Wellington Mgmt. Co., 154 F.3d 97 (3d Cir. 1998); Valentini v. Citigroup, Inc., 837 F. Supp. 2d 304 (S.D.N.Y. 2011); Oliver v. Black Knight Asset Mgmt., 812 F. Supp. 2d 2 (D.D.C. 2011); Clark v. Nevis Capital Mgmt., No. 04 Civ. 2702 (RWS), 2005 WL 488641 (S.D.N.Y. Mar. 2, 2005).

62 154 F.3d at 99.

63 *Id.*

64 *Id.*

65 *Id.* at 100.

66 *Id.*

67 *Id.*

68 *Id.*

69 *Id.* at 101.

70 *Id.* at 102.

Wellington under § 215, it has a cause of action," but it has no cause of action for any other remedy.[71] But, Russell had voluntarily canceled its contracts with Wellington prior to initiating its suit.[72] Therefore, because there were no contracts, the suit could not be to void a contract and could not be brought under the limited right of action found in Section 215.[73]

In *Valentini v. Citigroup, Inc.*, the court reached a similar conclusion in holding that no right of action exists for any party not subject to an investment adviser contract.[74] There, the court held that merely providing the plaintiffs with investment advice in the course of their professional duties as brokers of the plaintiff's non-discretionary investment accounts was not enough to establish an investment adviser contract.[75]

A Section 215 Claim May be Premised on Contracts Formed or Performed in Violation of the IAA

In addition to clarifying the type of plaintiff eligible to sue under Section 215, courts have also clarified the type of conduct on which a Section 215 suit may be based. It is not necessary that the contract itself violate the IAA.[76] Instead, a private party may bring suit under Section 215 to void an investment adviser contract, even if the contract was validly formed, as long as the performance of the contract violates the IAA.[77] These decisions do nothing to expand the reach of Section 215. They merely clarify the outer edges of the private right of action based on the statute's text.

But, investors are not left without a remedy for violations of other sections of the IAA, such as Section 206. Because the private right of

---

[71] *Id.*

[72] *Id.*

[73] *Id.*

[74] 837 F. Supp. 2d at 324 (citing Norman v. Salomon Smith Barney, 350 F. Supp. 2d 382, 388 (S.D.N.Y. 2004)).

[75] Valentini, 837 F. Supp. 2d at 325 (citing Bogart v. Shearson Lehman Bros., No. 91 Civ. 1036, 1993 WL 33643, *5 (S.D.N.Y. Feb. 3, 1993)); *see also* Oliver, 812 F. Supp. 2d at 13–14 (employer-employee relationship is not sufficient to support claim under § 215); Clark, 2005 WL 488641, at *13–14 (being a shareholder of a fund does not create an investment adviser contract for purposes of § 215).

[76] In re Evergreen Mut. Funds Fee Litig., 423 F. Supp. 2d 249, 262 (S.D.N.Y. 2006) (citing Clark, 2005 WL 488641, at *12–13; Norman, 350 F. Supp. 2d 382).

[77] Evergreen, 423 F. Supp. 2d at 262.

action under Section 215 allows rescission of contracts where performance, in addition to formation, violates the IAA, violation of any section of the IAA will support a claim under Section 215. For example, despite courts having repeatedly held that no private right of action exists under Section 206,[78] the Eastern District of Virginia used the Section 215 right of action to allow a remedy for a Section 206 violation.[79] In *Morris v. Wachovia Securities, Inc.*, after first holding that any private right of action under the IAA must arise under Section 215,[80] it then held that any violation of the IAA may allow a private party to void its investment adviser contract under Section 215.[81] The court then found that the broker had violated Section 206 and that the Section 206 violation was sufficient to trigger Section 215 and allow the investor to seek rescission.[82]

No Money Damages are Available in Section 215 Claims

Regardless of the conduct giving rise to the Section 215 claim, the remedies available to private parties remain the same: rescission of the contract, injunction against continued enforcement, and restitution.[83] When a party seeks to rescind the contract, "the rescinding party may seek 'consideration given under the contract, less any value conferred by the other party.'"[84] And, "[r]estitution does not include compensation for any losses from an investment alleged to have been made as a result of an investment adviser's conduct."[85]

---

78 Transamerica, 444 U.S. at 19–10; *see also* In re Bayou Hedge Fund Litig., 534 F. Supp. 2d 405, 420 (S.D.N.Y. 2007) ("It is well-settled that 'no implied private right of action for damages exists under Section 206 of the IAA'").

79 Morris v. Wachovia Sec., Inc., 277 F. Supp. 2d 622, 646.

80 277 F. Supp. 2d at 643.

81 *Id.* at 644 (in order to determine whether a contract is voidable under Section 215, there must first be a violation of the IAA).

82 *Id.* at 645–46.

83 *Id.* at 643 (citing Transamerica, 444 U.S. at 17–18).

84 Clark, 2005 WL 488641, at *13.

85 *Id.*

UNCERTAIN FUTURE OF SECURITIES CLASS ACTIONS

Another means for investors to seek redress for violations of the securities laws is the class action. However, because of recent developments in the U.S. Supreme Court and within FINRA itself, the future of securities class actions is in jeopardy.

Attack on FINRA Rules Protecting Availability of Class Litigation

FINRA rules on customer v. member class litigation

Arbitration of disputes between FINRA members and their customers[86] proceeds according to the Code of Arbitration Procedure for Customer Disputes (the "Code"), which comprises the 12000 Series of FINRA Rules. FINRA Rule 2268(d) provides that "[n]o predispute arbitration agreement shall include any condition that: (1) limits or contradicts the rules of any self-regulatory organization ... (3) limits the ability of a party to file any claim in court permitted to be filed in court under the rules of the forums in which a claim may be filed under the agreement."

Rule 12204(a) provides that "[c]lass action claims may not be arbitrated under the Code." Rule 12204(d) provides as follows:

> A member or associated person may not enforce any arbitration agreement against a member of a certified or putative class action with respect to any claim that is the subject of the certified or putative class action until:
>
> - The class certification is denied;
> - The class is decertified;
> - The member of the certified or putative class is excluded from the class by the court; or
> - The member of the certified or putative class elects not to participate in the class or withdraws from the class according to conditions set by the court, if any.

---

[86] A member is defined as "any broker or dealer admitted to membership in FINRA, whether or not the membership has been terminated or cancelled; and any broker or dealer admitted to membership in a self-regulatory organization that, with FINRA consent, has required its members to arbitrate pursuant to the Code and/or to be treated as members of FINRA for purposes of the Code, whether or not the membership has been terminated or cancelled." Rule 12100(o). "Customer" is defined simply as excluding brokers and dealers. Rule 12100(i).

Thus, although FINRA will not provide a forum for class actions, by expressly barring its members from enforcing arbitration agreements against members of class actions, it ensures that securities class actions in court are available to investors. When it proposed the above rule in 1992, FINRA-predecessor NASD stated that "the bar on class actions in arbitration was designed to provide investors with access to the courts, which already have developed the procedures and the expertise for managing class actions."[87] The SEC approved the rule and stated that it "believes that investor access to the courts should be preserved for class actions. …"[88]

Federal Arbitration Act and its application to securities disputes

For centuries, arbitration was strongly disfavored and courts routinely threw out arbitration agreements, requiring parties to settle their disputes through litigation.[89] To counter this judicial hostility toward arbitration and "place arbitration agreements 'upon the same footing as other contracts,'"[90] the Federal Arbitration Act ("FAA") was enacted in 1925.[91] Since then, courts have become increasingly favorable to arbitration, with many viewing it as a fair, cost-effective, and efficient alternative to litigation.[92] Indeed, the U.S. Supreme Court has repeatedly praised the benefits of arbitration in its decisions applying the FAA and "rigorously enforce[s]"[93] arbitration agreements.[94] Under the FAA, courts must put

---

[87] SEC approving release for amendments to NASD Code of Arbitration Procedure and Rules of Fair Practice, Exchange Act Rel. No. 31371 at *5–6, 1992 SEC LEXIS 2767, 57 Fed. Reg. 42659 (Oct. 28, 1992).

[88] *Id.* at *9.

[89] *See, e.g.*, Scherk v. Alberto-Culver Co., 417 U.S. 506, 510 n. 4 (1974) (explaining that "English courts traditionally considered irrevocable arbitration agreements as 'ousting' the courts of jurisdiction, and refused to enforce such agreements for this reason. This view was adopted by American courts as part of the common law up to the time of the adoption of the Arbitration Act.").

[90] *Id.* at 510–11 (quoting H.R. Rep. No. 96, 68th Cong., 1st Sess., 1, 2 (1924)).

[91] 9 U.S.C. § 1 et seq.

[92] *See, e.g.*, Shearson/American Express Inc. v. McMahon, 482 U.S. 220, 233 (1987) ("[T]he mistrust of arbitration that formed the basis for the *Wilko* opinion in 1953 is difficult to square with the assessment of arbitration that has prevailed since that time.").

[93] Dean Witter Reynolds Inc. v. Byrd, 470 U.S. 213, 221 (1985) (preeminent concern of Congress requires courts to "rigorously enforce agreements to arbitrate").

[94] *See, e.g.*, AT&T Mobility LLC v. Concepcion, 563 U.S. ___, 131 S. Ct. 1740, 1749 (2011) ("[T]he informality of arbitral proceedings is itself desirable,

arbitration agreements on equal footing with other contracts and enforce them according to their terms.[95]

In *Shearson/American Express Inc. v. McMahon*,[96] the Supreme Court held an arbitration agreement between a brokerage firm and its customers enforceable in the context of the customers' claims under Section 10(b) of the Securities Exchange Act of 1934.[97] Departing from its holding in *Wilko v. Swan*,[98] the Court made it clear that the FAA applies to claims based upon securities statutes with as much force as it applies to any other legal dispute in which Congress has not expressly overridden the FAA's command.[99] Since then, the rule in the securities industry has been that disputes must be arbitrated, rather than litigated unless the securities industry decides to create an exception.

AT&T Mobility and Charles Schwab's class action waiver

In *AT&T Mobility LLC v. Concepcion*,[100] the U.S. Supreme Court held that the FAA preempted California law (dubbed the *Discover Bank Rule*)[101] prohibiting class action waivers in consumer contracts of adhesion where disputes between the parties typically involve small sums. The Ninth Circuit had ruled that the *Discover Bank Rule* fell within the FAA's exception to enforcement "upon such grounds as exist at law or in equity for the revocation of any contract."[102] In doing so, the Ninth Circuit rejected the argument that the *Discover Bank Rule* put arbitration

---

reducing the cost and increasing the speed of dispute resolution"); Stolt-Nielsen SA v. AnimalFeeds Int'l, 559 U.S. ___, 130 S. Ct. 1758, 1776 (2010) ("In bilateral arbitration, parties forgo the procedural rigor and appellate review of the courts in order to realize the benefits of private dispute resolution: lower costs, greater efficiency and speed, and the ability to choose expert adjudicators to resolve specialized disputes").

[95] AT&T Mobility, LLC v. Concepcion, 131 S. Ct. at 1745.

[96] 482 U.S. 220 (1987).

[97] 15 U.S.C. § 78j(b).

[98] 346 U.S. 427 (1953) (holding that an arbitration agreement could not be enforced in a dispute involving a claim based on Section 12(2) of the Securities Act of 1933, 15 U.S.C. § 771(2)).

[99] 482 U.S. at 231–32 (noting that "the reasons given in *Wilko* reflect a general suspicion of the desirability of arbitration and the competence of arbitral tribunals—most apply with no greater force to the arbitration of securities disputes than to the arbitration of legal disputes generally. It is difficult to reconcile *Wilko*'s mistrust of the arbitral process with this Court's subsequent decisions involving the [FAA]").

[100] 131 S. Ct. 1740.

[101] Discover Bank v. Super. Ct. of L. A., 113 P.3d 1100, 1110 (Cal. 2005).

[102] 584 F.3d 849, 856–59 (2009) (quoting 9 U.S.C. § 2).

agreements on a different footing than other contracts, noting that the *Discover Bank Rul*e applied equally to class action waivers in litigation and arbitration.[103]

The Supreme Court disagreed, stating that the *Discover Bank Rule* "interferes with arbitration" by allowing "any party to a consumer contract to demand [classwide arbitration] *ex post*," which "makes the process slower, more costly, and more likely to generate procedural morass than final judgment."[104] Because this defeats the very purpose of arbitration, which is by its nature "poorly suited to the higher stakes of class litigation," a class procedure in arbitration "is not arbitration as envisioned by the FAA, lacks its benefits, and therefore may not be required by state law."[105] Thus, the *Discover Bank Rule* was preempted by the FAA,[106] and class action waivers in arbitration agreements—even those that are part of consumer contracts of adhesion—appeared to be completely enforceable under the FAA.

Emboldened by this decision, Charles Schwab inserted class action waivers into its customer agreements (the "Class Waiver").[107] Schwab also added a provision denying arbitrators the ability to consolidate the claims of more than one party in one arbitration proceeding (the "Anti-Consolidation Provision").[108] In response to these additions, FINRA's Department of Enforcement brought a disciplinary action against Schwab through FINRA's internal disciplinary mechanisms, seeking sanctions and an order that the Class Waiver and Anti-Consolidation Provision are unenforceable and must be removed from its customer agreements.[109]

---

[103] *Id.* at 857–58 (discussing Shroyer v. New Cingular Wireless Servs., Inc., 498 F.3d 976, 990 (9th Cir. 2007)).

[104] AT&T Mobility, 131 S. Ct. at 1750–51.

[105] *Id.* at 1752–53.

[106] *Id.* at 1753.

[107] Dep't of Enforcement v. Charles Schwab & Co., FINRA Disc. Pro. No. 2011029760201, Hearing Panel Decision Granting in Part and Denying in Part the Parties' Cross-Motions for Summary Disposition, at 23 (Feb. 21, 2013) (McConathy, Arb.) (hereinafter "Charles Schwab"), available at http://www.finra.org/web/groups/industry/@ip/@enf/@ad/documents/industry/p210893.pdf.

[108] *Id.* at 19.

[109] Dep't of Enforcement v. Charles Schwab & Co., FINRA Disc. Pro. No. 2011029760201, Complaint (Feb. 1, 2012), http://www.finra.org/web/groups/industry/@ip/@enf/@ad/documents/industry/p125516.pdf.

FINRA hearing panel's decision on Schwab's class action waiver

On February 21, 2013, the hearing panel presiding over the disciplinary action granted summary disposition for FINRA as to the Anti-Consolidation Provision, ordering Schwab to remove the provision and send out revised customer agreements, and also to notify customers that consolidation remains available pursuant to FINRA's rules and to pay a $500,000 fine.[110] However, the hearing panel dismissed the causes of action relating to the Class Waiver. Despite finding that the Class Waiver violated FINRA's rules, the hearing panel concluded that the violated rules were preempted by the FAA.[111]

Specifically, the hearing panel found that the Class Waiver violated Rule 2268(d)(1) and (d)(3) by depriving customers of the right to bring or participate in a class action, as provided by Rule 12204.[112] The panel then went on to discuss whether FINRA's rules providing for the availability of judicial class actions were unenforceable because they conflicted with the FAA. First, the panel decided that the FAA did apply, under its own express terms, to Schwab's customer agreement because the agreement related to "transactions involving commerce."[113] The decision next discussed the rule that only Congress can create exceptions to the FAA and Supreme Court precedent reiterating this rule and emphasizing the federal policy in favor of arbitration.[114] Law and rules created by government entities other than Congress, such as state governments, that hinder that policy are necessarily preempted.

Although this is unquestionably true, it leaves open the question of why FINRA's rules are preempted. If the point of the FAA is to give full effect to private agreements to arbitrate, then it is unclear why an exception to the general requirement—contained within the agreement itself—is invalid. This is the linchpin of the hearing panel's decision, but it is given surprisingly little discussion. The issue was briefly discussed as follows:

---

110 Charles Schwab, at 10–11, 48.

111 *Id.* at 9–10.

112 *Id.* at 23–26 (the panel also found violation of NASD Rule 3110(f)(4)(A) and (C), which applied prior to December 5, 2011, but as noted in footnote 6 on p. 6, FINRA Rule 2268 and NASD Rule 3110 are identical).

113 *Id.* at 33–34 (the panel also noted that Schwab's customer agreements expressly provided that the FAA governs).

114 *Id.* at 34–39 (discussing Nitro-Lift Techns., L.L.C. v. Howard, 568 U.S. __, 133 S. Ct. 500 (2012); Marmet Health Care Ctr. v. Brown, 565 U.S. __, 132 S. Ct. 1201 (2012); Compucredit Corp. v. Greenwood, 132 S. Ct. 655 (2012); KPMG LLP v. Cocchi, 565 U.S. __, 132 S. Ct. 23 (2011)).

> That FINRA's Rules are in issue here instead of state or federal statutes or regulations does not make a difference. FINRA promulgates its Rules pursuant to delegated authority from the SEC and subject to the SEC's oversight and approval, as part of its mission to protect investors and promote market integrity. While the Rules have the force and effect of federal regulation and may preempt state law, FINRA's Rules can only be enforced to the extent that they are not inconsistent with federal law. Federal law includes the FAA. Accordingly, FINRA's Rules may not be enforced to the extent they are inconsistent with the FAA, unless *Congress* has created a relevant exception.[115]

In this section, the decision cites case law providing that federal regulations conflicting with federal statutes are invalid.[116] Thus, because of the SEC's oversight of FINRA's rulemaking, the hearing panel treats FINRA's rules as de facto SEC regulations. And, since the SEC cannot do anything inimical to the federal policy favoring arbitration without express congressional mandate, neither can FINRA. The decision then explains that nothing in the federal securities laws indicates a "congressional intent to preserve judicial class actions as an option in customer securities claims even where there is a predispute arbitration agreement," and that case law supports the opposite conclusion.[117] Therefore, FINRA's rules preserving securities class actions are preempted by the FAA.

The decision acknowledges in a footnote that "despite the Supreme Court decisions described above, the interplay of arbitration and class actions remains controversial."[118] This footnote then describes the Second Circuit's decision, *In re American Express Merchants' Litigation, Italian Colors Restaurant v. American Express Travel Related Services Co.*,[119] which the hearing panel presumably saw as supporting a more restrictive view of the FAA's scope than did the hearing panel. It noted that "[t]he Hearing Panel doubts that *AMEX III* can stand in the fact of *Concepcion* and subsequent Supreme Court decisions … ."[120] As it turns out, the Hearing Panel was right.

---

115 *Id.* at 39–40 (emphasis in original) (citations omitted).

116 *Id.* at 40 n. 91.

117 *Id.* at 41.

118 *Id.* at 39 n. 89.

119 667 F.3d 204, 219 (2d Cir. 2012).

120 Charles Schwab, at 39 n. 89 (further noting that even if the Second Circuit's decision in *AMEX III* survived Supreme Court review, it still would not provide a basis for holding that securities class actions in court must be preserved notwithstanding the FAA).

Italian Colors

In *American Express Co. v. Italian Colors Restaurant*,[121] the Supreme Court was faced with the question of "whether a contractual waiver of class arbitration is enforceable under the FAA when the plaintiff's cost of individually arbitrating a federal statutory claim exceeds the potential recovery."[122] It answered in the affirmative.

The parties' contract required arbitration of all disputes and contained a class action waiver.[123] The plaintiffs, suing under federal antitrust laws, resisted defendant's motion to compel individual arbitration on the grounds that the class waiver could not be enforced because the maximum recovery that any individual plaintiff might obtain was far less than the cost of proving their claim.[124] Disagreeing with the plaintiffs, the Court first stated that the text of the FAA "reflects the overarching principle that arbitration is a matter of contract" and that only Congress can override the FAA's mandate such to be contracts strictly enforced.[125] The Court found no such congressional command in the antitrust laws, and noted that those laws were in fact enacted decades before Federal Rule of Civil Procedure 23 was promulgated to provide for class actions.[126] The Court also downplayed the importance of class actions generally by noting that they are an exception to the "usual rule" of litigation between individual parties and that "congressional approval of Rule 23 [does not] establish an entitlement to class proceedings for the vindication of statutory rights."[127]

The plaintiffs, however, argued that their situation fell within the ambit of a judicially-crafted exception to the FAA known as the "effective vindication" exception.[128] This exception (which, the Court noted had its roots in dicta) provided for the possibility of invalidation of arbitration agreements on public policy grounds where such agreements "operat[e] ... as a prospective waiver of a party's *right to pursue* statutory remedies."[129] The Court noted that this might include arbitration filing and administrative fees so high that the forum would, as a practical

---

[121] 570 U.S. ___, 133 S. Ct. 2304 (2013).
[122] 133 S. Ct. at 2307.
[123] *Id.* at 2308.
[124] *Id.*
[125] *Id.* at 2309.
[126] *Id.*
[127] *Id.*
[128] *Id.* at 2310.
[129] *Id.* (quoting Mitsubishi Motors Corp. v. Soler Chrysler-Plymouth, Inc., 473 U.S. 614, 637 n. 19) (emphasis in original).

matter, be inaccessible, and that it would definitely include a waiver of the right to bring certain statutory claims at all. But, "the fact that it is not worth the expense involved in *proving* a statutory remedy does not constitute elimination of the *right to pursue* that remedy."[130] The Court then stated that the class-action waiver "no more eliminates [the] parties' right to pursue their statutory remedy than did federal law before its adoption of the class action for legal relief in 1938."[131]

The Court further held that "our decision in AT&T all but resolves this case."[132] In fact, a footnote in the ensuing discussion is particularly revealing, describing the holding of *AT&T Mobility* as follows:

> [T]he FAA's command to enforce arbitration agreements trumps any interest in ensuring the prosecution of low-value claims. The latter interest, we said, is "unrelated" to the FAA. Accordingly, the FAA does ... favor the absence of litigation when that is the consequence of a class-action waiver, since its "principal purpose" is the enforcement of arbitration agreements according to their terms.[133]

The Court concluded that requiring a court to determine whether an individual arbitration claim would be cost-prohibitive to bring would create "a preliminary litigating hurdle [that] would undoubtedly destroy the prospect of speedy resolution that arbitration in general and bilateral arbitration in particular was meant to secure. The FAA does not sanction such a judicially created superstructure."[134]

After Italian Colors

Italian Colors thus forecloses another avenue of attacking the enforceability of class-action waivers (i.e., a cost-benefit imbalance rendering arbitration pointless), and in some ways arguably vindicates the FINRA Hearing Panel's decision regarding the Schwab class-action waiver. In addition to the fact that the Court ruled as the Hearing Panel predicted,[135] the Panel devoted several pages of its decision to discussion of four

---

130 Italian Colors, 133 S. Ct. at 2310–11 (emphasis in original).

131 *Id.* at 2311 (citing Fed. Rule Civ. Pro. 23, 28 U.S.C., 864 (1938 ed., Supp. V)).

132 Italian Colors, 133 S. Ct. at 2312.

133 *Id.* at 2312, n. 5 (internal citations omitted).

134 *Id.* at 2312.

135 Charles Schwab, at 39, n. 89.

recent Supreme Court cases mandating enforcement of arbitration agreements notwithstanding various policy concerns militating against arbitration.[136] *Italian Colors* provides yet another example.

Additionally, any arguments based upon the importance of class actions for the protection of rights provided by the securities laws, or upon the likelihood that individual lawsuits alleging violations of those rights will not be pursued because the costs of such litigation outweigh any potential recovery, will be unavailing. The Court rejected the idea that class actions are necessary to protect statutory rights when it stated that "the FAA's command to enforce arbitration agreements trumps any interest in ensuring the prosecution of low-value claims."[137] Thus, the National Adjudicatory Council may find the Hearing Panel's rationale reinforced by *Italian Colors* and thereby find support for affirming the Hearing Panel. And, if the National Adjudicatory Council does so, that may be the end of it. Class waivers in arbitration agreements between broker-dealers and customers will become standard and the number of securities class actions will therefore drop dramatically.

However, should the National Adjudicatory Council agree with the Department of Enforcement and find FINRA's Rules prohibiting class waivers not preempted by the FAA, it is fairly likely that this matter will head to federal court. Given the Supreme Court's apparent eagerness to grant certiorari in cases implicating the FAA (six such cases in the past three years),[138] it would not be surprising if the issue eventually made its way to the Supreme Court. And, if the Court did address the issue, it would give a sense of finality to the question of whether FINRA's Rules prohibiting class-action waivers was preempted by the FAA.

One recent opinion from the Southern District of New York answered that very question in the negative.[139] *Zeltser v. Merrill Lynch & Co.* involved a class action brought by employees of the defendants for alleged violations of the Fair Labor Standards Act and New York Labor

---

[136] *Id.* at 36–39 (discussing Nitro-Lift Techns., 133 S. Ct. 500; Marmet Health Care Ctr. v. Brown, 132 S. Ct. 1201; Compucredit Corp., 132 S. Ct. 655; Cocchi, 132 S. Ct. 23).

[137] Italian Colors, 133 S. Ct. at 2311, 2312, n. 5.

[138] *See* American Express Co. v. Italian Colors Restaurant, 570 U.S. ___, 133 S. Ct. 2304 (2013); Nitro-Lift Techns., LLC v. Howard, 568 U.S. __, 133 S. Ct. 500 (2012); Marmet Health Care Ctr. v. Brown, 565 U.S. __, 132 S. Ct. 1201 (2012); Compucredit Corp. v. Greenwood, 565 U.S. __, 132 S. Ct. 655 (2012); KPMG LLP v. Cocchi, 565 U.S. __, 132 S. Ct. 23 (2011)); AT&T Mobility LLC v. Concepcion, 563 U.S. ___, 131 S. Ct. 1740, 1749 (2011).

[139] Zeltser v. Merrill Lynch & Co., Inc., 13 CV 1531 (HB), 2013 WL 4857687 (Sept. 11, 2013).

Law. The specific FINRA rule at issue applied to industry disputes.[140] Although it discusses the SEC's interpretation of the rule vis-à-vis Fair Labor Standards Act actions,[141] nothing in the opinion's treatment of the preemption issue suggests that the holding would be any different in the context of customer disputes involving FINRA's analogous rule[142] (ignoring, of course, the Hearing Panel's Decision finding such Rule preempted by the FAA). The opinion states:

> Although recent opinions from the Supreme Court and this Circuit address arbitration in the context of FLSA claims and express a favorable view towards that modality, none of these opinions touch on whether arbitration should be compelled for class and collective actions where FINRA rules bind the parties. … Neither the Supreme Court nor the Second Circuit has held that FINRA is preempted by the FAA in a fact pattern such as the one before me.[143]

A federal court facing the question of whether FINRA can bar its members from including a class action waiver in their arbitration agreements may well hold, as the Southern District of New York did in *Zeltser*, that FINRA's rules are not preempted by the FAA. Such a court might reason that FINRA, a non-governmental entity, can require its members to play by its own rules if they wish to remain members, and that this requirement is simply part of a private agreement to arbitrate—one that binds members just as the members' own arbitration agreements bind customers. As the FINRA Hearing Panel itself noted, "courts have recognized that FINRA's Arbitration Rules themselves constitute an agreement to arbitrate that is covered by the FAA, even separate from a customer-member agreement."[144] If the purpose of the FAA is to require courts to "'rigorously enforce' arbitration agreements *according to their terms*,"[145] then the terms of FINRA's private agreement with its members should also be enforced. As the Supreme Court has explained, "[t]he Act, after all, does not mandate the arbitration of all claims, but merely the

140 *Id.* at *1 (citing FINRA Rule 13204).

141 *Id.*

142 FINRA Rule 12204. Rule 12204(d) and Rule 13304(a)(4) are identical, both barring the enforcement of arbitration agreements against members of a certified or putative class except in limited circumstances.

143 Zeltser, s*upra* note 140, at *3 (citations omitted).

144 Charles Schwab, at 34 (citing Wash. Square Sec., Inc. v. Aune, 385 F.3d 432, 435 (4th Cir. 2004), and Morgan Keegan & Co. v. Silverman, 2013 U.S. App. LEXIS 2412, *3–4 (4th Cir. Feb. 4, 2013)).

145 Italian Colors, 133 S. Ct. at 2309 (quoting Dean Witter Reynolds, 470 U.S. at 221) (emphasis added).

enforcement—upon the motion of one of the parties—of privately negotiated arbitration agreements."[146]

A court finding that the FAA does preempt FINRA's rules on this issue would probably respond, as the FINRA Hearing Panel suggested, that because "FINRA promulgates its Rules pursuant to delegated authority from the SEC and subject to the SEC's oversight and approval,"[147] FINRA is a sort of quasi-governmental entity and its rules are therefore not a private agreement with its members. Thus, should the issue of whether FINRA can prohibit its members from including class-action waivers in their arbitration agreements with customers or from enforcing such agreements against customers end up in federal court, the outcome will likely hinge upon the court's determination of whether or not FINRA is a de facto government entity, at least for purposes of the FAA.

Threat to the Fraud-on-the-Market Presumption

Another threat to securities class actions comes in the form of the U.S. Supreme Court possibly overruling the fraud-on-the-market presumption.

History of the presumption

First acknowledged by the Supreme Court in *Basic, Inc. v. Levinson*,[148] the fraud-on-the-market theory is a method through which an investor may satisfy the reliance element of a Rule 10b-5 claim. Reliance is essential to the Rule 10b-5 claim because reliance makes certain that a plaintiff's injury actually stems from the defendant's misrepresentation.[149] But, given the difficulty many investors would face in showing actual reliance, the courts developed the fraud-on-the-market theory, which creates a rebuttable presumption of reliance. The theory is especially important in class litigation because it allows for a presumption of reliance by the entire class where certification would otherwise generally be precluded due to individual issues of reliance outnumbering those common to the class.[150]

The fraud-on-the-market theory grew out of the realization that "average investors in a developed market do not personally need to access the

---

146 Dean Witter Reynolds, 470 U.S. at 219.

147 Charles Schwab, at 39.

148 485 U.S. 224 (1988).

149 Amgen v. Conn. Retirement Plans & Trust, 568 U.S. ___, 133 S. Ct. 1184, 1192 (2013).

150 *Id.* at 1193.

elaborate disclosure of documents and accounting data required by our securities laws."[151] Because investors do not personally review specific disclosures, they are "presumed under the fraud-on-the-market theory to rely on the integrity of information reflected in the market price of the security."[152]

The theory is an extension of the efficient capital markets hypothesis, which posits that "in an open and developed securities market, the price of a company's stock is determined by the available material information regarding the company and its business."[153] This concept of an efficient market was expressly relied upon by Congress in drafting the 1934 Act.[154] And, just as an efficient market assumes the market price reflects all available information, it also assumes that "artificial manipulation tends to upset the true function of an open market [and]… the hiding and secreting of important information obstructs the operation of the markets as indices of real value."[155]

The Supreme Court also found support for the theory in "common sense and probability."[156] In an efficient market, the security's price is presumed to reflect all available information; therefore, "few investors in such markets, if any, can consistently achieve above-market returns by trading based on public available information alone, for if such above-market returns were readily attainable, it would mean that market prices were not efficiently incorporating the full supply of public information."[157] And, because most investors know they cannot beat the market in the long run based solely on public information, common sense suggests they "will rely on the security's market price as an unbiased assessment of the security's value in light of all public information."[158]

Plaintiffs invoking the fraud-on-the-market theory do not have to "show that they actually knew of the communication that contained the

---

151 In re Verifone Sec. Litig., 784 F. Supp. 1471, 1479 (N.D. Cal. 1992).

152 *Id.* (citing Basic, 485 U.S. at 247).

153 Basic, 485 U.S. at 241 (quoting Peil v. Speiser, 806 F.2d 1154, 1160–61 (3d Cir. 1986)).

154 Basic, 485 U.S. at 245–46.

155 *Id.* at 246 (citing H. R. Rep. No. 1383, at 11).

156 Basic, 485 U.S. at 246.

157 Amgen, 133 S. Ct. at 1192.

158 *Id.*

misrepresentation or omission."[159] They must only "allege that the stock in question traded on an open and efficient market."[160]

However, implicit in the theory is a requirement of reasonableness. It requires that the market be reasonable in reacting to the alleged misrepresentation.[161] "Thus, a claim that a fraud was perpetrated on the market can draw no sustenance from allegations that defendant made overly-optimistic statements, if those statements are ones that … [the market] … would easily recognize as nothing more than a kind of self-directed corporate puffery."[162] Just because some investors may be "easily duped," does not mean that the market is equally gullible.[163]

But, assuming the standard of reasonableness is met, the defendant will be "held liable for any material misrepresentation which is proved to have caused the price of a security traded on an open and developed securities market to deviate from the securities efficient price."[164] Though, a defendant will generally not be liable for silence as "silence is not misleading in the absence of a duty to disclose."[165] If a plaintiff is attempting invoke the fraud-on-the-market theory in a case of non-disclosure, the plaintiff "must show both that the 'information would have been helpful to investors [and]… that the information was of a kind which the defendants had a legally cognizable duty to disclose."[166]

While the fraud-on-the-market theory creates a presumption of reliance, that presumption may be rebutted. And, one means of rebuttal is the truth-on-the-market corollary. Under this theory, "a misrepresentation is immaterial if the information is already known to the market because the misrepresentation cannot then defraud the market."[167] But, this defense is only effective if the truthful information correcting the prior misrepresentation is "conveyed to the public 'with a degree of intensity and

---

159 In re Burlington Coat Factory Sec. Litig., 114 F.3d 1410, n. 8 (3d Cir. 1997) (citing Basic, 485 U.S. at 241–42).

160 Burlington Coat Factory, 114 F.3d at n. 8 (citing Hayes v. Gross, 982 F.2d 104, 107 (3d Cir. 1992); Peil, 806 F.2d at 1161 (3d Cir. 1986)).

161 Shaw v. Digital Equip. Corp., 82 F.3d 1194, 1218 (1st Cir. 1996).

162 *Id.* (emphasis original).

163 *Id.*

164 In re Verifone Sec. Litig., 784 F. Supp. 1471, 1478 (N.D. Cal. 1992).

165 *Id.* at 1479.

166 *Id.* (citing Basic, 485 U.S. at 239 n. 17) (alteration original).

167 Ganino v. Citizens Utils. Co., 228 F.3d 154, 167 (2d Cir. 2000) (citing Provenz v. Miller, 102 F.3d 1478, 1492 (9th Cir. 1996); Associated Randall Bank v. Griffin, Kubik, Stephens & Thompson, Inc., 3 F.3d 208, 213–14 (7th Cir. 1993)).

credibility sufficient to counter-balance effectively any misleading information created by' the alleged misstatements."[168] This defense is also "intensely fact-specific and is rarely an appropriate basis for dismissing a § 10(b) complaint."[169]

Halliburton

Despite its quarter-century history, the future of the fraud-on-the-market theory is in jeopardy. In November 2013, the Supreme Court granted certiorari in *Halliburton Co. v. Erica P. John Fund, Inc.*[170] The *Halliburton* case involved a putative class action filed against Halliburton and its CEO. Plaintiffs, who had purchased Halliburton stock, alleged that the company misrepresented its potential exposure in asbestos litigation, its expected revenue, and its expected benefits from a merger. Plaintiffs further alleged that these misrepresentations injured them when they were revealed to be false, resulting in a decline of Halliburton's stock price. In a prior 2011 appeal, the Supreme Court remanded the case to the Fifth Circuit, holding that it was not necessary that the plaintiffs show the misstatement affected the stock price before the class could be certified.

Following the 2011 decision, the case ended up back in the district court, where Halliburton argued that, in order to invoke the fraud-on-the-market theory and establish a class-wide basis for proving reliance, the plaintiff needed to show there had been a change in stock price based on the misrepresentations. This argument failed and the class was certified with the decision being affirmed by the Fifth Circuit. Halliburton then sought review by the Supreme Court where it challenged whether it was necessary for the plaintiff to show a change in stock price before class certification and, more generally, the fraud-on-the-market theory previously accepted in *Basic*.

Implications of overruling *Basic*

If the Supreme Court were to overrule *Basic* and eliminate or severely limit the fraud-on-the-market presumption, the impact on securities class litigation would be immense. The presumption of reliance is essentially the only way that class litigation is feasible, as indicated by Justice Thomas's dissent in *Amgen*.[171] Without the presumption, it would be

---

[168] Ganino, 228 F.3d at 167 (quoting In re Apple Computer Sec. Litig., 886 F.2d 1109, 1116 (9th Cir. 1989)).

[169] Ganino, 228 F.3d at 167.

[170] No. 13–317.

[171] 133 S. Ct. at 1209.

necessary to make individual findings of reliance for each class member, which would thwart the commonality requirement for class certification. And, given that the economic costs of securities litigation are generally only justified by the potential aggregate recovery, in which each individual investor may only recover a small amount, reform in how courts handle securities litigation will likely follow if claims must be litigated on an individual basis.

16. Comparative analysis of global securities regulation

Jerry W. Markham

INTRODUCTION

This chapter will compare the "functional" system of regulation in the United States with the single regulator and "twin peaks" approaches used elsewhere.[1] Under "functional" regulation, different regulators are appointed to regulate particular financial services, even if the same firm offers those services. This has resulted in much overlap and regulatory conflict in the U.S., and proved to be troublesome during the Financial Crisis in 2008. Although elsewhere in the world financial services regulation is mostly consolidated into a single regulator, that model also proved to be wanting during that crisis.

That the functional regulatory system in the U.S. was flawed should not have been a surprise. It is a haphazard system that is not the result of a design or reasoned blueprint. Rather, it is a set of accumulated responses to a long history of financial crises, scandals, happenstance, personalities, and compromises among a broad and competing array of industry and governmental bodies.

Under functional regulation, financial service firms are regulated at the state level by 50 state bank regulators, 50 insurance commissioners (plus the District of Columbia) acting collectively through the National Association of Insurance Commissioners ("NAIC"), 50 state securities commissioners acting collectively through the North American Securities Administrators Association ("NASAA"), and 50 state attorneys general who operate in wolf packs when attacking financial service firms. New York has also created a Department of Financial Services that is now

[1] This chapter is drawn in part from Jerry W. Markham, *Merging the SEC and CFTC—A Clash of Cultures*, 78 U. CINN. L. REV. 537 (2009) & Jerry W. Markham, *Regulating Credit Default Swaps in the Wake of the Subprime Crisis*. A Working Paper Prepared for the International Monetary Fund Seminar on Current Developments in Monetary and Financial Law (Dec. 2009).

seeking to become a national and international regulator of financial firms operating in that state.

At the federal level, functional financial services regulators for banks include the Federal Reserve Board ("Fed"), the Office of the Comptroller of the Currency in the Treasury Department ("OCC"), the Federal Deposit Insurance Corporation ("FDIC"), the Office of Thrift Supervision ("OTS"). A new Bureau of Consumer Financial Protection was created by the Dodd-Frank Wall Street Reform and Consumer Protection Act of 2010 ("Dodd-Frank Act"). The Dodd-Frank Act also created the Financial Stability Oversight Council that is tasked with identifying and specially regulating systemically important financial services firms

In addition, FinCEN is the Treasury Department's anti-money laundering group, and the Office of Foreign Asset Control ("OFAC"), which is also in the Treasury Department, handles financial embargoes on troublesome countries. Functional federal financial services regulators also include the Securities and Exchange Commission ("SEC") and the Commodity Futures Trading Commission ("CFTC"). Self-regulatory organizations ("SROs") such as the Financial Industry Regulatory Authority ("FINRA") and the National Futures Association ("NFA") also regulate various aspects of the financial services industry.

Adding to this incredible list of financial services regulators are the Federal Trade Commission (FTC), and (believe it or not) the Occupational Safety & Health Agency (OSHA) (for Sarbanes-Oxley Act whistleblower claims). The Justice Department, together with the FBI and Postal Inspectors, has also become a financial services regulator by criminalizing much of what had previously been viewed to be only civil violations.

THE TREASURY BLUEPRINT

Secretary of the Treasury Henry Paulson warned in 2006 that the country was "creating a thicket of regulation that impedes competitiveness."[2] The Treasury Department conducted a broad based study of financial services regulation in the U.S., and elsewhere, and its flaws. The Department sought public comment on regulatory efficiency issues involving functional regulation. The Department received over 350 letters in response to that request.[3] Of particular interest was the Department's request for

---

[2] Deborah Solomon, *Treasury's Paulson Warns of the Costs of Rules Overlap*, WALL ST J., Nov. 21, 2006, at A2.

[3] U.S. Treasury Assistant Secretary for Financial Institutions David G. Nason, Remarks Before the City of London Corporation, Redesigning U.S.

comment on whether the "increasing convergence of products across the traditional 'functional' regulatory lines of banking, insurance, securities, and futures" justifies changes in the regulatory system to ensure that regulatory boundary lines do not unnecessarily inhibit competition.[4]

The Treasury Department published its report in March 2008 ("Treasury Blueprint").[5] The Treasury Blueprint was the first effort to undertake a comprehensive review of financial services regulation in the United States since the 1984 report by the Task Group on Regulation of Financial Services that was headed by then Vice President George H.W. Bush. Its members included Donald T. Regan, Treasury Secretary and former Merrill Lynch CEO, the chairman of the Federal Reserve Board, representatives from the Attorney General's office, the Office of Management and Budget, and the heads of several agencies responsible for regulating financial services.

The Bush taskforce concluded that financial services in the United States were the "central nervous system of the economy" and that this industry was suffering from too much regulation. The Bush taskforce recommended reducing federal bank regulators from three to two, creating a new Federal Banking Agency in the Treasury Department and reducing financial services regulators. Those recommendations were not implemented.[6] Instead, Congress further embraced "functional" regulation in the Gramm-Leach-Bliley Act in 1999.[7]

The 2008 Treasury Blueprint recommended changes to the U.S. functional regulatory system. The Treasury Blueprint sought more centralized and rational regulation because of concern that functional regulation was ineffective and was undermining America's traditional

---

Financial Regulation for a Global Marketplace (Dec. 11, 2007), available at http://www.treas.gov/press/releases/hp726.htm (accessed Dec. 2007).

[4] 72 Fed. Reg. 58939 (Oct. 17, 2007).

[5] Department of the Treasury, *Blueprint for a Modernized Financial Regulatory Structure* (Mar. 2008).

[6] U.S. Task Group on Regulation of Financial Services, Blueprint for Reform: The Report of the Task Group on Regulation of Financial Services (1984).

[7] (Pub. L. No. 106–102, 113 Stat. 1338), which also repealed the provisions of the Glass-Steagall Act (Pub. L. No. 73–66, 48 Stat. 162). *See* Lissa L. Broome & Jerry W. Markham, Regulation of Banking Financial Service Activities, Cases and Materials 239–240 (3d ed. 2008) (discussing functional regulation). Still another study, this one entitled Financial Institutions and the Nation's Economy ("FINE"), was undertaken by the House Committee on Banking Currency and Housing in 1975. FINE recommended that all depository institutions be regulated by a single regulator, a recommendation ahead of its time.

competitive advantage in financial services.[8] The Treasury Blueprint found that functional regulation "exhibit[ed] several inadequacies, the most significant being the fact that no single regulator possesses all of the information and authority necessary to monitor systemic risk, or the potential that events associated with financial institutions may trigger broad dislocation or a series of defaults that affect the financial system so significantly that the real economy is adversely affected.[9]

The Treasury Blueprint contrasted the functional regulatory approach in America with regulatory mechanisms abroad. England, Germany, Japan, and dozens of other countries use a single consolidated regulator, along with a central bank, to regulate. Those countries also eschewed the "rules-based" approach used by most regulators in the United States.[10] Rather, foreign regulators generally use a "principles-based" approach that sets broad regulatory goals and permits the industry to decide how to meet those goals.

A principles-based approach reduces the need for volumes of regulations that seek to control every aspect of financial services operations—which is the approach taken by the SEC. The SEC has an institutional culture that is purely rule based. The agency thus seeks to dictate every aspect of corporate behavior. In contrast, the CFTC administers a principles-based regulatory structure put in place by the Commodity Futures Modernization Act of 2000.[11] However, in the wake of the Dodd-Frank Wall Street Reform and Consumer Protection Act of 2010, the CFTC has adopted a more rules-based approach and is starting to follow the SEC's regulatory model.

---

[8] Treasury Blueprint, *supra* note 5, at 2 noted

> Due to its sheer dominance in the global capital markets, the U.S. financial services industry for decades has been able to manage the inefficiencies in its regulatory structure and still maintain its leadership position. Now, however, maturing foreign financial markets and their ability to provide alternate sources of capital and financial innovation in a more efficient and modern regulatory system are pressuring the U.S. financial services industry and its regulatory structure.

[9] Treasury Blueprint, *supra* note 5, at 4.

[10] Treasury Blueprint, *supra* note 5, at 141.

[11] Commodity Futures Modernization Act of 2000, Pub. L. No. 106–554, 114 Stat. 2763.

THE FINANCIAL SERVICES AUTHORITY

Before the subprime crisis, the Financial Services Authority ("FSA"), Great Britain's single regulator, was a model for regulatory agencies around the world. That agency was created after earlier regulatory reform efforts in London failed.[12] The FSA was given regulatory authority over all financial services in the UK, and in the process, assumed the duties of nine other regulatory bodies. In so doing, Great Britain abolished self-regulatory organizations, such as those in the United States.[13]

Among other things, the FSA consolidated six separate insurance funds for compensating investors who suffer losses from failed financial institutions into one.[14] The FSA also merged 14 separate rulebooks governing various financial activities into one.[15] The single rulebook approach taken by the FSA was appealing, at least compared with the multitude of regulators in the United States.

FSA regulation initially appeared successful. Despite the reduced regulation under the FSA, Great Britain was spared the Enron-era scandals that occurred under functional regulation in the United States. Nevertheless, critics contended that the FSA was understaffed and remained a weak regulator that deferred to the industry. Critics also argued that FSA unified regulations still imposed significant costs. Indeed, principles-based regulation under the FSA still required many

---

12 For a description of the background that led to the creation of the FSA see Jerry W. Markham, *Super-Regulator: A Comparative Analysis of Securities and Derivatives Regulation in the United States, Great Britain & Japan*, 28 BROOKLYN J. INT'L L. 319, 37–378 (2003) (hereinafter "Super-Regulator").

13 The FSA was a mixture of private and government initiative:

> The FSA is an independent non-governmental body, given statutory powers by the Financial Services and Markets Act 2000. We are a company limited by guarantee and financed by the financial services industry. The Treasury appoints the FSA Board, which currently consists of a Chairman, a Chief Executive Officer, three Managing Directors, and 9 non-executive directors (including a lead non-executive member, the Deputy Chairman). This Board sets our overall policy, but day-to-day decisions and management of the staff are the responsibility of the Executive.

Available at http://www.fsa.gov.uk/Pages/About/Who/index.shtml.

14 FSA, Introduction to the Financial Services Authority 18 (2001), available at http://www.fsa.gov.uk/pubs/other/fsa_intro.pdf.

15 Super-Regulator, *supra* note 12, at 379–380.

rules. The FSA handbook, which consolidated the rulebooks of earlier regulators, still totaled over 8,000 pages.[16]

The FSA also had some controversial powers. It could veto decisions by large financial institutions to hire executives with "significant influence." The FSA also had authority to monitor the performance of such executives through regular reviews and was authorized to require an executive be fired if its appraisal was negative.[17] Additionally, the FSA interviewed and approved hiring senior executives at "high impact" firms.[18] This meant, of course, that financial institutions had to kowtow to their regulators because if, for any reason, they displeased the FSA their executives could be fired. Nevertheless, the FSA remained the most popular regulatory model, which was adopted by numerous countries. However, as described below, that favorable impression was lost when the FSA failed to prevent and deal with the financial services problems that arose during the Financial Crisis in 2008, and it was disbanded.

Twin Peaks

In seeking to abandon functional regulation, the Treasury Blueprint did not advocate a single regulator system for the United States. The Treasury Blueprint rejected a single regulator model for many reasons:

> While the consolidated regulator approach can deliver a number of benefits, several potential problems also arise. First, housing all regulatory functions related to financial and consumer regulation in one entity may lead to varying degrees of focus on these key functions. Limited synergies in terms of regulation associated with financial and consumer protection may lead the regulator to focus more on one over the other. There may also be difficulties in allocating resources to these functions. Second, a consolidated regulatory approach to financial oversight might also lead to less market discipline as the same regulator would regulate all financial institutions, whether or not they have explicit government guarantees. This would seem to be particularly important in the United States where a number of financial institutions have access to explicit government guarantees of varying degrees. Third, since regulatory reform must consider the role of the central bank, the consolidated regulatory approach must maintain some degree of close coordination with the central bank if the central bank is going to be ultimately responsible for

[16] Jerry W. Markham & Thomas Lee Hazen, Broker-Dealer Operations Under Securities and Commodity Law § 2:54 (2008).

[17] http://www.fsa.gov.uk/pages/Library/Communication/PR/2008/153.shtml (accessed on Jan. 9, 2009).

[18] http://www.fsa.gov.uk/pages/Doing/Regulated/Approved/index.shtml (accessed on Jan. 9, 2009).

> some aspect of market stability … . Finally, the scale of operations necessary to establish a single consolidated regulator in the United States could make the model more difficult to implement in comparison to other jurisdictions.[19]

Instead of a single regulator, the Blueprint recommended that the United States adopt a "Twin Peaks"-style regulatory approach that is used in Australia and the Netherlands.[20] This concept is attributed to Michael Taylor, a former official at the Bank of England who wrote a 1995 article entitled *'Twin Peaks': A Regulatory Structure for the New Century*.[21] The Twin Peaks approach is objectives-based and focuses on specific regulatory goals.

Twin Peaks envisions a central bank that focuses on prudential supervision, and a single business practices regulator that focuses on business conduct and consumer protection. From this model, the *Treasury Blueprint* constructed what might best be described as a "Three Peaks" approach. This proposed the creation of three separate regulatory bodies in which financial services regulation would be consolidated. Those three regulators would implement three specific regulatory goals: (1) market stability regulation, (2) prudential financial regulation and (3) business conduct regulation.

The objectives-based approach in the Treasury Blueprint thus sought the consolidation and reshuffling of the existing functional regulators in the United States into essentially three principal regulators who would implement and oversee regulatory goals. The market stability regulator would be the Federal Reserve Board. A new agency would be created for prudential financial regulation that would regulate financial institutions with a government guarantee, such as banks insured by the FDIC and broker-dealers insured by Securities Investors Protection Corporation ("SIPC"). A new agency would also have to be created for the business conduct regulator, which would create and apply principles-based regulation.[22]

The Treasury Blueprint recommended that in the interim, the SEC and CFTC be merged. It also recommended that the SEC adopt a principles-based regulatory approach, like that of the CFTC, to make the merger more workable.[23] However, prior efforts to merge the two agencies had

---

19 Treasury Blueprint, *supra* note 5, at 141.

20 Treasury Blueprint, *supra* note 5, at 142.

21 Regulators Back Taylor's Twin Peak Theory, BNet, http://findarticles.com/p/articles/mi_qn4158/is_/ai_n14085198 (Oct. 29, 1996).

22 Treasury Blueprint, *supra* note 5, at 144.

23 Treasury Blueprint, *supra* note 5, at 106–111.

revealed strongly entrenched constituencies willing to battle to keep them separate. There was also a vast gulf in the two agencies' regulatory approaches, creating differing cultures that often clashed.

THE NEED FOR REFORM GROWS

The Treasury Blueprint encountered much opposition and only mild support when it was published.[24] Among those opposing the Treasury Blueprint were the Consumer Federation of America and the Democratic leader of the Senate Finance Committee, Christopher Dodd of Connecticut.[25] The regulatory structure proposed by the Blueprint would also preempt most state regulation of financial institutions, which the states would not accept without a fight. This would have cut off the career paths of many budding state politicians who witnessed the rise of Eliot Spitzer to the New York governor's office as a result of his attacks on Wall Street.[26] Spitzer's successor as New York's attorney general, Andrew Cuomo, also became nationally known for taking on Wall Street by investigating the financial services industry, including student loans, auction rate securities, rating agencies, and even bonuses paid to Merrill Lynch executives.[27] Like Spitzer, those efforts catapulted him into the New York governor's seat.

The North America Securities Administrators Association ("NASAA") announced its own plan for reform in November 2008, which recommended preserving state regulation, but admitted that some streamlining might be in order. The NASAA advocated that all financial products and

---

[24] The author attended a banking conference sponsored by the University of North Carolina law school shortly after the Blueprint was published. The general counsel for Wachovia noted that Secretary Paulson had stated that the recommendations in the Treasury Blueprint were only "aspirational." The general counsel stated that he looked that word up in the dictionary and that it appeared to be a derivative of the Latin term for "not a snowball's chance in hell." That was a fair assessment at the time. Subsequent events, however, overtook Wachovia, which had to be rescued during the Financial Crisis by Well Fargo.

[25] David Cho, Neil Irwin, & Carrie Johnson, *Long Fight Ahead for Treasury Blueprint*, Wash. Post, Mar. 30, 2008, at AO1.

[26] I have described those events in Jerry W. Markham, A Financial History of Modern U.S. Corporate Scandals: From Enron to Reform *passim* (2005).

[27] Amir Efrati and Aaron Lucchetti, *U.S. News: Cuomo Blazes Own Trail as Wall Street Cop*, Wall St. J., Aug. 11, 2008 at A3; Michael J. de la Merced and Louise Story, *Nearly 700 at Merrill in Million-Dollar Club*, N.Y. Times, Feb. 12, 2009, at B1.

markets be subjected to regulation so that there would be no regulatory gaps. It was in favor of principles-based regulation, but only as an additional layer to existing rules. The NASAA also advocated tougher enforcement and stronger private remedies.[28]

THE FINANCIAL CRISIS OF 2008

That Treasury Blueprint study was commenced at a time when inefficient regulation was thought to be impairing financial services. However, even while the Treasury study was ongoing, a sea change was occurring as the subprime crisis arose and intensified, resulting in demands for more regulations and regulators. The *Wall Street Journal* declared in a front-page article on March 24, 2008, that a new era of increased regulation could be expected due to problems then occurring in the subprime mortgage securities market.[29] The Treasury Blueprint, which recommended a broad restructuring of the chaotic financial services regulatory structure, was published a few days after the *Wall Street Journal* article.[30]

The Financial Crisis, which began in 2007 and heightened in 2008, exposed a number of flaws in financial regulation. The credit default swaps that were thought to be at the center of the crisis were virtually unregulated. As described in an earlier chapter, a credit default swap involves an arrangement whereby a swap dealer agrees to pay the value of a credit instrument should it default. In exchange for that obligation, the party receiving the credit protection agrees to make payments to the credit swap dealer that act as an insurance premium payment.[31] The growth of the credit default swaps market was phenomenal. The notional amount of outstanding credit default swaps in 2000 was $900 billion. That figure increased to $62 trillion by 2008.[32]

---

[28] *NASAA to Host Financial Services Regulatory Reform Roundtable*. http://www.North America Securities a. org/NASAA_Newsroom/Current_NASAA_Headlines/9910.cfm (accessed on Jan. 10, 2009).

[29] Elizabeth Williamson, *Political Pendulum Swings Toward Stricter Regulation—Safety Scares, Crisis In Housing Rupture A Long Consensus*, WALL ST J., Mar. 24, 2008, at A1.

[30] Treasury Blueprint, *supra* note 5.

[31] *See* Jerry W. Markham, A Financial History of the United States From the Subprime Crisis to the Great Recession (2006–2009) 406 (2011) (defining credit default swaps).

[32] Nat'l Ass'n of Professional Ins. Agents, *Congress Exempted Credit Default Swaps From State Gaming Laws in 2000*, http://www.pianet.com/NewsCenter/BizPolitics/10–15–08–7.htm (accessed on July 3, 2011).

Credit default swaps were unregulated because the Commodity Futures Modernization Act of 2000 had barred the CFTC from regulating those and other over-the-counter derivative markets.[33] Commercial markets trading swaps were also exempted from regulation. This allowed the IntercontinentalExchange Inc. ("ICE") in Atlanta Georgia to become a major unregulated market for trading swaps.

The Financial Crisis of 2008 resulted in the destruction of two of the largest firms regulated by the SEC, i.e., Bear Stearns and Lehman Brothers. Another large firm, Merrill Lynch, was rescued by the Bank of America. Goldman Sachs and Morgan Stanley converted to bank holding companies so that they could have access to Federal Reserve Board funding. More regulatory flaws were revealed after a panic in the money market mutual funds occurred following the failure of Lehman Brothers. That failure caused the Reserve fund, one of the largest money market funds, which was holding Lehman Brothers paper, to "break-the-buck," which meant that its investors were facing a loss of their funds. The government was forced to guarantee the money market funds in order to quell the resulting panic.

Emergency restrictions were placed on short sales that were thought to be crashing the market in 2008, but proved to be ineffective.[34] TARP and other bailout programs were used to rescue faltering financial institutions and to restore faith in the financial system. The bailouts stopped the panic in the markets but those programs also stirred deep resentment by populist politicians who did not think taxpayer funds should be used to bail out elitist banks and Wall Street firms.

Congress reacted to that criticism with the Dodd-Frank Act, a statute totaling 2,300 pages, and which affected nearly every aspect of financial regulation. Dodd-Frank chose to ignore the Treasury Blueprint's recommendations. Instead, that legislation sought to buttress regulatory oversight by more functional regulation. As a part of that effort, Dodd-Frank created a Financial Stability Oversight Council ("FSOC") and designated a host of regulators for its membership. The purpose of the Council is to identify risks to the financial stability of the United States that could arise from the distress, failure, or on-going activities, of large, interconnected bank holding companies or nonbank financial companies, or that could arise outside the financial services marketplace. FSOC is to be responsible for eliminating any belief on the part of shareholders,

---

[33] Pub. L. No. 106–544, 114 Stat. 2763 (2000).

[34] Jerry W. Markham, A Financial History of the United States, From the Subprime Crisis to the Great Recession (2006–2009) (2011) (describing those events).

creditors and counterparties that in the future large financial service firms will be viewed by federal government to be "too big to fail."

The voting members of FSOC are the heads of the Fed, OCC, FDIC, SEC, CFTC, Federal Housing Finance Agency, National Credit Union Administration, the new Bureau of Consumer Financial Protection, and an independent member appointed by the President and knowledgeable about insurance. Membership on FSOC also includes a number of non-voting (advisory) members, including the heads of a new Federal Insurance Office (which is to monitor all aspects of the insurance industry and to identify any issues that could pose a systemic risk to the industry or to the financial system as a whole), a new Office of Financial Research (which supports FSOC by collecting information, conducting research, analyzing data, and making it accessible to regulators), and delegates selected by state insurance, banking and securities commissions.

FSOC is to act by majority vote, except for some actions a two-thirds vote is required including the affirmative vote of the chair, which is the Secretary of the Treasury. FSOC was given oversight authority over large financial institutions that pose systemic risk to the financial system. Once identified, those institutions may be the subject of special regulation. In the event of the failure of such an institution they will be "resolved" by an orderly liquidation like other banks, avoiding the need for future federal bailouts.[35]

Dodd-Frank also created a Bureau of Consumer Financial Protection ("BCFP") that is housed under the umbrella of the Fed, but is headed by an independent director appointed by the President and confirmed by the Senate. The BCFP will implement and enforce federal consumer financial laws for the purpose of ensuring that all consumers have access to markets for consumer financial products and services and that markets for consumer financial products and services are fair, transparent, and competitive. The BCFP will further regulate the offering and provision of consumer financial products or services under existing Federal consumer financial laws. It has independent authority to write rules governing consumer protection for customers of all financial institutions that offer consumer financial services or products.

Dodd-Frank also regulated the previously unregulated swaps market. The SEC was given jurisdiction over security-based swaps and the CFTC

---

[35] *See* Jerry W. Markham, *The Financial Stability Oversight Council—Risk Manager or Debating Society?*, 33 J. FIN. TRANS. 3 (Dec. 2011) (describing the role and flaws in this new regulator).

jurisdiction over commodity swaps. Joint regulatory authority was given to both agencies for "mixed" swaps that have elements of both securities and commodities. Most swaps will now be exchange traded and cleared through a regulated central counterparty. The customer funds associated with exchange-traded swaps must be held in segregated accounts. The legislation required registration of, and allowed the SEC and CFTC to impose capital and margin requirements on, swap dealers and major swap participants, but not end-users. It directed the CFTC to establish position limits on swaps traders.

Dodd-Frank required hedge fund managers to register with the SEC as investment advisers if the assets they manage in the United States exceed $150 million. Registered hedge fund managers must keep books and records that disclose the amount of assets under management, the degree of leverage in the funds they manage, any side pocket arrangements giving some investors greater rights than others and trading practices. The SEC is authorized to make periodic and surprise examinations of registered hedge funds.

Dodd-Frank required a massive rule-making effort by the financial services regulators involving thousands of rules, some with tight deadlines for adoption that were frequently missed.

THE FUTURE OF MARKET REGULATION IN THE U.S.

Another factor affecting the future course of financial services regulation has been the growth of electronic trading that is shuttering the trading floors of the traditional exchanges. A market phenomenon, and a matter of intense regulatory scrutiny, was the growth of the so-called "high frequency traders." Those algorithmic traders generate rapid-fire orders to take advantage of even the most transient market inefficiencies.[36] The rapidity of this trading gave rise to its label as "high frequency trading."

High frequency trading has been driving trading volumes on both the stock and commodity markets in this century.[37] By 2009, some two-thirds of stock-market volume was attributable to "high-frequency traders, who can buy or sell in less than 400 microseconds, or nearly a thousand times

---

[36] *See* Jerry W. Markham and Daniel J. Harty *For Whom the Bell Tolls: The Demise of Exchange Trading Floors and the Growth of ECNs*, 33 IOWA J. CORP. L. 865 (2008) (describing growth of this trading).

[37] Dennis K. Berman, *The Game: Saving the Stock Market Only to Destroy It*, WALL ST. J., Aug. 24, 2010, at C1.

faster than you can blink your eye."[38] However, there has been no effort toward substantive regulation of these traders through registration requirements, as is commonly the case for regulated entities.[39]

In response to concerns over high frequency trading, the SEC issued a concept release in January 2010 ("Market Concept Release"). It sought comment on whether and how high frequency traders should be defined and regulated. The Market Concept Release noted that:

> One of the most significant market structure developments in recent years is high frequency trading ("HFT"). The term is relatively new and is not yet clearly defined. It typically is used to refer to professional traders acting in a proprietary capacity that engage in strategies that generate a large number of trades on a daily basis. These traders could be organized in a variety of ways, including as a proprietary trading firm (which may or may not be a registered broker-dealer and member of FINRA), as the proprietary trading desk of a multi-service broker-dealer, or as a hedge fund (all of which are referred to hereinafter collectively as a "proprietary firm").[40]

These high frequency traders interact with other investors in various ways, including the use of "flash" orders that are cancelled immediately upon communication or which are withdrawn if not executed immediately after communication.[41] As the SEC has noted, "[f]or those seeking liquidity, the flash mechanism may attract additional liquidity from market participants who are not willing to display their trading interest publicly."[42] The SEC has deferred a decision on whether to ban flash trades. Instead, its Market Concept Release launched a broad-based review of the current equity market structure. The SEC was seeking to determine whether its rules had kept pace with the growth of electronic

---

[38] Jason Zweig, *The Intelligent Investor: Staying Calm in a World of Dark Pools, Dark Doings*, WALL ST. J., Oct. 24, 2009, at B1.

[39] The SEC has noted that:

Unlike years ago, trades today are transacted in milliseconds or faster and dispersed among many trading centers. These changes have allowed large market participants to employ sophisticated trading methods to trade electronically on multiple venues in huge volumes at very fast speeds. SEC, *SEC Adopts Large Trader Reporting Regime*, Release No. 2011–154 (July 26, 2011), available at http://www.sec.gov/news/press/2011/2011–154.htm (accessed on Mar. 17, 2011).

[40] SEC, *Concept Release on Equity Market Structure*, 75 Fed. Reg. 3594, 3606 (Jan. 21, 2010).

[41] 74 Fed. Reg. 48632 (Sept. 23, 2009).

[42] 74 Fed. Reg. 48632, 48638 (Sept. 23, 2009). Securities Exchange Act Release No. 34–60684, 74 Fed. Reg. 48632 (Sept. 23, 2009).

trading, including the role of flash and other orders like "pinging" orders.[43]

For a time, high frequency traders were allowed to have "naked" or "sponsored" access to market centers. This allowed those traders to have direct access to exchanges and other market centers where they interfaced with customer orders. Naked access thus allowed unregistered high frequency traders to access an exchange's trading facilities without broker-dealer intermediation or supervision.[44] The SEC imposed risk supervision requirements on the broker-dealers that had offered naked access.[45] That rule effectively curbed naked access.

"Dark pools" also allow active traders to engage in high volume securities trading.[46] As the SEC's Market Concept Release noted, "[i]n general, dark pools offer trading services to institutional investors and others that seek to execute large trading interest in a manner that will minimize the movement of prices against the trading interest and thereby

---

[43] SEC, *Concept Release on Equity Market Structure*, 75 Fed. Reg. 3594 (Jan. 21, 2010).

[44] As the SEC noted:

> Over the past decade, the proliferation of sophisticated, high-speed trading technology has changed the way broker-dealers trade for their own accounts and as agent for their customers. In addition, customers—particularly sophisticated institutions—have themselves begun using technological tools to place orders and trade on markets with little or no substantive intermediation by their broker-dealers. This, in turn, has given rise to the increased use and reliance on "direct market access" or "sponsored access" arrangements. Under these arrangements, the broker-dealer allows its customer–whether an institution such as a hedge fund, mutual fund, bank or insurance company, an individual, or another broker-dealer—to use the broker-dealer's market participant identifier ("MPID") or other mechanism for the purposes of electronically accessing the exchange or ATS [Alternative Trading System]. With "direct market access," as commonly understood, the customer's orders flow through the broker-dealer's systems before passing into the markets, while with "sponsored access" the customer's orders flow directly into the markets without first passing through the broker-dealer's systems. In all cases, however, whether the broker-dealer is trading for its own account, is trading for customers through more traditionally intermediated brokerage arrangements, or is allowing customers direct market access or sponsored access, the broker-dealer with market access is legally responsible for all trading activity that occurs under its MPID.

See Risk Management Controls for Brokers or Dealers With Market Access, 75 Fed. Reg. 4007, 4008 (Jan. 26. 2010) (footnotes omitted).

[45] *See* 17 C.F.R. § 240.15c3–5.

[46] *See* Scott Patterson, Dark pools (2012) (describing these trading venues).

reduce trading costs."[47] Dark pools are anonymous trading platforms for trading stock listed on public markets.[48] Orders placed through an exchange are visible to the public and all other market participants. In contrast, an order or an indication of interest entered on a dark pool is revealed only to other dark pool participants. This gives dark pool participants access to information unavailable to the public.

As the SEC has stated:

> As a result, dark pool participants are able to have their orders filled, while those on publicly displayed markets go unfilled, even though dark pools use the information from publicly displayed markets to price the dark pool transactions. When dark pools share information about their trading interest with other dark pools, they can function like private networks that exclude the public investor.[49]

The SEC has proposed rules to limit such exclusions by dark pools but has not acted to date on those proposals.[50] The SEC did create a large trader reporting system that requires high frequency traders to report their trading to the SEC on Form 13H.[51] The SEC advised in connection with this requirement that "an institutional investment manager that is required to report is an entity that either invests in, or buys and sells, securities for its own account."[52]

These were all weak measures and the SEC seemed always behind on market developments, including numerous computer glitches that frequently halted or disrupted trading on electronic trading platforms. The SEC seemed to be unable to deal with its dual role as a market regulator and as a cop on the beat. This is because the SEC views itself to be foremost a law enforcement agency. It does not seem willing to assume

---

47 75 Fed. Reg. at 3599 (footnote omitted).

48 Austin J. Sandler, T*he Invisible Power Of Machines: Revisiting The Proposed Flash Order Ban In The Wake Of The Flash Crash*, 2011 DUKE L. & TECH REV. 3, n. 18.

49 SEC Fact Sheet, Strengthening the Regulation of Dark Pools (Oct. 21, 2009), available at http://www.sec.gov/news/press/2009/2009–223-fs.htm (accessed on Apr. 21, 2012).

50 SEC Fact Sheet, Strengthening the Regulation of Dark Pools (Oct. 21, 2009), available at http://www.sec.gov/news/press/2009/2009–223-fs.htm (accessed on Apr. 21, 2012).

51 *Id.*

52 SEC Division of Investment Management: Frequently Asked Questions About Form 13F (June 2011), available at http://www.sec.gov/divisions/investment/13ffaq.htm (accessed on Mar. 25, 2013).

the role of a prudential regulator, a role that dominates bank regulation in the U.S.

Prudential regulation is less adversarial than law enforcement. Prudential regulation seeks to identify unsafe and unsound financial practices. The regulator then works with the financial institution to correct those deficiencies. A law enforcement agency plays a "gotcha" game of seeking out violations for the purpose of punishment, not correction. Such actions are highly publicized and are, therefore, preferred by the SEC to prudential regulatory efforts that do not draw the attention of the press.

It may be that the SEC needs to be split into two agencies, thereby adding still another regulator, that would separately act, one in the role of prudential regulator and one as law enforcement. More realistic, and less burdensome, is the possibility of combining the SEC with a prudential bank regulator or the CFTC. The CFTC has, at least until recent years traditionally focused more on prudential regulation than law enforcement.

Such a combination of the CFTC and SEC was recommended in the Treasury Blueprint, but congressional action on that recommendation seemed unlikely until recent years. This was because the agricultural committees in congress had jurisdiction over the commodity exchanges while the banking committees had jurisdiction over the securities markets. Both sets of committees had jealously guarded their respective jurisdictions.[53] As described in an earlier chapter, the SEC and CFTC have repeatedly clashed over the scope of their respective jurisdictions in court and elsewhere. However, the importance once attributed to this jurisdictional division is all but gone.

The commodity markets have for decades been dominated by derivative products that involve underlying financial instruments, many of which are regulated by the SEC. Even trading in derivatives on agricultural commodities has been said to be "financialized" by professional traders. The growth of electronic trading also evidences that the two markets are increasingly trading and operating in similar manner.[54]

---

[53] *See* Jerry W. Markham, *Merging the SEC and CFTC—A Clash of Cultures*, 78 U. CINN. L. REV. 537 (2009) & *Super-Regulator: A Comparative Analysis of Securities and Derivatives Regulation in the United States, Great Britain & Japan*, 28 BROOKLYN J. INTL. LAW 319 (2003) (describing those issues).

[54] *See* Jerry W. Markham & Daniel J. Harty, *For Whom the Bell Tolls: The Demise of Exchange Trading Floors and the Growth of ECNs*, 33 J. CORP. L. 865 (2008) (describing the growth of electronic trading).

Economic reports were claiming that the financialization of the commodity markets by high frequency and index traders was causing a correlation of prices that varied from fundamental factors affecting those commodities.[55]

The SEC and CFTC are also increasingly becoming co-regulators of financial services products. That began with the duties to consult on their regulation in some areas, to have joint regulation of narrow-based indexes and to allow single stock futures on narrow-based indexes. Dodd-Frank took that effort considerably further with the agencies splitting regulation of some swaps and jointly regulating others.

Still another event that will affect future regulation is the demutualization of both the stock and commodity exchanges and the shuttering of their trading floors. This means that the power once exercised by the floor members on those exchanges is much diluted. It was those members who had led the crusade against an agency merger. Today, the exchanges are shareholder owned and political fights over SEC regulation are less appealing to that constituency. The cost of dealing with dual regulators is also a matter of concern to shareholders.

The proposed merger between ICE and the NYSE-Euronext may be still another game changer, since it is the combining of two of the largest stock and commodity exchanges.[56] This will undoubtedly lead to more such consolidation and more joint product offerings. An exchange operating dual markets will unlikely want dual regulation that differs in scope and format. In sum, keeping two regulators over a combined industry is making less and less sense.

THE FINANCIAL SERVICES AUTHORITY FAILS

The Financial Services Authority ("FSA") in London encountered a host of problems during the Financial Crisis in 2007–2008. The favorable impression of FSA regulation had increased after it adopted a unified approach to capital requirements and risk management.[57] That program, however, proved to be an empty shell during the Financial Crisis. The FSA was strongly criticized for failing to prevent a bank run on Northern Rock PLC during that event. That was the first run on a bank in England

---

[55] Gregory Meyer, *Challenge to Conventional Wisdom on Speculators*, FIN. TIMES (LONDON), Aug. 30, 2011.

[56] *See* Jacob Bunge, *Buying the Big Board—The Ice Chief: A 'Chess Master' With Sharp Elbows*, WALL ST. J., Dec. 21, 2012, at A8.

[57] http://www.fsa.gov.uk/pubs/cp/cp06_09.pdf (accessed Jan. 9, 2009).

in over 100 years. The British government nationalized that bank and put up $30 billion to rescue it and stop the panic.[58] The British government also rescued the Royal Bank of Scotland and Lloyds at a tremendous cost.[59]

The House of Commons Treasury Committee subsequently issued a report criticizing the FSA for its laxness in regulating Northern Rock. The report asserted that the FSA had failed to allocate sufficient resources to monitor the bank whose "business model was so clearly an outlier."[60] The committee recommended that the Bank of England be the lead regulator when a bank faces financial difficulties. That recommendation was an apparent effort to turn back the clock on the single regulator concept that had given the Bank of England's regulatory authority to the FSA because of perceived inadequacies in the Bank of England's own regulatory abilities.

The FSA promised more stringent regulation in March 2009. Its head, Hector Sants, also vowed that London would no longer be friendly to the financial services industry and that he intended to take strong action to assure that the business community would be "frightened" of the FSA.[61] The FSA's proposals included a regulatory wish list of massively increased capital requirements for banks, and closer scrutiny of their business models, products, and compensation schemes. The FSA also proposed regulation of credit rating agencies and hedge funds.[62] FSA chairman Lord Jonathan Adair Turner weighed in with a lengthy report in March 2009 that also advocated abandoning London's light-touch regulation. He wanted to impose requirements that would restrict excessive

---

[58] Julie Werdigier, *A Nationalized Northern Rock Curtails Its Products as Deposits Surge*, N.Y. TIMES, Oct. 3, 2008 at C7.

[59] Landon Thomas, Jr., *British Bank Adapts to Life On a Leash*, N.Y. TIMES, Feb. 6, 2009, at B1. The UK government effectively nationalized the Royal Bank of Scotland, which suffered the largest ever quarterly loss by any company in the history of the U.K. in 2008. Sara Schaefer Munoz, *et al.*, *U.K. Moves to Save Bank on the Brink*, WALL ST. J., Feb. 27, 2009 at A1.

[60] Diana B. Henriques, *Lehman Loss Just the Start for Money Fund,* N.Y. TIMES, Feb. 27, 2009, at B9.

[61] Peter Thal Larsen, *Gloves to Come Off as FSA Ends "Light Touch" Era*, FIN. TIMES (London), Mar. 13, 2009, at 17.

[62] Julia Werdigier, *British Regulator Takes a Tougher Line*, N.Y. TIMES, Mar. 19, 2009, at B8.

risks taken by banks through increased capital liquidity measures. Lord Turner also sought a pan-European regulatory body.[63]

The FSA then tried to become a more forceful regulator. It strongly supported the objective of achieving robust and resilient central clearing party ("CCP") arrangements for credit default swaps ("CDS") clearing.[64] The March 2009 Turner Report recognized, however, that the impact of central clearing arrangements should not be overstated because "clearing and CCP systems will only be feasible for the roughly 50–75 percent of the CDS which is accounted for by standardized contracts."[65] This statement acknowledged that a large volume of CDSs might continue to trade OTC.

The British government subsequently announced that it was dropping its single regulator approach in favor of a "twin peaks" model.[66] This involved the creation of a new Consumer Protection and Markets Authority ("CPMA") that would begin operations in 2012 and that would assume the functions of the FSA. "The CPMA will have the primary objective of promoting confidence in financial services and markets, with particular focus on ensuring that consumers of financial services are protected and that financial markets work effectively."[67]

The CPMA underwent a name change before it began operations and is now called the Financial Conduct Authority ("FCA"). It did not begin its operations until April 1, 2013. The FCA has stated that:

---

63 Peter Thal Larsen *et al.*, *Turner to End Light-Touch Regulation*, FT.com (FIN. TIMES), Mar. 18, 2009, http://www.ft.com/cms/s/0/68397782–13b7–11de-9e32–0000779fd2ac.html.

64 Financial Services Authority, The Turner Review: A Regulatory Response to the Global Banking Crisis 82 (2009), available at http://www.fsa.gov.uk/pubs/other/turner_review.pdf [hereinafter Turner Review]. The FSA is also taking a more aggressive approach to dealings in CDS, including references to the Serious Fraud Office. Harry Wilson, FSA Looks Into Trading in Penrod Credit Default Swaps, DowJones Online, Aug. 24, 2009, available at http://www.efinancial news.com/investment banking/regulation/content/1055002340.

65 *Id.*

66 Bank of England, Prudential Regulatory Authority, accessible at http://www.bankofengland.co.uk/pra/Pages/default.aspx (accessed on Apr. 1, 2013).

67 Bank of England, Government announces CEO-designate of new Consumer Protection and Markets Authority available at http://www.hm-treasury.gov.uk/press_11_11.htm (accessed on Apr. 1, 2013).

> We regulate the financial services industry in the UK. Our aim is to protect consumers, ensure our industry remains stable and promote healthy competition between financial services providers. We have rule-making, investigative and enforcement powers that we use to protect and regulate the financial services industry. We are fair and principled in our approach to regulation.[68]

A new Prudential Regulatory Authority (PRA) was created in the Bank of England, which will now take back FSA's former control of prudential regulation. The PRA has stated that it is:

> responsible for the prudential regulation and supervision of banks, building societies, credit unions, insurers and major investment firms. In total the PRA regulates around 1,700 financial firms.
>
> The PRA's role is defined in terms of two statutory objectives to promote the safety and soundness of these firms and, specifically for insurers, to contribute to the securing of an appropriate degree of protection for policyholders.
>
> In promoting safety and soundness, the PRA focuses primarily on the harm that firms can cause to the stability of the UK financial system. A stable financial system is one in which firms continue to provide critical financial services—a precondition for a healthy and successful economy.
>
> The PRA will make forward-looking judgments on the risks posed by firms to its statutory objectives. Those institutions and issues which pose the greatest risk to the stability of the financial system will be the focus of its work.[69]

The FCA and PRA started off with some aggressive actions, including a requirement that financial service firm officers sign an attestation that made them personally responsible if any regulatory concerns were not corrected.[70] These regulators were also more carefully vetting executives with "significant influence functions."[71]

---

[68] FCA, *About Us*, available at http://www.fca.org.uk/about (accessed on Apr. 1, 2013).

[69] Bank of England, *Prudential Regulatory Authority*, available at http://www.bankofengland.co.uk/pra/Pages/default.aspx (accessed on Apr. 1, 2013).

[70] Brooke Masters, *Top Executives Targeted on Compliance*, FIN. TIMES, May 27, 2013 at 1.

[71] Brooke Masters, *Watchdogs Keep Up the Pressure Over Responsibility*, FIN. TIMES, May 27, 2013 at 18.

THE EUROPEAN UNION

The European Union ("EU") is increasingly playing a broader role in financial regulation. A 1993 EU Directive decreed that securities firms and banks licensed in one member state had to be recognized in all other member states. Regulation of such firms, however, is the responsibility of the bank's home state. The EU adopted a Financial Services Action Plan in 1999 that sought complete integration of financial services among member states.[72] The EU issued a Markets in Financial Instruments Directive ("MiFid") that seeks to develop a single market in member states in all financial transactions.[73] That directive sought a best execution requirement, which like the SEC National Market System in the U.S. seeks to assure that customers receive the best available price quoted in all market centers.[74]

More EU regulation followed. In 2009, the EU had three committees that exercised "advisory powers" over financial services in member states. They were the Committee of European Banking Supervisors ("CEBS"), the Committee of European Insurance and Occupational Pensions Committee ("CEIOPS") and the Committee of European Securities Regulators ("CESR"). "These are often known as the 'Lamfalussy level Committees' because of the role which they play in the EU framework for financial services legislation, created following a report by a group chaired by Alexandre Lamfalussy."[75]

---

[72] For a description of the background of financial services regulation in the EU, see Jerry W. Markham & Thomas Lee Hazen, Broker-Dealer Operations Under Securities and Commodity Law § 16:5 (2008). For a comparison of U.S. and EU regulation, see Stavros Gadinis, *Market Structure for Institutional Investors: Comparing the U.S. and E.U. Regimes*, 3 VA. L. & BUS. REV. 311 (2008).

[73] Council Directive 2004/39, 2004 O.J. (L 145) 1–44 (EC).

[74] For a discussion of the best execution obligation in the U.S., see Joseph M. Furey & Beth D. Kiesewetter, *On-Line Broker-Dealers: Conducting Compliance Reviews in Cyberspace*, 56 BUS. LAW. 1461 (2001); Thomas J. McGonigle, Rochelle S. Hall & N. Elizabeth Clark, *NASDR Examinations: Priorities and Procedures*, 34 SEC. & COMM. REG. 165, 167–168 (Aug. 2001); Francis J. Facciolo, *A Broker's Duty of Best Execution in the Nineteenth and Early Twentieth Centuries*, 26 PACE L. REV 155 (2005); and David A. Lipton, *Best Execution: The National Market System's Missing Ingredient*, 57 NOTRE DAME L. REV. 449 (1982).

[75] European Commission, Financial Services Committee Architecture, http://ec.europa.eu /internal%market/'nances/committees/index%en.htm (Nov. 13, 2009).

A matter of increasing concern is the cross-border regulation of financial services firms that operate in both the United States and the EU. An EU directive issued in 2002 required foreign financial services firms with operations in the EU to demonstrate holding company supervision that is equivalent to EU consolidated supervision. The SEC and CFTC reacted to that directive by allowing such entities to use risk-based capital requirements as substitutes for their existing net capital requirements. That proved to be an unfortunate decision because it allowed those firms to increase substantially their leverage. The firms choosing that model either failed (Lehman Brothers, Merrill Lynch and Bear Stearns) or converted to bank holding company status (Goldman Sachs and Morgan Stanley) during the Financial Crisis in 2008.[76]

Cross-border regulation has raised other issues. The merger of the NYSE and Euronext in 2007 was arranged so that the merger would remain in place only so long as each institution was not subject to the regulatory jurisdiction of the other.[77] The Financial Crisis in 2008 resulted in sometimes coordinated action by U.S. and EU central banks, but at other times regulation was disjointed. The regulation of credit default swaps, which were thought to be at the heart of the causes of that crisis were a matter of contention.

A report issued by the High-Level Group on Financial Supervision in the EU (the de Larosière Report) in 2009 recommended that credit default swaps and other over-the-counter derivatives be simplified, standardized and made more transparent. The de Larosière Report recommended strengthening the Level 3 committee's coordination of national regulators. It also urged the creation of a European Banking Authority, a European Insurance Authority and a European Securities Authority. The de Larosière Report envisioned that these regulators would coordinate national supervision of cross-border financial institutions and develop a single a European rulebook for financial services.[78]

The de Larosière Report thought that the Financial Stability Forum (FSF) should be tasked with the duty of coordinating the convergence of international financial regulation. The FSF was an international group of regulators, but it was later replaced by a new Financial Stability Board

---

[76] *See* Jerry W. Markham, *Merging the SEC and CFTC—A Clash of Cultures*, 78 U. CINN. L. REV. 537, 576–580 (2009) (describing those events).

[77] Eric J. Pan, *A European Solution to the Regulation of Cross-Border Markets*, 2 BROOK. J. CORP., FIN. AND COMM. L. 133, 137 (2007).

[78] European Commission, Financial Services Committee Architecture, http://ec.europa.eu/internal%market/fnances/committees/index%en.htm (Nov. 2009).

("FSB") by the Group of Twenty in 2009. The FSB was expanded to include all Group of Twenty countries plus the European Commission.[79]

Banks in the EU had been badly damaged by the same triple-A rated "Super-Senior" subprime collateralized debt obligations ("CDOs") that caused much of the damage to financial institutions in the U.S. during the Financial Crisis.[80] The de Larosière Report had recommended the creation of at least one well-capitalized CCP, a.k.a. clearinghouse, to be supervised by the Committee of European Securities Regulators ("CESR") and the European Central Bank ("ECB").[81]

Charlie McCreevy, the European Commissioner in charge of the Internal Market and Services, declared in October 2008 that an immediate goal of the Commission was to require central clearing of credit default swaps. The Commission required the creation of a central registry for CDS that would record credit derivative instruments after trades have been confirmed. This would create a "golden" copy of those transactions.[82] That goal was accomplished on July 31, 2009, when CDS on European reference entities began clearing through central counterparties regulated in the EU.[83]

The EU then put a new system of regulation in place:

> On 1 January 2011, the new European Supervisory Authorities, namely the European Banking Authority (EBA), the European Insurance and Occupational Pensions Authority (EIOPA) and the European Securities and Markets Authority (ESMA), as well as the Joint Committee of the European Supervisory Authorities (Joint Committee) commenced operation. Additionally, the European Systemic Risk Board (ESRB) was established. Together with

---

[79] Financial Stability Board, History, http://www.financialstabilityboard.org/about/history.htm (=Nov. 13, 2009).

[80] By August 2008, write-offs at European banks included $44.2 billion at UBS; IKB Deutsche $12.6 billion; Royal Bank of Scotland $14.9 billion; Credit Suisse $10.5 billion; Credit Agricole $8 billion; Societe Generale $6.8 billion; Bayerische Landesbank $6.4 billion; ING Groep $5.8 billion; Lloyds TSB $5 billion; Dresdner $4.1 billion; and BNP Paribas $4 billion, to name a few. *See* Yalman Onaran, *Banks Subprime Losses Top $500 Billion on Writedowns*, BLOOMBERG.COM, Aug. 12, 2008, http://www.bloomberg.com/apps/news?pid=20601087&sid=a8sW0n1Cs1tY (accessed on Nov. 13, 2009).

[81] *See* de Larosière Report, *supra* note 78, at 25.

[82] *See* Jeremy Grant, *Watchdogs Call for Central Registry*, FIN. TIMES (London), Feb. 27, 2009, at 7. *See also* European Central Bank, Credit Default Swaps and Counterparty Risk (2009).

[83] *See* Sebastian Hrovatin, et al,. *Derivatives and the Financial Crisis*, FUTURES INDUS. MAGAZINE, Sept. 2009, at 43.

national supervisory authorities, the new authorities are meant to ensure improved and harmonized financial supervision in the EU.[84]

The European Commission adopted a European Market Infrastructure Regulation (EMIR) that became effective on August 16, 2012. EMIR will require entities that enter into any form of derivative contract, including interest rate, foreign exchange, equity, credit and commodity derivatives, to:

- report every derivative contract that they enter to a trade repository;
- implement new risk management standards, including operational processes and margining, for all bilateral over-the-counter (OTC) derivatives i.e. trades that are not cleared by a CCP [central counterparty]; and
- clear, via a CCP, those OTC derivatives subject to a mandatory clearing obligation.[85]

The new European Securities and Marketing Authority ("ESMA") began operations in 2012. Its mission is to create a multi-dimensional supervisory approach to financial services regulation in the EU and to build a single rulebook for Europe. ESMA will seek to drive the convergence of national supervisory activities with EU regulations. ESMA will also supervise Trade Repositories under the terms of the European Market Infrastructure Regulation ("EMIR") and will coordinate supervisory colleges for central counterparties.[86]

The European Commission published proposals for a MiFiD 2 in October 2011. It specifically targeted the over-the-counter market in financial instruments for increased regulation. It also proposed a new Markets in Financial Instruments Regulation ("MiFiR"). The Commission was also seeking transparency in dark pools and would create a new Organized Trading Facility category for regulation.

On September 26, 2012, the Economics and Monetary Affairs Committee of the European Parliament unanimously voted its approval (45–0) of legislation that would restrict high-frequency traders ("HFT") in the European Union. The proposed legislation would require HFT orders to

---

84 BaFin, *International*, available at http://www.bafin.de/EN/International/international_node.html (accessed on Apr. 1, 2013).

85 FSA, *EMIR—What You Need to Know*, available at http://www.fsa.gov.uk/about/what/international/emir (accessed on Apr. 1, 2013).

86 ESMA, *2013 Work Program*, available at http://www.esma.europa.eu/fr/system/files/2012–631_0.pdf (accessed on Apr. 1, 2013).

be posted for at least one half second, which would considerably reduce the speed of HFT. That committee also sought controls that would curb commodity price speculation by position limits like those used in the United States. It also sought to restrict bank proprietary trading and to push derivative trading in bonds and commodities onto electronic trading platforms that would be separate from the equity exchanges.[87]

GERMANY

Historically, in Germany the largest banks, rather than broker-dealers and exchanges, dominated finance, including equities and lending. Speculation was strictly limited, which prevented commodity futures trading from developing there until the 1990s. After that ban lifted, that trading became an important part of German financial markets.[88]

Until 2002, the German Financial Supervisory Authority was responsible for licensing banks, broker-dealers and other financial institutions. That Authority was divided into three separate units that separately regulated banking, insurance and securities. In 2002, those units were consolidated into a single regulator, a new German Financial Supervisory Authority, generally referred to as BaFin. That regulator is contained within the portfolio of the German Federal Ministry of Finance.

Several large German banks suffered large losses from investments in U.S. collateralized debt obligations during the Financial Crisis in 2008. Among other things, the German government implemented a $750 billion rescue package for its financial institutions and approved a $40 billion economic stimulus package in 2008. BaFin required German banks to avoid compensation plans that encouraged undue risk. It also required stress testing of trading positions at all levels, increased risk management controls and required banks' directors to be given greater control over management.[89]

---

87 Huw Jones, *EU Lawmakers Back Curbs on High Frequency Share Trade*, Reuters, Sept. 26, 2012, http://www.reuters.com/article/2012/09/26/us-eu-mifid-idUSBRE88P1A920120926 (accessed on Sept. 27, 2012).

88 *See* William P. Rogers & Jerry W. Markham, *The Application of West German Statutes to United States Commodity Futures Contracts: An Unnecessary Clash of Policies*, 19 GEORGETOWN J. OF L. & POLICY IN INTERN. BUS. 273 (1987) (describing those restrictions and their effects).

89 *See* Lissa L. Broome & Jerry W. Markham, Regulation of Bank Financial Services Activities 994 (4th ed. 2011) (describing those events).

BaFin also sent out a directive to firms engaging in high frequency trading and directed them to take actions to prevent manipulative trading practices called "spoofing" and "layering."[90] Germany was also considering a legislative proposal that would require HFTs to register with BaFin. This proposal would assess fees against HFTs that trade "excessively," and they could also be required to disclose their algorithms to the government.[91]

JAPAN

General Douglas MacArthur required the Japanese government to adopt a number of U.S. laws while he was in command of the occupying forces at the conclusion of World War II. Those measures included the U.S. federal securities laws. That legislation established a Securities Commission for the Supervision of Securities Business, and it was modeled after the SEC in the U.S. The Bank of Japan acted as the country's central bank, setting monetary policy, while the Ministry of Finance ("MoF") was responsible for financial policy.[92]

The MoF abolished the Securities Commission for the Supervision of Securities Business in 1952 and replaced it with its own Securities Bureau. Other aspects of the U.S.-style regulatory system were also abandoned in later years. The MoF then assumed a dual role of regulator and business promoter. Though it was the sole governmental financial regulator, SROs, including the exchanges and the Japanese Securities Dealers Association, also provided some minimal regulatory functions.[93]

Japan developed a bubble economy in the 1980s that collapsed in the early 1990s. The Japanese economy then collapsed after several large financial institutions failed. The Japanese economy also suffered from a serious bout of deflation. In response, the Japanese Diet passed the Financial Reform Act of 1992, which allowed the MoF to establish capital requirements for banks and allowed banks to own securities affiliates. A new Securities Exchange and Surveillance Commission

---

90 BaFin, BaFin Publishes Information on the Prevention of Market Manipulation in an Automated Trading Environment, available at http://www.bafin.de/SharedDocs/Veroeffentlichungen/EN/Meldung/2012/meldung_121218_layering_en.html (accessed on Apr. 1, 2013).

91 Christopher Lawton & Andreas Kissler, *Germany to Tap Brakes on High-Speed Trading*, WALL STREET JOURNAL, Sept. 26, 2012, at C1.

92 *Super-Regulator*, *supra* note 12, at 389–393 (describing this history).

93 *Id.*

("SESC") was created in 1992 to police the securities markets. This legislation was supposed to reduce MoF's role as financial services regulator. In fact, it failed to do so.[94]

More reform was sought in 1996 that would adopt the UK regulatory model and deregulate Japan's financial services. The SESC was transferred out of the MoF in 1998, along with an independent Financial Supervisory Agency, which was succeeded by the Financial Services Agency ("FSA-Japan") in 2000. FSA-Japan was also given the power, previously held by the MoF, to set securities regulatory policy and to regulate securities and banking. The SESC continued its operations under authority from the FSA-Japan, which in turn was supervised by the Financial Reconstruction Commission.[95]

Japan enacted a new Financial Instruments and Exchange Law ("FIEL") just in time for the subprime crisis.[96] The FIEL consolidated four other statutes including those regulating financial futures and the mortgage-backed securities.[97] The Japanese Financial Services Authority ("JFSA") was given authority over, "not only derivatives related to securities but also derivatives related to other financial instruments, and the FIEL covers derivatives that are transacted on a Japanese or foreign exchange or over the counter."[98]

FIEL did not address central clearing of derivatives.[99] A committee of the Tokyo Financial Exchange ("TFX")[100] did consider the issue of using

---

[94] *Id.*

[95] *Id.*

[96] For a description of FIEL see Japan Financial Services Authority, New Legislative Framework for Investor Protection, available at http://www.fsa.go.jp/en/policy/fiel/20061010.pdf.

[97] *Id.* at 10, 19, 21.

[98] Tetsuya Itoh, *Pay Careful Attention*, 2007 INT'L FIN. L. REV. 67–69 (2007). (supp. to the 2007 Global Report, Oct. 1, 2007), *available at* http://www.iflr.com/Article/1984203/Pay-careful-attention.html.

[99] FIEL had been under discussion for years, and the nature and scope of the subprime crisis was largely unforeseen at the time FIEL was enacted. Even a subsequent amendment to the FIEL promulgated on June 13, 2008, did not seem to adopt any measures related to regulation of financial derivatives. *See* Japan Financial Services Authority, Outline of the Bill for Amendment of the Financial Instruments and Exchange Act, Etc., *available at* http://www.fsago.jp/en/ refer/measures/20080606/02.pdf.

[100] Tokyo Financial Exchange, Study Committee on Central Counterparty for OTC Derivatives Transactions (Apr. 2009), available at http://www.tfx.co.jp/en/newsfile/pdf/clearing200904_e.pdf.

a central counterparty to clear OTC derivatives.[101] The committee's report identifies the TFX as the most likely institution for clearing OTC transactions, given it "is the only exchange in Japan that specializes in trading and clearing financial derivatives"[102] and its members (including major financial institutions in Japan, the United States, and Europe) have the credit quality required to successfully establish a CCP at the TFX.[103] The report identified the following benefits of having a CCP: (1) reduced counterparty risk and thus less use of credit lines; (2) reduction of the risk portion of the capital adequacy ratio; (3) standardized processing reducing operational risk; and (4) reduced systemic market risk.[104]

The conclusion of the committee was to proceed with setting up a clearinghouse for interest rate swaps and CDSs.[105] The TFX committee resolved to set the schedule to establish a functioning CCP for OTC transactions in Japan in 2010.[106] Interest rate swaps will be cleared immediately, but the committee was more cautious about CDS, stating that it would be better to wait and see what kind of CCP system is successfully adopted and supported by the market place in Europe and the US.[107]

IOSCO

The Final Report of IOSCO's Technical Committee of the Task Force on Unregulated Financial Markets and Products ("TFUMP") addressed the regulation of CDS.[108] This committee was formed at the behest of the Group of Twenty to "review the scope of financial regulation with 'a

---

[101] *Id.* at 3.
[102] *Id.*
[103] *Id.*
[104] *Id.* at 5.
[105] *Id.* at 6.
[106] *Id.* at 8.
[107] *Id.* at 7.
[108] This effort was co-chaired by the Autorité des Marchés Financiers ("AMF") of France and the Australian Securities and Investments Commission (ASIC). *See* International Organization of Securities Commissions, Unregulated Financial Markets and Products—Final Report (Sept. 2009), available at http://www.fsa.go.jp/inter/ios/20090911/02.pdf.

special emphasis on institutions, instruments and markets that are currently unregulated, along with ensuring all systemically important institutions are appropriately regulated.'"[109] The committee's report identified three main issues related to CDS: counterparty risk, lack of transparency and operational risk.[110] The recommendations of the committee echo many of those made by U.S., UK and EU officials concerning the regulation of financial derivatives, including the use of a central counterparty for CDS.

CONCLUSION

In the U.S. the creation of new financial instruments and repeated financial crises inevitably led to another layer of functional regulation that does nothing to prevent the next crisis. The FSA created a new model for more streamlined regulation that appeared to be more effective than the U.S. model. The FSA, however, appeared to have failed in preventing and dealing with the Financial Crisis in 2008. As a result, it was stripped of its role and replaced by dual "twin peak" regulators. The EU went further and appears to have adopted the U.S. model of "functional" layer upon layer of regulation. That seems strange in view of the failure of U.S. functional regulation in allowing the conditions that led to the Financial Crisis of 2008.

---

[109] G20 Communiqué Declaration on the Summit of Financial Markets and the World Economy (Nov. 15, 2008), available at http://www.g20.org/Documents/g20_summit_declaration.pdf.

[110] *Id.* at 29.

Index